Small Claims Court Practice and Procedure in Ontario

Revised Edition

Laurence M. Olivo
B.A., M.A., J.D. of the Ontario Bar

DeeAnn M.P. Gonsalves
B.A., J.D. of the Ontario Bar
(Deputy Judge of the Ontario Small Claims Court)

Captus Press

Small Claims Court Practice and Procedure in Ontario, Revised Edition

© 2011–2013 Laurence M. Olivo, DeeAnn M.P. Gonsalves, and Captus Press Inc.

Captus Press Inc.
Mail: Units 14 & 15
          1600 Steeles Avenue West
          Concord, Ontario
          Canada L4K 4M2
Telephone: (416) 736–5537
Fax: (416) 736–5793
Email: info@captus.com
Internet: http://www.captus.com

Library and Archives Canada Cataloguing in Publication

Olivo, Laurence M., author
    Small claims court practice and procedure in Ontario / Laurence M. Olivo, DeeAnn M.P. Gonsalves. – Revised edition.

Includes bibliographical references and index.
ISBN 978-1-55322-288-0 (pbk.)

    1. Small claims courts — Ontario — Textbooks. 2. Civil procedure — Ontario — Textbooks. 3. Debtor and creditor — Ontario — Textbooks. I. Gonsalves, DeeAnn, author II. Title.

KEO1090.O45 2013   347.713'04   C2013-904446-9
KF8769.O45 2013

Canada ▌▌ *We acknowledge the financial support of the Government of Canada through the Canada Book Fund for our publishing activities.*

0 9 8 7 6 5 4 3
Printed in Canada

Dedication

To Joyce Moore, as always, and to my students, who for over a quarter-century have provided me with both insight and inspiration.

To Brian, for his patience and support, and to my students and past clients for their inspiration. Also to Grandma Hattie for inspiring my love of books.

Contents

I
Preliminary Matters

II
Small Claims Court Proceedings:
From Commencement of Proceedings to Trials

III
Judgment and Enforcement

Appendices, Glossary, Bibliography, Index

Preface

Since the colonial period, the Small Claims Court has been the established workhorse of the Ontario court system. Historically it has been
accessible to citizens all over Ontario and, the citizenry has not been
slow to use it. Yet it has been largely ignored by the legal profession
and those who write on legal topics. But with the increase in the monetary jurisdiction of this court to $25,000, the Small Claims Court
began to attract more attention from lawyers. More importantly, after
two decades of discussion, the provincial government decided to allow
paralegals to practice as advocates in lower courts, including the Small
Claims Court. Licensing and training of paralegals was made the
responsibility of the Law Society But even before the Law Society took
over formal control of the paralegal profession, we at the Colleges of
Applied Arts and Technology saw the need to provide paralegal training and education for independent paralegals. This text was closely connected to those efforts and was initially developed with these students
in mind.

In addition to focusing on practice and procedure, we recognized
the major role played by the Small Claims Court in collection cases
involving unpaid consumer debts. Special attention is paid to debtor
creditor law and the calculation of a creditor's claims. There is also a
discussion of other preliminary matters including how damages in various types of cases are determined and calculated. Once that foundation
is laid, we then proceed with a discussion of practice and procedure,
starting at the beginning of the process with the claim, and ending with
enforcement of a judgment. Along the way there are opportunities to
analyze and understand the rules of the court, look at practical examples, use court forms and solve problems that students are likely to

encounter in the field. References, including useful web sites are provided for students who wish to or need to obtain updated information or pursue an issue in more depth. Review questions in each chapter help the student to check his or her knowledge, and discussion questions and case studies help the student to assess their ability to apply that knowledge to situations they are likely to encounter in practice. We also include in the appendices, the Small Claims Court Rules, the list of court fees, pre and post judgments interest tables, and a days-of-the-year chart that is useful for interest calculations.

Since the first edition of this text was published in 2010, the law, as ever, has continued to be a moving target. There have been a number of changes to the rules of procedure, the forms, and the law itself. We also discovered that some judges in this court, as well as practitioners, used the text as a guide and procedural reference. That has led us to focus even more on the requirements of practitioners as well as students. In the new edition, we have been very alert to practices and procedures that are used in these courts that are not apparent from the rules of procedure: the use of sheriffs to enforce writs of seizure and sale of personal property, the issuance of writs of delivery prior to judgment, are but two examples.

This edition then updates both the formal law and procedural changes since the first edition, but also tracks various practices, techniques and strategies used in day to day practice in these courts. We could not have caught all of this for inclusion without the help of our students in the Paralegal Program at Seneca College, and without the help of practitioners, many of them our former students. In particular we would like to thank Neal Schoen, Tony Falcitellia, and Fredrick Goodman, among others, for their suggestions.

We hope this text will continue to meet students' needs as we intended, and that practitioners will find it useful. Students and practitioners have never been shy about telling us what works and what doesn't. We encourage them — and you — to help us to make this text as useful as it can be by passing on comments and suggestions to the publisher.

Laurence M. Olivo and DeeAnn Gonsalves
August 2013

I
Preliminary Matters

Chapter 1

Introduction to the Ontario Small Claims Court

LEARNING OBJECTIVES

⇨ Understand the role of the Small Claims Court and how it evolved to its present position as a branch of the Superior Court of Justice

⇨ Know the differences between the types of judges of the Small Claims Court

⇨ Understand how a judge hears cases in a summary manner

⇨ Know who can represent someone in the Small Claims Court

⇨ Understand the limits of the court's monetary, legal, and territorial jurisdiction

⇨ Obtain a general sense of the various steps and stages in a Small Claims Court case from commencement to enforcement of a judgment

INTRODUCTION

The Small Claims Court has been part of the Ontario court system since colonial times. In this chapter we will examine its historical roots and its place in the present court system. We will also examine the role of its judges and discuss who can represent a party in the Small Claims Court. The court's summary hearing procedure and its monetary, legal, remedial, and territorial jurisdictions are also examined. The chapter concludes with a complete overview of a hypothetical Small Claims Court case from its commencement to the enforcement of the judgment.

HISTORICAL OVERVIEW

The Small Claims Court, under a variety of names, has been part of the legal system in Ontario since the early colonial period, well before Ontario was a province.[1] It was designed to settle minor civil disputes, with parties often representing themselves or being represented by agents rather than by lawyers. The procedures in the Small Claims Court were simple and relatively informal compared to the superior courts. This made it possible to hear and decide a case relatively quickly and at a low cost that ordinary people could afford to pay. The unique features of this court, described here, that characterized it in the past continue to characterize it today.

Mr. Justice Zuker, appointed to the Small Claims Court of Ontario in 1978, has remarked that, "The Small Claims Court is not a building or a courtroom, but a special procedure, established by provincial statute, that simplifies the court process for a specific monetary range for small civil disputes."[2]

The popularity of the Small Claims Court is apparent from the number of cases filed in it. In 2009–2010, 64,254 new cases were filed in the Ontario Small Claims Court.[3] The claims filed concerned minor civil disputes for no more than $10,000 excluding interest and costs.[4]

---

[1] Prior to the enactment of the *Small Claims Court Act*, R.S.O. 1970, c. 439, small claims were heard in the Division Courts. The *Small Claims Court Act* created a Small Claims Court. Figure 1.1 in this chapter outlines the progression of the Small Claims Court from the Provincial Court (Civil Division) to the present Superior Court of Justice. Courts of Request were established in 1792 (Upper Canada) 32 Geo. III, c. 6, to hear and deterine small debt matters.

[2] Mr. Justice Marvin A. Zuker, *Ontario Small Claims Court Practice 2007* (Toronto, Ont.: Thomson Carswell, 2006), p. 9.

[3] Ministry of the Attorney General, *The Ministry of Attorney General, Court Services Division Report 2009–2010*, p. 35. Available online at <http://www.attorneygeneral.jus.gov.on.ca>.

[4] The monetary jurisdiction of the court was increased to $10,000 from $6,000 in 2001. The *Osborne Report* (Ministry of the Attorney General, *Civil Justice Reform*

The Small Claims Court is a branch of the Ontario Superior Court of Justice established under s. 22(1) of the *Courts of Justice Act*, R.S.O. 1990, c. C.43 (*CJA*):[5]

> **22.**(1) The Small Claims Court is continued as a branch of the Superior Court of Justice under the name Small Claims Court in English and Cour des petit créances in French.

The *CJA* establishes the organization of Ontario's courts. Regulations made under the *CJA* contain rules for various courts, including the Small Claims Court. The *Rules of the Small Claims Court*, O. Reg. 258/98, as am. by O. Reg. 400/12, provide directions for commencing and completing procedures in the Small Claims Court.

As illustrated in Figure 1.1, the Small Claims Court has been part of a variety of courts during its history. The organizational history of the court demonstrates that a court to hear minor civil claims has always been a necessary part of the judicial system. However, the Ontario Small Claims Court, with its low ranking in the court system and the makeup of its judiciary, which consists of only two full-time judges with over 400 deputy judges drawn from the ranks of lawyers in private practice, functions as more of a judicial afterthought than as a primary court.[6]

JUDGES IN THE SMALL CLAIMS COURT

Judges in the Small Claims Court fall into one of three categories. They may come from the Superior Court of Justice or they may be Provincial Court (Civil Division) judges appointed prior to the 1990 change in the structure of the courts; however, the largest contingent of Small Claims Court judges are lawyers appointed by the court to sit as deputy judges. We shall look at each of these categories of judges in turn.

Project, November 2007, available online at <http://www.attorneygeneral.jus.gov.on.ca/english/about/pubs/cjrp/CJRP-Report_EN.pdf>) recommended an increase to $25,000, beginning with an increase to $15,000, followed by a second increase to $25,000. The Ontario government by-passed an increase to $15,000. As of January 1, 2010, the court's monetary jurisdiction increased from $10,000 to $25,000. For a complete history of the court's monetary jurisdiction, consult Zuker, *supra*.

[5] When the words "section" or "subsection" and "sections" or "subsections" (or s. and ss., respectively) are used in the text or footnotes, unless otherwise indicated, the reference is to the *CJA*. When the term, "Rule" or "Rules" is used, unless otherwise indicated, the reference is to the *Rules of the Small Claims Court* ("the Rules"). When "Paralegal Rules" is used, the reference is to the *Paralegal Rules of Conduct*.

[6] The *Osborne Report*, *supra* note 4, Ch. 3, pp. 15–16.

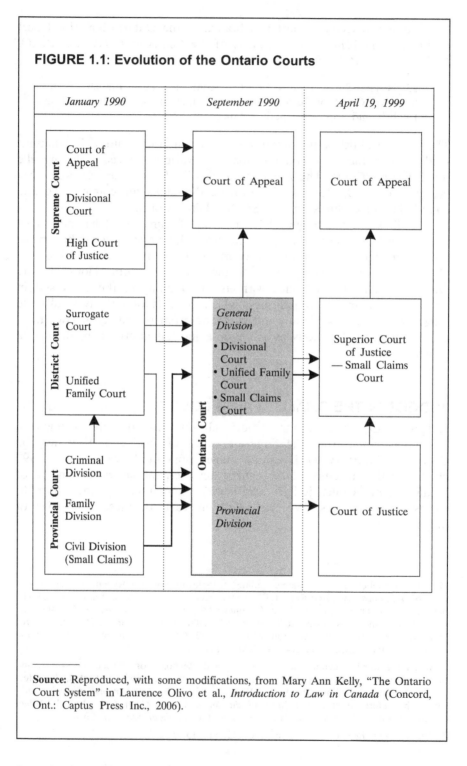

FIGURE 1.1: Evolution of the Ontario Courts

Source: Reproduced, with some modifications, from Mary Ann Kelly, "The Ontario Court System" in Laurence Olivo et al., *Introduction to Law in Canada* (Concord, Ont.: Captus Press Inc., 2006).

Superior Court of Justice Judges

Under s. 22(2), the Small Claims Court has as its president the Chief Justice of the Superior Court of Justice:

> **22.**(2) The Small Claims Court consists of the Chief Justice of the Superior Court of Justice who shall be president of the court and such other judges of the Superior Court of Justice as the Chief Justice designates from time to time.
>   (3) Every judge of the Superior Court of Justice is also a judge of the Small Claims Court.

From time to time, the Chief Justice may designate other judges of the Superior Court of Justice to sit in the Small Claims Court. Under s. 22(3), every judge of the Superior Court of Justice is also a judge of the Small Claims Court. Although Superior Court judges could sit in Small Claims Court, in practice most of them do not. They do, however, hear cases in the Superior Court that come within the small claims monetary jurisdiction.[7] Under s. 32(1), which can be found on the following page, a regional senior judge of the Superior Court of Justice may, with the approval of the Attorney General, appoint lawyers to act as Small Claims Court deputy judges. These deputy judges are the backbone of the system, without them it could not operate.

Judges from the Former Provincial Court (Civil Division)

Under s. 24(2)(a), a provincial judge who was assigned to the Provincial Court (Civil Division) immediately before the first day of September 1990 may hear proceedings in the Small Claims Court.

> **24.**(2) A proceeding in the Small Claims Court may also be heard and determined by,
>   (a) a provincial judge who was assigned to the Provincial Court (Civil Division) immediately before the 1st day of September, 1990;

The Provincial Court (Civil Division) was the Small Claims Court in Ontario for a time prior to September 1, 1990. The last full-time

---

[7] Litigants should be aware of the possible adverse costs consequences of bringing a matter before the Superior Court of Justice when the monetary value of the claim falls within the jurisdiction of the Small Claims Court. See Rule 57.05 of the *Rules of Civil Procedure*, R.R.O. 1990, Reg. 194, as amended. Some exceptions apply whereby certain matters under the monetary jurisdiction of the Small Claims Court, such as construction lien matters and most matters seeking equitable relief, must be brought in the Superior Court because the Small Claims Court lacks jurisdiction to deal with such matters.

Small Claims Court provincial judge retired from full-time service in the fall of 2009. There are two supernumerary provincial judges who sit on a per diem basis in Small Claims Court (one in Toronto and one in Ottawa).[8] Generally, there is no practical significance to the type of judge sitting in the court as far as lawyers, paralegals or self-represented parties are concerned when appearing in court. However, if a superior court of justice judge is presiding, he or she can hear all contempt matters. A deputy Small Claims Court judge mainly deals with contempt *in facie* (i.e., a contempt made directly in front of a judge). An example of contempt *in facie* is the refusal of a judgment debtor to answer a question at an examination in aid of execution. Beginning January 2011, deputy judges will have a limited *ex facie* contempt power they can exercise if a judgment debtor misses a second examination in aid of execution. The deputy judge will be able to order a jail sentence of five days or less. A Superior Court judge can make a sentence of 40 days or less. Contempt is covered in detail in Chapter 13.

Deputy Judges of the Small Claims Court

Deputy judges are usually lawyers in private practice who sit part-time, sometimes in the evenings. There are also retired higher court judges who are now deputy judges of the Small Claims Court.[9] Lawyers are appointed to act as deputy judges of the Small Claims Court. Under s. 32(9), any appointments or renewals made after January 1, 2010, must end when the deputy judge turns 75.

> **32.**(1) A regional senior judge of the Superior Court of Justice may, with the approval of the Attorney General, appoint a lawyer to act as a deputy judge of the Small Claims Court.
>
> (2) The appointment of a deputy judge is for a term of three years, subject to subsections (3) and (7).
>
> (3) If the deputy judge is 65 years of age or older and under 75 years of age, the appointment shall be for a term of one year, subject to subsection (8).
>
> (4) The appointment of a deputy judge who is under 65 years of age may be renewed by a regional senior judge of the Superior Court of Justice for a term of three years, subject to subsection (7).
>
> (5) The appointment of a deputy judge who is 65 years of age or older and under 75 years of age may be renewed by a regional

---

[8] The *Osborne Report*, *supra* note 4, p. 16. Note that supernumerary judges are judges nearing retirement age who have accumulated enough service to elect a reduced workload. Given this fact, these judges are expected to retire within a few years.

[9] A complete list of all Ontario Small Claims Court deputy judges is available, by region, at <http://www.ontariocourts.on.ca>; follow the Superior Court of Justice link to the Small Claims Court.

senior judge of the Superior Court of Justice for a term of one year, subject to subsection (8).

(6) Subject to subsections (7) to (9), there is no limit to the number of times the appointment of a deputy judge can be renewed under subsection (4) or (5).

(7) If the deputy judge is 63 years of age or older and under 65 years of age, an appointment under subsection (2) or a renewal under subsection (4) shall provide for a term that expires when he or she reaches 65 years of age.

(8) If the deputy judge is 74 years of age, an appointment under subsection (3) or a renewal under subsection (5) shall provide for a term that expires when he or she reaches 75 years of age.

(9) No person shall be appointed as a deputy judge, or have an appointment renewed, once he or she reaches 75 years of age.

(10) For greater certainty, nothing in this section shortens or otherwise affects an appointment or renewed appointment that is in effect immediately before the day subsection 20(11) of Schedule 2 to the *Good Government Act, 2009* comes into force, but any renewals of the appointment on and after that day are subject to this section.

Deputy judges are generally appointed for a term of three years, which may be renewed on a three-year term basis. However, for deputy judges between the ages of 63 and 65, their term of appointment or renewal ends at the time they turn 65 at which time it can be renewed for one-year terms up to age 75. Deputy judges between the ages of 65 and 75 are appointed for a term of one year, which may be renewed yearly, up to age 75. The number of deputy judges far outweighs that of permanent full-time judges.[10] There used to be limits on the monetary level of cases a deputy judge could hear, compared to Provincial Court judges, but such limits have been eliminated.[11]

Appointment, Compensation, and Regulation of Deputy Judges

Section 32 and the lengthy s. 33 govern the appointment, compensation, and regulation of deputy judges. Much of the detail results from the need to supervise, compensate, and oversee deputy judges without interfering with their judicial independence, a delicate balancing act:

---

[10] The *Osborne Report, supra* note 4, p. 16.

[11] For example, in 1979 when the Small Claims Court in Toronto became a Provincial Court under a three-year pilot project, the monetary jurisdiction of that court was raised to $3,000 for cases heard in Toronto. The limit for cases outside Toronto remained at $1,000. Only Provincial Court judges could hear cases between $1,000 and $3,000. Deputy judges were limited to hearing cases up to $1,000.

33.(1) A council known as the Deputy Judges Council in English and as Conseil des juges suppléants in French is established.

...

(6) The functions of the Deputy Judges Council are,

(a) to review and approve standards of conduct for deputy judges as established by the Chief Justice;

(b) to review and approve a plan for the continuing education of deputy judges as established by the Chief Justice; and

(c) to make recommendations on matters affecting deputy judges.

Complaints against Deputy Judges

Section 33.1(1) allows any person to make a written complaint alleging misconduct by a deputy judge. A Superior Court judge shall review the complaint and may dismiss it or refer it to a committee for investigation and recommendations:

Complaints
33.1(1) Any person may make a complaint alleging misconduct by a deputy judge, by writing to the judge of the Superior Court of Justice designated by the regional senior judge in the region where the deputy judge sits.

Dismissal
(2) The judge shall review the complaint and may dismiss it without further investigation if, in his or her opinion, it falls outside the jurisdiction of the regional senior judge, is frivolous or an abuse of process, or concerns a minor matter to which an appropriate response has already been given.

Notice of dismissal
(3) The judge shall notify the regional senior judge, the complainant and the deputy judge in writing of a dismissal under subsection (2), giving brief reasons for it.

Committee
(4) If the complaint is not dismissed, the judge shall refer it to a committee consisting of three persons chosen by the regional senior judge.

...

Recommendations
(7) The committee shall make a report to the regional senior judge, recommending a disposition in accordance with subsections (8), (9) and (10).

Disposition
(8) The regional senior judge may dismiss the complaint, with or without a finding that it is unfounded, or, if he or she con-

cludes that the deputy judge's conduct presents grounds for imposing a sanction may,

(a) warn the deputy judge;

(b) reprimand the deputy judge;

(c) order the deputy judge to apologize to the complainant or to any other person;

(d) order that the deputy judge take specified measures, such as receiving education or treatment, as a condition of continuing to sit as a deputy judge;

(e) suspend the deputy judge for a period of up to 30 days;

(f) inform the deputy judge that his or her appointment will not be renewed under subsection 32(2);

(g) direct that no judicial duties or only specified judicial duties be assigned to the deputy judge; or

(h) remove the deputy judge from office.

Same

(9) The regional senior judge may adopt any combination of the dispositions set out in clauses (8)(a) to (g).

Example 1.1: Initiating a Complaint against a Deputy Judge

Ellen Grant is the defendant in a case before the Small Claims Court. When giving his oral judgment, the deputy judge stated, "Miss Grant, you are as thick as a plank. Your defence was stupid. It is whiners like you who are clogging up the court system." Judgment was then made in favour of the plaintiff. Ellen Grant believes that the judge was biased against her and did not read or listen to her defence. She can file a complaint against the deputy judge. In accordance with s. 33.1(1), she must submit a complaint, in writing, to the Superior Court Judge, assigned by the Regional Senior Judge to handle complaints. Ellen can call the office of the Regional Senior Judge to find out the name of the judge assigned to receive complaints.

SMALL CLAIMS COURT HEARINGS

Composition of the Small Claims Court for a Hearing

Small Claims Court proceedings, under s. 24(1), are heard by one judge. There are no civil jury trials in this court:

24.(1) A proceeding in the Small Claims Court shall be heard and determined by one judge of the Superior Court of Justice.

(2) A proceeding in the Small Claims Court may also be heard and determined by,

(a) a provincial judge who was assigned to the Provincial Court (Civil Division) immediately before the 1st day of September, 1990;

(b) a deputy judge appointed under section 32.

Court Hearings

The *Rules of the Small Claims Court* provide for hearings that are less formal than those in the Superior Court of Justice. The Rules begin with the overriding principal that all of the rules should be construed in a manner that provides for the just, most expeditious, and least expensive determination of every proceeding. In plain English, the court is directed to use straightforward and non-technical procedures to reduce costs and delays in delivering fair results:

> 1.03(1) These rules shall be liberally construed to secure the just, most expeditious and least expensive determination of every proceeding on its merits in accordance with section 25 of the *Courts of Justice Act*.

Although proceedings in the Small Claims Court are not as formal as in other courts, the court is required to act in a just manner. The court, under Rule 1.04, may impose terms and give directions that are just. Rule 1.03(1) discussed above and s. 25 discussed below also speak of just determinations and just orders:

> 1.04 When making an order under these rules, the court may impose such terms and give such directions as are just.

Summary Hearings

Matters in the Small Claims Court are determined in a summary manner in accordance with s. 25:

> **25.** The Small Claims Court shall hear and determine in a summary way all questions of law and fact and may make such order as is considered just and agreeable to good conscience.

A **summary hearing** is one in which justice is to be done relatively quickly and inexpensively. In the Small Claims Court, this means "cutting to the chase" without cutting out just results. Litigants are expected to get to the point, not engage in trying to make proceedings more complicated than they need to be, and not play procedural games or try to defeat opponents through technical tricks and strategies.

This section, despite its language, is not an invitation for judges to decide cases however they feel like deciding them. Judges here are still bound by substantive common law and statute law.[12] However, the section does authorize the court to conduct proceedings in a "summary way", which means that justice should be done quickly and not be hindered or delayed by overly technical procedures that would raise costs and cause delay. Section 25 is also authority for the proposition that the technical requirements of procedural rules should not stand in the way of achieving a just result. This underlies provisions in the Rules that allow a judge to dispense with the application of any rule if justice so requires.[13] It also justifies a relaxation of the technical aspects of the rules of evidence. Of great importance is the fact that the section authorizes judges to take an interventionist approach in these courts where people often represent themselves. Judges often find it necessary to assist the litigants, determining applicable law for them, where the litigants set out the facts of the case. In *Gardiner v. Mulder*,[14] for example, the court noted that litigants are often unrepresented and that legal concepts, such as the many varieties of causes of action and the technicalities of pleading them, are unknown to the parties. In such cases the judge must determine what the law is, advise the litigants, and assist them in applying the relevant law to the facts of their case. This kind of intervention would not be permitted in the Superior Court, where judges are expected to be passive and act like referees, leaving the quality of advocacy to the parties.

Representation in the Small Claims Court

Section 26 provides that a party may be represented in the Small Claims Court by a person authorized under the *Law Society Act*, R.S.O. 1990, c. L.8, to represent the party:[15]

> **26.** A party may be represented in a proceeding in the Small Claims Court by a person authorized under the *Law Society Act* to represent the party, but the court may exclude from a hearing anyone,

---

[12] *Wittenberg v. Fred Geisweiller/Locomotive Investments Inc.* (1999), 44 O.R. (3d) 626 (Sup. Ct. J.).

[13] Rule 2.

[14] Unreported, March 9, 2007, Superior Court of Justice, Divisional Court (007/072/182).

[15] The Law Society licenses lawyers and paralegals who have completed law school or college programs (in the case of non-grandfathered paralegals) and have passed the bar admission exams for lawyers and the licensing exam for paralegals. At the time of writing, the LSUC has announced that it will introduce an integrated paralegal licence program for experienced collection agents and certain other professionals presently exempted from licensing. For up-to-date details, consult LSUC website: <www.lsuc.on.ca>.

other than a person licensed under the *Law Society Act*, appearing on behalf of the party if it finds that such person is not competent properly to represent the party, or does not understand and comply at the hearing with the duties and responsibilities of an advocate.

The section also provides that the court has the power to exclude non-licensed persons from appearing on a party's behalf if they are not competent to do so or do not understand and comply with an advocate's duties and responsibilities. This section was amended as a result of the legislative requirement that **paralegals** be licensed by the Law Society of Upper Canada ("Law Society"), and hence the Law Society will deal with any inappropriate behaviour.

Under By-Law Number 4, made under the *Law Society Act*,[16] paralegals have a right to appear in Small Claims Courts, and judges cannot simply exclude licensed paralegals from appearing in Small Claims Court, any more than they can exclude a lawyer.

BY-LAW 4 — LICENSING (EXCERPTS)
(MADE UNDER THE *LAW SOCIETY ACT*, current as of July 17, 2013)

PART I
...

LICENCE TO PROVIDE LEGAL SERVICES
Classes of licence
5. There shall be the following classes of licence to provide legal services in Ontario:
    1. Class P1.

Scope of Activities
Class P1
Interpretation
6.(1) In this section, unless the context requires otherwise,

"claim" means a claim for statutory accident benefits within the meaning of the *Insurance Act*, excluding a claim of an individual who has or appears to have a catastrophic impairment within the meaning of the Statutory Accident Benefits Schedule;

"party" means a party to a proceeding;

"proceeding" means a proceeding or intended proceeding,
    (a) in the Small Claims Court,
    (b) in the Ontario Court of Justice under the *Provincial Offences Act*,
    (c) in a summary conviction court under the *Criminal Code* (Canada),

---

[16] The By-Laws can be found online at the Law Society's website, <http://www.lsuc.on.ca/regulation/a/by-laws/>.

(d) before a tribunal established under an Act of the Legislature of Ontario or under an Act of Parliament, or

(e) before a person dealing with a claim or a matter related to a claim, including a mediator, a person performing an evaluation, an arbitrator or the Director acting under section 280, 280.1, 282 or 283 or 284, respectively, of the *Insurance Act*;

"Statutory Accident Benefits Schedule" means the Statutory Accident Benefits Schedule within the meaning of the *Insurance Act*.

Activities authorized

(2) Subject to any terms, conditions, limitations or restrictions imposed on the class of licence or on the licensee and subject to any order made under the Act, a licensee who holds a Class P1 licence is authorized to do any of the following:

1. Give a party advice on his, her or its legal interests, rights or responsibilities with respect to a proceeding or the subject matter of a proceeding.
2. Represent a party before,
   i. in the case of a proceeding in the Small Claims Court, before the Small Claims Court,
   ii. in the case of a proceeding under the *Provincial Offences Act*, before the Ontario Court of Justice,
   iii. in the case of a proceeding under the *Criminal Code*, before a summary conviction court,
   iv. in the case of a proceeding before a tribunal established under an Act of the Legislature of Ontario or under an Act of Parliament, before the tribunal, and
   v. in the case of a proceeding before a person dealing with a claim or a matter related to a claim, before the person.
3. Anything mentioned in subsection 1(7) of the Act, provided the activity is required by the rules of procedure governing a proceeding.
4. Select, draft, complete or revise, or assist in the selection, drafting, completion or revision of, a document for use in a proceeding.
5. Negotiate a party's legal interests, rights or responsibilities with respect to a proceeding or the subject matter of a proceeding.
6. Select, draft, complete or revise, or assist in the selection, drafting, completion or revision of, a document that affects a party's legal interests, rights or responsibilities with respect to a proceeding or the subject matter of a proceeding.

Exemptions from Paralegal Licensing

Certain groups of persons, exempted from paralegal licensing under Parts IV and V of By-law Number 4, may appear on someone's behalf in the Small Claims Court from time to time. These persons include in-house paralegals working for one client, friends (limited to three cases per year for friends), relatives, articling students, legal aid and quasi-

legal aid clinic workers, and Aboriginal court workers.[17] A judge, however, may exclude such persons from appearing if they are not competent to represent someone or do not understand or comply with an
advocate's duties and responsibilities.

BY-LAW 4 — LICENSING (EXCERPTS)
(MADE UNDER THE *LAW SOCIETY ACT*, current as of July 17, 2013)

PART IV
NOT PRACTISING LAW OR PROVIDING LEGAL SERVICES
Not practising law or providing legal services
28. For the purposes of this Act, the following persons shall be
deemed not to be practising law or providing legal services:

Aboriginal Courtwork Program
  1. A person who delivers courtworker services to Aboriginal peo-
     ple through an Aboriginal delivery agency that has contracted
     with the Government of Ontario or the Government of Canada
     to deliver courtworker services as part of the Aboriginal Court-
     work Program.

Other profession or occupation
  2. A person whose profession or occupation is not the provision
     of legal services or the practice of law, who acts in the normal
     course of carrying on that profession or occupation, excluding
     representing a person in a proceeding before an adjudicative
     body.

Committee of adjustment
  3. A person whose profession or occupation is not the provision
     of legal services or the practice of law, who, on behalf of
     another person, participates in hearings before a committee of
     adjustment constituted under section 44 of the *Planning Act*.

PART V
PROVIDING LEGAL SERVICES WITHOUT A LICENCE
Interpretation
29. In this Part,

"accredited law school" means a law school in Ontario that is
accredited by the Society;

---

[17] A place on the "exemptions" list is in large measure a reflection of the lobbying abilities of various organizations whose employers had traditionally been heard in the Small
Claims Court. Some persons exempt from licensing may qualify for an integrated licensing
program now offered by the Law Society as detailed in note 15. Those persons who qualify for the Law Society's integrated licensing program have until September 30, 2011, to
apply and until December 31, 2014 to finish.

"accredited program" means a legal services program in Ontario approved by the Minister of Training, Colleges and Universities that is accredited by the Society;

"law firm" means,

(a) a partnership or other association of licensees each of whom holds a Class L1 licence,

(b) a professional corporation described in clause 61.0.1(a) of the Act, or

(c) a multi-discipline practice or partnership described in section 17 of By-Law 7 [Business Entities] where the licensee mentioned therein is a licensee who holds a Class L1 licence;

"legal services firm" means,

(a) a partnership or other association of licensees each of whom holds a Class P1 licence,

(b) a professional corporation described in clause 61.0.1(b) of the Act, or

(c) a multi-discipline practice or partnership described in section 17 of By-Law 7 [Business Entities] where the licensee mentioned therein is a licensee who holds a Class P1 licence;

"licensee firm" means a partnership or other association of licensees, a partnership or association mentioned in Part III of By-Law 7 [Business Entities] or a professional corporation.

Providing Class P1 legal services without a licence
30.(1) Subject to subsection (2), the following may, without a licence, provide legal services in Ontario that a licensee who holds a Class P1 licence is authorized to provide:

In-house legal services provider
1. An individual who,
    i. is employed by a single employer that is not a licensee or a licensee firm,
    ii. provides the legal services only for and on behalf of the employer, and
    iii. does not provide any legal services to any person other than the employer.

Legal clinics
2. An individual who,
    i. is any one of the following:
        A. An individual who is enrolled in a degree program at an accredited law school and volunteers in or is completing a clinical education course at a clinic, within the meaning of the *Legal Aid Services Act, 1998*, that is funded by Legal Aid Ontario,
        B. An individual who is employed by a clinic, within the meaning of the *Legal Aid Services Act, 1998*, that is funded by Legal Aid Ontario,
        C. An individual who is enrolled in an accredited program and is completing a field placement approved by the

educational institution offering the program at a clinic, within the meaning of the *Legal Aid Services Act, 1998,* that is funded by Legal Aid Ontario,

ii. provides the legal services through the clinic to the community that the clinic serves and does not otherwise provide legal services, and

iii. has professional liability insurance coverage for the provision of the legal services in Ontario that is comparable in coverage and limits to professional liability insurance that is required of a licensee who holds a Class L1 licence.

Student legal aid services societies

3. An individual who,

i. is enrolled in a degree program at an accredited law school,

ii. volunteers in, is employed by or is completing a clinical education course at a student legal aid services society, within the meaning of the *Legal Aid Services Act, 1998,*

iii. provides the legal services through the clinic to the community that the clinic serves and does not otherwise provide legal services, and

iv. provides the legal services under the direct supervision of a licensee who holds a Class L1 licence employed by the student legal aid services society.

Student pro bono programs

3.1 An individual who,

i. is enrolled in a degree program at an accredited law school,

ii. provides the legal services through programs established by Pro Bono Students Canada, and

iii. provides the legal services under the direct supervision of a licensee who holds a Class L1 licence.

Not-for-profit organizations

4. An individual who,

i. is employed by a not-for-profit organization that is established for the purposes of providing the legal services and is funded by the Government of Ontario, the Government of Canada or a municipal government in Ontario,

ii. provides the legal services through the organization to the community that the organization serves and does not otherwise provide legal services, and

iii. has professional liability insurance coverage for the provision of the legal services in Ontario that is comparable in coverage and limits to professional liability insurance that is required of a licensee who holds a Class L1 licence.

Acting for friend or neighbour

5. An individual,

i. whose profession or occupation is not and does not include the provision of legal services or the practice of law,

ii. who provides the legal services only for and on behalf of a friend or a neighbour,

iii. who provides the legal services in respect of not more than three matters per year, and

iv. who does not expect and does not receive any compensation, including a fee, gain or reward, direct or indirect, for the provision of the legal services.

Acting for family

5.1. An individual,

i. whose profession or occupation is not and does not include the provision of legal services or the practice of law,

ii. who provides the legal services only for and on behalf of a related person, within the meaning of the *Income Tax Act* (Canada), and

iii. who does not expect and does not receive any compensation, including a fee, gain or reward, direct or indirect, for the provision of the legal services.

Member of Provincial Parliament

6. An individual,

i. whose profession or occupation is not and does not include the provision of legal services or the practice of law,

ii. who is a member of Provincial Parliament or his or her designated staff, and

iii. who provides the legal services for and on behalf of a constituent of the member.

Other profession or occupation

7. An individual,

i. whose profession or occupation is not the provision of legal services or the practice of law,

ii. who provides the legal services only occasionally,

iii. who provides the legal services as ancillary to the carrying on of her or his profession or occupation, and

iv. who is,

A. a member of the Human Resources Professionals Association of Ontario in the Certified Human Resources Professional category,

B. a member of the Board of Canadian Registered Safety Professionals, or

C. a member of the Appraisal Institute of Canada in the designated membership category.

...

Interpretation

31.(1) In this section,

"employer" has the meaning given it in the *Workplace Safety and Insurance Act, 1997*;

"injured workers' group" means a not-for-profit organization that is funded by the Workplace Safety and Insurance Board to provide specified legal services to workers;

"public servant" has the meaning given it in the *Public Service of Ontario Act, 2006*;

"survivor" has the meaning given it in the *Workplace Safety and Insurance Act, 1997*;

"worker" has the meaning given it in the *Workplace Safety and Insurance Act, 1997*.

Office of the Worker Adviser

(2) An individual who is a public servant in the service of the Office of the Worker Adviser may, without a licence, provide the following legal services through the Office of the Worker Adviser:

1. Advise a worker, who is not a member of a trade union, or the worker's survivors of her or his legal interests, rights and responsibilities under the *Workplace Safety and Insurance Act, 1997*.

2. Act on behalf of a worker, who is not a member of a trade union, or the worker's survivors in connection with matters and proceedings before the Workplace Safety and Insurance Board or the Workplace Safety and Insurance Appeals Tribunal or related proceedings.

Office of the Employer Adviser

(3) An individual who is a public servant in the service of the Office of the Employer Adviser may, without a licence, provide the following legal services through the Office of the Employer Adviser:

1. Advise an employer of her, his or its legal interests, rights and responsibilities under the *Workplace Safety and Insurance Act, 1997* or any predecessor legislation.

2. Act on behalf of an employer in connection with matters and proceedings before the Workplace Safety and Insurance Board or the Workplace Safety and Insurance Appeals Tribunal or related proceedings.

Injured workers' groups

(4) An individual who volunteers in an injured workers' group may, without a licence, provide the following legal services through the group:

1. Give a worker advice on her or his legal interests, rights or responsibilities under the *Workplace Safety and Insurance Act, 1997*.

2. Act on behalf of a worker in connection with matters and proceedings before the Workplace Safety and Insurance Board or the Workplace Safety and Insurance Appeals Tribunal or related proceedings.

Interpretation

32.(1) In this section,

"dependants" means each of the following persons who were wholly or partly dependent upon the earnings of a member of a trade union at the time of the member's death or who, but for the member's incapacity due to an accident, would have been so dependent:

1. Parent, stepparent or person who stood in the role of parent to the member.
2. Sibling or half-sibling.
3. Grandparent.
4. Grandchild;

"survivor" means a spouse, child or dependant of a deceased member of a trade union;

"workplace" means,

(a) in the case of a former member of a trade union, a workplace of the former member when he or she was a member of the trade union; and

(b) in the case of a survivor, a workplace of the deceased member when he or she was a member of the trade union.

Trade unions

(2) An employee of a trade union, a volunteer representative of a trade union or an individual designated by the Ontario Federation of Labour may, without a licence, provide the following legal services to the union, a member of the union, a former member of the union or a survivor:

1. Give the person advice on her, his or its legal interests, rights or responsibilities in connection with a workplace issue or dispute.
2. Act on behalf of the person in connection with a workplace issue or dispute or a related proceeding before an adjudicative body other than a federal or provincial court.
3. Despite paragraph 2, act on behalf of the person in enforcing benefits payable under a collective agreement before the Small Claims Court.

...

Student under articles of clerkship

34.(1) A student may, without a licence, provide legal services in Ontario under the direct supervision of a licensee who holds a Class L1 licence who is approved by the Society.

Other law student

(2) A law student may, without a licence, provide legal services in Ontario if the law student,

(a) is employed by a licensee who holds a Class L1 licence, a law firm, a professional corporation described in clause 61.0.1(c) of the Act, the Government of Canada, the Government of Ontario or a municipal government in Ontario;

(b) provides the legal services,

(i) where the law student is employed by a licensee, through the licensee's professional business,

(ii) where the law student is employed by a law firm, through the law firm,

(iii) where the law student is employed by a professional corporation described in clause 61.0.1(c) of the Act, through the professional corporation, or

(iv) where the law student is employed by the Government of Canada, the Government of Ontario or a municipal government in Ontario, only for and on behalf of the Government of Canada, the Government of Ontario or the municipal government in Ontario, respectively; and

(c) provides the legal services,

    (i) where the law student is employed by a licensee, under the direct supervision of the licensee,

    (ii) where the law student is employed by a law firm, under the direct supervision of a licensee who holds a Class L1 licence who is a part of the law firm,

    (iii) where the law student is employed by a professional corporation described in clause 61.0.1(1)(c) of the Act, under the direct supervision of a licensee who holds a Class L1 licence who practise[s] law as a barrister and solicitor through the professional corporation, or

    (iv) where the law student is employed by the Government of Canada, the Government of Ontario or a municipal government in Ontario, under the direct supervision of a licensee who holds a Class L1 licence who works for the Government of Canada, the Government of Ontario or the municipal government in Ontario, respectively.

Same

(3) A law student may, without a licence, provide legal services in Ontario that a licensee who holds a Class P1 licence is authorized to provide if the law student,

(a) is employed by a licensee who holds a Class P1 licence, a legal services firm or a professional corporation described in clause 61.0.1(1)(c) of the Act;

(b) provides the legal services,

    (i) where the law student is employed by a licensee, through the licensee's professional business,

    (ii) where the law student is employed by a legal services firm, through the legal services firm, or

    (iii) where the law student is employed by a professional corporation described in clause 61.0.1(1)(c) of the Act, through the professional corporation; and

(c) provides the legal services,

    (i) where the law student is employed by a licensee, under the direct supervision of the licensee,

    (ii) where the law student is employed by a legal services firm, under the direct supervision of a licensee who holds a Class P1 licence who is a part of the legal services firm, or

    (iii) where the law student is employed by a professional corporation described in clause 61.0.1(1)(c) of the Act, under the direct supervision of,

        (A) a licensee who holds a Class P1 licence who provides legal services through the professional corporation, or

(B) a licensee who holds a Class L1 licence who practises law as a barrister and solicitor through the professional corporation.

Interpretation: "law student"
(4) For the purposes of subsections (2) and (3), "law student" means an individual who is enrolled in a degree program at a law school in Canada that is accredited by the Society.

Paralegal student completing a field placement
34.1 A student enrolled in an accredited program and completing a field placement approved by the educational institution offering the program may, without a licence, provide legal services in Ontario that a licensee who holds a Class P1 licence is authorized to provide if the student,
  (a) is completing the field placement with a licensee who holds a Class P1 licence or a Class L1 licence, a legal services firm, a law firm, a professional corporation described in clause 61.0.1(1)(c) of the Act, the Government of Canada, the Government of Ontario or a municipal government in Ontario;
  (b) provides the legal services,
    (i) where the student is employed by a licensee, through the licensee's professional business,
    (ii) where the student is employed by a legal services firm or a law firm, through the legal services firm or the law firm,
    (iii) where the student is employed by a professional corporation described in clause 61.0.1(1)(c) of the Act, through the professional corporation, or
    (iv) where the student is employed by the Government of Canada, the Government of Ontario or a municipal government in Ontario, only for and on behalf of the Government of Canada, the Government of Ontario or the municipal government in Ontario, respectively; and
  (c) provides the legal services,
    (i) where the field placement is with a licensee, under the direct supervision of the licensee,
    (ii) where the field placement is with a legal services firm, under the direct supervision of a licensee who holds a Class P1 licence who is a part of the legal services firm,
    (iii) where the field placement is with a law firm, under the direct supervision of a licensee who holds a Class L1 licence who is a part of the law firm,
    (iv) where the field placement is with a professional corporation described in clause 61.0.1(1)(c) of the Act, under the direct supervision of,
      (A) a licensee who holds a Class P1 licence who provides legal services through the professional corporation, or
      (B) a licensee who holds a Class L1 licence who practises law as a barrister and solicitor through the professional corporation, or

(v) where the field placement is with the Government of Canada, the Government of Ontario or a municipal government in Ontario, under the direct supervision of a licensee who holds a Class L1 licence or a Class P1 licence and who works for the Government of Canada, the Government of Ontario or the municipal government in Ontario, respectively.

PART VI

PRACTISING LAW WITHOUT A LICENCE

Practising law without a licence

35. The following may, without a licence, practise law in Ontario:
  1. An individual who,
      i. is authorized under Part VII of this By-Law to practise law in Ontario, and
      ii. practises law in Ontario in accordance and in compliance with Part VII of this By-Law.
  2. An individual,
      i. who is authorized to practise law in a jurisdiction outside Ontario, and
      ii. whose practice of law in Ontario is limited to practising law as counsel to a party to a commercial arbitration that is conducted in Ontario and that is "international" within the meaning prescribed by the *International Commercial Arbitration Act*.

SMALL CLAIMS COURT JURISDICTION

When we talk about jurisdiction of a civil court, we are usually talking about the following:

- *Jurisdiction over subject matter:* On what matters, things, or issues does the court have the power to decide?
- *Monetary jurisdiction:* What are the upper and lower limits, if any, of the monetary amount that can be sued for in the court?
- *Territorial jurisdiction:* In what geographical areas is the court allowed to exercise its authority?
- *Jurisdiction to grant remedies:* What types of orders can the court make?

Jurisdiction over Subject Matter

Superior Courts have their jurisdiction determined by statutes, but they also have an inherent jurisdiction based on custom, convention, and common law. That is, Superior Courts have a broad range of powers they may exercise because they are Superior Courts and the judges in them are Superior Court judges. For example, a Superior Court is given the power to decide child custody issues by statute. But if the statute leaves a gap that results in a child's welfare being put at risk, the law recognizes that the Superior Court has an inherent power (known as *parens patrie* jurisdiction) to look after the welfare of children. This power will permit the Superior Court, despite a lack of statutory authority, to step in and make orders affecting the child. Courts like the Small Claims Court, on the other hand, have only the jurisdiction and authority given by statutes. If you cannot find the authority for one of these courts to act in a statute, then the court does not have the authority, and any order it makes would be invalid and a nullity, of no force or effect. For this reason, courts that derive all of their authority to act from statutes are called inferior courts. In the case of the Small Claims Court, its jurisdictional authority is derived primarily from the *CJA*. If you cannot find in this statute the authority for the Small Claims Court to do something, then the court has no jurisdiction to act in the matter unless authorized to do so under another statute.[18]

Monetary Jurisdiction

The Small Claims Court is a civil court that may hear actions between parties for the payment of money or for the recovery of property with a value that is within the monetary limits of the court. You will note that the *CJA* does not set out what the monetary limit is. Because that is expected to change from time to time, the limit is set by a regulation under the *CJA*, in this case, O. Reg. 626/00, which sets the maximum amount of a claim at $25,000, exclusive of interest and costs.[19] This means that you could get judgment for more than this amount, once interest and costs are added in, but that you cannot sue for an amount that exceeds this amount. Nor can you take on an action for more than $25,000 and split it into two separate lawsuits by the same plaintiff in order to come within the court's monetary jurisdiction. Rule 6.02 clearly prohibits a plaintiff from doing this:

---

[18] An example of a statute giving authority concerning the Small Claims Court is the *Parental Responsibility Act, 2000*, S.O. 2000, c. 4, s. 2(1).

[19] Regulation 626/00 has been amended by O. Reg. 439/08, raising the monetary maximum of the court to $25,000, effective January 1, 2010. Note that the court will permit claims filed before January 1, 2010 to be revised to claim up to $25,000. The change to the amount claimed can be made by serving and filing an amended plaintiff's claim or by asking the court for an order to amend the plaintiff's claim or, if the parties agree, by filing a Request for a Clerk's Order. The court can also be asked at the settlement conference for an order to change the amount claimed. There is no charge for this.

6.02 A cause of action shall not be divided into two or more actions for the purpose of bringing it within the court's jurisdiction.

The courts look to see whether the cause of action or causes of action arise from the same facts, events, or series of facts or events or transactions. If there is a common fact situation, the court will hold that the plaintiff's actions must be consolidated into one action, with the excess claim over the court's $25,000 limit being abandoned. Alternatively, the plaintiff could sue for the entire amount in one action, but it would have to move to Superior Court. However, if there are two plaintiffs with causes of action arising from the same set of facts, and if each plaintiff has a separate cause of action so that each could sue independently, then each may sue separately, even though the total claims of both would exceed $25,000.[20]

Because this is a statutory court, it can do what the *CJA* says it can do and, by implication, cannot do other things that civil courts do. So, for example, a plaintiff who wishes to sue for $26,000 cannot do it in the Small Claims Court because it is outside the court's monetary jurisdiction.

Transfer of an Action to the Small Claims Court from the Superior Court

If you sue in the Superior Court and later discover that the actual amount of the claim is within the Small Claims Court's monetary jurisdiction, s. 23 allows a transfer to the Small Claims Court from the Superior Court. If your claim in the Superior Court of Justice was commenced before January 1, 2010, and is for $25,000 or less as of January 1, 2010, the matter can be transferred to the Small Claims Court.

23.(2) An action in the Superior Court of Justice may be transferred to the Small Claims Court by the local registrar of the Superior Court of Justice on requisition with the consent of all parties filed before the trial commences if,
(a) the only claim is for the payment of money or the recovery of possession of personal property; and
(b) the claim is within the jurisdiction of the Small Claims Court.

---

[20] *KNP Headwear Inc. v. Levinson* (2005), 205 O.A.C. 291, 144 A.C.W.S. (3d) 699 (Div. Ct.); *Kent v. Conquest Vacations Co.* (2005), 194 O.A.C. 302, 136 A.C.W.S. (3d) 831 (Div. Ct.). Both cases support the proposition that a single plaintiff is prevented from dividing a cause of action when it arises from the same facts, but where two plaintiffs on the same facts have distinct and separate causes of action they may sue separately on their causes of action in the same proceeding where the amounts claimed by both plaintiffs are in excess of the court's monetary jurisdiction.

(3) An action transferred to the Small Claims Court shall be titled and continued as if it had been commenced in that court.

This means that you don't have to terminate the Superior Court action and re-start it in Small Claims Court. If the parties agree to the transfer, the following steps must be taken:

1. All parties must sign a consent to transfer the case to the Small Claims Court.
2. A Superior Court of Justice (SCJ) Form 4E, Requisition, must be completed.
3. The Form 4E, Requisition, and the written consent must be filed with the Superior Court of Justice accompanied by a $75 court fee for the transfer.

If the parties do not agree on the transfer, the following steps must be taken by the party seeking the transfer:

1. Obtain a motion hearing date from the Superior Court of Justice.

2. If the case is under the simplified procedure, complete an SCJ motion Form 76B and serve it on the other parties, then file the motion form and an Affidavit of Service with the court at least seven days before the hearing.

3. If the case is under the ordinary procedure, prepare an SCJ Form 37A, Notice of Motion, and an Affidavit. Serve the notice and affidavit of the other parties and file them along with an Affidavit of Service at least seven days before the motion date. Note that motions can also be made in writing under Rule 37.12.1.

4. File the notice of motion and affidavit with the Superior Court of Justice along with a $127 filing fee.

If you do have to terminate the Superior Court action and re-start it, there could be problems if the limitation period has expired. The defendant could argue that, technically speaking, you could not commence the proceeding in the Small Claims Court because the time for doing so had run out under the *Limitations Act, 2002*, S.O. 2002, c. 24, Sched. B.

Note, however, that the Superior Court has an unlimited monetary jurisdiction. There is no maximum amount you can sue for; neither is there a minimum. You can sue in the Superior Court for $5.00 if you wish to do so. Sometimes there is good reason to do so. If there is an important public policy issue or other important legal issue that might affect many people, and there is a need to establish a precedent, there may be merit in bringing such a proceeding to the Superior Court, despite the low monetary amount of the claim. After all, the precedent value of Small Claims Court reasons for judgment is negligible — at best, it is persuasive for other Small Claims Courts, but it is not binding on any judge in any court. However, if a Superior Court judge finds that the case should have gone to Small Claims Court, he or she can make an order denying the plaintiff any costs.[21] This could result in a loss of thousands of dollars in costs for the plaintiff. If the plaintiff obtains a default judgment in the Superior Court that is within the monetary jurisdiction of the Small Claims Court, costs shall be assessed in accordance with the tariff of the Small Claims Court.[22]

Territorial Jurisdiction

Judges in the Ontario Small Claims Court can deal only with cases where the cause of action arose in Ontario.[23] Rule 6.01 states that an action shall be commenced in the territorial division in which the cause of action arose or in which the defendant resides or carries on business or at the court nearest to where the defendant resides or carries on business. A judge has the power to hold the trial at another place where the balance of convenience favours the new location:

> 6.01(1) An action shall be commenced,
>   (a) in the territorial division,
>   (i) in which the cause of action arose, or
>   (ii) in which the defendant or, if there are several defendants, in which any one of them resides or carries on business; or
>   (b) at the court's place of sitting that is nearest to the place where the defendant or, if there are several defendants, where any one of them resides or carries on business.
>
>   (2) An action shall be tried in the place where it is commenced, but if the court is satisfied that the balance of convenience substantially favours holding the trial at another place than those described in subrule (1), the court may order that the action be tried at that other place.

Jurisdiction to Grant Remedies

The last jurisdictional matter concerns remedies that may be granted by a Small Claims Court judge. It is clear from s. 23(1) that the Small Claims Court may award monetary relief and order the recovery of

---

[21] Rule 57.05(1) of the *Rules of Civil Procedure*.

[22] Rule 57.05(3) of the *Rules of Civil Procedure*.

[23] *Xerox Canada Inc. v. Neary* (1984), 47 O.R. (2d) 776 (Prov. Ct. (Civ. Div.)).

property within its monetary limit of $25,000 or less, excluding interest and costs:

> **23.**(1) The Small Claims Court,
> (a) has jurisdiction in any action for the payment of money where the amount claimed does not exceed the prescribed amount exclusive of interest and costs; and
> (b) has jurisdiction in any action for the recovery of possession of personal property where the value of the property does not exceed the prescribed amount.

Other issues about jurisdiction are less clear. While principles of equity can be applied in Small Claims Courts, it was generally thought that equitable remedies were not available. But in some recent small claims appeal cases heard in the Divisional Court, it has been held that so long as the initial claim appears to be within the jurisdiction, the application of equitable principles and remedies to give effect to a judgment within the court's jurisdiction is permissible. In practical terms, this means that if your pleadings show a claim that is within the court's jurisdiction, equitable principles may be used to support the claim (or defence), and in some cases equitable remedies that will enforce a within-jurisdiction claim may be used. For example, although trust law, the area of law dealing with property held by one person for the benefit of another person, is based on equitable principles, a Small Claims Court has jurisdiction to hear such claims if the original claim was within the monetary jurisdiction of the court.[24] Another case states that the Small Claims Court is entitled to grant equitable remedies to give effect to a monetary judgment within the court's jurisdiction. In this case, where the claim was for a breach of contract, the court awarded judgment on a *quantum meruit* basis (where a formal contract with all its elements was not established, but where there was a quasi-contractual debt established). Without the equitable remedy or device of *quantum meruit*, the plaintiff's action would have been dismissed.[25] Mr. Justice Osborne recommended in his report that Small Claims Court deputy judges be permitted to grant equitable relief.[26]

How far one can go in applying these appellate rulings is not entirely clear. Because they are provincially appointed, the Small Claims Court judges are not Superior Court judges with power to make orders

---

[24] *Brighton Heating & Air Conditioning Ltd. v. Savoia* (2006), 79 O.R. (3d) 386, 207 O.A.C. 1 (Sup. Ct. J. (Div. Ct.)).

[25] *936464 Ontario Ltd. v. Mungo Bear Ltd.* (2003), 258 D.L.R. (4th) 754, 74 O.R. (3d) 45 (Sup. Ct. J. (Div. Ct.)).

[26] The *Osborne Report, supra* note 4, p. 3.

in both law and equity.[27] While it appears that Small Claims Court judges can call on the law of equity in limited circumstances as a tool to make an order that is within their jurisdiction, they cannot use the law of equity independently. For example, they can order damages for breach of contract, but they cannot use the equitable remedy of specific performance to require a party to actually perform the contract. On the other hand, a Superior Court judge sitting as a Small Claims Court judge may have the full range of equitable relief available in a Small Claims Court under s. 96(3), which gives a Superior Court judge the power to grant equitable relief. In the future, the Ontario government may act upon Mr. Justice Osborne's recommendation to give deputy judges the power to grant equitable relief.

Making the Small Claims Court part of the Superior Court broadened the jurisdiction over subject matter. So long as the court operates within its monetary jurisdiction, it is possible to sue the federal Crown or maintain an action in admiralty (involving issues such as ship collisions arising on navigable waterways). Formerly these kinds of actions were outside the Small Claims Court's jurisdiction.

The Small Claims Court has been granted authority under some statutes to make orders other than the payment of money or the return of property. For example, under section 55(10) of the Ontario *Condominium Act, 1998*, S.O. 1998, c. 19, authority is given to the Small Claims Court to make an order that the condominium produce records.

An Overview of the Small Claims Court Process: A Tale of Love Derailed

In this section, using a hypothetical fact situation, we will see how the court process actually works.[28] This will provide both an overview and a context to understand and appreciate how the court's procedural rules work when we consider them in more detail. The steps in a Small Claims Court action are illustrated in Figure 1.2.

The Sad Tale of Albert Oryx

Albert Oryx and Ophelia Foot became engaged last year, pledging eternal love to each other. Albert bought Ophelia an engagement ring, which cost him $2,000. Recently, Ophelia announced to Albert that the engagement was off as she had fallen out of love with Albert and

---

[27] *Courts of Justice Act*, s. 96(3).

[28] The hypothetical situation provided is for procedural purposes only. No representation is made as to the success of such a claim. In all cases, the parties, prior to making a claim, should review applicable federal and provincial legislation and relevant case law.

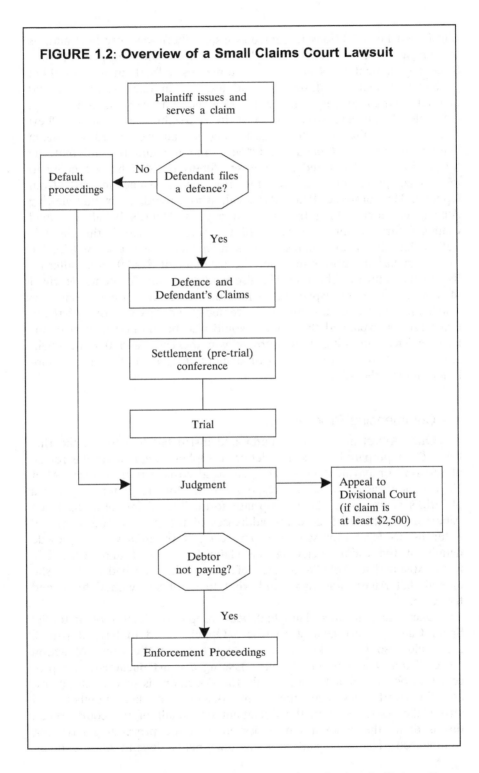

FIGURE 1.2: Overview of a Small Claims Court Lawsuit

transferred her affections to someone else. Albert was very hurt and, as the engagement was off, asked her to return the engagement ring. Since engagement rings are not like tomatoes, Albert knew it wouldn't go bad and could be dusted off and used again later when he found another woman to get engaged to. Ophelia, however, liked the ring, and told Albert she would keep it in remembrance of him. Albert responded that that was the tackiest thing he had ever heard, and again demanded the ring. Ophelia said "No", and it could be said that the former lovers had reached an impasse. Albert decided he was going to take legal proceedings to get the ring or its value in cash from Ophelia. He consulted Peter Paralegal, who agreed, after interviewing Albert, and ascertaining the facts, to act on Albert's behalf in Small Claims Court. Because the value of the ring was $2,000, the claim is well within the Small Claims Court's monetary jurisdiction of $25,000. The court has the power to order the payment of $2,000 as an alternative to the return of the ring. He also wanted to sue for being deprived of a wife, but Peter explained to him that there are some wrongs for which the court does not provide a remedy, and this was one of them. Peter further explained that Albert would also be entitled to part of his legal expenses in suing if he were to win the case, and that he might also be entitled to pre- and post-judgment interest at the rates established under the *CJA*.

Commencing Proceedings

Once Albert had retained Peter and instructed him to get the ring back, Peter prepared and sent a letter to Ophelia demanding the return of the ring or payment of $2,000 plus legal costs within 10 days. After 10 days had passed without a response from Ophelia, Peter prepared a plaintiff's claim, using the appropriate form. The claim form identified Albert as the plaintiff, gave the addresses of the parties, and identified Peter as his legal representative. The claim form asks you to provide details of the claim, including the claim for interest and costs. The form explained to Ophelia, as the defendant, what she had to do if she agreed that Albert was right, and what to do if she wished to defend the case.

Once the plaintiff's claim had been prepared, Peter took it to the Small Claims Court nearest to where Ophelia lived to have it issued. He could also have taken it to the court where the cause of action arose, if that was a different court. **Issuing a court document** is a process that occurs when the fee to file the document is paid to the court, and the court clerk signs the claim, assigns it a claim number, and affixes the court's seal to the document on behalf of the court. When this is done, the claim has been issued, and the proceeding has been commenced. The fees paid to issue documents depend on the document and, in the case of a plaintiff's claim, the fee varies depending on how many claims the plaintiff has filed in that court since January 1 of that year. The fees are listed in a schedule of court fees and allowances that is available on the Attorney General's website (see the Bibliography section at the end of this book for this information). In this case, if Albert had not filed more than 10 claims since January 1, the fee would have been $75.00. If, however, he had sued in that court more than 10 times since January, he would be considered a "frequent claimant" and would have to pay $145.00. There is a fee waiver program in place for individuals who are acting on their own and finding it difficult to pay a fee.[29]

Serving the Plaintiff's Claim

After the claim was issued, Peter made copies of it. He gave a copy of the claim to a private process server, who personally served a copy of the claim on Ophelia. Note that documents can be served on any day of the week.

The process server swore an affidavit of service to prove to the court that Ophelia was properly served and had notice of the proceeding.

The rules of procedure also allow for documents to be served by alternatives to personal service such as sending the document by courier or registered mail if the recipient verifies receipt of the document by his or her signature. If service had proven to be difficult or impractical, or if Ophelia had evaded service, Peter could have brought a **motion** for an order for substitutional service, allowing him to serve Ophelia by any means that the court permits. To do this, Peter would have prepared a **notice of motion** and supporting affidavit, setting out the procedural issue and the reasons why the order he requested should be made. He would also set out the facts and evidence he relied on to support the request.

Defending a Claim

After Ophelia had been served with the plaintiff's claim, she had some choices: she could have admitted that Albert was right and returned the ring, or paid the monetary claim if there was one. If she had opted to pay, but could not pay all at once, she could have asked the court to let her pay by instalments. If she had a defence, she could have filed a defence setting out the facts upon which she had

---

[29] Financial guidelines for the fee waiver program are found in O. Reg. 2/05, as am. by O. Reg 671/05 made under the *Administration of Justice Act*, R.S.O. 1990, c. A.6.

relied, or she could have hired a legal representative to prepare and
file a defence for her. If a defence is filed with the court, the court
will send a copy to the plaintiff or the plaintiff's legal representative. A
defendant generally has 20 days from the time she is served with the
claim to file her defence. If she does not do so in time, the plaintiff
has the right to bring a motion for **default judgment**. At this point, she
is deemed to have admitted liability, and the only issue is to determine
the damages and the amount, including costs and interest, that she
must pay. However, if she has a good reason why she could not file a
defence within the 20 days provided by the Rules (for example, she
was in hospital and unable to prepare a defence), she can bring a
motion to the court to set the default judgment aside, with leave, or
permission, to defend against Albert's claim.

Defendant's Claims: Counterclaims, Crossclaims, and Third Party Claims

In addition to defending against Albert's claim, Ophelia could have
made her own claim against Albert if she had one. If, for example, she
had loaned him the money to buy the engagement ring and he had
never repaid her, she would have had a **counterclaim**. Along with her
defence, she would have filed a defendant's claim setting out her counterclaim against Albert. Albert would then have had to file a defence
to the defendant's claim. At trial a judge hears and decides both claims
in the same proceeding.

Although unlikely in Ophelia's case, she could have used a defendant's claim to bring others into Albert's lawsuit who she thought were
responsible for either Albert's loss or her own, if she had sustained a
loss. For example, if she thought someone other than her had caused
Albert's damages, and he had not sued that person, she could have
made a **third party claim** against that person, saying the third party,
not her, was responsible for the loss. If Albert had also sued another
defendant in addition to Ophelia and if Ophelia had her own claim
against that defendant or claimed that he or she was totally responsible,
she could have made a **crossclaim** against that defendant.

Case Management — Control of the Progress of the Case by the Court

If Albert filed a claim, and Ophelia did not defend, and Albert did
not move for default judgment within 180 days of the commencement
of his claim, a court clerk would give 45 days notice to Albert that the
case would be dismissed as abandoned if he did not take steps to proceed. The same thing would happen if Ophelia filed a defence and
nothing further happened for 150 days afterwards. The purpose of this

rule is to give the court some control over case management to ensure that the volume of cases heading for trial is both predictable and steady, allowing for efficient use of court resources to try cases.

Settlement Conferences

Where an action is defended, the court clerk shall set up a settlement conference within 90 days of the first defence being filed. Most settlement conferences are conducted in person; however, the Rules permit a conference by video or phone.[30] The purpose of a settlement conference in Albert's case would be to bring Albert and Ophelia and their representatives together to see if a settlement could be worked out prior to trial. It is important to note that most cases settle before trial; and by requiring settlement discussions, the court can further reduce the number of cases going to trial, saving both parties and the courts unnecessary expense and leaving the courts available for those who really do require their cases to be heard. Even if Albert and Ophelia were unable to reach a settlement, the conference could be used to narrow the issues, determine what evidence will be used, and resolve other procedural matters. This would result in a more efficient use of everyone's time, reducing cost and delay for the parties and the courts. Offers to settle do not have to wait for a settlement conference, however; they can be made at any time. To make sure they are carefully considered, the Rules permit offers to be made before trial, where there may be cost penalties for those who refuse to accept what turns out to be a good offer. In this case, if an offer were to be made, in the time permitted by the Rules,[31] but not accepted, at the end of the trial the judge would look at the offer and compare it to the actual judgment. In general, if a defendant's offer is as good as or better than the judgment or if a plaintiff's offer is as good as or less than the judgment, there may be cost penalties for the party who refused what turned out to be a good offer. Either the plaintiff or defendant may make an offer to settle.

Notice of Trial

Once a settlement conference has been held, the court clerk will send out a notice to all parties stating that if the action is not disposed of within 30 days after the settlement conference, one of the parties

---

[30] Rule 1.07(11).

[31] Rule 14.07 stipulates that offers to settle made seven or more days before trial will be considered when costs are set.

must request a trial date. Either Albert or Ophelia could also request a date for trial and require a notice of trial to be issued.

Trial

Albert and Ophelia and their legal representatives are expected to attend trial on the appointed date. If they have witnesses, they are expected to issue summonses to have those witnesses attend court.

The strict rules of evidence used in the Superior Court are relaxed somewhat in the Small Claims Court so that it is often easier, faster, and cheaper to present a case in Small Claims Courts. Witness statements, if properly served and if there are no objections, may be used as evidence in court instead of calling the witness to give oral evidence. In our example, Albert might have considered filing a statement from a jeweller to establish the value of the ring. He would have had to serve the defendant with the statement at least 30 days prior to trial.[32]

The court may also decide to admit documents in evidence that normally would not be admitted because they were not properly served. In fact, the judge has very broad powers to admit evidence, including evidence that would be hearsay and inadmissible in the Superior Court.[33]

The trial, in other respects, looks like a Superior Court trial. in our example, Peter, the plaintiff's legal representative, might have made an opening statement,[34] and then called and questioned his witnesses (or filed their witness statements). Ophelia, or her legal representative if she had one, could have then cross-examined those witnesses. After all of Albert's evidence had been heard, Ophelia could have made an opening statement and called her witnesses to present the defence version of the case. Peter could have then cross-examined her witnesses. At the end, each party could have made a closing summary statement. The judge would have then decided the case, noting his or her judgment on an endorsement record. If Albert failed to prove his case, it would have been dismissed. If, however, he did prove his case, he would have obtained a judgment permitting him to recover the ring from Ophelia, or alternatively, a judgment for the payment by Ophelia

---

[32] Rule 18.02(1).

[33] *CJA*, s. 27.

[34] Some judges in Small Claims Court, particularly if unrepresented parties are involved, bypass opening statements and ask the plaintiff to simply call their first witness. An unrepresented party may be unaware of the nature of an opening statement and simply use the opportunity to start relating their entire case to the court without yet having been sworn in. In some cases if both parties are represented, a judge may permit both to make opening statements at the beginning of the case.

of damages for the monetary value of the ring. If the judgment was for the payment of money, then Albert would have also likely been awarded pre-judgment and post-judgment interest on the amount of the judgment. He would have also been awarded costs.

Costs

A successful party, whether it was Albert or Ophelia, would have likely recovered all reasonable **disbursements** from the unsuccessful party. These are actual amounts paid by the successful party to serve documents (limited to $60.00),[35] summon witnesses, obtain experts' reports, and make photocopies, provided those payments were reasonable in the circumstances. The successful party can also recover all fees paid to the court and may recover a $100.00 fee for preparing and filing **pleadings**.[36] If a party has a legal representative, he or she is entitled to a representation fee that is capped at up to 15% of the monetary claim, or the value of the property to be recovered. Costs may be awarded at trial or at an assessment hearing.[37]

Enforcement of Judgments

Assuming Albert was successful, and obtained a judgment to recover the ring or the value of it from Ophelia, it would not mean that the ring was returned or the payment made the next day. A judgment is an order from the court, but until steps are taken to enforce it, it is merely words on paper. If Ophelia did not return the ring, Peter, the paralegal, on Albert's behalf, could obtain a **writ of delivery** authorizing the Small Claims Court bailiff, the court's officer for enforcing most orders and judgments of the court, to go and seize the ring from Ophelia. If she did not produce it, Albert could have, on a motion, obtained a further order directing the bailiff to seize other property belonging to Ophelia of equivalent value, and hold it "hostage" until the ring was returned.[38] If Albert obtained a judgment for the payment of money, he would have been entitled to **garnish** any sum that would otherwise be owing to Ophelia, compelling the garnishee (the person who owes money to Ophelia) to pay the money to the court for Albert's benefit. Albert would have required a **notice of garnishment** from the court. Usually, the garnishee is the

---

[35] Rule 19.01(3).

[36] Rule 19.01(4).

[37] While Rule 19 of the *Rules of the Small Claims Court* sets out the costs that may be awarded, s. 29 of the *CJA* limits costs to be awarded in Small Claims Court.

[38] Rule 20.05(2).

judgment-debtor's employer. If more than one notice of garnishment had been filed, the court would have distributed payment equally among creditors who had filed a garnishment in that territorial court division.[39] Albert might have also directed the bailiff to seize Ophelia's personal property, using a **writ of seizure and sale** of personal property. The seized property could then have been sold, with the after-sale profit paid to Albert, although it might have had to be shared with other creditors who had filed writs of seizure and sale against Ophelia. If Ophelia owned an interest in land, Albert might also have asked the sheriff of the county or region where the land was located to seize and sell the interest in land (the sheriff is the enforcement officer of the Superior Court).[40] A writ of seizure and sale of land could have been filed even if Ophelia did not have any real estate. If she owns property, the writ in such cases would have to be paid off if she sought a mortgage or refinancing. If she does not own property at the time the writ is filed but she subsequently applies for mortgage financing to purchase real estate, she will have to pay the judgment in order to have the writ removed and financing approved. Lastly, if Albert did not know what assets Ophelia had that would satisfy the judgment, he might have asked the court to hold an examination in aid of execution, sometimes called a judgment debtor examination, where he and the court could have questioned Ophelia on her means, assets, and expenses with a view to finding assets to satisfy the judgment.[41]

Where a judgment debtor has two or more judgments against him or her, and has difficulty paying them, the court may make a **consolidation order** so that the judgment debtor can make a single payment to the court, to be distributed amongst judgment creditors.[42] The court can also order payment by instalments in some circumstances.[43]

Appeals and Motions for a New Trial

If the loser thinks the trial judge made a serious error in law or fact, he or she can appeal to the Divisional Court of the Superior Court provided the judgment in the Small Claims Court was for the payment of money or the recovery of property worth more than $2,500

---

[39] Rule 20.08(10).

[40] Rule 20.07(1).

[41] Rule 20.10(1).

[42] Rule 20.09(1).

[43] Rule 20.02(1)(b).

excluding costs.[44] Because the costs of an appeal are high, compared to the amounts being sued for, appeals are very rare.

A motion for a new trial may be granted if an error was made in the judgment due to a mathematical mistake in determining the amount of damages, or if there is relevant evidence found after trial and that evidence could not reasonably have been expected to be available at the time of the original trial.[45]

CHAPTER SUMMARY

In this chapter we looked at the historical origins of the Small Claims Court. The progress of the court as a branch of various courts in Ontario to its present position as a branch of the Superior Court of Justice was then examined.

The various judges permitted to hear matters in the court, particularly the deputy judges, were described. The summary hearing process used in the court was explained. We then looked at who can represent someone in the Small Claims Court.

We then looked at the jurisdiction of the court as it pertains to subject matter, monetary value, territorial area, and types of remedies.

At the end of the chapter, we used a hypothetical fact situation to give an overview of how the Small Claims Court process actually works.

---

[44] Section 31 of the *CJA*.

[45] Rule 17.04(5).

REVIEW QUESTIONS

1. Doofus Tinamou wants to sue in Small Claims Court. He thinks it will cost nothing and that he can do it in a week. Briefly describe to Doofus what is involved, what costs might be involved, and whether it will take a week.

2. Explain the position of the Small Claims Court in Ontario's present court system.

3. What kinds of cases can the Small Claims Court decide?

4. Describe the types of judges that can sit in the Small Claims Court.

5. Explain who can represent a party in the Small Claims Court.

6. What amount can you sue for in the Small Claims Court?

7. Where do you commence your Small Claims Court case?

8. Tell Doofus what a counterclaim, a crossclaim, and a third party claim are.

9. Can Doofus file documents, including copies, as evidence in Small Claims Court?

10. Can Doofus give hearsay evidence in Small Claims Court?

11. If Doofus sues for $10,000, what is likely the most he can expect to get for a representation fee if he is represented by a lawyer? A paralegal?

12. If Doofus wins his case, and the defendant refuses to pay, what can Doofus do to collect what is owing to him?

13. Does a judge have the power to waive or adjust the Rules?

14. If Doofus loses, does he have an automatic right of appeal to the Court of Appeal?

DISCUSSION QUESTIONS/CASE STUDIES

1. Dolores Henry is an avid hunter of big and small game. She is also a paralegal. She was out in the woods in Algonquin Park. She saw a snark and took a shot at it. To her knowledge no licence was required to shoot a snark, but in any case she missed and the snark bounded off into the woods, unharmed. However, she was observed by a federal wildlife officer, who apprehended her and charged her with attempting to shoot a rare and protected species. In fact, the snark was not on the list of protected species, and Dolores told him so. He said, "I couldn't care less; you're the type that shoots at everything, and the sooner you are behind bars the better". In fact, Dolores is careful about observing hunting regulations. Further, if it was a hunting offence, she

was of the view that only a provincial official under the *Game and Fish Act* had authority to charge her with a hunting offence, not a federal officer. The charge was thrown out of court, as Dolores knew it would be, and the judge had some things to say about federal officials who need to investigate properly and not just make assumptions about people without evidence.

Dolores had been put to a lot of time and trouble and, given the judge's comments, formed the idea that she had been maliciously prosecuted, there having been no reasonable basis to charge her. Also her picture was in the paper, and she was described by the federal official in an accompanying article as a bloodthirsty menace to animal life. She was hurt by this and subjected to ridicule and nasty remarks from all sorts of people. She wants to sue the wildlife officer and the federal government in Small Claims Court.

Discuss the following:

(a) Can Dolores sue the federal Crown, which is responsible for the acts of its employees?

(b) Can Dolores sue for defamation and demand an order for an apology from the federal official?

(c) Can Dolores raise the issue of the federal *Endangered Species Act* being *ultra vires* (beyond the powers of the federal government) insofar as it applies to hunting offences of animals not listed under the Act?

(d) Can Dolores obtain an injunction in Small Claims Court to prevent the federal official coming within 100 metres of her house?

(e) Can Dolores serve her claim on the defendant on any day she feels like, including Christmas Day?

(f) Suppose that the limitation period for suing a federal official ran out before Dolores issued her claim — can she have her claim revived under the *Rules of the Small Claims Court*?

2. Rule 7 requires that the plaintiff set out all claims clearly in the plaintiff's claim. The plaintiff claimed interest under a contract but did not claim pre- and post-judgment interest under the *Courts of Justice Act* in the claim. At trial, the plaintiff did not succeed in proving he was owed interest under the contract. If at trial the defendant argues that the plaintiff should not get post-judgment interest under the *CJA* because he didn't claim it, what rules can the plaintiff use to argue that he should get post-judgment interest despite the technical failure to plead it in his claim?

Chapter 2

The Small Claims Court Client and the Client File

LEARNING OBJECTIVES

⇨ Know how to formalize the contractual relationship with the client

⇨ Understand the importance of effective interview techniques

⇨ Understand and be able to use various interview techniques

⇨ Appreciate the need to manage the advocate–client relationship

⇨ Know how to establish with the client a communications protocol to keep the client informed of the progress of the case

⇨ Know how to acquire and manage case documents, generally

⇨ Know how to set up a litigation file

⇨ Know how to handle closed files

⇨ Appreciate the importance of limitation periods

⇨ Know how to set up a tickler or reminder system

⇨ Understand and be able to effectively use various reminder systems to keep track of notice and limitation periods

INTRODUCTION

In the preceding chapter you acquired an overview of the Small Claims Court. In this chapter you will look at how to formalize the contractual relationship with your client. You will be introduced to concepts and techniques involved in gathering information from clients, including interview techniques, and acquiring and managing client documents. You will also be introduced to key litigation administration systems, particularly those concerned with the observation of deadlines and the establishment of a positive contractual and working relationship with the client.

COMPETENCY TO ACT

There are a number of matters to consider when someone retains you to represent them on a Small Claims Court matter. You should ensure that you do not undertake work that you lack the competence to complete. You should only take on matters that you are competent to handle. If, for example, you never studied tort law and are unfamiliar with personal injury law, you should not take on a personal injury case on your own. Rule 3.01 of the Paralegal Rules sets out the duty of competence owed to clients. If you lack the competence for the task, you must decline to act or obtain the client's consent to transfer the file to someone competent to perform the task.

Required Standard

3.01(1) A paralegal shall perform any services undertaken on a client's behalf to the standard of a competent paralegal.

(2) A paralegal shall be alert to recognize any lack of competence for a particular task and the disservice that would be done to the client by undertaking that task and shall not undertake a matter without being competent to handle it or being able to become competent without undue delay or expense to the client.

(3) If a paralegal discovers that he or she lacks the competence to complete the task for which he or she has been retained, the paralegal shall either decline to act or obtain the client's consent to retain, consult or collaborate with another licensee who is competent and licensed to perform that task.

Who is Competent

(4) For the purposes of this rule, a competent paralegal is one who has and applies the relevant skills, attributes, and values appropriate to each matter undertaken on behalf of a client including,

(a) knowing general legal principles and procedures and the substantive law and procedures for the legal services that the paralegal provides;

(b) investigating facts, identifying issues, ascertaining client objectives, considering possible options, and developing and advising clients on appropriate courses of action;

(c) implementing, as each matter requires, the chosen course of action through the application of appropriate skills, including,

(i) legal research,
(ii) analysis,
(iii) application of the law to the relevant facts,
(iv) writing and drafting,
(v) negotiation,
(vi) alternative dispute resolution,
(vii) advocacy, and
(viii) problem-solving ability;

(d) representing the client in a conscientious, diligent, and cost-effective manner;

(e) communicating with the client at all stages of a matter in a timely and effective manner that is appropriate to the age and abilities of the client and engaging the services of an interpreter when necessary;

(f) answering reasonable client requests in a timely and effective manner;

(g) ensuring that all applicable deadlines are met;

(h) managing one's practice effectively;

(i) applying intellectual capacity, judgment, and deliberation to all functions;

(j) pursuing appropriate training and development to maintain and enhance knowledge and skills;

(k) adapting to changing requirements, standards, techniques and practices; and

(l) complying in letter and in spirit with these Rules.

(**THE PARALEGAL RULES**)

INITIAL CONSULTATIONS

Many lawyers and paralegals provide prospective clients with a free consultation. If someone comes in for a consultation and does not retain you, it is wise to write a letter to that person, stating that you provided a free consultation during which no legal advice was provided and only general information was given. Confirm that you have not been retained. You can remind the person that they can in the future retain you if they wish to do so. Mail the letter to the person and keep a copy in a file for yourself. You will not be able to bill anyone for this letter, but if someone tries to sue you or complain to the Law Society about "advice" given at and relied on from a free consultation, you will have a letter stating that no such information was provided at the time (see Figure 2.1).

FIGURE 2.1: Letter Confirming Legal Advice Not Given and Firm Not Retained Following a Free Consultation

PARALEGAL SERVICES
200 — 4392 NORTH STREET
TORONTO, ON M64 2P1
Tel. 416-123-4567 Fax 416-123-8910
paralegalservices@email.com

August 18, Yr. 0

Watta Boar
123 Evergreen Drive
Smalltown, ON K3T 2P4

Dear Ms. Boar:

Re: Consultation of August 18, Yr 0

I confirm that you attended our office today for a free consultation. During the course of the consultation, we provided you with general background information but we did not provide you with legal advice. As you did not retain us, please be advised that you are not my client, nor are you a client of Paralegal Services.

Should you wish to retain our firm to act for you, please phone our office. We would be happy to assist you.

Yours very truly,
PARALEGAL SERVICES

M. Bolsomova

Maurizio Bolsomova

FORMALIZING THE CONTRACTUAL RELATIONSHIP WITH THE CLIENT

If a client does retain you, a written retainer agreement should always be executed. In the event of a dispute over fees or scope of services, having the written retainer to fall back on is essential. A paralegal may have many clients but a client generally has only one paralegal, so judges and assessment officers (in fee disputes) are more likely to believe the client's recollection over that of the paralegal unless there was a written retainer agreement.

Retainer Agreements

Once you have met with the client and it has been agreed that you will do the work, formalize the contractual relationship by having the client sign a **retainer** (Figure 2.2). The retainer will note that there is a contract in which you represent the client in the Small Claims Court. It will also describe the matter for which you have been retained, and describe what you are to do. It should also go on to describe the basis on which fees are to be paid: this could be an hourly rate, a flat fee, or a contingency fee, where you are paid a percentage of the amount recovered from the defendant. Practices vary, but note that as the regulations for licensed paralegals are interpreted, some billing practices may be controlled or prohibited. If the client is a corporation (particularly in the case of a one-person corporation), the retainer agreement can include a personal guarantee signed by a director of the corporation. In the event of non-payment by the corporation, a payment demand can be made against the personal guarantor. Rule 5.01 of the Paralegal Rules sets out the conditions concerning fees and retainers, including contingency fees and referral fees:

> ### Reasonable Fees and Disbursements
> 5.01(1) A paralegal shall not charge or accept any amount for a fee or disbursement unless it is fair and reasonable and has been disclosed in a timely fashion.
>
> (2) What is a fair and reasonable fee will depend upon such factors as,
> (a) the time and effort required and spent;
> (b) the difficulty and importance of the matter;
> (c) whether special skill or service was required and provided;
> (d) the amount involved or the value of the subject matter;
> (e) the results obtained;
> (f) fees authorized by statute or regulation; and
> (g) special circumstances, such as the loss of other retainers, postponement of payment, uncertainty of reward, or urgency.
>
> (3) No fee, reward, costs, commission, interest, rebate, agency or forwarding allowance, or other compensation related to his or her employment may be taken by the paralegal from anyone other than the client, without full disclosure to, and the consent of, the client.
>
> (4) In a statement of account delivered to the client, a paralegal shall clearly and separately detail amounts charged as fees and as disbursements.
>
> (5) A paralegal shall not appropriate any funds of the client held in trust, or otherwise under the paralegal's control, for or on account of fees, except as permitted by the by-laws under the *Law Society Act*.

FIGURE 2.2: Retainer

CONTRACT OF RETAINER
BETWEEN
CARL CLIENT
AND
PARALEGAL SERVICES

1. I, Carl Client, retain you, Paralegal Services, as my representative to collect the money due and owing to me from Daniel Debtor on a loan agreement dated January 10, Yr. 0. I authorize Paralegal Services to send a demand letter and, if it does not produce payment, to commence proceedings in the Small Claims Court. If there is a settlement of the case at any time it is to be only on instructions in writing from me to do so.

2. I understand that paralegals and other staff of the firm may work on my case. I further understand that the paralegals at Paralegal Services are licensed by the Law Society of Upper Canada but are not lawyers and could not represent me on an appeal.

3. I agree to pay a deposit of $500 to Paralegal Services, in trust at the time of signing this retainer agreement. I understand that accounts rendered for legal fees and disbursements will be paid from this and future deposits. I agree to pay further deposits as may be required and demanded from time to time. I understand that no work will be done until a requested deposit has been paid.

4. I understand that I will be billed for time spent on this case by Paralegal Services and for all disbursements related to this matter. The paralegal's present hourly fee is $75. HST is payable on all fees and on some disbursements. I will be given 30 days advance notice of any fee changes, and after that time such changes shall be applied to my account.

5. Payment is due when accounts are rendered. If any account is not paid within 30 days, interest will be charged on the outstanding balance at the rate permitted by the Law Society of Upper Canada.

6. In the event of settlement, I agree that settlement funds shall be paid to Paralegal Services in trust and that they may deduct any outstanding fees, HST, and disbursements when an account is rendered for services. The funds in trust shall then first be applied to any outstanding accounts.

7. I understand that it is my obligation, upon receiving advice and being asked to provide instructions, to provide Paralegal Services with instructions as requested.

continues....

Figure 2.2 (continued)

8. By my signature below I authorize Paralegal Services or their delegate to search my credit bureau record now or in the future for the purposes of collecting information for any lawsuits brought on my behalf or against me and for enforcement of any debts or judgments against me. I understand that Paralegal Services will protect my personal information and will only use it for the aforementioned purposes. If I require any further information about the use of my personal information, I agree to contact Peter Paralegal.

May 1, Yr. 0

Signed: _____
Carl Client

Signed: _____
Peter Paralegal

Contingency Fees

(6) Except in quasi-criminal or criminal matters, a paralegal may enter into a written agreement that provides that the paralegal's fee is contingent, in whole or in part, on the successful disposition or completion of the matter for which the paralegal's services are to be provided.

(7) In determining the appropriate percentage or other basis of a contingency fee under subrule (6), the paralegal shall advise the client on the factors that are being taken into account in determining the percentage or other basis, including the likelihood of success, the nature and complexity of the claim, the expense and risk of pursuing it, the amount of the expected recovery, who is to receive an award of costs and the amount of costs awarded.

(8) The percentage or other basis of a contingency fee agreed upon under subrule (6) shall be fair and reasonable, taking into consideration all of the circumstances and the factors listed in subrule (7).

Joint Retainers

(9) If a paralegal is acting for two or more clients, the paralegal shall divide the fees and disbursements equitably between them, unless there is an agreement by the clients otherwise.

Division of Fees

(10) Fees for a matter may be divided between licensees who are not in the same firm if the client consents and the fees are divided in proportion to the work done and the responsibilities assumed.

Fee Splitting
(11) A paralegal shall not,
(a) directly or indirectly share, split, or divide his or her fees with any person who is not a licensee, including an affiliated entity; or
(b) give any financial or other reward to any person who is not a licensee, including an affiliated entity for the referral of clients or client matters.

(12) Subrule (11) does not apply to multi-discipline practices of paralegal and non-licensee partners where the partnership agreement provides for the sharing of fees, cash flows or profits among members of the firm.

Referral Fees
(13) A paralegal who refers a matter to another licensee because of the expertise and ability of the other licensee to handle the matter may accept, and the other licensee may pay, a referral fee if,
(a) the referral was not made because of a conflict of interest,
(b) the fee is reasonable and does not increase the total amount of the fee charged to the client; and
(c) the client is informed and consents. (**THE PARALEGAL RULES**)

Financial Retainers

If the client provides a financial retainer as a deposit for services to be carried out, By-law 9 from the Law Society of Upper Canada must be adhered to in respect of the handling of such a deposit. In general, such funds must first be paid into the firm's trust account. Note that under the by-law, a paralegal cannot, subject to a couple of exceptions, accept more than $7,500 in cash from a client.

BY-LAW 9 — FINANCIAL TRANSACTIONS AND RECORDS (EXCERPTS)
(MADE UNDER THE *LAW SOCIETY ACT*, current as of July 17, 2013)
...

PART III
CASH TRANSACTIONS

Definition
3. In this Part,

"funds" means cash, currency, securities and negotiable instruments or other financial instruments that indicate the person's title or interest in them;

"public body" means,
(a) a department or agent of Her Majesty in right of Canada or of a province;

(b) an incorporated city, metropolitan authority, town, township, village, county, district, rural municipality or other incorporated municipal body or an agent of any of them; and

(c) an organization that operates a public hospital and that is designated by the Minister of National Revenue as a hospital under the *Excise Tax Act* (Canada) or agent of the organization.

Cash received

4.(1) A licensee shall not receive or accept from a person, in respect of any one client file, cash in an aggregate amount of 7,500 or more Canadian dollars.

...

Exceptions

6. Despite section 5, section 4 does not apply when the licensee,

(a) receives cash from a public body, an authorized foreign bank within the meaning of section 2 of the *Bank Act* (Canada) in respect of its business in Canada or a bank to which the *Bank Act* (Canada) applies, a cooperative credit society, savings and credit union or caisse populaire that is regulated by a provincial Act, an association that is regulated by the *Cooperative Credit Associations Act* (Canada), a company to which the *Trust and Loan Companies Act* (Canada) applies, a trust company or loan company regulated by a provincial Act or a department or agent of Her Majesty in right of Canada or of a province where the department or agent accepts deposit liabilities in the course of providing financial services to the public;

(b) receives cash from a peace officer, law enforcement agency or other agent of the Crown acting in an official capacity;

(c) receives cash pursuant to an order of a tribunal;

(d) receives cash to pay a fine or penalty; or

(e) receives cash for fees, disbursements, expenses or bail provided that any refund out of such receipts is also made in cash.

PART IV
TRUST ACCOUNT
TRUST ACCOUNT TRANSACTIONS

Money received in trust for client

7.(1) Subject to section 8, every licensee who receives money in trust for a client shall immediately pay the money into an account at a chartered bank, provincial savings office, credit union or a league to which the *Credit Unions and Caisses Populaires Act, 1994* applies or registered trust corporation, to be kept in the name of the licensee, or in the name of the firm of licensees of which the licensee is a partner, through which the licensee practises law or provides legal services or by which the licensee is employed, and designated as a trust account.

Interpretation

(2) For the purposes of subsection (1), a licensee receives money in trust for a client if the licensee receives from a person,

(a) money that belongs in whole or in part to a client;

(b) money that is to be held on behalf of a client;

(c) money that is to be held on a client's direction or order;

(d) money that is advanced to the licensee on account of fees for services not yet rendered; or

(e) money that is advanced to the licensee on account of disbursements not yet made.

...

Withdrawal of money from trust account

(4) A licensee who pays into a trust account money described in paragraph 2 of subsection (3) shall as soon as practical withdraw from the trust account the amount of the money that belongs to him or her.

One or more trust accounts

(5) A licensee may keep one or more trust accounts.

Money not to be paid into trust account

8.(1) A licensee is not required to pay into a trust account money which he or she receives in trust for a client if,

(a) the client requests the licensee in writing not to pay the money into a trust account;

(b) the licensee pays the money into an account to be kept in the name of the client, a person named by the client or an agent of the client; or

(c) the licensee pays the money immediately upon receiving it to the client or to a person on behalf of the client in accordance with ordinary business practices.

Same

(2) A licensee shall not pay into a trust account the following money:

1. Money that belongs entirely to the licensee or to another licensee of the firm of licensees of which the licensee is a partner, through which the licensee practises law or provides legal services or by which the licensee is employed, including an amount received as a general retainer for which the licensee is not required either to account or to provide services.

2. Money that is received by the licensee as payment of fees for services for which a billing has been delivered, as payment of fees for services already performed for which a billing will be delivered immediately after the money is received or as reimbursement for disbursements made or expenses incurred by the licensee on behalf of a client.

Record keeping requirements

(3) A licensee who, in accordance with subsection (1), does not pay into a trust account money which he or she receives in trust for a client shall include all handling of such money in the records required to be maintained under Part V.

Withdrawal of money from trust account

9.(1) A licensee may withdraw from a trust account only the following money:

1. Money properly required for payment to a client or to a person on behalf of a client.

2. Money required to reimburse the licensee for money properly expended on behalf of a client or for expenses properly incurred on behalf of a client.

3. Money properly required for or toward payment of fees for services performed by the licensee for which a billing has been delivered.

4. Money that is directly transferred into another trust account and held on behalf of a client.

5. Money that under this Part should not have been paid into a trust account but was through inadvertence paid into a trust account.

Send a letter to the client as a follow up to the meeting. The letter should acknowledge receipt of the case, briefly summarize what the matter is about for which you have been retained, outline the action to be taken, and set out the agreed billing arrangements. This letter confirms your instructions, and helps to establish a professional and businesslike relationship with the client. If the client did not receive a copy of the retainer agreement at the meeting, a copy should be included with this letter. In the event that there is a dispute later with the client about the nature of the retainer or the billing arrangements, the letter can provide you with useful protection. At common law, where instructions to a lawyer were given orally, and the client later complained that the lawyer did not follow instructions, the presumption was that the client's version of what was said orally was correct. For this reason, communications with clients, particularly concerning instructions and terms of the retainer, should always be in writing or, if oral, confirmed in writing. In that way, you can overcome the common law presumption in favour of the client's version of events.

CASE INFORMATION

Information on the case will come from what the client tells you in interviews and meetings, and from the documents that he or she supplies.

Interviewing Clients

The client interview can accomplish several tasks — it can be used to establish an advocate–client relationship, to obtain information, and to assess the client as a potential witness. While interview techniques and styles vary, listed below are some useful suggestions for you to use in developing interview techniques and skills with clients (and others, such as witnesses):

- When clients come for a meeting, be sure you see them in private, using your office or an interview room.

- An interview room can be a small room with a table and some comfortable chairs; a client may find an interview room less intimidating and formal than an office setting with you sitting behind a desk and the client in front of you. However, there may be situations where you need to be the dominant person in the room, in which case the office setting may be more appropriate than the interview room.

- The interview time should not be interrupted by staff, telephone calls, e-mails, or text messages; clients should have the sense that they have your undivided attention.

- Ask a client or witness **open-ended questions** to get him or her started in telling the story. "Is there anything more about your contract with X that you would like to tell me?" is an open-ended question. It allows the client to tell the story in his or her own way, emphasizing what is important. It may result in more detail than necessary, but you can re-direct the client back to the issues by asking, for example, "So, to sum up, what you are saying is......" This may help the client to refocus on what is essential.

- Once the client has finished telling you his or her story, you can ask a close-ended, **narrow question** to isolate issues and focus on what is important. A narrow question will provide more detail on specific issues or facts. "When you met Lucy in her office on May 29, what did she tell you about the contract with X?" is an example of a close-ended question.

- When the client is telling his or her story, you may jot down the occasional note on what is important, and what further clarification or information might be required. You can then refer to these notes to ask narrow questions to clarify points in the story. But avoid trying to take verbatim notes when the client is telling the story. This often distracts the client, makes him or her self-conscious, and interrupts the narrative. If that happens, you can encourage the client by saying things like, "I see, please go on." This will help the client get back on track.

- If the client becomes emotional or angry, empathize by saying something like, "I understand this made you very angry." Don't ignore the client's emotional state.

In interviewing, there are some common errors that you should avoid:

- Jumping into the middle of a client's story with comments of your own
- Fidgeting, shuffling papers, tapping pens while the client is speaking
- Answering the client's question with a question
- Pretending to understand what the client is saying, when you are not clear (It is OK to ask the client to clarify a statement.)

Obtaining Client Documents

Civil litigation, particularly in debtor/creditor cases, is often based largely on documentation, such as contracts, account records, and so on. It is important to obtain all of the documents that the client relies on to support the claim, and to retain them in your file.

Client Documents as Evidence

If possible, the *original* documents along with copies should be kept in the file. If it is necessary to prove a fact in court with the use of a document, rules of evidence generally require that the original document, rather than a copy of it, be produced. However, in Small Claims Court, the rules on this are relaxed considerably, and copies can often be filed with the court, unless there are issues about whether the document is authentic. A paralegal must preserve and keep safe the client's property, including documents. Rule 3.07 of the Paralegal Rules requires a paralegal to care for a client's property in the same manner as a careful and prudent owner would when dealing with his or her own property:

> *Preservation of Client's Property*
> 3.07(1) A paralegal shall care for a client's property as a careful and prudent owner would when dealing with like property and shall observe all relevant rules and law about the preservation of property entrusted to a fiduciary.
>
> *Notification of Receipt of Property*
> (2) A paralegal shall promptly notify the client of the receipt of any money or other property of the client, unless satisfied that the client is aware they have come into the paralegal's custody.
>
> *Identification of Property*
> (3) A paralegal shall clearly label and identify the client's property and place it in safekeeping, distinguishable from the paralegal's own property.
> (4) A paralegal shall maintain such records as necessary to identify a client's property that is in the paralegal's custody.

Accounting and delivery

(5) A paralegal shall account promptly for a client's property that is in the paralegal's custody and upon request, shall deliver it to the order of the client.

(6) If a paralegal is unsure of the proper person to receive a client's property, the paralegal shall apply to a tribunal of competent jurisdiction for direction.   (**THE PARALEGAL RULES**)

If documents have been produced from an electronic source such as a computer disk, flash drive, or CD, then the electronic source should be available, if required, to authenticate the document produced from it. The trend in civil litigation in the Superior Court is toward electronic discovery, where, in order to determine relevance to the case, you may have to examine everything on a hard drive, CD, disk, flash drive, or other electronic device. With the advent of electronic records, the volume of records seems to have increased, simply because it is easier to make voluminous records electronically. This may result in a considerable amount of client document hard copy in your case file.

Client Documents and Case Information

Your client's records may provide you with useful background information about the debtor, including address, phone number, assets owned, banks where the debtor does business, and about whether the debtor is in financial difficulty. The debtor's address is required in order to send out a demand letter. In addition, the information obtained from the client allows you to locate the debtor when it is time to sue, and the information may also tell you what assets may be available to satisfy the debt owed to your client and help you to decide what strategy to take in pursuing the claim. Tort cases may result in fewer documents than debt and contract cases, but they can still be considerable, particularly with respect to documenting damages. When interviewing the client, use a checklist to ensure that you have obtained all the relevant and required information and documents. (See Figure 2.3 for a sample checklist.)

Client Documents for Identification and Verification Purposes

The Law Society of Upper Canada's By-Law 7.1 requires licensees to obtain every client's name, address, phone number, and occupation(s). If the case involves the receipt, payment, or transfer of funds, in addition to obtaining information from the client, actual identification must be obtained and copied for the file in order to verify the information provided by the client. It is a good practice in every case

---

FIGURE 2.3: Client Information Checklist

Client Information:

1. Client's full name and any other names client is known by:
   _____

2. Address (home and business):
   _____

3. Telephone number(s): _____

4. Fax number: _____

5. E-mail address: _____

6. Can we leave messages and send faxes and e-mails to the above numbers/addresses on a confidential basis? _____

7. Occupation and employer's address (list all that apply):
   _____
   _____

8. Bank and address: _____
   _____

9. Credit card (type, number, and expiry date): _____
   _____

10. Date of birth and place of birth: _____

List and copy driver's licence information and one other piece of identification to verify client information:

_____

_____

[Note: In all cases, obtain the client's driver's licence number if he or she has one, along with one of the following documents (documents should be reviewed and copied): an original government-issued identification that is valid and has not expired, such as a birth certificate, provincial or territorial health card (if volunteered, as we cannot demand a health card due to privacy legislation), or passport. If non–face-to-face instruction is provided from a client in Canada, then the review and verification of the identification documents can be provided by attestation from a person listed under By-Law 7.1, including a commissioner of oaths or a guarantor (doctor, pharmacist, lawyer, etc.). If the client is outside of Canada, an agent who can provide an attestation must be retained: see by-law for details and/or call the Law Society at 416-947-3315, ext. 3315 for confidential assistance.]

continues....

Figure 2.3 (continued)

Date identity verified: _____

Identity verified by: _____

Reviewing lawyer: _____

For Clients that are a Business or Organization:

11. Incorporation or Business Identification Number: _____

12. Place of issuance of Incorporation/Business Identification Number:

_____

13. Type of business: _____

14. Name, position, and contact information for those individuals authorized to give instructions with respect to the matter for which the licensee is retained (in the case of an organization, we must make reasonable efforts to record the names, addresses, and occupations of all directors and of those who own 25% or more of the shares of a corporation):

_____

_____

_____

15. Give details of identification reviewed and copied to verify client information:

_____

_____

_____

[Note: The following documents, where applicable, should be reviewed and copied: a certificate of corporate status issued by a public body for corporations, articles of association or a trust or partnership agreement, or any other similar record that confirms the unincorporated organization's existence. For directors' information, consult corporate minute books or online corporate registry services.]

continues....

Figure 2.3 (continued)

Where the client is acting for or representing a third party beneficiary or a principal:

16. Information about the beneficiary or principal as set out in paragraphs 1 to 14, as applicable:

_____

_____

Information about Debtor/Defendant:

17. Full name/Business name: _____

18. Business type (sole prop., corp., partnership) if applicable:

_____

19. Address of defendant: _____

20. Phone number of defendant: _____

21. Fax/e-mail of defendant: _____

22. Defendant's representative (if any) and his/her contact information:

_____

23. Marital status of defendant and name of spouse if applicable:

_____

24. Employer of defendant:

_____

Defendant's assets:

25. Real estate (address, lot, plan no. if known):

_____

26. Vehicles(s) (licence, VIN, description): _____

_____

27. Bank account numbers and bank address:

_____

28. Investments (type, number, company, address of company):

_____

_____

continues....

Figure 2.3 (continued)

Details of claim:

29. Type of case (tort, collections, etc.): _____

_____

_____

If collection matter:

30. Original amount: _____

31. Terms, including interest: _____

32. Evidence of debt (contract, invoice, note, security agreement):

_____

33. Payment history/Default history: _____

34. Co-signor or guarantor information (name, address, phone no.):

_____

35. Collateral given as security, if any (type and location):

_____

Documents delivered by client:
(Obtain and secure originals and make copies.)

36. Invoices: _____

37. Account records: _____

38. Promissory notes: _____

39. Guarantees: _____

40. Security agreements: _____

41. Demand letters sent by client: _____

42. Other documents (list): _____

43. Searches carried out by client: _____

continues....

Figure 2.3 (continued)

Client retainer, instructions, and action taken:

44. Name of lawyer/paralegal assigned to case: _____

45. Retainer agreement reviewed and signed (write date and copy for file, put retainer funds into trust account):
_____

46. Reporting frequency (monthly or details of other): _____

47. Billing frequency (monthly or details of other): _____

48. Conflicts check carried out: _____

49. Tickler date system established: _____

50. Client account opened: _____

51. File number assigned: _____

52. Details of searches carried out (credit bureau, driver's licence, business name, executions, PPSA, and title):
_____
_____

53. Demand letter sent and date of letter: _____

54. Time given for payment in demand letter: _____

55. Authority given to discuss settlement and details as to what client will accept: _____

56. Authority to commence litigation: _____

57. Authority to retain outside counsel if needed: _____

58. Authority to retain experts: _____

59. Date Claim issued: _____

60. Date Claim served: _____

61. Date default judgment may be requested: _____

62. Date of settlement conference: _____

63. Case management deadlines: _____

64. Trial date: _____

65. Judgment date: _____

66. Examination in aid of execution date: _____

continues....

Figure 2.3 (continued)

67. Date writ of seizure and sale obtained and type of writ(s):

    _____

68. Date for renewal of writ(s) of seizure and sale: _____

69. Date garnishment obtained: _____

70. Date for renewal of garnishment: _____

71. Details of any other enforcement action taken: _____

    _____

72. Final account and reporting letter to client: _____

73. Client documents and any property on hand returned to client:

    _____

    _____

74. Other: _____

75. Date file closed: _____

NOTE: This form and copies of any identification verification documents must be kept on file for six years following completion of the matter.

to review and copy identification verifying the client's name and address. Independent source identification documents, such as a driver's licence and passport, should be reviewed and copied. These requirements are designed as safeguards against fraud and criminal activity on behalf of clients who may turn out to be fictional or non-existent. If the licensee discovers, in the course of identity verification, that he or she may be assisting the client with illegal conduct, he or she must withdraw from the case as set out in Section 24 of the by-law. Section 22(2) of the by-law sets out exemptions from the client identification and verification requirements. If, for example, the licensee is engaged in activities on behalf of his or her employer or is acting as an agent for another licensee who has already complied with the identification and verification provisions, the licensee does not have to obtain and verify identification. Section 22(3) of the by-law provides exemptions where the funds were obtained from sources such as financial institutions and other licensees.

BY-LAW 7.1 — OPERATIONAL OBLIGATIONS AND RESPONSIBILITIES (EXCERPTS)

(MADE UNDER THE *LAW SOCIETY ACT*, current as of July 17, 2013)

Application of client identification and verification requirements

22.(1) Subject to subsections (2), (3) and (4), a licensee shall,

(a) when the licensee is retained to provide her or his professional services to a client, comply with the client identification requirements set out in subsection 23(1); and

(b) when the licensee engages in or gives instructions in respect of the receiving, paying or transferring of funds,

    (i) comply with the client identification requirements set out in subsection 23(2), and

    (ii) comply with the client verification requirements set out in subsection 23(4).

Exemption re certain licensees

(2) A licensee is not required to comply with the client identification and verification requirements set out in section 23 if,

(a) the licensee is engaged in the activities described in subsection (1) on behalf of her or his employer;

(b) the licensee is engaged in the activities described in subsection (1) as agent for another licensee or a lawyer who has already complied with the client identification and verification requirements set out in section 23;

(c) the licensee is engaged in the activities described in subsection (1) for a client referred to the licensee by another licensee or a lawyer who has already complied with the client identification and verification requirements set out in section 23; or

(d) the licensee is engaged in the activities described in subsection (1), other than the activities described in clause (1)(b), as a duty counsel under the *Legal Aid Services Act, 1998*, as a duty counsel providing professional services through a duty counsel program operated by a not-for-profit organization or as a provider of legal aid services through the provision of summary advice under the *Legal Aid Services Act, 1998.*

Exemptions re certain funds

(3) A licensee is not required to comply with the client identification requirements set out in subsection 23(2) or the client verification requirements set out in subsection 23(4) in respect of funds,

(a) paid to or received from a financial institution, public body or reporting issuer;

(b) received from the trust account of another licensee or a lawyer;

(c) received from a peace officer, law enforcement agency or other public official acting in an official capacity;

(d) paid or received pursuant to a court order;

(e) paid to pay a fine or penalty;

(f) paid or received as a settlement in a proceeding;

(g) paid or received for professional fees, disbursements, expenses or bail; or

(h) paid, received or transferred by electronic funds transfer.

Exemptions re certain clients

(4) A licensee is not required to comply with the client identification requirements set out in subsection 23(2) or the client verification requirements set out in subsection 23(4) in respect of any of the following clients:

1. A financial institution.
2. A public body.
3. A reporting issuer.

Client identification

23.(1) When a licensee is retained to provide her or his professional services to a client, the licensee shall obtain the following information about the client:

1. The client's full name.
2. The client's business address and business telephone number, if applicable.
3. If the client is an individual, the client's home address and home telephone number.
4. If the client is an organization, other than a financial institution, public body or reporting issuer, the organization's incorporation or business identification number and the place of issue of its incorporation or business identification number, if applicable.
5. If the client is an individual, the client's occupation or occupations.
6. If the client is an organization, other than a financial institution, public body or reporting issuer, the general nature of the type of business or businesses or activity or activities engaged in by the client.

7. If the client is an organization, the name, position and contact information for each individual who gives instructions with respect to the matter for which the licensee is retained.

8. If the client is acting for or representing a third party, information about the third party as set out in paragraphs 1 to 7, as applicable.

Same

(2) When a licensee is engaged in the activities described in clause 22(1)(b) and the client or any third party that the client is acting for or representing is an organization, in addition to complying with the client identification requirements set out in subsection (1), the licensee shall make reasonable efforts to obtain the following information about the client and the third party:

1. The name and occupation or occupations of each director of the organization, other than an organization that is a securities dealer.

2. The name, address and occupation or occupations of each person who owns twenty-five percent or more of the organization or of the shares of the organization.

Client identification, identification by others in licensee's firm

(2.1) A licensee complies with the identification requirements set out in subsections (1) and (2) if an employee of the licensee's firm or another licensee who practises law or provides legal services through the licensee's firm, acting on behalf of the licensee, complies with the requirements.

Client identification, previous identification

(3) A licensee complies with the identification requirements set out in subsection (2) if the licensee or another individual acting on behalf of the licensee under subsection (2.1) has previously complied with the identification requirements and has also previously complied with the verification requirements set out in subsection (4) in respect of the organization.

Client verification requirements

(4) When a licensee is engaged in the activities described in clause 22(1)(b), the licensee shall take reasonable steps to verify the identity of the client and any third party that the client is acting for or representing using what the licensee reasonably considers to be reliable, independent source documents, data or information.

Timing of verification, individuals

(5) A licensee shall verify the identity of an individual mentioned in subsection (1), including an individual mentioned in paragraph 7, immediately after first engaging in the activities described in clause 22(1)(b).

Timing of verification, organizations

(6) A licensee shall verify the identity of an organization mentioned in subsection (1) by not later than 60 days after first engaging in the activities described in clause 22(1)(b).

Examples of independent source documents

(7) The following are examples of independent source documents for the purposes of subsection (4):

1. If the client or third party is an individual, an original government issued identification that is valid and has not expired, including a driver's licence, birth certificate, provincial or territorial health card (if such use of the card is not prohibited by the applicable provincial or territorial law), passport or similar record.

2. If the client or third party is an organization such as a corporation or society that is created or registered pursuant to legislative authority, a written confirmation from a government registry as to the existence, name and address of the organization, which includes the names of the organization's directors, if applicable, such as,

    i. a certificate of corporate status issued by a public body,
    ii. a copy obtained from a public body of a record that the organization is required to file annually under applicable legislation, or
    iii. a copy of a similar record obtained from a public body that confirms the organization's existence.

3. If the client or third party is an organization other than a corporation or society, such as a trust or partnership which is not registered in any government registry, a copy of the organization's constating documents, such as a trust or partnership agreement, articles of association or any other similar record that confirms its existence as an organization.

Client verification, non–face-to-face

(8) When a licensee is engaged in the activities described in clause 22(1)(b) and the licensee is not receiving instructions from an individual face-to-face, the licensee complies with the verification requirements set out in subsection (4) if the licensee obtains an attestation from a person described in subsection (9) that the person has seen the appropriate independent source documents.

Persons from whom attestations may be accepted

(9) For the purposes of section (8), a licensee may obtain an attestation from the following persons:

1. If the client whose identity is being verified is present in Canada,

    i. a person entitled to administer oaths and affirmations in Canada, or
    ii. any of the following persons:
        A. a dentist,

      B. a physician,

      C. a chiropractor,

      D. a judge,

      E. a magistrate or a justice of the peace,

      F. a lawyer,

      G. a licensee (in Ontario)

      H. a notary (in Quebec),

      I. a notary public,

      J. an optometrist,

      K. a pharmacist,

      L. an accountant,

      M. a professional engineer,

      N. a veterinarian,

      O. a police officer,

      P. a nurse,

      Q. a school principal.

2. If the client whose identity is being verified is not present in Canada, a person acting on behalf of the licensee under clause (11)(b).

Attestation, form

(10) For the purposes of subsection (8), an attestation shall be endorsed on a legible photocopy of the document and shall include,

(a) the name, occupation and address of the person providing the attestation;

(b) the signature of the person providing the attestation; and

(c) the type and number of the document seen by the person providing the attestation.

Client verification, use of agent, etc.

(11) A licensee complies with the verification requirements set out in subsection (4) if,

(a) an employee of the licensee's firm or another licensee who practises law or provides legal services through the licensee's firm, acting on behalf of the licensee, complies with the requirements; or

(b) an individual who is not an individual mentioned in clause (a), acting on behalf of the licensee, complies with the requirements, provided that the licensee and the individual, prior to the individual acting on behalf of the licensee, enter into a written agreement specifying the steps that the individual will be taking on behalf of the licensee to comply with the verification requirements.

Client verification, previous verification

(12) A licensee complies with the verification requirements set out in subsection (4),

(a) in the case of an individual mentioned in subsection (1), if the licensee has previously complied with the verification requirements set out in subsection (4) in respect of the individual and recognizes the individual; and

(b) in the case of an organization mentioned in subsection (1), the licensee or an individual acting on behalf of the licensee under subsection (11) has previously complied with the identification requirements set out in subsection (2) and the verification requirements set out in subsection (4) in respect of the organization.

Copies to be obtained

(13) The licensee shall obtain a copy of every document used to verify the identity of any individual or organization for the purposes of subsection (4), including a copy of every document used by an individual acting on behalf of the licensee under subsection (11).

Record retention

(14) The licensee shall retain a record of the information obtained for the purposes of subsections (1) and (2) and copies of all documents received for the purposes of subsection (4) for the longer of,

(a) the duration of the licensee and client relationship and for as long as is necessary for the purpose of providing service to the client; and

(b) a period of at least six years following completion of the work for which the licensee was retained.

Criminal activity, duty to withdraw at time of taking information

24. If a licensee, in the course of complying with the client identification or verification requirements set out in section 23, knows or ought to know that he or she is or would be assisting a client in fraud or other illegal conduct, the licensee shall,

(a) immediately cease to and not further engage in any activities that would assist the client in fraud or other illegal conduct; and

(b) if the licensee is unable to comply with clause (a), withdraw from the provision of the licensee's professional services to the client.

Commencement

25. This Part comes into force on December 31, 2008.

In debt collection cases, your client's accounting records will often tell you how much is owing, including interest, at a point in time prior to suing. You will need those records to prove the basis of the debt claim. You also need them to calculate damages from that point on so that you can determine pre- and post-judgment interest at trial. In other kinds of cases, note that some damages will continue to accrue after the suit begins. For example, if a client has been injured and is on medication for a prolonged period, the amounts claimed for medication costs may continue to accrue up to trial. To claim all of the damages right up to judgment, you will need to have not only the documentation the client gave you at the beginning of the case, but you must also have the client continue to provide the documentation that supports the claim right up until judgment.

FILE ORGANIZATION

Once you have been retained, and the client has handed over relevant documents, it is important that all documents relating to the case are stored in a systematic way so that documents can easily be found and retrieved as required. In some practices, paralegals simply open a file folder and drop everything related to the case into it. This is fine if you have only one or two open files, but when you have many, a more systematic approach is required. The following are suggestions for effective file organization:

- *Case file folder.* For each case or matter, you should have a separate retainer and a separate case file, even if you have multiple case files for the same client. Once a case file is set up, all subfiles are placed inside the case file. The case file folder contains the name of the client, for example, "ORYX v. Foot" (if you act for the defendant, it might be "FOOT ats Oryx". The short form "ats" stands for "at the suit of"). The file also should contain, on the inside file cover, a form with the client's name, address, phone and fax numbers, e-mail address, and other essential information. This can be set out on the client information checklist, which can be stapled to the inside cover of the file. The checklist is also useful to check off steps in the proceeding as they are completed, and anyone picking up the file for the first time will know what stage the proceedings have reached. The file name should also have a file number — the file number can include codes for the type of file (collection, contract, tort, etc.), the staff person responsible for the file, the date it was opened, and so on. Some offices use different colours of file folders for different types of legal work. It is wise to give careful thought to the filing system you set up. A simple one might do for now, but as your practice gets busier, and your system requirements change, changing a file system may be complicated. Choosing with the future in mind is advisable.

- *Correspondence subfile.* All correspondence related to the file should go here — the most recent on top. A quick glance at this file should tell you what the matter is about, how it has progressed, the stage the proceeding has reached, and what problems need to be addressed. When you send out an original letter, e-mail, or fax, remember to include a copy of it in this file. Some paralegals and lawyers use a steel brad instead of a subfile for correspondence. They punch letters, memos, e-mails, and other correspondence on to the brad with the oldest at the bottom and the most recent on the top. Brads are not generally used for litigation documents or documents that may become evidence as punching a hole in such documents alters their original state.

- *Notes subfile.* Notes written by you or others in your office concerning the matter should be filed here. If the client later hires someone else to finish the matter for which you were originally retained, you may remove your notes from any materials you return to the client or send to another representative.

- *Client documents subfile.* Client documents, including copies, should be kept separate from other documents because they may be required to be filed as evidence in the proceeding. These documents are the property of the client and must be returned to the client when the matter is concluded, although you may keep copies for your file before you close it. In fact, it is wise to keep copies of closed file client notes. For example, if a client complained to the Law Society that you had neglected to include an important fact in a pleading, you might, in some cases, have a copy of the client's original notes telling you "the facts" to put in the claim and "the fact" in question had never been mentioned.

- *Pleadings subfile.* All court documents, including copies, should be kept in this file. These will include the plaintiff's claim, the defence, affidavits of service, motions, and any supporting affidavits.

- *Miscellaneous subfile.* Documents that do not fit into the preceding categories should be placed here. When this file gets crowded, consider whether additional specific subfiles should be created.

STORAGE OF CLOSED FILES

Care should be taken with the storage of files. The Law Society of Upper Canada has information on closed files in the Resource Centre/Knowledge Tree section of its website at <http://www.lsuc.on.ca>. When a matter has been completed, the client's original documents should be returned to the client when you send the final reporting letter and account. The material remaining should then be stored among the inactive files. Because further work may need to be done, or in case a client becomes dissatisfied and sues for negligence, the file should not be destroyed. Many lawyers used to keep closed files indefinitely. The Law Society currently suggests that there is no fixed rule about file retention. LawPro, the lawyers' errors and omissions insurance carrier suggests a 10- to 15-year file retention period.[1] There are a number of factors to consider. Certainly you should keep closed files until after the limitation period for a negligence claim against you by the client has expired. By-law 7.1(14)(b) stipulates that client identification and verification documents must be retained for at least six years following completion of the work. Other factors include the nature of the actual legal work performed, the working life of the legal document(s), the outcome of the case, and the client's attitude and capacity, or lack thereof. When setting up a storage area for closed files, factors to consider are accessibility, easy retrieval of a closed file, and safety. You should use a storage area that is not prone to fire, theft, flooding, or extremes of temperature. You should also be aware that there may be problems storing electronic versions of paper records. It is possible that some electronic records will deteriorate over time. There is also the problem that given the evolution of hardware and record storage formats, you may end up with records for which there is no hardware available to read them. For example, you are likely to have a problem reading a 5-¼ inch floppy disk from the 1980s, considering disk drives for such disks have been unavailable since the mid-1990s.

KEEPING ON TOP OF THE FILE

In any litigation, deadlines must be carefully noted in the file and in a "tickler" system. A **tickler system** is a date recording system that alerts you to upcoming deadlines, using either a date book, a calendar, a pocket diary, or a computer system. Maintaining a backup system is also advisable, in case a computer crashes or a date book is misplaced. In order for these systems to work, the relevant deadlines must be diarized or entered in the tickler system. The careful and methodical use of a tickler system is absolutely essential because a missed deadline can be detrimental to a client's case. If you fail to record a limitation period, there is a good chance that the client will sue you for professional negligence. If a limitation period is missed, there is a positive obligation to notify the Law Society and your errors and omissions insurance carrier of the negligence. The Small Claims Court can waive time limits on procedural rules, but limitation periods are substantive, and if you miss one deadline, it cannot be waived or excused.

---

[1] "File retention: What and for how long?" *LAWPRO Magazine* 98:4 (December 2010), online: practicePRO <www.lawpro.ca/magazinearchives>.

Limitation Periods

Limitation periods are found in federal and provincial legislation, including the Ontario *Limitations Act, 2002*. Limitation periods usually set out the time period during which a plaintiff must start proceedings; if the plaintiff does not start proceedings within the time period, he or she is "**statute barred**" and may not proceed with the lawsuit at all. The limitation period begins when the right to sue (sometimes called a "cause of action") arises.

Under the *Limitations Act, 2002*, the basic limitation period for almost all causes of action, including actions in debt, contract, and tort, is two years from the time the debt was past due or the contract was breached or all the elements that constitute the tort have occurred (s. 4) or could reasonably be determined to be past due or to have occurred (s. 5). There are some exceptions to this general rule that may affect a debt action.

Limitations Act Exceptions and Qualifications

- *Minors and persons under disability:* The limitation period begins to run only when a litigation guardian is appointed (ss. 6 to 9).

- *Victims of assault and sexual assault:* The limitation period begins to run when the victim has recovered from physical and psychological injuries and is able to act (s. 10).

- *Discoverability rule:* The Act codifies the common law rule that a limitation period does not run until the plaintiff knew or reasonably ought to have known that the cause of action was complete.

- *Some debt actions not subject to any limitation period:* Proceedings to enforce a family law domestic agreement for support and proceedings by the Crown to collect taxes, reclaim welfare benefits, or recover on defaulted student loans (s. 1) are not subject to a limitation period.

- *Limitations Act overrides limitation periods in other statutes:* A limitation period set out in another Ontario statute does not apply unless it is set out as an exception to the general provisions of the *Limitations Act, 2002* in the schedule at the back of the Act (s. 19).

There are a number of reasons given for having limitation periods. By requiring an action to be commenced within a specific time period, the defendant does not have the threat of a lawsuit constantly hanging over him or her. Also, in an action brought soon after the events giving rise to it, witnesses' memories are fresher, and evidence is probably more reliable than it would be if recalled long after the event.

In addition to limitation periods, there are also notice periods that should be diarized or noted in the tickler system. For example, when you issue a claim in the Small Claims Court, Joe the defendant has 20 days from the time he is served to file a defence, or you can request that he be noted in default and a default judgment can be obtained against him. Noting the 20-day period is therefore important for both the plaintiff and defendant. Unlike a limitation period, where failure to observe the timelines will be detrimental to the action, missing a notice period may be merely a procedural irregularity that can be cured. Overcoming an irregularity may, however, result in a delay and increased costs for the client. Some statutes also have notice periods. If you wish to sue a government department or agency, statutes governing such lawsuits often require the plaintiff to serve a written notice of intention to sue on the relevant government defendant as a condition precedent to suing. These statutes may also impose relatively short limitation periods for taking action.

Aside from limitation periods and notice periods, there are other important deadlines or dates that need to be "brought forward" so that you will be able to accomplish the tasks before the time for doing so has passed. Many of these dates are based on common sense rather than on rules. Of particular importance are the timing of the demand letter and the commencement of proceedings. The older a debt is, the harder it is to collect. If the client did not send a letter demanding payment as part of the initial collection efforts, one should be sent as soon as possible. A demand letter should indicate the date on which payment is required. If payment is not made by that date, diarize commencement of proceedings for the next day, and issue the claim on that date. If the action is not defended, diarize the date for signing the default judgment, and sign the default judgment on that date. It is important to diarize and adhere to a litigation schedule. Delay generally does not favour a creditor, or a plaintiff, because the debtor's assets may be shrinking rapidly. Also, sticking firmly to dates sends a psychological message to the debtor or defendant that the plaintiff or creditor is determined to pursue the matter diligently and that the matter is not going to fade away.

If the plaintiff plans to take action against a guarantor, the legal representative must remember to first make a demand for payment on the guarantor. A demand on the guarantor is a condition precedent to an action on the collateral obligation. The Ontario Court of Appeal considered the issue in *Bank of Nova Scotia v. Williamson*, 2009 ONCA 754 and affirmed that making a demand on a guarantor is a condition precedent to such an action.

PROTOCOLS FOR CLIENT COMMUNICATION

During the time it takes to get a small claims case to trial, there will be periods when nothing happens. However, it doesn't mean you stop communicating with your clients.

Maintaining Communication with the Client

The first protocol for client communication is to maintain communication with the client so that he or she realizes that silence from you does not mean the client is forgotten. In Chapter 1 there is a walk-through of the small claims process that explains the steps between issuing a claim and getting to trial. It is a good idea to give that kind of information to clients so that they will know what happens next and when it is likely to happen. An informed client is a less anxious client, and is less likely to be constantly calling your office to find out what is happening.

In this connection you should also tell clients when you will be updating them and why. Be sure you have their information and ask them how they wish to receive information — by phone, fax, regular mail, e-mail, or some combination of these methods. If the client wants phone contact, it is a good idea to confirm the phone conversations that you have with the client in writing, or at least put a note of the conversation in the file. This is some assurance that there is a record of who said what to whom, should the content of the conversation become an issue either in the case or between you and the client.

Confidentiality

The second protocol for client communication is to maintain confidentiality. If you phone a client and someone else answers and takes a message, be careful what you say to the person who answers. Unless you have the client's written consent to communicate the client's legal business with other persons, all communications should be treated as confidential. In this circumstance, leave a message for the client to call you. There is no need to identify yourself as a paralegal. Leaving your name and number is sufficient. If communicating by e-mail or fax, ensure that you have the client's personal fax number or e-mail address and add a warning to your fax cover sheet or at the bottom of your e-mail stating that "This document is confidential and is intended only for the person it is addressed to." A paralegal must at all times hold in strict confidence all information concerning the affairs of a client. The duty to maintain confidentiality is set out in Rule 3.03 of the *Paralegal Rules of Conduct* ("The Paralegal Rules"):

Confidential Information

3.03(1) A paralegal shall, at all times, hold in strict confidence all information concerning the business and affairs of a client acquired in the course of their professional relationship and shall not disclose any such information unless expressly or impliedly authorized by the client or required by law to do so.

(2) The duty of confidentiality under subrule (1) continues indefinitely after the paralegal has ceased to act for the client, whether or not differences have arisen between them.

(3) The paralegal shall keep the client's papers and other property out of sight, as well as out of reach, of those not entitled to see them.

Justified or Permitted Disclosure

(4) A paralegal shall disclose confidential information when required by law or by order of a tribunal of competent jurisdiction.

(5) If a paralegal believes upon reasonable grounds that there is an imminent risk to an identifiable person or group of death or serious bodily harm, including serious psychological harm that substantially interferes with health or well-being, the paralegal may disclose, pursuant to judicial order where practicable, confidential information if it is necessary to do so in order to prevent the death or harm.

(6) In order to defend against the allegations, a paralegal may disclose confidential information if it is alleged that the paralegal or his or her employees are,

(a) guilty of a criminal offence involving a client's affairs;

(b) civilly liable with respect to a matter involving a client's affairs; or

(c) guilty of malpractice or misconduct.

(7) A paralegal may disclose confidential information in order to establish or collect his or her fees.

(8) A paralegal shall not disclose more information than is necessary when he or she discloses confidential information as required or permitted by subrules (4), (5), (6) and (7).

(**THE PARALEGAL RULES**)

Example 2.1 Confidentiality

Albert Oryx's mother thinks that Albert would be happier and better able to move on with his life if his case against Ophelia Foot could be wrapped up as soon as possible. She calls Peter Paralegal, Albert's legal representative, and asks him to do what he can to move things along. In order to maintain the confidentiality owed to his client, Peter cannot confirm that he represents Albert, nor can he discuss the case or take instructions from Albert's mother.

Circumstances for Client Communication

The third protocol for client communication is that you and the client should agree on the circumstances in which the client should expect to hear from you. A suggested communication schedule might be as follows:

- Tell the client when the claim has been issued. Send a copy of the claim to the client.

- Tell the client that the defence has been received. Send a copy of the defence to the client. It may also be wise to schedule a meeting with the client to discuss issues and facts alleged in the defence.

- Tell the client the date for the settlement conference, and set up a meeting to explore settlement and narrow issues for trial. At this meeting, a list of proposed witnesses should be finalized as this must be served on the other side at least 14 days before the settlement conference. If there are any documents or other evidence not yet disclosed, these will need to be agreed upon and served as well.

- Tell the client the date for trial, and arrange a meeting with the client to prepare the client as a witness and to familiarize the client with the trial process.

Generally, unless the client indicates otherwise in your discussion of the communication protocol, it is advisable to forward copies of all correspondence sent and received, copies of court documents, and copies of **memos to the file**. An informed client is generally a contented client.

CHAPTER SUMMARY

In this chapter we focused on obtaining information from the client through oral interviews, using various interview techniques, and through data gathering, using client documents. We then turned to techniques for storing documents so that they can be easily found and retrieved through the use of an effectively organized litigation file and file system. As communicating with the client on an ongoing basis is important, we looked at elements of a communication protocol that might be used with a client to establish the nature of the relationship, including the use of a retainer. We also considered various elements that should be employed to keep on top of the file and the case, including the use of tickler systems to monitor limitation periods and notice periods and to bring forward dates.

REVIEW QUESTIONS

1. In what sort of physical setting should you interview a client or witness?

2. Give two examples of open-ended questions.

3. Give two examples of close-ended questions.

4. Why should you set up a communication protocol with clients?

5. What are your obligations with respect to original client documents and any property held by the legal representative that belongs to the client?

6. What should you do with the clients' files after the work has been completed?

7. How should a litigation file be set up?

8. What is a tickler system, and why is it important?

9. What are the main provisions of the Ontario *Limitations Act, 2002*?

10. What special problems might arise with respect to time limitations when suing governments?

DISCUSSION QUESTIONS/CASE STUDIES

1. Your paralegal firm has decided that it wants to provide clients with an information handout that will include contact information, a description of the likely process, and a communication protocol, so clients know what they can expect by way of future communication during the period leading up to trial. Draft the information handout.

2. Your paralegal firm, Paralegal Services, has been retained by Hieronymous Bosch, who is trying to recover $4,000 from the Peasant's Cooperative for a painting he did in May of Yr. 0 of the cooperative's board of directors. Bosch hasn't yet sent a demand letter, and he wants to sue. You and Bosch agree on a flat fee of $1,500, inclusive of disbursements, to be paid at the end of trial or on settlement, with a deposit of $500 to your firm's trust account on the execution of the retainer. Draft a retainer.

Chapter 3

Background Searches for the Small Claims Court File

LEARNING OBJECTIVES

⇨ Know the types of information available and how to conduct searches on the following databases:
  - Driver's Record Abstract
  - Plate History and Vehicle History Abstracts
  - Canada411 and reverse directories
  - Online commercial search engines and "people finders"
  - Business name searches at the Companies and Personal Property Security Branch
  - Online business name searches
  - Corporate searches at the Companies and Personal Property Security Branch
  - Online corporate searches
  - Execution searches
  - *Personal Property Security Act* searches: phone and online
  - *Bank Act* searches online
  - *Bulk Sales Act* searches online
  - *Bankruptcy and Insolvency Act* searches through the Superintendent of Bankruptcy: phone and online
  - Credit Bureau searches

⇨ Know how to use public database information to verify the identity and location of the debtor or defendant in order to name the party properly and serve the claim

⇨ Know how to use and analyze public and private database information to identify whether the defendant has enough assets to make him or her worth suing, and to determine whether the defendant's situation is deteriorating

⇨ Know how to obtain, read, understand, and analyze a credit report on a defendant or debtor

INTRODUCTION

In the previous chapter you learned how to obtain information from client interviews and documents and how to organize, manage, and use it. In this chapter you will learn how to obtain further information about a debtor or potential defendant from a variety of public databases. We identify the various databases in the context of identifying the debtor or defendant as a legal entity that can be sued, and we locate the party so that we know where to serve the claim. We also use these databases to determine whether the debtor or defendant has sufficient assets to be worth suing, or, if sued, whether collecting on a judgment is likely. If the debtor is bankrupt or is heading in that direction, it may not be worthwhile to spend time and money in court. The databases are identified with detailed information as to how data is obtained from them, what kind of data they supply, and how that data can be used.

OBTAINING BACKGROUND INFORMATION: PUBLIC RECORD SEARCHES

When plaintiffs come to you, it is because someone has caused them damage for which they have not been paid, or they have tried and failed to collect a debt and expect you to do it for them, usually by suing the debtor. However, that may not be the best strategy. Consider the following possibilities:

- Joe (the plaintiff) went to look for Matthew (the defendant) at the address he had in his records and discovered that Matthew had cancelled his phone and Internet account, and Matthew had moved without leaving a forwarding address.

- Mark (the plaintiff) just discovered that Jason (the defendant) has recently transferred or encumbered his car, house, and boat, all of which might otherwise be available to satisfy the debt or claim.

- Jay (the plaintiff) has heard that Mary (the defendant) was sued by other creditors who have been unsuccessful in collecting on their judgments.

- Jill (the plaintiff) has heard that Martin (the defendant) has had some of his assets seized by other creditors.

- Marvin (the plaintiff) has learned that Jenny (the defendant) recently suffered personal or business financial losses.

- Jack (the debtor) had assets seized by secured creditors who have a collateral interest in those assets and a right to seize them to satisfy the debt when there is default.

In cases like these, there may be little or no purpose in suing the defendant because he or she has vanished or because there may be no assets available to satisfy the debt and, generally, no hope of payment. To obtain the necessary information about the debtor or to confirm information supplied by the client, or by others, there are a number of public and private searches and databases that can yield useful information to help you to find and to decide whether to sue or to pursue another strategy or remedy. Many of these searches can be done online, as well as by phone, fax, mail, or in person.

IDENTIFYING AND LOCATING THE DEBTOR

We begin the discussion with an examination of database tools that allow us to verify the identity of a debtor, to be sure we have the right person, and that we have the correct name of the individual or business by which that person can be sued. We can also use these databases to physically locate the debtor so that we will be able to serve the person with the plaintiff's claim in accordance with the requirements of the Rules for service of court documents.[1]

Searches by Name: Consumer Debtors

If you are suing an individual consumer rather than a business, you should verify the debtor's legal name. Suing in the wrong name can result in an unenforceable judgment. For example, if you are suing John Deadbeat and you obtain a judgment in that name, the judgment will be useless if it turns out that John's legal first name is really Giovanni, but that he informally changed it to John years ago. Legally, Giovanni Deadbeat exists, but John Deadbeat does not, at least for the purposes of obtaining and enforcing a judgment. Getting the debtor's name right at the outset is important, both to obtain a judgment against the debtor in the right name and to conduct searches to determine whether the debtor is worth suing.

There are several ways in which you can verify a debtor's correct name.

---

[1] The process of locating a debtor is sometimes referred to as skip tracing. Often a collection agency will have a person known as a skip-tracer whose job is to locate a debtor, using online sources and address and phone directories.

Ministry of Transportation Driver and Vehicle Searches

If the debtor drives or owns a vehicle, you can carry out various searches through the Ministry of Transportation to find out information about the debtor. In Ontario, the Ministry of Transportation offers pay-for-fee online searches. To access the search site, go directly to the Ministry of Transportation site at <http://www.mto.gov.on.ca/english/> and click on the link for "online services". This link will bring you to the Service Ontario site <http://www.ontario.ca/en/services_for_residents/index.htm>, where you select "driver and vehicle services". Payment is made by credit card. The following types of searches, among others, are available through the site:

- Three-year Statement of Driving Record (abstract — certified)
- Vehicle identification number search by date (certified)
- Plate search — recent owner (certified)
- Plate search by date (certified)

The most common searches are the three-year statement of driving record (abstract) and the recent owner search.

Due to privacy legislation, the driver/owner's address is not shown on searches carried out by the general public. The ministry will, however, include address information on searches ordered by registered authorized users. Various parties, including lawyers, paralegals, collection agents, private investigators, security guards, process servers, and insurance agents, among others, can become authorized users. These parties are usually permitted to register as their work involves the following activities:

- Conducting searches for the purposes of legal service or for the purposes of contacting people with respect to "claims, litigation, and accidents"
- Debt collection

For further information on becoming a registered authorized user, contact the ministry by writing or calling the following:

Supervisor
Driver and Vehicle Licensing Call Centre
Licensing Administration Office
Ministry of Transportation
2680 Keele Street
Downsview ON M3M 3E6
Tel. 416-235-2999
Toll-free Tel. 1-800-387-3445

Driving Record Abstract

If you have the debtor's driver's licence number, you can request a three-year driving record search, known as a Driving Record Abstract, which will provide the name of the driver, licence status information (including gender, height, hair and eye colour, and date of birth), and a record of driving offence convictions. If you are a registered authorized user, the driver's address will also be shown. The information provided by a Driving Record Abstract can help you to

• verify the debtor's name;

• verify that you have the right person by comparing height, eye, hair colour, gender, and age to match the description your client has of the debtor;

• instruct the process server as to the physical description of the debtor for the purposes of personal service;

• carry out other searches (for example, having the debtor's date of birth makes it easier to verify who a debtor is on a *Personal Property Security Act* search).

A Driving Record Abstract may be especially useful with someone who has a common last name, such as Smith or Wong. This search is useful *only* if you have the driver's licence number. Ideally, your client obtained the debtor's driver's licence number on a credit application form at the time the parties entered into a creditor and debtor relationship.

To see what a Statement of Driving Record Abstract looks like, see Figure 3.1.

Plate History, Vehicle Identification Number, and Vehicle History Abstracts

If you have the vehicle identification number (VIN) or the licence plate number for a vehicle you think is owned by the debtor, you can use either number to do a plate or VIN search, either of which will provide the name of the owner, his or her driver's licence number, the date the vehicle was registered, and whether it has changed owners recently.

Again, the address of the owner will not be provided unless you are a registered authorized user as described in the previous section on driver's abstract searches. You may do plate, vehicle identification number, and vehicle history searches online using the URL provided in the previous section.

You can see what a Certified Plate Search — Recent Owner Report looks like in Figure 3.2 on page 86. The VIN search record is similar.

FIGURE 3.1: Statement of Driving Record Abstract

	Ministry of Transportation	Ministère des Transports	Safety and Regulation Division	Division de la sécurité et des règlements

Ontario

Ministry No./No. Du Ministère   Search Date/Date de recherche (Y/A M D/J)
0000-0000-0   1994/08/19

STATEMENT OF DRIVING RECORD/RELEVÉ DU DOSSIER DE CONDUITE PAGE 01

DRIVER INFORMATION/DONNÉE DE CONDUCTEUR

Name/Nom **PUBLIC, JOHN, Q.**
Address/Adresse *

Reference No. or Driver's Licence No./
No de référence ou du permis de conduire **P0000-00000-00000**
Date of Birth/Date de naissance (Y/A M D/J) **1962/12/10**
Sex/Sexe **MALE/HOMME**
Height/Taille **175**
Class/Catégorie **G*****
Condition/Restriction ***
Expiry Date/Date d'expirition (Y/A M D/J) **1985/08/31**
STATUS/STATUT **UNLICENCED/PERMIS DE CONDUIRE EXPIRÉ UNRENEWABLE/NON RENOUVELABLE SUSPENDED/SUSPENDU**

DATE CONVICTIONS, DISCHARGES AND OTHER ACTIONS
Y/A M D/J CONDAMNATIONS, LIBÉRATIONS ET AUTRES ACTIONS

93/10/12 NO DRIVERS LICENCE OR IMPROPER CLASS OF LICENCE
ABSENCE OU MAUVAISE CATÉGORIE DE PERMIS DE CONDUIRE
93/10/26 NO DRIVERS LICENCE OR IMPROPER CLASS OF LICENCE
ABSENCE OU MAUVAISE CATÉGORIE DE PERMIS DE CONDUIRE
93/11/10 SPEEDING 82 KMH IN 50 KMH ZONE
EXCÈS DE VITESSE 82KMH DANS ZONE DE 50 KMH
93/11/10 NO DRIVERS LICENCE OR IMPROPER CLASS OF LICENCE
ABSENCE OU MAUVAISE CATÉGORIE DE PERMIS DE CONDUIRE
93/11/15 SPEEDING 100 KMH IN 70 KMH ZONE
EXCÈS DE VITESSE 100 KMH DANS ZONE DE 70 KMH
93/11/15 NO DRIVERS LICENCE OR IMPROPER CLASS OF LICENCE
ABSENCE OU MAUVAISE CATÉGORIE DE PERMIS DE CONDUIRE
93/12/04 SUSPENDED UNTIL JAN. 3, 1994, DEMERIT POINT
TOTAL - PROBATIONARY DRIVER
SUSPENDU JUSQU'AU 3 JANV. 1994, TOTAL DES
POINTS D'INAPTITUDE, STAGIAIRE

Source: Ontario Ministry of Transportation website: <https://www.apps.rus.mto.gov.on.ca/jtips/drivingrecord3YCertIllustrationRecord.jsp>

FIGURE 3.2: Certified Plate Search — Recent Owner

| Ministry of Transportation | Ministère des Transports | Safety and Regulation Division | Division de la sécurité et des règlements |

Ontario

MINISTRY CONTROL NO./NO. DE CONTRÔLE DU MINISTÈRE SEARCH DATE/DATE DE RECHERCHE
000000 94/10/24

SEARCH TYPE/TYPE DE RECHERCHE INQUIRY KEY/ CRITÈRE DE RECHERCHE

PLATE/PLAQUE PLATE/PLAQUE - **AAAAAA**
==

REGISTRANT/CONDUCTEUR
NAME/NOM - **PUBLIC, JOHN, Q.**
ADDRESS/ADRESSE - *** STAGGER/ÉCHELONNER - 0509**
--VEHICLE/VÉHICULE
VEHICLE IDENTIFICATION NO./NO D'IDENTIFICATION DU VÉHICULE - **OAOAAOOAOAAOOOOOO**
CLASS/CATÉGORIE - **PASSENGER/VOITURE PARTICULIÈRE** MAKE/MARQUE - **PONT**
MODEL/MODÈLE - **FRS**
BODY TYPE/TYPE DE CARROSSERIE - **2 DOOR SEDAN/COUPÉ**
NO. OF CYLINDERS/NO DE CYLINDRÉE-**04**
MOTIVE POWER/FORCE MOTRICE - **GASOLINE/ESSENCE**
COLOUR/COULEUR - **WHITE/BLANC** YEAR/ANNÉE - **84**
STATUS/STATUT - **FIT/EN ÉTAT DE MARCHE** WEIGHT EMPTY/POIDS À VIDE -
NO. OF AXLES/NO D'ESSIEUX -
--PLATE/PLAQUE
PLATE/PLAQUE - **000YYY** YEAR/ANNÉE -
SERIES/SÉRIE - **OWN CHOICE PASSENGER/PERSONNALISÉE VOITURE PARTICULIÈRE**
STATUS/STATUT - **ATTACHED/FIXÉE**
FORMAT -
PLATE REGISTRATION DATE/DATE D'ENREGISTREMENT DES PLAQUES - **910122**
--VALTAG NO./NO DE VIGNETTE
0000000 REGISTERED WEIGHT/POIDS ENREGISTRÉ -
DECLARATION/DÉCLARATION -
STAGGER/ÉCHELONNER - **93/05/10** EXPIRY/EXPIRATION - **94/05/09**
PERMIT NO./NO DE CERTIFICAT - **49815715** DATE ISSUED/DATE DE DÉLIVRANCE - **91/05/09**

Source: Ontario Ministry of Transportation website: <https://www.apps.rus.mto.gov.on.ca/jtips/plSearchRecOwnerIllustration.jsp>

Online Name and "People Finder" Private Searches

In the past several years there has been an expansion and refining of Internet search engines and other online sources. You can now use the name of the defendant or debtor to obtain addresses, telephone numbers, and other information about an individual. Such information can help you verify a name and obtain other identifying information to locate the person so that you can serve a claim on him or her. These searches can be used to find both individual consumer debtors and business debtors operating under a business name. **Reverse searches** may be conducted on many of these sites by submitting a telephone number, address, e-mail address, or other information that will help you to obtain the correct name of a debtor, as well as other information.

These searches should reveal some information, provided the debtor subscribes to a phone service and/or is a home owner or a tenant in a residence. Reverse searches of phone numbers will often identify the subscriber of unlisted landlines and cell phones. Many sites are free, but some charge for information, in which case you can pay by credit card. The following are examples of useful sites, current at the time of publication. Note that sites come and go, and change Web addresses. You may find more sites by using a search engine such as Google, or Mamma, found at <http://www.google.com>, and <http://www.mamma.com>, and typing in "directory" or "search people".

Yahoo People Canada: <http://www.yahoo.ca>. Click on People Finder. You may search by name, with or without the city or province. This may turn up addresses and other information, some of which may be useful. A broad search of a common name that has not been narrowed by city or province may turn up too much information to be useful.

Pipl: <http://www.pipl.com>. You can submit a person's name or business name to this site. The site can be used for various countries. This site searches the "deep web", including online databases, to find references to the name submitted.

CanPages: <http://www.CanPages.ca>. You can submit a person's name or business name to this site, which may turn up an address and telephone number. Reverse searches are also possible.

Canada411: <http://www.canada411.ca>. You can submit a name to this site, which may turn up a telephone number of the phone subscriber.

Telus: <http://www.mytelus.com/phonebook/>. This site allows you to submit names to obtain phone numbers, including unlisted cell phone numbers, and addresses. You may also do reverse searches of phone numbers and addresses to identify and locate individuals.

Search Detective: <http://www.searchdetective.net/phone.html>. This site is useful for U.S. addresses. This site allows you to search by a phone number and will turn up account holder names and addresses, including those for unlisted landlines and cell phones. Searches may also be done by name to find a location.

Lycos Search: <http://www.whowhere.com>. This site can find individuals via a name search. You can also do reverse searches by submitting an address, a telephone number, or an e-mail address. The information submitted will yield information about who has the phone or e-mail account or who owns premises or lives at an address. It may also provide other personal information.

Searches by Name: Business Debtors

If the debtor is a business debtor, it is important to know the form of business organization used by the debtor. The debtor may be an individual (referred to in law as a natural person) carrying on business in her own name. In that case, the consumer name search techniques discussed in the previous section can be used to verify the name of the debtor. However, if the individual carries on business using a trade name (Hieronymous Bosch carrying on business as "Bosch Paint-by-Numbers") or as a partnership or a corporation, it may be difficult initially to determine the debtor's identity as an entity or party worth suing. You need to get the name right to ensure that you sue the party you intend to sue. If you sue using an incorrect name, at a minimum, an amendment costing time and money will be required. In some cases a new lawsuit will be required if you are still within the limitation period. Consider the following:

Sole proprietorships: If you are dealing with a sole proprietorship, you can sue the individual who is the sole proprietor in his or her own name; in addition you may wish to sue the sole proprietorship in the name in which it carries on business. Suing in both names may make enforcement of a judgment easier if assets are in either or both names. Note that Rule 5 makes it possible to sue in the business name and obtain information about the sole proprietor that will allow you to expand your enforcement rights against all available assets, as is the case with partnerships, as detailed below and on the next page.

> 5.06(1) If a person carries on business in a business name other than his or her own name, a proceeding may be commenced by or against the person using the business name.
> (2) Rules 5.01 to 5.05 apply, with necessary modifications, to a proceeding by or against a sole proprietor using a business name, as though the sole proprietor were a partner and the business name were the firm name of a partnership.

Partnerships: If the debtor or defendant is a partnership, you may sue in the partnership's name or sue the partners individually in their own names. Even if you sue in the partnership name, you will want to know the names of individual partners so that you can expand your enforcement rights to include a claim against their personal assets. In addition to the options discussed here, as is the case for sole proprietorships, Rule 5 allows you to sue in the partnership name and find out who the partners are so as to enforce a judgment against both the individual partners and the partnership through the use of a Notice to Alleged Partner form. How the plaintiff uses Rule 5 is discussed further in Chapter 6.

Partnerships
5.01 A proceeding by or against two or more persons as partners may be commenced using the firm name of the partnership.

Defence
5.02 If a proceeding is commenced against a partnership using the firm name, the partnership's defence shall be delivered in the firm name and no person who admits being a partner at any material time may defend the proceeding separately, except with leave of the court.

Notice to Alleged Partner
5.03(1) In a proceeding against a partnership using the firm name, a plaintiff who seeks an order that would be enforceable personally against a person as a partner may serve the person with the claim, together with a notice to alleged partner (Form 5A).

(2) A person served as provided in subrule (1) is deemed to have been a partner at the material time, unless the person defends the proceeding separately denying having been a partner at the material time.

Disclosure of Partners
5.04(1) If a proceeding is commenced by or against a partnership using the firm name, any other party may serve a notice requiring the partnership to disclose immediately in writing the names and addresses of all partners constituting the partnership at a time specified in the notice; if a partner's present address is unknown, the partnership shall disclose the last known address.

Partnership's Failure to Comply
(2) If a partnership fails to comply with a notice under subrule (1), its claim may be dismissed or the proceeding stayed or its defence may be struck out.

Enforcement of Order
5.05(1) An order against a partnership using the firm name may be enforced against the partnership's property.

(2) An order against a partnership using the firm name may also be enforced, if the order or a subsequent order so provides, against any person who was served as provided in rule 5.03 and who,
(a) under that rule, is deemed to have been a partner at the material time;
(b) has admitted being a partner at that time; or
(c) has been adjudged to have been a partner at that time.

Against Person not Served as Alleged Partner
(3) If, after an order has been made against a partnership using the firm name, the party obtaining it claims to be entitled to enforce it against any person alleged to be a partner other than a person who was served as provided in rule 5.03, the party may make a

motion for leave to do so; the judge may grant leave if the person's liability as a partner is not disputed or, if disputed, after the liability has been determined in such manner as the judge directs.

Corporations: If the business is incorporated, you must sue the corporation in its legal corporate name, as that name appears in the corporate registration documents kept by the Companies and Personal Property Security Branch.

Special care must be taken in determining who the party or entity to be sued is, particularly if a corporation has been used as the business entity to carry on business.

Example 3.1 Sue the Corporation, Not the Individual Manager

Suppose you are the manager of Video Supplies Inc. (a corporation), and you have always dealt face-to-face with Gary Gameman, the manager and president of Gary's Great Games Ltd. (also a corporation). Gary always places orders, writes the cheques, accepts delivery, and complains if the product isn't suitable. The cheques are on Gary's Great Games Ltd.'s account, and the invoices are always made out to Gary's Great Games Ltd. But in practical terms Gary Gameman owns the shares of the company and is its only employee and officer. In this situation it is easy to think of the business transactions as being between Video Supplies Inc. and Gary Gameman personally. Suppose Gary tells you, the manager of Video Supplies Inc., that "I'm not paying for that order." Video Supplies Inc. might be tempted to sue Gary Gameman in order to collect the debt; and if it did, it might very well lose on the ground that Gary Gameman had no *personal* liability in this transaction:

- At all times the sales were between Video Supplies Inc. and Gary's Great Games Ltd.
- Accounts were rendered to Gary's Great Games Ltd.
- Accounts were paid on the Gary's Great Games Ltd. account.
- Gary may have been president, sole shareholder, and sole employee of Gary's Great Games Ltd. He may even be the directing mind, but his actions were all through and on behalf of the company, which he used to do business. It does not make him personally liable. At best he can be described as acting as an agent for the company or as acting on its behalf.

So, if you sue Gary, the defendant in Example 3.1, instead of the corporation, you are likely to meet with the defence that he did not incur the debt and that he has no personal liability. The correct entity to be sued is the company. Many people have difficulty seeing why this should be so. But remember why limited liability companies were allowed to be formed in the first place. They permitted individuals to put capital into a legal but artificial person called a limited liability company. As this was a legal person with power to carry on business, it was responsible for its actions, as if it were an individual. The investors who "owned" it (through shares) could not be personally liable for the company's debts and defaults, so that their personal assets were not at risk beyond what they had invested in the company. If the company failed or its assets were seized, the investors could lose their capital investment in the company; but that was the limit of their liability, hence the term, "limited liability company". The rationale for permitting investors to do this was to encourage investments and various economic ventures and activities by limiting the investors' risk. So, if you deal with a company, sue the company. There may be some situations where you can sue the "owner" personally when the courts permit the "corporate veil" to be lifted to make an owner/manager of a company directly liable; but in the absence of fraud or other illegal behaviour, this rarely happens, particularly in Small Claims Court, where the effort would be so costly as to cancel out any gain, given the court's relatively low monetary jurisdiction.

If the business had simply been called "Gary's Great Games", it would most likely have been a partnership or a sole proprietorship. When the words "limited", "ltd.", "incorporated", or "inc." appear in a business name, as in "Gary's Great Games Ltd.", the business is incorporated. If Gary's Great Games was a partnership, you would need to know the name the partnership uses to carry on business, as well as who the partners are. While you can sue the partnership in its business name, that judgment would only bind partnership assets, such as the video games held in inventory, office furniture, and equipment owned by the business. If you also wanted to expand enforcement to include each individual partner's assets, such as land, cars, and personal bank accounts, you would need to know the correct name of each partner so that each could be given notice that you intend to use Rule 5, as noted earlier, to go after his or her assets, as well as those of the business in order to satisfy the judgment.

If Gary's Great Games were a sole proprietorship, you would have to verify who the owner of the business is. Although you have been dealing with Gary Gameman, you don't know for sure who the owner of Gary's Great Games is. If you wish to sue a sole proprietorship and you know, as in this example, the name it uses to carry on business without knowing who the individual sole proprietor is, you can do a **business name search**, which will turn up the name of the sole proprietor (or the name of the partners if it is a partnership, or the corporation's name if it is a numbered company or a company using a trade name different from its registered corporate name). All businesses being carried on in Ontario in a name other than the owner's name(s) must register their business name with the Companies and Personal Property Security Branch of the Ministry of Government Services.

In order to determine if Gary's Great Games is a corporation, you can carry out a Corporation Profile Report search (see Figure 3.5 on page 96) or a search for the Articles of Incorporation for Gary's Great Games. Submission of the name under which a corporation carries on business will result in the correct corporate name. Unlike with sole proprietorships and partnerships, remember that when a corporation is legally responsible, you must sue the corporation, not its officers, managers, or shareholders, unless those persons as individuals have acted so as to create a cause of action that is separate and distinct from the one against the corporation.

When you perform a search on a corporation using a business name, you may come up with a corporate name that is different from the name under which it carries on business. The name may well be an assigned registration number given by the Companies Branch, and it may appear, for example, as 12358 Ontario Limited — a so-called "numbered company". There is nothing sinister about a numbered company. For example, if Gus Al-Said decides to buy and operate a McDonald's franchise, he may run it as a corporation. If so, there is no point in getting a business name for the company because the company will be carrying on business under the well-known and highly marketable name of the franchisor. In this case, Al-Said may simply use the number that the Companies Branch assigns to the company he creates to run the franchise when it is incorporated without a name.

Conducting a Business Name Search

A business name search can be done in two ways. You can attend in person at the Companies and Personal Property Security Branch at 393 University Avenue, Toronto, Ontario M5G 2M2, or you can conduct an online search of the Ontario Business Information System (ONBIS), which is a public record database. An online search is easy and inexpensively done provided the name has been registered with the Companies and Personal Property Security Branch. The search site is available through Service Ontario. This site is most easily reached through <http://www.mgs.gov.on.ca/>: click on the Starting a Business link, and follow with another click on the ServiceOntario — Register a Business link. This search can be a bit of a fishing expedition if you do not know the name exactly. You can search the exact business name or words within the name, or use the business identification number that all registered businesses are given. You can pay for

FIGURE 3.3: Sample Online Business Name Search Form

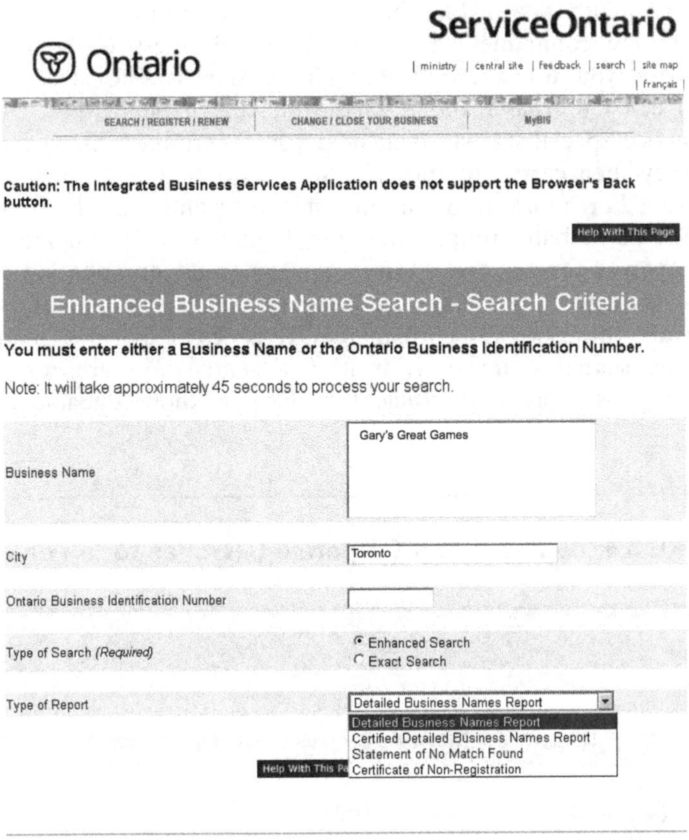
ServiceOntario

Ontario

| ministry | central site | feedback | search | site map | français |

SEARCH / REGISTER / RENEW | CHANGE / CLOSE YOUR BUSINESS | MyBIG

Caution: The Integrated Business Services Application does not support the Browser's Back button.

Help With This Page

Enhanced Business Name Search - Search Criteria

You must enter either a Business Name or the Ontario Business Identification Number.

Note: It will take approximately 45 seconds to process your search.

Business Name: Gary's Great Games

City: Toronto

Ontario Business Identification Number:

Type of Search *(Required)*: Enhanced Search / Exact Search

Type of Report: Detailed Business Names Report

Detailed Business Names Report
Certified Detailed Business Names Report
Statement of No Match Found
Certificate of Non-Registration

Help With This Pa

Source: ServiceOntario, Services for Businesses, <https://www.ibsa.serviceontario.ca/ibsa/servlet/com.visionmax.servlet.CommandServlet?command=screenflownoscript&screenid=26>

the search online by credit card. A sample online search application form is set out in Figure 3.3.

The business names report will set out the names and addresses of the individual persons using that business name. This information can assist you in carrying out further searches and in preparing and serving court documents. If the business name is not registered, you can obtain a certificate of non-registration showing that a business name that may be in use has not been registered. (There are penalties for failure to register a business under the *Business Names Act*, R.S.O. 1990, c. B.17. Although this will not directly affect a creditor's lawsuit against the debtor, the lawsuit will be **stayed** until the name is registered if the creditor is suing in a name that is not registered.)

There are companies that will conduct Business Name and other searches for you for a fee. Cyberbahn Group is one such company. You can call Cyberbahn and discuss your search needs with their customer service specialists, who will help you determine which searches to order. They then carry out the searches and e-mail you the results and an invoice. For more information on Cyberbahn, see its website at <http://www.cyberbahngroup.com> (see Figure 3.4). If you know which searches you want to carry out, you can conduct your own online searches through Cyberbahn, or through other companies such as OnCorp at <http://www.oncorp.com/>. It is less expensive to do your own online searches; however, if it is a search you are not familiar with, it may be more cost efficient to have a knowledgeable company

FIGURE 3.4: Business and Corporate Searches for a Fee

Source: Screen shot of Cyberbahn Service Web page. Reprinted with permission of Cyberbahn Group.

carry out the search for you. In any event, you should include the cost as a disbursement to the client on your account.

For most search sites, start at the homepage and follow the directions and links. These search sites will also allow you to conduct a variety of searches of other public business records maintained by the federal and provincial governments.

Conducting a Corporation Profile Report Search

If you are dealing with a corporation, you can verify the correct corporate name, registered office address, and information concerning officers and directors by obtaining a Corporation Profile Report. A sample report is found at Figure 3.5. This report can also be used to verify information about your own corporate client, as required by By-law 7.1 of the Law Society of Upper Canada. At the present time, you need to use a private search company such as Cyberbahn or OnCorp to obtain Corporation Profile Reports. Note that these searches are limited to the Ontario ministry records and will yield information related only to companies incorporated in Ontario. If a corporation is carrying on business in Ontario but was incorporated in another province or is a federally incorporated company, an Ontario corporation search will not provide any information. For searches that include information on corporations incorporated federally or in another province, you can use a private search company, such as those set out earlier, to carry out extra-provincial and/or federal corporate searches.

INFORMATION ABOUT THE DEBTOR'S ASSETS AND DEBTS

Up to this point our discussion has been about identifying the debtor accurately for litigation purposes. You are now able to sue the debtor by its proper name, and you have obtained information to locate the debtor for service of the plaintiff's claim. Having an accurate version of the debtor or defendant's name will now permit you to conduct a second set of searches about the defendant's assets and debts.

Is the Defendant Worth Suing?

When you conduct searches concerning the debtor's assets, consider the following questions:

- Does the debtor have assets worth seizing to satisfy a Small Claims Court judgment?

FIGURE 3.5: Sample Corporation Profile Report

Request ID:	010738912	Province of Ontario	Date Report Produced:	2010/11/30
Transaction ID:	36732459	Ministry of Consumer and Business Services	Time Report Produced:	16:43:49
Category ID:	UN/E	Companies and Personal Property Security Branch	Page:	1

CORPORATION PROFILE REPORT

Ontario Corp Number	Corporation Name		Incorporation Date
456789	GARY'S GREAT GAMES LTD.		1981/06/30
			Jurisdiction
			Ontario

Corporation Type	Corporation Status		Former Jurisdiction
ONTARIO BUSINESS CORP.	ACTIVE		NOT APPLICABLE

Registered Office Address		Date Amalgamated	Amalgamation Ind.
123 YONGE STREET		NOT APPLICABLE	NOT APPLICABLE
		New Amal. Number	Notice Date
TORONTO		NOT APPLICABLE	NOT APPLICABLE
ONTARIO			
CANADA M6C 1L3			Letter Date
Mailing Address			NOT APPLICABLE
		Revival Date	Continuation Date
123 YONGE STREET		NOT APPLICABLE	NOT APPLICABLE
TORONTO		Transferred Out Date	Cancel/Inactive Date
ONTARIO			
CANADA M6C 1L3		NOT APPLICABLE	NOT APPLICABLE
		EP Licence Eff.Date	EP Licence Term.Date
		NOT APPLICABLE	NOT APPLICABLE

		Number of Directors		Date Commenced in Ontario	Date Ceased in Ontario
		Minimum	Maximum		
Activity Classification		UNKNOWN	UNKNOWN	NOT APPLICABLE	NOT APPLICABLE
NOT APPLICABLE					

continues....

Figure 3.5 (continued)

Request ID:	010738912	Province of Ontario	Date Report Produced:	2010/11/30
Transaction ID:	36732459	Ministry of Consumer and Business Services	Time Report Produced:	16:43:49
Category ID:	UN/E	Companies and Personal Property Security Branch	Page:	2

CORPORATION PROFILE REPORT

Ontario Corp Number
456789

Corporation Name
GARY'S GREAT GAMES LTD.

Corporate Name History
GARY'S GREAT GAMES LTD.

Effective Date
1981/06/30

Current Business Name(s) Exist: NO

Expired Business Name(s) Exist: NO

Administrator:
Name (Individual / Corporation)

GARY
HENRY
GAMEMAN

Address

36 GAME COURT

THORNHILL
ONTARIO
CANADA   L4J 7X7

Date Began	First Director	
1981/06/30	NOT APPLICABLE	
Designation	Officer Type	Resident Canadian
DIRECTOR		Y

continues....

Figure 3.5 (continued)

Request ID:	010738912	Province of Ontario
Transaction ID:	36732459	Ministry of Consumer and Business Services
Category ID:	UN/E	Companies and Personal Property Security Branch

Date Report Produced:	2010/11/30
Time Report Produced:	16:43:49
Page:	3

CORPORATION PROFILE REPORT

Ontario Corp Number
456789

Corporation Name
GARY'S GREAT GAMES LTD.

Administrator:
Name (Individual / Corporation)

GARY
HENRY
GAMEMAN

Address

36 GAME COURT

THORNHILL
ONTARIO
CANADA   L4J 7X7

Date Began	**First Director**	
1981/06/30	NOT APPLICABLE	
Designation	**Officer Type**	**Resident Canadian**
OFFICER	PRESIDENT	Y

Administrator:
Name (Individual / Corporation)

GARY
HENRY
GAMEMAN

Address

36 GAME COURT

THORNHILL
ONTARIO
CANADA   L4J 7X7

Date Began	**First Director**	
1981/06/30	NOT APPLICABLE	
Designation	**Officer Type**	**Resident Canadian**
DIRECTOR		Y

continues....

Figure 3.5 (continued)

Request ID:	010738912	Province of Ontario	Date Report Produced: 2010/11/30
Transaction ID:	36732459	Ministry of Consumer and Business Services	Time Report Produced: 16:43:49
Category ID:	UN/E	Companies and Personal Property Security Branch	Page: 4

CORPORATION PROFILE REPORT

Ontario Corp Number
456789

Corporation Name
GARY'S GREAT GAMES LTD.

Administrator:
Name (Individual / Corporation)
GARY
HENRY
GAMEMAN

Address
36 GAME COURT

THORNHILL
ONTARIO
CANADA   L4J 7X7

Date Began
1981/06/30

First Director
NOT APPLICABLE

Designation
OFFICER

Officer Type
PRESIDENT

Resident Canadian
Y

Administrator:
Name (Individual / Corporation)
GARY
HENRY
GAMEMAN

Address
36 GAME COURT

THORNHILL
ONTARIO
CANADA   L4J 7X7

Date Began
1981/06/30

First Director
NOT APPLICABLE

Designation
DIRECTOR

Officer Type
SECRETARY

Resident Canadian
Y

continues....

Figure 3.5 (continued)

Request ID:	010738912	Province of Ontario	Date Report Produced:	2010/11/30
Transaction ID:	36732459	Ministry of Consumer and Business Services	Time Report Produced:	16:43:49
Category ID:	UN/E	Companies and Personal Property Security Branch	Page:	5

CORPORATION PROFILE REPORT

Ontario Corp Number
456789

Corporation Name
GARY'S GREAT GAMES LTD.

Last Document Recorded

Act/Code	Description	Form	Date
CIA	ANNUAL RETURN 2009	1C	2010/01/23

THIS REPORT SETS OUT THE MOST RECENT INFORMATION FILED BY THE CORPORATION ON OR AFTER JUNE 27, 1992, AND RECORDED IN THE ONTARIO BUSINESS INFORMATION SYSTEM AS AT THE DATE AND TIME PRINTING. ALL PERSONS WHO ARE RECORDED AS CURRENT DIRECTORS OR OFFICERS ARE INCLUDED IN THE LIST OF ADMINISTRATORS.

ADDITIONAL HISTORICAL INFORMATION MAY EXIST ON THE COMPANIES AND PERSONAL PROPERTY SECURITY BRANCH MICROFICHE.

The issuance of this report in electronic form is authorized by the Director of Companies and Personal Property Security Branch.

continues....

Figure 3.5 (continued)

INVOICE

Cyberbahn Inc.
60 Adelaide Street East, 5th Floor
Toronto, Ontario
M5C 3E4

Invoice#:   3001000100087035

Date: 11/30/2010

Sold To: CREDIT CARD USER

Attention:
Client #: 30010001
Your P.O.: 13285
GST# 89040 4288 RT
Terms: NET30

RE: GARY'S GREAT GAMES LTD.

Item		Price
ONB100000	ONBIS SEARCH - CYBERBAHN FEE	25.00
DIS100000	GOV'T DISB. - PROFILE REPORT	8.00
	GROSS AMOUNT:	$33.00
	HST:	$ 3.25
	TOTAL:	$36.25

Source: A paid search conducted by Cyberbahn.

- Are there secured creditors who will get all the valuable assets before you ever get near them with your judgment?

- Are you the only creditor suing the debtor, or are there 15 others, circling the debtor like sharks closing in for the kill?

- Does the debtor have a long history of defaulting on debts where creditors have had little success in recovering anything on their judgments?

- Will the costs of enforcing a judgment be so expensive, relative to the limited amounts that can be recovered in Small Claims Court, that proceeding with a lawsuit is simply not worth it?

The answers to these questions may indicate how you should advise the creditor. If the debtor has few assets or has assets that are subject to the security interests of other creditors, or if many other creditors have judgments and are closing in, or if no creditor has been successful in enforcing a judgment, then the best advice to the potential plaintiff may be to not sue at all. While you might obtain a judgment, it would be more money and time thrown away on what is likely to be an unrecoverable debt. It might be best for the creditor at this point to simply write off the debt as a business loss. If the debt is written off, the loss can be claimed against other income for tax purposes. The taxpayer must be able to document the reasons for writing off the debt, especially if he or she decides not to sue.

In order to get to the point where you can properly advise a client, you may need to conduct some or all of the following searches, which can tell you whether there are likely to be assets to seize, whether the debtor is about to or has become insolvent, and whether collection efforts are likely to be successful.

Execution Search

When a plaintiff obtains a judgment in a lawsuit, the judgment orders the defendant to pay money to the plaintiff, but that command from the court is not self-enforcing. If the defendant does not pay, it is necessary for the plaintiff to enforce the judgment. He or she can do this in a number of ways: one way to is file a writ of seizure and sale (also referred to as a "writ of execution"). If you are a judgment creditor filing a writ of execution and you are not sure where the debtor has assets, you might have to file duplicate writs of execution in sheriff's offices in more than one county or district. You usually file a writ or a duplicate writ in the county or region where the judgment was obtained and in the counties or regions where the debtor lives, works, and/or carries on business and where you know or suspect the debtor has property. Once filed, a creditor can use a writ of execution in two ways:

- The judgment creditor can direct the sheriff to seize and sell the judgment debtor's land if he or she knows of land that can be seized and sold so that the proceeds of sale can be used to satisfy the judgment.

- The judgment creditor can simply leave the execution sitting on file. Businesses often search executions to assure themselves that the person they are dealing with is a good credit risk. Others who do business with the debtor or who may be lending the debtor money may be reluctant to lend or extend credit to a business once they learn of an outstanding writ of execution. In these circumstances, the debtor may be pressured to pay off the execution creditor. A writ simply left on file may also produce money for the judgment creditor if another judgment creditor enforces his or her writ because the proceeds of sale of any property recovered by the bailiff or sheriff must be shared among execution creditors, in that jurisdiction, on a pro-rata basis under the *Creditors' Relief Act, 2010*, S.O. 2010, c. 16, Sch. 4, ss. 3, 4, and 5.[2] The writ, once filed, is enforceable for six years and can be renewed.

In a Small Claims Court action, if the writ is to be used to seize personal property, it is filed with the court that gave judgment, or with another Small Claims Court where the property might be located. Then, the bailiff, an officer of the Small Claims Court whose duty is to enforce that court's orders, will execute the writ and try to seize and then arrange the sale of personal property of the judgment debtor. If a Small Claims Court judgment is to be enforced against an interest in real property, it must be filed with the Office of the Sheriff of the county, region, or district where the land is located. The sheriff is the officer who enforces civil orders of the Superior Court.

Execution searches of Small Claims Court files are rarely conducted through the courts, as there are no easily used search systems. Execution searches for Small Claims Court writs of seizure and sale of personal property are filed with the individual courts, making searches time consuming. In the past, with monetary levels so low in the Small Claims Court, such searches were often skipped. Fortunately, information about small claims judgments is often obtained through the reports

---

[2] The *Creditor's Relief Act, 2010*, in most cases, extends the proportionate sharing of funds collected by the sheriff to execution creditors who file with the sheriff within one month after funds from the seizure are received by the sheriff.

from credit bureaus. Private search companies can be hired to conduct Ontario-wide execution searches. These reports and private searches are discussed later in this chapter.

It is customary to search Superior Court of Justice writs of execution to see if there are writs filed against a named debtor in respect of Superior Court judgments and whether they remain unsatisfied. Unfortunately, the province has no centralized file of all writs of seizure and sale in all the counties, regions and districts of Ontario. This means that you must search executions in the sheriff's office in each county, region, or district where you think the debtor has or had assets. You can search on your own through the applicable sheriff's offices, or more commonly you can hire a private search company, as set out in the next section, to conduct a province-wide search for you.[3]

A Superior Court of Justice execution search against the name of the debtor may show any of the following:

- An execution that can be used to verify the name of the debtor or the spelling of the debtor's name, and may identify aliases (appears as "also known as").

- A number of outstanding writs of execution, which may indicate that the debtor has been sued before and that the judgment creditors have not been able to collect on the judgment.

- Recently filed writs of execution, which may indicate that all of the creditors are closing in and that the debtor is likely to be "**judgment proof**", with little likelihood that assets will be available to satisfy the judgment by the time you sue and obtain a judgment. This pattern may also indicate that the debtor has just gone, or is about to go, bankrupt. Suing may be a waste of time as a court claim against a person going through a bankruptcy will be stayed. In such circumstances the creditor must file a claim with the trustee in bankruptcy.

- Many outstanding writs that are several years old, which may indicate that the debtor has successfully avoided paying creditors for some time and that the debtor either has no assets or is adept at hiding them. This is particularly true if the debtor has not gone bankrupt.

- No executions against the debtor, which may be an indication that there are no prior unsatisfied judgments and that there will be assets

------

[3] It is hoped that changes to the *Execution Act* arising from Bill 68, Ontario *Open for Business Act, 2010*, will result in the establishment of a provincial index of executions.

available to seize; it may also indicate that the debtor's assets are not located in the county or district where you searched executions.

Conducting an Execution Search

As mentioned earlier, you an conduct an execution search yourself or you can hire a private search company.

EXECUTION SEARCHES THROUGH THE SHERIFF'S OFFICE

To conduct a search of executions against the name of a debtor, you can attend at the local sheriff's office to complete a form to request a certificate indicating whether there are writs of seizure and sale on file in that office. Forms are available from the local sheriff's office. The sheriff's office for each county, region, or district is usually located in the local Superior Court of Justice courthouse. The local court office and the sheriff's office are listed in the blue government pages of the local telephone directory.

In Toronto, execution searches at the sheriff's office may be done online after payment of the prescribed fee. You key in the same kind of information you would provide for the certificate, and the system produces an on-screen response and, if desired, a printout of that response. In time, this system will extend to other parts of Ontario. Hopefully, one day soon, it will be available online from your office computer and, like the Personal Property Security Register, be province wide.

In completing the request for a certificate, you must do the following:

- Give the full name of the debtor; if the debtor is an individual, give middle names as well as the first name, if possible.

- If the debtor is a business, be sure to give the business's proper legal name. With sole proprietorships and partnerships, it may be wise in most cases to list the name of the individual who is the sole proprietor or the names of the partners, as well as the business name. You can then learn whether expansion of your enforcement rights to partners and individual proprietors is worthwhile.

File the request for a certificate in the sheriff's office in the area where the debtor is likely to have assets, or where the debtor lives or carries on business.

Once you have results, you can ask for copies of the writs to find out the particulars, such as the name of the judgment creditor, the amount owing, and the length of time the debt has been unsatisfied.

You can also call the judgment creditor's lawyer, whose name appears on the writ, to find out about attempts to collect.

EXECUTION SEARCHES USING PRIVATE SEARCH COMPANIES

To efficiently search for executions filed anywhere in Ontario, you can use the search services of a private search company, such as Cyberbahn Group at <http://www.cyberbahngroup.com/>, Teranet® at <http://www.teranet.ca>, or BAR-eX Communications Inc. at <http://www.bar-ex.com>. A sample OWL® report, an Ontario-wide executions search, from BAR-eX® is found in Figure 3.6.

Personal Property Security Act Search

In order to determine if the debtor has pledged any of his or her property as security to other creditors, a search should be conducted under the Personal Property Security Registration System (PPSR), which is set up under Ontario's *Personal Property Security Act*, R.S.O. 1990, c. P.10 (PPSA). The registration system permits a secured creditor to register a notice of security interest in an asset otherwise owned and in the possession of the debtor. Registration is notice to strangers of that creditor's interest in the asset and that this interest must be satisfied before the interests of other creditors, including some of those who later take an interest in the same security. In other words, whoever registers first generally has priority over those who come afterwards.

At this stage, a PPSA search will reveal what assets the debtor owns that are pledged as collateral to other creditors. The nature and range of assets will tell you something about the debtor's business or, if the debtor is a consumer, his spending habits. It will also identify assets that may not be available for you to seize once you obtain a judgment, as the secured creditor has priority over unsecured judgment creditors. If the amount of secured debt is so high that none of the assets appears to be available for seizure, it may not be advisable for your client to sue at all because there may be no assets available to be seized and sold to satisfy a judgment. As the secured creditor is likely to have priority over a judgment creditor, proceeds of sale after seizure of a secured asset by an unsecured judgment creditor would be used first to pay the secured creditor(s) before proceeds would be available for an ordinary judgment creditor.

After you have obtained a judgment, you have a right under the PPSA to ask the secured creditor questions about the security agreement with the debtor, including how much the debtor has to pay to the secured creditor. You may also write to the secured creditor and ask questions before a judgment has been obtained, but the secured

FIGURE 3.6: Sample Ontario-wide OWL® Search

WRITS OF EXECUTION

OWL® Report

www.bar-ex.com

For BAR-eX Customer Service,
please email info@bar-ex.com
or call 1-877-GO-BAR-eX
(1-877-462-2739)

Requested By: MB, Reference Number: DOE

Date of Search:
March 01, 2007

Total Cost(including GST):
$52.45

Name Searched:
DOE, JOHN

The following writs of execution were retrieved:

ENFORCEMENT OFFICE: NEWMARKET

WRIT NUMBER:
06-0002045
06-0003692

ENFORCEMENT OFFICE: HAMILTON

WRIT NUMBER:
06-0000991
95-0001491
97-0002027

ENFORCEMENT OFFICE: ST CATHARINES

WRIT NUMBER:

GST Registration No.: 858 632 003 RT0001

All 49 Ontario enforcement offices were searched to obtain this result, unless otherwise noted above.
This report may not be copied or resold except under license from Teranet Enterprises Inc.
The information in this report is provided on an "as is" basis and is not to be relied upon for land registration purposes.
Access to and use of the BAR-eX web site, and the services and products available through the web site, are subject to terms,
conditions, availability and pricing at www.bar-ex.com, all of which can be changed without notice.

page 1 of 5   ©2006 Teranet Enterprises Inc. BAR-eX, the BAR-eX design and OWL are registered trademarks and Ontario Writs Locator is a
trademark of Teranet Enterprises Inc. All rights reserved.

continues....

Figure 3.6 (continued)

WRITS OF EXECUTION
OWL® Report
www.bar-ex.com

For BAR-eX Customer Service,
please email info@bar-ex.com
or call 1-877-GO-BAR-eX
(1-877-462-2739)

04-0000069

ENFORCEMENT OFFICE: WELLAND

WRIT NUMBER:
03-0000638

ENFORCEMENT OFFICE: KITCHENER

WRIT NUMBER:
95-0003348

ENFORCEMENT OFFICE: LINDSAY

WRIT NUMBER:
05-0000399
92-0000155

ENFORCEMENT OFFICE: PARRY SOUND

WRIT NUMBER:
95-0000346
95-0000632
96-0000200

ENFORCEMENT OFFICE: GODERICH

WRIT NUMBER:
06-0000162

GST Registration No.: 858 632 003 RT0001

All 49 Ontario enforcement offices were searched to obtain this result, unless otherwise noted above.
This report may not be copied or resold except under license from Teranet Enterprises Inc.
The information in this report is provided on an "as is" basis and is not to be relied upon for land registration purposes.
Access to and use of the BAR-eX web site, and the services and products available through the web site, are subject to terms, conditions, availability and pricing at www.bar-ex.com, all of which can be changed without notice.
page 2 of 5   ©2006 Teranet Enterprises Inc. BAR-eX, the BAR-eX design and OWL are registered trademarks and Ontario Writs Locator is a trademark of Teranet Enterprises Inc. All rights reserved.

continues....

Figure 3.6 (continued)

WRITS OF EXECUTION
OWL® Report

www.bar-ex.com

For BAR-eX Customer Service,
please email info@bar-ex.com
or call 1-877-GO-BAR-eX
(1-877-462-2739)

ENFORCEMENT OFFICE: TORONTO

WRIT NUMBER:
01-0001805
04-0004225
05-0000456
05-0002676
05-0003457
06-0003569
06-0003569
92-0017879
95-0010570
95-0020997
96-0004837
98-0002986

ENFORCEMENT OFFICE: BARRIE

WRIT NUMBER:
05-0000667

ENFORCEMENT OFFICE: PEMBROKE

WRIT NUMBER:
99-0000355

ENFORCEMENT OFFICE: KINGSTON

WRIT NUMBER:
05-0000106

GST Registration No.: 858 632 003 RT0001

All 49 Ontario enforcement offices were searched to obtain this result, unless otherwise noted above.
This report may not be copied or resold except under license from Teranet Enterprises Inc.
The information in this report is provided on an "as is" basis and is not to be relied upon for land registration purposes.
Access to and use of the BAR-eX web site, and the services and products available through the web site, are subject to terms,
conditions, availability and pricing at www.bar-ex.com, all of which can be changed without notice.

page 3 of 5

continues....

Figure 3.6 (continued)

WRITS OF EXECUTION
OWL® Report

www.bar-ex.com

For BAR-eX Customer Service,
please email info@bar-ex.com
or call 1-877-GO-BAR-eX
(1-877-462-2739)

ENFORCEMENT OFFICE: WINDSOR

WRIT NUMBER:
05-0001588

ENFORCEMENT OFFICE: PETERBOROUGH

WRIT NUMBER:
04-0000105

ENFORCEMENT OFFICE: ST THOMAS

WRIT NUMBER:
95-0010536

ENFORCEMENT OFFICE: BRAMPTON

WRIT NUMBER:
05-0004841
96-0005039

ENFORCEMENT OFFICE: COCHRANE

WRIT NUMBER:
93-0000924

ENFORCEMENT OFFICE: BRACEBRIDGE

WRIT NUMBER:

GST Registration No.: 858 632 003 RT0001

All 49 Ontario enforcement offices were searched to obtain this result, unless otherwise noted above.
This report may not be copied or resold except under license from Teranet Enterprises Inc.
The information in this report is provided on an "as is" basis and is not to be relied upon for land registration purposes.
Access to and use of the BAR-eX web site, and the services and products available through the web site, are subject to terms,
conditions, availability and pricing at www.bar-ex.com, all of which can be changed without notice.
©2006 Teranet Enterprises Inc. BAR-eX, the BAR-eX design and OWL are registered trademarks and Ontario Writs Locator is a
trademark of Teranet Enterprises Inc. All rights reserved.

page 4 of 5

continues....

Figure 3.6 (continued)

WRITS OF EXECUTION

www.bar-ex.com

OWL® Report

For BAR-eX Customer Service,
please email info@bar-ex.com
or call 1-877-GO-BAR-eX
(1-877-462-2739)

05-0000346
95-0000813
97-0000032
97-0000032

ENFORCEMENT OFFICE: WHITBY

WRIT NUMBER:
06-0002176
94-0002106

ENFORCEMENT OFFICE: BRANTFORD

WRIT NUMBER:
07-0000088

ENFORCEMENT OFFICE: NORTH BAY

WRIT NUMBER:
00-0000461

GST Registration No.: 858 632 003 RT0001

All 49 Ontario enforcement offices were searched to obtain this result, unless otherwise noted above.
This report may not be copied or resold except under license from Teranet Enterprises Inc.
The information in this report is provided on an "as is" basis and is not to be relied upon for land registration purposes.
Access to and use of the BAR-eX web site, and the services and products available through the web site, are subject to terms,
conditions, availability and pricing at www.bar-ex.com, all of which can be changed without notice.

page 5 of 5

©2006 Teranet Enterprises Inc. BAR-eX, the BAR-eX design and OWL are registered trademarks and Ontario Writs Locator is a
trademark of Teranet Enterprises Inc. All rights reserved.

Source: Teranet is a registered trademark of Teranet Inc. and BAR-eX and OWL are registered trademarks and Ontario Writs Locator is a trademark of Teranet Enterprises Inc. All rights reserved.

creditor does not have to answer your questions. However, asking questions at this stage sometimes causes the secured creditor to contact the debtor, which may cause the debtor to pay your client. But it could also warn the debtor to try to *judgment-proof* himself or herself.

Conducting a PPSA Search

In order to conduct a PPSA search, you must know the full name of the debtor, including, if possible, the person's middle name. Supplying the debtor's date of birth will narrow the search. A search under the name "John Smith" without an accompanying date of birth will result in a report that will overwhelm you with all the registrations against every John Smith in the system. Having the right date of birth will help eliminate the John Smiths you are not interested in. You may also search for automobiles owned by the debtor by supplying the VIN. You may be able to obtain the debtor's proper name and date of birth from a driving record search, as detailed earlier in this chapter.

Filing a PPSA inquiry request results in a report that will identify the category of asset secured along with the secured creditor's name and address. To obtain details about the asset and the debt, it is necessary to contact the secured creditor identified in the report. If there are no registrations against the debtor, the report will state this.

PPSA searches may be done by phone by calling 1-800-267-8847 (in Toronto, 416-325-8847). You may also conduct searches online at the Ministry of Government Services site at <http://www.mgs.gov.on.ca> and click on "services for residents", then "more online services" and follow the link to search or register a personal property lien. There is a fee for the search, and you can order a report that is either certified (can be filed as evidence in court) or uncertified. Payment is by credit card, but if you do many PPSA searches you can open an account and be billed periodically. Searches may also be conducted online for a fee through private search companies such as Cyberbahn Group or OnCorp. You may do several types of PPSA searches:

- *Individual non-specific:* Submit the last name and the first name. You may search for all possible registrations or registrations within a specific time period.

- *Individual specific:* Submit the last name, first name, and middle initial along with the date of birth.

- *Business debtor inquiry:* Submit the business name.

- *Motor vehicle search:* Submit the VIN. This allows you to track a vehicle given as collateral, no matter who owned the car or what licence plate was on it.

Bank Act Search

Under s. 427 of the federal *Bank Act*, S.C. 1991, c. 46, Canadian banks providing financing to wholesalers, retailers, shippers, and dealers in "products of agriculture, products of aquaculture, products of the forest, products of the quarry and mine, products of the sea, lakes, and rivers, of goods, wares and merchandise, manufactured or otherwise" can take security in the form of a first preferential lien on the goods or equipment. Such security is usually taken in bank financing arrangements with farmers, fisherfolk, and those involved in transporting agriculture or forestry products. The assigning of security under the *Bank Act* results in a transfer of **title** of the debtor's property to the bank until the loan is repaid. During this time, the debtor remains in possession of the collateral and may use it in the ordinary course of business. For example, a forestry company may pledge its fleet of delivery trucks as collateral under s. 427. The bank has title and is the legal owner; the company continues to use the trucks to deliver goods without interference by the bank unless the loan goes into default. When the loan is repaid, title to the trucks passes back to the debtor.

A *Bank Act* search would normally be conducted only if the debtor carried on business in any of the areas specified under s. 427.

Searching under the *Bank Act*

A *Bank Act* search is done by examining the register under the name of the business debtor at the offices of the Bank of Canada. In Ontario, such a search is done through Canadian Securities Registration Systems (CSRS). Anyone can request searches by CSRS. However, you must first register with CSRS by sending a fax to 604-637-4015 setting out your name and address and the type of account you want. For occasional searches, you can elect to establish a credit account, whereby you pay, in advance, each time you request a search. For more information on types of accounts, call 416-204-3000.

If you only require a *Bank Act* search occasionally, you can avoid the time and expense involved in setting up a CSRS account by using a private search firm, such as Cyberbahn Group at <http://www.cyberbahngroup.com> or CorporateSearchers at <http://corporatesearchers.com>. There is a fee for the search report, which may be paid by credit card. An entry in the Bank of Canada register will give a file number that can be used to obtain further particulars of the loan. If most or all of the business's assets are pledged as security under s. 427, there may be very few assets available to satisfy the claims of an ordinary judgment debtor; therefore, suing the business may not be worthwhile.

Section 427 provides for a secured credit registration system similar to that of the PPSA. In fact, assets may be pledged as collateral under both systems. If it is advisable to conduct a *Bank Act* search, it is probably a good idea to do a PPSA search as well; the reverse, however, is not necessarily true because a PPSA search may be used with consumer debtors and small businesses, whereas a *Bank Act* search would usually be unnecessary for those classes of debtors.

Because creditors may register against the same debtor in both systems, there can be problems in sorting out which creditor has priority over the other. Where two creditors use the PPSA, for example, the PPSA's internal priority-ranking rules will determine which of two PPSA creditors of the same debtor has priority. There is, however, no statutory solution to resolve a priority conflict between a PPSA registration and a *Bank Act* registration, which has its own separate rules for determining priorities among competing s. 427 registrants.[4]

Bulk Sales Act Searches

If a business is selling its assets and equipment "in bulk", an affidavit must be registered under the Ontario *Bulk Sales Act*, R.S.O. 1990, c. B.14, stating that all creditors have been paid or will be paid from the proceeds of the sale. This search should be carried out when the debtor is a business and there is some risk that the business has just sold all of its assets or is about to sell all of its assets, resulting in the business's ceasing to operate or to have assets.

While there is nothing wrong with selling the assets of a business, a debtor could sell all of her assets to a **purchaser in good faith**, take the sale proceeds, and leave the jurisdiction, making it difficult or impossible for creditors to obtain payment of what the debtor owes them. The *Bulk Sales Act* requires that a purchaser complete documentation that gives details of the sale in order to protect himself against claims by the vendor's creditors that the purchaser knew the vendor was disposing of assets to defraud his creditors. This documentation is filed in the bulk sales register, which is kept in the court offices of

---

[4] In the case of *Bank of Montreal v. Innovation Credit Union*, 2010 SCC 47, the Supreme Court of Canada upheld that although provinces cannot legislate in order to oust the bank's rights, they can alter the law as it relates to property and civil rights in each province. A province therefore can, as Saskatchewan has done, add in priority provisions to its provincial PPSA legislation.

the Superior Court of Justice in the county, region, or district where the purchase occurred. A purchaser who has complied with the act is protected from claims by the seller's creditors against the assets sold by the debtor to the purchaser. A search of the register will determine if the act has been complied with. If it has not, the purchaser's interest in the assets of the debtor can be attacked by the creditor.

Searching under the *Bulk Sales Act*

Unfortunately there is no centralized registry for Ontario of all *Bulk Sales Act* registrations. Therefore a search must be done in the Superior Court of Justice office for the county, region, or district where the purchase occurred. The easiest way to conduct a *Bulk Sales Act* search is through a private search company such as Cyberbahn Group or CorporateSearchers.

Bankruptcy and Insolvency Act Search

A bankruptcy search is useful to determine if the debtor has gone bankrupt or is about to go bankrupt. If a debtor is bankrupt, there is no point suing the debtor because any action would be automatically stayed, and once the bankrupt is discharged from bankruptcy, the debt will usually be extinguished. Instead, the creditor will file proof of the debt claim with the debtor's trustee in bankruptcy. The trustee will review the claim and, if it is in order, the creditor may recover some of the money owing, but probably not all of it.

Secured creditors are entitled to seize their secured property to sell it to satisfy the debt owing to them and to do so ahead of the claims and rights of unsecured creditors claiming through the trustee. Unsecured creditors, which include ordinary judgment creditors, get what is left over after secured and priority creditors, such as Canada Revenue Agency, have realized on their security. After all of the bankrupt's creditors, both secured and unsecured, have had their interests attended to, the debtor is usually discharged from bankruptcy, free and clear of the debts incurred before bankruptcy, with some exceptions, such as family law support obligations.

As a result of the bankruptcy rules, there is often little of value left for unsecured creditors of the bankrupt. For this reason, unsecured creditors may recover no more than 10 or 20 cents on each dollar owed because the secured creditors have already taken major assets.

There are two ways to go bankrupt: an unpaid creditor can put a debtor into bankruptcy using a petition for bankruptcy, or the debtor can make an assignment in bankruptcy. As an alternative to bankruptcy, in some cases, a debtor can make a consumer proposal to his creditors. A proposal can be made when consumer debts, excluding a mortgage, are over $1,000 and under $250,000 in total. In some cases, a proposal known as a divisional proposal can be made for debts over $250,000.[5] A proposal is a plan for repayment made by the debtor, through a trustee in bankruptcy, to his creditors.

A search through the Superintendent of Bankruptcy at its national office can be made by phoning 613-941-2863 or by fax at 613-941-9490 or online at the Industry Canada website: <http://www.strategis.ic.gc.ca/>. Search on the homepage and follow the link for bankruptcy. A credit bureau search will also show if a debtor is bankrupt or is making a consumer proposal.

Credit Bureau Search

Licensed credit bureaus, which can be found in the Yellow Pages, can give you a credit history for the debtor. With this information you can contact other lenders to obtain more detailed information, although they are under no obligation to provide it; and they may be breaching privacy legislation requirements if they do provide it. Credit bureaus themselves come under an exception in privacy legislation. They rely on members reporting information about loans, defaults, and payments made by a debtor to get an accurate sense of what kind of credit risk the borrower is. Some credit bureaus have inexpensive online services available to members that allow them to gather information using an office computer, and some let you search online for a fee. In order to obtain a credit bureau report on someone other than yourself, you have to become a member of that particular credit bureau and obtain the consent of the person you are searching against to carry out the search. Because lawyers and paralegals extend services to the public for a fee, they are considered creditors and can join a credit bureau by registering and abiding by the terms of membership. One of the most commonly used credit bureaus is Equifax. More information on Equifax can be found at <http://www.equifax.com/>. Another major credit bureau is TransUnion at <http://www.transunion.ca>.

You may order a debtor's credit report online using the business name or the individual's name. The more identifying information you provide, the more likely you are to obtain an accurate credit report. A credit report provides broader and more detailed information than the other searches we have examined so far. However, the information in the report comes from a variety of sources: some of which may be less than accurate, and some of which are the result of subjective interpretation. Thus, caution should be observed with respect to report contents.

---

[5] *Bankruptcy and Insolvency Act*, R.S.C. 1985, c. B-3, s. 66.11 and 2(b).

You can obtain commercial and personal credit reports from Equifax or other credit bureaus. We will first examine the contents of a commercial credit report.

Commercial Credit Reports

Among the types of information such reports will likely provide are the following, which are found in reports from Equifax:

- *Identification:* The debtor is identified by name, address, phone number, the date the file was established, and the reporting agency's file number.

- *Summary:* This provides an overview of the degree of risk as well as the contents of the report. It may include information on how creditors have been treated and may describe negative information, if there is any. This part can be very subjective and should be used with caution. Note that debtors have a right to have incorrect information corrected by the reporting agency. Information about how to do this is available on the agency website.

- *Creditor Information:* This section identifies the industry or reporting creditors for this debtor. It should include the date the information was posted, because some of the information may be ancient history and irrelevant. This section often provides information about the "ageing" of receivables, which describes how long it takes a debtor to pay creditors. The most recently posted information appears first.

- *Payment Trends:* The speed with which payments are received is reported over a two-year period. This allows creditors to view trends and cyclical fluctuations in payment delays, which can result from cash flow fluctuations due to the nature of the business.

- *Returned Cheques:* This reports details on **NSF cheques**. NSF means "not sufficient funds". When a creditor deposits into his or her bank account a cheque payment from a debtor and the cheque is rejected and returned by the bank as an NSF cheque, it means that the debtor's bank account does not have enough money to cover the amount of the cheque.

- *Collection Claims:* This reports creditors' collection claims for a five-year period.

- *Legal Information:* This sets out legal information about lawsuits and judgments over a five-year period. Note that not every lawsuit has to do with debts.

- *Information on Bankruptcy:* Information about the creditor for a five-year period is noted here. This information comes from the Superintendent of Bankruptcy.

- *Banking Information:* When available, information about bank accounts, loans, and lines of credit are reported here.

- *Company Information:* The date of incorporation and information about officers and directors is reported here if available.

- *Other Files:* If the business has had name changes or is linked to other business entities, any previous credit files about predecessor business entities will be included, providing a longer historical payment trail. However, assumptions about current behaviour based on the behaviour of predecessors is risky, as past behaviour may be only remotely linked to present behaviour due to changes in the nature of the business and in its management and control.

- *Recent Inquiries:* There will be a record here of recent inquiries by other creditors about this debtor.

- *Scoring:* From all of this detail a credit reporting agency will provide a credit information score indicating overall risk in dealing with the debtor, and a payment index score indicating the percentage of the total amount owing that is past due. These scores are important to creditors in determining the steps they take with respect to a debtor and how quickly they take them. These two scores, as used by Equifax, are discussed below. Other credit reporting agencies use similar scoring techniques. But be sure to read how their scoring system works before trying to interpret the score.

  - *Credit Information Score:* The higher the score, the greater the risk factor. The lowest possible risk score is zero. A zero score is characteristic of less than 1% of all businesses, and would describe a business that pays all debts when accounts are presented. A company with a score higher than 40 is considered to be a high risk. Only about 1.06% of all businesses score higher than 40.

    New companies automatically default to a factor of 20, indicating they are neither very safe nor very risky. As time goes by, and there are few or no negative reports, the risk factor will drop toward 0. If there is a bad payment history it will rise toward 40.

    If the Superintendent of Bankruptcy reports a company, it automatically gets a score of 70, indicating insolvency proceedings.

    A company that scores between 1 and 10 is considered a very good risk. Only about 15% of all businesses fall into this low-risk group, however. A score of 20 represents a "neutral" risk assessment, but a score of over 20 represents increased risk.

The score is calculated using the seven factors shown in the matrix at the end of the report.

- *Payment Index Score:* This index forms part of the total credit information score and takes the amounts owed in the current, first, second, third, and fourth payment periods past due and calculates these amounts as percentages of the total amount owed. It then uses a formula to work out the average number of days payment is past the due date. In Canada the average score is 22. Accounts are often sent to collection when they reach a score of 60. The highest score would be 100, which would mean that everything owing would have to be in the third period past due. This would indicate that all of the amounts owing have been unpaid for months, which would be evidence of insolvency. The lowest score would be zero, which indicates that all bills are paid before the due date. Note that the long-term trend of the scores is more important than the score at the moment. Of interest is whether the risk is increasing, indicating financial problems, or decreasing, indicating that the business is doing well. Equifax provides nine quarters, or just over two years, of scores to give you access to long-term trends.

A sample Equifax commercial credit report, using the elements discussed here, is set out in Figure 3.7.

Consumer Credit Reports

If you are trying to obtain information on a non-business debtor, you may obtain a consumer credit report, which is different in its focus from a commercial credit report. The following description of a consumer credit report, based on the Equifax Consumer Credit Report, indicates the kind of information the report provides:

- It identifies the consumer's name, address, and other contact information. The information comes from other creditors and may be inaccurate.
- It lists credit bureau members who have obtained copies of this report in the past three years.
- Banking information about the consumer is provided, but the information is automatically deleted six years after it is entered.
- Credit history is provided. Each creditor gives the date of the last report, the balance outstanding, the date indebtedness began, and the highest amount owing. The credit rating assigned by the creditor is reported. These are referred to as "R" ratings, and are North American Standard Account Ratings, which is a scale widely used in

FIGURE 3.7: Sample Equifax Commercial Credit Report

EQUIFAX   Commercial Credit Report

```
ABC HOMES LTD
12345 FORGE RD SE                     Report date     : Feb 05, 1999
CALGARY, AB                           File opened     : Dec 31, 1979
T2H 0S9
                                      File Number     : 0000199943
Telephone : 403-555-0581              Subject Number  : A13999
Fax       : 403-555-1284              Reference Number : New Business
                                      Requestor ID    : John Test

Primary SIC number - 1521 - (Gen Con, Home Improvement)
```

```
                         * * * SUMMARY * * *
                                     Credit Info  Scores  Payment
9    Trade Suppliers  Owed    220K           * 23   Current  12 *
3rd Period Past Due   Owed   9,006 or  4%    * 12   4Q1998   14 *
Current               Owed    160K or 72%    *  5   4Q1997   16 *
Highest Credit Limit  Rptd    116K           * 15   4Q1996   11 *


Returned Cheques .....  1 for    275  Last Returned Cheque .. Dec 01, 1998
Collection Claims ....  1 for    500  Last Claim ............ Jan 12, 1998
Legal Suits .........   2 for   492K  Last Legal Suit ....... Feb 26, 1998
Judgments ..........    1 for      0  Last Judgment ........ Jun 12, 1998
Other Items .........   1 for      0  Last Other Item ....... Jul 31, 1998

                        * * * TRADE ITEMS * * *
```

Supplier's Name/Industry	Terms Amount/Comments/Habits					
Rptd Open	High	Total	Current	Past Due/Pay Period		
Date Date	Credit	Owing	$	1st	2nd	3rd
Mfr-Auto & Parts: DLA-1998/10/01, 839						
Jan* Jun/1997	30,211	20,520	20,520	0	0	0
REVELSTOKE HOME CTRE: 604-899-5555						
Nov*	36,150	36,150	19,521	16,629	0	0
Retail-Bldg/Hardware:						
Nov*	57,347	6,144	553	5,591	0	0
P.I. = 12 90 Days	123K	62,814	40,594	22,220	0	0
Reported						
Mfr-Fabricated Mtl:						
Nov*	116K	116K	90,495	21,488	1,681	3,106
Contr,Masonry,Stone:						
Oct*	33,955	33,955	23,769	3,396	1,019	5,771
SHELL CANADA (WEST): 403-691-2622						
Oct*	2,724	2,724	2,724	0	0	0
Mfr-Paint, Varnishes:						
Oct*	2,000	919	680	110	0	129
Services-Employment:						
Aug*	707	707	707	0	0	0
CANADIAN TURBO INC: 403-294-6431						
Mar*	5,154	3,007	1,594	1,413	0	0
P.I. = 12 Total	285K	220K	160K	48,627	2,700	9,006
Reported						

Note: * Indicates the data was supplied by an accounts receivable submission.

continues....

Figure 3.7 (continued)

```
Note: # indicates Long Term Secured Debt which is NOT included in the PI and
      CI calculation.
              * * * PAYMENT TRENDS * * *
      -----------------------------------------------------------------------
         Payment C.I.  Number Of  Total                    - $ Overdue -
Quarters Index   Score Suppliers  Owing    Current    1st     2nd      3rd
      -----------------------------------------------------------------------
4 Qtr/1998  14     12       7     483,240  326,251  130,191   8,737   18,061
3 Qtr/1998  12     15       8     483,583  352,171  100,601  19,906   10,905
2 Qtr/1998  15     20       4     305,839  171,552  130,204   1,468    2,615
1 Qtr/1998  17     17       6     173,488  120,544   33,907   4,055   14,982
4 Qtr/1997  16      5       5     495,333  321,001  134,057  13,521   26,754
3 Qtr/1997  15     15       4     237,619  178,573   34,266   3,802   20,978
2 Qtr/1997  17     23       8     311,722  172,597  128,078       0   11,047
1 Qtr/1997  58     25       4       5,134    1,849      513       0    2,772
4 Qtr/1996  11     15       5      25,566   22,498      256       0    2,812

              * * * RETURNED CHEQUES * * *
      -----------------------------------------------------------------------
Sys. Date   Bank date          Amount  Reason Returned  Status
      -----------------------------------------------------------------------
Feb 05, 1999 Dec 01, 1998      275.00  NSF              Not Replaced

              * * * COLLECTION CLAIMS RECEIVED * * *
Debtor    ABC HOMES LTD                  Date Placed   Jan 12, 1998
Creditor  ABC Publishing                 Amount Placed          500
Agency    Equifax Accounts Receivable    Amount Paid              0
Comment   In Collection

              * * * LEGAL INFORMATION SECTION * * *
Statement of Claim:
Defendant  ABC HOMES LTD                 Date        Feb 26, 1998
Plaintiff  SMART, WARREN                 Court       Queen's Bench
Amount     16,364                        Location    Calgary
Reason     Damages                       File Number 960324546

Statement of Claim:
Defendant  ABC HOMES 1997 LTD            Date        Oct 05, 1995
Plaintiff  VAN SMITH HOMES               Court       Queen's Bench
Amount     476,000                       Location    Calgary
Reason     Damages                       File Number 970312904

Judgment, Order:
Defendant  ABC HOMES LTD                 Date        Jun 12, 1998
Plaintiff  JONES, MARK                   Court       Queen's Bench
Amount     0                             Location    Calgary
Reason     Damages                       File Number 970345560


              * * * OTHER LEGAL INFORMATION * * *
Notice of Discontinuance:
Defendant  ABC HOMES 1997 LTD            Date        Jul 31, 1998
Plaintiff  123658 ALBERTA INC            Court       Queen's Bench
                                         Location    Calgary
```

continues....

Figure 3.7 (continued)

```
                                        File Number 960355797
                          * * * BANKING INFORMATION * * *


Reported on: ABC HOMES LTD
Date: 1999/02/05                            File Number: 0000199943
                                           Subject Number: A13999
CANADIAN IMPERIAL BANK OF COMMERCE
628-8TH AVE S.W.
CALGARY, ALBERTA, T2P1G4
Branch: 010, Transit: 00019
Ref. Phone: (403) 544-1234            Ref. Fax: (403) 544-0988

     Account Information:
          Number of Accounts: 2, Current account, US account,
          Opened: For more than 3 years
          Total Balance: Low 6 figures

     *** Returned Cheque Details:
          Quantity: None, Frequency: In the last 3 months

     Line of Credit Details:
          Opened: 1980/12/03
          Authorized Amount: Low 7 figures
          Utilized: 80%
          Rating: Paid as agreed
          Secured: yes, Equipment, Mortgage

     Loan Details:
          Term loan, Opened: 1980/12/04
          Authorized Amount: $ 180,000
          Balance Owing: $ 25,000
          Terms: Monthly, $ 1,280
          Rating: Paid as agreed
          Secured: yes, Mortgage, Inventory

     Signing officer(s):
          WILSON JOHN, WILSON WILMA, WILSON SAMANTHA
          2 signatures required

                    * * * COMPANY INFORMATION * * *

Incorporation  Number: 12345667, Effective Date: 1978/05/01
Provincial Charter / Alberta

1999/02/05, ALBERTA CORPORATE REGISTRY:REGISTERED OFFICE AND RECORDS
          ADDRESS:12345 FORGE RD SE,CALGARY,AB,T2H0S9.LAST ANNUAL REPORT
          1998-12-01.

Premises: Owned, Land Only (Reported: 1999/02/26)
          12345 FORGE RD SE CALGARY AB T2H0S9
          Valuation Srce: Municipal Evaluation, Value: $ 500,000

Number Employees: Full Time: 25, (Reported: 1999/02/05)
              Part Time: 25, (Reported: 1999/02/05)

Finances: Sales: $ 1,500,000, (Reported: 1999/02/05)
          Net Worth: $ 2,500,000, (Reported: 1999/02/05)
          A/R Amount: $ 75,000, (Reported: 1999/02/05)
          A/P Amount: $ 50,000, (Reported: 1999/02/05)
```

continues....

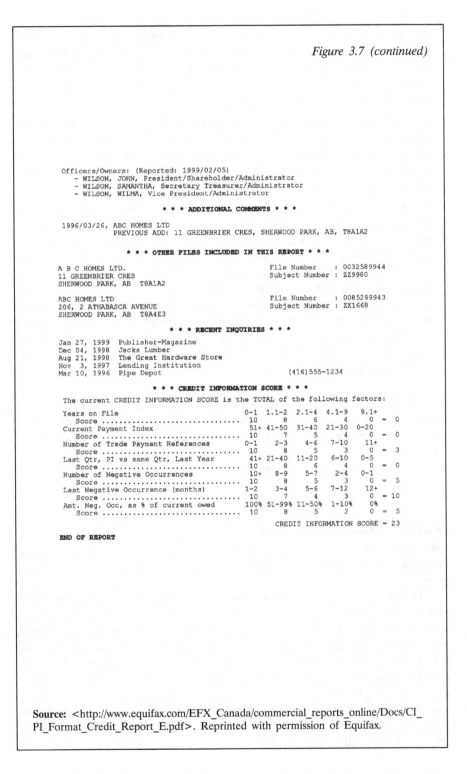

Figure 3.7 (continued)

```
Officers/Owners: (Reported: 1999/02/05)
     - WILSON, JOHN, President/Shareholder/Administrator
     - WILSON, SAMANTHA, Secretary Treasurer/Administrator
     - WILSON, WILMA, Vice President/Administrator

             * * * ADDITIONAL COMMENTS * * *

1996/03/26, ABC HOMES LTD
           PREVIOUS ADD: 11 GREENBRIER CRES, SHERWOOD PARK, AB, T8A1A2

          * * * OTHER FILES INCLUDED IN THIS REPORT * * *

A B C HOMES LTD.                      File Number   : 0032589944
11 GREENBRIER CRES                    Subject Number : ZZ9980
SHERWOOD PARK, AB  T8A1A2

ABC HOMES LTD                         File Number   : 0085299943
206, 2 ATHABASCA AVENUE               Subject Number : ZX1668
SHERWOOD PARK, AB  T8A4E3

                * * * RECENT INQUIRIES * * *

Jan 27, 1999  Publisher-Magazine
Dec 04, 1998  Jacks Lumber
Aug 21, 1998  The Great Hardware Store
Nov  3, 1997  Lending Institution
Mar 10, 1996  Pipe Depot                    (416)555-1234

             * * * CREDIT INFORMATION SCORE * * *

The current CREDIT INFORMATION SCORE is the TOTAL of the following factors:

Years on File                    0-1  1.1-2  2.1-4  4.1-9  9.1+
    Score .............................  10    8      6      4     0   =  0
Current Payment Index            51+  41-50  31-40  21-30  0-20
    Score .............................  10    7      5      4     0   =  0
Number of Trade Payment References  0-1  2-3    4-6    7-10   11+
    Score .............................  10    8      5      3     0   =  3
Last Qtr, PI vs same Qtr, Last Year 41+ 21-40  11-20  6-10   0-5
    Score .............................  10    8      6      4     0   =  0
Number of Negative Occurrences   10+  8-9    5-7    2-4    0-1
    Score .............................  10    8      5      3     0   =  5
Last Negative Occurrence (months) 1-2  3-4    5-6    7-12   12+
    Score .............................  10    7      4      3     0   = 10
Amt. Neg. Occ, as % of current owed 100% 51-99% 11-50% 1-10%  0%
    Score .............................  10    8      5      2     0   =  5
                           CREDIT INFORMATION SCORE = 23

END OF REPORT
```

the United States and Canada. These accounts focus on revolving credit or running accounts, such as credit cards. The rating spectrum runs from R0, indicating no information; followed by R1, indicating debts always paid on time; through to R9, which indicates a bad debt that has gone to collection.

- The report may also provide information on past judgments, executions, consumer proposals (an offer by a debtor owing less than $250,000, excluding mortgages, to settle with all creditors under the *Bankruptcy and Insolvency Act*), bankruptcies, and discharges from bankruptcy.

- A credit score is assigned to each file. Lenders use the score to assess how likely the person is to repay a debt. The score is based on payment history, the number of debts, the balances outstanding, and factors such as how long your accounts have been open and used and any bankruptcies, consumer proposals, or debt management plans. The amount of credit you have or have applied for is also considered. The highest possible score is 900. The lowest possible score is 300. A score of 600 is considered good, while a score of 800 is considered very good. You can read more about credit scores on the Financial Consumer Agency of Canada website, <www.fcac-acfc.gc.ca/>.

Credit bureaus, upon receipt of a written request, will provide a person with a copy of their credit report at no charge. However, you must pay a fee (usually $20.00) to obtain online access to your credit score.

A sample Equifax consumer credit report is set out in Figure 3.8.

POST-SEARCH STRATEGIES

After completing the searches, evaluate with your client the information you have obtained, and get his or her instructions about how to proceed.

If the debtor is transferring assets to others and judgment-proofing himself or herself, there are remedies available in the Superior Court, with injunctions and receiving orders being two of the more common ones. **Injunctions** are mandatory court orders directing a party to do or refrain from doing something. For example, if a debtor appears to be moving inventory out of the province and the creditor is concerned that there will not be any assets left to satisfy a judgment, the creditor can ask the court for an injunction ordering the defendant to hold and preserve all inventory on site until further order of the court. Injunctions are equitable relief and as such cannot be granted by Small Claims

FIGURE 3.8: Sample Equifax Consumer Credit Report

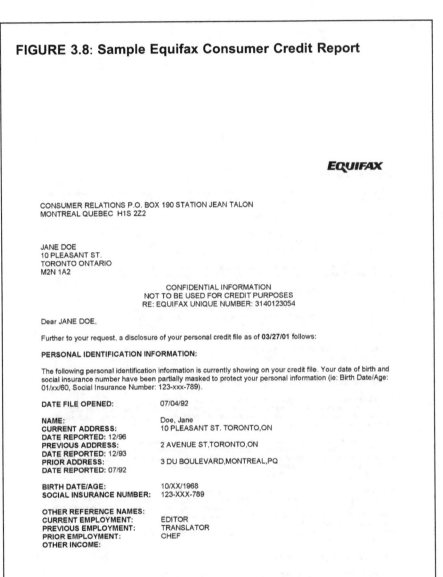

EQUIFAX

CONSUMER RELATIONS P.O. BOX 190 STATION JEAN TALON
MONTREAL QUEBEC H1S 2Z2

JANE DOE
10 PLEASANT ST.
TORONTO ONTARIO
M2N 1A2

CONFIDENTIAL INFORMATION
NOT TO BE USED FOR CREDIT PURPOSES
RE: EQUIFAX UNIQUE NUMBER: 3140123054

Dear JANE DOE,

Further to your request, a disclosure of your personal credit file as of **03/27/01** follows:

PERSONAL IDENTIFICATION INFORMATION:

The following personal identification information is currently showing on your credit file. Your date of birth and social insurance number have been partially masked to protect your personal information (ie: Birth Date/Age: 01/xx/60, Social Insurance Number: 123-xxx-789).

DATE FILE OPENED:	07/04/92
NAME:	Doe, Jane
CURRENT ADDRESS:	10 PLEASANT ST. TORONTO,ON
DATE REPORTED: 12/96	
PREVIOUS ADDRESS:	2 AVENUE ST,TORONTO,ON
DATE REPORTED: 12/93	
PRIOR ADDRESS:	3 DU BOULEVARD,MONTREAL,PQ
DATE REPORTED: 07/92	
BIRTH DATE/AGE:	10/XX/1968
SOCIAL INSURANCE NUMBER:	123-XXX-789
OTHER REFERENCE NAMES:	
CURRENT EMPLOYMENT:	EDITOR
PREVIOUS EMPLOYMENT:	TRANSLATOR
PRIOR EMPLOYMENT:	CHEF
OTHER INCOME:	

continues....

Figure 3.8 (continued)

CREDIT INQUIRIES ON YOUR FILE:

Following is a list of Equifax members who have received a copy of your credit file for credit granting or other permissible purposes. Addresses are available by calling Equifax at 1-800-465-7166.

DATE	REQUESTOR NAME	TELEPHONE
03/02/00	CANADA TRUST MTG	(416) 361-8518
02/22/00	TD BANK	(800) 787-7065
01/16/00	BQE NATIONALE	(450) 677-9122

The following inquiries are for your information only and are not displayed to others. They include requests from authorized parties to update their records regarding your existing account with them.

DATE	REQUESTOR NAME	TELEPHONE
03/23/00	SOC ALCOOLS (not displayed)	(514) 873-6281
03/22/00	CANADA TRUST MTG (not displayed)	(416) 361-8518
02/16/00	CMHC SCHL (not displayed)	(888) 463-6454
01/16/00	AMERICAN EXPRESS (not displayed)	(416) 123-4567

CONSUMER INTERVIEWS AND OTHER SERVICES:
You contacted our office in 12/98 to request a review of your credit file.

CREDIT HISTORY AND/OR BANKING INFORMATION:

The following information was reported to us by organizations listed below.
Information is received every 30 days from most credit grantors. All account numbers with your creditors have been masked to protect your personal account information and only the last three digits will be displayed (i.e.: xxx...123).

GMAC last reported to us in 01/01 rating your installment account as I1, meaning paid as agreed and up to date. The reported balance of your account was $1000. Your account number: xxx...345. The account is in the subject's name only. Date account opened: 04/99. Credit limit or highest amount of credit advanced: $4400. **DATE OF LAST ACTIVITY** meaning the last payment or transaction made on this account was in 12/00. Additional comments: auto loan. Monthly payments.

CANADA TRUST MC last reported to us in 01/01 rating your revolving account as R1, meaning paid as agreed and up to date. At the time the reported balance of your account was $285. Your account number: xxx...234. Date account opened: 06/99. Credit limit or highest amount of credit advanced $2000. **DATE OF LAST ACTIVITY** meaning the last payment or transaction made on this account was in 12/00. **PREVIOUS PAYMENT STATUS:**
30 DAYS: 1 time (s) account previously R2 meaning one payment past due

PUBLIC RECORDS AND OTHER INFORMATION:

The following information was reported to your file on the date indicated.

A COLLECTION was assigned in 10/96 to Commercial Credit by Transamerica Financial in the amount of:$2675. Date reported paid: 07/97. Collection status: PAID. **DATE OF LAST ACTIVITY** was in 04/96. Collection agency reference number: 222222.

continues....

Figure 3.8 (continued)

A JUDGEMENT was FILED IN 01/96 in Min Govt Serv. Plaintiff and/or case number: Chrysler Canada 4444. Defendant/other info: joint with Dossier. Amount reported: $7525. Status reported: Satisfied. Date satisfied: 09/97.

A BANKRUPTCY was FILED IN 08/97 in SC Newmarket. Case number and/or trustee: 5555555 SYNDIC & ASS. Liabilities: $250000.Assets: $8900000.Item classification: individual. Information reported on: The subject only. The item is reported as: DISCHARGED. DATE SETTLED: 05/98. Additional comments: absolute discharge from bankruptcy.

THE CONSUMER PROVIDED A PERSONAL STATEMENT to us in 12/98. The statement has been recorded as follows:

RE: BANKRUPTCY, CONSUMER DECLARED BANKRUPTCY DUE TO DIVORCE
This statement is to be removed from the file in: 12/04.

RETENTION PERIOD OF DATA:

CREDIT INQUIRIES TO THE FILE
- An Inquiry made by a Creditor will automatically purge three (3) years from the date of the inquiry. The system will keep a minimum of five (5) inquiries.

CREDIT HISTORY AND BANKING INFORMATION
- A credit transaction will automatically purge from the sytem six (6) years from the date of last activity.
- All banking information (checking or saving account) will automatically purge from the system six (6) years from the date of registration.

VOLUNTARY DEPOSIT - ORDERLY PAYMENT OF DEBTS, CREDIT COUNSELING
- When voluntary deposit – OPD – credit counseling is paid, it will automatically purge from the sytem three (3) years from the date paid.

REGISTERED CONSUMER PROPOSAL
- When a registered consumer proposal is paid, it will automatically purge three (3) years from the date paid.

BANKRUPTCY
- A bankruptcy automatically purges six (6) years from the date of discharge in the case of a single bankruptcy. If the consumer declares several bankruptcies, the system will keep each bankruptcy for fourteen (14) years from the date of each discharge. All accounts included in a bankruptcy remain on file indicating "included in bankruptcy" and will purge six (6) years from the date of last activity.

JUDGMENTS, SEIZURE OF MOVABLE/IMMOVABLE, GARNISHMENT OF WAGES
- The above will automatically purge from the system six (6) years from the date filed.

COLLECTION ACCOUNTS
- A collection account under public records will automatically purge from the sytem six (6) years from the date of last activity.

SECURED LOANS
- A secured loan will automatically purge from the system six (6) years from the date filed.

(Exception: P.E.I. Public Records: seven (7) to ten (10) years.)

The attached Reference Update Form is included for your convenience. If you wish to update your file with more current information or to request a change in the information provided above, please complete this form and return it to Equifax. We will ensure that appropriate measures will be applied if corrections are required.

continues....

Figure 3.8 (continued)

Please be advised that the file you have received is for your information only and may not be used for credit purposes.

INFORMATION ABOUT YOUR CREDIT FILE

Every day Canadians purchase goods and services using credit. The decision to extend credit to you, the buyer, is made by the seller - commonly referred to as the "credit grantor". Most often, this decision involves reviewing your personal credit file, which is obtained from a credit reporting agency such as Equifax. The agency is a clearinghouse for credit information. Credit grantors provide the agency with factual information about your credit history.

The reporting agency then assembles this information into your personal file. In return, credit grantors can access your files before granting credit to you or identifying you for security purposes. Only you and the credit grantor can have you personal file modified.

WHAT IS AN INQUIRY?

When you apply for credit a credit grantor carries out an account inquiry. Account inquiries are also done routinely by organizations based on their client lists. If you have dealt with certain organizations, your name would likely be on their client list. At times, they may monitor client accounts or update their client information prior to making promotional offerings. This second type of inquiry is confidential and is not shown to other organizations that may offer you credit.

WHY WAS I DENIED CREDIT?

Equifax neither grants nor denies any application for credit. We simply provide a factual account of your credit history to credit grantors. Each credit granting organization reviews this information and makes an independent decision based on its own individual criteria. If an account/business transaction is joint or you have co-signed, both parties are held equally responsible.

WHY HAS SOMETHING I PAID OFF STILL SHOWS ON MY CREDIT FILE?

The fact that you have paid an account on time or did not pay as agreed is of interest to any potential credit grantor because it reflects your ability to pay your bills. A credit file shows past and present transactions.

WHAT CAN BE DONE IF I SUSPECT I AM A VICTIM OF IDENTIFY FRAUD?

If you have lost or had your personal identification stolen or an institution has contacted you regarding suspected fraud activity, please call Equifax toll free at 1 800 465-7166 or (514) 493-2314. A statement will be added to your file to alert credit grantors that you may be a victim of fraud activity.

CREDIT CLINICS: SHOULD I USE THE SERVICE OF COMPANIES WHO INDICATE THEY CAN HELP FIX MY CREDIT?

That is your choice. Remember, however, that these companies cannot have accurate information removed from your credit file. If there is inaccurate information on you file; Equifax will amend it, at no charge to you.

Consumer Department

Source: <http://www.equifax.com/EFX_Canada/consumer_information_centre/docs/ Consumer_Friendly_File_e.pdf>. Reprinted with permission of Equifax.

Court judges. They must be sought and obtained from a Superior Court of Justice judge. **Receiving orders** allow for the appointment of a receiver to run the debtor's business, with a view to managing it or selling it. Some secured loan agreements permit the creditor to appoint a receiver without a court order if the agreement is breached by the debtor. Interim receivers can be appointed under the *Bankruptcy and Insolvency Act* where there is a danger that an asset, otherwise available to creditors in bankruptcy proceedings, might be dissipated. In other cases a motion can be made to the Superior Court of Justice for an order appointing a receiver. Small Claims Court judges cannot make an order appointing a receiver. Injunctions and receiving orders are expensive remedies to pursue, and it may simply not be worth spending large sums on a Superior Court action to collect a debt within the Small Claims Court monetary jurisdiction.

If the creditor has a secured interest in the debtor's assets, it may not be necessary to sue at all. In most secured transactions, the creditor retains the right, in the parties' security agreement or through the PPSA if they have registered under the Act, to seize and sell an asset if there is a default by the debtor without going to court. Using a private bailiff to seize and privately sell a car on a conditional sale contract where the debtor has defaulted on the car loan is one obvious example. Exercising the right of a private power of sale on a land mortgage is another.

Although these private law remedies are attractive because they are fast and inexpensive, those using them must comply with both the letter and spirit of the law. Because the courts do not supervise the process and allow the creditor to run it, if it is not done properly, the debtor can apply to the Superior Court for relief from forfeiture. If the court finds unfair or inequitable treatment, oppressive behaviour, or failure to comply exactly with required procedure, the court may order return of the asset to the debtor and stay further proceedings.

If the debtor's situation is hopeless and he is insolvent, the creditor may wish to consider petitioning the debtor into bankruptcy, although this is risky if most assets are secured and may be removed by the secured creditors ahead of bankruptcy claimants. The process can also be expensive. A creditor with a claim within the Small Claims Court's monetary jurisdiction might be better advised to simply write off the claim as a business loss for tax purposes.

CHAPTER SUMMARY

In this chapter we examined a variety of database sources, available through governments and private organizations, that are accessible for searches in a variety of ways: in person, by phone, by fax, and online.

Some searches focus on accurately identifying the defendant/debtor and verifying his or her location. Other searches focus on whether or not the debtor has sufficient assets and a payment history to make him or her worth suing.

We began with various government and private databases that are used to verify the names of individual and business debtors, including a determination of which party might be the appropriate party to sue. In this section we also examined various databases, particularly private ones, that could help you to find a debtor or defendant who preferred not to be found. (A list of commonly used search websites is provided in Figure 3.9.)

FIGURE 3.9: List of Commonly Used Search Websites

People finder searches
Search Detective: <http://www.searchdetective.net/phone/html>
Yahoo People Canada: <http://www.yahoo.ca>
Canada411: <http://www.canada411.ca>
Lycos Search: <http://www.whowhere.com>
Telus: <http://www.mytelus.com/phonebook/>
Canpages: <http://www.Canpages.ca>

Consumer credit information searches
Financial Consumer Agency of Canada: <http://www.fcac-acfc.gc.ca/>

Driver and vehicle searches
Ministry of Transportation: <http://www.mto.gov.on.ca/english/>

Business name, corporate, bankruptcy searches, PPSA searches
Bar-ex: <http://www.bar-ex.com>
Corporate Searchers: <http://www.corporatesearchers.com>
Cyberbahn Group: <http://www.cyberbahngroup.com/>
OnCorp: <http://www.oncorp.com/>
Dye & Durham: <http://www.eservicedd.ca/searchaccess/>
Equifax (Credit Bureau Search): <http://www.equifax.com/>
TransUnion (Credit Bureau Search): <http://www.transunion.ca>
ServiceOntario: <http://www.ontario.ca/en/services_for_business/index.htm>

From there we turned to databases that provided information about a debtor's assets and likely ability to pay a judgment if one was obtained. In this connection we examined the use of execution searches, *Personal Property Security Act* searches, bankruptcy searches, *Bank Act*, *Bulk Sales Act*, and credit bureau searches as a means of discovering if the debtor has assets available to satisfy a judgment, has a history as a judgment debtor who resisted paying previous judgments, has creditors chasing him, and whether the debtor is on the verge of bankruptcy (or over the verge, and actually bankrupt). Throughout this examination, we identified situations and scenarios where it might be advisable or not advisable to sue in the Small Claims Court, to resort to other remedies, or to write off the debt.

REVIEW QUESTIONS

1. For the following databases, indicate whether the database will provide information to identify and locate the debtor, or provide information about the debtor's assets and solvency, or both.

   (a) Driver's record search

   (b) Credit bureau report

   (c) PPSA search

   (d) Execution search

   (e) Lycos search

   (f) Bankruptcy search

2. After you obtain a judgment, a PPSA search reveals that Don Debtor owns a car, a motor home, a 10-year-old motorcycle, and an aluminum boat with a motor. All are subject to registered security agreements. The loan on the car is $10,000, and the car is worth about $6,000. The motor home is worth $50,000, and the loan on it was for $10,000. The boat is worth about $2,000, and the loan on it was for $5,000. The motorcycle is sitting in pieces in Don's yard, and was subject to a loan for $6,000. What information do you obtain from the search to assist you?

3. What is indicated by a search of executions that shows the following results?

   (a) Seven writs filed in the past three weeks

   (b) Seven writs filed four years ago

   (c) No executions

   (d) One execution, three years ago

4. Boris Gudinov is the general manager of Gudinov 4 U, a bakery. You have always dealt directly with Boris when he ordered flour from you, and he often paid you in cash out of the till. Last week he said your flour was defective, and he wasn't paying. You know the flour was fine, so you want to sue to collect. Whom or what do you sue?

5. Suppose Gudinov 4 U turns out to be a partnership between Boris Gudinov and Marko Bolsemov. Whom or what do you sue?

6. If you think Gudinov 4 U has been petitioned into bankruptcy, describe how you would conduct a search to find out. Would it make a difference if Gudinov 4 U had made an assignment in bankruptcy?

7. What is a reverse directory or database?

DISCUSSION QUESTIONS/CASE STUDIES

1. You act for Everflowing Brewery. One of its customers, The Walrus and the Whatever, is way behind in its beer payments. This is a relatively recent pattern, and Everflowing has some concerns. You have been asked to collect the debt. In order to find out information you have commissioned a credit report from Equifax. The report has just come in and has, among other things, the following information:

   • Overall Credit Information score: 32
   • Most Recent Payment Index score: 40

   Interpret these scores for the client.

2. You have now conducted some further searches on the Walrus and the Whatever, and you discovered the following:

   • A PPSA search reveals that all of the furniture, kitchen equipment, beer glasses, and the big screen TVs, permanently tuned to an all-sports station, are subject to a security interest in favour of the Caring Bank. None of the business assets appears to be unsecured.
   • An execution search indicates that there are four creditors who obtained judgments for amounts from $25,000 to $50,000 in the past two years. There is no indication that any have been paid.
   • A bankruptcy search indicates that there has been no filing for bankruptcy by any creditor or by the debtor.

   What advice would you give to the creditor based on all this information, including the Equifax Report noted above?

Chapter 4

Introduction to Credit
Transactions and Collections

LEARNING OBJECTIVES

⇨ Know how lenders protect themselves from non-payment

⇨ Know how lenders administer credit transactions

⇨ Know how lenders determine which collection procedures to use when there is a default

⇨ Know the difference between secured and unsecured debts

⇨ Understand how creditors are ranked in priority when they are collecting from the same debtor

⇨ Know the requirements of the *Collection Agencies Act* and the Act's impact on paralegal practice

INTRODUCTION

Debt collection cases are a large part of a Small Claims Court practice. In this chapter we examine matters relating to collection proceedings. Included in this chapter is a discussion of features and characteristics of secured and unsecured debt, and an examination of the strategies and procedures used by creditors, including an examination of how creditors administer credit transactions. The chapter also examines the requirements of the *Collection Agencies Act* for those who carry on a collection practice.

THE SMALL CLAIMS COURT AND CREDIT COLLECTION

Many of the cases filed in the Small Claims Court are collection matters, with a creditor suing a debtor for an unpaid account or other debt. Often these are consumer debts for personal loans, consumer purchases financed by the seller through a **conditional sale contract** and credit card debts. While the personal consumer debt load carried by Canadians is not as high as that carried by Americans, it is significant and gives rise to much of the case volume in the Small Claims Court. It follows that a paralegal with a Small Claims Court practice can expect to be frequently involved in debt collection cases, acting for either creditors or debtors. So, before we start to look at court procedures and practices, we will provide a context by looking at some of the background issues that are important to a debt collection practice and to the determination of damages generally.

COLLECTION PROCEDURES AND STRATEGIES

How creditors act with respect to creditor's remedies depends on a variety of factors. In particular, whether a debt is secured or unsecured will determine the kinds of actions a creditor will take. So, we will begin with an introduction to how secured and unsecured credit works, both for consumer and commercial transactions.

Secured and Unsecured Debt

Lawyers and paralegals use the term "collections" to describe cases in which the task is to collect an amount owing on a contract or a loan. Debts fall into two main categories, unsecured and secured debts.

An unsecured debt is a type of debt that a borrower has agreed to and is a simple promise to repay the borrowed amount when it is due. The promise may be oral or in writing and, in either case, the law recognizes it as being enforceable, unless there are particular formality requirements that stipulate that certain types of promises must be in writing. For example, a contract to sell land must be made in writing. If the borrower breaches the loan agreement, the lender can sue for the amount due and for interest on that amount. If the lender obtains judgment from the court, he or she may then use court enforcement mechanisms to enforce the judgment. These include **garnishment**, in which the creditor can require someone who owes money to the debtor to pay that amount to the creditor rather than to the debtor through the court. The creditor can also ask an officer of the court, called a **bailiff**, to seize and sell assets belonging to the debtor, and pay money from the sale to the creditor to satisfy the debt. The court can also order that property wrongfully held be returned to its legal owner. Examples of unsecured loans are credit card debts, simple promissory notes, and bills for goods or services.

A secured debt features a promise by the debtor to pay the debt when it is due, but it also includes a right given to the creditor to seize a specific asset or class of assets of the debtor to satisfy the debt if the debtor does not pay when the debt is due. The asset is said to secure payment of the debt, and is referred to as **collateral** for repayment of the debt. The creditor and debtor involved in a secured transaction usually sign a **general security agreement** or a **specific security agreement** setting out the terms of financing and the details of the collateral and its possible seizure in the event of non-payment or other breach of the agreement.

In a secured transaction, the creditor can sue on the promise to pay or seize the collateral. In most secured transactions, the creditor does not have to sue first because he or she has a contractual right under the security agreement to use private bailiffs to seize the collateral and sell it without direct court supervision. Usually the creditor is entitled to collect only what he or she is owed from the sale monies. If there is a surplus it goes to other creditors of the debtor or to the debtor. The creditor is not entitled to a windfall profit. If there is a shortfall, the creditor can sue the debtor for that amount.

The right to seize and sell the collateral is a private, contractual right. The terms governing the process are agreed to by the parties and set out as terms of the contract. This means that the creditor does not have to obtain a court order or have the court supervise the seizure of the asset and its sale. If there is a default by the debtor, the creditor can exercise the right to seize and sell the collateral set out in the contract itself. But because there is no oversight by the courts, the law requires that the creditor follow the sale procedure exactly as it is set out in the agreement. If the creditor cuts corners, or behaves unfairly, the Superior Court can stop oppressive conduct with injunctions or other equitable remedies. But if the amount of the debt is at the Small

Claims Court level, then equitable remedies are not available, but the debtor can sue for damages sustained as the result of an improper exercise of a sale remedy by the creditor.

If a secured creditor is going to be able to maintain a right to seize collateral when it becomes necessary to do so, the creditor has to have some way of informing the rest of the world that he or she has an interest in the asset. The reason this is necessary is that the secured asset is usually in the possession and control of the debtor, not the creditor. For example, if you buy a new car and the car dealer lends you the money to purchase it on a **conditional sale contract**, the car becomes security for the loan. But the secured creditor does not have physical control of the car; you do. It is registered in your name, your child's baby shoes hang from the rear-view mirror, and you have possession and control over the car. You could turn around and sell it, or use it for security for a loan from a different creditor. So, the creditor has to have some way of making sure others know that if they buy the car, or accept it as collateral, their interest in the collateral is subject to the superior interest of the car dealer, who is the first secured creditor with respect to the car. In Ontario, and in most other provinces, a creditor can register notice of his or her interest in the collateral by using a government registration system. In Ontario, *The Personal Property Security Act* (PPSA) sets up the Personal Property Security Registration System (PPSR). Once the creditor has registered a notice of security interest, it is protected from most other creditors dealing with the asset in a way that would deprive other creditors of their rights in the collateral.

We will use your car purchase on a conditional sale contract as an example of how the registration system works. Once you, the debtor, and the bank, your creditor, have created a conditional sale contract, the bank must complete a financing statement and register it in the PPSR registration system. From the moment it is registered, the financing statement constitutes notice to strangers of the creditor's (i.e., the bank's) interest. Any later registration by another creditor with an interest in the same collateral is subordinate to the interest of the first registrant. The earliest registrant has priority over later registrants. This means that if the subordinate secured creditor seizes and sells the collateral (i.e., your car), he or she must first pay off the secured creditor, the bank, which has registered its interest first and therefore has a superior interest in the collateral. If you sell your car, you will have to pay what is owing to the lenders who registered security interests in the car, paying off the creditors in the order of priority based on who registered first. If you didn't make enough from the sale to cover the amounts owing to all of the secured creditors, you will have to dig into your pocket and find the money to pay them off. This is similar to the land registration system, where the first mortgagee has priority over the second or third mortgagee because he or she registered the mortgage ahead of the others and, therefore, gets paid off first if the land is sold by the owner or one of the mortgagees. Here is an example of how the registration system would work if you were to sell your car.

Example 4.1 Sale of PPSA Registered Security

You buy your car for $25,000.

The seller lends you $20,000 on a conditional sale contract.

The seller registers a financing statement under the PPSA.

You borrow $4,000 from your bank, which requires you to give it a security interest in the car as collateral for the loan.

The bank registers a financing statement under the PPSA.

You sell your car to X for $4,000.

At the time of the sale, assume you still owe the original seller $3,500 on the conditional sale contract, and you owe the bank $2,000 on its financing agreement.

The original seller has the right to collect the $3,500 from you before the bank is paid anything.

The bank has the right to collect the remaining $500 left over from the sale, and will sue you for the outstanding balance on the loan.

You, of course, get nothing from the sale, and you still have to pay the bank $1,500.

From this example, you might wonder when a secured lender has a right to seize your car. Generally, if you default on your loan by missing a payment, the loan agreement will **accelerate** the debt, making you liable not just for the missed payment but for the entire amount of the loan that remains to be paid. For consumer car loans, under the *Consumer Protection Act, 2002*, S.O. 2002, c. 30, Sched. A, s. 25, the vehicle cannot be seized if more than two-thirds of the loan has been paid off.

The secured lender can use private bailiffs to seize and sell your car. But the contract is likely to define "default" in other ways as well, such as the following:

- Destruction of the car in a crash
- Sale of the car to a third party
- Failure to maintain and service the car, resulting in increased depreciation
- Going bankrupt or defaulting on loans to other lenders

In order to obtain a secured priority interest under the PPSA, a creditor must attach and perfect his or her security interest. Attachment can be achieved in two ways: by having the creditor maintain possession of the secured asset or by having the parties execute a security agreement. The secured interest is then perfected by the registration of a financing statement in the PPSR system.

The PPSR registration system is an online system, so financing statements can be registered and searched via computer. In this connection, because registration **perfects** an interest in collateral, it is incumbent on creditors to conduct a PPSA search before accepting collateral as a security. If the creditor discovers a prior registration against the same collateral, the creditor will know that he or she does not have first priority; this increases the risk that the lender may not be able to look to the collateral for payment in full if there is a default. The subordinate creditor will have to consider whether there is enough value in the collateral to pay off the prior registered creditor and the subordinate creditor if the asset has to be sold after a default by the debtor. Usually, if the subordinate creditor does go ahead with the loan, it is likely to be at a higher interest rate, in recognition of the second lender's subordinate interest in the collateral and of the greater risk in granting the loan.

Administration of Credit Transactions: Debt, Interest, Terms of Payments

Where payment on a contract is due at a future date or over a period of time, there has been an extension of credit by one party to another. As noted in the previous discussion, it may be secured or unsecured. Consumer credit and commercial credit are administered differently. We will start with an examination of how consumer credit works.

Consumer Credit Administration

Consumer credit is remarkably easy to obtain. Many retail sellers offer credit to finance purchases or allow payments on easy terms. Although many of these credit transactions may go into default and require collection, retail sellers rely on the high volume of such sales to generate profits. In the absence of a downturn in the economy with rapidly rising unemployment, this approach usually works. Unfortunately, many consumers take on a debt load that they cannot discharge, and they find themselves being sued or having their secured property seized.

Many retail and consumer transactions, particularly for less expensive items, are on bank credit cards or based on immediate cash payments for the full price. In the case of coffee shops or convenience stores, the transactions are almost always for cash, and payment is made in full at the point of sale. In these cases, merchants do not really have to worry about collecting debts from customers. Problems may arise for a retail seller if payment is made by cheque, though this is becoming increasingly rare because merchants seek to avoid having to chase a non-paying customer on an NSF cheque; in addition, most customers find it easier to use cash, a debit card, or a credit card. Similarly, the practice of extending credit and sending out periodic accounts to steady retail customers is a practice more likely to be encountered in a 19th century novel than in real life. Today, for many retail transactions, enforcement of debt payment is done by credit card companies, such as VISA or MasterCard, that pay the retailer what the customer charged to his or her credit card (less a retailer service fee) and deal with their cardholder who doesn't pay the minimum monthly charge on the credit card account. The banks love this arrangement as they make their profit from people who pay the minimum amount required, which includes interest at a very high rate. The banks have no great love of their more prudent customers who pay the monthly balance in full every month. Even if there is an annual fee for the cardholder, banks make very little money on this kind of customer. Only if a customer fails to pay the minimum amount due each month does the bank take action. The bank will then sue its customer for the amount owing, including accrued interest, with interest continuing to run on unpaid amounts.

Where consumer transactions involve "big ticket" items, such as automobiles, furniture, large appliances or recreational vehicles, few people can pay by credit card or directly out of their pocket. However, in most cases, it is likely that a seller will lend the money to the purchaser to buy the seller's product. This is done with a conditional sale contract, as discussed earlier in this chapter. For example, if a consumer buys a car and does not have all of the cash to pay the purchase price, the seller will give the buyer credit, allowing the buyer to pay a down payment on the purchase price and pay the balance of the purchase price plus interest in monthly instalments over a period of time. Because this loan may be quite large, the seller may require the purchaser to pledge the car as security for repayment of the loan. This means that if the purchaser misses an instalment payment on the debt, the lender has the right to seize and sell the car and apply the sale proceeds to pay off the loan. Usually, if the debtor still owes money after that happens, the seller has the right to then sue the debtor to collect the balance that remains outstanding. Under this arrangement, in addition to paying the purchase price, the buyer will pay interest on the credit extended, allowing the seller to make both a profit on the goods sold and on the credit extended. As noted previously, if the purchaser is an ordinary consumer (as opposed to a commercial purchaser), the *Consumer Protection Act* provides that the vehicle cannot be seized by the creditor if the debtor has paid two-thirds or more of the loan. The Act does, however, state in s. 25 that the creditor may go to the Superior Court of Justice for an order permitting him or her to seize the vehicle.

Many retail sellers in this situation sell or assign their right of payment to financial institutions. They do this for the following reasons:

- To improve cash flow, obtaining most of the purchase price in a lump sum
- To avoid having to administer a credit transaction or enforcing credit remedies against a defaulting debtor

A document that permits the right to payment to be assigned to a third party is called a **negotiable instrument**. In the trade, a consumer's conditional sale contract or other credit document is referred to as a **consumer note** or **consumer paper**.

Example 4.2 shows how it works.

Example 4.2 Purchase of a Consumer Note

If Henry buys a car from Quick Motors, Quick might sell the credit contract to Friendly Bank at a discount. If Quick is owed $20,000 by Henry over a period of time, Quick sells the credit contract to the Friendly for $15,000, receiving that amount from the bank immediately. Friendly Bank then notifies Henry and tells him to make payments directly to the bank rather than to Quick Motors. Having purchased the consumer note or paper, the Friendly Bank is guessing there will be no default and that it will clear a profit, representing the difference between what it will receive from Henry and what it paid Quick Motors for the right to collect the debt. In this case, Friendly will make a profit of $5,000, assuming Henry does not default. Of course, if Henry does default, it is the bank that will now have to enforce payment rights and remedies against Henry and run the risk of not recovering the debt in full. Quick Motors has been paid and is now out of the picture.

At common law, a party to a contract could sell its rights or benefits under the contract to a third party. However, the party's liabilities under the contract could not be transferred. Now, suppose Henry discovers the car he bought is defective. Normally, Quick Motors would be liable; and if it doesn't provide Henry with a suitable remedy, Henry could argue that Quick breached the contract and that the breach relieved Henry of the obligation to continue paying.

Example continues....

Example 4.2 (continued)

However, if Quick had assigned its interest in the conditional sale contract to Friendly Bank, Henry could have some problems:

- Friendly Bank has the right to be paid by Henry even though the car is defective.
- Henry cannot raise the problems with the car as a defence to a claim for payment by Friendly Bank.
- Henry can make a claim against Quick for the car's defects, but he will still have to continue to pay Friendly Bank.
- If Quick is no longer in business or has gone bankrupt, Henry will have no one to remedy the situation, and he will still have to pay the bank.

Not surprisingly, this legal approach is popular with assignees but not with debtors, particularly if the original seller is no longer in business or has disappeared. It is still an accurate description of the law for commercial, business transactions involving negotiable instruments where rights to payment have been assigned. But it is no longer the law governing negotiable instruments where the consumer bill or note has been sold to an assignee.

Today, Henry would have a remedy against both the seller and the assignee for defective goods.

Under amendments to the federal *Bills of Exchange Act*, R.S.C. 1985, c. B-4, in the 1970s, a negotiable instrument, such as a conditional sale contract or other consumer bill, note, or paper, used in a consumer transaction had to be marked "consumer note". In our example, this would be deemed to be notice to assignee Friendly Bank that it took the assignment of the right to payment, subject to Henry's right to look to Friendly for remedies if the goods were defective. In effect, this would mean that Henry's refusal to pay the Bank until the defect was remedied could be a defence if the Bank sues Henry for payment. In commercial transactions not involving a consumer, the common law continues to prevail, so the right of payment can be assigned free of liability claims by the debtor against the assignee. But that is no longer the case for consumers.

Commercial Credit Administration

Commercial credit arrangements are handled somewhat differently from consumer credit transactions. Businesses often have long-term relationships with suppliers, in addition to customers, where purchases of goods and services are made on an ongoing basis, often involving large amounts of money. In this context, cash sales or sales by credit card do not work very well. Instead, a more likely and customary business arrangement for the sale of goods and services is to offer payment terms of "net 30 days". This means that the debtor has 30 days, commencing with the date of the invoice, to pay the invoiced amount without having to pay interest. This provides the debtor with a 30-day "interest free" period. Interest starts to accrue on the 31st day after purchase at the percentage per month stated on the invoice, usually in the range of 1 to 2%. Although that may not sound like much, it works out to between 12 and 24% per year, which adds substantially to the debt and makes it more difficult to pay off. As a matter of practice, a knowledgeable debtor may negotiate a late payment by trying to reduce or eliminate the interest component. A creditor may well accept this, knowing that the older a debt is the harder it is to collect, and take what is offered rather than run the risk of collecting nothing or ending a long-term relationship with a customer.

Many creditors and some lawyers assume that if there is a provision for interest in the invoice, the creditor is legally entitled to payment. This is usually not the case. Unless the debtor specifically agreed to the interest provision at the time of sale or extension of credit, simply including it afterwards in an invoice does not make interest an enforceable part of the contract. Terms cannot be inserted by one party into a contract or on an invoice *after* the contract has been formed.

Most commercial extenders of credit will not immediately demand payment on the 31st day after the debt was incurred (see Figure 4.1). Often, there is a continuing business relationship that has gone on for some time and is expected to go on in the future. In the interest of continuing the relationship, most creditors will allow the 30th day to pass without taking action. Instead, the overdue debt, called a **receivable**, begins to earn interest. Most businesses will review the receivable

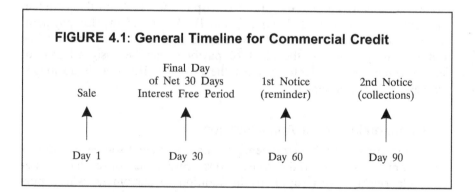

FIGURE 4.1: General Timeline for Commercial Credit

Sale	Final Day of Net 30 Days Interest Free Period	1st Notice (reminder)	2nd Notice (collections)
↑	↑	↑	↑
Day 1	Day 30	Day 60	Day 90

at the end of 60 days and again at 90 days. Depending on the nature of the relationship, the extender of credit may automatically send a letter in the form of a gentle reminder that payment is due when 60 days have elapsed. When 90 days have elapsed, most lawyers and most businesses will consider that there is a problem with the account, and there may be difficulties with collecting. Now is the time for creditors to make personal contact with the debtor and find out why payment has not been made. Sometimes the reasons are quite innocent — for example, the person responsible for payment has been ill, or is on vacation, or the matter has simply been overlooked. At other times, the creditor may learn that the debtor has a cash flow problem — that is, business has fallen off, other creditors are demanding payment, or the debtor's own customers have been slow to pay. In times of recession, this can have a rippling effect, as one debtor fails to pay his creditor, who, in turn, does not have the cash to pay his creditor, and so on. Whatever the reason, the creditor needs to make some decisions — that is, alter the terms of payment; extend further time to pay; or turn the matter over to a lawyer, paralegal, or collection agency. This decision requires a balancing of the desire to continue a commercial relationship with the desire to be paid. In the interests of preserving the relationship and profits from it over time, a creditor may choose to forgo all that he is entitled to and relax the terms for payment.

With a new customer, before extending credit, a business, with the customer's consent, may order a credit report from a credit reporting agency such as Equifax. This report will provide information about payment history, previous defaults, and lawsuits. The report includes scales that measure and predict the likelihood of late payment or default. If a potential payer appears to be a credit risk, a business can always insist on payment up front in full, often referred to as C.O.D. (cash on delivery). Later, if the payer seems to be reliable, other more permissive trade terms such as "net 30" may be extended. Credit reports and how to read them are discussed in the previous chapter.

CREDIT COLLECTION: TIME AND MONETARY CONSIDERATIONS

When a debtor has defaulted, large lenders such as banks often have formulas they apply in deciding how much time and money should be spent trying to collect the debt. Creditors are not in the morals business. They are not really interested in punishing debtors for failing to pay a debt. Rather, they are interested in collecting a debt as efficiently as possible. It makes little sense to spend $10,000 to collect a $10,500 debt. As well, the longer a debt is outstanding, the less likely it is to be collected. At some point, a creditor will decide that a bird in the hand is worth two in the bush and will negotiate with the debtor and accept a fraction of what is owing as payment in full of the debt. If the debt is uncollectible, the creditor may choose to write the debt off as a business expense. This means that it can be deducted from gross profits along with other expenses, thereby reducing the creditor's taxable income.

You should also be aware that what sometimes looks like a debt collection problem is actually a civil dispute. In this situation, a debtor may not have paid because he or she thinks the creditor is liable for something, either in contract or tort. For example, the debtor may refuse to pay the balance due for a piece of assembly line equipment because the piece caused the line to stop several times and resulted in reduced production and lost profits. When you are unable to collect and eventually sue, you may find that the action is defended with a real, substantive defence.

THE *COLLECTION AGENCIES ACT*

Debt collectors are regulated under the *Collection Agencies Act*, R.S.O. 1990, c. C.14. Although this may change with the licensing of paralegals and the Law Society's plans to introduce an integrated licensing program for experienced collection agents, at present, if you wish to act as a paralegal for creditors on a regular basis in debt collection cases, you should register your business as a collection agency. Employees of a paralegal practising in this area must also be registered. Lawyers in a regular practice and their employees do not have to register.

Under R.R.O. 1990, Reg. 74, made under the *Collection Agencies Act*, collection agents are prevented from harassing debtors. The regulation ensures that creditors who use a collection agency are paid what they are entitled to out of amounts collected from debtors. A collection agency is prohibited from engaging in any of the following tactics:[1]

- Attempting to collect payment without having sent a notice to the debtor to advise that the agency is acting on behalf of the creditor to collect the debt

- Phoning the debtor before the sixth day after mailing the above-mentioned notice

- Commencing proceedings without first giving notice to the debtor of its intention to sue on behalf of the creditor

---

[1] Sections 21–25 of R.R.O. 1990, Reg. 74.

- Threatening proceedings or other collection activity without authorization in writing by the creditor
- Continuing to contact a debtor when the debtor or the debtor's lawyer has sent a registered letter directing the collector to go to court
- Phoning the debtor with such frequency as to constitute harassment
- Phoning the debtor on Sunday before 1:00 pm or after 5:00 pm, or on any other day other than between the hours of 7:00 a.m. to 9:00 p.m. local time, or on a statutory holiday
- Contacting the debtor more than three times in a 7-day period
- Giving false information about a debtor to anyone
- Failing to give full particulars of the debt when contacting a debtor
- Contacting the debtor's spouse, relatives, friends, or employer, except in situations permitted by the Regulation (i.e., that person is a guarantor or the debtor has consented)
- Publishing or threatening to publish the debtor's failure to pay
- Using threatening, profane, intimidating or coercive language, or undue, excessive or unreasonable pressure
- Continuing to contact a person who has stated that he or she is not one and the same person as the debtor the agency is seeking, unless the agency is reasonably sure that the person is the debtor
- Commencing proceedings in its own name, unless it has paid the creditor for the right to collect and keep the amount owing to the creditor
- Commencing proceedings without written authorization from the creditor

In order to register as a collection agency, a person must meet certain conditions, including

- payment of the required fees;
- residence of the agency in Ontario;[2]
- posting a bond, the amount of which is based on the amount of money collected by the agency;
- mandatory filing of copies of all forms and form letters sent to debtors, and all contracts used with creditor-clients, for review by the registrar;

---

[2] The location of the agency cannot be in a dwelling house and must be in a permanent place of business open to the public during normal business hours: Reg. 74, s. 13(10).

- residence by the agent in Ontario and at least two years in the collection business or related experience that is equivalent to this experience, in the opinion of the registrar;[3] and
- writing an examination.

All monies collected by the agency are deemed to be held in trust for the creditor in accordance with the collection contract. The required bonding of agencies is designed to provide some assurance that money collected for a creditor is turned over to the creditor. If an agency fails to do this, the bond may be forfeited and its proceeds used to pay creditors.

Catch 22: Complying with the *Collection Agencies Act*

The *Collection Agencies Act*'s requirement of two years' experience as a prerequisite for registration as a collection agency is a problem for paralegals: a paralegal cannot have a collection practice unless he or she has had two years of experience in a collection practice. The actual wording is found in ss. 12(1), (2) of Regulation 74, made under the Act:

> **12.**(1) No person shall be registered as a collection agency unless the person,
> - (a) has had at least two years of actual experience in all phases of the collection agency business, or has related experience that in the opinion of the Registrar, is equivalent to that actual experience; and
> - (b) is 18 years of age or over, if the applicant for registration is an individual.
>
> (2) No person shall be registered as a collector unless the person,
> - (a) is an individual who is a Canadian citizen or has been lawfully admitted to Canada for permanent residence and who is ordinarily resident in Canada, and
> - (b) is 18 years of age or over.

A person who makes an isolated collection and whose regular business is not collecting debts for others is exempt from the Act and its registration requirements. However, any paralegal who acts on behalf of creditors as part of a paralegal practice must at the present time

---

[3] The LSUC is now offering an integrated paralegal licensing program for collection agents with three or more years of experience. As the *Collection Agencies Act* stands now, after two years you can obtain a collection agency licence. With integrated licensing, after a third year you could become a licensed paralegal as well.

register as a collection agency under the Act, and he or she must have two years' experience in order to do this.

This problem should disappear as paralegals are now members of a profession licensed and regulated by the Law Society. Paralegals are subject to rules of professional conduct and to audit controls over monies handled for others, and they are required to have taken a prescribed education program. Additional control by the Registrar under the Act is not required. In effect, the argument is that paralegals should be treated like lawyers under the Act. Recent steps by the Law Society to license experienced collection agents through a Law Society-run integrated paralegal program suggests that in the future the government may respond by dropping the *Collection Agencies Act* registration requirement.

But it is clear at present that a paralegal cannot ignore the Act if he or she wishes to establish a Small Claims Court practice that includes collections. Note, however, that a paralegal can act on behalf of debtors without having to register or do anything else under the Act.

CHAPTER SUMMARY

In this chapter you were introduced to debt collection issues, including key concepts and approaches. We began with an examination of the distinction between secured and unsecured debts, and noted how the difference affects remedies and defences, and the strategies and approaches of creditors and debtors to collection issues. We focused on the administration of credit transactions, both consumer and commercial, noting distinctions and differences in the various forms debt takes, and pointing out how debtor and creditor rights and remedies are enforced. We then considered collection strategies, noting the factors that will determine whether a creditor pursues a claim, negotiates a settlement, or writes off a debt. Last, we considered the requirements of the *Collection Agencies Act* for those who intend to make collections a significant part of their paralegal practice.

REVIEW QUESTIONS

1. What are the principal differences between a secured and unsecured transaction?

2. What problem might arise if a debtor has used an asset as collateral for credit advances from two different creditors? How is that problem resolved?

3. What constitutes "default" so as to trigger creditor remedies?

4. Describe briefly how credit is often arranged for consumer purchases of "big ticket" items like cars.

5. What is the significance of 30–60–90 days in commercial credit transactions?

6. What can creditors do to assure themselves of the creditworthiness of a customer?

7. What are the requirements of the *Collection Agencies Act* that a paralegal must be aware of?

DISCUSSION QUESTIONS/CASE STUDIES

1. You sell computer software to business customers. A new customer has approached you to supply software for Big D, a chain of 30 drugstores. The product you sell is expensive, about $200 per software package, including installation and post-installation servicing. Your business is based on a continuing relationship with customers over long periods of time. What factors do you need to consider to protect yourself against default by this customer, and what steps do you take if there is a default?

2. You know you have to be currently registered under the *Collection Agencies Act*. What argument can you make before the registrar that may minimize the imposition of the Act's requirements on you as a paralegal?

Chapter 5

Determining Damages and the Amount Owing

LEARNING OBJECTIVES

⇨ Understand the difference between simple and compound interest

⇨ Be able to calculate the amount of interest owing on a debt
  → that is due on a fixed date
  → that is due on terms of "net 30"
  → that is due on a simple running account
  → that has interest accumulated for more than a year

⇨ Know and distinguish between the different types of damages that a court can award

⇨ Be able to calculate the amount of damages that should be included in a claim

⇨ Understand the basic heads of damage, and the ways in which damages are determined

INTRODUCTION

In this chapter, we examine the factors that we must consider to determine the amount owing, including how simple and compound interest is calculated and how to determine whether there is a right to interest, generally, and to a particular type of interest. Examples of different types of interest calculations are given. We also examine generally the kinds of damages that are available in Small Claims Court that are recognized by law, including how damages, generally, are determined and calculated.

CALCULATING THE INTEREST OWING

We know that debts normally include a claim for principal and interest. If your client is a creditor who advances credit in the ordinary course of business, the interest owing on a debt would have been calculated prior to a claim being issued. But with a client who is a smaller creditor, you will have to calculate the interest owing on the debt. In any event, you should always verify a client's calculation to ensure it is correctly done. Once you start a lawsuit, you will have to keep track of the interest that is accruing and that will be payable, both before and after a judgment. Post-judgment interest issues are discussed in more detail in Chapter 13 on enforcement of judgments.

As we will see, interest is either compound or simple interest. With simple interest, you calculate the annual interest on the outstanding balance. The debtor will have to pay both the principal amount and any interest that has accrued. With compound interest, annual interest is calculated for a compounding period (a day, a month, quarterly, etc.) and then added to the principal at the end of the compounding period. Interest is then charged on the combined principal and interest for the next compounding period, and then added to the principal, and so on. You will see that in Example 5.1 the debtor will have to pay more to a creditor if interest is compounded than if it is simple interest.

Example 5.1 Interest Calculation

(a) Simple Annual Interest
Assume there is a debt of $10,000, and it is 1, 2, 3, and 15 months overdue. The interest is 21% **per annum**.

To calculate the interest that is owing, we use the following formula for simple interest:

$$I = P \times R \times T$$

Example continues....

Example 5.1 (continued)

where

I = interest,

P = principal on which interest is calculated,

R = rate of interest charged (show your interest rate in decimal places, so 21% would become .21),

T = time during which interest is accruing. This is expressed as a fraction of a year. If you are using days, the fraction is days/365 (even in a leap year, which has 366 days, you still divide by 365, as the average year has 365 days in it); if you are using weeks, it is number of weeks/52; if you are using months, it is the number of months/12. In our example, we are using months the debt is overdue, so we will use 1/12, 2/12, 3/12, and 15/12 as the measurement of time.

Interest for 1 month:	$10,000 × .21 × 1/12	= $ 175.00
Interest for 2 months:	$10,000 × .21 × 2/12	= $ 350.00
Interest for 3 months:	$10,000 × .21 × 3/12	= $ 525.00
Interest for 15 months:	$10,000 × .21 × 15/12	= $2,625.00

At the end of the 15-month period, the total amount owing would be 15 months of interest ($2,625) added to the principal ($10,000), or $12,625.00.

(b) Compound Interest

Using the same facts, but substituting compound interest for simple interest, results in a higher amount due from the debtor, as compounded interest is added to the principal at the end of each compounding period. Compound interest is calculated using the following formula:

$$S = P (1 + i)^n$$

where

S = amount owing (principal and interest),

P = principal (amount of the original debt),

i = interest rate for each compounding period (remember to show interest as a decimal, so 21% would be .21),

n = the number of compounding periods.

As the compounding period is 1 month, i will be the monthly interest rate, which we calculate by dividing the annual interest rate (21%) by the number of months in a year (12), or .21/12 = .0175.

The amount owing (S), at the end of

Interest for 1 month:	$10,000 (1 + .0175)^1	= $10,175.00
Interest for 2 months:	$10,000 (1 + .0175)^2	= $10,353.06
Interest for 3 months:	$10,000 (1 + .0175)^3	= $10,534.24
Interest for 15 months:	$10,000 (1 + .0175)^{15}	= $12,972.28

If you compare the amounts owing using simple and compound interest, you will see that compound interest yields a much higher amount because of the interest on the interest that is added to the principal at the end of each compounding period. If you tried out these calculations using a simple calculator, you may have gotten an "error" message because the calculator is not able to handle or display the kinds of large numbers the formula generates. You can use a scientific calculator to assist with the calculation of compound interest. It is easier to do these calculations using specialized financial bookkeeping or other financial service software. You can also use Excel or other office software to do the calculations for you.

Calculating Overdue "Net 30" Accounts

Creditors will often make accounts payable on a "net 30 days" basis. In fact, lawyers and paralegals bill their own clients on a "net 30 days" basis as permitted by the Law Society. The term "net 30" means that debtors have 30 days, interest free, before they have to pay the creditor. Day 1 of the net 30-day period is the date of purchase of the goods or services or the day the account is rendered. A business person will want to start to run the net 30-day period as soon as possible so that interest can be charged on late payments as soon as possible. On Day 31, interest on the amount billed begins to be charged.

Example 5.2 Net 30-day Simple Interest Calculation

On January 3, Year 0 (which is not a leap year), Billy Bob purchased an industrial freezer from Apple Appliances for $2,500. Billy made a down payment of $300 at the time of purchase and agreed to pay the remaining $2,200 on a net 30-day basis. His contract provided that overdue accounts were subject to interest of 10% per annum. It is now June 17, Year 0, and Billy has not paid any of the $2,200. Apple Appliances would like to know how much Billy owes it.

Step 1: Ensure that you give Billy his 30 interest-free days. Day 1 would be the date of purchase, January 3. You can use a calendar, or the Days of the Year Chart in Appendix 1 found at the end of this book, to count out 30 full days. Day 30 would be February 1. Accordingly, interest would run from Day 31, which is February 2, up to and including June 17.

Example continues....

Example 5.2 (continued)

Step 2: Determine how many days of interest there are.

You now need to calculate how many days the period February 2 to June 17 includes. You may count the days on a calendar (starting with February 2 and ending with June 17) or use the Days of the Year Chart found in Appendix 1 to calculate the number of days. The Days of the Year Chart is a simple, effective, and efficient means of calculating a large number of days in a single year or in multiple years. To calculate the number of days in this example using the Days of the Year Chart, you take the number of the day of the year of the end date (here June 17, which is Day 168 of the year) and subtract from it the day BEFORE your interest start date. To make the table "work", unless your interest start date is January 1, you always "back up" a day from your interest start date and look up that date on the table. Here you would look up February 1, being the day before the interest start date of February 2. On the Days of the Year Chart, February 1 is Day 32 of the year. When you calculate Day 168 minus Day 32, you find that there are 136 days for which interest should be charged.

Step 3: Apply your simple interest formula.

The formula for calculating simple interest is

$$I = P \times R \times T$$

So here: $I = \$2,200 \times .10 \times 136/365$
$I = \$81.97$

In most cases it is helpful to work out the **per diem** amount of interest, which is the amount of interest being added to the account each day. That way if the debtor calls on a particular day to come in and pay off the debt, you can quickly let him or her know the total due with interest. A simple way to calculate the per diem is to divide the interest you calculated by the number of days you worked with, so here $\$81.97/136 = 60$ cents per day.

Step 4: Add the interest to the principal for the total amount owed.

Here you would add $\$2,200 + \$81.97 = \$2,281.97$, which is the amount owed by Billy to Apple Appliances.

Calculating Simple Interest When There Is a Fixed Date for Repayment

Sometimes the parties agree on a fixed date for repayment. If repayment is not made on that date, then interest begins to be charged. The calculation of interest for an agreement with a fixed repayment date is illustrated in Example 5.3.

Example 5.3 Calculating Simple Interest on an Amount Due on a Fixed Date

---

Lucy borrowed $5,000 from MoneyMan on January 1, Year 0. Interest would not be charged if she paid the loan back in full on or before June 30, Year 0. If she did not pay, interest of 30% per year would be charged, starting July 1, Year 0. It is now August 1, Year 0, and Lucy has not paid back MoneyMan. MoneyMan would like to know how much Lucy owes him.

Step 1: Calculate when interest starts to be charged.
Here, Lucy has up to and including June 30, Year 0, to pay without interest. Interest starts to be charged on July 1, Year 0.

Step 2: Determine how many days of interest there are.
You now need to calculate how many days the period from July 1 to August 1 inclusive includes. You may use a calendar (starting with July 1 and ending with August 1 to count) or the Days of the Year Chart found in Appendix 1 to calculate the number of days. Using the table, August 1 is Day 213. For the start date, you "back up" a day from the day interest begins, so you would look up June 30, not July 1. June 30 on the table is Day 181. When you subtract the two dates, you get Day 213 – Day 181 = 32 days of interest.

Step 3: Apply your simple interest formula.
The formula for calculating simple interest is
$$I = P \times R \times T$$
So here:

I = $5,000 × .30 × 32/365
I = $131.51

Step 4: Add the interest to the principal for the total amount owed.
Here you would add $5,000 + $131.51 = $5,131.51, which is the amount owed to MoneyMan.

Calculating Simple Interest over a Period of Years

Sometimes a debt may carry over for more than a year. In those situations, you will be required to calculate interest over a period of years.

The quickest way to do this, as illustrated in Example 5.4, is to use the Days of the Year Chart.

**Example 5.4 Calculating Simple Interest Owed Over
a Period of Years That Includes a Leap Year**

Jennifer obtained judgment in the amount of $10,000 inclusive of costs on February 14, 2006. Post-judgment interest of 6% was awarded. It is now May 13, 2008, and Jennifer would like to know what she is owed.

Step 1: Calculate when interest starts to be charged.
With post-judgment interest, the interest starts to be charged the day of judgment. In this case, that would be February 14, 2006.

Step 2: Determine how many days of interest there are.
You now need to calculate how many days there are from February 14, 2006, to May 13, 2008, inclusive. You may use calendars (starting with February 14, 2006, and ending with May 13, 2008) or the Days of the Year Chart found in Appendix 1 to calculate the number of days. The "trick", when using the table to count multiple years, is to "back up" a day only *once* for the first year and not for subsequent years — it may help to think of the table as one long revolving table that you only need to "back up a day" once to use. Also remember that when your start date is January 1, you do not back up a day. It is helpful to break down your calculation of days year by year and add all the days together at the end.

Here, for 2006, when using the Days of the Year Chart, start from the day before interest starts, which is February 13, up to and including the end of the year, being December 31, 2006. Using the table, December 31 is Day 365, and February 13 is Day 44. Day 365 – Day 44 = 321 days in 2006.

For 2007 you do not back up any days as you already did the one "back up" required. Calculating 2007 is easy as interest ran all year, being 365 days.

For 2008 you calculate interest from January 1 to May 13. You do not need to back up a day as you already did your one "back up" in 2006. For 2007 and 2008 you began with January 1. Whenever you begin with January 1, you do not need to "back up a day" to make the table work. So, in 2008, you simply go to May 13, which is Day 133, and you would have your number of days for 2008. However, 2008 is a leap year, which means there is one extra day to add on in this situation, so you add 133 + 1 = 134 days in 2008. Note that you only add on the

Example continues....

Example 5.4 (continued)

extra day (for February 29) in a leap year if your calculation period in a leap year actually includes February 29. In this example, February 29 falls in the period of January 1 to May 13. However, if our calculation period was January 1 to February 20, we would not add a day. To use another example, if our calculation period in a leap year was from March 3 to July 5, we would not add a day. An extra day is not added in the latter two examples as February 29 was not included in those periods.

After determining if you need to add an extra day in a leap year, you then add all your days for all of the years together, in this case being 321 + 365 + 134 = 820 days in total.

Step 3: Apply your simple interest formula.
The formula for calculating simple interest is

$$I = P \times R \times T$$

So here:
I = \$10,000 × .06 × 820/365
I = \$1,347.95

Step 4: Add the interest to the principal for the total amount owed.
Here, you would add \$10,000 + \$1,347.95 for a total of \$11,347.95, which is the amount owed to Jennifer.

Determining What Kind of Interest to Charge

In order to decide what to do with interest you have to determine if there is a contract that governs your dispute. If there is, you can then see whether the parties agreed to interest. Note that the parties must agree to interest under a contract as a term of the contract at the time it is made. One party cannot insert it as a condition after the contract is made, unless both parties consent. Some businesses will enter into a contract without mentioning interest, and then send an invoice in which a rate of interest is specified. Defendants have been successful in arguing that if they did not agree to a term or condition of the contract providing for interest in the first place, then the other party cannot simply insert one into a contract by setting out an interest provision in an invoice. However, if the parties have agreed to interest, the contract will determine what the rate is, when interest begins to run, whether it is simple or compound, whether the rate changes, and so on.

If there is no contractual term providing for interest, or if the legal dispute arises from a tort or some other non-contractual matter, a party may still make a claim for interest under ss. 127–129 of the *CJA*.

- There are two separate sets of interest rates posted: the first one is for post-judgment interest and the second one is for pre-judgment interest rates.

- The latest rates, as well as past interest rates, can be found online on the Ontario Ministry of the Attorney General website (http://www.attorneygeneral.jus.gov.on.ca, click on "Court Services", and follow the links to pre- and post-judgment interest).[1]

- The rates for both types of interest change each **quarter**, using formulas in s. 127 of the *Courts of Justice Act*, based on the interest charged by the Bank of Canada to the chartered banks. You need not concern yourself with working through the statutory formulas; that work is done for you by the Attorney General's office, and the results posted in the pre-/post-judgment interest tables — don't make it more complicated than it is, just use the tables.

- The post-judgment interest rate is higher than the pre-judgment rate.

- The rate is announced and posted at least one month prior to the beginning of each quarter.

- Pre-judgment interest *starts on and includes the date the cause of action arose and runs up to and including* the **day before judgment**. The **cause of action** is the legal basis or reason for suing someone. When a legal right is breached and legally recognized damages have occurred, the cause of action is complete with interest running from that date.

- Pre-judgment interest is calculated using *either* the rate set out in the parties' contract *or* the *Courts of Justice Act* interest rate (if the parties do not have a contract or the contract is silent concerning interest) for the quarter in which the court issues the claim. Do not use the interest rate for the quarter in which the cause of action arose.

- Post-judgment interest *starts on and includes the date of judgment and runs up to and including the date of payment.*

- Post-judgment interest is *usually* calculated based on the *Courts of Justice Act* interest rates as parties rarely address the issue of post-judgment interest in their contract. When using the *Courts of Justice Act* interest rate for post-judgment interest, use the rate for the quarter in which judgment is given.

---

[1] The tables can be found at <http://www.attorneygeneral.jus.gov.on.ca/english/courts/interestrates.asp>.

Pre- and post-judgment interest is not automatic; you must claim interest in your plaintiff's claim (or defendant's claim for a counterclaim or crossclaim). If you do not, the other party may object to its being awarded because the other party had no notice that you wished to claim interest. Judges have discretion to refuse to grant pre- or post-judgment interest under the *Courts of Justice Act*, or to grant it at a rate other than the official rate, but this is done rarely.

DETERMINING THE AMOUNT OWING ON A DEBT

Now that you know how to calculate interest and when to claim it, we can look at the issues of determining what to include in the amount claimed on a debt. On a debt, the client's accounts will usually provide you with information about how much to claim, including interest. Then you need only update by calculating further accrued interest up to the point where a claim is issued. If you get a judgment, it will include pre-judgment interest. After judgment, you will continue to add on accrued post-judgment interest, beginning with the date of judgment. All of this is done either as a result of a contractual right to interest, or under the *Courts of Justice Act*.

Determining the Amount Owing on Simplified Interest Running Accounts

A **running account** is one where the debtor is a regular customer who keeps an account with the creditor. The customer will buy goods or services from the creditor and have the cost added to his or her account, increasing the customer's account balance. From time to time, the customer may make payments, which decreases or eliminates the balance. This kind of account is common in commercial activities, where running accounts may be kept by those who provide goods or services on a regular basis. Special care should be taken when making calculations on a running account. The best practice to follow in calculating simple interest on a running account is to calculate interest on each invoice on its own and then to tally them up at the end.

Running accounts usually allow a grace period to pay, usually 30 days from the date of purchase or from when the account is invoiced, and many running accounts are not paid off in full every month; as a result, there is often some kind of outstanding balance. While the creditor may appear to be "carrying" the debtor, the debtor will be paying interest on overdue amounts. When determining how much is owing on a running account, remember the following:

- Go through the debits and credits to find a nil balance to start your calculations. Begin with the next purchase following the nil balance.

- Calculate the interest on each purchase from the time it is due (i.e., after the grace period) until there is a credit received.

- Credits (i.e., payments made) are used to reduce the balance, but, unless the contract otherwise provides, the following will occur:
  - A payment on the account is first applied to reduce outstanding interest, starting with the "oldest" interest first. This means that if there is a debit from Yr. –1, and one from Yr. 0, the payment is applied first to the interest on the Yr. –1 debt, and then to the interest on the debt from Yr. 0, and finally to the principal balance outstanding.
  - If the payment is not enough to cover both, it is used to pay off or reduce the interest on the Yr. –1 debt.
  - Only after all of the accrued interest is paid off is the payment used to reduce the principal amount outstanding.

See Example 5.5 for an illustration of a manual simple interest running account calculation. Running accounts that involve compound interest are more complicated to tabulate. Reference must be made to the compounding period (i.e., weekly, monthly, or otherwise), and interest must be added to the principal and past interest. (Most businesses use software programs to calculate simple or compound interest running accounts.)

INTEREST: HOW MUCH IS TOO MUCH?

In the medieval period it was illegal to charge interest on a loan; over time, interest became legal. However, s. 347 of the *Criminal Code* of Canada prohibits an effective interest rate greater than 60% per year. There have been a number of charges laid against companies that make cash advances against paycheques, credit card companies, and utilities companies. The rates in contract documents, on their face, do not appear to describe annual rates of over 60%. The key here is the term "effective rate of interest", where what appears to be legal may appear to be less so when you do the calculations. A number of cases concerning lender interest rates, repayment fees, and calculation fees have been brought to court across Canada. However, the issue is complicated, and the case law is mixed. In some provinces the government has been successful in such cases.[2] In Ontario, under the *Payday Loans*

---

[2] The B.C. government was successful in *Instaloans Financial Solution Centres (BC) Ltd.*, 2008 BCSC 669 May 29/08 Docket L051076.

Example 5.5 Running Accounts — Simple Interest

(a) *Application of a Payment to Outstanding Principal and Interest*

- Yr. 0 debit — $450 accrued interest
- Yr. 1 debit — $300 accrued interest
- Yr. 1 payment of $200
- Yr. 0 debit — accrued interest is reduced to $250 with interest continuing to run on this amount
- Yr. 1 debit — accrued interest remains at $300, with interest continuing to run on this amount.

The outstanding principal remains the same as it was before payment. Only some of the interest has been paid off.

(b) *A Sample Calculation Using a Running Account*

We act for Fly by Night Construction Ltd. It has a running account with Shoddy Building Supplies Ltd. Orders are phoned in by Fly by Night, and debited by Shoddy to Fly by Night's account, and invoiced to them by Shoddy. Fly by Night makes monthly payments, sometimes paying off the balance due, sometimes not. There was some activity in June Yr. 0, but there has been no activity since that time. Fly by Night's ledger card in Shoddy's bookkeeper's office shows the following transactions:

DATE	INVOICE	DEBIT	CREDIT	BALANCE
June 3	0113	$20,000		$20,000.00
June 4			$20,000	$0.00
June 15	0893	$32,000		$32,000.00
June 21	0896	$20,000		$52,000.00
July 28			$20,000	$32,199.88*

* This amount results from using the payment to first pay off the outstanding amount of interest before applying the balance to reduce the principal amount.

No further orders have been placed or payments received. The original agreement stated that payments were due within 30 days of billing, after which interest would be charged at the rate of 12% per annum. Calculate the amount owing for inclusion in a demand letter that requires the debt to be paid by September 25, Yr. 0.

Example continues....

Example 5.5 (continued)

Solution

Note: Amounts have been rounded off while working through the solution to this problem to make it more easily readable.

Step 1: Determine the rate of interest and type of interest to use. The agreement indicates that there is a contractual interest rate of 12%; there is no clear indication that compound interest is required, so assume that it is simple interest and use the simple interest formula:

$$I = P \times R \times T$$

Step 2: Calculate the number of days of interest and the interest. Because there is a nil balance on June 4, start with the debit of $32,000 on June 15. Interest runs from July 15 (30-day interest-free period ended on July 14) to the date when payment is made on July 28, which results in 14 days' interest:

$$\$32,000 \times .12 \times 14/365 = \$147.28 \text{ (interest)}$$

Step 3: Calculate the number of days and the interest on the next debit of $20,000 on June 21. Interest runs from July 21 (30-day interest-free period ended on July 20) to date when the payment is made on July 28, which results in 8 days' interest:

$$\$20,000 \times .12 \times 8/365 = \$52.60 \text{ interest}$$

Step 4: From the payment of $20,000, subtract the outstanding interest:

Total accrued interest
= $147.28 + $52.60 = $199.88
Payment portion for outstanding principal
= $20,000 – $199.88 = $19,800.12

Step 5: Allocate the remainder of the $20,000 payment to outstanding principal:

$$\$52,000 – \$19,800.12 = \$32,199.88$$

This is the outstanding balance as of July 28.

Step 6: Calculate the interest on the outstanding principal from July 29 to September 25, and add it to the outstanding principal to determine the amount owing as of September 25:

Interest	$32,199.88 × .12 × 59/365 =	$ 624.59
Add principal		$32,199.88
Total due on September 25		$32,824.47

Act, 2008, S.O. 2008, c. 9, the maximum amount that can be charged on a payday loan is now $21 per $100 borrowed. "Rollover loans", where the borrower takes out a second loan before the first loan is paid, are not allowed, and borrowers have a two-day period in which to cancel a loan without incurring a penalty. Aside from the criminal charges, remember that even if the debtor agreed to the interest terms in a contract, if the terms are illegal, they may be unenforceable and may provide a debtor with a defence. Because illegal interest provisions may affect thousands of customers, many of the civil actions are class proceedings, which must be brought in the Superior Court. However, an individual may wish to sue on his or her own, and if the damages are within the Small Claims Court monetary jurisdiction, a case may be brought there.

Aside from the *Criminal Code* limits on excessive interest and the *Payday Loans Act* restrictions, where applicable, any rate agreed to by the parties is allowable. However, there are some protections for debtors in the federal *Interest Act*, R.S.C. 1985, c. I-15. If a contract stipulates interest but does not clearly set out an annual rate of interest, the rate will be limited to 5% per year. Where invoices set out a monthly rate, such as 1.5% per month, there must be a reference in the agreement between the parties to an annual rate that corresponds to the monthly rate. If there isn't one, then interest is limited to 5% per year. Remember that if the only statement of interest is in the invoice (whether annual or otherwise), interest may not be enforceable if both parties have not clearly agreed to it. An invoice is a statement by one party to the other. It is not an agreement between them.

MEASURING DAMAGES IN TORT AND CONTRACT

When we talk about "damages", we are talking about using a legal remedy to provide compensation to someone who has suffered a legal wrong. So far we have been talking about damages in the context of repayment of a debt. The measure of damages is simply the amount owing. Similarly, where the harm done causes you to incur expenditures, for example, to repair property damaged by another, it is usually easy enough to find out what it cost you to repair the property and then claim damages for the amount spent. In other cases, determining the monetary value of damages is going to be more difficult. How much is the pain and suffering worth for someone who is physically injured? In the Small Claims Court, we will have to somehow determine a monetary value for the pain and estimate the value of other types of damages, where they cannot be precisely and objectively determined.

While the superior courts have some leeway in fashioning a broad range of remedies, the Small Claims Court can compensate only with money, or order the return of property wrongfully taken. In the Superior Court, the court may order a party to do something, order a party to refrain from doing something, order a party to meet a contractual obligation, and so on. These equitable remedies are not, however, available in Small Claims Court. Aside from ordering the return of property, a damage claim must be expressed in dollars.[3]

In the Small Claims Court you may make a claim for damages for $25,000 or less, exclusive of costs and pre-judgment interest. For example, if you have damages of $24,999 and interest of $2,000, and costs of $800, you can still sue in Small Claims Court, even though the total judgment will exceed $25,000. This is because the monetary jurisdiction of the court is based on the damage claim alone and does not include accrued interest or costs, which are collateral to the claim.

You may also make a claim for the return to you of property wrongfully withheld from you, if the value of the property is within the monetary jurisdiction of the court. If you borrow my $2,000 lawnmower and refuse to return it, I can sue you in Small Claims Court to get it back.

Remember that not every wrong is a legal wrong giving rise to a damage claim. If I invite you for dinner for social reasons and spend money on making the dinner and you fail to show up, my feelings may be hurt, but the law does not recognize this as a legal wrong entitling me to damages, even though I suffered a monetary loss (the cost of making dinner). Another thing to remember is that although you may have been legally wronged, if there were no damages or the damages were trifling, the law refuses to recognize the claim. There is a legal maxim here to bear in mind: *de minimis non curat lex* — the law does not concern itself with trifling matters. For example, if a tenant removes and takes with him three light bulbs, that is technically wrongful taking of property. But the court may not see its way to giving judgment for the cost of three light bulbs.

---

[3] In *Grover v. Hodgins*, [2011] O.J. No. 310 (C.A.), the Court of Appeal for Ontario resolved the question as to whether or not the Small Claims Court could give equitable relief. The court stated, in par. 31, that the Small Claims Court may grant equitable relief within the limits of jurisdiction set out in s. 23 of the *CJA*: namely, to order the payment of money or the return of property. Accordingly, the Small Claims Court can now give relief in equity, including relief for *quantum meruit* and unjust enrichment situations and order restitution to be paid. However, the remedy must always be a judgment for the return of property or for a monetary sum. There is no jurisdiction to grant equity-based orders such as injunctions or orders for specific performance.

Heads (Categories) of Damages

We divide damages into general damages and special damages. General damages are those that do not have an obvious monetary value that can be determined objectively. Special damages are those whose monetary value can be measured with precision by objective means such as a formula.

General or Unliquidated Damages

These are damages that cannot be given a monetary value with precision or by objective means. Instead, a judge must establish a value subjectively, although he or she will try to look at damage awards in cases with similar facts on the damages issue. For example, if a broken nose in a barroom brawl resulted in damage awards in the $2,000 range in previous cases, then it is likely that a judge considering such a case will make a damage award in that range. Sometimes general damages cannot be readily quantified, as in the case of pain and suffering. In other situations, damages can be quantified but must be estimated because they cannot be measured precisely or by a formula. In cases of mental suffering, evidence of psychological or psychiatric care should be provided to the court. The following is a list of general damages, each provided with an illustrative example.

- Physical pain and suffering

   Victor is walking through the park and is run over by a cyclist. Victor is injured, with sprains and bruises, and is in pain for a week, and he has trouble sleeping. Victor is entitled to general damages for pain and suffering.

- Mental suffering

   Horace really hates George. It is hard to put in words how much he hates him. Horace knows George is an avid gardener. One night he steals into George's garden and stomps the garden to a pulp. George sees the garden the next morning and is in shock. He is unable to sleep for weeks, has nightmares, can't eat, is unable to enjoy any aspect of life, and is in mourning for his wrecked garden and can't concentrate on anything. He may obtain general damages for nervous shock and mental suffering (and also special damages for destruction to his property measured by the estimated cost of restoring it).

- Loss of business opportunity

  Axel damages machinery that Belinda needs to do contract work she is going to bid on. She likely would have won the contract, but because she lost the use of the machinery she was not able to win the bid. She has suffered general damages for the loss of a business opportunity; the measure of the damages is the estimated profit from the contract. Note that it is not the amount of the total bill she would have sent, because she never did the work or incurred the costs, but she did lose the profit. So, if the contract had been worth $12,000 if she had billed it, and the expected, estimated profit would have been $2,000, she would sue for the $2,000.

- Loss of enjoyment of life

  Niccolo was an avid amateur violinist; Martine accidentally slammed a door on Niccolo's hand. Niccolo can no longer play the violin, and he really misses the pleasure he got from playing it. He is entitled to general damages for the loss of enjoyment of life, measured by the importance of the activity to his income or well-being and by the length of time that he is deprived of the ability to perform the activity. If he were a professional and damages involved loss of income, he would need to prove his income from playing the violin in recent years and show his future engagements that had to be cancelled in order to prove his damages. If damages are loss of the pleasure of playing, the estimates are more open ended, and the process resembles fixing damages for pain and suffering. He is also, on these facts, likely to be entitled to damages for pain and suffering.

- Loss of earning potential and reduction of earning capacity

  Mariana is an expert pancake flipper at Flapjack Fred's. She was in a car crash and, as a result, suffered injuries that resulted in reduced eye–hand coordination. As a result, when she flips a pancake, it is as likely to end up on the floor as in the pan, so she is no longer able to do this work. She will have to accept other work, but it will never pay as well as the pancake-flipping job did. Mariana has suffered general damages for loss of earning potential and reduction of earning capacity, measured by the difference between what she earned before the injury and the estimated earning potential she now has, over her working lifetime. She also is entitled to damages for pain and suffering.

- Loss of enjoyment of possession
  In addition to ordering the return of property to its rightful owner, the court may also award general damages for loss of enjoyment of the property. This includes enjoyment in the sense of pleasure, but it also includes enjoyment in the sense of having the use of a thing, including the convenience it gives to the owner. The measure of damage is the estimated value resulting from the inconvenience or loss of pleasure that results from the deprivation, and it can include the estimated loss of income or profit from the thing.

  > If I lent you the lawn mower that I use not only to cut my own grass but also use to cut other people's lawns for profit and you did not return the mower to me in the agreed upon time period, you may have to pay me for loss of enjoyment of my property and loss of income for the lawns I could not cut.

- Repairs to bring property to the state it was in at the time of the damage

  > If Dan's car was five years old at the time it was damaged, he has a right to damages to bring the car into the state it was in prior to the damage; Dan does not have the right to have repairs done to make it like new.

Special or Liquidated Damages

Special damages (also called liquidated damages), on the other hand, have a monetary value that can be measured objectively by use of simple mathematical formulas, where there is no subjectivity or discretion: everyone who plugs in the values comes up with the same answer. The amount of a debt due usually fits the definition of special damages, as does the actual cost of repairs to damaged property, the cost of medications for someone who has been injured, wage losses for someone who is off work because of injury, and so on. The following is a list of special damages, each provided with an illustrative example.

- Out of pocket expenses (the most common form of special damages arising from a legal wrong, and including things like the costs of all medications prescribed as the result of an injury)

  > Victor, who suffered general damages for pain and suffering, could include his prescription drug costs as special damages.

- Loss of income

  Victor used to be employed and earn a salary or wage, but he is now unable to work. Measurable income loss from employment may be calculated and claimed. If he is an hourly worker, multiply the hours lost by the hourly rate. If he is on salary, then divide the annual salary by 365 to get a per diem salary amount, and multiply the per diem amount by the number of days lost. When calculating income loss, use gross pay, not net pay.

- Costs of repairs actually carried out or agreed to by contract

  George, the gardener, whose property was damaged, may claim the costs of repairs if it is an actual price rather than an estimate as special damages.

Different types of general and special damages can arise out of a single lawsuit. We refer to the two main types and the subtypes as heads of damage; each head of damage is assessed separately, and while nothing may be recovered under one head of damage, other heads may result in damage awards. When we add up all the amounts awarded under the heads of damages relevant to a particular case, we arrive at the total damages assessed. Judges will usually break down the total judgment into specific amounts for each head of damage assessed on the facts of a particular case.

Aggravated and Punitive Damages

This is a form of damages that is not often seen in Small Claims Court, but it is available in appropriate cases. Aggravated damages are awarded to a successful plaintiff over and above general damages to compensate the plaintiff for the malice, callousness, or high-handedness of the defendant. For example, if Abbot fires Bill, and Abbot is merely wrong about the reasons for firing Bill, Bill gets general damages for wrongful dismissal. But if Abbott announced the firing to other workers in front of Bill and made Bill leave the workplace immediately, publicly humiliating Bill because he really wanted to make Bill feel bad, then Bill may get extra compensation for the extra aggravation and distress caused by the way in which Abbott fired him. Where something is not only done wrong but done in a way that was unnecessarily nasty, causing extra aggravation and hurt feelings, then extra damages should be paid to compensate for it.

Punitive damages are used in the same type of situation but for a different purpose. Where aggravated damages are used to compensate a plaintiff who has suffered from high-handed behaviour, punitive damages are awarded to punish a defendant for unnecessarily nasty behaviour. Punitive damages send a message to the public that such behaviour will not be tolerated. If a court awards aggravated damages, it will not also hand down punitive damages; it is either one or the other in an appropriate case.

Harm With No Damages

While someone might suffer a legally recognized harm, there must be damages that connect to or flow from that harm in order to have a complete cause of action. If you suffer harm but not damages, your lawsuit will not succeed. Note that if Mariana, the former pancake flipper, was injured and could no longer work as a pancake flipper but found a job that paid twice as much, she would suffer no damages for loss of earning potential. However, if pancake flipping was so important to her self-esteem and sense of well-being that she suffered from anxiety, sleeplessness, and other mental health issues, she might still recover damages for mental suffering, even though she would recover nothing for loss of earning potential. And, of course, she is entitled to damages for pain and suffering.

The Duty to Mitigate Damages

If you suffer damages as a result of the act of another, you have a duty to take action to prevent the damages from getting worse. For example, Dan's car is damaged by Peter. Dan does nothing about repairing the car, and the damage gets worse to the point that it now costs more to fix the car than it did right after the damage was done. Dan will not be able to obtain damages for the full cost of repairs because of his failure to mitigate his damages by making repairs promptly caused part of the loss. He will only be able to obtain damages for the harm done by Peter, prior to the additional deterioration occurring.

Apportioning Damages

So far we have discussed various issues concerning the assessment of damages against a defendant. But what happens if there are several defendants who are or might be liable for damages to a plaintiff?

The answer to this question can be determined by reference to principles derived from cases at common law, or by reference to statute law. Where there is a conflict between common law and statute law, statute law prevails.

At common law we need to distinguish between defendants who are **jointly liable**, **concurrently liable**, or **individually liable**. The common law may deem defendants to be acting jointly or together if they have a common intention or design to cause the harm giving rise to damages. If two persons decide to assault a third person, they would be jointly liable for the whole of the damage. They may also be seen to be jointly liable because of the nature of their relationship — for example, an employer is deemed to be responsible for unlawful acts of an employee done in the course of employment, even though the employer has done nothing wrong personally or even knew about the act of the employee. Or if two persons jointly by contract promise to repay a loan and do not: each is jointly responsible for repayment of the loan. Even if two persons act independently of each other, but cause harm to a third person in a single event or incident or series of events or incidents where it is not possible to tell which of them caused specific damage, then they are referred to as defendants who are concurrently liable. For example, if two drivers hit a car driven by a third person, although each acted independently and without a common plan or design, they would both be liable for all of the damage caused because it would be difficult or impossible to factually determine which of them caused specific harm or damage to the plaintiff. By contrast, a defendant is individually liable if he/she acted independently, and it is possible to identify the damage done by him/her, from that done by other defendants involved in the same event, transaction, or series of transactions and events.

Acting independently or jointly or concurrently determines how defendants are treated with respect to their obligation to pay for the harm done, both with respect to the plaintiff and with respect to each other. If the defendants are deemed to be jointly liable, then each is held to be liable for all the harm done by the others. This can be a great help to a plaintiff who is unable to show which joint defendant is responsible for which element of damage. In this case, if the plaintiff can show that all the defendants are responsible for the harm done, the plaintiff may not have to deal with causation problems he/she might face to apportion damages among the defendants. In practice, once a finding is made against jointly liable defendants, a judge will usually apportion liability on a 50–50 basis, as a practical matter.

As well, at common law, if defendants are deemed to be jointly liable, there is usually deemed to be one cause of action. At common law, it is then important to sue all possible defendants in one action, as suing and collecting a judgment from one might serve to release all the others if they had not been sued. That is not a problem if the plaintiff can recover the full judgment from one; however, if the plaintiff recovers only some of what is owing, the others may be released from further obligations since they had not also been sued in the same action. Similarly, if the plaintiff releases one defendant, where several defendants are jointly liable, it releases the others as well unless they have all been sued in one action. However, this should not be a problem for a plaintiff, for as we note elsewhere in the text, it is generally good practice to sue all of those involved in an event, transaction, or series of events and transactions in one lawsuit.

If there are defendants who are concurrently liable, at common law each is deemed to be acting independently, even if we cannot sort out who among them caused what damage. A plaintiff therefore would have a separate cause of action against each defendant and could sue each of them separately. Settlement with one would not release the other; nor would payment by one release the other. As with jointly liable defendants, a judge would likely apportion liability on a 50–50 basis.

The common law has been modified by statute, particularly with respect to tort law. In Ontario, and in other provinces, the *Negligence Act* now overrides the common law with respect to torts, generally. Under statute law, if a plaintiff is found to be partly responsible for the harm done, then under the doctrine of contributory negligence, the court can divide the responsibility for the damage between the plaintiff and the defendants, making the latter responsible only for the amount attributed to them. The plaintiff has to absorb the loss attributable to him/her. If the defendants are separately or individually liable, the court can determine the proportion of damages each defendant is deemed to owe the plaintiff. If the defendants are jointly liable to the plaintiff, then the statute provides that the plaintiff, having sued all of the possible defendants, may recover the full amount from any one of them, although the plaintiff may not recover from the defendants more than the amount in the judgment. A defendant who paid the plaintiff, can take proceedings to determine how much the other jointly liable defendants have to contribute to reimburse the defendant who paid the plaintiff. A plaintiff is also free to pursue all jointly liable defendants for whatever he/she can collect, until the judgment is satisfied. Part payment by one does not release the others.

Damages in breach of contract cases do not generally raise the same issues as tort actions do about several defendants being liable for harm done. Privity of contract rules will generally confine the claim to parties to the contract who will be liable for whatever damages flow from the breach. In many contracts, the consequences of the breach are spelled out in the contract terms, including how liability is apportioned when there are several defendants. For example, if a guarantor promises to pay a contract debt when the debtor does not, then the guarantor is liable for any amount not paid by the debtor in accordance with the terms of the contract. However, when the facts justify the plaintiff suing several defendants for breach of contract, apportionment of damages tends to follow the rules that now apply under statute to tort cases.

Dependants' Claim for Damages

If an individual is injured by someone, the individual's family members may claim damages under the *Family Law Act*, R.S.O. 1990, c. F.3, Part V, ss. 61–63:

Right of dependants to sue in tort

61.(1) If a person is injured or killed by the fault or neglect of another under circumstances where the person is entitled to recover damages, or would have been entitled if not killed, the spouse, as defined in Part III (Support Obligations), same-sex partner, as defined in Part III (Support Obligations), children, grandchildren, parents, grandparents, brothers and sisters of the person are entitled to recover their pecuniary loss resulting from the injury or death from the person from whom the person injured or killed is entitled to recover or would have been entitled if not killed, and to maintain an action for the purpose in a court of competent jurisdiction.

Damages in case of injury

(2) The damages recoverable in a claim under subsection (1) may include,

(a) actual expenses reasonably incurred for the benefit of the person injured or killed;

(b) actual funeral expenses reasonably incurred;

(c) a reasonable allowance for travel expenses actually incurred in visiting the person during his or her treatment or recovery;

(d) where, as a result of the injury, the claimant provides nursing, housekeeping or other services for the person, a reasonable allowance for loss of income or the value of the services; and

(e) an amount to compensate for the loss of guidance, care and companionship that the claimant might reasonably have expected to receive from the person if the injury or death had not occurred.

Contributory negligence

(3) In an action under subsection (1), the right to damages is subject to any apportionment of damages due to contributory fault or neglect of the person who was injured or killed.

(4) Repealed.

Offer to settle for global sum

62.(1) The defendant may make an offer to settle for one sum of money as compensation for his or her fault or neglect to all plaintiffs, without specifying the shares into which it is to be divided.

Apportionment

(2) If the offer is accepted and the compensation has not been otherwise apportioned, the court may, on motion, apportion it among the plaintiffs.

Payment before apportionment

(3) The court may direct payment from the fund before apportionment.

Payment may be postponed

(4) The court may postpone the distribution of money to which minors are entitled.

Assessment of damages, insurance

63. In assessing damages in an action brought under this Part, the court shall not take into account any sum paid or payable as a result of the death or injury under a contract of insurance.

Sections 61–63 in Part V of the *Family Law Act* set out provisions that state that if a person is killed or injured by the act of another, where the person could recover damages, the person's spouse (including unmarried spouse or same-sex partner), children, grandchildren, parents, grandparents, brothers and sisters are entitled to recover their pecuniary (monetary) loss resulting from the harm done to the person injured from whomever caused the injury. To do this, they may commence proceedings or, more usually, join in a proceeding brought by the person who was injured (or if the person was killed, by his estate). The dependants have no independent right of action; their right to sue depends on the injured person's right to sue successfully. If the person's action fails, then the claims of the dependants must fail as well.

The dependants' claim is available in tort actions in Small Claims Court, provided the claim of each plaintiff in the action does not exceed the court's monetary jurisdictional limit. Because this type of claim is often found where the injured person's claim is likely to exceed $25,000, it is seen most often in the Superior Court. But it is a claim that could be made before the Small Claims Court.

The dependants may claim damages, including the following:

- Actual expenses reasonably incurred for the benefit of the person injured
- Actual reasonable funeral expenses
- Travel expenses to visit the person during his or her recovery
- A reasonable allowance for a dependant who provides nursing, housekeeping, or other services (The measure of damages is either loss of income where someone has to take off time from work, or an amount based on the costs of such services if they were provided commercially.)
- An amount to compensate for the loss of guidance, care and companionship that the dependant might reasonably have been expected to receive (Although this is usually claimed for children and spouses who suffer these losses, it is available to other dependants.)

If there is contributory negligence, the amount of the award for dependants is reduced by the extent to which the person was responsible for the damages he or she sustained. If the defendant settles by offering a global sum to all parties, the person and dependants can divide the settlement among themselves or ask the court to determine the division on a motion. In assessing the damages sustained by dependants, the court may not take into account any sums received by the dependants or by the injured persons from insurance payable as a result of injury to the person.

CHAPTER SUMMARY

In this chapter we discussed the components that must be considered to determine how much a plaintiff is owed. We began with definitions of the type of interest available — simple or compound — and discovered how both types of interest are calculated. We then examined the situations where interest is or is not available to be claimed, and noted that when it is not available under contract it may be available under the *Courts of Justice Act* when a party sues for monetary damages. Examples of various types of interest calculations for both compound and simple interest were provided. We then commenced an examination of the different types or heads of damages available at law and in the Small Claims Court, distinguishing between general and special damages, and giving examples of each. We also noted some types of damages available in particular situations: aggravated and punitive damages where conduct is high-handed, and damages for the dependants of someone injured by another.

REVIEW QUESTIONS

1. Ace Artists Shop bought supplies from Canary Crafters on February 18, this year, on terms of net 30. On what day does interest start to be charged?

2. Belinda lent Davina some money. Davina signed a promissory note in favour of Belinda, stating that the loan would be paid in full on June 30, Year 0. If the loan was not paid on or before June 30, interest would start to run on July 1, Year 0. Davina finally came forward to pay Belinda on September 24, Year 0, on the terms as agreed. How many days of interest are owed?

3. Puccini owes Mayerbeer $1,000. It was due on May 10. It is now May 30, and you are calculating the interest, which is at the rate of 11% per year, to add to the principal for collection purposes. Calculate the interest.

4. Handel has lent Bach $1,000, at an interest rate of 11% per year, compounded monthly. Payment is due on May 10, with interest on overdue amounts. Calculate the interest at the end of one, two, and three months.

5. Identify the following types of damages as either special or liquidated damages, or as general or unliquidated damages.
   (a) Abigail Boar's damages for pain and sleeplessness resulting from a fall on a slippery sidewalk
   (b) Damages for a lost business opportunity
   (c) Damages for wages lost due to an injury
   (d) Damages for loss of enjoyment of personal property
   (e) Damages for the repair of property where you have a firm price for which the work will be done

6. Henry's house caught fire and burned down. He filed an insurance claim. The fire appeared to have been caused by an electrical fault. The insurance company investigated and decided that Henry had started the fire, and it refused to pay. The insurance company produced no evidence to support the claim, and the Fire Marshall's office indicated that this was not an arson case. What kind of damages can Henry recover if he sues and wins?

7. Barbara Boodle was injured and suffered damages. She was in the hospital for several days, and then home for a week. Her husband, Abraham, had to stay home and look after her for that week. She was listless, unresponsive, and unable to engage in her usual interaction with her husband. Does Abraham have damages the law recognizes?

DISCUSSION QUESTIONS/CASE STUDIES

1. Stradivarius has a running account with Fine Woods Ltd., from which he orders wood to make violins. The contract terms state that a customer has 30 days from the day an order was placed to pay the amount on the invoice. Thereafter, interest runs at 10% per year until payment. Here is Stradivarius's ledger card:

Date of Order	Amount	Debit	Credit	Balance
January 10, Yr. 0	1,000	1,000		1,000
January 20, Yr. 0			1,000	nil
January 30, Yr. 0	2,000	2,000		2,000
March 5, Yr. 0			1,000	
March 6, Yr. 0	3,000	3,000		

It is now April 10, Yr. 0. Calculate the balance that is now due and owing, including interest on overdue amounts.

2. Watta Bore is a 25-year-old security analyst who slipped on a banana peel on December 1, Yr. 0. She broke her arm, sustained a concussion, and had various bruises and a lot of lower back pain. She landed in a puddle, soiling her expensive suit. She was also off work for a week and had a lot of trouble doing things for herself with a cast on her arm. She was in a lot of pain and was gobbling prescription pain killers. The codeine base to the medication gave her terrible constipation, so she also had to gobble ExLax in vast quantities. Her boyfriend had to drive her to medical appointments, buy her groceries, and listen to her complain about her lot in life. You are trying to determine her damage claim and have asked her to produce any documents or other evidence that show the nature of her damages claim and the quantum or amount of those damages. She has the following documents:

    1. Prescriptions for pain killers $80.00
    2. Receipt for ExLax $12.00
    3. Drycleaners bill for suit $15.00
    4. Weekly pay stub showing gross pay $1,500.00
    5. Boyfriend's parking stubs $25.00
    6. Boyfriend's grocery receipts $90.00
    7. Boyfriend's signed statement about how annoying it was to have to listen to Watta complain.

    You have done some research and found three recent cases that indicated that slip and falls on fruit peels, with the kinds of injuries Watta sustained, generated damages for pain and suffering of about $7,000.

Write a short memo identifying damages and amounts for them.

II
Small Claims Court Proceedings: From Commencement of Proceedings to Trials

Unless otherwise specified, all rules discussed in this section are Small Claims Court Rules.

Chapter 6

Commencing Proceedings for the Plaintiff

LEARNING OBJECTIVES

⇨ Know how to prepare and draft a collection letter, also known as a demand letter

⇨ Know how to choose the proper forum before commencing proceedings

⇨ Know how to determine the appropriate party to sue, and know how to name that party correctly for the purposes of the lawsuit

⇨ Understand the types of disabilities that require a plaintiff or defendant to take appropriate steps if one or the other or both are persons under disability

⇨ Know how to complete the necessary steps required when suing or being sued by a person under disability

⇨ Know how to name and to sue various business entities, such as corporations, partnerships, sole proprietorships, and various government bodies

⇨ Know how to take steps to ensure the broadest possible enforcement rights against partnerships and sole proprietorships

⇨ Know and understand alternative style approaches to drafting claims

⇨ Understand some of the basic rules and principles that lie behind clearly drafted claims

⇨ Know how to accurately and completely prepare a plaintiff's claim

⇨ Know how to issue and serve a claim

⇨ Know how to choose the appropriate form of service

⇨ Know how to carry out a service procedure and complete an affidavit of service

INTRODUCTION

In the previous chapters, you learned how to deal with debt collections, determine the cause of action, and determine the type and amount of damages; you also learned what sorts of cases the Small Claims Court can hear, and you were introduced to the *Rules of the Small Claims Court* and the forms.

Having decided to sue in the Small Claims Court, we first need to prepare and send a demand for payment in the form of a collection letter. If that is not productive, we proceed with the lawsuit. But before doing this, we have some preliminary matters to decide: which Small Claims Court to sue in, which party to sue, and how to name the party properly. We will also deal with some specific problems that may arise when you sue certain parties. Persons with certain types of disabilities are entitled to certain safeguards and protections when involved in a lawsuit. Suing corporations, partnerships, and sole proprietorships may require you to take certain steps in order to ensure that your lawsuit and any judgment obtained are effective against these parties. It is good practice, before commencing any type of collection action, to review any agreements that the parties have entered into to determine if there are any prerequisites that must be met before collection action can be taken. For example, there is sometimes a requirement that one party must give the other party 30 days written notice of any dispute prior to commencing litigation. An agreement may also contain a clause wherein the parties have agreed, in advance, to attend mediation or arbitration to resolve any disputes. Loan guarantees often require that notice of default by the primary lender be given, prior to a lawsuit demanding payment from the guarantor.

Having identified the proper parties to sue and problems that may arise in suing them, and having named them properly, we then proceed to draft a plaintiff's claim and have the court issue it. Following that, we take the necessary steps to serve the defendants with the plaintiff's claim.

SENDING A COLLECTION LETTER

In a debt collection matter, the client will have usually sent a polite reminder when an account is past due; if that is not productive, the creditor may have sent a stronger demand, usually when the account is 60 days past due. If that is not productive, the client usually turns the matter over to a legal representative to start proceedings. If the creditor's last letter to the debtor already indicated that proceedings would be taken if the bill was not paid by a certain date and that date has passed, there is little point in sending another letter demanding payment — the faster you issue and serve your claim, the better. By acting promptly, the message is conveyed that the client means to collect the account and is serious about it. As well, as covered in Chapter 4, if you are an agent covered by the *Collection Agencies Act*, you are required, prior to attempting to collect on a debt, to advise the debtor, in writing, that you are acting on behalf of the creditor to collect the debt.

If the client did not send a letter indicating proceedings would be taken, or if you are required under the *Collection Agencies Act* to give the debtor a written notice that you have been hired to collect the debt, you should do so once you are retained, unless on the facts there is no point in doing so. For example, if your searches indicate that the debtor is in the process of going bankrupt, another collection letter would not be very helpful. In such a circumstance, you should get in touch with the trustee in bankruptcy to file a proof of claim. If you are drafting a collection letter, it should cover the following points:

- State that you are the paralegal/legal representative of the creditor and that you have been instructed to collect what is owing from the debtor.

- Identify the debt in question, the amount involved, and the fact that there is a default in payment.

- Indicate and demand how much the debtor must pay as of a particular date, which should be ten days to two weeks from the date of the letter: include the principal amount, costs, and interest to that date. It is not necessary to show detailed calculations, provided the specific debt is identified. Costs may be included in an amount that is reasonable, reflecting the cost to the client, such as searches, courier charges, etc. The sum of $100 to $200 is often added to the amount owing to cover legal costs and disbursements incurred to open the file, carry out some searches, and prepare and send the letter. Example 6.1 sets out how you might calculate the total amount for the collection letter.

- Indicate that payment should be made to the paralegal firm in trust if the client's retainer permits the firm to present its account and deduct its fees before paying the balance to the client. The payment to the firm in trust also permits the paralegal to quickly verify that the cheque will be honoured. If there is some doubt about that, you can require that the cheque be certified, although even that is not necessarily a guarantee that the cheque will be honoured, as the certifier can order that the certification be removed so long as the cheque has not been presented for payment. A creditor who requests rapid payment from your trust account immediately after payment by

Example 6.1 Collection Letter Calculation

Suppose you have been instructed to sue Gudinov 4 U for an unpaid bill from Fred's Flour Ltd. for $4,000. The bill was due on May 1, Yr. 0, and was on terms of net 30 days. Interest is at 12% per year. No payment has been received, and it is now June 10, Yr. 0, the day on which the letter will be written and dated.

There is no interest until May 31, as the terms are net 30 days (May 1–30). Interest begins to run on the first day after the interest-free period expires, being May 31, until and including the day of payment demanded in the letter, which will be June 20 (21 days in total). You have decided to also ask for collection costs to date, which are $200. So the amount you will claim is as follows:

- $4,000.00   unpaid account
- $ 27.62   interest ($4,000 × .12 × 21/365)
- $ 200.00   collection costs
- $4,227.62   total for demand letter

The demand letter for this example is shown in Figure 6.1.

Note: The term of "net 30" in business usually begins with Day 1 being the date of purchase and the interest-free period running up to and including Day 30. Interest starts to be charged on Day 31. Business people want the 30 days to pass as quickly as possible so that they can get paid or start earning interest, which is why they start the net 30-day count on the date of purchase.

a debtor using a certified cheque should be treated with suspicion! Allow a few days for clearance of funds and call the bank named on the cheque to verify the account. In the last few years, some lawyers have been "duped" into paying phony creditors from their trust accounts, only to discover the so-called certified cheque was a forgery on a non-existent account.[1]

- State that if payment is not made, proceedings will be commenced without further notice.

---

[1] *LawPro*, Summer 2008.

FIGURE 6.1: Demand Letter

PARALEGAL SERVICES
200 — 4392 NORTH STREET
TORONTO, ON M6R 2P1
TEL. 416-123-4567   FAX 416-123-8910
paralegalservices@email.com

Via Registered and Ordinary Mail

June 10, Yr. 0

Gudinov 4 U
1750 Finch Ave. E.
Toronto ON   M2J 2X5

Attn: Boris Gudinov, Manager

Dear Sir:

Re: Fred's Flour Ltd. — unpaid account (Invoice #1234)

We represent Fred's Flour Ltd. We have been instructed by our client to collect from you our client's account for flour sold but not yet paid for. The amount of the debt outstanding is $4,227.62, including the principal on account, accrued interest, and costs, as of June 20, Yr. 0.

In order to avoid legal proceedings, please forward a certified cheque to us in the amount of $4,227.62, payable to "Paralegal Services, in Trust" by June 20, Yr. 0. If we have not received your payment by that date we will commence civil legal proceedings to collect what is owing to our client without any further notice to you. Please note that you will be liable for further accrued interest and court costs.

Yours very truly,

PARALEGAL SERVICES

M. Bolsomova

Maurizio Bolsomova

c. Fred's Flour Ltd.

It is important not to threaten criminal proceedings if payment is not made. If you do this, you will have committed the criminal act of extortion and could be charged. However, it is quite permissible to threaten "civil proceedings" or just "proceedings" to collect the debt. Your client could lay charges for theft or fraud in some cases, but that rarely happens, as clients are much more interested in payment than they are in getting mixed up in the criminal court system.

Send the letter by registered mail with a return acknowledgement card, and also send it by ordinary mail. You can also send it by courier with a recipient's signature required. If you have a fax number or an e-mail address, the letter can also be sent by either or both of those methods.

In all forms of communication, including letters, you should ensure that the firm name and any firm marketing meets the requirements of Rule 8.03 of the Paralegal Rules. Rule 8.03 provides that firm names, advertisements, and other similar communications must be demonstrably true, accurate, and verifiable. Such communications must not be misleading, confusing, or deceptive and should be in the best interests of the public and consistent with a high standard of professionalism.

Marketing

8.03(1) In this Rule, "marketing" includes advertisements and other similar communications in various media as well as firm names (including trade names), letterhead, business cards and logos.

(2) A paralegal may market legal services if the marketing
(a) is demonstrably true, accurate and verifiable,
(b) is neither misleading, confusing, or deceptive, nor likely to mislead, confuse or deceive, and
(c) is in the best interests of the public and is consistent with a high standard of professionalism.

Advertising of Fees

(3) A paralegal may advertise fees charged by the paralegal for legal services if
(a) the advertising is reasonably precise as to the services offered for each fee quoted,
(b) the advertising states whether other amounts, such as disbursements and taxes will be charged in addition to the fee, and
(c) the paralegal adheres to the advertised fee.

(**THE PARALEGAL RULES**)

COMMENCEMENT OF PROCEEDINGS IN SMALL CLAIMS COURT

If the demand letter did not produce the desired response from the debtor, it is necessary to commence proceedings. Once the decision has been made with the client to sue in the Small Claims Court, it is not simply a matter of pulling down a plaintiff's claim, filling it out, and issuing it. There are a number of matters that must first be considered before preparing and issuing a claim.

Choice of Forum: The Basic Rule Is
Sue Where the Defendant Resides or
Where the Cause of Action Arose

Suppose there is a Small Claims Court office right around the corner. Should you file your claim there? It would certainly be convenient for you. But it might de-rail or delay your lawsuit. Although the right to choose the forum is the plaintiff's, it must be exercised within the limits imposed by Rule 6.01:

> 6.01(1) An action shall be commenced,
> (a) in the territorial division,
>   (i) in which the cause of action arose, or
>   (ii) in which the defendant or, if there are several defendants, in which any one of them resides or carries on business; or
> (b) at the court's place of sitting that is nearest to the place where the defendant or, if there are several defendants, where any one of them resides or carries on business.
>
> (2) An action shall be tried in the place where it is commenced, but if the court is satisfied that the balance of convenience substantially favours holding the trial at another place than those described in subrule (1), the court may order that the action be tried at that other place.
>
> (3) If, when an action is called for trial or settlement conference, the judge finds that the place where the action was commenced is not the proper place of trial, the court may order that the action be tried in any other place where it could have been commenced under this rule.

Sue Where the Defendant Resides or
Carries on Business

The default rule is Rule 6.01(1)(a)(ii): you commence your action in the territorial division where the defendant, or any one of them if more than one, resides or carries on business.

"Territorial Division" is defined in Rule 1.02(1)(a) as a county, a district, or a regional municipality, and each of the specific geographical areas listed under Rule 1.02(1)(b). For example, the Toronto Small Claims Court, under Rule 1.02(1)(b)(ix), would be the correct court to sue a defendant in who lives or carries on business at an address in the City of Toronto. All of the Small Claims Court offices, including satellite offices, can be found on the Attorney General's website at

<http://www.attorneygeneral.jus.gov.on.ca> (follow the Court Addresses link, and after choosing a municipality, select Small Claims from the "Choose a court office" drop-down menu). You will note that the address list does not clearly indicate a court's territorial boundaries, particularly where there is more than one court office in the county, region, or municipality. You can always call the clerk's office to have the issue clarified. This can be a useful heads-up, as it is the clerk examining your claim who may first question whether you are suing in the right **forum**. If that becomes an issue later, it will have to be resolved if the clerk or the defendant raises it. The court addresses website does not contain a separate list of Small Claims Courts in Ontario. A list of all Ontario Small Claims Courts, current as of June 24, 2013, is included as Appendix 6 of this book. You can use the assistance of a Small Claims Court Gazetteer to determine, by place, which Small Claims Court to use.[2]

Alternatively, under Rule 6.01(1)(b), you can commence your action in the court that is nearest to the place where any defendant resides or carries on business. A defendant, for example, who lives on the western side of Toronto may be closer to the Brampton Small Claims Court than to the Toronto Court office; if Brampton is a convenient forum for you, then you might start your action there, as the Rules permit you to.

Commencing the Proceeding Where the Cause of Action Arose: Rule 6.01(1)(a)(i)

This is the alternative to the defendant's residence/place of business when determining the proper forum. It requires the plaintiff to identify the geographical place where all the acts occurred that make up a complete cause of action. For example, Harrinder lives in Toronto. She parked her car in a lot in Hamilton, where Harrison, who lives in Oshawa, backed into it and damaged it. The actions that constitute the tort of negligence took place in the parking lot in Hamilton. All of the damage was done there. So Harrinder could sue Harrison in the Hamilton Small Claims Court (or, relying on Rule 6.01(1)(a)(ii), she could also sue in Whitby, which is the court for the region in which the defendant, Harrison, resides). However, consider the situation in Example 6.2.

---

[2] The *Ontario Legal Directory* published by University of Toronto Press contains a Small Claims Court Gazetteer.

> **Example 6.2 Determining Where to Sue**
>
> Roseann, who lives in Toronto, ordered a custom-made desk chair from Comfybutt Ltd. in Windsor. She paid by cheque when the chair was delivered to her in Toronto. The cheque was cashed by Comfybutt in Windsor. A day after delivery, the chair fell apart. On inspection, it is clear that there were both defective parts and improper manufacturing. It would be convenient for Roseann to sue in Toronto rather than in Windsor where the defendant carries on business. But did the cause of action arise in Toronto?

While the chair in Example 6.2 fell apart in Toronto, that may be no more than the last action required to **perfect the cause of action** of negligent manufacture or breach of contract. Many of the other acts that help to make up either negligent manufacture or breach of contract, such as the installation of defective parts, or the faulty manufacturing process, occurred in Windsor. So, it might be difficult to argue that the cause of action arose solely in any one court's territorial division or location.

Proper forum problems also may arise where the defendant resides or carries on business outside of Ontario. The plaintiff must show that all of the elements of the cause of action, on the facts, took place within the court's territorial jurisdiction. For example, where a contract is signed outside the court's territorial jurisdiction and payments under the contract were to be made in Ontario, it has been held that the court did not have jurisdiction because all of the elements that constitute the whole cause of action did not take place in Ontario.[3]

Unless your case is clear, like Harrinder's, it would be wise to avoid relying on where a cause of action arose as a basis for choosing the proper forum. A challenge by the defendant can result in lengthy

---

[3] *Xerox Canada v. Neary* (1984), 47 O.R. (2d) 776 (Prov. Ct. (Civ. Div.)). But note that where a foreign defendant had a sales manager in Ontario to solicit business, then the complete cause of action may, on the facts, be said to have occurred in Ontario: *Interamerican Transport Systems v. Grand Trunk Western Railroad* (1985), 51 O.R. (2d) 568 (Div. Ct.). When the tort of inducing a breach of contract was started by a phone call from outside Ontario, the court held that the elements of the cause of action occurred wholly within Ontario. Though the phone call may have started outside Ontario, it was received and heard inside Ontario; the other necessary elements clearly occurred in Ontario: *Elguindy v. Core Laboratories Canada Ltd.* (1987), 60 O.R. (2d) 151, 21 C.P.C. (2d) 281 (Div. Ct.).

delays as the issue has to be determined on a motion to challenge jurisdiction, and that motion can stop the action from moving forward until it is resolved.

Often a contract will specify the forum where any legal dispute is to be heard. If the parties have so agreed, they may well be bound just as they are by other terms of the agreement. However, as we shall see, the court has wide latitude to deal with territorial jurisdiction issues.

Filing Requirements for An Action Commenced in the Jurisdiction in Which a Defendant Resides or Carries on Business

Generally, if you start your action in the court located in the territorial division where any defendant resides or carries on business, the court will not interfere with your choice. The court will usually be satisfied as to jurisdiction by the filing of an affidavit of service on one or more defendants that showed you served the defendant at a residence or place of business within the territorial division of the court that issued the claim. In such cases, an affidavit to prove jurisdiction may not be required. Some courts, however, make it a practice to require an affidavit for jurisdiction in all cases. When in doubt, contact the court office to find out what is required.

Filing Requirements for An Action Commenced in the Court Located Nearest to Where a Defendant Resides or Carries on Business

If you are relying on Rule 6.01(1)(b) by using the court nearest to where a defendant resides or carries on business, an affidavit for jurisdiction attesting to the facts that would bring you within Rule 6.01(1)(b) must usually be sworn and filed along with your affidavit of service. A sample affidavit for jurisdiction can be viewed at Illustration 7.1 on page 270. The affidavit for jurisdiction allows you to check off a statement that the proposed issuing court is nearest to the place where the defendant resides or carries on business and that this place is where the defendant was served.

Filing Requirements for An Action Commenced in the Jurisdiction in Which the Cause of Action Arose

If you follow Rule 6.01(1)(a)(i) and serve a defendant where the cause of action arose, you should file an affidavit for jurisdiction with the court along with your affidavit of service. If the defendant brings a motion challenging the forum, the court will usually require you to file an Affidavit for Jurisdiction (Form 11A) if you have not already done so. As noted, a defendant can always challenge the plaintiff by serving and filing a motion for an order to require the action to be moved to another court, on the grounds that the plaintiff has not complied with Rule 6.01.

The Balance of Convenience and Judicial Override

Note the provisions of Rule 6.01(2) and (3). Subrule (2) gives the court the power to order the trial of an action to be held somewhere other than where the case is commenced on the **balance of convenience**. This test requires a factual analysis of where the cause of action arose, where witnesses and parties have to come from, and whether one party is much more disadvantaged in costs and inconvenience than another. It is clear that whatever the default rules say in subrule (1), the court has the power to override them and order the trial in a more convenient forum. Any party, though it is usually the defendant, can invoke the subrule by bringing a motion, and it can be combined with a motion challenging the choice of forum on other Rule 6 grounds.

Subrule (3) gives the court the power, either at the settlement conference or when the action is called for trial, to review the plaintiff's choice of forum, whether the defendant raises the issue or not. This means that the judge, on his or her own motion, may order the trial to proceed in a forum other than the one the plaintiff chose, in any other place that it could be tried under Rule 6.01. That clearly allows the court to correct a plaintiff's error under Rule 6.01(1), but it also allows the judge to consider the forum of convenience test in Rule 6.01(2) even if the defendant has not requested it.

The power under Rules 6.01(2) and 6.01(3) is worth noting if you act for a defendant. It is another illustration of a principle previously discussed with respect to Rule 2 — that the technical requirements of the Rules will not be allowed to hinder the delivery of just decisions in an expeditious and inexpensive way. For example, credit card companies often require, as a term of a revolving credit contract, that payment disputes be tried where the credit card companies' offices are, usually in Toronto. A defendant in Thunder Bay would then have to come to Toronto for trial, even if witnesses and evidence of payment were in Thunder Bay. Using Rule 6.01(2) it is possible to argue that a defendant in this situation will be much more inconvenienced than the plaintiff, who has more money and resources, and a motion under Rule 6.01(2) to change the venue might well be appropriate in a case like this.

Suing the Proper Party

Having chosen the right forum, you next have to choose the right party to sue. (See Figure 6.2.) There are two aspects to this:

- Choosing the person who is legally responsible for the breach of a right and for the damages that flow from the breach
- Naming that party correctly as an entity to be sued

Choosing the Proper Party

Sometimes choosing the person to sue is easy, as in the case of Albert Oryx and Ophelia Foot. In their dispute over an engagement ring, Albert and Ophelia were the only actors involved, and it is clear that Ophelia is the actor who allegedly breached the legal rights of Albert. As she is, in law, a natural person, or individual, she can be sued in her own name.

But sometimes it is not so simple. Suppose Paula was standing next to a weigh scale on a station platform. When a crowded commuter train arrived, a conductor helped a passenger to board the train by

---

FIGURE 6.2: Who Do You Sue?

If the party is	*Style to Use*
A limited company	Sue the company exactly how its name appears in government Companies Branch records. Do not sue officers, managers, or shareholders unless there are special circumstances where they are individually and personally liable.
A partnership	Sue in the name under which the partnership carries on business (you can also sue the individual partners). Note that Rule 5 allows you to sue in the partnership name; but to enforce a judgment against the assets of the partnership and the assets of individual partners, the partners must be served with a claim and a Notice to Alleged Partner.
Sole proprietorship	Sue in the business name or sue the individual who is the sole proprietor. Rule 5 allows you to sue the sole proprietor in the business name, and enforce a judgment against the business and personal assets of the sole proprietor.

---

pushing. As a result, the passenger dropped a package containing fire-works, and the fireworks exploded. The blast knocked over the scale, which fell on Paula, injuring her. You may recognize the situation from your tort law course as an illustration of problems in determining causation — who is legally responsible to the victim. Who do you sue: the passenger with the fireworks, the conductor, the railway company, the manufacturer or owner of the scale?[4] You may have to do some research to determine the answer to this.

In other cases, statutes or regulations may determine who the relevant party is for the purpose of a lawsuit. This is often the case if you are suing the Crown or its employees or agencies.

When a lawsuit involves a business, think carefully about the legal entity that is responsible for the breach. While those associated with a business may engage in acts that cause harm or violate a right, if they are acting on behalf of or through an incorporated business, then it is the corporation that is legally responsible for the harm done, and it is the corporation that is sued. For example, if Gary Gameman, the President of Gary's Great Games Ltd., refused to pay your account sent to Gary's Great Games Ltd., it is Gary's Great Games Ltd. that is the defendant because it has the contractual relationship with you that has been breached, even though it is Gary's action in refusing to have the company pay its account that creates liability. Similarly, if the business is a sole proprietorship or a partnership, the same principles apply. However, because the owners of unincorporated businesses are personally liable for the legal obligations of the business, you can sue either the business or the individual partners or sole proprietor, as the case may be. And, as we shall see, if you sue an unincorporated business in its name, you can expand your enforcement rights on a judgment to include the individual partners or the sole proprietor.

Fixing Mistakes If You Start An Action Against the Wrong Party

What if you are not sure which party is legally responsible for the harm done to the plaintiff? In this case, a conservative approach would be, when in doubt, sue everybody in sight. This is particularly good advice in the early stages of an action, where all of the facts might not be known. If it becomes clear that some persons ought not to be parties to the action, you can, on a motion, consent to dismissal of the action as against those persons. You may have to pay some costs, but

---

[4] *Palsgraf v. Long Island Railroad Co.* 248 N.Y. 339 162 N.E. 99 (N.Y.S. Ct. App., 1928).

this is probably less expensive than trying to add a party in the middle of a lawsuit. And if the limitation period has expired, you will not be able to add a party at that stage, and your lawsuit could well be lost.

Naming the Party Correctly

In Chapter 3 we focused on searches to verify the identity of a party. If a party is an individual and was named incorrectly or inaccurately, your attempt to enforce a judgment in the wrong name might fail. The judgment must be against a person that legally existed. So it is important to name an individual by his or her real or "legal" name, not by aliases or nicknames or anglicized versions of their real names. Conducting one of the motor vehicle searches to verify a name, or doing an online "people finder" search, may be necessary to be sure you name the individual correctly in the lawsuit.

If you are suing a business, a business name search is essential if you are suing a partnership or sole proprietorship or limited company in its business name. You may also find out through these searches who the partners or the sole proprietor is if you seek to expand enforcement rights to include these individuals. These searches will also lead you to the address of the business. This information will be needed when you serve the claim.

Take care when suing municipalities, government departments, Crown agencies, other public agencies, or the government generally; they are often legally called something quite different from what they are ordinarily called. See Figure 6.3 for some examples.

How a government body is named in a lawsuit is often dictated by legislation. For example, statutes that establish a government ministry or department often tell you how the department is named or styled officially. In other cases, the answer may lie in the regulations, and you can always call the body you are suing and ask how it is named for the purposes of a legal action.

Fixing "Naming" Mistakes

Suppose you misnamed a party. Do you have to discontinue your action and start again? As we will see, the Small Claims Court Rules allow you to amend your pleading up until trial. If it is a simple case of misnaming a party who is properly a party to the action and there is no prejudice to that party, the name of the party can be amended. As noted, however, if you have not just misnamed a party but named the wrong party, adding the right party can be complicated. If it is permitted, the party added has to be served, and the party has the right to file a defence, which will involve extra time and costs. If the limitation period has expired, adding the "right" party may not be possible.

FIGURE 6.3: How to Name Governments, Crown Agencies, or Public Agencies When Suing Them

The party you think you are suing	How the party is named or styled in a lawsuit
The federal government	Her Majesty the Queen in Right of Canada
The provincial government	Her Majesty the Queen in Right of Ontario
Government departments	Her Majesty the Queen in Right of Ontario (or Canada) as represented by the Minister of xxx[1] (If the minister is a Cabinet minister, it would be the Honourable Minister of xxx.[2])
The City (Town) of xxx	The Corporation of the City (or the Town) of xxx
Seneca College	The Board of Governors of Seneca College of Applied Arts and Technology

Notes:
1. You can find Canadian forms of address on the Heritage Canada website at <http://www.pch.gc.ca/pgm/ceem-cced/prtcl/address2-eng.cfm>
2. Most ministers are in Cabinet and are referred to as "the Honourable", but a few, such as ministers without portfolio, form a class of junior ministers and are not Cabinet ministers.

Parties Under Disability — Rule 4

The law presumes that persons who fall into one of three categories do not have the capacity to conduct or defend a lawsuit on their own:

- **A Minor:** This is an individual who is under 18. (This does not include a minor who wishes to sue for a sum that is $500 or less.[5])

- **Mentally incapable persons:** This is an individual who is intellectually impaired to the extent that he or she cannot handle his or her financial affairs and other demands of day-to-day living, or who is

---

5 Rule 4.01(2) provides that a minor may sue for any sum not exceeding $500.

unable to understand the advice given by a legal representative to the extent that he or she can give the representative rational and coherent instructions. Examples of a mentally incapable person would include persons suffering from dementia, those with severe memory loss, or those with impaired intellectual ability. Note that persons suffering from mental illness do not, for that reason, necessarily lack capacity. A person who is severely depressed, or who suffers from delusions, may still be able to pay his or her bills on time, handle financial affairs, and act on the advice of counsel and give counsel rational and coherent instructions.

A mentally incapable person may have been subject to guardianship proceedings, where friends or relatives have applied to the court to have a guardian appointed to manage the person's affairs. Or a person, who had been mentally capable at some point, may have given a power of attorney to someone to manage his or her affairs in the event that he or she becomes unable to do so.

- **Absentees:** An absentee is an individual who resides or is **domiciled** in Ontario but has disappeared and whose whereabouts is unknown, and there is no knowledge as to whether the individual is dead or alive. At the end of seven years, if an individual is an absentee, there is a presumption that the person is dead. In Ontario absentee actions are governed by the *Absentees Act*, R.S.O. 1990, c. A.3.

Litigation Guardians

The primary requirement for those who lack capacity is that they have a litigation guardian appointed to conduct or respond to the litigation by giving instructions to counsel and generally making the decisions that clients normally make. Rule 4.03(1) indicates that litigation guardians cannot themselves be under disability:

> 4.03(1) Any person who is not under disability may be a plaintiff's or defendant's litigation guardian, subject to subrule (2).

As in the case of a trustee, litigation guardians have a **fiduciary** duty to the party on whose behalf they act. In making decisions, litigation guardians must have the best interests of the party they act for in mind, which means that there can be no conflict of interest, and the interests of the party always take precedence over the interests of the litigation guardian.

LITIGATION GUARDIAN FOR A MINOR PARTY

If the party is a minor, Rule 4.03(2)(a)(i) and (ii) state that the litigation guardian shall be the person who has custody of the minor, usually a parent. But a close relative, friend, or other "suitable person" may also act as litigation guardian:

> 4.03(2) If the plaintiff or defendant,
> (a) is a minor, in a proceeding to which subrule 4.01(2) does not apply,
>> (i) the parent or person with lawful custody or another suitable person shall be the litigation guardian, or
>> (ii) if no such person is available and able to act, the Children's Lawyer shall be the litigation guardian;

The court, ultimately, will determine the suitability of the person who shall be the litigation guardian. If no such person can be found, then the Office of the Children's Lawyer may act as litigation guardian. This public office is responsible for looking after the interests of children in civil legal matters. For more information on the Office of the Children's Lawyer, see <http://www.attorneygeneral.jus.gov.on.ca/english/family/ocl/>.

LITIGATION GUARDIAN FOR A MENTALLY INCAPABLE PARTY

If the party is mentally incapable, the situation is more complex, depending on whether the party had given a **power of attorney** authorizing someone to act on his or her behalf with respect to financial and other affairs, or whether the person had been found incapable in a court proceeding where a guardian had been appointed to oversee his or her affairs:[6]

> 4.03(2) If the plaintiff or defendant,
> (b) is mentally incapable and has a guardian with authority to act as litigation guardian in the proceeding, the guardian shall be the litigation guardian;
> (c) is mentally incapable and does not have a guardian with authority to act as litigation guardian in the proceeding, but has an attorney under a power of attorney with that authority, the attorney shall be the litigation guardian;
> (d) is mentally incapable and has neither a guardian with authority to act as litigation guardian in the proceeding nor an attorney under a power of attorney with that power,
>> (i) a suitable person who has no interest contrary to that of the incapable person may be the litigation guardian, or
>> (ii) if no such person is available and able to act, the Public Guardian and Trustee shall be the litigation guardian;

---

[6] In some cases, a person may not have made a power of attorney or had a guardian appointed by the court but has a statutory guardian approved by the Public Guardian and Trustee to act in their interests.

The Rules define who should be litigation guardian for a mentally incapable party:

- If the mentally incapable person was the subject of a court process appointing a guardian, where the guardian is given the power to act as litigation guardian, the guardian shall be litigation guardian.

- If the mentally incapable person did not have a guardian, but while capable had given a power of attorney to someone, which included the power to act as litigation guardian in the event of incapacity, then the attorney shall act as litigation guardian.

- If the mentally incapable person had neither a guardian nor attorney with litigation guardian powers, then "a suitable person" who has no conflict of interest in the matter may be appointed by the court as litigation guardian. A suitable person may be a friend or a relative. Such people are not appointed unless they volunteer.

- If "a suitable person" cannot be found, then the litigation guardian of last resort is the office of the Public Guardian and Trustee. For more information on the Public Guardian and Trustee, see <http://www.attorneygeneral.jus.gov.on.ca/english/family/pgt/>.

LITIGATION GUARDIAN FOR AN ABSENTEE PARTY

As provided by Rule 4.03(2)(e), if the person is an absentee and someone has applied to have a committee of the absentee's estate appointed to manage the absentee's property and financial interests, then the committee is the litigation guardian. (Note that the committee is usually a single person, not a group.) If there is no committee, then a "suitable person" may be appointed. The appointed person should have no interest contrary to that of the absentee. If there is no committee or suitable person, the litigation guardian of last resort is, again, the Public Guardian and Trustee:

> 4.03(2) If the plaintiff or defendant,
> (e) is an absentee,
>> (i) the committee of his or her estate appointed under the *Absentees Act* shall be the litigation guardian,
>> (ii) if there is no such committee, a suitable person who has no interest contrary to that of the absentee may be the litigation guardian, or
>> (iii) if no such person is available and able to act, the Public Guardian and Trustee shall be the litigation guardian;

DUTIES OF A LITIGATION GUARDIAN

A litigation guardian is required to diligently attend to the interests of the person under disability. A guardian owes a duty of care to the person to take all steps reasonably necessary to protect his or her interests, including commencing and conducting or defending a claim. Rule 4.04(1) sets out the guardian's duties:

> 4.04(1) A litigation guardian shall diligently attend to the interests of the person under disability and take all steps reasonably necessary for the protection of those interests, including the commencement and conduct of a defendant's claim.

Litigation Guardian Consent

A litigation guardian must consent to act and must file with the court a consent in Form 4A. (The Children's Lawyer and the Public Guardian and Trustee, being public bodies, do not have to file this consent.) The plaintiff's consent must cover the matters set out in Rule 4.01(3)(a)–(f):

> 4.01(3) A plaintiff's litigation guardian shall, at the time of filing a claim or as soon as possible afterwards, file with the clerk a consent (Form 4A) in which the litigation guardian,
>   (a) states the nature of the disability;
>   (b) in the case of a minor, states the minor's birth date;
>   (c) sets out his or her relationship, if any, to the person under disability;
>   (d) states that he or she has no interest in the proceeding contrary to that of the person under disability;
>   (e) acknowledges that he or she is aware of his or her liability to pay personally any costs awarded against him or her or against the person under disability; and
>   (f) states whether he or she is represented by a lawyer or agent and, if so, gives that person's name and confirms that the person has written authority to act in the proceeding.

The defendant's consent must cover the matters set out in Rule 4.02(2)(a)–(e):

> 4.02(2) A defendant's litigation guardian shall file with the defence a consent (Form 4A) in which the litigation guardian,
>   (a) states the nature of the disability;
>   (b) in the case of a minor, states the minor's birth date;
>   (c) sets out his or her relationship, if any, to the person under disability;
>   (d) states that he or she has no interest in the proceeding contrary to that of the person under disability; and
>   (e) states whether he or she is represented by a lawyer or agent and, if so, gives that person's name and confirms that the person has written authority to act in the proceeding.

In both cases the consent states the nature of the disability with a very brief description. If the party is a minor, it sets out the minor's birth date. The litigation guardian must describe the relationship to the party and state that there is no conflict of interest with the party. The consent also indicates whether there is a lawyer or paralegal or other agent acting for the party; if there is one, the consent must indicate that the legal representative has authority to act. Usually it will be the litigation guardian's task to retain a legal representative and be advised by, and give instructions to, the legal representative.

The plaintiff's litigation guardian, however, unlike the defendant's, is obliged to acknowledge that he or she is aware that (i) if costs are awarded against him or her personally, he or she shall be obliged to pay them personally, and (ii) he or she may also have to pay costs awarded against the plaintiff. Ordinarily, costs awards are not made against the litigation guardian personally unless they behave improperly in the course of the lawsuit. It is not unusual to have a costs award against a minor paid by the litigation guardian, as the minor may have no means of paying a costs order. It is less usual in the case of a mentally incapable plaintiff. A plaintiff's litigation guardian consent in Form 4A is set out in Illustration 6.1. (For the purposes of this illustration, we assume Albert Oryx is 17 years old and a minor. This fact applies only to this illustration.)

SUPERVISION AND REMOVAL OF A LITIGATION GUARDIAN BY THE COURT

While a litigation guardian may consent to act, the court maintains overall supervision and control over what the litigation guardian does; a litigation guardian who is incompetent, dishonest, or who has a conflict of interest may be removed by the court under Rule 4.05 at any time, and the court may appoint someone else as a replacement:

> 4.05 The court may remove or replace a litigation guardian at any time.

LITIGATION GUARDIAN FOR A DEFENDANT

While a plaintiff is unlikely to start an action without first having a litigation guardian to get it underway, a defendant does not ask to be sued and, therefore, may not have a litigation guardian or even know one is needed. In this situation, under Rule 4.02(3), if it appears to the court that the defendant is a person under disability with no litigation guardian and there is someone who can act as a proposed litigation guardian, the court may appoint that person, provided he or she has no conflict of interest with the defendant:

ILLUSTRATION 6.1: Sample Consent to Act as Litigation Guardian Consent (Form 4A)

ONTARIO
Superior Court of Justice
Cour supérieure de justice

Consent to Act as Litigation Guardian
Consentement pour agir en qualité de tuteur à l'instance
Form / Formule 4A Ont. Reg. No. / Règl. de l'Ont. : 258/98

Toronto
Small Claims Court / Cour des petites créances de

SC-00-47669-00
Claim No. / N° de la demande

47 Sheppard Avenue E., 3rd Floor
Toronto, ON M2N 5N1

Address / Adresse

416-326-3554
Phone number / Numéro de téléphone

BETWEEN / ENTRE

Albert Oryx

Plaintiff(s) / Demandeur(s)/demanderesse(s)

and / et

Ophelia Foot

Defendant(s) / Défendeur(s)/défenderesse(s)

My name is *Je m'appelle*	Name / Nom **Allen Oryx**
And I live at *et j'habite à*	Street and number / Numéro et rue **111 First Ave.**
	City, province, postal code / Ville, province, code postal **Toronto, ON, M4R 1X6**
	Phone number and fax number / Numéro de téléphone et numéro de télécopieur **416-221-1234**

1. I consent to act as litigation guardian in this action for the
   Je consens à agir à titre de tuteur à l'instance dans la présente action au nom du

   ☒ plaintiff, named **Albert Oryx**
   demandeur suivant :   (Name of plaintiff / Nom du demandeur/de la demanderesse)

   (Check one box only. / Cochez une seule case.)
   and I acknowledge that I may be personally responsible for any costs awarded against me or against this person.
   et je reconnais que je peux être tenu(e) personnellement responsable des dépens auxquels moi-même ou cette personne pourrions être condamné(e)s.

   ☐ defendant, named
   défendeur suivant :   (Name of defendant / Nom du défendeur/de la défenderesse)

2. The above-named person is under the following disability:
   La personne susmentionnée est incapable parce qu'elle est :

   ☒ a minor whose birth date is **January 4, Yr. –17**
   un mineur dont la date de naissance est le   (State date of birth of minor / Indiquez la date de naissance du mineur)

   (Check appropriate box(es). / Cochez la ou les cases appropriées.)
   ☐ mentally incapable within the meaning of Section 6 or Section 45 of the *Substitute Decisions Act, 1992* in respect of an issue in a proceeding.
   mentalement incapable au sens de l'article 6 ou 45 de la Loi de 1992 sur la prise de décisions au nom d'autrui à l'égard d'une question dans une instance.

   ☐ an absentee within the meaning of the *Absentees Act.*
   une personne absente au sens de la Loi sur les absents.

SCR 4.01-4.02-4A (June 1, 2009 / 1er juin 2009) CSD

continues....

Illustration 6.1 (continued)

FORM / *FORMULE* 4A   PAGE 2   SC-00-47669-00
                                                                Claim No. / *N° de la demande*

3. My relationship to the person under disability is:
   Mon lien de parenté avec l'incapable est le suivant :
   (State your relationship to the person under disability. / Indiquez votre lien de parenté avec l'incapable.)
   Father of the plaintiff

4. I have no interest in this action contrary to that of the person under disability.
   Je n'ai dans la présente action aucun intérêt opposé à celui de l'incapable.

5. I am
   Je

   (Check one   ☒   represented and have given written authority to   **Peter Paralegal**
   box only. /   *suis représenté(e) et j'ai autorisé par écrit :*   (Name of lawyer/agent with authority to act in this
   Cochez une   proceeding / *Nom de l'avocat/du mandataire autorisé à
   seule case.)   agir dans la présente instance*)

                      of   **41 Yonge Street, #410, Toronto, ON   M5G 1S1**
                      de   (Address for service / *Adresse aux fins de signification*)

                      416-597-0048; 416-597-0049
                                  (Phone number and fax number / *Numéro de téléphone et numéro de télécopieur*)

                      to act in this proceeding.
                      à agir dans la présente instance.

                 ☐   not represented by a lawyer/agent.
                      ne suis pas représenté(e) par un avocat/un mandataire.

   January 2, Yr. 1

   Allen Oryx
   (Signature of litigation guardian consenting / *Signature du
   tuteur à l'instance qui consent*)

   Peter Paralegal
   (Signature of witness / *Signature du témoin*)

   Peter Paralegal
   (Name of witness / *Nom du témoin*)

NOTE: Within seven (7) calendar days of changing your address for service, notify the court and all other
             parties in writing.
REMARQUE : *Dans les sept (7) jours civils qui suivent tout changement de votre adresse aux fins de
             signification, veuillez en aviser par écrit le tribunal et les autres parties.*

SCR 4.01-4.02-4A (June 1, 2009 / *1er juin 2009*) CSD

> 4.02(3) If it appears to the court that a defendant is a person under disability and the defendant does not have a litigation guardian the court may, after notice to the proposed litigation guardian, appoint as litigation guardian for the defendant any person who has no interest in the action contrary to that of the defendant.

Knowledge of the defendant's incapacity may come to the court's attention through the plaintiff, as the result of contact with the defendant, or it may come to the court's attention later, at the settlement conference, where a judge first sees the parties in person. Typically it comes to the court's attention when the defendant fails to defend and the plaintiff obtains a default judgment. The Rules do not clearly indicate how the parties can proceed to appoint the defendant's litigation guardian. If the plaintiff becomes aware of the situation, he or she can bring a motion requesting the court to make an appointment, and it is in the interest of the plaintiff to do so to move the action along. In any case, if the court discovers that a default judgment has been obtained against a defendant who should have had a litigation guardian, the court will likely move under Rule 4.06 to set aside the judgment, appoint a litigation guardian, and then have the matter proceed.

> 4.06 If an action has been brought against a person under disability and the action has not been defended by a litigation guardian, the court may set aside the noting of default or any judgment against the person under disability on such terms as are just, and may set aside any step that has been taken to enforce the judgment.

Court Supervision of Settlements Where Party under Disability

Normally if the parties settle a case, the court rubber-stamps the decision. However, if the person is under disability, two things happen:

- The settlement must be approved by the court.
- The money is not simply paid to the party or legal representative but must be paid only as the court directs.

Rule 4.07 requires any settlement to be approved by the court:

> 4.07 No settlement of a claim made by or against a person under disability is binding on the person without the approval of the court.

The parties must bring a motion to approve the settlement by way of an order. If the settlement does not appear to be **improvident**, it will likely be approved without a detailed examination by the judge. Rule 4.08 indicates that the settlement is not then simply paid to the party under disability on the theory that if the person is deemed incapable of managing his or her affairs, the person is presumed to be incapable of properly handling the settlement funds:

> 4.08(1) Any money payable to a person under disability under an order or a settlement shall be paid into court, unless the court orders otherwise, and shall afterwards be paid out or otherwise disposed of as ordered by the court.
>
> (2) If money is payable to a person under disability under an order or settlement, the court may order that the money shall be paid directly to the person, and payment made under the order discharges the obligation to the extent of the amount paid.
>
> (3) A motion for an order under this rule shall be supported by an affidavit in Form 4B rather than an affidavit in Form 15A.
>
> (4) In making an order under this rule, the court may order that costs payable to the moving party be paid out of the money in court directly to the person representing that party in the proceeding.

The court has wide discretion under the rule: it can order the settlement to be paid into court to be held until the court decides how it is to be disbursed and on what terms. A minor's settlement is likely to be held in court until the minor reaches the age of majority, at which point the minor can apply to the court for payment out. An older minor, however, may receive some or all of the settlement directly, as ordered by the court. A mentally incapable person may have money held by the guardian, the attorney under a power of attorney, or the public trustee, who then disburses the money as the court orders or in accordance with his or her authority under the guardian's order or power of attorney, as the case may be.[7]

Procedure for Making Payments Into or Out of Court

As of January 1, 2013, the rules committee established a new rule, Rule 22, which provides a specific procedure for making payments into and out of court with respect to a proceeding.

It applies to payments with respect to persons under disability, and other payments in the course of a proceeding, but specifically does not apply to the following:

---

[7] As a result of amendments made in 2013, when bringing a motion for payment out of court for money held in court on behalf of a person under disability, in addition to the usual motion form, you should use Form 4B, Affidavit (Motion for Payment Out of Court), which is a specialized affidavit form for use on this type of motion. Note that money held in court can also be used to pay the court costs incurred on this type of motion, under Rule 4.08(4). Once an order is made, payments out of court are governed by the procedure set out in Rule 22.

(a) a proposal by a defendant to admit all or part of a claim and pay by instalments under Rule 9.03;

(b) an offer to settle a claim in return for the payment of money; and

(c) enforcement of an order for payment by way of garnishment or otherwise, under Rule 20.

Using the example of Albert Oryx, the minor whose father, Allen Oryx is acting as his litigation guardian, we can see how the rule would work. If Ophelia Foot was prepared to pay money into court she would have to file a written request with the clerk of the court or with the Accountant of the Superior Court — although as a practical matter it is probably advisable to file the request with the clerk in a small claims matter. The request should refer to the statutory provision or rule that permits payment to be made, and it should include Ophelia by name and include her mailing address. If the request is made pursuant to an order, there should be a reference to the order, and a copy of the order should be attached. There is no prescribed form for the written request.

The clerk, on receipt of the request, provides Ophelia with a direction to receive the money as a deposit, addressed to the chartered bank and identifying the account under the name of the Accountant of the Superior Court into which the money is to be paid.

Ophelia now has two choices as to how she makes the payment:

1. She can pay the money into court directly, depositing it with the bank, according to the direction.

2. She can mail the request to pay into court and a cheque or money order to the Accountant of the Superior Court whose mailing address is available from the clerk's office.

Depending on how she made her payment, either the Accountant of the Superior Court or the bank will provide her with a receipt. She should then mail a copy of the receipt to Albert Oryx's litigation guardian and file a copy with the clerk, as evidence that the payment into court has been made.

If Allen Oryx, as litigation guardian, wishes to obtain a payment out of court on behalf of Albert, he will need to obtain the court order as was previously discussed, by filing a motion and the prescribed affidavit in Form 4B. Allen then has to file with the Accountant of the Superior Court a written request for payment out and a supporting affidavit in the form prescribed by the Ministry together with a copy of the order with a seal on it (obtained from the clerk).

An example of Form 4B, Affidavit (Motion for Payment Out of Court), is set out in Illustration 6.2.)

ILLUSTRATION 6.2: Sample Affidavit (Motion for Payment Out of Court) (Form 4B)

ONTARIO
Superior Court of Justice
Cour supérieure de justice

Affidavit (Motion for Payment Out of Court)
Affidavit *(Motion en vue du versement d'une somme d'argent consignée)*
Form / *Formule* 4B Ont. Reg. No. / *Règl. de l'Ont.* : 258/98

Toronto
Small Claims Court / *Cour des petites créances de*

SC-00-47669-00
Claim No. / *N° de la demande*

47 Sheppard Avenue E., 3rd Floor
Toronto, ON M2N 5N1
Address / *Adresse*

416-326-3554
Phone number / *Numéro de téléphone*

BETWEEN / ENTRE

Albert Oryx
Plaintiff(s)/Creditor(s) / *Demandeur(s)/demanderesse(s)/créancier(s)/créancière(s)*

and / et

Ophelia Foot
Defendant(s)/Debtor(s) / *Défendeur(s)/défenderesse(s)/débiteur(s)/débitrice(s)*

My name is **Allen Oryx**
Je m'appelle
(Full name / *Nom et prénoms*)

I live in **Toronto, Ontario**
J'habite à
(Municipality & province / *Municipalité et province*)

I make this affidavit to support my motion for payment out of court of money belonging to
Je fais le présent affidavit à l'appui d'une motion en vue du versement d'une somme d'argent consignée qui appartient à

Albert Oryx
(Name of person under disability / *Nom de l'incapable*)

of **102 Finch Avenue East, Toronto ON**
de
(Address / *Adresse*)

who is **a minor**
qui est
(State the nature of the disability / *Indiquez la nature de l'incapacité*)

and who was born on **January 4, -17**
et qui est né(e) le
(Date)

I am **The father of the plaintiff**
Je suis
(State your connection with the person under disability / *Indiquez votre rapport avec l'incapable*)

The Accountant has informed me that $ **$2,000.00** , including interest accrued to
Le comptable m'a informé(e) que la somme de
$, *y compris les intérêts courus au*

August 14, Yr. -1 , is in court.
(Date)
est consignée au tribunal

There has been previously paid out the sum of $ **nil** on
Il a déjà été versé sur ce montant la somme de
$ *le*
(Date)

I propose that the sum of $ **2,000.00** should be paid out of court to **Albert Oryx**
Je propose que la somme de
soit versée à
(Name of person / *Nom de personne*)

for the following purpose: *(Set out what the person you named will do with the money.)*
aux fins de
(Précisez ce que la personne que vous avez nommée fera de l'argent)

to pay the plaintiff's college tuition

SCR 4.08-4B (November 1, 2012 / *1er novembre 2012*) CSD

continues....

Illustration 6.2 (continued)

FORM / *FORMULE* 4B   PAGE 2   SC-00-47669-00
....
Claim No. / *N° de la demande*

I believe that this money should be paid out of court for the following reasons:
J'estime que cet argent doit être versé pour les raisons suivantes :

Set out your reasons in numbered paragraphs.
Indiquez vos raisons sous forme de dispositions numérotées.

1. The plaintiff has decided to commence his post-secondary education following his graduation from secondary school in June, Yr. -1.
2. This is a decision that will benefit the plaintiff as it will advance his education and therefore employment prospects, and of which I approve.
3. Without the payment of the monies currently held in court, he will not have enough funds on his own to pay tuition when it is due in mid-September of Yr. -1.
4. With the funds held in court, I will be able to pay the tuition fees on the plaintiff's behalf.

If more space is required, attach and initial extra pages. / Si vous avez besoin de plus d'espace, annexez une ou des feuilles supplémentaires et paraphez-les.

Sworn/Affirmed before me at **Toronto**	
Déclaré sous serment/Affirmé (Municipality / *municipalité*)	
solennellement devant moi à	
in **Ontario**	
en/à/au (Province, state or country / *province, État ou pays*)	Signature
	(This form is to be signed in front of a lawyer, justice of the peace, notary public or commissioner for taking affidavits.)
on **August 20, Yr. -1**	
le Commissioner for taking affidavits	*(La présente formule doit être signée en présence d'un avocat, d'un juge de paix, d'un notaire ou d'un commissaire aux affidavits.)*
Commissaire aux affidavits	
(Type or print name below if signature is illegible.)	
(Dactylographiez le nom ou écrivez-le en caractères d'imprimerie ci-dessous si la signature est illisible.)	

WARNING:	**IT IS AN OFFENCE UNDER THE *CRIMINAL CODE* TO KNOWINGLY SWEAR OR AFFIRM A FALSE AFFIDAVIT.**
AVERTISSEMENT :	*FAIRE SCIEMMENT UN FAUX AFFIDAVIT CONSTITUE UNE INFRACTION AU CODE CRIMINEL.*

SCR 4.08-4B (November 1, 2012 / *1ᵉʳ novembre 2012*) CSD

However, if the applicant is the Children's Lawyer or the Public Guardian and Trustee, the rules for payment out are more relaxed. The request need not be accompanied by an affidavit, and the request filed may deal with more than one proceeding, allowing these public guardians to act more efficiently by combining many requests with respect to various files, in one application.

There is also a simplified procedure for a minor who has reached the age of majority and wishes to apply to obtain money held on her behalf. She has to provide to the Accountant of the Superior Court a letter of request for payment, together with an affidavit proving her identity and that she has reached the age of majority. In any of these cases, if the request for payment out follows the procedure in Rule 22, the Accountant is obliged to pay out the amount named in the order, together with any accrued interest, unless the court orders otherwise.

Definitions

22.01 In this Rule,

"Accountant" means the Accountant of the Superior Court of Justice; ("comptable")

"clerk" means the clerk in the location where the proceeding was commenced. ("greffier")

Non-Application of Rule

22.02 This Rule does not apply to money paid or to be paid into court,

   (a) under an order or proposal for payment made under rule 9.03;

   (b) under an offer to settle a claim in return for the payment of money; or

   (c) for the enforcement of an order for the payment or recovery of money under Rule 20, including enforcement by garnishment.

Payment into Court

22.03(1) Subject to subrule (7), a party who is required to pay money into court shall do so in accordance with subrules (2) to (6).

Filing with Clerk or Accountant

(2) The party shall file the following documents with the clerk or the Accountant:

  1. If the payment into court is under a statutory provision or rule, a written request for payment into court that refers to that provision or rule.

  2. If the payment into court is under an order, a written request for payment into court and a copy of the order that bears the court's seal.

Direction

(3) On receiving the documents required to be filed under subrule (2), the clerk or Accountant shall give the party a direction

to receive the money, addressed to a bank listed in Schedule I or II to the *Bank Act* (Canada) and specifying the account in the Accountant's name into which the money is to be paid.

Clerk to Forward Documents

(4) If the documents are filed with the clerk, the clerk shall forward the documents to the Accountant.

Payment

(5) On receiving the direction referred to in subrule (3), the party shall pay the money into the specified bank account in accordance with the direction.

Bank's Duties

(6) On receiving the money, the bank shall give a receipt to the party paying the money and immediately send a copy of the receipt to the Accountant.

Payment to Accountant by Mail

(7) A party may pay money into court by mailing to the Accountant the applicable documents referred to in subrule (2), together with the money that is payable; the written request for payment into court referred to in that subrule shall include the party's name and mailing address.

Accountant to Provide Receipt

(8) On receiving money under subrule (7), the Accountant shall send a receipt to the party paying the money.

Proof of Payment

(9) A party who pays money into court shall, immediately after receiving a receipt from the bank under subrule (6) or from the Accountant under subrule (8), as the case may be, send to every other party a copy of the receipt and file a copy of the receipt with the court.

Payment Out of Court

22.04(1) Money may only be paid out of court under an order.

Documents to be Filed

(2) A person who seeks payment of money out of court shall file with the Accountant,
  (a) a written request for payment out and supporting affidavit, in the form provided by the Ministry; and
  (b) a copy of the order for payment out that bears the court's seal.

Payment Out, Children's Lawyer or Public Guardian and Trustee

(3) If the person seeking payment out is the Children's Lawyer or the Public Guardian and Trustee,
  (a) the written request need not be in the form provided by the Ministry and a supporting affidavit is not required; and

(b) a single written request that deals with more than one proceeding may be filed.

Payment Out, Minor Attaining Age of Majority

(4) Despite subrule (2), money in court to which a party is entitled under an order once the party attains the age of majority may be paid out to the party on filing with the Accountant, in the forms provided by the Accountant,

(a) a written request for payment out; and

(b) an affidavit proving the identity of the party and that the party has attained the age of majority.

Accountant's Duties

(5) If the requirements of subrule (2) or (4), as the case may be, are met, the Accountant shall pay the money to the person named in the order for payment out, and the payment shall include any accrued interest, unless a court orders otherwise.

Transition

22.05 This Rule applies to the payment into and out of court of money paid into court on and after the day on which Ontario Regulation 400/12 comes into force.

23. Omitted (provides for coming into force of provisions of this Regulation).

Suing or Being Sued by Partnerships and Sole Proprietorships — Rule 5

As noted in previous chapters, you can sue a partnership or sole proprietorship in the firm name and/or you can sue the individual partners or the sole proprietor. Similarly, a partnership or sole proprietorship may also sue in the firm name. If you are suing a partnership or sole proprietorship, Rule 5 permits you to find out information about who is behind a partnership or sole proprietorship, and then permits you to expand your enforcement rights to include both the assets of the business and the personal assets of the individuals who own it. Unlike limited liability companies, those with ownership interests in partnerships and sole proprietorships have unlimited liability for the debts and obligations of these businesses.

Rule 5, which sets out procedures for suing partnerships and sole proprietorships and for identifying partners and expanding enforcement rights, is set out below:

Partnerships

5.01 A proceeding by or against two or more persons as partners may be commenced using the firm name of the partnership.

Defence

5.02 If a proceeding is commenced against a partnership using the firm name, the partnership's defence shall be delivered in the firm name and no person who admits being a partner at any material time may defend the proceeding separately, except with leave of the court.

Notice to Alleged Partner

5.03(1) In a proceeding against a partnership using the firm name, a plaintiff who seeks an order that would be enforceable personally against a person as a partner may serve the person with the claim, together with a notice to alleged partner (Form 5A).

(2) A person served as provided in subrule (1) is deemed to have been a partner at the material time, unless the person defends the proceeding separately denying having been a partner at the material time.

Disclosure of Partners

5.04(1) If a proceeding is commenced by or against a partnership using the firm name, any other party may serve a notice requiring the partnership to disclose immediately in writing the names and addresses of all partners constituting the partnership at a time specified in the notice; if a partner's present address is unknown, the partnership shall disclose the last known address.

Partnership's Failure to Comply

(2) If a partnership fails to comply with a notice under subrule (1), its claim may be dismissed or the proceeding stayed or its defence may be struck out.

If the plaintiff decides to sue a partnership in the firm name, the defendant must defend in the firm name, and no partner may defend separately in his or her own name without permission from the court. This reflects the common law presumption that a person who is partner at "the relevant time" is jointly and severally liable with other partners and with the partnership for the partnership's obligations, and must defend together. However, Rule 5.02 allows for exceptions in circumstances where an individual partner has a separate defence or, possibly, a crossclaim against another partner or the partnership. This exception to the general rule is likely to be resorted to if there is an internal dispute between the partners.

The Importance of Being a "Partner at Any Material Time"

When you sue a partnership or when a partnership sues someone, there may be two or three partners who have been partners for decades and who were partners before, during, and after the time when the plaintiff had dealings with the partnership. In that case there is no issue about who was a partner at the material time. However, sometimes partners come and go, and not all the current partners are necessarily liable with the partnership for a breach that occurred in the past. A large law firm may have hundreds of partners, as new associates become partners and old partners retire or move on to other firms. Partners who were not partners at the material time may have no personal liability, and they may defend separately on that basis if you sue them personally or try to enforce a judgment against the partnership against them personally.

In Figure 6.4, the material time begins to run when the partnership performed the acts that created the complete cause of action in tort. The time ends when the cause of action is complete. Partners who were members of the partnership during this period are personally liable together with the partnership; those who were not are not liable personally. So, *A* and *B* are not personally liable, because they joined and left the partnership before the tort occurred. *C* and *D* are liable because they were members of the partnership at the material time, even though *C* later leaves. *E*, *F*, *G*, and *H* are not personally liable, because they joined after the tort occurred; although as current partners when the lawsuit is launched, they will be affected by the impact of the suit on the partnership itself. But how they are affected depends on the internal arrangements in the partnership agreement. They may have the right to be indemnified by the partnership or by those who were partners at the relevant time. Another way of thinking about this is to imagine a group photograph of the partners that is taken on the day the tort occurred. The partners in the photo are the ones with personal liability.

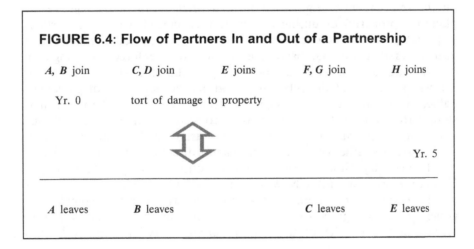

FIGURE 6.4: Flow of Partners In and Out of a Partnership

A, B join	*C, D* join	*E* joins	*F, G* join	*H* joins
Yr. 0	tort of damage to property			
				Yr. 5
A leaves	*B* leaves		*C* leaves	*E* leaves

Expanding Enforcement Rights:
Notice to Alleged Partner

When you sue a partnership in the firm name, if you also seek to enforce your judgment against individual partners, under Rule 5.03 you must serve the alleged partners with a Notice to Alleged Partner (Form 5A).

Example 6.3 Suing a Partnership

Carol Creditor catered a luncheon for Jacobs and Partners. She is now suing Jacobs and Partners for payment of her final invoice for catering services rendered. Her contact at Jacobs and Partners for the luncheon was Cameron Saint-Saëns. Carol does not know if Cameron is a partner; but if he is, Carol wants to enforce any judgment against him individually. Carol can put Cameron on notice that she will be seeking to enforce any judgment against him personally by serving a Notice to Alleged Partner on Cameron. A sample Notice to Alleged Partner form is set out at Illustration 6.3.

Carol thinks that there are other partners that she would like to enforce judgment against but has no idea who the partners were when she catered the luncheon. She can serve a notice on the partnership to disclose the names and address of the partners at the time that the luncheon was held. A sample Notice to Disclose Names and Addresses of Partners is set out at Figure 6.5.

In the sample Form 5A, Notice to Alleged Partner, set out in Illustration 6.3, the notice states that the individual is or was a partner on the relevant date (e.g., when the partnership caused damage to the plaintiff's property) or during a specific time period (when the partnership had a running account, incurred debt, and then defaulted on it). It also states that, on that basis, the plaintiff may enforce any judgment or order against the individual personally. If the individual denies he or she was a partner at the relevant period and is therefore not personally liable, he or she must file a separate defence from that of the partnership, setting out that defence. This is consistent with the general rule that defendants with separate defences must defend separately as they likely have a conflict of interest and cannot therefore defend together.

In deciding whom to serve with a Notice to Alleged Partner, you have to know who actually was a partner at the relevant time. This can be complicated, as Figure 6.4 indicates, with partners coming and going. Rule 5.04 gives some assistance here, in that it allows you to serve a notice on the partnership, requiring it to immediately furnish

ILLUSTRATION 6.3: Sample Notice to Alleged Partner (Form 5A)

ONTARIO
Superior Court of Justice
Cour supérieure de justice

Notice to Alleged Partner
Avis au prétendu associé
Form / *Formule* 5A Ont. Reg. No. / *Règl. de l'Ont.* : 258/98

Toronto
Small Claims Court / *Cour des petites créances de*

47 Sheppard Ave. E., 3rd Fl.
Toronto, ON M2N 5N1
Address / *Adresse*

416-326-3554
Phone number / *Numéro de téléphone*

SC-08-12345-00
Claim No. / *N° de la demande*

BETWEEN / *ENTRE*

Carol Creditor
Plaintiff(s) / *Demandeur(s)/demanderesse(s)*

and / *et*

Jacobs and Partners
Defendant(s) / *Défendeur(s)/défenderesse(s)*

TO: *DESTINATAIRE :*	Name of alleged partner / *Nom du (de la) prétendu(e) associé(e)* **Cameron Saint-Saëns**
	Street and number / *Numéro et rue* **17 Doofus Drive**
	City, province, postal code / *Ville, province, code postal* **Toronto, ON, M3R 1A8**

YOU ARE ALLEGED TO HAVE BEEN A PARTNER on
IL EST ALLÉGUÉ QUE VOUS ÉTIEZ UN(E) ASSOCIÉ(E) le

(or during the period) **August 2, Yr. 0**   to **September 15, Yr. 0**
(ou pendant la période du)   *au*

in the partnership/business of **Jacobs and Partners**
de la société en nom collectif/l'entreprise de   (Firm name / *Raison sociale*)

a party named in this proceeding.
désignée comme partie à l'instance.

IF YOU WISH TO DENY THAT YOU WERE A PARTNER at any material time, you must defend this proceeding separately from the partnership, denying that you were a partner at the material time. If you fail to do so, you will be deemed to have been a partner on the date (or during the period) set out above.
SI VOUS SOUHAITEZ NIER QUE VOUS ÉTIEZ UN(E) ASSOCIÉ(E) à l'époque en cause, vous devez présenter dans l'instance une défense distincte de celle de la société en nom collectif, selon laquelle vous niez avoir été un(e) associé(e) à cette époque. À défaut de ce faire, vous serez réputé(e) avoir été une(e) associé(e) à la date (ou pendant la période) susmentionnée.

CAUTION: *AVERTISSEMENT :*	**AN ORDER AGAINST THE PARTNERSHIP MAY BE ENFORCED AGAINST YOU PERSONALLY** if you are deemed to have been a partner, if you admit that you were, or if the court finds that they were at the material time. *UNE ORDONNANCE CONTRE LA SOCIÉTÉ EN NOM COLLECTIF PEUT ÊTRE EXÉCUTÉE CONTRE VOUS PERSONNELLEMENT si vous êtes réputé(e) avoir été un(e) associé(e), si vous admettez ce fait ou si le tribunal conclut que vous étiez un(e) associé(e) à l'époque en cause.*

November 10, Yr. 0

Carol Creditor

(Signature of plaintiff or representative / *Signature du demandeur/de la demanderesse ou du/de la représentant(e)*)

SCR 5.03-5A (June 1, 2009 / *1er juin 2009*) CSD

FIGURE 6.5: Notice to Disclose Names and Addresses of Partners

ONTARIO

SUPERIOR COURT OF JUSTICE

File no. SC-00-12345-00

Toronto Small Claims Court

B E T W E E N:

CAROL CREDITOR

Plaintiff

and

JACOBS AND PARTNERS

Defendant

NOTICE TO DISCLOSE THE NAMES AND ADDRESSES OF
PARTNERS

TAKE NOTICE that under the provisions of Rule 5.04(1) of the Small Claims Court Rules, the Plaintiff demands that the defendant partnership disclose immediately in writing the names and addresses of all partners constituting the partnership from August 2, Yr. 0, to September 15, Yr. 0.

If a partner's present address is unknown, you must disclose the last known address of that partner.

AND TAKE NOTICE that if the partnership fails to provide the information demanded in this notice, its defence may be struck out.

Dated at Toronto November 10, Yr. 0.

Petrus Paralegal, LSUC #P05761
1750 Finch Avenue E
Toronto, ON M2J 2X5
Tel 416 123 4567
Fax 416 123 4568

TO:
Jacobs and Partners
17 Doofus Drive
Toronto, ON M3R 1A8

the names and addresses of those who were partners at the material time. Failure to provide the information will result in the partnership's claim or defence being struck out.[8]

There is no prescribed form for giving notice to a partnership to provide the names and addresses of partners, so you have to make up your own. It can take the form of a letter, or you can develop your own form format, as in the example in Figure 6.5. There is no need to re-invent the wheel — simply use the language in the relevant rule, and use the rule as a checklist for what you need to include in the notice.

> ### Enforcement of Order
> 5.05(1) An order against a partnership using the firm name may be enforced against the partnership's property.
>
> (2) An order against a partnership using the firm name may also be enforced, if the order or a subsequent order so provides, against any person who was served as provided in rule 5.03 and who,
> - (a) under that rule, is deemed to have been a partner at the material time;
> - (b) has admitted being a partner at that time; or
> - (c) has been adjudged to have been a partner at that time.

Adding Individual Parties after Trial

What happens if you discover, after obtaining a judgment, that there are other individuals who allegedly were partners at the relevant time, against whom you would like to enforce the judgment? They weren't served with a Notice to Alleged Partner. Are you too late? Rule 5.05(3) permits you to bring a motion to the court for permission to enforce the judgment against an alleged partner who was not previously served with a Notice to Alleged Partner. The judge will grant the order on the motion if there is no dispute about membership in the partnership at the relevant time, or, if there is a dispute, the court will decide whether the individual was a partner at the relevant time. If he or she was found to be a partner, then a judgment against the partnership may now be enforced against the partner who was added under Rule 5.05(3). This rule also applies to sole proprietorships where the plaintiff sued in the business name and obtained a judgment without identifying or having sought to bind the sole proprietor's personal

---

[8] Although Rule 5.04 can be applied to partnerships and sole proprietorships that are either suing or being sued in the firm name, Rule 5 is used primarily to fix liability on relevant individuals to expand enforcement rights. This is of less importance where a partnership is a plaintiff — although there are situations where enforcement rights against a plaintiff might be relevant, for example, where the action is dismissed and the defendant seeks to expand the right to enforce a costs award, or where there is a counterclaim in the form of a defendant's claim.

assets. With self-represented plaintiffs, this happens frequently, and this rule provides an easy way to add proper parties against whom the plaintiff can enforce the judgment.

> *Against Person not Served as Alleged Partner*
> 5.05(3) If, after an order has been made against a partnership using the firm name, the party obtaining it claims to be entitled to enforce it against any person alleged to be a partner other than a person who was served as provided in rule 5.03, the party may move before a judge for leave to do so; the judge may grant leave if the person's liability as a partner is not disputed or, if disputed, after the liability has been determined in such manner as the judge directs.

Rule 5.06 — Sole Proprietors

Although the procedure set out in Rule 5 focuses on partnerships, Rule 5.06 clearly states that Rule 5 applies to sole proprietorships, which can sue or be sued in the business name; notice may be given to the individual sole proprietor to expand enforcement rights, and notice may be sent to the business requiring production of the name and address of the sole proprietor. Another way of looking at this is to consider a sole proprietorship to be a partnership with only one partner. This is one of the rules that invite you to create a procedure by analogy to an existing rule. Similarly, you have to adapt to sole proprietorships the forms used with respect to partnerships.

> *Sole Proprietorships*
> 5.06(1) If a person carries on business in a business name other than his or her own name, a proceeding may be commenced by or against the person using the business name.
> (2) Rules 5.01 to 5.05 apply, with necessary modifications, to a proceeding by or against a sole proprietor using a business name, as though the sole proprietor were a partner and the business name were the firm name of a partnership.

PREPARATION AND DRAFTING OF THE CLAIM

We can now turn to the drafting of the plaintiff's claim. The relevant rule governing the process is Rule 7, and the plaintiff's claim is Form 7A — the form that is used to start every proceeding in Small Claims Court.

> *Plaintiff's Claim*
> 7.01(1) An action shall be commenced by filing a plaintiff's claim (Form 7A) with the clerk, together with a copy of the claim for each defendant.

Contents of Claim, Attachments

(2) The following requirements apply to the claim:

1. It shall contain the following information, in concise and non-technical language:
   i. The full names of the parties to the proceeding and, if relevant, the capacity in which they sue or are sued.
   ii. The nature of the claim, with reasonable certainty and detail, including the date, place and nature of the occurrences on which the claim is based.
   iii. The amount of the claim and the relief requested.
   iv. The name, address, telephone number, fax number if any, and Law Society of Upper Canada registration number if any, of the lawyer or agent representing the plaintiff or, if the plaintiff is self-represented, the plaintiff's address, telephone number and fax number if any.
   v. The address where the plaintiff believes the defendant may be served.

2. If the plaintiff's claim is based in whole or in part on a document, a copy of the document shall be attached to each copy of the claim, unless it is unavailable, in which case the claim shall state the reason why the document is not attached.

Issuing Claim

7.03(1) On receiving the plaintiff's claim, the clerk shall immediately issue it by dating, signing and sealing it and assigning it a court file number.

(2) The original of the claim shall remain in the court file and the copies shall be given to the plaintiff for service on the defendant.

The purpose of the plaintiff's claim is to

- provide notice to the defendant that an action has been commenced;

- name the plaintiff, the defendant, and the plaintiff's legal representative, and give their addresses and contact information;

- tell the defendant what the case is about and what requirements of the case have to be met, giving the plaintiff's version of the facts, the breach of the plaintiff's legal right, the consequences of the breach, and the amount of the damages.

The Plaintiff's Claim (Form 7A)

The Plaintiff's Claim (Form 7A) for Video Supplies Inc. set out in Illustration 6.4 is based on the situation described in Example 3.1 on page 90.

ILLUSTRATION 6.4: Plaintiff's Claim (Form 7A)

ONTARIO

Superior Court of Justice
Cour supérieure de justice

Plaintiff's Claim
Demande du demandeur

Form / *Formule* 7A Ont. Reg. No. / *Règl. de l'Ont.* : 258/98

Seal / *Sceau*

Toronto
Small Claims Court / *Cour des petites créances de*

SC-00-31547-00
Claim No. / *N° de la demande*

47 Sheppard Ave. E, 3rd Floor
Toronto, ON M2N 5N1
Address / *Adresse*

416-326-3554
Phone number / *Numéro de téléphone*

Plaintiff No. 1 / *Demandeur n° 1*

☐ Additional plaintiff(s) listed on attached Form 1A.
Le ou les demandeurs additionnels sont mentionnés sur la formule 1A ci-jointe.

☐ Under 18 years of age.
Moins de 18 ans.

Last name, or name of company / *Nom de famille ou nom de la compagnie*		
Video Supplies Inc.		
First name / *Premier prénom*	Second name / *Deuxième prénom*	Also known as / *Également connu(e) sous le nom de*
Address (street number, apt., unit) / *Adresse (numéro et rue, app., unité)*		
c/o Peter Paralegal, 41 Yonge Street, #410		
City/Town / *Cité/ville*	Province	Phone no. / *N° de téléphone*
Toronto	**ON**	**416-597-0048**
Postal code / *Code postal*		Fax no. / *N° de télécopieur*
M5G 1S1		**416-597-0049**
Representative / *Représentant(e)*		LSUC # / *N° du BHC*
Peter Paralegal		**P02952**
Address (street number, apt., unit) / *Adresse (numéro et rue, app., unité)*		
41 Yonge Street, #410		
City/Town / *Cité/ville*	Province	Phone no. / *N° de téléphone*
Toronto	**ON**	**416-597-0048**
Postal code / *Code postal*		Fax no. / *N° de télécopieur*
M5G 1S1		**416-597-0049**

Defendant No. 1 / *Défendeur n° 1*

☐ Additional defendant(s) listed on attached Form 1A.
Le ou les défendeurs additionnels sont mentionnés sur la formule 1A ci-jointe.

☐ Under 18 years of age.
Moins de 18 ans.

Last name, or name of company / *Nom de famille ou nom de la compagnie*		
Gary's Great Games Ltd.		
First name / *Premier prénom*	Second name / *Deuxième prénom*	Also known as / *Également connu(e) sous le nom de*
Address (street number, apt., unit) / *Adresse (numéro et rue, app., unité)*		
123 Yonge Street		
City/Town / *Cité/ville*	Province	Phone no. / *N° de téléphone*
Toronto	**ON**	
Postal code / *Code postal*		Fax no. / *N° de télécopieur*
M6C 1L3		
Representative / *Représentant(e)*		LSUC # / *N° du BHC*
Address (street number, apt., unit) / *Adresse (numéro et rue, app., unité)*		
City/Town / *Cité/ville*	Province	Phone no. / *N° de téléphone*
Postal code / *Code postal*		Fax no. / *N° de télécopieur*

SCR 7.01-7A (September 1, 2010 / *1ᵉʳ septembre 2010*) CSD

continues....

Illustration 6.4 (continued)

FORM / *FORMULE* 7A   PAGE 2   SC-00-31547-00
....
Claim No. / *N° de la demande*

REASONS FOR CLAIM AND DETAILS / *MOTIFS DE LA DEMANDE ET PRÉCISIONS*

Explain what happened, including where and when. Then explain how much money you are claiming or what goods you want returned.
Expliquez ce qui s'est passé, en précisant où et quand. Ensuite indiquez la somme d'argent que vous demandez ou les biens dont vous demandez la restitution, explication à l'appui.

If you are relying on any documents, you **MUST** attach copies to the claim. If evidence is lost or unavailable, you **MUST** explain why it is not attached.
Si vous vous appuyez sur des documents, vous **DEVEZ** *en annexer des copies à la demande. Si une preuve est perdue ou n'est pas disponible, vous* **DEVEZ** *expliquer pourquoi elle n'est pas annexée.*

What happened? The defendant has failed to pay the plaintiff for goods purchased.
Where?   The goods were sold in the province of Ontario.
When?   The parties entered into a contract on September 11, Yr. 0 and the goods were delivered on September 14, Yr. 0.

Que s'est-il
passé?
Où?
Quand?

1. The plaintiff claims:
a) the sum of $3,000
b) pre-judgment interest at the rate of 6% per year
   or in the alternative under the Courts of Justice Act
c) post-judgment interest in accordance with the Courts of Justice Act
d) such further and other relief as this Honourable Court may deem just.

2. The plaintiff, Video Supplies Inc., is a company incorporated under the laws of Ontario with its head office in Toronto. It carries on business as a wholesaler of video games and equipment.

3. The defendant, Gary's Great Games Ltd., is a company incorporated under the laws of Ontario with its head office in Toronto. It carries on business as a retailer of video games and equipment.

4. The plaintiff's claim is against the Defendant for breach of contract for goods sold and delivered to the Defendant.

5. On September 11, Yr. 0, the defendant purchased from the plaintiff 10 Sony Play stations and 20 games at a purchase price of $4,000. The terms of purchase were that the defendant pay a cash deposit of $1,000.00 and the balance of $3,000 on delivery of the goods on September 14, Yr. 0. A true copy of the parties' contract is attached as Document "1" to this claim.

6. The plaintiff delivered the goods on September 14, Yr. 0.

7. Despite repeated demands for payment, the defendant has refused to pay the balance outstanding on the account.

8. The principal amount of $3,000 claimed is based on the purchase price of $4,000 less the deposit of $1,000. Pre-judgment interest of 6% in accordance with the parties' contract is claimed from September 15, Yr. 0, the date after payment was due.

SCR 7.01-7A (September 1, 2010 / *1er septembre 2010*) CSD   Continued on next page / *Suite à la page suivante*

continues....

Illustration 6.4 (continued)

FORM / FORMULE 7A   PAGE 3   SC-00-31547-00
                                                              Claim No. / *N° de la demande*

How much? $ 3,000.00
Combien?   (Principal amount claimed / *Somme demandée*) $

☐   ADDITIONAL PAGES ARE ATTACHED BECAUSE MORE ROOM WAS NEEDED.
    DES FEUILLES SUPPLÉMENTAIRES SONT ANNEXÉES EN RAISON DU MANQUE D'ESPACE.

The plaintiff also claims pre-judgment interest from September 15, Yr. 0   under:
Le demandeur demande aussi des intérêts   (Date)   conformément à :
antérieurs au jugement de

(Check only   ☐ the *Courts of Justice Act*
one box /   la *Loi sur les tribunaux judiciaires*
Cochez une
seule case)   ☒ an agreement at the rate of 6.0   % per year
                     un accord au taux de   % par an

and post-judgment interest, and court costs.
et des intérêts postérieurs au jugement, ainsi que les dépens.

Prepared on: November 3, Yr. 0   *Peter Paralegal*
Fait le :   (Signature of plaintiff or representative / *Signature du*
                                                   demandeur/de la demanderesse ou du/de la représentant(e))

Issued on: November 4, Yr. 0   *T. M. Clerk*
Délivré le :   (Signature of clerk / *Signature du greffier*)

CAUTION TO DEFENDANT:	IF YOU DO NOT FILE A DEFENCE (Form 9A) with the court within twenty (20) calendar days after you have been served with this Plaintiff's Claim, judgment may be obtained without notice and enforced against you. Forms and self-help materials are available at the Small Claims Court and on the following website: www.ontariocourtforms.on.ca.
AVERTISSEMENT AU DÉFENDEUR :	SI VOUS NE DÉPOSEZ PAS DE DÉFENSE *(formule 9A) auprès du tribunal au plus tard vingt (20) jours civils après avoir reçu signification de la présente demande du demandeur, un jugement peut être obtenu sans préavis et être exécuté contre vous. Vous pouvez obtenir les formules et la documentation à l'usage du client à la Cour des petites créances et sur le site Web suivant : www.ontariocourtforms.on.ca.*

SCR 7.01-7A (September 1, 2010 / *1er septembre 2010*) CSD

How to Complete the Plaintiff's Claim

1. Insert the location of the court (e.g., Toronto) and the full address. Court addresses may be obtained from the Attorney General's website or by calling the court at the number listed in Appendix 6. Most courts will have automated messages, one of which gives the court's address. Choose your court on the basis of the criteria for choice of forum in Rule 6.

2. Leave the claim number blank. The clerk will fill that in when you issue the claim.

3. For the plaintiff, insert his or her legal name, including middle name, and "also known as" if relevant (this is useful for someone who has shortened his or her name and is commonly known by that nickname). If the plaintiff is a limited company, include the full name as it is registered with the Companies Branch. If the plaintiff is a partnership or sole proprietorship, it may sue or be sued in its business name as that name appears as registered with the Companies Branch. If there are multiple plaintiffs and defendants, check the box on the top of the form, and attach Form 1A to the first page of the claim form, which allows you to list additional parties. Check off the second box if the plaintiff is a minor. Include address, phone, and fax numbers for the plaintiff if the plaintiff is self-represented. If the plaintiff is represented, insert the name of the representative and the address and other contact information where documents can later be served on the representative by the defendant. The address can include the paralegal firm name if it is, for example, a partnership and has a registered business name.[9] Also include phone and fax numbers. Lawyers and paralegals must also include their Law Society registration number.

4. List the same information in the boxes provided for the defendant to the extent that you know such information. You may not know who the representative is, for example, so just leave it blank. If there is more than one defendant, use Form 1A and attach it to the first sheet of the claim form. If there are errors about the defendant's information, the defendant can note the correct information on the first page of the defence when it is filed.

5. On Page 2, you can set out in three short sentences what happened, where it happened, and when the cause of action arose.

---

[9] The Law Society regulates the form of business name used by paralegal firms in the *Paralegal Rules of Conduct*, Rule 8.03.

You should then set out in numbered paragraphs the details of the claim. The reasons for claim and details section requires you to tell a story, and it gives some minimal instructions:

- To make it easy for the judge to follow the claim, you should set out in your reasons the following: what is claimed; who the parties are; and the facts, usually in chronological order, that gave rise to the claim. Finish off with information as to how you calculated your claim, including details of the calculation of the pre-judgment interest — the rate and start date of pre-judgment interest. The claim in Illustration 6.4 follows this format. Such a format allows the judge to have all the information in one section of the claim, without having to flip back and forth between the pages of the claim.[10] In some cases you may not be able to insert all the details for pre-judgment interest because your damages have not yet been determined in full. For example, where a claim for general damages for pain and suffering is made, the exact amount of damages may not yet be known because the plaintiff continues to suffer from her injuries. In such cases, the plaintiff can state that full damages, including pre-judgment interest, have yet "to be determined".
- When you describe the damages, you can indicate if they are general damages or special damages, and for each head of damages, give the amount and, where relevant, show the calculation of your claim. (For example, for special damages for the cost of medications, list the cost of each item and show the total.)
- If you are suing to recover property, you may also wish to claim damages for the value of the property as an alternative remedy. That amount can be included here. You should state that this is an alternative remedy claimed if you are unable to recover the property.
- If you rely on or have relevant documents, attach copies of them to the claim. You should refer to each document that you attach. You can refer to them as "Document 1", "Document 2", etc. Attach a photocopy of the original copy of these documents to the back of the claim, and write or type at the top of the document "Document '1' ", and "Document '2' ", etc., if there is more than one document.[11] If you made your

---

[10] The suggestions as to how to lay out the reasons for claim were suggested by Deputy Judge Lynn Wheatley of the Toronto Small Claims Court.

[11] In some cases, a party calls the documents attached Exhibit "A", Exhibit "B", etc. This is improper as Exhibits are documents attached to sworn affidavits. A plaintiff's claim is not a sworn document.

copy using the original document, you can refer to this copy in your claim as a "true copy". If you refer to a document in your explanation of your claim, identify it by its document number in the body of the claim. If a document has become lost, list it and indicate why it is not attached. As Page 2 of the Plaintiff's Claim form states, "If you are relying on any documents, you MUST attach copies to the claim. If evidence is lost or unavailable, you MUST explain why it is not attached."

- If you need additional space for your claim, ensure that you check off the Box on Page 3 of the claim to indicate that additional pages are attached.

6. The reasons for claim and details section requires some clear thinking and literacy skills. In the hands of amateurs, the section may turn out to be unclear, incoherent, and in some cases full of unnecessarily inflammatory material. Paralegals are not amateurs; their pleadings should look well-crafted and professional. Some suggestions on how to do that are set out in the next section.

7. On Page 3 of the claim, set out the principal amount claimed, which is the amount sued for without interest and costs added on. If you are claiming relief in the alternative to money, such as the return of property, you can note this here as well, along with a request, on Page 2, for an order allowing the bailiff to use reasonable force pursuant to the *Execution Act*, R.S.O. 1990, c. E.24, as am. by 2010, c. 16, Sched. 2, s. 3, to secure the return of the property. In our case study example, Albert Oryx might seek such an order to facilitate the return of the engagement ring.

8. Next, set out the date from which pre-judgment interest is claimed. This is normally the day interest starts to be charged (e.g., the first day money owing is overdue).

9. Note that the printed form includes a claim for costs and for interest. There are two ways to determine pre-judgment interest: (i) if you have a contract in which there is an agreement on the rate of interest, insert the rate agreed upon, or (ii) if there is no agreement, you will claim interest under the *CJA*. If relying on the *CJA* interest rate, insert the rate of pre-judgment interest shown for the quarter in which the claim is issued.

10. When the claim form has been completed, fill in the preparation date and sign it or have your client sign it.

11. Do not fill in the issuing date, even if it is to be the same day the claim is prepared. The clerk will fill in this part when the claim is issued.

Some Suggestions for Drafting the Reasons for Claim and Details

While some of the claim involves checking off boxes or filling in blanks, on Page 2 you do actually have to draft something — the story of what this claim is about. Crafting this carefully and professionally is important. This page is read by your opponent, by the judge or referee at the settlement conference, and by the judge who hears the case. It is meant to persuasively tell your side of the story, without going overboard.

The Small Claims Court Rules do not contain any guidelines on how to draft claims. Form 7A does contain an instruction sheet at the beginning and some pointers on Page 2 of the form. The Ministry of the Attorney General also publishes various guides concerning Small Claims Court procedures. There is a guide available on making a claim. All of the guides can be viewed online at <http://www.attorneygeneral.jus.gov.on.ca/english/courts/guides/>. There is a Forms Assistant Program on the court forms site <www.ontariocourtforms.on.ca> that may assist unrepresented persons in drafting court documents.

Presented here are two approaches to drafting claims (and other pleadings). The primary approach is to follow the drafting conventions used by lawyers in drafting claims and other pleadings. This type of drafting sets out a concise statement of material facts without setting out evidence. The second approach involves presenting a much more detailed case in the claim and other pleadings setting out both the facts and the evidence, and providing all relevant documents.[12] We will discuss each one in turn. But first we need to look at how to organize a claim.

Organizing Your Claim

Before you draft the details of the claim, you need to know what the relevant facts are — what the cause of action is, where the cause of action arose and where the parties reside, and whether or not any of the parties are under a disability. You also need to identify the type and amount of damages, and have a theory of the case.

---

[12] See Marcel Mongeon, "Small Claims Court — Initiating the Paperwork" in *The Small Claims Court Rules: Hot Spots One Year Later* (Continuing Legal Education: The Law Society of Upper Canada: 2007) pp. 1–44. Mongeon makes a case for a much more detailed presentation of a case in pleadings than one commonly sees from lawyers or paralegals. His argument is based on the proposition that because there is no pre-trial discovery, a party is obliged to plead not only the facts but also the evidence — in effect, presenting the full case on paper.

THE FACTS OF THE CASE

In order to determine the relevant facts of the case you should review all of your evidence, such as contracts and invoices. You should also review your notes from client meetings and the results of your searches. You may need to contact your client or other witnesses to confirm relevant facts. The relevant facts will be set out on Page 2 of the claim under "Reasons for Claim and Details".

THE CAUSE OF ACTION

You should determine your cause of action: for example, the plaintiff has been wronged by a tort or has experienced a breach of contract. In Albert Oryx's case against Ophelia Foot over the engagement ring, the cause of action is the tort of wrongfully withholding and refusing to return Albert's ring. The plaintiff should indicate the cause of action in the Reasons for Claim section on the plaintiff's claim form. You can insert the cause of action in the "what happened" section.

WHERE THE CAUSE OF ACTION AROSE AND WHERE THE DEFENDANTS RESIDE

For all claims, you will need to determine which court to start your claim in. Generally, a claim should be commenced in the jurisdiction in which the cause of action arose or the jurisdiction in which one or more of the defendants reside or carry on business.[13] You should review the information you have regarding where the cause of action arose and where the defendants reside or carry on business to ensure that you select the correct court. In the reasons for claim you should set out the residence of each of the parties. Stating the town(s) they reside in is sufficient. For a business the location of the head office should be stated. For example, in the claim at Illustration 6.4 the locations of the head office of the plaintiff and defendant corporations are stated in paragraphs 2 and 3 in the Reasons for Claim section.

PARTIES UNDER DISABILITY

You should review the facts prior to issuing your claim to ensure that none of the parties are minors or under a disability that might require the appointment of a litigation guardian. If the plaintiff or defendant is a minor or under a disability, reference should be made to Rule 4, provisions of which are set out in detail earlier in this chapter.

---

[13] Rule 6 of the Small Claims Court Rules.

TYPE AND AMOUNT OF DAMAGES

Prior to commencing your claim you must calculate the damages sought. For example, if the case is a collection matter you must set out the amount owed to you. For details on calculating outstanding accounts see Chapter 5. The monetary amount claimed should be set out on Page 3 of the claim form. If calculations are involved, you should set them out in the last paragraph of your Reasons for Claim section. If they are lengthy, you could attach a schedule setting out your calculations as to how the figures were arrived at. If you attach a schedule, fill in the box on Page 3 for additional pages. The form is preprinted to claim interest and court costs.

THEORY OF THE CASE

The theory of the case is the basis on which you organize and present information in a persuasive way.

Although Albert's cause of action is the tort of wrongfully withholding and refusing to return his ring, his theory of the case may be that Ophelia is selfish, greedy, and opportunistic, with an eye for the main chance. In her defence, she may maintain that the ring was a gift and therefore her property, but her theory of the case for her defence may be that Albert is demanding the ring because he is an angry, malicious male who can't handle rejection. If the evidence shows that the theory is wrong, you need to adjust the theory to fit the evidence, not the evidence to fit the theory. If the facts show that Ophelia really thought the gift was unconditional, then Albert has to abandon the theory that she is merely grasping and greedy, and change it to a theory that she misunderstood the conditions under which she obtained the ring. Then he must focus on evidence to show his intent was that the gift was conditional on her marrying him. Similarly, if the facts show Albert to be reasonable and rational in requiring the ring to be returned, then Ophelia will have to abandon the theory that he is merely an angry male who can't handle rejection, and abandon attempts to prove facts that support that theory.

Drafting the Claim

Assemble and review all of your client and witness interview notes from your discussions with Albert. Also review any documents he has. Summarize your evidence on the facts that you will plead in the claim. If there is not enough evidence to support a factual allegation, don't plead it. Now, having worked out what our claim is about and what facts and evidence support it, we can consider how we actually draft the claim, taking either the lawyer's approach to drafting claims concisely or the more detailed approach.

The Lawyer's Approach

Lawyers who appear in Small Claims Courts tend to do what they know: they draft small claims pleadings by following the conventions for drafting Superior Court pleadings. There are some advantages to this approach:

- It promotes concise, clear statements of the facts and the relevant law.
- Judges, who are lawyers, understand the style and format.

The style is based on conventions that are set out in the *Rules of Civil Procedure* of the Superior Court. Rule 25 of the *Rules of Civil Procedure* sets out guidelines that can be very useful in drafting clear, coherent, useful pleadings. Rule 1.03(2) of the Small Claims Court Rules states that if the rules do not cover a matter, you may look to the *Rules of Civil Procedure* as a reference. So we will look to Rule 25, particularly Rules 25.02 and 25.06, for some of the suggestions made in the next section on organizing and drafting claims and pleadings generally. In Chapter 8, on defences, we will also examine some drafting conventions that are specific to defences.

Don't try to re-invent the wheel; check your firm's precedent binders if there are some for claims or defences that are similar. These can be useful for suggestions on organization of the claim and choice of language in expressing a fact or an issue of law. But don't use precedents uncritically or simply copy them — read them carefully. Remember you are unlikely to find a claim exactly the same, on its facts, as the one you are doing, where you can simply plug in the name of the plaintiff or defendant. Many paralegals, particularly in collection matters, tend to use precedents, sometimes uncritically, with confusing and sometimes harmful results. Always read precedents carefully, and use them as suggestions rather than templates.

When using precedents, you will find that older ones use the common law drafting style: full of jargon, pompous and complex sentences, and repetition. This style is being slowly replaced by plain language drafting techniques (sometimes referred to as the Citibank style) originated from consumer loan agreements for the First National City Bank of New York — a major American commercial bank. The simpler and clearer language used by the bank has been credited with reducing ambiguity in the documents and reducing the amount of litigation those documents generated.

Lawyers drafting contracts, pleadings, and legislation now commonly use plain language drafting. Don't be afraid to use clear, simple language to express your meaning. Cut to the chase. Avoid legal jargon such as the "plaintiff states and the fact is . . .", and replace it with "the plaintiff states . . ." The basic principle to remember in drafting is that you should provide a concise statement of material facts.

Use an outline to prepare the first draft. A framework for the claim might follow these steps, though there is no magic to this particular form of organizing a claim:

1. Set out what you are claiming. This should include principal, interest, costs, along with any other relief, such as the return of property wrongly held by the defendant.
2. Identify the parties by legal status and geographical location. In the case of a business, set out the type of business. For example, "The plaintiff is a limited company incorporated under the laws of Ontario having its head office in Toronto, Ontario. The company manufactures fish tanks."
3. Describe the cause of action. For example, "The plaintiff's claim is against the defendant for a breach of contract for goods sold and delivered."
4. Set out the facts that support the cause of action.
5. Set out the law that you rely on if it is not apparent.
6. Set out the damages or losses sustained as a result of the defendant's acts.
7. Set out how you calculated the amounts that you are claiming.

Prepare a first draft. Send it to the client for comment and feedback. After getting feedback, revise and polish the draft. Check for internal consistency: e.g., if you refer to a statement in another paragraph, make sure the reference is there. Give the document a final, fast read to see that it flows logically and that the facts and law support the theory of the case. Figure 6.6 shows a completed Form 7A using this approach.

Pleading Suggestions from the Rules of Civil Procedure

The *Rules of Civil Procedure* provide some guidance in writing pleadings, especially if you are using the lawyer's approach. In particular, Rule 25.06 provides rules of pleadings applicable to Superior Court pleadings and guidance for drafting pleadings in the Small Claims Court.

RULES OF PLEADING — APPLICABLE TO ALL PLEADINGS
(*RULES OF CIVIL PROCEDURE*, current as of July 17, 2013)

Material Facts
25.06(1) Every pleading shall contain a concise statement of the material facts on which the party relies for the claim or defence, but not the evidence by which those facts are to be proved.

FIGURE 6.6: Oryx Return of Property — Lawyer's Format

ONTARIO
Superior Court of Justice
Cour supérieure de justice

Plaintiff's Claim
Demande du demandeur
Form / *Formule* 7A Ont. Reg. No. / *Règl. de l'Ont.* : 258/98

Seal / *Sceau*

Toronto
Small Claims Court / *Cour des petites créances de*

**47 Sheppard Avenue E., 3ʳᵈ Fl.
Toronto, ON M2N 5N1**

Address / *Adresse*

416-326-3554
Phone number / *Numéro de téléphone*

SC-00-47669-00
Claim No. / *N° de la demande*

Plaintiff No. 1 / *Demandeur n° 1* ☐ Additional plaintiff(s) listed on attached Form 1A.
Le ou les demandeurs additionnels sont mentionnés sur la formule 1A ci-jointe. ☐ Under 18 years of age.
Moins de 18 ans.

Last name, or name of company / *Nom de famille ou nom de la compagnie*		
Oryx		
First name / *Premier prénom*	Second name / *Deuxième prénom*	Also known as / *Également connu(e) sous le nom de*
Albert		
Address (street number, apt., unit) / *Adresse (numéro et rue, app., unité)*		
c/o Peter Paralegal, 41 Yonge Street, #410		
City/Town / *Cité/ville*	Province	Phone no. / *N° de téléphone*
Toronto	**ON**	**416-597-0048**
Postal code / *Code postal*		Fax no. / *N° de télécopieur*
M5G 1S1		**416-597-0049**
Representative / *Représentant(e)*		LSUC # / *N° du BHC*
Peter Paralegal		**P02952**
Address (street number, apt., unit) / *Adresse (numéro et rue, app., unité)*		
41 Yonge Street, #410		
City/Town / *Cité/ville*	Province	Phone no. / *N° de téléphone*
Toronto	**ON**	**416-597-0048**
Postal code / *Code postal*		Fax no. / *N° de télécopieur*
M5G 1S1		**416-597-0049**

Defendant No. 1 / *Défendeur n° 1* ☐ Additional defendant(s) listed on attached Form 1A.
Le ou les défendeurs additionnels sont mentionnés sur la formule 1A ci-jointe. ☐ Under 18 years of age.
Moins de 18 ans.

Last name, or name of company / *Nom de famille ou nom de la compagnie*		
Foot		
First name / *Premier prénom*	Second name / *Deuxième prénom*	Also known as / *Également connu(e) sous le nom de*
Ophelia		
Address (street number, apt., unit) / *Adresse (numéro et rue, app., unité)*		
83 Greengrove Rd.		
City/Town / *Cité/ville*	Province	Phone no. / *N° de téléphone*
Toronto	**ON**	**416-484-1234**
Postal code / *Code postal*		Fax no. / *N° de télécopieur*
M6R 4Q5		
Representative / *Représentant(e)*		LSUC # / *N° du BHC*
Address (street number, apt., unit) / *Adresse (numéro et rue, app., unité)*		
City/Town / *Cité/ville*	Province	Phone no. / *N° de téléphone*
Postal code / *Code postal*		Fax no. / *N° de télécopieur*

SCR 7.01-7A (September 1, 2010 / *1ᵉʳ septembre 2010*) CSD

continues....

Figure 6.6 (continued)

FORM / *FORMULE* 7A   PAGE 2   SC-00-47669-00
                                                                     Claim No. / *N° de la demande*

REASONS FOR CLAIM AND DETAILS / *MOTIFS DE LA DEMANDE ET PRÉCISIONS*

Explain what happened, including where and when. Then explain how much money you are claiming or what goods you want returned.
Expliquez ce qui s'est passé, en précisant où et quand. Ensuite indiquez la somme d'argent que vous demandez ou les biens dont vous demandez la restitution, explication à l'appui.

If you are relying on any documents, you **MUST** attach copies to the claim. If evidence is lost or unavailable, you **MUST** explain why it is not attached.
Si vous vous appuyez sur des documents, vous DEVEZ en annexer des copies à la demande. Si une preuve est perdue ou n'est pas disponible, vous DEVEZ expliquer pourquoi elle n'est pas annexée.

What happened? **Where?** **When?** *Que s'est-il passé?* *Où?* *Quand?*	The defendant ended the parties' engagement and is wrongfully withholding and refusing to return the plaintiff's ring. The events occurred in Toronto. The defendant ended the engagement on December 10 and the plaintiff demanded the ring back.

1. The plaintiff claims:
a) an order that the defendant return to the plaintiff an engagement ring given to the defendant by the plaintiff or, in the alternative, an order that the defendant pay to the plaintiff the sum of $2,000 (the value of the ring).
b) pre-judgment interest at the rate of 6% per year in accordance with the Courts of Justice Act
c) post-judgment interest in accordance with the Courts of Justice Act
d) court costs
e) an order that the bailiff may use reasonable force, pursuant to the Execution Act to secure the return of the property

2. The plaintiff, ALBERT ORYX, is an individual who resides in Toronto and was the fiancé of the defendant, Ophelia Foot.

3. The defendant, OPHELIA FOOT, is an individual who resides in Toronto.

4. On or about February 10, Yr. 0, the plaintiff and defendant agreed to become engaged to be married.

5. The plaintiff purchased an engagement ring for $2,000 and gave it to the defendant on February 28, Yr. 0, as a sign of his love and commitment. A true copy of the receipt for the purchase of the ring is attached as Document "1".

6. At all times, it was understood that the gift to the defendant was conditional on the defendant marrying the plaintiff.

7. On December 10, Yr. 0, the defendant broke off the engagement to the plaintiff.

8. On December 10, Yr. 0, the plaintiff demanded the return of the engagement ring, on the ground that the defendant had failed to fulfill the condition that would entitle her to keep the ring. The defendant refused to return the ring.

9. Despite repeated demands, the defendant has continued to refuse to return the ring, and continues to wrongfully withhold the plaintiff's property from him.

SCR 7.01-7A (September 1, 2010 / *1ᵉʳ septembre 2010*) CSD   Continued on next page / *Suite à la page suivante*

continues....

Figure 6.6 (continued)

FORM / *FORMULE* 7A   PAGE 3   SC-00-47669-00
                                                              Claim No. / *N° de la demande*

10. The plaintiff demands return of the ring or in the alternative payment to him for the price of the ring, $2,000.00.

11. The plaintiff bases his claim for $2,000 on the value of the ring. Pre-judgment interest at the CJA prejudgment interest rate is claimed from December 11, Yr. 0.

An order that the defendant return to the plaintiff his engagement ring and an order that the baliff may use reasonable force, pursuant to the Execution Act to secure return of the ring or in the alternative the sum of

How much? $ _____ 2,000.00
Combien?   (Principal amount claimed / *Somme demandée*) $

☐   ADDITIONAL PAGES ARE ATTACHED BECAUSE MORE ROOM WAS NEEDED.
    DES FEUILLES SUPPLÉMENTAIRES SONT ANNEXÉES EN RAISON DU MANQUE D'ESPACE.

The plaintiff also claims pre-judgment interest from   December 11, Yr. 0   under:
Le demandeur demande aussi des intérêts   (Date)   *conformément à :*
antérieurs au jugement de

(Check only   ☒ the *Courts of Justice Act*
one box /   la *Loi sur les tribunaux judiciaires*
Cochez une
seule case)   ☐ an agreement at the rate of _____ % per year
                    un accord au taux de   % par an

and post-judgment interest, and court costs.
et des intérêts postérieurs au jugement, ainsi que les dépens.

Prepared on: January 15, Yr. 0   *Peter Paralegal*
Fait le :   (Signature of plaintiff or representative / *Signature du
                                                    demandeur/de la demanderesse ou du/de la représentant(e)*)

Issued on: January 16, Yr. 0   *T. M. Clerk*
Délivré le :   (Signature of clerk / *Signature du greffier*)

| CAUTION TO DEFENDANT: | **IF YOU DO NOT FILE A DEFENCE** (Form 9A) with the court within twenty (20) calendar days after you have been served with this Plaintiff's Claim, judgment may be obtained without notice and enforced against you. Forms and self-help materials are available at the Small Claims Court and on the following website: www.ontariocourtforms.on.ca. |
| *AVERTISSEMENT AU DÉFENDEUR :* | *SI VOUS NE DÉPOSEZ PAS DE DÉFENSE (formule 9A) auprès du tribunal au plus tard vingt (20) jours civils après avoir reçu signification de la présente demande du demandeur, un jugement peut être obtenu sans préavis et être exécuté contre vous. Vous pouvez obtenir les formules et la documentation à l'usage du client à la Cour des petites créances et sur le site Web suivant : www.ontariocourtforms.on.ca.* |

SCR 7.01-7A (September 1, 2010 / *1er septembre 2010*) CSD

Pleading Law

(2) A party may raise any point of law in a pleading, but conclusions of law may be pleaded only if the material facts supporting them are pleaded.

Condition Precedent

(3) Allegations of the performance or occurrence of all conditions precedent to the assertion of a claim or defence of a party are implied in the party's pleading and need not be set out, and an opposite party who intends to contest the performance or occurrence of a condition precedent shall specify in the opposite party's pleading the condition and its non-performance or non-occurrence.

Inconsistent Pleading

(4) A party may make inconsistent allegations in a pleading where the pleading makes it clear that they are being pleaded in the alternative.

(5) An allegation that is inconsistent with an allegation made in a party's previous pleading or that raises a new ground of claim shall not be made in a subsequent pleading but by way of amendment to the previous pleading.

Notice

(6) Where notice to a person is alleged, it is sufficient to allege notice as a fact unless the form or a precise term of the notice is material.

Documents or Conversations

(7) The effect of a document or the purport of a conversation, if material, shall be pleaded as briefly as possible, but the precise words of the document or conversation need not be pleaded unless those words are themselves material.

Nature of Act or Condition of Mind

(8) Where fraud, misrepresentation, breach of trust, malice or intent is alleged, the pleading shall contain full particulars, but knowledge may be alleged as a fact without pleading the circumstances from which it is to be inferred.

Claim for Relief

(9) Where a pleading contains a claim for relief, the nature of the relief claimed shall be specified and, where damages are claimed,

  (a) the amount claimed for each claimant in respect of each claim shall be stated; and

  (b) the amounts and particulars of special damages need only be pleaded to the extent that they are known at the date of the pleading, but notice of any further amounts and particulars shall be delivered forthwith after they become known and, in any event, not less than ten days before trial.

Avoid jargon and legalese: In accordance with Rule 25.06(1), use short, concise statements of fact. Use simple language and simple, short, blunt sentences. State facts simply as facts — no need to search for a pile of colourful adjectives.

Don't plead evidence: Just stick to the basic facts and relevant law. For example, if Albert's statement of claim states, "The defendant wrongfully refused to return the ring. She knew she was wrong because she told her friends she had no legal right to it", Albert is pleading evidence. "The defendant wrongfully refused to return the ring" is a statement of fact (refusal to return the ring) and law (that she wrongfully withheld it). But what she told her friends is evidence of her act being wrongful. In keeping with Rule 25.06(1), the second sentence should be left out of the pleading.

Pleading law: Rule 25.06(2) provides that if you rely on a rule of law, after reciting the facts that support it, state the legal principle or law. For example, if you claim that Jim, a truck driver for Fly by Night Delivery, damaged your car while driving the employer's truck, the employer is liable for Jim's tortious act as an employee in the course of employment. But you need to clearly set out the employer–employee relationship if you are suing the employer and relying on this doctrine. Here you might state, after reciting the necessary facts, "The employer is liable on the grounds that it is vicariously liable for the acts of its agents." If the legal rule is in a statute, refer to the statute and the relevant section: "The plaintiff relies on s. 13 of the *Sale of Goods Act*, R.S.O. 1990, c. S.1, as amended."

Pleading conditions precedent: Under Rule 25.06(3) you can plead a condition precedent, but you do not have to. For example, if you are suing the guarantor on a loan, the guarantee may require that you give notice of default to the guarantor before making a demand for payment by the guarantor. If you plead that the defendant guarantor is in breach of his obligation to pay, it is presumed that you fulfilled the condition precedent to suing, of giving notice of default first. It is not necessary for you to include a statement that notice was given. If there is an issue about notice, the guarantor can raise that in the defence.

Inconsistent pleadings: Sometimes when you are not sure how damage occurred or how an event occurred, you may, in accordance with Rule 25.06(4), plead several alternative versions, even if they are inconsistent. For example, it is quite appropriate in a negligence case, where damage to a vehicle occurs, to plead how it occurred in the alternative: "The defendant failed to apply his brakes in time, or in the alternative, his brakes were not in good working order, or in the further alternative, he was talking on a cell phone and not paying attention to the road." It could be any one of the three facts as pleaded that was the cause of the damage, or it could have been a combination of all three. In the beginning of the case when the claim is filed, you simply may not know. But when the evidence is given at trial, it should support one or more of the alternatives presented. If the evidence shows a completely different act from those pleaded, the defendant could argue that you failed to prove the case as pleaded and that the action should be dismissed. Note, however, that a judge will recognize that the standard of pleading in this court is not high; consequently, a judge is unlikely to give much credit to such a technical approach to pleadings. So pleading broadly in the alternative can be a good strategy in certain cases.

Where inconsistent pleading is not permitted: If you allege a fact in your defence, you cannot contradict it in a later pleading, such as a defendant's claim. The fact allegations in all of your pleadings must be consistent.

Pleading notice: Under Rule 25.06(6), stating that notice was given is sufficient, without pleading the form of notice. If there was a defect in form, the defendant should raise it in the defence.

Pleading conversations: Rule 25.06(7) provides that you need only plead that the conversation occurred, and briefly, in so far as it is relevant, you can say what it is about. But you need not plead the whole conversation in detail. For example, if Albert is pleading, "The plaintiff had a conversation with the defendant in which she indicated she would not return the ring", that is sufficient. We don't need a detailed script or a verbatim quote, unless the exact language is in issue.

Pleading a state of mind: If Ophelia wishes to plead in her defence that Albert was in a rage, under Rule 25.06(8), that is sufficient — no detail is required, and she will have to prove the allegation at trial by giving evidence of his rage: that he banged his fist on the table, yelled, and turned purple. However, where fraud, misrepresentation, or breach of trust is alleged, the plaintiff needs to set out the facts in more detail than is ordinarily the case.

The Detailed Approach

Against the lawyer's style, where bare facts are pleaded, there is the more detailed approach. This approach is based primarily on the observation that because there is no discovery process where the opposite parties get full disclosure of the evidence, disclosure should take place through the pleadings. This in turn requires that pleadings be more detailed, setting out not only the facts but, contrary to the Superior Court approach, also the evidence. It is suggested that when attaching documents, don't just attach a contract or an invoice, but include all documents in your power, possession, or control that are not privileged that are relevant to the issues. These should be attached to the claim. If there are many documents, instead of attaching them to the claim, consider numbering them, creating a table of contents, and placing them in a binder to be served and filed with the claim.

In other respects, the two approaches require similar preparation — you should develop a theory of the case and prepare an outline of the pleading that is sequential and logical so that the story can be followed.

The detailed approach is not all that dissimilar to the lawyer's approach to drafting, except that it provides more detail and takes a broader view of what documents should be attached to a claim. There are some advantages to this approach:

- Although it leads to longer, wordier documents, this approach presents a complete case and, for that reason, may promote earlier settlements.

- If there is to be a default judgment, the claim is easily used as a model for an assessment hearing or an affidavit in support of a motion for default judgment.

- Your documents[14] can be used, particularly in a binder, as an exhibit and reference at the settlement conference and as an exhibit at trial.

- A detailed claim is useful in presenting the case at the settlement conference. With enough detail up front, the court will not require much in the way of further disclosure.

See Figure 6.7 for a claim drafted using the detailed approach.

The danger with this approach is that the pleading may become overly long and detailed and stray off into irrelevancy. There is already an oversupply of this kind of pleading from unrepresented parties. If you do follow this approach, edit your drafts carefully.

---

[14] Documents attached to the plaintiff's claim should be called Documents or Appendices and numbered if more than one. They should not be called Exhibits. Exhibits are only attached to affidavits.

FIGURE 6.7: Oryx Return of Property — Detailed Format

ONTARIO

Superior Court of Justice
Cour supérieure de justice

Plaintiff's Claim
Demande du demandeur
Form / *Formule* 7A Ont. Reg. No. / *Règl. de l'Ont.* : 258/98

Toronto	**SC-00-47669-00**
Small Claims Court / *Cour des petites créances de*	Claim No. / *N° de la demande*

Seal / *Sceau*

47 Sheppard Avenue E., 3rd Fl.
Toronto, ON M2N 5N1

Address / *Adresse*

416-326-3554

Phone number / *Numéro de téléphone*

Plaintiff No. 1 / *Demandeur n° 1*   ☐ Additional plaintiff(s) listed on attached Form 1A.   ☐ Under 18 years of age.
Le ou les demandeurs additionnels sont mentionnés   *Moins de 18 ans.*
sur la formule 1A ci-jointe.

Last name, or name of company / *Nom de famille ou nom de la compagnie*		
Oryx		
First name / *Premier prénom* **Albert**	Second name / *Deuxième prénom*	Also known as / *Également connu(e) sous le nom de*
Address (street number, apt., unit) / *Adresse (numéro et rue, app., unité)* **c/o Peter Paralegal, 41 Yonge Street, #410**		
City/Town / *Cité/ville* **Toronto**	Province **ON**	Phone no. / *N° de téléphone* **416-597-0048**
Postal code / *Code postal* **M5G 1S1**		Fax no. / *N° de télécopieur* **416-597-0049**
Representative / *Représentant(e)* **Peter Paralegal**		LSUC # / *N° du BHC* **P02952**
Address (street number, apt., unit) / *Adresse (numéro et rue, app., unité)* **41 Yonge Street, #410**		
City/Town / *Cité/ville* **Toronto**	Province **ON**	Phone no. / *N° de téléphone* **416-597-0048**
Postal code / *Code postal* **M5G 1S1**		Fax no. / *N° de télécopieur* **416-597-0049**

Defendant No. 1 / *Défendeur n° 1*   ☐ Additional defendant(s) listed on attached Form 1A.   ☐ Under 18 years of age.
Le ou les défendeurs additionnels sont mentionnés   *Moins de 18 ans.*
sur la formule 1A ci-jointe.

Last name, or name of company / *Nom de famille ou nom de la compagnie*		
Foot		
First name / *Premier prénom* **Ophelia**	Second name / *Deuxième prénom*	Also known as / *Également connu(e) sous le nom de*
Address (street number, apt., unit) / *Adresse (numéro et rue, app., unité)* **83 Greengrove Rd.**		
City/Town / *Cité/ville* **Toronto**	Province **ON**	Phone no. / *N° de téléphone* **416-484-1234**
Postal code / *Code postal* **M6R 4Q5**		Fax no. / *N° de télécopieur*
Representative / *Représentant(e)*		LSUC # / *N° du BHC*
Address (street number, apt., unit) / *Adresse (numéro et rue, app., unité)*		
City/Town / *Cité/ville*	Province	Phone no. / *N° de téléphone*
Postal code / *Code postal*		Fax no. / *N° de télécopieur*

SCR 7.01-7A (September 1, 2010 / *1er septembre 2010*) CSD

continues....

Figure 6.7 (continued)

FORM / *FORMULE* 7A   PAGE 2   SC-00-47669-00
                                                            Claim No. / *N° de la demande*

REASONS FOR CLAIM AND DETAILS / *MOTIFS DE LA DEMANDE ET PRÉCISIONS*

Explain what happened, including where and when. Then explain how much money you are claiming or what goods you want returned.
Expliquez ce qui s'est passé, en précisant où et quand. Ensuite indiquez la somme d'argent que vous demandez ou les biens dont vous demandez la restitution, explication à l'appui.

If you are relying on any documents, you **MUST** attach copies to the claim. If evidence is lost or unavailable, you **MUST** explain why it is not attached.
*Si vous vous appuyez sur des documents, vous **DEVEZ** en annexer des copies à la demande. Si une preuve est perdue ou n'est pas disponible, vous **DEVEZ** expliquer pourquoi elle n'est pas annexée.*

What happened? **Where?** **When?** *Que s'est-il passé?* *Où?* *Quand?*	The defendant ended the parties' engagement and is wrongfully withholding and refusing to return the plaintiff's ring. The events occurred in Toronto. The defendant ended the engagement on December 10 and the plaintiff demanded the ring back.

1. The plaintiff claims:
a) An order that the defendant return to the plaintiff an engagement ring given to the defendant by the plaintiff or, in the alternative, an order that the defendant pay to the plaintiff the sum of $2,000 (the value of the ring)
b) pre-judgment interest at the rate of 6% per year
c) post-judgment interest in accordance with the Courts of Justice Act
d) court costs
e) an order that the bailiff may use reasonable force, pursuant to the
   Execution Act to secure the return of the property

2. The Plaintiff (Oryx) is an individual who resides in Toronto and was the fiancé of the defendant (Foot).

3. Foot is an individual who resides in Toronto.

4. Oryx met Foot through mutual friends at a party in Toronto in the winter of Yr. -3.

5. Foot and Oryx began dating in Yr. -3 and within a few months were spending most of their time together.

6. On February 10, Yr. 0, Oryx asked Foot to marry him.

7. Foot agreed to do so but did not want to set a wedding date.

8. On February 28, Yr. 0, Oryx took Foot out to dinner at Il Porcino, an expensive restaurant in Toronto. At the end of a romantic evening, over liqueurs, Oryx presented Foot with an engagement ring, telling her that it was a symbol of his undying love for her and a symbol of his agreement to marry her. Foot accepted the ring and reaffirmed her willingness to marry him, but said she wanted to think about the date.

9. The ring cost Oryx $2,000; it is silver with a single 1K diamond in a contemporary setting. Attached as Document "1" to this claim is a true copy of the receipt for the purchase of the ring.

SCR 7.01-7A (September 1, 2010 / *1ᵉʳ septembre 2010*) CSD   Continued on next page / *Suite à la page suivante*

continues....

Figure 6.7 (continued)

FORM / *FORMULE* 7A   PAGE 3   SC-00-47669-00

Claim No. / *N° de la demande*

10. There was an implied agreement between Oryx and Foot that by accepting the ring Foot was agreeing to marry Oryx and that if she refused to do so, she was obliged to return the ring to him.

11. In her conversations with Oryx, Foot revealed that she expected to live lavishly on the income from his business.

12. In December Yr 0, Oryx's business income began to fall due to softening markets for his financial advising services.

13–18. See attached sheet.

An order that the defendant return to the plaintiff his engagement ring and an order that the bailiff may use reasonable force, pursuant to the Execution Act to secure return of the ring or in the alternative the sum of

How much? $ 2,000.00
Combien?   (Principal amount claimed / *Somme demandée*) $

☒   ADDITIONAL PAGES ARE ATTACHED BECAUSE MORE ROOM WAS NEEDED.
      DES FEUILLES SUPPLÉMENTAIRES SONT ANNEXÉES EN RAISON DU MANQUE D'ESPACE.

The plaintiff also claims pre-judgment interest from   December 11, Yr. 0   under:
Le demandeur demande aussi des intérêts   (Date)   *conformément à :*
antérieurs au jugement de

(Check only   ☒   the *Courts of Justice Act*
one box /   la *Loi sur les tribunaux judiciaires*
Cochez une
seule case)   ☐   an agreement at the rate of   % per year
               un accord au taux de   % *par an*

and post-judgment interest, and court costs.
et des intérêts postérieurs au jugement, ainsi que les dépens.

Prepared on: January 15, Yr. 1   *Peter Paralegal*
Fait le :   (Signature of plaintiff or representative / *Signature du*
                                demandeur/de la demanderesse ou du/de la représentant(e))

Issued on: January 16, Yr. 1   *T. M. Clerk*
Délivré le :   (Signature of clerk / *Signature du greffier*)

CAUTION TO DEFENDANT:	**IF YOU DO NOT FILE A DEFENCE** (Form 9A) with the court within twenty (20) calendar days after you have been served with this Plaintiff's Claim, judgment may be obtained without notice and enforced against you. Forms and self-help materials are available at the Small Claims Court and on the following website: www.ontariocourtforms.on.ca.
AVERTISSEMENT AU DÉFENDEUR :	***SI VOUS NE DÉPOSEZ PAS DE DÉFENSE*** *(formule 9A) auprès du tribunal au plus tard vingt (20) jours civils après avoir reçu signification de la présente demande du demandeur, un jugement peut être obtenu sans préavis et être exécuté contre vous. Vous pouvez obtenir les formules et la documentation à l'usage du client à la Cour des petites créances et sur le site Web suivant : www.ontariocourtforms.on.ca.*

SCR 7.01-7A (September 1, 2010 / *1er septembre 2010*) CSD

continues....

Figure 6.7 (continued)

**Attachment to
the Plaintiff's Claim of Albert Oryx**

13. From December Yr. 0 onwards, Foot began to make excuses not to spend time with Oryx, claiming the pressures of work.

14. On December 10, Yr 0, Foot phoned Oryx to tell him that although she loved him and would always remember him fondly, she was breaking off the engagement as she intended to marry Cosimo di Medici, a wealthy banker. In an aside, she also told him that she intended to keep the ring as a reminder of their time together.

15. At that time Oryx reminded Foot that it was an engagement ring and that she was now bound to return it because she broke off the engagement. He also told her she was a greedy, avaricious gold digger. In response, Foot laughed.

16. Foot refused to return the ring.

17. Oryx made a further demand for the return of the ring on December 11, Yr. 0 but to the date of this claim, Foot has refused to return the ring, and wrongfully retains it in her possession.

18. The plaintiff bases his claim for $2,000 on the value of the ring. Pre-judgment interest at the Courts of Justice Act rate is claimed.

ISSUING THE PLAINTIFF'S CLAIM

The action is commenced, or starts, when you have the claim issued by the clerk of the court. The act of issuing a claim has some consequences:

- It stops the clock on the running of a limitation period. If you issue the claim before the limitation period has expired, that puts an end to limitation issues, even if you don't serve the claim on the defendant right away.

- It starts the clock running on some deadlines concerning the action itself. For example, under Rule 11.1 a clerk may dismiss an action:

    Dismissal — Undefended Actions
    11.1.01(1) The clerk shall make an order dismissing an action as abandoned if the following conditions are satisfied, unless the court orders otherwise:
    1. More than 180 days have passed since the date the claim was issued or an order was made extending the time for service of the claim under subrule 8.01(2).
    2. No defence has been filed.
    3. The action has not been disposed of by order and has not been set down for trial.
    4. The clerk has given 45 days notice to the plaintiff that the action will be dismissed as abandoned.

Dismissal — Defended Actions

(2) The clerk shall make an order dismissing an action as abandoned if the following conditions are satisfied, unless the court orders otherwise:

1. More than 150 days have passed since the date the first defence was filed.
2. All settlement conferences required under Rule 13 have been held.
3. The action has not been disposed of by order and has not been set down for trial.
4. The clerk has given 45 days notice to all parties to the action that the action will be dismissed as abandoned.

Transition

(3) If an action was started before July 1, 2006, the following applies:

1. The action or a step in the action shall be carried on under these rules on or after July 1, 2006.
2. Despite paragraph 1, if a step in the action is taken on or after July 1, 2006, the timetable set out in subrules (1) and (2) shall apply as if the action started on the date on which the step was taken.

Same

(4) If an action was commenced before July 1, 2006 and no step is taken in the action on or after that date, the clerk may make an order dismissing it as abandoned if,

(a) where an action is undefended, more than two years have passed since the date the claim was issued and the conditions set out in paragraphs 2, 3 and 4 of subrule (1) are satisfied; or
(b) more than two years have passed since the date the first defence was filed and the conditions set out in paragraphs 3 and 4 of subrule (2) are satisfied.

Exception Where Terms of Settlement Signed

(5) Subrules (1), (2) and (4) do not apply if terms of settlement (Form 14D) signed by all parties have been filed.

Exception Where Admission of Liability

(6) Subrule (2) and clause (4)(b) do not apply if the defence contains an admission of liability for the plaintiff's claim and a proposal of terms of payment under subrule 9.03(1).

Service of Orders

(7) The clerk shall serve a copy of an order made under subrule (1) or clause (4)(a) on the plaintiff and a copy of an order made under subrule (2) or clause (4)(b) on all parties to the action.

- Under Rule 11.1.01(1) an action may be dismissed if, after 180 days have passed since the claim was issued, no defence has been filed and no move has been made to seek a default judgment, and the action is not on the trial list. It is a good idea to diarize these dates at the time the claim is issued.

- It starts the clock running on service of the claim; the plaintiff has, under Rule 8.01(2), six months from the date the claim is issued to serve it on the defendant:

  Service of Particular Documents Plaintiff's or Defendant's Claim
  8.01(1) A plaintiff's claim or defendant's claim (Form 7A or 10A) shall be served personally as provided in rule 8.02 or by an alternative to personal service as provided in rule 8.03.

  Time for Service of Claim
  (2) A claim shall be served within six months after the date it is issued, but the court may extend the time for service, before or after the six months has elapsed.

The Issuing Process

After you have drafted the claim, you have to take the claim and a copy for each defendant to the court office in the territorial division where the defendant lives or carries on business, or where the cause of action arises, as required by Rule 6. As permitted by Rule 6, in some cases you will want to use the court closest to where a defendant resides or carries on business, even if it is outside that territorial division, as it is closer and as such maybe more convenient and cheaper to access due to reduced transportation costs. At the court, the clerk will sign and date the original, assign it a claim number, and affix a court seal. The clerk will keep the original, and you will receive a copy. The copy must be a true copy of the original.

At the time of writing, a procedure is being introduced where clerks will stamp copies of the claim, showing that the claim has been issued and indicating which court issued it. This practice is designed to prevent creditors from presenting a copy of an unissued claim to an unsophisticated debtor, creating an impression that a lawsuit has been started when in fact it has not, thereby threatening and intimidating a debtor into paying, even where there might not be anything owing. A photocopy of the claim as issued will meet the requirements for making a true copy.

Formerly, the practice was for you to take your prepared copy and make your own "true" copy of the original. To do this, on the original copy you drew a circle on the front page where the court seal was and wrote "seal" inside the circle, and then copied the file number from the original onto the top, upper right-hand side of the copy. On the last page of the copy you wrote in the clerk's signature and the date, in quotes. You could then photocopy as many "true" copies of the original as you needed for your file. A true copy was then served on the defendant.

Court Fees to Issue Claims — Frequent and Infrequent Claimants

The plaintiff will also pay the court fee for issuing a claim. For those who use the Small Claims Court system regularly, such as consumer lenders suing defaulting debtors, the fees are higher than they are for those who use the courts less often. To find the current court fee schedule, see O. Reg. 432/93, as amended, *Small Claims Court — Fees and Allowances*. You may access this from the Attorney General's website, <http://www.attorneygeneral.jus.gov.on.ca/english/>; click on More ... under Court Services, and follow the links to Court Fees. A fees schedule current at the time of publication is found at Appendix 4.

The rationale for the differential fee is that "frequent flyers", instead of getting points, or a discount, pay more of the actual costs of running the court system, as court fees traditionally do not cover the actual system operating costs. If the plaintiff uses the court infrequently, the fee for an infrequent claimant as of July 17, 2013, is $75.00. If, however, the plaintiff files more than 10 claims in that court office in the year beginning on January 1, the fee for the 11th claim, and any that come after, is $145.00. Note that the "frequent flyer" designation is based on the filings in the same court office, not on filings in court offices in Ontario generally. So, if there are five claims filed in office *A*, five in office *B*, and five in office *C*, the party is still an infrequent claimant in each office because there are not more than 10 claims filed in any one office. Note that the frequent claimant category count does not include defendant's claims. The fee is always the same as for an infrequent plaintiff's claim.

There is a fee waiver program in place for low income plaintiffs. For further information and allowable gross monthly household income limits for the fee waiver program, consult O. Reg. 2/05 of the *Administration of Justice Act*, R.S.O. 1990, c. A.6. An unrepresented party using the Toronto Small Claims Court may seek assistance from the Law Help Ontario office located in the Toronto small claims courthouse. For more information on Law Help Ontario, including financial assistance cut-offs, see <www.lawhelpontario.org/civil>. There are self-help videos and tip sheets on the site as well.

SERVICE OF THE CLAIM AND LATER DOCUMENTS — RULE 8

Now that the claim has been issued, it is ready to be served. Rule 8, which governs service of court documents, and Form 8A, the Affidavit of Service, are both lengthy and complex. However, they are easier to deal with once you are familiar with the nature of the service requirements and the various optional methods of service that are available:

- The purpose of service is to ensure that a party receives notice of, and copies of, important court documents to alert the party to what he or she must do to preserve legal rights.

- Personal service, where a document is handed directly to the person to whom it is directed, is the "highest" form of service.

- The rule also provides for alternatives to personal service.

- The rule provides for substituted service, available with a court order, where other modes of service are impractical or are likely to be ineffective.

- There are various modes of service: by mail, by courier, by hand-delivery to residences, by fax, or by service on representatives of the party being served. Each mode of service has its own procedural rules, which is one of the things that make the rule seem so complicated. But if you are using one of the modes of service, you have to concentrate only on the procedural requirements of that particular mode of service and complete Form 8A only for that method.

- In addition to the modes of service, there are also a number of rules about how certain parties are to be served. For example, an artificial person, such as a limited liability company, cannot have a document handed to it. So the rules tell you who, in the case of a company or other artificial body, you deliver a document to.

- Because issues may arise over whether service was effective in reaching the party served, it is important to follow the Rules carefully, and complete the affidavit of service accurately.[15]

The type of document sometimes determines how it is to be served. As you will see, once you get beyond the **originating documents**, the rules of service are somewhat relaxed — personal service often is not required — and the clerk may be responsible for serving many of the subsequent documents. However, in the case of a summons to a witness, personal service is required, as a witness who is properly served a summons and who fails to show up is in contempt of court and can be jailed for contempt. But before the court jails someone for contempt, it will have to be satisfied that the party was personally served with the summons. A notice of contempt for failure to attend an

---

[15] See Rule 8.06 and Form 8A regarding requirements for the affidavit of service.

examination in aid of execution also requires personal service, for the same reasons.

Where rules indicate that a document is served by the clerk, it is up to the party to get the document to the clerk within the time period prescribed by the Rules. For example, if the defendant has 20 days to file a defence, he or she must get the defence to the clerk by that time period so that it can be served on the plaintiff by the clerk.

Personal Service — On Whom? Rule 8.02

Personal service on an individual of full age and capacity is relatively straightforward (see Figure 6.8). Rule 8.02 sets out the particulars:

> 8.02 If a document is to be served personally, service shall be made,
>
> Individual
> (a) on an individual, other than a person under disability, by leaving a copy of the document with him or her;

Documents can be served on any day of the week.

Once you find the person, leave a copy of the document with him or her. If, having been served, the party rips the document up and throws the pieces in the process server's face, it doesn't matter — what the party does with the document after it is served is irrelevant in determining whether it was properly served.

The Rules are silent on who may serve a document. You may have a friend or relative serve a document for you, if you wish, or you could even do it yourself. However, it is advisable to use a private process server (see the Internet or the yellow pages of your phone book) or some neutral third party who has no interest in the action. The reason for this is that if there is a dispute about whether a document was properly served or served at all, the server's affidavit of service is much more credible, or other evidence about service is much more credible, if the server is a person who is in the business of serving court documents and who has no personal interest in the proceedings. Note that Small Claims Court bailiffs do not serve documents as part of their duties. Also, if you are a successful litigant and are awarded costs, reasonable disbursements are usually recovered on a dollar-for-dollar basis, but the recovery on the disbursements for personal service of documents is limited to $60.00 per person served, no matter how much you actually paid. However, if service was particularly difficult, the court can increase the amount payable (Rule 19.01(3)); and if you serve a defendant who resides outside of Ontario with a claim, you may recover reasonable costs incurred to serve the party (Rule 8.05).

FIGURE 6.8: Service Requirements for Different Types of Documents

Document	Who Serves It	Mode of Service	On Whom
Plaintiff's claim or defendant's claim	Plaintiff (or plaintiff by defendant's claim)	P — r. 8.02, or A — r. 8.03	Defendant (defendant by defendant's claim) within 6 months of claim being issued
Defence	Clerk	M or F — r. 8.01(3)	All parties
Motion	Moving party	M, C, F, P, or A — r. 8.01 and r. 15.01(3)	All parties, unless it is a motion done without notice
Default judgment	Clerk	M or F — r. 11.01(3) *as per* r. 8.01(4)	All parties named in the claim
Order for assessment of damages where the motion was in writing	Clerk	M, if moving party provides stamped, self-addressed envelope — r. 11.03(6) *as per* r. 8.01(5)	Moving party (usually the plaintiff where the defendant is in default)
Notice of Settlement Conference (together with a blank List of Proposed Witnesses forms)	Clerk	M, F, C, or A — r. 13.01(2) *as per* r. 8.01(14)	Plaintiff and defendant
Settlement conference order	Clerk	M or F — r. 8.01(6)	All parties who did not attend settlement conference
Summons to a witness	Party requiring the witness to be present	P, 10 days before trial date and includes attendance money for witness — r. 8.01(7)	Witness
List of proposed witnesses	Plaintiff and defendant	M, C, F, P, or A — r. 13.03(2)(b) *as per* r. 8.01(14)	Other party, 14 days or more before settlement conference
Notice of garnishment + blank garnishee's statement	Judgment creditor	M, C, P, A — r. 8.01(8) and r. 8.01(14)	Garnishee
Notice of garnishment	Judgment creditor	M, C, P, A — r. 8.01(8) and r. 20.08(6.1)	Judgment debtor, within 5 days of service on garnishee
Notice of garnishment hearing	Person requesting the hearing	M, C, P, A — r. 8.01(9)	Judgment creditor, judgment debtor, garnishee, co-owner of a debt, and any other interested party

continues....

Note: Mail (M); Fax (F); Courier (C); Personal (P); Alternative to personal service (A)

Figure 6.8 (continued)

Document	Who Serves It	Mode of Service	On Whom
Garnishee's statement	Garnishee	M, C, P, A — r. 20.08(13)	Judgment creditor and judgment debtor
Notice to co-owner of debt and garnishee's statement	Creditor served with garnishee's statement	M, C, P, A — r. 20.08(14) *as per* r. 8.01(14)	Co-owner(s) of the debt
Notice of examination of a judgment debtor	Judgment creditor	M, C, P, A — r. 20.10(3) *as per* r. 8.01(10),(11),(12)	Judgment debtor or other person to be examined; if debtor is an individual, also include blank financial information form; 30 days before the examination date
Notice of contempt for failure to attend examination	Judgment creditor	Personal service — r. 8.01(13) and r. 20.11(3)(b)	Judgment debtor or person to be examined
Any other documents (e.g., change of address under r. 8.09)	Party or clerk	Mail, courier fax, personally, or alternative to personal service, as per Rules or as court directs — r. 8.01(14)	Party to whom document to be served

Note: Mail (M); Fax (F); Courier (C); Personal (P); Alternative to personal service (A)

> 8.05 If the defendant is outside Ontario, the court may award as costs of the action the costs reasonably incurred in effecting service of the claim on the defendant there.

A problem arises with personal service on a party who is not an individual but an artificial person. How, after all, do you hand a document to General Motors of Canada Ltd.? Or to Her Majesty the Queen in Right of Ontario? Rule 8.02 provides direction (as shown in Figure 6.9). For example, a corporation can be served by leaving a copy of the document with an officer, director or agent of the corporation, or a person who appears to be in control of the place of business (Rule 8.02(c)).

> 8.02 If a document is to be served personally, service shall be made,
> Corporation
>   (c) on any other corporation, by leaving a copy of the document with,
>   (i) an officer, director or agent of the corporation, or
>   (ii) a person at any place of business of the corporation who appears to be in control or management of the place of business;

A final word on personal service: although the rule provides options for service, consider using personal service even where it is not required. With most other forms of service, you do not have a direct way of knowing if a document actually reached the intended party. This makes it easy for a party to deny being served and may result in a re-opening of proceedings, with attendant cost and delay. With personal service, on the other hand, it will be much more difficult for a party to deny service, when the affidavit from the process server clearly states that the person was actually handed the document. It may cost more to personally serve a document, but with an evasive or dishonest opponent or where a document really was lost in the mail, it may be money well spent. (A sample affidavit of service is provided in Illustration 6.5.)

Alternatives to Personal Service: Rule 8.03

In most cases where personal service is required, you also have the option of using an alternative to personal service. Generally, where personal service is practical, particularly for the first document in the lawsuit, use it. The person is deemed to be served at the moment of service, and there are less likely to be arguments later about whether the party actually received the document. However, if you elect to use alternatives to personal service, they are usually more convenient to carry out and less costly than personal service. There are several alternatives to personal service, and they are governed by Rule 8.03:

FIGURE 6.9: Personal Service on Artificial Persons and Parties under a Disability

PARTY TO BE PERSONALLY SERVED	PERSON OR PROCEDURE FOR SERVICE
Municipality	Leave copy with mayor, chair, warden [of a county], reeve, municipal clerk or deputy, or counsel for the municipality
Corporation	Leave copy with officer, director, or agent, or with a person at any place of business of the corporation who appears to be in control of or management of the place of business
Government board or commission	With a member or officer of the board or commission
Person outside Ontario who carries on business inside Ontario	Leave a copy with anyone who carries on business for the corporation in Ontario
Her Majesty the Queen/Crown in Right of Canada	Follow the directions in s. 23(2) of the *Crown Liability and Proceedings Act*, R.S.C. 1985, c. C-50
Her Majesty the Queen/Crown in Right of Ontario	Follow the directions in s. 10 of the *Proceedings Against the Crown Act*, R.S.O. 1990, c. P.27
Absentee	Leave a copy with Absentee's committee, if there is one; if not, leave a copy with the office of the Public Guardian and Trustee
Minor	Leave a copy with the minor, and if the minor resides with a parent or person who has custody, leave another copy with that person
Mentally incapable person — where there is a guardian or an attorney under a validated power of attorney with power to act in the proceeding	Leave a copy with a guardian or the attorney, as the case may be
Mentally incapable person — where there is an attorney under a power of attorney with power to act in the proceeding	Leave a copy with the attorney and with the mentally incapable person
Mentally incapable person — where there is no guardian or attorney under any power of attorney	Leave a copy, showing the person's name and address, with the Public Guardian and Trustee, and leave a copy with the mentally incapable person
Partnership	Leave a copy with any partner, or with a person who appears to be managing or in charge of the principal place of business of the partnership
Sole proprietorship	Leave a copy with the sole proprietor, or with a person who appears to be managing or in charge of the principal place of business of the sole proprietorship

Source: Rule 8.02.

ILLUSTRATION 6.5: Sample Affidavit of Service (Form 8A)

ONTARIO
Superior Court of Justice
Cour supérieure de justice

Affidavit of Service
Affidavit de signification
Form / *Formule* 8A Ont. Reg. No. / *Règl. de l'Ont.* : 258/98

Toronto
Small Claims Court / *Cour des petites créances de*

SC-00-47669-00
Claim No. / *N° de la demande*

**47 Sheppard Ave., 3rd Fl.
Toronto, ON M2N 5N1**
Address / *Adresse*

416-326-3554
Phone number / *Numéro de téléphone*

BETWEEN / *ENTRE*

Albert Oryx
Plaintiff(s) / *Demandeur(s)/demanderesse(s)*

and / *et*

Ophelia Foot
Defendant(s) / *Défendeur(s)/défenderesse(s)*

My name is **Samuel Server**
Je m'appelle
(Full name / *Nom et prénoms*)

I live in **Toronto, Ontario**
J'habite à
(Municipality & province / *Municipalité et province*)

and I swear/affirm that the following is true:
et je déclare sous serment/j'affirme solennellement que les renseignements suivants sont véridiques :

1. **I served** **Ophelia Foot**
, on **April 2, Yr. 1**
   J'ai signifié à (Full name of person/corporation served / *Nom et prénoms*   , *le*   (Date)
   *de la personne/nom au complet de la personne morale
   qui a reçu la signification)*

   at **83 Greengrove Rd., Toronto, ON**
   au (Address (street and number, unit, municipality, province) / *Adresse (numéro et rue, unité, municipalité, province)*)

   which is ☒ the address of the person's home
   soit   *l'adresse du domicile de la personne*

   ☐ the address of the corporation's place of business
   l'adresse du lieu de travail de l'établissement de la personne morale

   ☐ the address of the person's or corporation's representative on record with the court
   l'adresse du/de la représentant(e) de la personne ou de la personne morale figurant au dossier du tribunal

   ☐ the address on the document most recently filed in court by the party
   l'adresse figurant sur le document déposé le plus récemment au tribunal par la partie

   ☐ the address of the corporation's attorney for service in Ontario
   l'adresse du fondé de pouvoir de la personne morale aux fins de signification en Ontario

   ☐ other address:
   autre adresse :   (Specify. / *Précisez.*)

   with **Plaintiff's Claim**
   ce qui suit :   (Name(s) of document(s) served / *Titre(s) du ou des documents signifiés*)

SCR 8.06-8A (September 1, 2010 / *1ᵉʳ septembre 2010*) CSD

continues....

Illustration 6.5 (continued)

FORM / *FORMULE* 8A   PAGE 2   SC-00-47669-00
                                                                Claim No. / *N° de la demande*

2. I served the document(s) referred to in paragraph one by the following method:
   J'ai signifié le ou les documents mentionnés au numéro un de la façon suivante :
   (Tell how service took place by checking appropriate box(es).)
   (Indiquez la façon dont la signification a été effectuée en cochant la ou les cases appropriées.)

Personal ☒ leaving a copy with the person.
service /   *en laissant une copie à la personne.*
Significa-
tion à   ☐ leaving a copy with the _____ of the corporation.
personne   *en laissant une copie au/à la*   (Office or position / *Charge ou poste*)   *de la personne morale.*

             ☐ leaving a copy with: _____
                en laissant une copie à :   (Specify person's name and office or position. / *Indiquez le nom de la personne ainsi que*
                                                                              sa charge ou son poste.)

Service at ☐ leaving a copy in a sealed envelope addressed to the person at the person's place of residence with
place of   a person who appeared to be an adult member of the same household, and sending another copy of
residence /   the same document(s) to the person's place of residence on the same day or the following day by:
Significa-   *en laissant une copie au domicile de la personne, dans une enveloppe scellée adressée à celle-ci,*
tion au   *auprès d'une personne habitant sous le même toit qui semblait majeure et en envoyant une autre*
domicile   *copie du ou des mêmes documents au domicile de la personne le même jour ou le jour suivant :*

                ☐ regular lettermail.
                   par courrier ordinaire.

                ☐ registered mail.
                   par courrier recommandé.

                ☐ courier.
                   par messagerie.

Service by ☐ registered mail.
registered   *par courrier recommandé.*
mail /
Significa-   *(If a copy of a plaintiff's claim or defendant's claim was served by registered mail, attach a copy of the Canada Post*
tion par   *delivery confirmation, showing the signature verifying delivery, to this affidavit.)*
courrier   (Si une copie de la demande du demandeur ou de la demande du défendeur a été signifiée par courrier recommandé,
recom-   annexez au présent affidavit une copie de la confirmation de livraison remise par Postes Canada sur laquelle figure une
mandé   signature qui confirme la livraison.)

Service by ☐ courier.
courier /   *par messagerie.*
Significa-
tion par   *(If a copy of a plaintiff's claim or defendant's claim was served by courier, attach a copy of the courier's delivery confirmation,*
messa-   *showing the signature verifying delivery, to this affidavit.)*
gerie   (Si une copie de la demande du demandeur ou de la demande du défendeur a été signifiée par messagerie, annexez au
                   présent affidavit une copie de la confirmation de livraison remise par le service de messagerie sur laquelle figure la signature
                   du destinataire de la signification.)

Service on ☐ leaving a copy with a lawyer who accepted service on the person's behalf.
lawyer /   *en laissant une copie avec l'avocat qui a accepté la signification au nom de la personne.*
Significa-
tion à   *(Attach a copy of the document endorsed with the lawyer's acceptance of service.)*
l'avocat   (Annexez une copie du document, sur lequel l'avocat a inscrit qu'il a accepté la signification.)

Service by ☐ regular lettermail.
regular   *par courrier ordinaire.*
lettermail /
Significa-
tion par
courrier
ordinaire

SCR 8.06-8A (September 1, 2010 / *1ᵉʳ septembre 2010*) CSD   Continued on next page / *Suite à la page suivante*

continues....

Illustration 6.5 (continued)

FORM / *FORMULE* 8A   PAGE 3   **SC-00-47669-00**

Claim No. / *N° de la demande*

Service by fax / *Significa-tion par télécopie*

☐ fax sent at .... at the following fax number:
par télécopie   (Time / *heure*)   *au numéro de télécopieur*   (Fax number / *numéro de*
envoyée à   *suivant :*   *télécopieur*)

Service to last known address of corporation or attorney for service, and to the directors / *Significa-tion à la dernière adresse connue de la personne morale ou de son fondé de pouvoir aux fins de signification et aux administra-teurs*

☐ mail/courier to the corporation or attorney for service at last known address recorded with the Ministry of Government Services, and
d'une part, par la poste/par messagerie à la personne morale ou à son fondé de pouvoir aux fins de signification, à la dernière adresse connue figurant dans les dossiers du ministère des Services gouvernementaux;

☐ mail/courier to each director, as recorded with the Ministry of Government Services, as set out below:
d'autre part, par la poste/par messagerie à chaque administrateur mentionné dans les dossiers du ministère des Services gouvernementaux et dont le nom et l'adresse sont indiqués ci-dessous :

Name of director / *Nom de l'administrateur*	Director's address as recorded with the Ministry of Government Services (street & number, unit, municipality, province) / *Adresse de l'administrateur figurant dans les dossiers du ministère des Services gouvernementaux (numéro et rue, unité, municipalité, province)*
....	....
....	....
....	....
....	....

(Attach separate sheet for additional names if necessary. /
Joignez au besoin une feuille séparée s'il y a d'autres noms à ajouter.)

Substituted service / *Significa-tion indirecte*

☐ substituted service as ordered by the court on .... ,
par signification indirecte ordonnée par le tribunal le   (Date)

as follows: (Give details.)
comme suit :   *(Précisez.)*

Sworn/Affirmed before me at **Toronto** ....
Déclaré sous serment/Affirmé   (Municipality / *municipalité*)
solennellement devant moi à

in **Ontario** ....
en/à/au   (Province, state, or country / *province, État ou pays*)

on **April 3, Yr. 1** .... *Lorenzo Lawyer*
le   Commissioner for taking affidavits
Commissaire aux affidavits
(Type or print name below if signature
is illegible.)
*(Dactylographiez le nom ou écrivez-le
en caractères d'imprimerie ci-dessous
si la signature est illisible.)*

Lorenzo Lawyer

Samuel Server
Signature

(This form is to be signed in front of a
lawyer, justice of the peace, notary public
or commissioner for taking affidavits.)
*(La présente formule doit être signée en
présence d'un avocat, d'un juge de paix,
d'un notaire ou d'un commissaire aux
affidavits.)*

SCR 8.06-8A (September 1, 2010 / *1ᵉʳ septembre 2010*) CSD

8.03(1) If a document is to be served by an alternative to personal service, service shall be made in accordance with subrule (2), (3) or (5); in the case of a plaintiff's claim or defendant's claim served on an individual, service may also be made in accordance with subrule (7).

1. At the Place of Residence (Individuals) Where Personal Service Ineffective (Rule 8.03(2))

If an attempt of personal service has been made but unsuccessful, an alternative is to

- leave a copy, in a sealed envelope addressed to the individual, with anyone who appears to be an adult member of the same household, and
- mail or courier another copy to the individual at the residence on the same or the next day.

On the fifth day after the document was mailed or couriered (as verified by the courier as delivered), service is deemed to have occurred.

At Place of Residence
8.03(2) If an attempt is made to effect personal service at an individual's place of residence and for any reason personal service cannot be effected, the document may be served by,
 (a) leaving a copy in a sealed envelope addressed to the individual at the place of residence with anyone who appears to be an adult member of the same household; and
 (b) on the same day or the following day, mailing or sending by courier another copy of the document to the individual at the place of residence.

When Effective
8.03(4) Service made under subrule (2) or (3) is effective on the fifth day after the document is mailed or verified by courier that it was delivered.

2. Corporations No Longer At the Last Known Business Address (Rule 8.03(3))

If the corporation's head office or the attorney for service for an extra-provincial corporation is no longer at the last known address listed on the corporation returns filed with the Companies Branch, then

- mail or courier a copy to the last known address of the corporation or to the attorney for service, as the case may be, and

- mail or courier a copy of the document to each director of the corporation at the address for that person on the corporation returns listing directors, filed with the Companies branch.

Service is deemed to have occurred on the fifth day after mailing or couriering (as verified by the courier as delivered) the document.

Corporation
8.03(3) If the head office or principal place of business of a corporation or, in the case of an extra-provincial corporation, the attorney for service in Ontario cannot be found at the last address recorded with the Ministry of Government Services, service may be made on the corporation,

(a) by mailing or sending by courier a copy of the document to the corporation or to the attorney for service in Ontario, as the case may be, at that address; and

(b) by mailing or sending by courier a copy of the document to each director of the corporation as recorded with the Ministry of Government Services, at the director's address as recorded with that Ministry.

When Effective
(4) Service made under subrule (2) or (3) is effective on the fifth day after the document is mailed or verified by courier that it was delivered.

3. Service on Lawyer Who Is Authorized to Accept Service (Rule 8.03(5))

If the lawyer has authority to accept service on behalf of a client, service may be made on the lawyer by leaving a copy with the lawyer or an employee in the lawyer's office. The lawyer or employee must note on a copy that they have accepted service on behalf of their client, with the date of service. This rule does not authorize a paralegal to accept service in the same way as a lawyer does.[16]

8.03(5) Service on a party who is represented by a lawyer may be made by leaving a copy of the document with the lawyer or an employee in the lawyer's office, but service under this subrule is effective only if the lawyer or employee endorses on the document or a copy of it an acceptance of service and the date of the acceptance.

(6) By accepting service the lawyer is deemed to represent to the court that he or she has the client's authority to accept service.

---

[16] This was the case as of July 17, 2013, but it would be reasonable to expect that this will be amended to allow paralegals to accept service on behalf of clients.

4. Service of Claim by Mail to the Last Known Address (Rule 8.03(7))

> 8.03(7) Service of a plaintiff's claim or defendant's claim on an individual against whom the claim is made may be made by sending a copy of the claim by registered mail or by courier to the individual's place of residence, if the signature of the individual or any person who appears to be a member of the same household, verifying receipt of the copy, is obtained.

A plaintiff's claim or defendant's claim may be served by registered mail or courier to the individual's residence, and the claim is considered served if the individual's signature or the signature of a person who appears to be a member of the household verifying receipt of the copy is obtained.

Service is effective on the date that a delivery confirmation from Canada Post or a commercial courier confirming receipt of the copy is made.

> 8.03(8) Service under subrule (7) is effective on the date on which receipt of the copy of the claim is verified by signature, as shown in a delivery confirmation provided by or obtained from Canada Post or the commercial courier, as the case may be.

Modes of Services: Rule 8.07 and Rule 8.08

In addition to personal service, some documents can be served by mail, courier, and fax. These modes of service have some special rules of which you need to be aware.

If you are using mail service, you may use ordinary letter mail or registered mail, unless the rule itself specifies that registered mail must be used. If you wish to verify receipt, registered mail with a return acknowledgement card (or computer tracking, see <http://www.canadapost.ca>) is advisable. Canada Post does not provide return acknowledgement cards; however, you can use Form 16A under the *Rules of Civil Procedure* to create your own Acknowledgement Card. Service must be to the last address known to the sender or to the address appearing on court documents, if served by the clerk of the court. Service by mail is deemed to be effective on the fifth day following the date of mailing.

> *Service by Mail*
> 8.07(1) If a document is to be served by mail under these rules, it shall be sent, by regular lettermail or registered mail, to the last address of the person or of the person's lawyer or agent that is,
>> (a) on file with the court, if the document is to be served by the clerk;

(b) known to the sender, if the document is to be served by any other person.

When Effective

(2) Service of a document by mail is deemed to be effective on the fifth day following the date of mailing.

Exception

(3) This rule does not apply when a claim is served by registered mail under subrule 8.03(7).

Service by commercial courier is deemed to occur on the fifth day after the day on which the courier has verified to the sender that the document has been delivered.

Service by Courier

8.07.1(1) If a document is to be served by courier under these rules, it shall be sent by means of a commercial courier to the last address of the person or of the person's lawyer or agent that is on file with the court or known to the sender.

When Effective

(2) Service of a document sent by courier is deemed to be effective on the fifth day following the date on which the courier verifies to the sender that the document was delivered.

Exception

(3) This rule does not apply when a claim is served by courier under subrule 8.03(7).

Service by fax is deemed to have been made on the day of transmission if sent before 5:00 p.m. on a day that is not a holiday. But if sent on a holiday, or after 5:00 p.m., it is deemed to be served on the next day that is not a holiday. Any document that is 16 pages or more can be faxed only between the hours of 5:00 p.m. and 8:00 a.m. so as not to jam up the recipient's fax machine during business hours, unless the recipient agrees to transmission during business hours.

Service by Fax

8.08(1) Service of a document by fax is deemed to be effective,
  (a) on the day of transmission, if transmission takes place before 5 p.m. on a day that is not a holiday;
  (b) on the next day that is not a holiday, in any other case.

(2) A document containing 16 or more pages, including the cover page, may be served by fax only between 5 p.m. and 8 a.m. the following day, unless the party to be served consents in advance.

Substitutional Service: Rule 8.04

Substituted service upon a party is permitted under Rule 8.04.

> 8.04 If it is shown that it is impractical to effect prompt service of a claim personally or by an alternative to personal service, the court may allow substituted service.

Suppose you knew the last known address of a party you wish to serve with a claim but then discovered that the party had moved and left no forwarding address. You spoke to a neighbouring business and learned that the plaintiff had moved to Philadelphia, but the neighbour did not know the new address there. Your "people finder" Internet search turned up nothing on the party's address there or anywhere. In this case you cannot meet the requirements of the Rules for alternatives to personal service. So you may apply to the court by motion for an order for substituted service. You need to show in your affidavit in support of the motion that it is impractical to effect prompt personal service, or service by an alternative to personal service, in which case the court may order substituted service. You must give the court some indication of how and where the person could be served. In this case, for example, you might suggest service by way of a legal notice in a Philadelphia newspaper of general circulation. If you propose to publish a legal notice in a newspaper as the form of substitutional service, it is a good idea to attach a copy of the proposed notice as an exhibit to the affidavit in support of your motion for substitutional service. In that way, the judge can see it and order service of a notice in the form of the exhibit filed in support of the motion. This can ensure that the form you actually use will conform to the court's requirements.

> **Example 6.4 Substituted Service and Change of Address**
>
> Carol Creditor has been unsuccessful in her attempts to serve her claim on Jacobs and Partners. She did hear a rumour that the business had relocated to Pennsylvania. She can obtain an order from the court to achieve service by means of a method of substituted service, such as placing an ad in a daily newspaper where the defendant resides or carries on business. A sample of Carol Creditor's substituted service by newspaper advertisement is found in Figure 6.10.

In any event, whatever form a substitutional service takes, there is no guarantee the party will see it, but even if he or she does not, this will be deemed to be good and effective service. The defendant cannot simply stop a lawsuit by disappearing.

FIGURE 6.10: Substituted Service by Newspaper Advertisement

ONTARIO

SUPERIOR COURT OF JUSTICE

File no. SC-00-12345-00

The Toronto Small Claims Court

B E T W E E N:

CAROL CREDITOR

Plaintiff

and

JACOBS AND PARTNERS

Defendant

LEGAL NOTICE

TO: Jacobs and Partners, Philadelphia, PA, USA

An action has been commenced against you in the Toronto Small Claims Court for damages in the amount of $8,000 plus pre-judgment interest and costs. A copy of the Plaintiff's claim may be obtained from the office of this court at 47 Sheppard Avenue East, 3rd Floor, Toronto, Ontario, Canada M2N 5N1, telephone: 416 326 3554

You or an Ontario lawyer or paralegal on your behalf, may defend this action by filing a defence in the office of the court at 47 Sheppard Avenue East, 3rd floor, Toronto, Ontario, Canada M2N 5N1, within 20 days of the date of the publication of this notice. If you do not file a defence, judgment may be entered without further notice to you, and may be enforced against you.

This notice is published in accordance with an order of this court.

A copy of the order may be obtained from the court at the above-noted address.

Dated at Toronto, Ontario November 12, Yr. 0.

Petrus Paralegal, LSUC #P05761
1750 Finch Avenue E
Toronto, ON M2J 2X5
Tel 416 123 4567
Fax 416 123 4568

Legal representative for the Plaintiff.

When Served Documents Fail to Reach a Party

Sometimes a document, although served in accordance with the Rules, fails to reach the intended party. In such a case the party can show on a motion that the document did not come to their notice or came to their notice at a time later than when it was served or deemed to be served.

> 8.10 A person who has been served or who is deemed to have been served with a document in accordance with these rules is nevertheless entitled to show, on a motion to set aside the consequences of default, on a motion for an extension of time or in support of a request for an adjournment, that the document,
> (a) did not come to the person's notice; or
> (b) came to the person's notice only at some time later than when it was served or is deemed to have been served.

Notice of Change of Address

Under Rule 8.09(1), if you change your address, you are obliged to serve a written notice of change of address on every other party and the court. There is no special form for this, so you can make up your own, which needs to set out the old and new address and the date on which the new address becomes effective. The notice must be sent within seven days of the address change becoming effective.

> 8.09(1) A party whose address for service changes shall serve notice of the change on the court and other parties within seven days after the change takes place.
> (2) Service of the notice may be proved by affidavit if the court orders that proof of service is required.

> **Example 6.5 Change of Address**
>
> Jacobs and Partners did in fact relocate to Pennsylvania and is required to serve notice of its change of address on Carol Creditor. A sample Notice of Change of Address is set out in Figure 6.11.

CHAPTER SUMMARY

In this chapter, we discussed steps and procedures that should be considered before you issue and serve a plaintiff's claim, as well as the process involved in preparing the claim, issuing it, and serving it. Prior

FIGURE 6.11: Notice of Change of Address

ONTARIO
SUPERIOR COURT OF JUSTICE

File no. SC-00-12345-00

The Toronto Small Claims Court

B E T W E E N:

CAROL CREDITOR

Plaintiff

and

JACOBS AND PARTNERS

Defendant

NOTICE OF CHANGE OF ADDRESS

TAKE NOTICE that the defendant, Jacobs and Partners, has changed its address for service from 17 Doofus Drive, Toronto, ON M3R 1A8 to 60 Wayout Rd. North, Unit 311, Philadelphia, PA, USA 66330-9123. This change of address is effective as of November 8, Yr. 0.

Toronto, Ontario, November 15, Yr. 0.

JACOBS AND PARTNERS
60 Wayout Rd. North, Unit 311
Philadelphia, PA, USA 66330-9123
Tel 291-491-4567
Fax 291-491-4568

To:
Carol Creditor
c/o Petrus Paralegal, 1750 Finch Avenue E, Toronto, ON M2J 2X5

and to:
The clerk of the court
47 Sheppard Ave. E., 3rd Fl., Toronto, ON M2N 5N1

to issuing the claim, the plaintiff should usually send a demand letter to attempt to obtain payment without having to sue. If the demand letter is unproductive, the plaintiff should prepare to issue a claim. Before doing that, several matters must be addressed. The plaintiff must choose the correct court to sue in, following Rule 6. The plaintiff must also take care to determine who the appropriate defendants are, and name them properly, using their legal or "official" names. If a party is a minor, an absentee, or mentally incapable, special procedures must be taken to protect the rights of a party under disability in the lawsuit. If a party is a partnership or sole proprietorship, it is particularly important to use the procedures available under Rule 5 to identify who the sole proprietor is, or who the individual partners are, with respect to expanding enforcement rights after judgment.

Having dealt with these preliminary matters, we turned our attention to preparing the claim. You are now ready to prepare the claim. Having assembled all your facts and information and having established a theory of the case, you are prepared to draft the claim, including particulars and details. Drafting a claim or other court document is an art, and suggestions on how to draft a clear, coherent claim were provided, including suggestions drawn from the *Rules of Civil Procedure* of the Superior Court. Having drafted a claim, we then examined the steps required to issue the claim, including payment of the appropriate fee. We then considered the service options available and the most effective way of serving the claim on a particular defendant.

REVIEW QUESTIONS

1. When should a demand letter be used? What points should be covered in a demand letter?

2. What determines which court you should use to start your proceeding?

3. Paul lives in Brampton. He was in a bar in Toronto, where he was punched out by Desmond and Darren, who took exception to Paul's presence. Desmond lives in Oshawa, and Darren lives in Windsor. Where does Paul have the right to sue Desmond and Darren?

4. Frederica is a fruit wholesaler and regularly sells her product line to Fred's Fruits Ltd. She always deals with Fred, who does all the ordering and who signs all the cheques. The cheques are on an account for Fred's Fruits Ltd., and Frederica always ships the orders to the store in the name of the company. One day Frederica insulted Fred. He was so mad he told her she could wait to be paid for the last order until hell freezes over. Who should she sue?

5. *A* and *B* were partners when the business started. Later *C* and *D* joined. Then *D* left. Later, the partnership borrowed money from *X*. *E* then joined. Then there was default on the loan, and *X* sued the partnership. What should *X* do if she wants to expand her enforcement rights, and who should be sued?

6. If individual partners wish to deny they were partners, what step should they take?

7. Who are deemed to be persons under disability with respect to conducting and defending actions?

8. If you are acting for a minor plaintiff, what steps must you take (i) before you can sue, and (ii) if the case settles?

9. Who can act as a litigation guardian for a mentally incapable person? For a minor? An absentee?

10. Indicate whether the following statements are true or false when you prepare a claim.
    (a) The plaintiff should not include the name and particulars of a legal representative on the claim.
    (b) If you are suing to recover property, it is a good idea to claim the monetary value of the property in the alternative.

(c) If you are claiming interest under the *Courts of Justice Act*, you should claim the rate in force for the quarter in which the cause of action arose.

(d) When you indicate the amount of damages in your claim, you need to provide calculations to show how each type of damages was determined.

(e) You are obliged to supply copies of all relevant documents in the plaintiff's possession and attach them to the claim.

11. Why is it important to develop a theory of a case? Use an example to illustrate your answer.

12. What is a frequent claimant?

13. What are the different ways in which a claim may be served?

14. How would you serve each of the following parties?
    (a) The government of Canada
    (b) A municipality
    (c) A corporation
    (d) A minor
    (e) A mentally incapable person who has a court-appointed guardian

15. You tried to serve Doofus at his residence. No one was home. You go back the next day. A woman opens the door. She tells you she is the wife of Doofus but that they are separated, and she threw him out weeks ago. You hand her a sealed envelope addressed to Doofus, and the next day you mail another copy to Doofus at that residence. Is this good service?

16. I faxed 87 pages of claim to you at your office at 1:00 p.m. I didn't get your prior consent. Is this effective service?

DISCUSSION QUESTIONS/CASE STUDIES

You are Paul Paralegal, and you were given the following information:

Memo to: Paul Paralegal,
27 Milkyway,
Somewhere, ON K2L 3T2

September 8, Yr. 0

RE: Freda's Linens — Nopay Windows account

Our client Freda's Linens, located in Somewhere, Ontario, sold $5,000 worth of curtain material to Nopay Windows on June 2, Yr. 0. Nopay's business is located at 12 South Mall, Nowhere, ON L2L 3T4. Payment was due on July 2, Yr. 0, after which interest was payable on overdue amounts at the rate of 10% per year. Freda has sent reminders, but has received nothing. Our instructions are to send out a demand letter today, giving Nopay Windows 10 days to pay in full, including $200 for our costs. If nothing happens, we are to sue for everything we can get.

---

1. Draft the demand letter.

2. Nopay Windows has failed to respond to the demand letter. On September 20, Yr. 0, prepare a plaintiff's claim.

3. Your searches indicate that Nopay Windows is a partnership, but the information on the Companies Branch files is not recent. So you will also serve a notice on the partnership, demanding the names of the partners. Prepare the notice.

4. You discover that the names of the partners are Norbert and Norella Nopay and that they live over their shop at 12 South Mall in Unit 2, Somewhere, ON K2L 4K7. Prepare the document that will give you expanded enforcement rights against the partners' personal assets.

5. You served the defendant by handing the claim to Norella Nopay on September 25, Yr. 0, at 6:00 p.m. at her residence in Unit 2, 12 South Mall. Prepare the affidavit of service.

Chapter 7

Default Proceedings

LEARNING OBJECTIVES

⇨ Know the situations when default proceedings are permitted

⇨ Know the legal consequences of being noted in default

⇨ Know how to note a defendant in default

⇨ Know when to have the clerk sign default judgment, and when to move to assess damages

⇨ Know how to complete the documentation to sign default judgment or assess damages, including detailed affidavits to prove damages

⇨ Know how to take the steps required to obtain a hearing to assess damages

⇨ Know in what circumstances a default judgment may be set aside

⇨ Know how to move to set aside a default judgment

INTRODUCTION

Once the plaintiff has served the claim, a defendant normally files a defence. But what happens if the defendant does not defend the action? In this chapter we examine what a plaintiff may do if no defence is filed, looking at the procedures to be followed, depending on the circumstances of the default situation, in order to obtain a default judgment. As we will also see, there are things a defendant may do, in certain circumstances, to set aside a default judgment.

DEFAULT PROCEEDINGS

The general rule is that if a defendant to a claim, or the defendant to a defendant's claim, does not file a defence to the claim, then the plaintiff may move for default judgment under Rule 11. If a defendant defends part of a claim but not all of it, then the plaintiff may move for default judgment on the part of the claim that was not defended, and the defended part will go on to trial. Partial defaults are unusual. In this situation it is more likely that a defendant will admit part of a claim and defend the rest. For example, a defendant may admit liability and the claim for special damages but defend the claim for general damages on the ground that the claim is excessive. But, usually, when a defendant defaults, he or she simply fails to defend at all, and default judgment is obtained on the whole claim.

When May a Default Judgment Be Signed?

Normally, a defence must be filed within 20 days of service, but the act that constitutes service of a claim may not start the 20-day count. For example, if you serve a defendant by mail under Rule 8.03(7), service is not effective until the date the receipt of the claim is verified by the signature of the defendant or of a member of the same household. You then have to wait 20 days from that date. A few more days may then pass before the clerk mails or faxes the defence to you. If service is carried out under Rule 8.03(2) by leaving a copy with an adult person at the same household, service is effective 5 days after for a total of 25 days from the date of delivery to the household. It is up to you to monitor the file and check with the court to see if a defence has been filed.

Conditions Precedent to Signing Default Judgment

There are conditions to be fulfilled before you can obtain a default judgment before trial. As set out in Rule 11.01(1), a defendant must have failed to defend on all or part of the claim and must have been noted in default:

> 11.01(1) If a defendant to a plaintiff's claim or a defendant's claim fails to file a defence to all or part of the claim with the clerk within the prescribed time, the clerk may, when proof is filed that the claim was served within the territorial division, note the defendant in default.

The plaintiff must have complied with Rule 6 and sued the defendant inside the territorial division of the court — usually this will be proved by an affidavit of service. If, for some reason, all of the defendants have been served outside of the territorial division, in order to comply with Rule 11.01(3) you will have to file an affidavit to prove jurisdiction in Form 11A to show why they were not sued where they live or carry on business:

> 11.01(3) If all the defendants have been served outside the court's territorial division, the clerk shall not note any defendant in default until it is proved by an affidavit for jurisdiction (Form 11A) submitted to the clerk, or by evidence presented before a judge, that the action was properly brought in that territorial division.

Illustration 7.1 is a sample Affidavit for Jurisdiction (Form 11A) for the following example:

Example 7.1 A Case Where an Affidavit for Jurisdiction Is Required

Cruel Credit Ltd. loaned Donald DeFaulter the sum of $6,000. DeFaulter failed to make his loan payment.

Cruel Credit Ltd. (the plaintiff) carries on business in Toronto. DeFaulter lives in Newmarket, York Region, Ontario. The contract between the parties states that in the event of a dispute, the entire transaction is deemed to have occurred in Toronto. In accordance with the parties' contract, both pre- and post-judgment interest and interest on costs were at the rate of 18% per year and ran from April 3, Yr. 0, to the day before the date of judgment.

On July 5, Yr. 0, the paralegal for the plaintiff, Paul Paralegal, filed a Request to the Clerk asking to note the defendant in default and for a default judgment, together with a draft default judgment, as the 20 days for the defendant to file a defence to the plaintiff's claim had expired. As the claim was issued in Toronto and DeFaulter lives in Newmarket, Paul Paralegal filed an Affidavit for Jurisdiction with the court.

ILLUSTRATION 7.1: Sample Affidavit for Jurisdiction (Form 11A)

ONTARIO
Superior Court of Justice
Cour supérieure de justice

Affidavit for Jurisdiction
Affidavit établissant la compétence
Form / *Formule* 11A Ont. Reg. No. / *Règl. de l'Ont.* : 258/98

Toronto
Small Claims Court / *Cour des petites créances de*

SC-00-42658-00
Claim No. / *N° de la demande*

47 Sheppard Avenue East, 3rd Fl.
Toronto, ON M2N 5N1
Address / *Adresse*

416-326-3554
Phone number / *Numéro de téléphone*

BETWEEN / *ENTRE*

Cruel Credit Ltd.
Plaintiff(s) / *Demandeur(s)/demanderesse(s)*

and / *et*

Donald DeFaulter
Defendant(s) / *Défendeur(s)/défenderesse(s)*

My name is Paul Paralegal
Je m'appelle
(Full name / *Nom et prénoms*)

I live in Somewhere, Ontario
J'habite à
(Municipality & province / *Municipalité et province*)

and I swear/affirm that the following is true:
et je déclare sous serment/j'affirme solennellement que les renseignements suivants sont véridiques :

1. In this action, I am the
   Dans la présente action, je suis le/la

   ☐ plaintiff
   demandeur/demanderesse

   ☒ representative of the plaintiff(s) **Cruel Credit Ltd.**
   représentant(e) du/de la/des (Name of plaintiff(s) / *Nom du/de la/des demandeur(s)/demanderesse(s)*)
   demandeur(s)/demanderesse(s)

2. I make this affidavit in support of the plaintiff's request to note the defendant(s) in default, where all the defendants have been or will be served outside the court's territorial division [R. 11.01 (3)].
   Je fais le présent affidavit à l'appui de la demande du demandeur de faire constater le ou les défendeurs en défaut étant donné que tous les défendeurs ont reçu ou recevront la signification en dehors de la division territoriale du tribunal [par. 11.01 (3)].

SCR 11.01-11A (June 1, 2009 / *1er juin 2009*) CSD

continues....

Illustration 7.1 (continued)

FORM / *FORMULE* 11A	PAGE 2	SC-00-42658-00
		Claim No. / *N° de la demande*

3. The plaintiff is entitled to proceed with this action in this territorial division because this is:
   Le demandeur a le droit de poursuivre cette action dans cette division territoriale parce que :

☒ where the event (cause of action) took place.
l'événement (cause d'action) a eu lieu dans cette division territoriale.

☐ where the defendant lives or carries on business.
le défendeur réside dans cette division territoriale ou y exploite une entreprise.

☐ the court nearest to the place where the defendant lives or carries on business [R. 6.01].
c'est dans cette division territoriale que se trouve le greffe du tribunal qui est le plus près de l'endroit où le défendeur réside ou exploite une entreprise. [règle 6.01].

Sworn/Affirmed before me at **Toronto**
Déclaré sous serment/Affirmé (Municipality / *municipalité*)
solennellement devant moi à

in **Ontario**
en/à/au (Province, state or country / *province, État ou pays*)

on **July 5, Yr. 0**
le

G. Smith
Commissioner for taking affidavits
Commissaire aux affidavits
(Type or print name below if signature is illegible.)
(Dactylographiez le nom ou écrivez-le en caractères d'imprimerie ci-dessous si la signature est illisible.)

G. Smith

Paul Paralegal
Signature

(This form is to be signed in front of a lawyer, justice of the peace, notary public or commissioner for taking affidavits.)
(La présente formule doit être signée en présence d'un avocat, d'un juge de paix, d'un notaire ou d'un commissaire aux affidavits.)

WARNING:	IT IS AN OFFENCE UNDER THE *CRIMINAL CODE* TO KNOWINGLY SWEAR OR AFFIRM A FALSE AFFIDAVIT.
AVERTISSEMENT :	*FAIRE SCIEMMENT UN FAUX AFFIDAVIT CONSTITUE UNE INFRACTION AU CODE CRIMINEL.*

SCR 11.01-11A (June 1, 2009 / *1ᵉʳ juin 2009*) CSD

In some situations you may not be able to obtain a default judgment prior to trial without fulfilling some additional conditions:

- If the defendant is a person under disability, he or she may not be noted in default without first bringing a motion, pursuant to Rule 11.01(2), to get the court's permission. Here, you will have to show the person was served and had a litigation guardian who was aware of the proceedings. Often, however, a defendant does not have a litigation guardian when you sue and may not, because of the disability, be able to defend. You may only become aware of the defendant's disability when someone surfaces to move to set aside the default judgment, and the disability is advanced as the reason for doing so. In that case the court will set aside the default judgment.

  > 11.01(2) A person under disability may not be noted in default under subrule (1), except with leave of the court.

- If you are suing several defendants and some filed defences and you seek to assess damages against a defaulting defendant (rather than requesting that judgment be signed on a claim for **liquidated damages**), perhaps for unliquidated damages, under Rule 11.03(7) default judgment will not be granted prior to trial and the matter will be dealt with at trial. In accordance with the rule, a settlement conference will be held prior to trial. This will allow the court to determine the extent to which and the amount for which each defendant is liable, including the defaulting defendant. If default judgment could be signed against the defaulting defendant alone, he or she would be liable for all of the damages and the court would be shut out of the process of accurately apportioning liability among all of the defendants.

  > 11.03(7) If one or more defendants have filed a defence, a plaintiff requiring an assessment of damages against a defendant noted in default shall proceed to a settlement conference under rule 13 and, if necessary, a trial in accordance with rule 17.

- If a defendant files both a defence and a defendant's claim and the plaintiff in the main action does not defend against the defendant's claim, under Rule 11.04, default judgment on the defendant's claim will be determined at trial of the main action or on a motion for judgment before trial. There are two reasons for this. First, defendant's claims and plaintiff's claims arise from the same fact situation, transactions, or events, so the court needs to examine both claims together in order to justly decide the case. Second, self-represented plaintiffs often believe (incorrectly) that having filed a claim they need not file a defence to a defendant's claim.

11.04 If a party against whom a defendant's claim is made has been noted in default, judgment may be obtained against the party only at trial or on motion.

Consequences of Being Noted in Default — Rule 11.05

A defendant who has been noted in default may take no further steps in the action. He or she is deemed to have admitted liability, and the plaintiff is entitled to a judgment once the damages have been determined. The action can move ahead without the defaulting defendant's consent. The defendant does have the right, however, to move to set aside the noting in default and the default judgment.

While the defendant cannot participate in the action, he or she is entitled to notice of certain procedures:

- **A Default Judgment must be served on the defaulting defendant:** Once the plaintiff obtains a default judgment, the clerk of the court, under Rule 11.02(3), must serve it on the defendant. Receipt of the judgment is often a trigger for a motion to set the judgment aside.

  11.02(3) A default judgment (Form 11B) shall be served in accordance with subrule 8.01(4).

- **An amended claim or defence must be served on a defaulting defendant:** Under Rule 12.01, if a party moves to amend a claim or defence so that the facts and law pleaded change, then the case the defendant thought he or she was meeting may also change, and the defendant may decide he or she has a good reason to defend.

  12.01(1) A plaintiff's or defendant's claim and a defence to a plaintiff's or defendant's claim may be amended by filing with the clerk a copy that is marked "Amended", in which any additions are underlined and any other changes are identified.
  (2) The amended document shall be served by the party making the amendment on all parties, including any parties in default, in accordance with subrule 8.01(14).

- **A Motion After Judgment must be served on a defaulting defendant:** A motion that is made after judgment to correct an error in a judgment or to otherwise vary a judgment may result in a changed situation. As a result, the defaulting defendant may find that he or she now has a claim or defence worth arguing. At the very least the amount found owing may change, and the defendant has the right to know that. Such a motion must, under Rule 15.01(6), be served on a party noted in default.

  15.01(6) A motion that is made after judgment has been signed shall be served on all parties, including those who have been noted in default.

- **Post-judgment proceedings must be served on a judgment debtor:** A judgment by default is no different from judgment after trial. Defendants in both situations are equally subject to enforcement proceedings. Defendants must be given notice of certain proceedings, such as examinations in aid of execution or garnishment hearings. In general, the enforcement proceedings set out in Rule 20 require that the judgment debtor be served with notice of the proceeding. Note, however, that some enforcement steps do not require notice to be given to judgment debtor. A judgment creditor, for example, may file a Writ of Seizure and Sale of Property in the sheriff's office, and let it sit. There is no need to give the debtor notice of the filing, unless the creditor actually takes steps to enforce the Writ by directing the seizing and selling of real property.

Obtaining Default Judgment —
Liquidated and Unliquidated Damages

The form of the default judgment procedure depends on the type of damages that arise from the claim. If the damages are **liquidated damages**, there is a simple and quick administrative procedure where the clerk will check your damage and interest calculations and, if satisfied with their accuracy, will sign the default judgment.[1] If the clerk has any doubt about how the damages were calculated or if they are clearly **unliquidated damages**, the damages must be assessed by a judge. This is a more complex procedure, where a judge will review the documents providing the evidence on the issue of damages and may hold a hearing prior to fixing the amount of the damages.[2]

Liquidated Damages

These are damages that are objectively determined, using an agreed upon formula or method of calculation, requiring simple arithmetic. No discretion or subjective weighing of factors is required to determine the amount precisely. Another way of looking at this is to

---

[1] It is the current practice of some clerks, including those in Toronto, to only sign default judgments that use the *Courts of Justice Act* rate as the rate of pre-judgment interest. A request for judgment based on a contractual rate of pre-judgment interest, such as an interest rate in a car lease contract, is put before a judge to review and assess without a hearing. There is a government initiative underway, however, to standardize clerk procedures across Ontario so that one day all clerks may sign a default judgment where the pre-judgment interest rate is not the *CJA* rate but is clearly set out in the parties' contract filed as part of the claim.

[2] Liquidated damages are also referred to as a liquidated claim or demand or as special damages. Unliquidated damages are sometimes referred to as general damages.

say that any two reasonable people, given all the information about the damages issue, should come up with the same monetary value of the damages. For this reason the clerk can sign judgment on liquidated damages, using, at most, a calculator to check your default judgment calculations for accuracy. No subjective discretionary judgment is required — or indeed permitted. If a clerk is not certain of the amount, he or she will not sign judgment. Below are some examples of liquidated damages:

- A list of medications and their cost in a personal injury case
- Calculation of wage loss, when we know the rate of pay and the hours that would have been worked normally for a specific period
- The price of goods sold and delivered in a debt action
- The cost of services rendered if the hourly rate and the hours worked are known
- An unpaid debt and accrued interest
- The disbursements on your account to clients but not necessarily the fee, unless it was fixed and agreed to beforehand

Unliquidated Damages

Unliquidated damages are subjectively determined by applying general principles to a fact situation that does not provide a basis for precise calculations of the amount owing. There is no formula or simple mathematical operation that will yield a precise answer. There will be as many different answers as persons examining the issue, but the answers should fall within a general range.

Generally, judges will look to precedent cases where the fact situation and the nature of the damages are similar to the case before the court (although this is difficult to do in Small Claims Court where there are so few reported cases). Because of the subjective nature of the process, a judge must weigh and assess these types of damages. Given below are some examples:

- Damages for pain and suffering
- Damages for loss of profits
- Damages for loss of the use of personal property
- The price of goods on a contract where no clear price is set out

OBTAINING A DEFAULT JUDGMENT — STEP BY STEP

How you obtain a default judgment depends on whether the defendant has defaulted on a claim for liquidated or unliquidated damages. If the damages were for a debt or liquidated damages (called a liquidated demand in the Rules), the clerk may sign the judgment. If the claim was for unliquidated damages, the plaintiff must move for assessment of damages by a judge.

Default Judgment for Damages for a Debt or Liquidated Claim

Obtaining default judgment for damages for a debt or liquidated claim is covered by Rule 11.02:

> 11.02(1) If a defendant has been noted in default, the clerk may sign default judgment (Form 11B) in respect of the claim or any part of the claim to which the default applies that is for a debt or liquidated demand in money, including interest if claimed.

Once the time has passed for the defence to be filed, you can take the following steps to obtain default judgment:

1. Request that the clerk note the defendant in default by filing a Form 9B, Request to Clerk. (A sample Form 9B for Example 7.1 is provided in Illustration 7.2.) This form is used to request the clerk to perform any administrative act, including noting a party in default.

    Note that in some cases you may not be in a position to obtain default judgment immediately after the time for a defence to be filed has passed. You should, however, consider noting the defendant in default by filing Form 9B and your affidavit of service with the court before you obtain default judgment. It is wise to request the noting in default in a timely fashion, as Rule 11.1.01(1) states that the action will be dismissed as abandoned if no defence has been filed and no request has been made to note in default within 180 days of the issuing of the claim. You might, for example, have a case where 20 days have passed since the defendant was personally served; however, you are waiting for receipts from your client that will prove damages in order to have default judgment signed. While waiting for the receipts, you can file Form 9B to have the defendant noted in default so that a defence can no longer be filed and to avoid dismissal of the case under the Small Claims Court case management rules.

2. File an Affidavit of Service of the claim (Form 8A). The affidavit of service of the claim is filed to show the defendant was served in the court's territorial division. If the affidavit of service does not show on its face that you complied with Rule 6, you also need to file an Affidavit for Jurisdiction (Form 11A) on which

ILLUSTRATION 7.2: Sample Request to Clerk (Form 9B)

ONTARIO

Superior Court of Justice
Cour supérieure de justice

Request to Clerk
Demande au greffier
Form / *Formule* 9B Ont. Reg. No. / *Règl. de l'Ont.* : 258/98

Toronto
Small Claims Court / *Cour des petites créances de*

SC-00-42658-00
Claim No. / *N° de la demande*

47 Sheppard Avenue East, 3rd Fl.
Toronto, ON M2N 5N1
Address / *Adresse*

416-326-3554
Phone number / *Numéro de téléphone*

BETWEEN / *ENTRE*

Cruel Credit Ltd.

Plaintiff(s) / *Demandeur(s)/demanderesse(s)*

and / *et*

Donald DeFaulter

Defendant(s) / *Défendeur(s)/défenderesse(s)*

TO THE CLERK OF THE Toronto
AU GREFFIER DE LA COUR
DES PETITES CRÉANCES DE
(Name of Small Claims Court location / *Emplacement de la Cour des petites créances*) :

SMALL CLAIMS COURT:

My name is Paul Paralegal
Je m'appelle
(Name of party/representative / *Nom de la partie ou du/de la représentant(e)*)

and I request that the clerk of the court:
et je demande au greffier du tribunal de faire ce qui suit :

(Check appropriate box(es). / Cochez la ou les cases appropriées.)

☒ note defendant(s) **Donald DeFaulter**
constater le ou les défendeurs
(Name of defendant(s) / *Nom du/de la/des défendeur(s)/défenderesse(s)*)

in default for failing to file a Defence (Form 9A) within the prescribed time period [R. 11.01(1)].
en défaut pour n'avoir pas déposé de défense (formule 9A) dans le délai prescrit [par. 11.01 (1)].

☐ schedule an assessment hearing (all defendants have been noted in default) [R. 11.03(2)(b)].
fixer la date d'une audience d'évaluation (tous les défendeurs ont été constatés en défaut) [alinéa 11.03 (2) b)].

☐ schedule a terms of payment hearing because I dispute the defendant's proposed terms of payment contained in the Defence (Form 9A) [R. 9.03(3)].
fixer la date d'une audience relative aux modalités de paiement parce que je conteste les modalités de paiement proposées par le défendeur dans la défense (formule 9A) [par. 9.03 (3)].

☐ schedule a trial [R. 16.01(1)(b)].
fixer une date de procès [alinéa 16.01 (1) b)].

SCR 4-9-11-14-16-9B (June 1, 2009 / *1er juin 2009*) CSD

continues....

Illustration 7.2 (continued)

FORM / *FORMULE* 9B   PAGE 2   SC-00-42658-00
                                                                Claim No. / *N° de la demande*

☐ accept payment in the amount of $ _____into court
   accepter que le paiement de (Amount / *montant*) *$ soit consigné au tribunal,*

   ☐ according to an order of the court, dated _____ .
      conformément à une ordonnance du tribunal datée du

   ☐ for a person under disability according to an order or settlement dated
      au nom d'un incapable, conformément à une ordonnance ou à une transaction datée du
      _____ [R. 4.08(1)].
                                 [par. 4.08 (1)].

   ☐ pursuant to the attached written offer to settle, dated_____[R. 14.05(2)].
      aux termes de l'offre de transaction écrite ci-jointe datée du *[par. 14.05 (2)].*

   ☐ according to the following legislation:
      conformément à la disposition législative suivante :

      _____ .
      (Name of statute or regulation and section / *Titre de la loi ou du règlement et mention de l'article*)

☐ Other: (Specify.)
  Autre : (*Précisez.*)

July 5, Yr. 0 _____   *Paul Paralegal*
                                      (Signature of party or representative / *Signature de la partie ou du/de la représentant(e)*)

CAUTION:	To obtain an assessment of damages, all defendants must be noted in default. If one or more defendants has filed a defence, the matter must proceed to a settlement conference. To bring a motion in writing for an assessment of damages, file a Notice of Motion and Supporting Affidavit (Form 15A). You can get forms at court offices or online at www.ontariocourtforms.on.ca.
AVERTISSEMENT :	*Pour obtenir une évaluation des dommages-intérêts, tous les défendeurs doivent être constatés en défaut. Si un ou plusieurs défendeurs ont déposé une défense, l'affaire doit passer à l'étape de la conférence en vue d'une transaction. Pour présenter une motion par écrit en vue d'une évaluation des dommages-intérêts, déposez un avis de motion et affidavit à l'appui (formule 15A). Vous pouvez obtenir les formules aux greffes des tribunaux ou en ligne à l'adresse www.ontariocourtforms.on.ca.*

SCR 4-9-11-14-16-9B (June 1, 2009 / *1er juin 2009*) CSD

you demonstrate compliance with the rule.[3] Samples of Form 8A and Form 11A are provided earlier in Illustration 6.5 and Illustration 7.1, respectively.

3. File a draft Default Judgment (Form 11B) in which you set out your damage calculation, including pre-judgment interest.[4] Pre-judgment interest is calculated from and including the day the cause of action arose (in a collection case, the day interest first starts to be charged), up to and including the day before judgment. The clerk will check your math and, if satisfied that it is correct, will sign the default judgment.

4. Submit the required fee for default judgment. The fee is lower for an infrequent claimant. At the time of writing, the fee was $35 for infrequent claimants and $50 for frequent claimants. You can consult the latest Small Claims Court fees tariff online at <http://www.e-laws.gov.on.ca> under the regulations to the *Administration of Justice Act*, R.S.O. 1990, c. A.6.

5. Keep a copy of the default judgment as signed for your file.

6. The clerk will serve the default judgment by mail or fax on all parties, whether they are in default or not, as required by Rule 8.04.

7. You now have a judgment that you may enforce in the same way as you could after a trial, using the enforcement tools in Rule 20. Enforcement is discussed later in Part III.

Illustration 7.3 shows Form 11B, Default Judgment, required to sign default judgment for Cruel Credit Ltd. in Example 7.1. In addition to the principal and pre-judgment interest, Illustration 7.3 also includes another item called "Costs to date".

The costs on a default judgment that may be added to the principal and interest on the judgment normally include the following:

• The fees paid to the court to issue the claim ($75.00 for an infrequent claimant, $145.00 for a frequent claimant)

• The fee for entering a default judgment ($35.00 for an infrequent claimant, $50.00 for a frequent claimant)

---

[3] If required, submit an affidavit proving jurisdiction, or other proof of proper service, and a draft Default Judgment (Form 11B), together with the fee required to enter a default judgment. See *Small Claims Court — Fees and Allowances*, Schedule 1, Clerk's Fees.

[4] If the defendant on the Plaintiff's Claim is shown as having two different names (an aka name), you should ensure that both names are listed on the judgment.

ILLUSTRATION 7.3: Sample Default Judgment (Form 11B)

ONTARIO

Superior Court of Justice
Cour supérieure de justice

Default Judgment
Jugement par défaut

Form / *Formule* 11B Ont. Reg. No. / *Règl. de l'Ont.* : 258/98

Seal / *Sceau*

Toronto
Small Claims Court / *Cour des petites créances de*

47 Sheppard Avenue East, 3rd Fl.
Toronto, ON M2N 5N1

Address / *Adresse*

416-326-3554
Phone number / *Numéro de téléphone*

SC-00-42658-00
Claim No. / *N° de la demande*

Plaintiff No. 1 / *Demandeur n° 1* ☐ Additional plaintiff(s) listed on attached Form 1A.
Le ou les demandeurs additionnels sont mentionnés sur la formule 1A ci-jointe.

Last name, or name of company / *Nom de famille ou nom de la compagnie*		
Cruel Credit Ltd.		
First name / *Premier prénom*	Second name / *Deuxième prénom*	Also known as / *Également connu(e) sous le nom de*
Address (street number, apt., unit) / *Adresse (numéro et rue, app., unité)*		
c/o Paul Paralegal, 27 Milkway		
City/Town / *Cité/ville*	Province	Phone no. / *N° de téléphone*
Somewhere	**ON**	**909-842-5678**
Postal code / *Code postal*		Fax no. / *N° de télécopieur*
K2L 3T4		**909-842-5679**
Representative / *Représentant(e)*		LSUC # / *N° du BHC*
Paul Paralegal		**P02953**
Address (street number, apt., unit) / *Adresse (numéro et rue, app., unité)*		
27 Milkway		
City/Town / *Cité/ville*	Province	Phone no. / *N° de téléphone*
Somewhere	**ON**	**909-842-5678**
Postal code / *Code postal*		Fax no. / *N° de télécopieur*
K2L 3T4		**909-842-5679**

Defendant No. 1 / *Défendeur n° 1* ☐ Additional defendant(s) listed on attached Form 1A.
Le ou les défendeurs additionnels sont mentionnés sur la formule 1A ci-jointe.

Last name, or name of company / *Nom de famille ou nom de la compagnie*		
DeFaulter		
First name / *Premier prénom*	Second name / *Deuxième prénom*	Also known as / *Également connu(e) sous le nom de*
Donald		
Address (street number, apt., unit) / *Adresse (numéro et rue, app., unité)*		
2340 Main Street		
City/Town / *Cité/ville*	Province	Phone no. / *N° de téléphone*
Newmarket	**ON**	
Postal code / *Code postal*		Fax no. / *N° de télécopieur*
L3Y 3H3		
Representative / *Représentant(e)*		LSUC # / *N° du BHC*
Address (street number, apt., unit) / *Adresse (numéro et rue, app., unité)*		
City/Town / *Cité/ville*	Province	Phone no. / *N° de téléphone*
Postal code / *Code postal*		Fax no. / *N° de télécopieur*

SCR 11.02-11B (September 1, 2010 / *1er septembre 2010*) CSD

continues....

Illustration 7.3 (continued)

FORM / *FORMULE* 11B   **PAGE 2**   SC-00-42658-00
                                                                          Claim No. / *Nº de la demande*

NOTICE TO THE DEFENDANT(S):
AVIS AU(X) DÉFENDEUR(S) :
(*Check one box only. / Cochez une seule case.*)

☒ You have been noted in default according to Rule 11.01.
   vous avez été constaté(e) en défaut aux termes de la règle 11.01.

☐ You have defaulted in your payment according to Rule 9.03(2)(b), pursuant to
   vous n'avez pas effectué vos paiements aux termes de l'alinéa 9.03 (2) b), conformément à/au

_____ dated _____
(Name of document / *Titre du document*)   *daté(e) du*

   and 15 days have passed since you were served with a Notice of Default of Payment (Form 20L).
   et 15 jours se sont écoulés depuis qu'un avis de défaut de paiement vous a été signifié (formule 20L).

DEFAULT JUDGMENT IS GIVEN against the following defendant(s):
UN JUGEMENT PAR DÉFAUT EST RENDU *contre le ou les défendeurs suivants :*

Last name, or name of company / *Nom de famille ou nom de la compagnie*		
DeFaulter		
First name / *Premier prénom*	Second name / *Deuxième prénom*	Also known as / *Également connu(e) sous le nom de*
Donald		

Last name, or name of company / *Nom de famille ou nom de la compagnie*		
First name / *Premier prénom*	Second name / *Deuxième prénom*	Also known as / *Également connu(e) sous le nom de*

Last name, or name of company / *Nom de famille ou nom de la compagnie*		
First name / *Premier prénom*	Second name / *Deuxième prénom*	Also known as / *Également connu(e) sous le nom de*

☐ Additional defendant(s) listed on attached page (*list in same format*).
   Défendeur(s) additionnel(s) mentionné(s) sur une feuille annexée (énumérez-les en suivant le même format).

THE DEFENDANT(S) MUST PAY to the plaintiff(s) the following sums:
LE OU LES DÉFENDEURS DOIVENT VERSER *au(x) demandeur(s) les sommes suivantes :*

(A) **DEBT** (principal amount claimed minus any payments received since the plaintiff's
     claim was issued) $ _____6,000.00_____
     LA CRÉANCE *(somme demandée moins tout paiement reçu depuis la délivrance* $
     de la demande du demandeur)

(B) **PRE-JUDGMENT INTEREST** calculated
     LES INTÉRÊTS ANTÉRIEURS AU JUGEMENT *calculés*

     on the sum of $ _____6,000.00_____ at the rate of **18** %
     sur la somme de   *$ au taux de*   *pour cent*

     per annum from **April 3, Yr. 0**   , to **July 4, Yr. 0** _____ ,
     par an du   *au*

     being **93** _____ days. $ _____275.18_____
     soit   *jours.* $

SCR 11.02-11B (September 1, 2010 / *1ᵉʳ septembre 2010*) CSD   **Continued on next page / *Suite à la page suivante***

continues....

Illustration 7.3 (continued)

FORM / *FORMULE* 11B   PAGE 3   SC-00-42658-00
                                                               Claim No. / *N° de la demande*

(C) **COSTS** to date (including the cost of issuing this judgment) $ 270.00
   LES DÉPENS *à ce jour (dont les frais afférents à la prononciation* $
   du présent jugement)

                                                          TOTAL $ 6,545.18
                                                                              $

This judgment bears post-judgment interest at __18_____ % per annum commencing this date.
Le présent jugement porte des intérêts postérieurs   *pour cent à partir de la date du présent jugement.*
au jugement calculés au taux annuel de

July 5, Yr. 0   "Court Clerk"
_____   _____
                                             (Signature of clerk / *Signature du greffier*)

CAUTION TO DEFENDANT:	**YOU MUST PAY THE AMOUNT OF THIS JUDGMENT DIRECTLY TO THE PLAINTIFF(S) IMMEDIATELY.** Failure to do so may result in additional post-judgment interest and enforcement costs.
AVERTISSEMENT AU DÉFENDEUR :	***VOUS DEVEZ VERSER DIRECTEMENT AU(X) DEMANDEUR(S) LE MONTANT DÛ AUX TERMES DU PRÉSENT JUGEMENT IMMÉDIATEMENT***, *à défaut de quoi d'autres intérêts postérieurs au jugement et dépens de l'exécution forcée pourront vous être imputés.*

SCR 11.02-11B (September 1, 2010 / *1ᵉʳ septembre 2010*) CSD

- The fee paid to the process server to serve the claim (limited to a maximum of $60.00 by Rule 19.01(3))[5]
- The fees paid for photocopying and for travel expenses

The party may claim a fee of up to $100 to prepare the claim, under Rule 19.01(4). However, in some courts, this cost item is given only where the party has incurred the cost of having a legal representative prepare the claim. Unrepresented litigants are unlikely to get this included in their costs. Representation fees are not awarded unless there is a trial or hearing. Signing default judgment does not require a hearing.

In Example 7.1 we have assumed that the plaintiff is represented by a paralegal, is an infrequent claimant, and that he spent at least $60.00 to serve the claim, and that he received the maximum for the preparation of the claim.

Disbursements that may be recovered on a default judgment are governed by Rule 19:

> **Disbursements**
> 19.01(1) A successful party is entitled to have the party's reasonable disbursements, including any costs of effecting service or preparing a plaintiff's or defendant's claim or a defence and expenses for travel, accommodation, photocopying and experts' reports, paid by the unsuccessful party, unless the court orders otherwise.
>
> (2) The clerk shall assess the disbursements in accordance with the regulations made under the *Administration of Justice Act* and in accordance with subrules (3) and (4); the assessment is subject to review by the court.
>
> (3) The amount of disbursements assessed for effecting service shall not exceed $60 for each person served unless the court is of the opinion that there are special circumstances that justify assessing a greater amount.
>
> (4) The amount of disbursements assessed for preparing a plaintiff's or defendant's claim or a defence shall not exceed $100.
>
> **Limit**
> 19.02 Any power under this rule to award costs is subject to section 29 of the *Courts of Justice Act*, which limits the amount of costs that may be awarded.

We have assumed that the plaintiff in Example 7.1 is not a frequent claimant, that he received nothing under Rule 19.01(4) for his time and effort in filing documents, and that he received the maximum under Rule 19.01(3).

---

[5] However, under Rule 8.05, if the default judgment was served outside of Ontario, the extra costs reasonably incurred to carry out such service may be claimed.

There is no representation fee in this illustration because there is no trial or assessment hearing required, but a party may claim a preparation fee of $100.00 under Rule 19.01(4). Some courts require the submission of a lawyer or a paralegal's account for the preparation of a claim before they will grant the $100 preparation fee.

Service of the Default Judgment

Under Rule 11.02(3), a default judgment shall be served by the court clerk by mail or fax, as required by Rule 8.01(4):

> 11.02(3) A default judgment (Form 11B) shall be served in accordance with subrule 8.01(4).

Proceeding with Other Parts of the Claim

Under Rule 11.02(2), the plaintiff retains a right to proceed with any part of his or her claim for which default judgment has not been signed or against any other defendant for all or part of the claim. In such a case, the plaintiff would proceed on to a settlement conference and/or trial.

> 11.02(2) The fact that default judgment has been signed under subrule (1) does not affect the plaintiff's right to proceed on the remainder of the claim or against any other defendant for all or part of the claim.

Default Judgment for an Unliquidated Claim

Obtaining default judgment for an unliquidated claim is covered by Rule 11.03:

> 11.03(1) If all defendants have been noted in default, the plaintiff may obtain judgment against a defendant noted in default with respect to any part of the claim to which rule 11.02 does not apply.

Where a claim is for an unliquidated claim (general damages) that must be determined subjectively, the amount of the claim must be assessed by a judge, either on the basis of documents filed with the court or after a hearing. If part of the claim was liquidated, the plaintiff may ask the clerk to sign judgment on the liquidated part of the claim and have the other parts of the claim assessed.

There are two alternative procedures available to assess damages: (i) assessment of damages on the basis of filed documents, and (ii) assessment based on a hearing to assess damages.

Assessment of Damages on the Basis of Filed Documents

The plaintiff uses Rule 11.03(2) to obtain default judgment on the basis of filed written documents to obtain judgment for unliquidated damages. The rule stipulates which documents are to be filed with the court for judgment:

> 11.03(2) To obtain judgment the plaintiff may,
> (a) file a notice of motion and supporting affidavit (Form 15A) requesting a motion in writing for an assessment of damages, setting out the reasons why the motion should be granted and attaching any relevant documents; or
> (b) file a request to clerk (Form 9B) requesting that an assessment hearing be arranged.

The plaintiff should take the following steps:

1. File with the clerk a Notice of Motion and Supporting Affidavit (Form 15A). The motion will tell the court what you want to do — just fill in Part B on Page 3 of the form for an assessment of damages on the basis of the documents filed.

2. Complete the supporting affidavit part of Form 15A, starting at Page 3 of the form, and attach any relevant documents, such as the invoice, bill, or account. The purpose of the affidavit is to provide evidence of the amount of the claim. For example, if you claim an amount for pain and suffering from a personal injury, your affidavit should describe how and when the defendant injured you, what your injuries were, how and where you were treated, the pain and discomfort the injury caused, and how the injury impacted on your daily life, limiting your pursuits and activities. You could also add a list of medications you had to take. From the affidavit, the judge will be able to see the nature and extent of the injury and assess your damages. Note that you are not required to prove liability — just the amount of the damages claimed. If the judge finds that the plaintiff's affidavit is inadequate or unsatisfactory, he or she may order, under Rule 11.03(3), that a further affidavit be filed or that an assessment hearing be held:

   > 11.03(3) On a motion in writing for an assessment of damages under clause (2)(a), a judge who finds the plaintiff's affidavit inadequate or unsatisfactory may order that,
   > (a) a further affidavit be provided; or
   > (b) an assessment hearing be held.

3. File the affidavit of service for the plaintiff's claim and, if required, an affidavit for jurisdiction.

4. Pay the fee required for a motion. The clerk, under Rule 11.03(6), shall serve the order for default judgment on the defendant, and, if the plaintiff supplies a stamped, self-addressed envelope, on the plaintiff as well:[6]

> 11.03(6) An order made on a motion in writing for an assessment of damages shall be served by the clerk in accordance with subrule 8.01(5).

Example 7.2 Scenario Requiring an Assessment of Damages

Henry Fallover, the plaintiff, was injured as a result of a fall and is claiming general damages for pain and suffering, which is described in some detail in terms of the effects of the injury. Note that there is a liquidated claim for special damages included in the claim. Although technically you could ask the clerk to sign judgment for the special damages, it is more efficient and less expensive to include the special damages in the assessment process.

Set out in Illustration 7.4 is a sample of a notice of motion and supporting affidavit for an assessment of damages in writing for Example 7.2 above. For the request to note the defendant in default, refer to the sample that appears in Illustration 7.2 earlier on page 277.

Hearing for the Assessment of Damages

If you prefer, or if you suspect a judge may wish to ask questions or require additional information about anything in the affidavit, you may, under Rule 11.03(2)(b), file a Request to Clerk (Form 9B) to note the defendant in default and require a hearing for the assessment of damages:

> 11.03(2) To obtain judgment the plaintiff may,
> (b) file a request to clerk (Form 9B) requesting that an assessment hearing be arranged.

---

[6] Under the Rules, the clerk must serve the defendant the order for default judgment but will only do so for the plaintiff if a stamped, self-addressed envelope is supplied, as stated in Rule 8.01(5). You should, therefore, always include a stamped, self-addressed envelope with your notice of motion and supporting affidavit.

ILLUSTRATION 7.4: Sample Notice of Motion and Supporting Affidavit (Form 15A) to Assess Damages

ONTARIO
Superior Court of Justice
Cour supérieure de justice

Notice of Motion and Supporting Affidavit
Avis de motion et affidavit à l'appui
Form / Formule 15A Ont. Reg. No. / Règl. de l'Ont. : 258/98

Toronto
Small Claims Court / Cour des petites créances de

47 Sheppard Ave. E., 3rd Fl.
Toronto, ON M2N 5N1
Address / Adresse

416-326-3554
Phone number / Numéro de téléphone

SC-00-23456-00
Claim No. / N° de la demande

Plaintiff No. 1 / *Demandeur n° 1* ☐ Additional plaintiff(s) listed on attached Form 1A.
Le ou les demandeurs additionnels sont mentionnés sur la formule 1A ci-jointe.

Last name, or name of company / Nom de famille ou nom de la compagnie		
Fallover		
First name / Premier prénom	Second name / Deuxième prénom	Also known as / Également connu(e) sous le nom de
Henry		
Address (street number, apt., unit) / Adresse (numéro et rue, app., unité)		
c/o Peter Paralegal, 41 Yonge Street, #410		
City/Town / Cité/ville	Province	Phone no. / N° de téléphone
Toronto	**ON**	**416-597-0048**
Postal code / Code postal		Fax no. / N° de télécopieur
M5G 1S1		**416-597-0049**
Representative / Représentant(e)		LSUC # / N° du BHC
Peter Paralegal		**P02952**
Address (street number, apt., unit) / Adresse (numéro et rue, app., unité)		
41 Yonge Street, #410		
City/Town / Cité/ville	Province	Phone no. / N° de téléphone
Toronto	**ON**	**416-597-0048**
Postal code / Code postal		Fax no. / N° de télécopieur
M5G 1S1		**416-597-0049**

Defendant No. 1 / *Défendeur n° 1* ☐ Additional defendant(s) listed on attached Form 1A.
Le ou les défendeurs additionnels sont mentionnés sur la formule 1A ci-jointe.

Last name, or name of company / Nom de famille ou nom de la compagnie		
Householder		
First name / Premier prénom	Second name / Deuxième prénom	Also known as / Également connu(e) sous le nom de
Morris		
Address (street number, apt., unit) / Adresse (numéro et rue, app., unité)		
101 Risk Rd.		
City/Town / Cité/ville	Province	Phone no. / N° de téléphone
Toronto	**ON**	
Postal code / Code postal		Fax no. / N° de télécopieur
M6R 1J6		
Representative / Représentant(e)		LSUC # / N° du BHC
Address (street number, apt., unit) / Adresse (numéro et rue, app., unité)		
City/Town / Cité/ville	Province	Phone no. / N° de téléphone
Postal code / Code postal		Fax no. / N° de télécopieur

SCR 15.01-15A (September 1, 2010 / 1er septembre 2010) CSD

continues....

Illustration 7.4 (continued)

FORM / *FORMULE* 15A   PAGE 2   SC-00-23456-00
                                                                 Claim No. / *N° de la demande*

THIS COURT WILL HEAR A MOTION on September 10, Yr. 0   , at 10:00 a.m. ,
LE TRIBUNAL PRÉCITÉ ENTENDRA UNE MOTION le   , *à*   (Time / *heure*)

or as soon as possible after that time, at 47 Sheppard Ave. E., Courtroom 3
ou dès que possible par la suite à/au   (Address of court location and courtroom number / *Adresse du tribunal et numéro de la salle d'audience*)

Complete Part A _or_ Part B below, then complete the affidavit in support of motion on page 3. / *Remplissez la partie A _ou_ la partie B ci-dessous. Remplissez ensuite l'affidavit à l'appui de la motion à la page 3.*

A.   **This motion will be made in person by** ....
     La motion sera présentée en personne par :   (Name of party / *Nom de la partie*)

     for the following order : / en vue d'obtenir l'ordonnance suivante :

☐   the court's permission to extend time to   (Specify)
     l'autorisation du tribunal de proroger le délai pour   *(Précisez)*

☐   set aside default judgment and noting in default.
     l'annulation du jugement par défaut et la constatation du défaut.

☐   set aside noting in default.
     l'annulation de la constatation du défaut.

☐   permission to file a Defence.
     l'autorisation de déposer une défense.

☐   permission to file a Defendant's Claim.
     l'autorisation de déposer une demande du défendeur.

☐   set aside order dismissing claim as abandoned.
     l'annulation d'une demande pour cause de renonciation

☐   terminate garnishment and/or withdraw writ(s).
     la mainlevée de la saisie-arrêt ou le retrait d'un ou de plusieurs brefs, ou les deux.

☐   Other:
     Autre :

☐   **ADDITIONAL PAGES ARE ATTACHED BECAUSE MORE ROOM WAS NEEDED.**
     DES FEUILLES SUPPLÉMENTAIRES SONT ANNEXÉES EN RAISON DU MANQUE D'ESPACE.

☐   **DOCUMENTS ARE ATTACHED.**
     PIÈCES JOINTES.

NOTE: **IF YOU FAIL TO ATTEND AN IN-PERSON MOTION,** an order may be made against you, with costs, in your absence. If you want to attend the motion by telephone or video conference, complete and file a Request for Telephone or Video Conference (Form 1B). If the court permits it, the clerk will make the necessary arrangements and notify the parties [R. 1.07(5)].

REMARQUE :   *SI VOUS NE VOUS PRÉSENTEZ PAS EN PERSONNE À L'AUDITION DE LA MOTION, une ordonnance peut être rendue contre vous en votre absence, avec dépens. Si vous voule z assister à l'audition de la motion par conférence téléphonique ou vidéoconférence, remplissez et déposez la Demande de conférence téléphonique ou vidéoconférence (formule 1B). Si le tribunal l'autorise, le greffier prendra les dispositions nécessaires et en avis era les parties [par. 1.07 (5)].*

SCR 15.01-15A (September 1, 2010 / *1er septembre 2010*) CSD   Continued on next page / *Suite à la page suivante*

continues....

Illustration 7.4 (continued)

FORM / *FORMULE* 15A	PAGE 3	SC-00-23456-00
		Claim No. / *N° de la demande*

B. This motion in writing for an assessment of damages is made by
La présente motion par écrit en vue d'une évaluation des dommages-intérêts est présentée par

Henry Fallover
(Name of plaintiff / *Nom du demandeur/de la demanderesse*)

who asks the court for an order assessing damages against
qui demande au tribunal de rendre une ordonnance d'évaluation des dommages-intérêts contre

Morris Householder
(Name of defendant(s) / *Nom du/de la/des défendeur(s)/défenderesse(s)*)

who have/has been noted in default.
qui a/ont été constaté(e)(s) en défaut.

AFFIDAVIT IN SUPPORT OF MOTION / *AFFIDAVIT À L'APPUI DE LA MOTION*

My name is Henry Fallover
Je m'appelle (Full name / *Nom et prénoms*)

I live in Toronto, Ontario
J'habite à (Municipality & province / *Municipalité et province*)

I swear/affirm that the following is true:
Je déclare sous serment/j'affirme solennellement que les renseignements suivants sont véridiques :

Set out the facts in numbered paragraphs. If you learned a fact from someone else, you must give that person's name and state that you believe that fact to be true.
Indiquez les faits sous forme de dispositions numérotées. Si vous avez pris connaissance d'un fait par l'entremise d'une autre personne, vous devez indiquer le nom de cette personne et déclarer que vous croyez que ce fait est véridique.

1. I am the plaintiff in this action
2. On April 1, Yr. 0, I was walking down a public passageway on the defendant's property. I tripped on uneven pavement and fell, landing on my shoulder and side.
3. As a result of the fall, I dislocated my clavicle on my right side. I was in severe pain for 3 days.
4. As a result of the fall, my sleep was disturbed, and I was anxious and irritable for a period of 3 days, during which I had to take prescription painkillers. My right arm and shoulder were difficult to move, and I found it very difficult to dress myself and perform normal and routine daily tasks for 2 weeks from the time of the fall.
5. I am advised by Doctor Donald Doofus, an orthopedic surgeon at GetWell Hospital in Toronto, and believe, that while the pain will abate, and movement will be normal within a 3-month period, the clavicle will stick up as it cannot be pinned or treated surgically. This injury and its effect on my physical appearance is permanent. Now shown to me and marked Exhibit "A" and attached hereto is a copy of a medical report from Dr. Doofus, dated June 15, Yr. 0.
6. As a result of the fall, my right shoulder is disfigured. I take great pride in my appearance, and dress with style and care. As a result of my injury, a lump now appears on my right shoulder, with the lump disrupting the natural shoulder line of my suits causing them to hang inelegantly. This has caused me great anxiety and unhappiness, as friends and acquaintances have commented on how it spoils my appearance.
7. In addition to pain, suffering and humiliation caused by my fall, I have also suffered special damages as follows:
   a. I have had to purchase prescription painkillers at a cost of $60.00. A true copy of the receipt for this medication is attached to this, my affidavit, marked as Exhibit "B".
   b. As a result of the fall, the suit I was wearing was soiled and had to be dry-cleaned at a cost of $20.00. A true copy of the dry-cleaner's bill is attached to this, my affidavit, marked as Exhibit "C".
8. I swear this affidavit in support of this motion and for no other purpose.

SCR 15.01-15A (September 1, 2010 / *1ᵉʳ septembre 2010*) CSD

Continued on next page / *Suite à la page suivante*

continues....

Illustration 7.4 (continued)

FORM / *FORMULE* 15A   PAGE 4   SC-00-23456-00
Claim No. / *N° de la demande*

AFFIDAVIT IN SUPPORT OF MOTION, continued / *AFFIDAVIT À L'APPUI DE LA MOTION, suite*

If more space is required, attach and initial extra pages. / Si vous avez besoin de plus d'espace, annexez une ou des feuilles supplémentaires et paraphez-les.

Sworn/Affirmed before me at **Toronto**
Déclaré sous serment/Affirmé (Municipality / *municipalité*)
solennellement devant moi à

in **Ontario**
en/à/au (Province, state or country / *province, État ou pays*)

on **July 31, Yr. 0** *Peter Paralegal*
le   Commissioner for taking affidavits
          Commissaire aux affidavits
          (Type or print name below if signature is illegible.)
          (Dactylographiez le nom ou écrivez-le en caractères d'imprimerie ci-dessous si la signature est illisible.)

Henry Fallover
Signature
(This form is to be signed in front of a lawyer, justice of the peace, notary public or commissioner for taking affidavits.)
(La présente formule doit être signée en présence d'un avocat, d'un juge de paix, d'un notaire ou d'un commissaire aux affidavits.)

WARNING: **IT IS AN OFFENCE UNDER THE** *CRIMINAL CODE* **TO KNOWINGLY SWEAR OR AFFIRM A FALSE AFFIDAVIT.**
AVERTISSEMENT : *FAIRE SCIEMMENT UN FAUX AFFIDAVIT CONSTITUE UNE INFRACTION AU* CODE CRIMINEL.

SCR 15.01-15A (September 1, 2010 / *1er septembre 2010*) CSD

continues....

Illustration 7.4 (continued)

EXHIBIT "A"

REPORT OF
DR. DONALD DOOFUS
June 15, Yr. 0

....

EXHIBIT "B"

This is Exhibit "B" to the
Affidavit of Henry Fallover,
Sworn July 31, Yr. 0.

Peter Paralegal
_____
Commissioner for taking Affidavits

PAIN-A-WAY DRUGS
123 Anywhere Place
Toronto, Ontario
M3Y 1C5
Phone: 416-222-1234

RECEIPT

April 2, Yr. 0
Receipt # M5335
Patient: Henry Fallover
           12 Maple Drive
           Toronto, Ontario M2M 1Y7

DESCRIPTION	QUANTITY	PRICE
Prescription Painkiller Drug No. 7	100	$60.00
TOTAL COST:		**$60.00**

EXHIBIT "C"

This is Exhibit "C" to the
Affidavit of Henry Fallover,
Sworn July 31, Yr. 0

Peter Paralegal
_____
Commissioner for taking Affidavits

QUEENSWAY CLEANERS INC.
200 The Queensway
Toronto, Ontario
M8M 1K4
416-222-1555

RECEIPT

April 2, Yr. 0

SERVICE	ITEM	COST
Dry-cleaning	Man's 2 piece suit	$20.00

A NOTE ABOUT AFFIDAVITS

While the subject of notices of motion and affidavits is covered in more detail in Chapter 9, note the following with respect to drafting affidavits:

- Affidavits are drafted like claims: set out the evidence or material facts in concise sentences, in sequentially numbered paragraphs, with one paragraph for each material fact and evidence relevant to it.

- Affidavits are written in the first person, using "I", as in "I observed the defendant getting up from the floor."

- If your affidavit relates something someone told you, state who told you and that you believe what they told you. For example, "I am advised by Henry Hearsay, and believe that the defendant told Henry Hearsay that......"

- If you refer in your affidavit to a document or other evidence, you should briefly describe it and include the date of it, or indicate when it was created, or sworn, or issued. It is a good idea to follow the Superior Court practice and make the document an exhibit to the affidavit. For example, "Ophelia Foot sent me a letter indicating that the engagement was off. Attached to my affidavit and marked Exhibit 'A' is a true copy of a letter to me from Ophelia Foot, dated December 10, Yr. 0." On the copy of the letter attached to the back of the affidavit should be a statement as follows: "This is Exhibit 'A' to the affidavit of Albert Oryx sworn the 12 day of May, Yr. 1"; underneath this statement the commissioner for taking oaths and affidavits signs his or her name. See the sample affidavit in Illustration 7.4 for format.

Alternatively, if you choose to prove damages by filing a notice of motion and supporting affidavit, and the affidavit is inadequate, the judge may order an assessment hearing. It is a good idea to provide as detailed as possible an affidavit, with copies of supporting documentary evidence attached as exhibits to avoid the extra time and cost involved in a hearing to assess damages. Under Rule 11.03(4), if a hearing is to be held, the clerk sets a date and notifies the plaintiff of the date:

> 11.03(4) If an assessment hearing is to be held under clause (2)(b) or (3)(b), the clerk shall fix a date for the hearing and send a notice of hearing to the plaintiff, and the assessment hearing shall proceed as a trial in accordance with rule 17.

The steps to be taken for a hearing for an assessment of damages are as follows:

1. File a Request to Clerk (Form 9B) to note the defendant in default and request a hearing for the assessment of damages.

2. File the Affidavit of Service (Form 8A). If none of the defendants was served in the court's territorial division, you also need to file an Affidavit for Jurisdiction (Form 11A).

3. Pay the required fee for an assessment hearing. At the time of writing, the fee for an infrequent claimant is $100, and for a frequent claimant it is $130.

4. The clerk will set a date for the assessment hearing and send you a notice of hearing.

5. The assessment hearing is conducted like a trial, except that it is a one-sided affair — the defendant is not present and is not entitled to be heard. You will bring the plaintiff with you as a witness to give oral evidence to prove the amount of the claim. You may also summon and call any other person as a witness to give evidence that will help determine the amount of the damages. You will cover, with your questions of each witness, the issues that you would have covered in an affidavit. When you are done examining your witnesses, the judge may question them. Based on the oral evidence and supporting documentary evidence that you may have introduced through your witnesses, the judge will give judgment for an appropriate monetary amount. The plaintiff is not required to prove liability. Under Rule 11.03(5), only the amount of the claim must be proven on an assessment hearing.

   > 11.03(5) On a motion in writing for an assessment of damages or at an assessment hearing, the plaintiff is not required to prove liability against a defendant noted in default, but is required to prove the amount of the claim.

Remember that if there are multiple defendants and at least one has filed a defence, you cannot assess damages against a defaulting defendant, and you must prove damages against that defendant at trial. The same is true if a defendant to a defendant's claim has failed to defend. The matter must proceed to a settlement conference and, if necessary, to trial.

A representation fee, in accordance with Rule 19.04, may be granted on an assessment hearing. The amount granted tends to vary from court to court. The upper limit would generally be 15% of the amount claimed as permitted under the *Courts of Justice Act* for trials; however, a lower fee is generally granted on assessment hearings.

SETTING ASIDE A DEFAULT JUDGMENT

If a plaintiff has obtained a default judgment, the defendant may move to set the judgment aside under Rule 11.06:

> 11.06 The court may set aside the noting in default or default judgment against a party and any step that has been taken to enforce the judgment, on such terms as are just, if the party makes a motion to set aside and the court is satisfied that,
>> (a) the party has a meritorious defence and a reasonable explanation for the default; and
>> (b) the motion is made as soon as is reasonably possible in all the circumstances.

If the judgment is set aside, all enforcement of it will cease. To set aside a default judgment,

- the defendant must file a Notice of Motion and Supporting Affidavit (Form 15A) and pay the required court fee for a motion; and

- the affidavit must show (i) that the defendant moved to set the judgment aside as soon as was reasonably possible in all the circumstances, (ii) that the defendant has an explanation for the default, and (iii) that he or she has a good defence to the claim. You may want to attach a draft defence as an exhibit to the affidavit to show you have a good defence.

The defendant will need to give reasons why there was a default — that he or she wasn't served properly or at all, that the defendant was ill, or on vacation, or away from home for some other reason, and that the claim did not come to his or her attention. The default cannot have been knowing and wilful. However, even if it was wilful, there are circumstances where the defendant may want to change his or her mind because the circumstances since the default judgment was made have changed. It may be the case, for example, that the plaintiff amended a claim that the defendant had defaulted on, and, as a result of the amendment, the defendant would now have a good defence and wish to have the default judgment set aside so that he or she can defend. (An example of the documentation for a motion to set aside a default judgment is set out in Figure 7.1.)

If the court orders the judgment to be set aside, it may be on terms. The plaintiff, for example, paid a court fee to file a default judgment. Those are costs thrown away if the judgment is set aside. The court may allow the plaintiff to recover those costs from the defendant as a condition of being allowed to defend. The defendant may also be required to meet deadlines for filing a defence, and attending a settlement conference and a trial. Generally, if the failure of the defendant to defend in a timely fashion was the defendant's

FIGURE 7.1: Documentation for a Motion to Set Aside a Default Judgment

ONTARIO
Superior Court of Justice
Cour supérieure de justice

Notice of Motion and Supporting Affidavit
Avis de motion et affidavit à l'appui
Form / *Formule* 15A Ont. Reg. No. / *Règl. de l'Ont.* : 258/98

Toronto	SC-00-23456-00
Small Claims Court / *Cour des petites créances de*	Claim No. / *N° de la demande*

47 Sheppard Ave. E., 3rd Fl.
Toronto, ON M2N 5N1

Address / *Adresse*

416-326-3554

Phone number / *Numéro de téléphone*

Plaintiff No. 1 / *Demandeur n° 1* ☐ Additional plaintiff(s) listed on attached Form 1A.
Le ou les demandeurs additionnels sont mentionnés sur la formule 1A ci-jointe.

Last name, or name of company / *Nom de famille ou nom de la compagnie*		
Fallover		
First name / *Premier prénom*	Second name / *Deuxième prénom*	Also known as / *Également connu(e) sous le nom de*
Henry		
Address (street number, apt., unit) / *Adresse (numéro et rue, app., unité)*		
c/o Peter Paralegal, 41 Yonge Street, #410		
City/Town / *Cité/ville*	Province	Phone no. / *N° de téléphone*
Toronto	**ON**	**416-597-0048**
Postal code / *Code postal*		Fax no. / *N° de télécopieur*
M5G 1S1		**416-597-0049**
Representative / *Représentant(e)*		LSUC # / *N° du BHC*
Peter Paralegal		**P02952**
Address (street number, apt., unit) / *Adresse (numéro et rue, app., unité)*		
41 Yonge Street, #410		
City/Town / *Cité/ville*	Province	Phone no. / *N° de téléphone*
Toronto	**ON**	**416-597-0048**
Postal code / *Code postal*		Fax no. / *N° de télécopieur*
M5G 1S1		**416-597-0049**

Defendant No. 1 / *Défendeur n° 1* ☐ Additional defendant(s) listed on attached Form 1A.
Le ou les défendeurs additionnels sont mentionnés sur la formule 1A ci-jointe.

Last name, or name of company / *Nom de famille ou nom de la compagnie*		
Householder		
First name / *Premier prénom*	Second name / *Deuxième prénom*	Also known as / *Également connu(e) sous le nom de*
Morris		
Address (street number, apt., unit) / *Adresse (numéro et rue, app., unité)*		
101 Risk Rd.		
City/Town / *Cité/ville*	Province	Phone no. / *N° de téléphone*
Toronto	**ON**	
Postal code / *Code postal*		Fax no. / *N° de télécopieur*
M6R 1J6		
Representative / *Représentant(e)*		LSUC # / *N° du BHC*
Address (street number, apt., unit) / *Adresse (numéro et rue, app., unité)*		
City/Town / *Cité/ville*	Province	Phone no. / *N° de téléphone*
Postal code / *Code postal*		Fax no. / *N° de télécopieur*

SCR 15.01-15A (September 1, 2010 / *1er septembre 2010*) CSD

continues....

Figure 7.1 (continued)

FORM / *FORMULE* 15A   PAGE 2   SC-00-23456-00
                                                                 Claim No. / *N° de la demande*

THIS COURT WILL HEAR A MOTION on September 14, Yr. 0 _____ , **at** 10:00 a.m. ,
LE TRIBUNAL PRÉCITÉ ENTENDRA UNE MOTION le _____ , *à* _____
                                                              (Time / *heure*)

or as soon as possible after that time, at 47 Sheppard Ave. E., Courtroom 3
ou dès que possible par la suite à/au   (Address of court location and courtroom number / *Adresse du tribunal et numéro de la salle d'audience*)

Complete Part A or Part B below, then complete the affidavit in support of motion on page 3. / *Remplissez la partie A ou la partie B ci-dessous. Remplissez ensuite l'affidavit à l'appui de la motion à la page 3.*

A.   This motion will be made in person by Morris Householder ,
       La motion sera présentée en personne par :   (Name of party / *Nom de la partie*)
       for the following order : / *en vue d'obtenir l'ordonnance suivante :*

☐   the court's permission to extend time to (Specify)
    l'autorisation du tribunal de proroger le délai pour *(Précisez)*

☒   set aside default judgment and noting in default.
    l'annulation du jugement par défaut et la constatation du défaut.

☐   set aside noting in default.
    l'annulation de la constatation du défaut.

☒   permission to file a Defence.
    l'autorisation de déposer une défense.

☐   permission to file a Defendant's Claim.
    l'autorisation de déposer une demande du défendeur.

☐   set aside order dismissing claim as abandoned.
    l'annulation d'une demande pour cause de renonciation

☐   terminate garnishment and/or withdraw writ(s).
    la mainlevée de la saisie-arrêt ou le retrait d'un ou de plusieurs brefs, ou les deux.

☐   Other:
    Autre :

☐   ADDITIONAL PAGES ARE ATTACHED BECAUSE MORE ROOM WAS NEEDED.
    DES FEUILLES SUPPLÉMENTAIRES SONT ANNEXÉES EN RAISON DU MANQUE D'ESPACE.

☒   DOCUMENTS ARE ATTACHED.
    PIÈCES JOINTES.

NOTE:	**IF YOU FAIL TO ATTEND AN IN-PERSON MOTION,** an order may be made against you, with costs, in your absence. If you want to attend the motion by telephone or video conference, complete and file a Request for Telephone or Video Conference (Form 1B). If the court permits it, the clerk will make the necessary arrangements and notify the parties [R. 1.07(5)].
REMARQUE :	*SI VOUS NE VOUS PRÉSENTEZ PAS EN PERSONNE À L'AUDITION DE LA MOTION,* une *ordonnance peut être rendue contre vous en votre absence, avec dépens. Si vous voulez assister à l'audition de la motion par conférence téléphonique ou vidéoconférence, remplissez et déposez la Demande de conférence téléphonique ou vidéoconférence (formule 1B). Si le tribunal l'autorise, le greffier prendra les dispositions nécessaires et en avisera les parties [par. 1.07 (5)].*

SCR 15.01-15A (September 1, 2010 / *1ᵉʳ septembre 2010*) CSD   Continued on next page / *Suite à la page suivante*

continues....

Figure 7.1 (continued)

FORM / *FORMULE* 15A   PAGE 3   SC-00-23456-00
                                                                                     Claim No. / *N° de la demande*

B. This motion in writing for an assessment of damages is made by
   La présente motion par écrit en vue d'une évaluation des dommages-intérêts est présentée par

_____
                              (Name of plaintiff / *Nom du demandeur/de la demanderesse*)

who asks the court for an order assessing damages against
qui demande au tribunal de rendre une ordonnance d'évaluation des dommages-intérêts contre

_____
                         (Name of defendant(s) / *Nom du/de la/des défendeur(s)/défenderesse(s)*)

who have/has been noted in default.
qui a/ont été constaté(e)(s) en défaut.

AFFIDAVIT IN SUPPORT OF MOTION / *AFFIDAVIT À L'APPUI DE LA MOTION*

My name is Morris Householder
Je m'appelle   (Full name / *Nom et prénoms*)

I live in Toronto, Ontario
J'habite à   (Municipality & province / *Municipalité et province*)

I swear/affirm that the following is true:
Je déclare sous serment/j'affirme solennellement que les renseignements suivants sont
véridiques :

Set out the facts in numbered paragraphs. If you learned a fact from someone else, you must give that person's name and state that you believe that fact to be true.
Indiquez les faits sous forme de dispositions numérotées. Si vous avez pris connaissance d'un fait par l'entremise d'une autre personne, vous devez indiquer le nom de cette personne et déclarer que vous croyez que ce fait est véridique.

1. I am the defendant in this proceeding.
2. The plaintiff obtained a default judgment on Sept. 10, Yr. 0.
3. From April 2, Yr. 0, until Sept. 11, Yr. 0, I was in Europe on business. Now shown to me and attached hereto and marked Exhibit "A" to my affidavit is a "true copy" of my Air Canada return ticket showing the dates of my departure and return to Canada.
4. On my return to Canada on Sept. 11, Yr. 0, I found a copy of the claim and a copy of the default judgment that had been served by courier.
5. Upon learning of the default judgment I moved promptly on Sept. 12, Yr. 0, to set it aside.
6. I have a good defence to the plaintiff's claim.
7. With respect to the plaintiff's claim, I observed the plaintiff walking on my property moments before he fell. He was staggering, and walking with difficulty. After he fell, I went to assist him. When I got close to him I could smell alcohol on his breath and he was clearly intoxicated.
8. The plaintiff in these circumstances was wholly responsible for his own injuries as a result of his intoxication.

SCR 15.01-15A (September 1, 2010 / *1ᵉʳ septembre 2010*) CSD   Continued on next page / *Suite à la page suivante*

continues....

Figure 7.1 (continued)

FORM / *FORMULE* 15A   PAGE 4   SC-00-23456-00
Claim No. / *N° de la demande*

AFFIDAVIT IN SUPPORT OF MOTION, continued / *AFFIDAVIT À L'APPUI DE LA MOTION, suite*

If more space is required, attach and initial extra pages. / Si vous avez besoin de plus d'espace, annexez une ou des feuilles supplémentaires et paraphez-les.

Sworn/Affirmed before me at **Toronto**
Déclaré sous serment/Affirmé   (Municipality / *municipalité*)
solennellement devant moi à

in **Ontario**
en/à/au   (Province, state or country / *province, État ou pays*)

on **Sept. 12, Yr. 0**   "Case Commissioner"
le   Commissioner for taking affidavits
Commissaire aux affidavits
(Type or print name below if signature is illegible.)
(Dactylographiez le nom ou écrivez-le en caractères d'imprimerie ci-dessous si la signature est illisible.)

Morris Householder
Signature

(This form is to be signed in front of a lawyer, justice of the peace, notary public or commissioner for taking affidavits.)
(La présente formule doit être signée en présence d'un avocat, d'un juge de paix, d'un notaire ou d'un commissaire aux affidavits.)

WARNING: **IT IS AN OFFENCE UNDER THE** *CRIMINAL CODE* **TO KNOWINGLY SWEAR OR AFFIRM A FALSE AFFIDAVIT.**
AVERTISSEMENT :   *FAIRE SCIEMMENT UN FAUX AFFIDAVIT CONSTITUE UNE INFRACTION AU CODE CRIMINEL.*

SCR 15.01-15A (September 1, 2010 / *1ᵉʳ septembre 2010*) CSD

fault, the defendant may expect to have to pay some of the plaintiff's costs in obtaining the default judgment in the first place. In some cases the court may order the defendant to pay into court the sum claimed by the plaintiff before a defence can be filed.

CHAPTER SUMMARY

In this chapter, we set out the consequences for a defendant who has not defended an action and who has been noted in default. We then noted the circumstances in which a plaintiff may move for a default judgment against the defendant and when, depending on the number of defendants and the nature of the claim, the plaintiff may not. We noted that the clerk might sign default judgment if the damages are liquidated. But if the damages are unliquidated, they must be assessed. In some cases, unliquidated damages may be assessed on the basis of affidavit evidence. However, if a judge orders it, or a plaintiff chooses, damages will be assessed after a hearing by a judge. Last, we looked at the circumstances in which a court will set aside a default judgment, and outlined the procedures that must be followed to do this.

REVIEW QUESTIONS

1. How may you obtain a default judgment on a liquidated claim?

2. What do you do to obtain a default judgment on an unliquidated claim?

3. What are liquidated damages?

4. What are unliquidated damages?

5. Indicate whether the types of damages listed below are likely to be liquidated or unliquidated:

   (a) Loss of quality and enjoyment of life due to a physical injury that makes it difficult for the plaintiff to sit for more than 10 minutes

   (b) Damage to your automobile, where you have paid for repairs and have the receipt for the cost of repairs

   (c) Loss of the use of your lawnmower due to Henry's borrowing it and refusing to return it

   (d) Same situation as in (c), above, except that you rented a replacement lawnmower and have a receipt for the rental costs

   (e) Demand for the return of a deposit where the other party breached a contract

6. Azrat sued Xeno for a debt. Xeno is 16 and did not defend the action. Can Azrat get the clerk to sign a default judgment?

7. Azrat sued three people who assaulted her. One of the three has defaulted on a defence, but the others have filed defences. Can Azrat obtain a default judgment against the defaulter?

8. What must a defendant do to set aside a default judgment?

DISCUSSION QUESTIONS/CASE STUDIES

1. Mucous von Mendacious (28 Squash Court, Elsewhere ON K2F 1A2) had an account with Brutus Building Supplies Ltd. (13 Main Rd., Elsewhere, ON K2R 1A3).

   Mucous had an account due on February 28, Yr. 0. On April 10, Yr. 0 Brutus sued for the unpaid balance of $4,000, with interest thereon as agreed to by contract of 18% per annum from and after March 1, Yr. 0. Mucous has not defended the claim. Brutus wishes to obtain a default judgment.

Assume Mucous was served within the court's territorial boundaries. Prepare the necessary documents for Brutus to obtain a default judgment. The court is located at 29 Main Rd., Elsewhere, ON K2R 1A3, telephone 809-456-7890. Documents are prepared and filed on the same day, May 20, Yr. 0. For costs you get the maximum for service, and you are an infrequent claimant. You did not get compensation for the work of filing documents.

2. Contractile C. Vacuole, of 26 Handball Court, Pigsear, ON L9A 2A2, walked into Harry's Inconvenience Store Ltd. (41 Calamity Way, Pigsnout, ON L4A 2R5) on January 15, Yr. 0. As Vacuole walked in, he slipped on some gooey stuff on the floor just inside the door. Vacuole fell to the ground, striking his right arm, spraining it, and wrenching his back, causing great pain. He was able to get up by himself and go home. He was in terrible pain in both his arm and his back, and was unable to sleep that night. He saw the doctor, Dr. Killjoy, on January 16, Yr. 0. He was X-rayed, but there were no broken bones. The doctor gave him a prescription for Killpain at a cost of $55.00 and wrote a medical report dated February 1, Yr. 0. The prescription dulled the pain, and Vacuole could sleep, but he was so dopey from the drugs that he was off work for four days. His normal daily earnings are $96.00 per day ($12.00 × 8 hours per day). He had a letter from his employer attesting to the wage loss attached to the claim. His arm was stiff for about three weeks, with limited mobility preventing him from curling on three successive Saturdays, an activity he enjoyed. He sued for general damages of $4,000 and special damages. The defendant did not defend, and on February 15, Vacuole decided to obtain a default judgment.

Draft the necessary documents to assess damages. Assume the defendant was served within the territorial boundaries of the court. The court office is at 21 Law Way, Pigsnout, ON, telephone 231-456-7890. Default documents are prepared and filed on March 15, Yr. 0.

Chapter 8

Preparing Defences and Defendant's Claims

LEARNING OBJECTIVES

⇨ Understand response options for a defence and a defendant's claim

⇨ Know how to organize facts and law to prepare the defence and a defendant's claim

⇨ Be aware of drafting conventions and practices for accurate and well-crafted defences and defendant's claims

⇨ Know how to accurately and completely prepare a defence and a defendant's claim

⇨ Know the procedure for filing a defence and issuing a defendant's claim

INTRODUCTION

In this chapter we consider the responses and options open to a defendant when served with a claim. The defendant, in addition to making a substantive defence, has some other options:

- Admitting liability while disputing the amount owing
- Acknowledging the debt, but asking to pay in instalments
- Making claims against the plaintiff with a defendant's claim
- Making claims against other defendants, and third parties in some circumstances, using a defendant's claim

Attention is paid here to approaches used to organize and draft defence documents that are accurate and persuasive when a defendant elects to use these options.

DEFENCES

When a plaintiff serves a claim, the defendant is required to file a defence within 20 days of being served. The defence gives the defendant the opportunity to present his or her version of the dispute, reply to allegations made by the plaintiff, and set out facts and defences consistent with the defendant's theory of the case.

Defence Options

A defendant has some options open to him or her when sued. The defendant may do nothing. If he or she has no defence, and perhaps no assets to seize or income to garnish to satisfy a judgment, there may be little point wasting time and effort on defending. However, if the defendant does nothing, the plaintiff will move, under Rule 11, to obtain default judgment. At the other extreme the defendant can dispute the entire claim, both on the issues of liability and damages. The defendant can also admit the entire claim, in which case he or she can either pay the admitted amount or ask to make a proposal to pay the damages by instalments. The defendant may also admit part of the claim and make a payment proposal with respect to the part admitted, but deny the rest of the claim and defend. Last, in addition to defending, the defendant may also make a claim against the plaintiff or against another defendant or another person not a party to the action (sometimes referred to as a **third party**, who the defendant thinks is responsible for the plaintiff's damages).

Organizing and Preparing a Defence

Once the claim has been received, review it with the defendant and obtain his or her version of the facts. Determine which facts in the claim you agree with, which you deny, and which you have no knowledge of. Review the client's documents to see which should be attached to and filed with the defence. Check with the client to see if there are other documents that may be relevant to the case after reading the claim. Review both liability and damage issues with the client. There may be no dispute that there is something owing, but rather a dispute about how much the damages should be or how the damages were computed.

Check jurisdictional issues. Review the claim to see that what the plaintiff is claiming is within the court's jurisdiction over subject matter, remedy, and amount. If the claim is not within the court's jurisdiction, then that is a useful defence in addition to any other substantive defence the defendant may have. Note that you can advance different defences together or in the alternative. Also, see if you were sued in the right court under Rule 6. If you have been sued in the wrong court, that fact should be set out in the defence. This won't cause the action to be dismissed, but it will cause the case and file to be moved to the right court, and the cost and delay to the plaintiff may give you some bargaining room to discuss settlement.

Has the claim been made on time, or has the limitation period expired? If the limitation period expired, that fact should be set out in the defence as that defence is a complete bar to the plaintiff's claim and will result in the dismissal of the action.

Review your theory of the case. Does it have to be revised in light of the facts in the plaintiff's claim? For example, your original theory on behalf of Ophelia Foot may have been that the engagement ring was an unconditional gift from Albert Oryx and that Albert knew this to be the case; but if it now appears that he never thought it was an unconditional gift, Ophelia will have to revise her theory of the case and marshal and prove facts to support the revised theory. Her new theory might be that the matter was never clearly discussed, but that there was no explicit requirement that she return the ring if she broke up with Albert. This would replace the theory that it was clearly an unconditional gift.

Drafting and Filing a Defence

The following matters should be considered as part of drafting and filing a defence.

Time for Filing a Defence

The procedure governing defences, in general, is set out in Rules 9.01 and 9.02. Rule 9.01 sets out the time for filing a defence:

> 9.01(1) A defendant who wishes to dispute a plaintiff's claim shall file a defence (Form 9A), together with a copy for each of the other parties with the clerk within 20 days of being served with the claim.
>
> (2) On receiving the defence, the clerk shall retain the original in the court file and shall serve a copy in accordance with subrule 8.01(3) on each of the other parties.

Once the claim has been served on a defendant, he or she has 20 days from the date of service to file a defence with the clerk. Remember that the day the defendant receives the claim is not necessarily the deemed date of service. The deemed date the claim was served may be later than the date the claim was actually received, giving a defendant more time. For example, if an alternative to personal service was carried out under Rule 8.03(2), which covers service by leaving a copy with an adult member of the household, followed by mailing or sending by courier a copy to the individual at his or her residence. In such a situation, subrule (4) says that service is effective the fifth day after the document is mailed or verified by a courier that it was delivered. Therefore, the defendant would have the usual 20 days to respond, plus an additional 5 days. In the event that a defendant needs more time to respond, it is always possible to ask for the time to be extended under Rule 3.02(1) or (2), by a motion, or with the consent of the plaintiff.

> *Computation*
> 3.01 If these rules or an order of the court prescribe a period of time for the taking of a step in a proceeding, the time shall be counted by excluding the first day and including the last day of the period; if the last day of the period of time falls on a holiday, the period ends on the next day that is not a holiday.

> *Powers of Court*
> 3.02(1) The court may lengthen or shorten any time prescribed by these rules or an order, on such terms as are just.

> *Consent*
> (2) A time prescribed by these rules for serving or filing a document may be lengthened or shortened by filing the consent of the parties.

What Happens If the Parties Do Not Move the Case Forward? Dismissal by Clerk of Abandoned Cases

Both parties should keep Rule 11.1.01 in mind and meet all filing deadlines in good time. The Rule provides that the clerk shall make an order dismissing an action as abandoned if no defence has been filed and more than 180 days have passed since the claim was issued. The clerk will give 45 days' notice to the plaintiff that the action will be dismissed as abandoned. For the defendant, if more than 150 days have passed since the date the first defence was filed and a settlement conference has been completed, the clerk shall make an order dismissing an action as abandoned. The clerk will give 45 days' notice to all parties in the action that the action will be dismissed.

Dismissal — Undefended Actions

11.1.01(1) The clerk shall make an order dismissing an action as abandoned if the following conditions are satisfied, unless the court orders otherwise:

1. More than 180 days have passed since the date the claim was issued or an order was made extending the time for service of the claim under subrule 8.01(2).
2. No defence has been filed.
3. The action has not been disposed of by order and has not been set down for trial.
4. The clerk has given 45 days notice to the plaintiff that the action will be dismissed as abandoned.

Dismissal — Defended Actions

(2) The clerk shall make an order dismissing an action as abandoned if the following conditions are satisfied, unless the court orders otherwise:

1. More than 150 days have passed since the date the first defence was filed.
2. All settlement conferences required under Rule 13 have been held.
3. The action has not been disposed of by order and has not been set down for trial.
4. The clerk has given 45 days notice to all parties to the action that the action will be dismissed as abandoned.

Transition

(3) If an action was started before July 1, 2006, the following applies:

1. The action or a step in the action shall be carried on under these rules on or after July 1, 2006.
2. Despite paragraph 1, if a step in the action is taken on or after July 1, 2006, the timetable set out in subrules (1) and (2) shall apply as if the action started on the date on which the step was taken.

Same

(4) If an action was commenced before July 1, 2006 and no step is taken in the action on or after that date, the clerk may make an order dismissing it as abandoned if,

(a) where an action is undefended, more than two years have passed since the date the claim was issued and the conditions set out in paragraphs 2, 3 and 4 of subrule (1) are satisfied; or

(b) more than two years have passed since the date the first defence was filed and the conditions set out in paragraphs 3 and 4 of subrule (2) are satisfied.

Exception Where Terms of Settlement Signed

(5) Subrules (1), (2) and (4) do not apply if terms of settlement (Form 14D) signed by all parties have been filed.

Exception Where Admission of Liability

(6) Subrule (2) and clause (4)(b) do not apply if the defence contains an admission of liability for the plaintiff's claim and a proposal of terms of payment under subrule 9.03(1).

Service of Orders

(7) The clerk shall serve a copy of an order made under subrule (1) or clause (4)(a) on the plaintiff and a copy of an order made under subrule (2) or clause (4)(b) on all parties to the action.

Contents of the Defence

Rule 9.02(1) sets out the content requirements for a defence, and conveniently, these requirements are also detailed in the Defence form (Form 9A).

9.02(1) The following requirements apply to the defence:

1. It shall contain the following information:
   i. The reasons why the defendant disputes the plaintiff's claim, expressed in concise non-technical language with a reasonable amount of detail.
   ii. If the defendant is self-represented, the defendant's name, address and telephone number, and fax number if any.
   iii. If the defendant is represented by a lawyer or agent, that person's name, address and telephone number, and fax number if any, and Law Society of Upper Canada registration number if any.

2. If the defence is based in whole or in part on a document, a copy of the document shall be attached to each copy of the defence, unless it is unavailable, in which case the defence shall state the reason why the document is not attached.

Illustrations 8.1 and 8.2 show two sample Defence forms (Form 9A): one for a non-debt action (*Oryx v. Foot*), and one for a debt action (*Video Supplies Inc. v. Gary's Great Games Ltd.*, in Example 3.1

ILLUSTRATION 8.1: Sample Defence Form (Form 9A) for a Non-debt Action

ONTARIO
Superior Court of Justice
Cour supérieure de justice

Defence / *Défense*
Form / *Formule* 9A Ont. Reg. No. / *Règl. de l'Ont.* : 258/98

Toronto
Small Claims Court / *Cour des petites créances de*

**47 Sheppard Ave. E., 3rd Fl.
Toronto, ON M2N 5N1**

Address / *Adresse*

416-326-3554
Phone number / *Numéro de téléphone*

SC-00-47669-00
Claim No. / *N° de la demande*

Plaintiff No. 1 / *Demandeur n° 1* ☐ Additional plaintiff(s) listed on attached Form 1A. / *Le ou les demandeurs additionnels sont mentionnés sur la formule 1A ci-jointe.*   ☐ Under 18 years of age. / *Moins de 18 ans.*

Last name, or name of company / *Nom de famille ou nom de la compagnie*		
Oryx		
First name / *Premier prénom* **Albert**	Second name / *Deuxième prénom*	Also known as / *Également connu(e) sous le nom de*
Address (street number, apt., unit) / *Adresse (numéro et rue, app., unité)* **c/o Peter Paralegal, 41 Yonge Street, #410**		
City/Town / *Cité/ville* **Toronto**	Province **ON**	Phone no. / *N° de téléphone* **416-597-0048**
Postal code / *Code postal* **M5G 1S1**		Fax no. / *N° de télécopieur* **416-597-0049**
Representative / *Représentant(e)* **Peter Paralegal**		LSUC # / *N° du BHC* **P02952**
Address (street number, apt., unit) / *Adresse (numéro et rue, app., unité)* **41 Yonge Street, #410**		
City/Town / *Cité/ville* **Toronto**	Province **ON**	Phone no. / *N° de téléphone* **416-597-0048**
Postal code / *Code postal* **M5G 1S1**		Fax no. / *N° de télécopieur* **416-597-0049**

Defendant No. 1 / *Défendeur n° 1* ☐ Additional defendant(s) listed on attached Form 1A. / *Le ou les défendeurs additionnels sont mentionnés sur la formule 1A ci-jointe.*   ☐ Under 18 years of age. / *Moins de 18 ans.*

Last name, or name of company / *Nom de famille ou nom de la compagnie*		
Foot		
First name / *Premier prénom* **Ophelia**	Second name / *Deuxième prénom*	Also known as / *Également connu(e) sous le nom de*
Address (street number, apt., unit) / *Adresse (numéro et rue, app., unité)* **c/o Digbert Fightback, 60 My Way**		
City/Town / *Cité/ville* **Toronto**	Province **ON**	Phone no. / *N° de téléphone* **416-491-5041**
Postal code / *Code postal* **M6R 8P1**		Fax no. / *N° de télécopieur* **416-491-5042**
Representative / *Représentant(e)* **Digbert Fightback**		LSUC # / *N° du BHC* **P05427**
Address (street number, apt., unit) / *Adresse (numéro et rue, app., unité)* **60 My Way**		
City/Town / *Cité/ville* **Toronto**	Province **ON**	Phone no. / *N° de téléphone* **416-491-5041**
Postal code / *Code postal* **M6R 8P1**		Fax no. / *N° de télécopieur* **416-491-5042**

SCR 9.01-10.03-9A (September 1, 2010 / *1er septembre 2010*) CSD

continues....

Illustration 8.1 (continued)

FORM / *FORMULE* 9A   PAGE 2   SC-00-47669-00

Claim No. / *N° de la demande*

THIS DEFENCE IS BEING FILED ON BEHALF OF: (Name(s) of defendant(s))
LA PRÉSENTE DÉFENSE EST DÉPOSÉE AU NOM DE : (Nom du/de la ou des défendeur(s)/défenderesse(s))

Ophelia Foot

and I/we: (Check as many as apply)
et je/nous : (Cochez la ou les cases qui s'appliquent)

☒ Dispute the claim made against me/us.
    conteste/contestons la demande présentée contre moi/nous.

☐ Admit the full claim and propose the following terms of payment:
    reconnais/reconnaissons être redevable(s) de la totalité de la demande et propose/proposons les modalités de paiement suivantes :

$ _____ per _____ commencing _____ .
(Amount / Montant) $ par   (Week/month / semaine/mois)   à compter du

☐ Admit part of the claim in the amount of $ _____ and propose the following terms of payment:
    reconnais/reconnaissons être redevable(s) (Amount / Montant) *$ et propose/proposons les modalités de d'une partie de la demande, soit   paiement suivantes :*

$ _____ per _____ commencing _____ .
(Amount / Montant) $ par   (Week/month / semaine/mois)   à compter du

REASONS FOR DISPUTING THE CLAIM AND DETAILS:
MOTIFS DE CONTESTATION DE LA DEMANDE ET PRÉCISIONS :

Explain what happened, including where and when. Explain why you do not agree with the claim made against you.
Expliquez ce qui s'est passé, en précisant où et quand. Expliquez pourquoi vous contestez la demande présentée contre vous.

If you are relying on any documents, you **MUST** attach copies to the Defence. If evidence is lost or unavailable, you **MUST** explain why it is not attached.
*Si vous vous appuyez sur des documents, vous **DEVEZ** en annexer des copies à la défense. Si une preuve est perdue ou n'est pas disponible, vous **DEVEZ** expliquer pourquoi elle n'est pas annexée.*

What happened?	The parties' engagement ended.
Where?	The engagement and the break-up took place in Toronto , Ontario.
When?	The engagement ended on December 10, Yr. 0. On that date, the plaintiff requested
Que s'est-il	the engagement ring; however, the defendant informed the plaintiff that as it was an
passé?	unconditional gift, she would be keeping the ring.
Où?	
Quand?	

SCR 9.01-10.03-9A (September 1, 2010 / *1er septembre 2010*) CSD   **Continued on next page / *Suite à la page suivante***

continues....

Illustration 8.1 (continued)

FORM / *FORMULE* 9A   PAGE 3   SC-00-47669-00
....
                                                              Claim No. / *N° de la demande*

Why I/we disagree   1. The defendant acknowledges she was engaged to the plaintiff and that she
with all or part of   received an engagement ring from him.
the claim: /   2. She has no knowledge of the value of the ring.
Je conteste/Nous   3. Due to differences between them, the defendant ended the engagement.
contestons la   4. At all relevant times the plaintiff told the defendant that the ring was "hers forever"
totalité ou une   and that it was an unconditional gift.
partie de la   5. The defendant at no time was under any duty to return the ring or pay its value to
demande pour les   the plaintiff.
motifs suivants :   6. The defendant asks that the claim be dismissed with costs.

☐   ADDITIONAL PAGES ARE ATTACHED BECAUSE MORE ROOM WAS NEEDED.
    DES FEUILLES SUPPLÉMENTAIRES SONT ANNEXÉES EN RAISON DU MANQUE D'ESPACE.

Prepared on: April 7, Yr. 1   *Digbert Fightback*
Fait le : ....
                                                           (Signature of defendant or representative /
                                                  Signature du défendeur/de la défenderesse ou du/de la représentant(e))

| NOTE: | Within seven (7) calendar days of changing your address for service, notify the court and all other parties in writing. |
| *REMARQUE :* | *Dans les sept (7) jours civils qui suivent tout changement de votre adresse aux fins de signification, veuillez en aviser par écrit le tribunal et les autres parties.* |

| CAUTION TO PLAINTIFF(S): | If this Defence contains a proposal of terms of payment, you are deemed to have accepted the terms **unless** you file with the clerk and serve on the defendant(s) a Request to Clerk (Form 9B) for a terms of payment hearing **WITHIN TWENTY (20) CALENDAR DAYS** of service of this Defence [R. 9.03(3)]. |
| *AVERTISSEMENT AU(X) DEMANDEUR(S) :* | *Si la présente défense comprend une proposition à l'égard des modalités de paiement, vous êtes réputé(e)(s) les avoir acceptées, **sauf** si vous déposez auprès du greffier et signifiez au(x) défendeur(s) une demande au greffier (formule 9B) pour la tenue d'une audience relative aux modalités de paiement **DANS LES VINGT (20) JOURS CIVILS** de la signification de la présente défense [par. 9.03 (3)].* |

SCR 9.01-10.03-9A (September 1, 2010 / *1ᵉʳ septembre 2010*) CSD

ILLUSTRATION 8.2: Sample Defence Form (Form 9A) for a Debt Action

ONTARIO

Superior Court of Justice
Cour supérieure de justice

Defence / *Défense*
Form / *Formule* 9A Ont. Reg. No. / *Règl. de l'Ont.* : 258/98

Toronto
Small Claims Court / *Cour des petites créances de*

SC-00-31547-00
Claim No. / *N° de la demande*

47 Sheppard Ave. E., 3rd Fl.
Toronto, ON M2N 5N1

Address / *Adresse*

416-326-3554
Phone number / *Numéro de téléphone*

Plaintiff No. 1 / *Demandeur n° 1* ☐ Additional plaintiff(s) listed on attached Form 1A. / *Le ou les demandeurs additionnels sont mentionnés sur la formule 1A ci-jointe.* ☐ Under 18 years of age. / *Moins de 18 ans.*

Last name, or name of company / *Nom de famille ou nom de la compagnie*		
Video Supplies Inc.		
First name / *Premier prénom*	Second name / *Deuxième prénom*	Also known as / *Également connu(e) sous le nom de*
Address (street number, apt., unit) / *Adresse (numéro et rue, app., unité)*		
c/o Peter Paralegal, 41 Yonge Street, #410		
City/Town / *Cité/ville*	Province	Phone no. / *N° de téléphone*
Toronto	**ON**	**416-597-0048**
Postal code / *Code postal*		Fax no. / *N° de télécopieur*
M5G 1S1		**416-597-0049**
Representative / *Représentant(e)*		LSUC # / *N° du BHC*
Peter Paralegal		**P02952**
Address (street number, apt., unit) / *Adresse (numéro et rue, app., unité)*		
41 Yonge Street, #410		
City/Town / *Cité/ville*	Province	Phone no. / *N° de téléphone*
Toronto	**ON**	**416-597-0048**
Postal code / *Code postal*		Fax no. / *N° de télécopieur*
M5G 1S1		**416-597-0049**

Defendant No. 1 / *Défendeur n° 1* ☐ Additional defendant(s) listed on attached Form 1A. / *Le ou les défendeurs additionnels sont mentionnés sur la formule 1A ci-jointe.* ☐ Under 18 years of age. / *Moins de 18 ans.*

Last name, or name of company / *Nom de famille ou nom de la compagnie*		
Gary's Great Games Ltd.		
First name / *Premier prénom*	Second name / *Deuxième prénom*	Also known as / *Également connu(e) sous le nom de*
Address (street number, apt., unit) / *Adresse (numéro et rue, app., unité)*		
c/o I.M. Power, 185 Yonge Street		
City/Town / *Cité/ville*	Province	Phone no. / *N° de téléphone*
Toronto	**ON**	**416-128-4567**
Postal code / *Code postal*		Fax no. / *N° de télécopieur*
M6C 1L3		
Representative / *Représentant(e)*		LSUC # / *N° du BHC*
I.M. Power		**P28453**
Address (street number, apt., unit) / *Adresse (numéro et rue, app., unité)*		
186 Yonge Street		
City/Town / *Cité/ville*	Province	Phone no. / *N° de téléphone*
Toronto	**ON**	**416-128-4567**
Postal code / *Code postal*		Fax no. / *N° de télécopieur*
M6C 1L3		

SCR 9.01-10.03-9A (September 1, 2010 / *1er septembre 2010*) CSD

continues....

Illustration 8.2 (continued)

FORM / *FORMULE* 9A   PAGE 2   SC-00-31547-00
....
Claim No. / *N° de la demande*

THIS DEFENCE IS BEING FILED ON BEHALF OF: (Name(s) of defendant(s))
LA PRÉSENTE DÉFENSE EST DÉPOSÉE AU NOM DE : (Nom du/de la ou des défendeur(s)/défenderesse(s))

Gary's Great Games Ltd.

and I/we: (Check as many as apply)
et je/nous : (Cochez la ou les cases qui s'appliquent)

☒ Dispute the claim made against me/us.
conteste/contestons la demande présentée contre moi/nous.

☐ Admit the full claim and propose the following terms of payment:
reconnais/reconnaissons être redevable(s) de la totalité de la demande et propose/proposons les modalités de paiement suivantes :

$ .... per .... commencing ....
(Amount / Montant) $ par   (Week/month / semaine/mois)   à compter du

☐ Admit part of the claim in the amount of $ .... and propose the following terms of payment:
reconnais/reconnaissons être redevable(s)   (Amount / Montant)   *$ et propose/proposons les modalités de paiement suivantes :*
d'une partie de la demande, soit

$ .... per .... commencing ....
(Amount / Montant) $ par   (Week/month / semaine/mois)   à compter du

REASONS FOR DISPUTING THE CLAIM AND DETAILS:
MOTIFS DE CONTESTATION DE LA DEMANDE ET PRÉCISIONS :

Explain what happened, including where and when. Explain why you do not agree with the claim made against you.
Expliquez ce qui s'est passé, en précisant où et quand. Expliquez pourquoi vous contestez la demande présentée contre vous.

If you are relying on any documents, you **MUST** attach copies to the Defence. If evidence is lost or unavailable, you **MUST** explain why it is not attached.
*Si vous vous appuyez sur des documents, vous **DEVEZ** en annexer des copies à la défense. Si une preuve est perdue ou n'est pas disponible, vous **DEVEZ** expliquer pourquoi elle n'est pas annexée.*

What happened?   The defendant received a late delivery of defective and unusable PlayStations.
Where?   The order for goods was made in Toronto, Ontario.
When?   The order was made on September 11, Yr. 0. The goods were delivered late
Que s'est-il   and were defective.
passé?
Où?
Quand?

SCR 9.01-10.03-9A (September 1, 2010 / *1er septembre 2010*) CSD   Continued on next page / *Suite à la page suivante*

continues....

Illustration 8.2 (continued)

FORM / *FORMULE* 9A   PAGE 3   SC-00-31547-00
                                                                Claim No. / *N° de la demande*

Why I/we disagree 1. The defendant acknowledges the order for the PlayStations as described in the
with all or part of claim.
the claim: / 2. The goods were not delivered on Sept. 14, Yr. 0.
Je conteste/Nous 3. The PlayStations delivered by the plaintiff on September 18, Yr. 0, were defective
contestons la and unusable. The images were unstable and jumped on the screen.
totalité ou une 4. As a result, the PlayStations were unusable.
partie de la 5. By delivering goods which were defective and by delivering them after the date
demande pour les they were promised for, the plaintiff breached its contract with the defendant.
motifs suivants : 6. As a result, the defendant owes no money to the plaintiff.
7. The defendant asks that the claim be dismissed with costs.

☐ ADDITIONAL PAGES ARE ATTACHED BECAUSE MORE ROOM WAS NEEDED.
DES FEUILLES SUPPLÉMENTAIRES SONT ANNEXÉES EN RAISON DU MANQUE D'ESPACE.

Prepared on: **November 15, Yr. 0**   *Gary Gameman*
Fait le :   (Signature of defendant or representative /
                                                       Signature du défendeur/de la défenderesse ou du/de la représentant(e))

| NOTE: | Within seven (7) calendar days of changing your address for service, notify the court and all other parties in writing. |
| REMARQUE : | *Dans les sept (7) jours civils qui suivent tout changement de votre adresse aux fins de signification, veuillez en aviser par écrit le tribunal et les autres parties.* |

| CAUTION TO PLAINTIFF(S): | If this Defence contains a proposal of terms of payment, you are deemed to have accepted the terms **unless** you file with the clerk and serve on the defendant(s) a Request to Clerk (Form 9B) for a terms of payment hearing **WITHIN TWENTY (20) CALENDAR DAYS** of service of this Defence [R. 9.03(3)]. |
| AVERTISSEMENT AU(X) DEMANDEUR(S) : | *Si la présente défense comprend une proposition à l'égard des modalités de paiement, vous êtes réputé(e)(s) les avoir acceptées, **sauf** si vous déposez auprès du greffier et signifiez au(x) défendeur(s) une demande au greffier (formule 9B) pour la tenue d'une audience relative aux modalités de paiement **DANS LES VINGT (20) JOURS CIVILS** de la signification de la présente défense [par. 9.03 (3)].* |

SCR 9.01-10.03-9A (September 1, 2010 / *1er septembre 2010)* CSD

on page 90). As demonstrated in both illustrations, the defence form must contain the following information:

- **Names of parties:** On Page 1, where the parties are named and identified, you should include the plaintiff's contact information or their representative's contact information as set out in the Claim. For the defendant's information, the defendant should provide accurate contact information for the defendant if the defendant is self-represented, and for the representative if the defendant has a lawyer or paralegal. If the plaintiff recorded the name of the defendant incorrectly, a defendant may simply plead that the defendant as named has no liability. In practical terms, both parties may know the right person has been sued, but technically, the different spellings are interpreted to mean that they are different people. It is then up to the plaintiff to bring a motion to correct the misnomer by substituting the name of the correct party. Remember that "Ophelia Foot" and "Ofelia Foote" are, in law, two different persons, even though in practical terms both parties know who the plaintiff intends to sue. If a plaintiff gets a judgment against a mis-named party, he or she may have difficulty enforcing the judgment against the party he or she seeks to collect from.

- **Contact information for the defendant:** If the plaintiff made errors in presenting this information on the claim, it is a good idea to correct it now on the defence. This will be the address used by the clerk and other parties to serve documents. It is in the defendant's interest that the address be accurate. If a paralegal or lawyer represents the defendant, the contact information should be that of the legal representative, not the defendant. On Page 2 there is a line to indicate which defendant is filing the defence. This is important if there is more than one defendant — it tells us which defendant or defendants are filing a particular defence. Remember that different defendants with different defences will file separate defences. Defendants who have identical defences can file a single defence setting out that defence for all of them, and be represented by the same legal representative, there being no conflict of interest among the defendants in this situation.

- **Information about the defence:** On Page 2 of the defence, there are check-off boxes. The first box is used where the defendant disputes the entire claim on any substantive or technical ground, ranging from "I didn't do whatever you said I did" to "the limitation period has expired, so your claim should be dismissed."

  The second box allows you to make a sort of defence along the lines of "I owe the money but I need to pay by instalments". The defendant that checks this box then sets out the proposed terms of payment. A defendant who does this does not have to set out his or her own version of the facts on Page 3 of the defence. Proposals are discussed in more detail in the next section.

The last box permits a defendant who admits part of the claim but disputes other parts to admit part and make a proposal to pay the part that is admitted.

In the next section, set out your reasons for disputing the claim. Occasionally you will see a defence that is a complete denial of the claim — admitting nothing, and denying all allegations in the claim without setting out a defendant's version of the facts. This kind of defence is known as a **traverse and denial**. This may result in a settlement with a plaintiff, who realizes that the defendant will be obstructive every step of the way. However, if the case gets to a settlement conference, a judge will not be impressed with this kind of stonewall defence, and the defence form clearly tries to compel the defendant to set out a defence if there is one.

- **Detailed reasons for disputing the claim:** On Page 3 of the defence, set out your version of the facts, in sequentially numbered paragraphs, one paragraph for each material fact you allege in reasonable detail, including the evidence on which you rely (unless you are following Superior Court rules of pleading, in which case you write succinctly and do not plead evidence). Set out why you disagree with all or part of a claim. As with the claim, the paragraphs should be relatively brief, consisting of two or three clear and brief sentences per paragraph. As with claims, if you have documents you rely on as part of the defence, you should attach copies; and if they are lost or unavailable, you should explain why you cannot produce them and attach your explanation. Remember that if you have the ability or right to obtain a document not in your possession, you should obtain a copy and attach it to the claim.

Some Suggestions for Drafting the Reasons for Disputing the Claim and Details

You will recall that in Chapter 6, there were various suggestions about organizing your material and using an outline to set up the details in the claim. You should review those comments and suggestions, as they apply generally to setting out the numbered paragraphs containing details in both claims and defences.

In organizing your presentation of the details, you may wish to prepare an outline that covers the following:

- Identify paragraphs in the claim as follows: (i) those the defendant agrees with, (ii) those the defendant disagrees with, and (iii) those the defendant has no knowledge of, if that is the case.

- For each allegation of fact that the defendant denies in the claim, set out the defendant's version of the facts.
- Provide a defence for each allegation that the defendant denies.
- Set out the facts you are relying on to support your position.
- Plead any legislation or common law rule that you rely on for your defence.
- Plead that the plaintiff's claim should be dismissed with costs.

The *Rules of Civil Procedure* and Defences

In the last two chapters, we have noted some of the practices and drafting conventions used in claims and in pleadings generally, many of them drawn from the *Rules of Civil Procedure*. These practices and conventions can be used for reference here too. In fact, some practices and conventions apply specifically to defences, which you may find contain helpful guidelines:

- **Plead affirmative defences.** Rule 25.07(4) of the *Rules of Civil Procedure* provides that if the defendant is doing more than denying the events as alleged by the plaintiff, he or she must set out an affirmative defence and the facts on which he or she relies:

  > In a defence, a party shall plead any matter on which the party intends to rely to defeat the claim of the opposite party and which, if not specifically pleaded, might take the opposite party by surprise or raise an issue that has not been raised in the opposite party's pleading.

  For example, if Ophelia Foot pleads that the ring is her property, she needs to set out the basis for that defence — that it was a unilateral gift.

- **Also plead in the alternative that the agreement lacks legality if you deny the existence of an agreement.** Rule 25.07(5) of the *Rules of Civil Procedure* states that if you deny the existence of an agreement, you are in effect denying there was any agreement; however, if you also wish to say that the agreement lacks legality, that should be stated clearly and explicitly. Unless you specifically deny the agreement has these characteristics and give reasons why, the agreement is also considered valid and legal if it is proved to exist:

  > Where an agreement is alleged in a pleading, a denial of the agreement by the opposite party shall be construed only as a denial of the making of the agreement or of the facts from which the agreement may be implied by law, and not as a denial of the legality or sufficiency in law of the agreement.

Admitting Liability and Proposing Terms of Payment

As noted earlier, if a defendant admits the plaintiff's claim but cannot pay all of the money owing immediately, he or she can make a payment proposal. This procedure is designed to encourage consumer debtors to pay debts rather than go into default. It also saves creditors the time and money necessary to obtain and then enforce a default judgment. However, when reviewing whether or not a consumer debtor should make a proposal, consideration should be given to the debtor's whole financial situation. If this is but one debt among many and the debtor cannot meet obligations as they fall due, it may be better for the debtor to consider bankruptcy than to tie himself or herself to a proposal on only one among many pressing debts.

Rule 9.03 sets out the procedure for making, administering, and enforcing a proposal.

> 9.03(1) A defendant who admits liability for all or part of the plaintiff's claim but wishes to arrange terms of payment may in the Defence admit liability and propose terms of payment.
>
> *Where No Dispute*
> (2) If the plaintiff does not dispute the proposal within the 20-day period referred to in subrule (3),
> (a) the defendant shall make payment in accordance with the proposal as if it were a court order;
> (b) the plaintiff may serve a notice of default of payment (Form 20L) on the defendant if the defendant fails to make payment in accordance with the proposal; and
> (c) the clerk shall sign judgment for the unpaid balance of the undisputed amount on the filing of an affidavit of default of payment (Form 20M) by the plaintiff swearing,
>   (i) that the defendant failed to make payment in accordance with the proposal,
>   (ii) to the amount paid by the defendant and the unpaid balance, and
>   (iii) that 15 days have passed since the defendant was served with a notice of default of payment.
>
> *Dispute*
> (3) The plaintiff may dispute the proposal within 20 days after service of the Defence by filing with the clerk and serving on the defendant a request to clerk (Form 9B) for a terms of payment hearing before a referee or other person appointed by the court.
>
> (4) The clerk shall fix a time for the hearing, allowing for a reasonable notice period after the date the request is served, and serve a notice of hearing on the parties.
>
> *Manner of Service*
> (4.1) The notice of hearing shall be served by mail or fax.

Financial Information Form, Defendant an Individual

(4.2) The clerk shall serve a financial information form (Form 20I) on the defendant, together with the notice of hearing, if the defendant is an individual.

(4.3) Where a defendant receives a financial information form under subrule (4.2), he or she shall complete it and serve it on the creditor before the hearing, but shall not file it with the court.

Order

(5) On the hearing, the referee or other person may make an order as to terms of payment by the defendant.

Failure to Appear, Default Judgment

(6) If the defendant does not appear at the hearing, the clerk may sign default judgment against the defendant for the part of the claim that has been admitted and shall serve a default judgment (Form 11B) on the defendant in accordance with subrule 8.01(4).

(6.1) Revoked.

Failure to Make Payments

(7) Unless the referee or other person specifies otherwise in the order as to terms of payment, if the defendant fails to make payment in accordance with the order, the clerk shall sign judgment for the unpaid balance on the filing of an affidavit by the plaintiff swearing to the default and stating the amount paid and the unpaid balance.

If the defendant has checked off the box for admitting some of the claim, or the box for admitting all of it, it is up to him or her to set out the proposal in the defence. The defendant needs to determine, based on ability to pay, how much he or she can afford in weekly or monthly payments. Being realistic about ability to pay is important because if the proposal is disputed by the plaintiff, a judge's decision to confirm a proposal or not will likely turn on whether the defendant can afford to pay more than he or she has proposed. Defendants in setting out the proposal are likely to avoid the subject of ongoing interest. As the form simply invites the defendant to set out the total amount in the claim at the time the claim was prepared and to base the instalments on paying that total, it does not seem to take into account post-judgment interest. However, there is nothing to stop a court from factoring that in on the declining balance because payments are made if the plaintiff requests it. But the complexity of the math makes this unlikely except for sophisticated commercial creditors, who know they can factor in interest and who know how to do it. Even so, a creditor who is dealing with a debtor in financial difficulty will often settle for less than the full amount if there is some assurance that the settlement amount will be paid, rather than risk getting a judgment for the full amount that turns out to be expensive or impossible to enforce. If the defendant admits liability for some of the money claimed but not all of it, the court will schedule the matter for a settlement conference as to the amount still in dispute.

The Plaintiff's Response to the Proposal

When the defendant makes a proposal in the defence, it must be filed with the clerk within 20 days of service of the claim on the defendant, just as is the case with any defence. The clerk will then serve the defence on the plaintiff. The plaintiff then has 20 days to consider the proposal. If the plaintiff is silent, the proposal is accepted, and the defendant begins to make payments as if the proposal were a court order. If the plaintiff disputes the proposal, then the court will schedule a hearing.

Procedure Where There Is No Dispute

Once the 20-day period ends and the plaintiff does not dispute the proposal, the defendant must treat the proposal as a court order. This means that if there is a default on any payment due, a quick and easy way exists under the proposal procedure for the plaintiff to obtain a default judgment. The defendant must begin paying on the first instalment date, continuing until the full amount in the proposal is paid. If there is a default, the plaintiff serves the defendant with a Notice of Default of Payment (Form 20L). The plaintiff then allows 15 days to pass, from the time the defendant was served with the notice of default, before filing with the clerk an Affidavit of Default of Payment (Form 20M), showing that the defendant failed to make a payment, what the amount paid to date is, and what the unpaid balance is. Note that this is different from a normal default judgment to the extent that if the proposal was for less than the full amount of the claim, the plaintiff is limited to enforcing a judgment on the balance outstanding on the proposed amount, even if it is less than the original claim. Note also that this procedure, using Forms 20L and 20M, is also used when there is a default in payment ordered by the court in other circumstances where instalment payments were made by the defendant.

The Notice of Default of Payment is prepared and served, and 15 days after the date of service, if there is no payment, the Affidavit of Default of Payment is prepared and filed. If the proposal originally had an interest component to each payment, interest must be calculated on a changing balance, like a running account. You need to attach an exhibit to the affidavit to show your calculations. Interest is calculated on the balance of the principal from time to time, but not added to the principal due. The situation might be different if you had a contractual agreement that allowed interest to be compounded. If the original proposal did not have an interest component, then you would simply enforce the proposal as it was made without calculating interest.

Example 8.1 Default on a Proposal

Suppose Ophelia Foot had made a proposal to pay Albert Oryx $1,500 in $150 instalments for 10 weeks. Interest was agreed to at the then *Courts of Justice Act* rate of 6% on the balance from time to time, with the first payment to be made on July 1, and the rest to follow on July 7, 14, 21, 28, August 4, etc. Suppose further that after making the first two payments on July 1 and 7, she defaulted.

Albert Oryx served Ophelia with a Notice of Default of Payment after the second default. Fifteen days later, he proceeded to file with the clerk an Affidavit of Default of Payment.

Illustrations 8.3 and 8.4 show the notice of default of payment and affidavit of default of payment, as you might see, in the above situation where Ophelia defaulted after two payments.

Plaintiff's Dispute of the Proposal

Within the 20-day period after service of the defence with a proposal on the plaintiff, the plaintiff may dispute the proposal by filing a Request to Clerk (Form 9B) requesting a terms of payment hearing. A sample Request to Clerk form is found in Illustration 7.2 on page 277. The clerk will set a date for hearing, and serve a Notice of Hearing on the parties by mail or fax. If you are disputing a proposal, you may wish to suggest some dates for the hearing that fit your schedule in order to avoid unnecessary adjournments. In addition to the Notice of Hearing, the clerk will also serve a blank Financial Information Form (Form 20I) on the defendant if the defendant is an individual. A sample Form 20I can be found in Illustration 13.5 on page 542. Corporate debtors do not have to complete this form. The individual debtor must complete the form and serve it on the plaintiff prior to the hearing, but does not file it with the court.

The form will enable the referee or other designated person at the hearing who rules on the proposal to see what the individual debtor's income and expenses are, which will help the referee to

ILLUSTRATION 8.3: Sample Notice of Default of Payment (Form 20L)

ONTARIO
Superior Court of Justice
Cour supérieure de justice

Notice of Default of Payment
Avis de défaut de paiement
Form / Formule 20L Ont. Reg. No. / Règl. de l'Ont. : 258/98

Toronto
Small Claims Court / *Cour des petites créances de*

SC-00-47669-00
Claim No. / *N° de la demande*

47 Sheppard Ave. E., 3rd Fl.
Toronto, ON M2N 5N1
Address / *Adresse*

416-326-3554
Phone number / *Numéro de téléphone*

BETWEEN / ENTRE

Albert Oryx
Plaintiff(s)/Creditor(s) / *Demandeur(s)/demanderesse(s)/Créancier(s)/créancière(s)*

and / et

Ophelia Foot
Defendant(s)/Debtor(s) / *Défendeur(s)/défenderesse(s)/Débiteur(s)/débitrice(s)*

TO: Ophelia Foot
DESTINATAIRE(S) :   (Name of defendant(s)/debtor(s) / *Nom du/de la/des défendeur(s)/défenderesse(s)/débiteur(s)/débitrice(s))*

TAKE NOTICE that you defaulted in your payment(s) to
VEUILLEZ PRENDRE NOTE *que vous n'avez pas effectué le ou les paiements que vous deviez verser à*

Albert Oryx
(Name of plaintiff(s)/creditor(s) / *Nom du/de la/des demandeur(s)/demanderesse(s)/créancier(s)/créancière(s))*

(Check appropriate box. / Cochez la case appropriée.)

☐ under an order for periodic payment, dated
   en vertu d'une ordonnance prescrivant des versements périodiques datée du

According to Rule 20.02(4) of the *Rules of the Small Claims Court*, the order for periodic payment terminates on the day that is 15 days after the creditor serves the debtor with this notice, unless before that date, a Consent (Form 13B) is filed in which the creditor waives the default.
Conformément au paragraphe 20.02 (4) des Règles de la Cour des petites créances, l'ordonnance prescrivant des versements périodiques prend fin le 15e jour qui suit la signification par le créancier au débiteur du présent avis, sauf si, avant cette date, le créancier dépose le consentement (formule 13B) dans lequel il renonce à la constatation du défaut.

☒ under a proposal of terms of payment in the Defence (Form 9A) dated **April 7, Yr. 1**
   en vertu d'une proposition à l'égard des modalités de paiement dans la défense (formule 9A) datée du

According to Rule 9.03(2)(c) the clerk may sign judgment for the unpaid balance of the undisputed amount on the day that is 15 days after the plaintiff serves the defendant with this notice.
Conformément à l'alinéa 9.03 (2) c), le greffier peut consigner un jugement relativement au solde impayé de la somme non contestée le 15e jour qui suit la signification par le demandeur au défendeur du présent avis.

SCR 20.02-20L (June 1, 2009 / *1er juin 2009*) CSD

continues....

Illustration 8.3 (continued)

FORM / *FORMULE* 20L   PAGE 2   SC-00-47669-00
                                                                   Claim No. / *N° de la demande*

You can get forms and self-help materials at the Small Claims Court or online at: www.ontariocourtforms.on.ca.
Vous pouvez obtenir les formules et la documentation à l'usage du client auprès de la Cour des petites créances
ou en ligne à l'adresse : www.ontariocourtforms.on.ca.

NOTE TO DEFENDANT/DEBTOR: / *REMARQUE AU DÉFENDEUR/DÉBITEUR :*

If you / *Si, selon le cas :*

- failed to make payments but intend to do so; or
  vous n'avez pas effectué de paiements mais vous avez l'intention de le faire;

- made payments but the payments were not received by the creditor;
  vous avez effectué des paiements mais le créancier ne les a pas reçus;

contact the plaintiff/creditor to make payment arrangements or correct the reason for non-receipt of payments.
You may obtain the plaintiff/creditor's written consent (Form 13B may be used) to waive the default and file it with
the court within 15 days of being served with this notice. Failure to do so may result in the following:
communiquez avec le demandeur/créancier pour prendre les dispositions de paiement ou pour régler le motif de la
non-réception des paiements. Vous pouvez obtenir le consentement écrit du demandeur/créancier (vous pouvez utiliser
la formule 13B) pour renoncer à la constatation du défaut et le déposer au tribunal dans les 15 jours de la signification
du présent avis. Si vous ne le faites pas, vous pourriez subir l'une ou l'autre des conséquences suivantes :

- in the case of default under a proposal of terms of payment in the Defence (Form 9A), the plaintiff may
  obtain default judgment for the unpaid balance of the undisputed amount; or
  si vous n'effectuez pas les paiements conformément aux modalités de paiement proposées dans la
  défense (formule 9A), le demandeur pourra obtenir un jugement par défaut relativement au solde impayé
  de la somme non contestée;

- in the case of default under an order for periodic payment, the order will terminate and the creditor may take
  other steps to enforce the order.
  si vous n'effectuez pas les paiements conformément à une ordonnance prescrivant des versements
  périodiques, l'ordonnance prendra fin et le créancier pourra prendre d'autres mesures en vue de
  l'exécution forcée de l'ordonnance.

July 22, Yr. 1   *Peter Paralegal*
                                   (Signature of plaintiff/creditor or representative / *Signature du demandeur/de*
                                   la demanderesse/du créancier/de la créancière ou du/de la représentant(e))

                                   Peter Paralegal, 41 Yonge Street, #410
                                   Toronto ON   M5G 1S1
                                   416-597-0048
                                   (Name, address and phone number of plaintiff/creditor or representative /
                                   Nom, adresse et numéro de téléphone du demandeur/de la
                                   demanderesse/du créancier/de la créancière ou du/de la représentant(e))

SCR 20.02-20L (June 1, 2009 / *1er juin 2009*) CSD

ILLUSTRATION 8.4: Sample Affidavit of Default of Payment (Form 20M)

ONTARIO
Superior Court of Justice
Cour supérieure de justice

Affidavit of Default of Payment
Affidavit de défaut de paiement
Form / *Formule* 20M Ont. Reg. No. / *Règl. de l'Ont.* : 258/98

Toronto
Small Claims Court / *Cour des petites créances de*

**47 Sheppard Ave. E., 3rd Fl.,
Toronto, ON M2N SN1**
Address / *Adresse*

416-326-3554
Phone number / *Numéro de téléphone*

SC-00-47669-00
Claim No. / *N° de la demande*

BETWEEN / *ENTRE*

Albert Oryx
Plaintiff(s)/Creditor(s) / *Demandeur(s)/demanderesse(s)/Créancier(s)/créancière(s)*

and / et

Ophelia Foot
Defendant(s)/Debtor(s) / *Défendeur(s)/défenderesse(s)/Débiteur(s)/débitrice(s)*

My name is **Peter Paralegal**
Je m'appelle (Full name / *Nom et prénoms*)

I live in **Toronto, Ontario**
J'habite à (Municipality & province / *Municipalité et province*)

and I swear/affirm that the following is true:
et je déclare sous serment/j'affirme solennellement que les renseignements suivants sont véridiques :

1. In this action, I am the
   Dans la présente action, je suis le/la

   (Check one box only. / *Cochez une seule case.*)

   ☐ plaintiff/creditor.
   demandeur/demanderesse/créancier/créancière.

   ☒ representative of the plaintiff(s)/creditor(s) **Albert Oryx**
   représentant(e) du/de la/des demandeur(s)/demanderesse(s) ou du/de la/des créancier(s)/créancière(s)
   (Name of plaintiff(s)/creditor(s) / *Nom du/de la/des demandeur(s)/demanderesse(s) ou du/de la/des créancier(s)/créancière(s)*)

2. To date, I have received from the defendant(s)/debtor(s) $ **300.00** , the last payment being made
   À ce jour, j'ai reçu du ou des défendeurs/débiteurs (Amount / *Montant*) *$, soit le dernier paiement ayant*
   on or about **July 7, Yr. 1** .
   été effectué le ou vers le

3. I make this affidavit in support of a request that:
   Je fais le présent affidavit à l'appui d'une demande visant à :

   (Check appropriate box and complete paragraph. / *Cochez la case appropriée et remplissez le point.*)

   ☒ the clerk of the court issue a Default Judgment (Form 11B) [R. 9.03(2)(c)]. The defendant(s)
   enjoindre au greffier du tribunal de rendre un jugement par défaut (formule 11B) [alinéa 9.03 (2) c)].
   Le ou les défendeurs
   Ophelia Foot
   (Name(s) of defendant(s) / *Nom du/de la/des défendeur(s)/défenderesse(s)*)

   failed to make payment in accordance with the proposed terms of payment in the Defence
   n'ont pas effectué les paiements conformément aux modalités de paiement proposées dans la défense
   (Form 9A) dated **April 7, Yr. 1** and fifteen (15) days have passed since the
   (formule 9A) datée du *et quinze (15) jours se sont écoulés depuis*
   defendant was served with a Notice of Default of Payment (Form 20L) at the following address(es):
   la signification de l'avis de défaut de paiement au défendeur (formule 20L) à l'adresse (aux adresses)
   suivante(s) :
   83 Greengrove Rd., Toronto, ON M6R 4O5
   (Address(es) of defendant(s) / *Adresse(s) du/de la/des défendeur(s)/défenderesse(s)*)

SCR 9.03-20M (April 11, 2012 / *11 avril 2012*) CSD

continues....

Illustration 8.4 (continued)

FORM / *FORMULE* 20M   PAGE 2   SC-00-47669-00
                                                          Claim No. / *N° de la demande*

☐ the clerk of the court issue a Default Judgment (Form 11B) [R. 9.03(7)]. The defendant(s)
   enjoindre au greffier du tribunal de rendre un jugement par défaut (formule 11B) [par. 9.03 (7)]. Le
   ou les défendeurs

   _____
   (Name of defendant(s) / *Nom du/de des défendeur(s)/défenderesse(s)*

   failed to make payment in accordance with the terms of payment order
   n'ont pas effectué les paiements conformément à l'ordonnance relative aux modalités de paiement

(Check   dated _____ .
appropriate   *datée du*
box and
complete
paragraph. /   ☐ I may enforce the judgment [R. 20.02(3)]. The debtor(s)
Cochez la   *m'autoriser à exécuter le jugement [par. 20.02 (3)]. Le ou les débiteurs*
case
appropriée
et   _____
remplissez   (Name(s) of debtor(s) / *Nom du/de la/des débiteur(s)/débitrice(s)*
le point.)
                   failed to make payment in accordance with the order for periodic payment dated
                   n'ont pas effectué les paiements conformément à l'ordonnance prescrivant des versements
                   périodiques datée du

                   _____ , and fifteen (15) days have passed since the debtor(s) has/have
                                                      et quinze (15) jours se sont écoulés depuis la signification de

                   been served with a Notice of Default of Payment (Form 20L) at the following address(es):
                   l'avis de défaut de paiement (formule 20L) au ou aux débiteurs à l'adresse (aux adresses) suivante(s) :

                   _____
                   (Address(es) of debtor(s) / *Adresse(s) du/de la/des débiteur(s)/débitrice(s))*

                   A Consent (Form 13B) in which the creditor waives the default has not been filed.
                   Un consentement (formule 13B) dans lequel le créancier renonce à la constatation du défaut n'a
                   pas été déposé.

4. The unpaid balance is calculated as follows:
    Le solde impayé est calculé de la façon suivante :

(A) **DEBT** $ 1,500.00
    LA CRÉANCE $

(B) **PRE-JUDGMENT INTEREST** calculated
    LES INTÉRÊTS ANTÉRIEURS AU JUGEMENT *calculés*
                        See Exhibit "A"
    on the sum of $ _____ attached _____ at the rate of **6.0** ____ %
    sur la somme de $ *au taux de*   *pour cent*

    per annum from _____ to _____ ,
    par an du   *au*

    being _____ days. $ 6.83
    soit   *jours.* $

    ┌───┐
    │ NOTE: Calculation of interest is always on the amount owing from time to time as payments are │
    │   received. This is true for both pre-judgment and post-judgment interest. Attach a separate │
    │   sheet setting out how you calculated the total amount of any pre/post-judgment interest. │
    │ REMARQUE : Les intérêts doivent toujours être calculés sur la somme due. Le calcul doit tenir │
    │   compte des paiements reçus de temps à autre. Ceci s'applique autant aux intérêts │
    │   antérieurs au jugement qu'aux intérêts postérieurs au jugement. Annexez une feuille │
    │   distincte indiquant comment vous avez calculé le montant total des intérêts │
    │   antérieurs et postérieurs au jugement. │
    └───┘

                                    SUBTOTAL (amount of judgment) $ 1,506.83
                                    TOTAL PARTIEL (*montant du jugement*) $

SCR 9.03-20M (April 11, 2012 / *11 avril 2012*) CSD   Continued on next page / *Suite à la page suivante*

continues....

Illustration 8.4 (continued)

FORM / *FORMULE* 20M	PAGE 3	SC-00-47669-00
		Claim No. / *N° de la demande*

(C) **COSTS** to date of judgment
LES DÉPENS à la date du jugement

$ 95.00

$

(D) **TOTAL AMOUNT OF PAYMENTS RECEIVED FROM DEBTOR**
after judgment (if any)
LE MONTANT TOTAL DES PAIEMENTS REÇUS DU DÉBITEUR
après le jugement (le cas échéant)

(minus) $ 300.00
(moins) $

(E) **POST-JUDGMENT INTEREST** to date calculated
LES INTÉRÊTS POSTÉRIEURS AU JUGEMENT à ce jour, calculés

on the sum of $ _____ at the rate of _____ %
sur la somme de $ *au taux de* *pour cent*

per annum from _____ to _____ '
par an du *au*

being _____ days.
soit *jours.*

$ 0.00
$

(F) **SUBSEQUENT COSTS** incurred after judgment (including the cost of serving
the Notice of Default of Payment (Form 20L))
LES DÉPENS SUBSÉQUENTS engagés après le jugement (y compris le coût de
signification de l'avis de défaut de paiement (formule 20L))

$ 35.00
$

TOTAL DUE $ 1,336.83
SOLDE DÛ $

Sworn/Affirmed before me at **Toronto**
Déclaré sous serment/Affirmé
solennellement devant moi à
(Municipality / *municipalité*)

in **Ontario**
en/à/au (Province, state, or county / *province, État ou pays*)

on **August 5, Yr. 1** "Case Commissioner"
le Commissioner for taking affidavits
Commissaire aux affidavits
(Type or print name below if signature is illegible.)
(Dactylographiez le nom ou écrivez-le en caractères d'imprimerie ci-dessous si la signature est illisible.)

Peter Paralegal
Signature
(This form is to be signed in front of a lawyer, justice of the peace, notary public or commissioner for taking affidavits.)
(La présente formule doit être signée en présence d'un avocat, d'un juge de paix, d'un notaire ou d'un commissaire aux affidavits.)

WARNING:	**IT IS AN OFFENCE UNDER THE CRIMINAL CODE TO KNOWINGLY SWEAR OR AFFIRM A FALSE AFFIDAVIT.**
AVERTISSEMENT :	*FAIRE SCIEMMENT UN FAUX AFFIDAVIT CONSTITUE UNE INFRACTION AU CODE CRIMINEL.*

SCR 9.03-20M (April 11, 2012 / *11 avril 2012*) CSD

continues....

Assumptions:

Costs to date of judgment (C): $75.00 to issue claim, $20.00 to serve claim
Subsequent costs (F): $35 to file default judgment

Illustration 8.4 (continued)

Exhibit "A" to the Affidavit of Default of Payment of Peter Paralegal sworn August 5, Yr. 1
Pre-judgment interest calculations
per item B, p. 2 of the Affidavit of Default

Interest rate: 6% per *Courts of Justice Act*

Date payment	Interest	Principal balance
July 1, Yr. 1 — $150	July 2–7: $1,350 \times .06 \times 5/365 = \$1.11$	$1,350
July 7, Yr. 1 — $150		$1,200
July 8–August 5 — $0	July 7–Aug. 5: $1,200 \times .06 \times 29/365 = \$5.72$	
	Total Interest as of Aug. 5 = $6.83	
	Total Principal as of August 5	$1,200

decide whether the proposed amount is suitable or not. It is open to the referee to amend the terms of the proposal, or reject it altogether, based on the submissions of the party, but the Financial Information Form is crucial to that decision. If it is not sufficiently informative, the referee can adjourn proceedings to require the defendant to produce specific information. Both the plaintiff and the referee may question the defendant on the contents of the form. Note that the form can also provide useful information for the plaintiff to use later to enforce a judgment.

If the defendant, having made a proposal, fails to appear at the hearing, the clerk may sign default judgment for the part of the claim that has been admitted, and shall serve the default judgment on the defendant. This judgment now becomes immediately enforceable through the usual enforcement methods in Rule 20.

DEFENDANT'S CLAIMS

When a plaintiff sues a defendant, the defendant may file a defence against that Claim. But based on the facts or events in the plaintiff's case, the defendant may also have a claim to make against the plaintiff (**counterclaim**), or the defendant may have a claim to make against a co-defendant (**cross claim**) or against a third party (**third party claim**). In these cases, in addition to filing a defence, the defendant should also file a defendant's claim against the plaintiff, or other defendants or third parties.

Here are some examples of situations where defendant's claims might be used:

• **Defendant's claim against the plaintiff**

> The plaintiff and defendant have a business relationship, each supplying the other with goods or services on account. The plaintiff sues the defendant for an unpaid account of $4,000. The defendant files a defence in which he states that the plaintiff owes him $5,000, and claims a **set off** of what is owed to him by the plaintiff, against the amount claimed in the plaintiff's claim. He also files a defendant's claim for the additional $1,000 still owing to him.

• **Defendant's claim against a co-defendant**

> The plaintiff claims two defendants are jointly liable for damage to the plaintiff's property when Defendant #1 drove Defendant #2's car into the wall of the plaintiff's house. Defendant #2 may defend the plaintiff's claim by denying liability; however, he may also make a defendant's claim called a crossclaim, against Defendant #1 for damage to his, Defendant #2's, car, when Defendant #1 drove the car into the plaintiff's wall.

• **Defendant's claim against a third party**

> The plaintiff claims the defendant is responsible for damage to his property. The defendant thinks that X caused the damage and states in his defence that X is liable and the defendant is not. However, because X was not sued and is not party to the judgment, he is not bound by any judgment on the plaintiff's claim. To make X a party so that he will be bound, and to also fix liability on X, the defendant makes a defendant's claim against X, adding him to the proceeding and claiming **relief and indemnity over** against X, who is now a third party.

There are several things to keep in mind when considering and trying to understand defendant's claims:

• Defendant's claims are really claims, and many of the rules and procedures that apply to plaintiff's claims apply to defendant's claims as well.

- Defendant's claims must be linked to the issues and facts in the plaintiff's claim. If the defendant's claim is not connected to the facts, transactions, events, and issues in the plaintiff's claim, it must proceed as a separate action.

- Defendant's claims make what may have started as a simple lawsuit more complicated. You need to be careful so that, as it unfolds, you are able to keep track of the issues involving different parties, noting which parties are subject to different claims or defences, and remember to serve the appropriate parties as the Rules require. It may be a good idea to make a drawing or diagram in which you identify the parties with arrows to show which claims and defences apply to each of the parties.

- The expanded case, with defendant's claims and defences to defendant's claims, will be tried together as one case unless it is too complex, in which case it may be split into separate proceedings to be tried separately. The decision to split the case, or not, is usually made at the settlement conference.

Procedure for Completing Defendant's Claims

A defendant who has a claim against the plaintiff, another defendant, or a third party may make a defendant's claim in Form 10A, following the procedure set out in Rule 10:

Defendant's Claim
10.01(1) A defendant may make a claim,
 (a) against the plaintiff;
 (b) against any other person,
   (i) arising out of the transaction or occurrence relied upon by the plaintiff, or
   (ii) related to the plaintiff's claim; or
 (c) against the plaintiff and against another person in accordance with clause (b).

 (2) The defendant's claim shall be in Form 10A and may be issued,
 (a) within 20 days after the day on which the Defence is filed; or
 (b) after the time described in clause (a) but before trial or default judgment, with leave of the court.

Copies
 (3) The defendant shall provide a copy of the defendant's claim to the court.

Contents of Defendant's Claim, Attachments
 (4) The following requirements apply to the defendant's claim:

1. It shall contain the following information:
   i. The full names of the parties to the defendant's claim and, if relevant, the capacity in which they sue or are sued.
   ii. The nature of the claim, expressed in concise non-technical language with a reasonable amount of detail, including the date, place and nature of the occurrences on which the claim is based.
   iii. The amount of the claim and the relief requested.
   iv. If the defendant is self-represented, the defendant's name, address and telephone number, and fax number if any.
   v. If the defendant is represented by a lawyer or agent, that person's name, address and telephone number, and fax number if any, and Law Society of Upper Canada registration number if any.
   vi. The address where the defendant believes each person against whom the claim is made may be served.
   vii. The court file number assigned to the plaintiff's claim.
2. If the defendant's claim is based in whole or in part on a document, a copy of the document shall be attached to each copy of the claim, unless it is unavailable, in which case the claim shall state the reason why the document is not attached.

(5) Revoked.

Issuance
(6) On receiving the defendant's claim, the clerk shall immediately issue it by dating, signing and sealing it, shall assign it the same court file number as the plaintiff's claim and shall place the original in the court file.

(7), (8) Revoked.

Service
10.02 A defendant's claim shall be served by the defendant on every person against whom it is made, in accordance with subrules 8.01(1) and (2).

Defence
10.03(1) A party who wishes to dispute the defendant's claim or a third party who wishes to dispute the plaintiff's claim may, within 20 days after service of the defendant's claim, file a defence (Form 9A) with the clerk, together with a copy for each of the other parties or persons against whom the defendant's or plaintiff's claim is made.

Service of Copy by Clerk
(2) On receiving a defence under subrule (1), the clerk shall retain the original in the court file and shall serve a copy on each party in accordance with subrule 8.01(3).

Defendant's Claim to be Tried with Main Action
10.04(1) A defendant's claim shall be tried and disposed of at the trial of the action, unless the court orders otherwise.

Exception
(2) If it appears that a defendant's claim may unduly complicate or delay the trial of the action or cause undue prejudice to a party, the court may order separate trials or direct that the defendant's claim proceed as a separate action.

Rights of Third Party
(3) If the defendant alleges, in a defendant's claim, that a third party is liable to the defendant for all or part of the plaintiff's claim in the action, the third party may at the trial contest the defendant's liability to the plaintiff, but only if the third party has filed a defence in accordance with subrule 10.03(1).

Application of Rules to Defendant's Claim
10.05(1) These rules apply, with necessary modifications, to a defendant's claim as if it were a plaintiff's claim, and to a defence to a defendant's claim as if it were a defence to a plaintiff's claim.

Exception
(2) However, when a person against whom a defendant's claim is made is noted in default, judgment against that person may be obtained only in accordance with rule 11.04.

Illustration 8.5 shows the defendant's claim filed by Gary's Great Games Ltd., in which Gary's Great Games made a counterclaim.

The defendant's claim must be issued in the same way as a plaintiff's claim — by filing it with the court to be issued by the clerk, and by paying the prescribed fee. The claim must be issued within 20 days after the date on which the defence was filed.[1] This will give a defendant the opportunity to deal with the defence and then give him or her an opportunity to work on the defendant's claim. In the event that a defendant becomes aware of the existence of a claim against the plaintiff or someone else after the 20-day period expires, but before trial or a default judgment has been obtained, he or she will have to bring a motion to explain to the court the reasons why the request is being made relatively late in the pre-trial process. A typical reason that would justify a defendant's claim would be that facts have been recently discovered.

The contents of the defendant's claim are very similar to the plaintiff's claim. It should set out the full names of the parties to the defendant's claim. Note that these will not necessarily be the same cast of characters as on the plaintiff's claim. For example, if the claim is only

---

[1] As a practical matter, some courts, including the Toronto Small Claims Court, will accept a defence and issue a defendant's claim at the same time, thereby avoiding two trips to the court by the defendant.

ILLUSTRATION 8.5: Sample Defendant's Claim (Form 10A)

ONTARIO
Superior Court of Justice
Cour supérieure de justice

Defendant's Claim
Demande du défendeur
Form / *Formule* 10A Ont. Reg. No. / *Régl. de l'Ont.* : 258/98

Seal / *Sceau*

Toronto	**SC-00-31547-01**
Small Claims Court / *Cour des petites créances de*	Claim No. / *N° de la demande*

47 Sheppard Ave. E., 3rd Fl.
Toronto, ON M2N 5N1

Address / *Adresse*

416-326-3554
Phone number / *Numéro de téléphone*

Plaintiff by Defendant's Claim No. 1 /
Demandeur dans la demande du
défendeur n° 1

☐ Additional plaintiff(s) listed on attached Form 1A.
Le ou les demandeurs additionnels sont
mentionnés sur la formule 1A ci-jointe.

☐ Under 18 years of age.
Moins de 18 ans.

Last name, or name of company / *Nom de famille ou nom de la compagnie*		
Gary's Great Games Ltd.		
First name / *Premier prénom*	Second name / *Deuxième prénom*	Also known as / *Également connu(e) sous le nom de*
Address (street number, apt., unit) / *Adresse (numéro et rue, app., unité)*		
c/o I.M. Power, 185 Yonge Street		
City/Town / *Cité/ville* **Toronto**	Province **ON**	Phone no. / *N° de téléphone* **416-128-4564**
Postal code / *Code postal* **M6C 1L3**		Fax no. / *N° de télécopieur*
Representative / *Représentant(e)* **I.M. Power**		LSUC # / *N° du BHC* **P28453**
Address (street number, apt., unit) / *Adresse (numéro et rue, app., unité)*		
185 Yonge Street		
City/Town / *Cité/ville* **Toronto**	Province **ON**	Phone no. / *N° de téléphone* **416-128-4564**
Postal code / *Code postal* **M6C 1L3**		Fax no. / *N° de télécopieur*

Defendant by Defendant's Claim No. 1 /
Défendeur dans la demande du
défendeur n° 1

☐ Additional defendant(s) listed on attached Form 1A.
Le ou les défendeurs additionnels sont mentionnés
sur la formule 1A ci-jointe.

☐ Under 18 years of age.
Moins de 18 ans.

Last name, or name of company / *Nom de famille ou nom de la compagnie*		
Video Supplies Inc.		
First name / *Premier prénom*	Second name / *Deuxième prénom*	Also known as / *Également connu(e) sous le nom de*
Address (street number, apt., unit) / *Adresse (numéro et rue, app., unité)*		
c/o Peter Paralegal, 41 Yonge Street, #410		
City/Town / *Cité/ville* **Toronto**	Province **ON**	Phone no. / *N° de téléphone* **416-597-0048**
Postal code / *Code postal* **M5G 1S1**		Fax no. / *N° de télécopieur* **416-597-0049**
Representative / *Représentant(e)* **Peter Paralegal**		LSUC # / *N° du BHC* **P02952**
Address (street number, apt., unit) / *Adresse (numéro et rue, app., unité)*		
41 Yonge Street, #410		
City/Town / *Cité/ville* **Toronto**	Province **ON**	Phone no. / *N° de téléphone* **416-597-0048**
Postal code / *Code postal* **M5G 1S1**		Fax no. / *N° de télécopieur* **416-597-0049**

SCR 10.01-10A (June 1, 2009 / *1er juin 2009*) CSD

continues....

Illustration 8.5 (continued)

FORM / *FORMULE* 10A	PAGE 2	SC-00-31547-01

Claim No. / *N° de la demande*

REASONS FOR CLAIM AND DETAILS / *MOTIFS DE LA DEMANDE ET PRÉCISIONS*

Explain what happened, including where and when. Then explain how much money you are claiming or what goods you want returned.
Expliquez ce qui s'est passé, en précisant où et quand. Ensuite indiquez la somme d'argent que vous demandez ou les biens dont vous demandez la restitution, explication à l'appui.

If you are relying on any documents, you **MUST** attach copies to the claim. If evidence is lost or unavailable, you **MUST** explain why it is not attached.
*Si vous vous appuyez sur des documents, vous **DEVEZ** en annexer des copies à la demande. Si une preuve est perdue ou n'est pas disponible, vous **DEVEZ** expliquer pourquoi elle n'est pas annexée.*

What happened?
Where?
When?
Que s'est-il passé?
Où?
Quand?

The Defendant by Defendant's Claim, Video Supplies Inc. ("Video") breached the parties' contract, causing the Plaintiff by Defendant's Claim, Gary's Great Games Ltd. ("Gary's") a loss of profit.
The parties' contract was entered into in Toronto, Ontario.
The parties' contract was breached when the goods ordered were not delivered by Video on September 14, Yr. 0, and when finally delivered, the goods were defective, thereby causing a loss of business to Gary's. Video has also refused to return Gary's deposit of $3,000.

1. Gary's claims:
a) Damages in the amount of $4,000 for breach of contract;
b) Its costs of defending the Plaintiff's claim;
c) Its costs of the Defendant's claim;
d) Such further and other relief as this Honourable court may deem just.

2. Gary's had a contract with Video for the supply of PlayStations to be delivered on Sept. 14, Yr. 0.

3. Video breached this contract by failing to deliver the PlayStations on time and by delivering products, as noted in the Defence to the Claim, that were so defective as to be unusable.

4. As a result of Video's breach, Gary's contract to re-sell the PlayStations to PETER PLAYFAIR ("PlayFair") was terminated because Gary's was unable to honour its agreement with Playfair to deliver saleable goods on time.

5. As a result, Gary's has suffered damages of $1,000 for loss of profit on the aborted sale to Playfair, and $3,000 for the deposit on the agreement with Video which Video has refused to return to Gary's despite demands for the return of the deposit.

6. Gary's also relies on the allegations in its Defence to the Plaintiff's claim.

7. Gary's proposes that this Defendant's claim be heard at the same time and place as the trial of the Plaintiff's claim.

SCR 10.01-10A (June 1, 2009 / *1er juin 2009*) CSD

Continued on next sheet / *Suite à la page suivante*

continues....

Illustration 8.5 (continued)

FORM / *FORMULE* 10A   PAGE 3   SC-00-31547-0001
                                                                  Claim No. / *N° de la demande*

How much? $ _____ 4,000.00 $
Combien?   (Principal amount claimed / *Somme demandée*)

☐   ADDITIONAL PAGES ARE ATTACHED BECAUSE MORE ROOM WAS NEEDED.
     DES FEUILLES SUPPLÉMENTAIRES SONT ANNEXÉES EN RAISON DU MANQUE D'ESPACE.

The plaintiff by defendant's claim also claims pre-judgment interest from Sept. 14, Yr. 0 _____ under:
Le demandeur dans la demande du défendeur demande aussi des   (Date)   *conformément à :*
intérêts antérieurs au jugement à compter du

(Check only   ☒   the *Courts of Justice Act*
one box /   la *Loi sur les tribunaux judiciaires*
Cochez une
seule case)   ☐   an agreement at the rate of _____ % per year
                    un accord au taux de   % par an

and post-judgment interest, and court costs.
et des intérêts postérieurs au jugement, ainsi que les dépens.

Prepared on: November 15, Yr. 0 _____   *Gary Gameman*
Fait le :   (Signature of plaintiff or representative / *Signature du*
                                                    demandeur/de la demanderesse ou du/de la représentant(e))

Issued on: _____
Délivré le :   (Signature of clerk / *Signature du greffier*)

CAUTION TO DEFENDANT BY DEFENDANT'S CLAIM: AVERTISSEMENT AU DÉFENDEUR DANS LA DEMANDE DU DÉFENDEUR :	**IF YOU DO NOT FILE A DEFENCE** (Form 9A) with the court within twenty (20) calendar days after you have been served with this Defendant's Claim, judgment may be obtained by Defendant's Claim without notice and enforced against you. Forms and self-help materials are available at the Small Claims Court and on the following website: www.ontariocourtforms.on.ca. *SI VOUS NE DÉPOSEZ PAS DE DÉFENSE (formule 9A) auprès du tribunal au plus tard vingt (20) jours civils après avoir reçu signification de la présente demande du défendeur, un jugement peut être obtenu par suite de cette demande sans préavis et être exécuté contre vous. Vous pouvez obtenir les formules et la documentation à l'usage du client à la Cour des petites créances et sur le site Web suivant : www.ontariocourtforms.on.ca.*

SCR 10.01-10A (June 1, 2009 / *1ᵉʳ juin 2009*) CSD

against a third party, only the third party's name will appear as a defendant to the defendant's claim. The defendant's claim should go on to set out the amount of the claim, including pre-judgment interest to the date of preparation. It should also indicate the type of claim being made, and go on to provide reasons for the claim, setting out a concise statement of material facts in consecutively numbered paragraphs without setting out evidence. You must also supply and attach copies of all documents relevant to the defendant's claim. The suggestions in Chapter 6 about how to organize material, outline the claim, use precedents, and follow drafting practices and conventions for plaintiff's claims apply equally to defendant's claims.

In identifying the parties when setting out the reasons for the claim, the person making the claim is the plaintiff by defendant's claim, and the person against whom the claim is made is the defendant by defendant's claim. In order to minimize the use of these cumbersome descriptions when giving the claim details, after the first time you use a description, put a shorter description in parentheses, and use the shorter description thereafter. For example, "The Plaintiff by Defendant's Claim (Foot)" allows you to simply use "Foot" instead of the longer phrase when you refer to that party in the details of the claim.

Remember that you must issue the defendant's claim in the same court that the main claim came from. The clerk will assign it the same court file number and file it with the plaintiff's claim so that all of the claims will proceed to trial together. The court may add the numbers 01 at the end of the claim number when issuing a Defendant's Claim to flag that it is a separate claim brought within an existing claim.

Service of Defendant's Claim

Because this is a claim, after you have it issued you have to serve it in the same way as you would serve a plaintiff's claim — personally, or by an alternative to personal service. It does not have to be served on everyone in the main action — only on those against whom the plaintiff by defendant's claim has made a claim.

Disputing a Defendant's Claim

A defendant by a defendant's claim does what any defendant does: he or she files a defence in Form 9A within 20 days of being served with the defendant's claim. This is the same form that defendants use to defend and respond to a plaintiff's claim. A copy must be provided to the court for each of the parties to the defendant's claim and the plaintiff's claim. The court clerk serves the defence.

Special Rules for Third Party Defences to Defendant's Claims

If a defendant in the main action files a defendant's claim stating that a third party is liable to the plaintiff for the entire claim made by the plaintiff against the defendant (a claim for indemnity and relief over), the third party may file a defence to the plaintiff's claim and a separate defence to the defendant's claim, both in Form 9A. If the third party does this, he or she may dispute the defendant's liability to the plaintiff, as well as his or her liability to the defendant for indemnity and relief over. If a third party defends only the defendant's claim, he or she will not be able to defend the original claim against the defendant by the plaintiff. If you act for a third party, it is important to remember this:

> To preserve your right to use every defence available, including defences the defendant in the main action had but didn't use, you should consider Rule 10.04(3) and file defences to both the main claim and the defendant's claim.

CHAPTER SUMMARY

This chapter focused on the ways in which a defendant may defend against a plaintiff's claim. It began by discussing options available for the preparation of a defence, including disputing the entire claim, admitting part and disputing part, and admitting the entire claim and making a proposal to pay by instalments. The proposal procedure was discussed in detail, including what happens if a plaintiff objects to and disputes the proposal, in which case a referee decides whether the proposal is acceptable or not. The procedure to be followed in filing a defence was outlined, as were the steps in preparing one, including the drafting of a detailed response to the claim. The chapter then discussed a defendant's claim, noting that it can be used to make a claim against the plaintiff, another defendant, or a third party, provided the claim is based on the same facts, transactions, or events as are found in the plaintiff's claim. The procedure to be followed in preparing, serving, and filing a defendant's claim was also discussed.

REVIEW QUESTIONS

1. What are the defendant's options when served with a plaintiff's claim?

2. How long do you have to file or issue the following:
   (a) Defence
   (b) Defendant's claim
   (c) Defence to the defendant's claim

3. Can you file a defence that simply denies the plaintiff's claim and says nothing further?

4. What are the advantages of a debtor making a proposal? A creditor?

5. (a) What happens if a plaintiff disputes a proposal?
   (b) If a proposal is accepted or approved, what happens if the defendant fails to pay the instalments agreed to in the proposal?

6. What is a counterclaim? A crossclaim? A third party claim?

7. Paul sues David for an unpaid debt. David says that Paul, in the year before, damaged David's computer and never paid the cost of repair. Can David file a defendant's claim against Paul for the cost of repairing the computer?

8. If you are sued in Toronto because the cause of action arose there, but you live in Brampton and have a defendant's claim, can you issue it in Brampton?

9. Does a defendant's claim have to be served on every party to the main lawsuit?

10. If a person is served with a defendant's claim against her as a third party, can she also defend the main claim?

DISCUSSION QUESTIONS/CASE STUDIES

FACTS

The Nopays, the partners who run Nopay Windows, have come to see you to ask you to handle a lawsuit. You are Delford Defendo, Paralegal, 123 Commerce Rd., Nowhere, Ontario L2L 3Y4, Tel. 909-765-4321, Fax 909-765-4322. Your Law society number is P09876. The claim indicates that Freda's Linens has sued them for $5,000 for curtain material sold on July 2, Yr. 0, to Nopay by Freda's Linens, but not paid for. However, the reason Nopay did not pay was that the curtain material was defective. It had defects in the weave, and was different in texture and colour from the sample the Nopays had seen when they ordered. They were going to use it to complete an order from the Hotel Nowhere, but when the hotel's manager saw the material he said it was not what he had bargained for with Nopay. The hotel, which would have paid on July 30, Yr. 0, cancelled the $20,000 contract on that date, and Nopay lost the sale and the profit it would have made of $6,000 on the sale. The Nopays want you to file a defence and also sue for the lost profit.

1. Prepare a defence to the plaintiff's claim.
2. Prepare a counterclaim on behalf of Nopay.

Chapter 9

Repairs, Amendments, Motions, and Discontinuance

LEARNING OBJECTIVES

⇨ Know, generally, how to use procedural rules to correct errors and handle collateral issues requiring court intervention prior to trial

⇨ Know how to amend pleadings

⇨ Know when and how to strike out improper pleadings

⇨ Know how to bring motions to resolve pre-trial disputes and issues

⇨ Know how to discontinue an undefended claim

INTRODUCTION

Up to this point, the parties have been investigating and developing their respective cases and positions and determining the facts and the applicable law they intend to rely on. They have stated their case in their pleadings. But what happens if one party thinks he or she has made an error and wants to correct it? Or the parties get entangled in a procedural dispute? Or a procedural issue arises that must be resolved before the action can proceed further? At this stage either party, having reviewed his or her own case or considered the position taken by the other party, may wish to either amend his or her pleadings or attack the other party's. In addition, if there are other issues or disagreements between the parties that arise before trial, the parties will need to bring motions before the court to have a judge resolve these issues or disputes. In this chapter we will examine some of the procedural tools available to correct errors and resolve disputes; we also look at the procedures used to bring a motion before the court for resolution of some procedural matters prior to trial.

THE RULES TOOLBOX

If you need to make amendments or repairs, or challenge the other parties on procedural issues, it is well to remember that there are some basic rules that provide the court with wide latitude in granting or denying requests. These rules, which we refer to as the "Rules Toolbox", can be used as the legal basis in a motion for the order you seek, either on their own or in combination with other rules focused on specific issues, giving added flexibility in interpreting specific procedural rules.

Rule 1.03: The General Principle

> 1.03(1) These rules shall be liberally construed to secure the just, most expeditious and least expensive determination of every proceeding on its merits in accordance with section 25 of the *Courts of Justice Act*.
>
> (2) If these rules do not cover a matter adequately, the court may give directions and make any order that is just, and the practice shall be decided by analogy to these rules, by reference to the *Courts of Justice Act* and the Act governing the action and, if the court considers it appropriate, by reference to the Rules of Civil Procedure.

This rule allows the court to interpret the Rules liberally and broadly, rather than literally, narrowly, or in an overly technical way, so as to ensure that justice is done by having a case heard on its merits, in as quick and inexpensive a manner as possible, consistent with reaching a just result. This rule can be used to overcome procedural delay by the other party and to prevent a procedure from being used to make the process more complex than it has to be. For example, this rule can be used to support a motion for separate trials in a case where there are multiple parties and one set of parties is ready to go to trial, but the others are not, even though normally the issues common to all parties are tried together. Here the rule would support an argument for determining the dispute quickly and without delay by ordering separate trials.

Note that subrule (2) of this rule provides that if a matter is not adequately covered by the *Rules of the Small Claims Court*, the court may determine which practice to use by analogy to any of the *Rules of the Small Claims Court* or by reference to the *Courts of Justice Act* and the Act governing the action. In some cases, if the court considers it appropriate, it may decide by reference to the *Rules of Civil Procedure* that govern proceedings in the Superior Court. As provided by the rule, the court's directions and orders made under this part must be "just".

Rule 2.01: Effect of Non-compliance with the Rules

> 2.01 A failure to comply with these rules is an irregularity and does not render a proceeding or a step, document or order in a proceeding a nullity, and the court may grant all necessary amendments or other relief, on such terms as are just, to secure the just determination of the real matters in dispute.

This rule says that if you fail to follow the Rules, it is not necessarily fatal to your case. The expectation is that if you make procedural errors, the court will allow you to correct them rather than dismiss a case on a procedural technicality. However, there is an assumption here that if you made a procedural mistake or forgot to do something, the error was one that was made inadvertently, or at least in good faith. If you intentionally misuse, abuse, or twist the rules, or act in bad faith or dishonestly, this rule will not bail out misconduct. But it will assist the litigant who made an inadvertent error through inexperience or ignorance. In that case, the court may suspend a rule's requirements and permit various amendments and repairs to be made so that the case can proceed on the merits. However, the right to make corrections may have a cost. If the opposing party has to do more work or repeat a step previously taken, the court may order the party who seeks the court's assistance to compensate the opposing party for any expense or inconvenience to which it is put as a result of a "repair" order under Rule 2.01. For example, if you should have attached documents to your claim but forgot to, you could bring a motion to disclose at a later date, rather than have your claim dismissed for non-compliance with the rules, although you may have to pay the opposing party for the inconvenience and delay, particularly if he or she has to attend court and/or amend his or her pleadings as a result of what your late disclosure revealed.

Rule 2.02: Dispensing with Compliance with the Rules

2.02 If necessary in the interest of justice, the court may dispense with compliance with any rule at any time.

This is the blockbuster rule in the toolbox. It permits the court, in appropriate cases, to dispense with or ignore any rule at any time in order that the case be allowed to proceed to trial on the merits.

Example 9.1 Using the Rules in the Rules Toolbox

Julie is 17 years old. She was hired by Maria to babysit her son Nathan for the month of August. On September 1, Maria was to pay Julie the sum of $600 for babysitting services provided. Julie completed the job on August 31, as agreed. It's now September 20 and Maria, despite Julie's calls to her, has failed to pay Julie as agreed. Julie decides to sue Maria in Small Claims Court.

As the claim in Example 9.1 exceeds $500 and Julie is under 18, she should have a litigation guardian. However, Julie can argue that she should be allowed to proceed on her own without a litigation guardian on the grounds that she is mature and almost an adult who is able to act without a litigation guardian, particularly as the claim is not far removed from $500 (the level at which she can represent herself anyhow).

If a judge is persuaded, he or she can dispense with the requirements of Rule 4. Julie can also use Rule 1.03 (the Rules should be given a broad and liberal interpretation in order to try the case on the merits) and Rule 2.01 (failure to follow the Rules is not necessarily fatal) to support her argument. Often, in fact, each of the rules in the rules toolbox will support different aspects of your argument, and you may use more than one.

Rule 3.02(1): Power of the Court to Lengthen or Shorten Time

> 3.02(1) The court may lengthen or shorten any time prescribed by these rules or an order, on such terms as are just.

This rule allows the court to lengthen or shorten the time set out in the Rules for doing something. In a motion, this is sometimes expressed as a request to extend (lengthen) or abridge (shorten) the time for doing something. For example, if a defendant needs time to investigate the facts for a defence, he may ask the court to extend the time for filing a defence beyond the normal 20 days given for this in Rule 9. By way of another example, if a party served the other side with a notice of motion and supporting affidavit three days before the motion, when seven days notice was required, the party could ask the court in their notice of motion, or orally at the hearing of the motion, to abridge the time for service.

AMENDING PLEADINGS

If Albert Oryx's claim against Ophelia Foot stated that the engagement ring he gave her had to be returned to him because she broke off the engagement but her defence stated that he said it was an unconditional gift as a symbol of his undying love, Albert may wish to consider whether or not he needs to amend his claim to deal with that allegation in the defence. He could just leave it be and present evidence to refute her version. But suppose he explicitly said that the gift was conditional upon her marrying him and that she knew this. If that is a fact he would now like to allege, given the allegation in her defence, he will have to amend his Claim.

Rule 12 allows a party to amend a claim, defendant's claim, or defence without obtaining the court's permission — that is, there is no need to bring a motion to do this, provided the amendment is made, served, and filed at least 30 days before trial so that the other side has time to respond or knows what the case is that he or she has to meet prior to trial.

Right to Amend
12.01(1) A plaintiff's or defendant's claim and a defence to a plaintiff's or defendant's claim may be amended by filing with the clerk a copy that is marked "Amended", in which any additions are underlined and any other changes are identified.

Service
(2) The amended document shall be served by the party making the amendment on all parties, including any parties in default, in accordance with subrule 8.01(14).

Time

(3) Filing and service of the amended document shall take place at least 30 days before the originally scheduled trial date, unless,
  (a) the court, on motion, allows a shorter notice period; or
  (b) a clerk's order permitting the amendment is obtained under subrule 11.2.01(1).

Service on Added Party

(4) A person added as a party shall be served with the claim as amended, except that if the person is added as a party at trial, the court may dispense with service of the claim.

No Amendment Required in Response

(5) A party who is served with an amended document is not required to amend the party's defence or claim.

How to Amend Pleadings

Rule 12.01(1) says that if you amend a pleading, you should mark the document at the top as amended, with additions underlined. Other changes must also be identified. For example, deletions may be identified with a line drawn through them. If you are using a word processing software, you can easily underline the additions and use the strikethrough function to cross out deleted text. All these changes, however, can also be made on a hard copy of the pleading by using a pen and a ruler.

Remember that you must allow enough time to file your amendments within the 30-day period before the trial. Allow enough time to make the amendments, serve them, and file them. If you do not have enough time or you discover an error just before trial, you will need to bring a motion permitting you to amend your claim or, with the consent of the other side, request a clerk's order permitting the amendment.

Note also that an amended pleading must be served on all parties, including a party who has defaulted, as the defaulter may, on seeing the amended pleading, also see a reason to defend a claim that seemed previously indefensible. Further, if the amendments result in a claim against a person who is not presently a party, it must be served on the new party, who then has the right to file a defence or a claim, as the case may be, and participate in the action. This will undoubtedly have the effect of delaying the action further.

Striking Out or Amending Improper Pleadings

In a court where parties often represent themselves, are not familiar with the conventions and rules governing pleadings, and have strong feelings about the issues or other parties, there is a tendency to include commentary in the pleadings that may be inappropriately inflammatory, or that may be designed to waste time, or that reveals no reasonable cause of action or defence.

A party has the right, under Rule 12.02, to ask the court to strike out or amend pleadings.

> 12.02(1) The court may, on motion, strike out or amend all or part of any document that,
> (a) discloses no reasonable cause of action or defence;
> (b) may delay or make it difficult to have a fair trial; or
> (c) is inflammatory, a waste of time, a nuisance or an abuse of the court's process.
>
> (2) In connection with an order striking out or amending a document under subrule (1), the court may do one or more of the following:
> 1. In the case of a claim, order that the action be stayed or dismissed.
> 2. In the case of a defence, strike out the defence and grant judgment.
> 3. Impose such terms as are just.

The rule allows a party to ask the court to strike out or amend all or part of a document on three grounds:

1. The pleading discloses no reasonable cause of action or defence. For example, I could sue you because you failed to show up for dinner after I had invited you and you had accepted. This may be a wrong done to me, but it is a breach of good manners, not a breach of a right of mine that the law recognizes. In this case, you could move to have my action dismissed as there is no reasonable cause of action known to the law. However, if I had left out facts that would create a cause of action, the court could **stay proceedings** until I made the necessary amendments. To illustrate, let's say I have left out of the claim the fact that when I invited you for dinner you said that you would come if I also invited a potential client that you were trying to attract to your business. You further told me that you would only come if I made your potential client's favourite meal, which consisted of lobster, sirloin steak, and caviar followed by chocolate soufflé. You told me that you would pay for the cost of the ingredients for the meal. Such a case would involve a cause of action in contract law for the reimbursement of the cost of the food as promised. However, the claim would have to be amended to include the above facts.

2. The pleadings may delay or make it difficult to try the action. This may occur in a variety of ways:

- The pleadings may be unnecessarily wordy, disorganized, or incoherent, to the extent that it is difficult to determine what the suit is about or what the fact allegations are.
- A wide variety of claims or defences are set out against many parties, and the case cannot be tried quickly or inexpensively and has to be divided into several different actions.
- There are so many overlapping claims or defences that the other party could not easily defend or pursue the claim in a coherent way at trial. In such a case, if amendments cannot resolve the problems, the claim or defence could be struck out.

3. The claim is inflammatory, a waste of time, a nuisance, or an abuse of the court's process. This is a hold-all or basket provision that can catch all kinds of improper pleadings.

   - An inflammatory pleading is one that contains unnecessary or irrelevant allegations that add heat and atmosphere but not much light. For example, Albert Oryx, having been spurned by Ophelia Foot when she broke off the engagement, may wish to comment on her character (or, in his view, lack of character) by stating that she is a "mercenary, money-grubbing liar". At first glance, this looks like name calling by an angry man who has been rejected by his former fiancée, and if that is the case, it is not relevant to the case as pleaded — that is, she had no legal right based on their relationship to keep the ring. Her actions are in issue, not her character. However, if Albert's pleading and the theory of his case support a claim that Ophelia kept the ring because of her greed and had never intended to marry him but had, instead, intended to defraud him, then the allegation may be relevant and could be allowed to stand. That is really the test — is the allegation or the statement or the language used by a party, which appears to be nasty and inflammatory, actually relevant to the case that is being presented? If it is, it may be left alone or, perhaps, amended to make it less inflammatory. But if it is simply an inflammatory diatribe, then it cannot be relevant to the case and the court may strike it out.
   - A waste of time, under the rule, is a case that, as pleaded, has no real chance of success or contains allegations that could never be proven. There is some overlap here with the two previous grounds discussed. A nuisance is an action that is clearly brought for an ulterior purpose designed to harass the other party. An example is where an action is brought on grounds and facts similar to one that has previously been dismissed.

- Nuisance and an abuse of the court's process are very similar. Abuse of process applies more specifically to a litigant who is clearly flouting a court's direction, where, for example, an action is clearly intended as a form of harassment. Note here that this is not just a question of the language used in or clarity of the pleadings. It goes to the substantive issues that the case is about and the behaviour of the parties in conducting the lawsuit.

MOTIONS

As you will have noticed in the first part of this chapter and in previous chapters, occasionally you need to ask the court to make an order to permit you to do something under the procedural rules. For example, you need to ask the court to strike out inflammatory pleadings or appoint a litigation guardian for a defendant who does not have one. The Rules usually give you some clues that indicate you need to bring a motion. Sometimes the Rules will be explicit, saying that a party may bring a motion to do something. At other times, the Rules use less direct language, such as "the court may", or "a party may, with leave of the court", or "the court may order."

Motion Documents

When it is necessary to ask the court to make an order before or after trial, the usual mechanism is the motion, made under Rule 15. As set out in Rule 15.01(1), a Notice of Motion and Supporting Affidavit (Form 15A) is the document used in the motion process:

> 15.01(1) A motion shall be made by a notice of motion and supporting affidavit (Form 15A).

The Notice of Motion and Supporting Affidavit

The Notice of Motion and Supporting Affidavit tells the court and your opponent what it is you want the court to do, and identifies documents and rules on which you rely. Sample Notices of Motion and Supporting Affidavits can be found in Illustration 7.4 (Motion to Assess Damages) and Figure 7.1 (Motion to Set Aside Default Judgment).

The Affidavit

The affidavit part of Form 15A sets out the facts and evidence on which you rely to obtain the order you seek. For example, if you bring a motion to set aside default judgment, you should see what the rule (in this case Rule 11.06) requires in order for you to obtain an order to set a judgment aside. Rule 11.06 indicates you need to show that you have a good defence, that you have a reasonable excuse for the default, and that you moved as quickly as reasonably possible in the circumstances to set the default judgment aside once you discovered it.

Affidavits can be filed in Form 15A or Form 15B. If you are the party bringing a motion, your affidavit would be contained in Form 15A. If you had additional information for the court after you filed your Form 15A, you could prepare another affidavit (a supplementary affidavit) using Form 15B. If you are the party responding to the motion and wish to provide evidence to the court, you would use Form 15B for your affidavit.

DRAFTING AFFIDAVITS

Affidavits provide the facts and evidence that support the request for the order sought in the motion. Affidavits are sworn statements in which the **deponent**, or maker of the affidavit, sets out a written statement of facts and evidence in consecutively numbered paragraphs, with one paragraph for each fact set out in the sworn statement. The statement is told in the first person singular, "I", as in "As soon as I found out there was a default judgment against me, I moved to set it aside". At the end, the deponent swears or affirms, before a Commissioner for Taking Oaths and Affidavits, that the contents are true. The court clerk can commission affidavits, as can lawyers, as all lawyers are commissioners upon call to the bar. Law clerks may apply for a commission if working under the supervision of a lawyer, as may other individuals who work in legal environments, such as Legal Aid clinic workers. However, these non-lawyers must use a stamp indicating that their commissionership is only with respect to the law office or clinic they work for. Paralegals, as a consequence of paralegal regulation, are able to become commissioners for taking oaths and affidavits in the areas in which they are authorized to practice. You can obtain an application form to become a Commissioner for Taking Oaths and Affidavits by calling the Legal Appointments Office of the Ontario Ministry of the Attorney General at 416-326-4064.

USE OF HEARSAY EVIDENCE IN AFFIDAVITS

If the deponent wishes to relate hearsay in an affidavit, he or she may do so, provided the deponent states the source of the information and that he or she believes the information to be true. The way this is usually expressed is as follows:

> "I am advised by Ophelia Foot, and believe that she agreed to become engaged to Albert Oryx in order to have access to his great wealth."

USE OF EXHIBITS IN AFFIDAVITS

If the deponent refers to a document, a true copy of the document (which can be a direct photocopy that you make of the original document, comparing it to the original to ensure it is an exact reproduction) should be marked as an exhibit to the affidavit and attached to the affidavit. If it is too large or cumbersome to attach, it should be marked as an exhibit and filed with the court. A reduced size copy of the original or photo of it should be attached to the affidavit to avoid introducing evidence in court that the other side has not had a chance to consider. A reduced size copy should be referred to as a copy, not a true copy. The original document should be maintained on hand for use as evidence at trial. The reference to a document in an affidavit is usually expressed as follows:

> "The price on the invoice for the frammix was $300.00.
> Attached to this, my affidavit, and marked as Exhibit
> 'A' is a true copy of invoice number 1234 for a model
> GT 4 frammix."

A sample exhibit to an affidavit is found in the affidavit to assess damages in Illustration 7.4 on page 287.

In an affidavit, you are telling a story, usually in a chronological or sequential order, using the first person singular, where the deponent says what he or she knows that is relevant to the relief requested in the motion. Remember that it is not necessary for the deponent to repeat all the allegations in the claim or defence. It is necessary to determine what facts are required to obtain the remedy requested (or, for the responding party, to prevent the remedy requested from being granted). As motions are often brought under a rule of the court, use the rule as an outline of what is required — for example, to set aside a default judgment, your outline should note the excuse for the default, such as the fact that you have a good defence and that you took prompt action to set the judgment aside.

Motion Procedure

Once you have prepared your motion documents, you will need to obtain a date from the court and serve and file your documents.

Obtaining a Motion Date

If you bring a motion, you should first obtain a date from the clerk in accordance with Rule 15.01(2) to have the motion heard:

15.01(2) The moving party shall obtain a hearing date from the clerk before serving the notice of motion and supporting affidavit under subrule (3).

You cannot usually choose any day you feel like doing the motion. Different courts may have particular "motion days" where a morning or a day in each week is reserved to hear motions. How they are scheduled depends on the volume of motions heard by a particular court.

Service of Motion Materials

Once you have obtained a date, in accordance with Rule 15.01(3)(a), you must serve a copy of the notice of motion and supporting affidavit on each party who has filed a claim or defence, whether the motion affects the party or not:

15.01(3) The notice of motion and supporting affidavit,
(a) shall be served on every party who has filed a claim and any defendant who has not been noted in default, at least seven days before the hearing date ...

All parties are entitled to notice of a motion brought before trial except for a party who has defaulted on his or her defence. However, if the motion is to amend a pleading, you must also serve parties who are in default in accordance with Rule 11.05(3):

11.05(3) A defendant who has been noted in default is not entitled to notice of any step in the proceeding and need not be served with any other document, except the following:
1. Subrule 11.02(3) (service of default judgment).
2. Rule 12.01 (amendment of claim or defence).
3. Subrule 15.01(6) (motion after judgment).
4. Postjudgment proceedings against a debtor under rule 20.

Service is required, in such a case, as the amendments might now provide the defaulting defendant with a reason to file a defence. Rule 11.05(3) also provides that if the motion is brought after judgment, all parties, including defaulting parties, must be served. In accordance with Rule 15.01(3)(a), the motion material must be served at least seven days before the motion date. Motion materials are usually served by an alternative to personal service, such as mail, courier, or fax. An affidavit of service, using Form 8A, must be completed following service. A sample affidavit of service is found in Illustration 6.5 on page 251.

Filing Motion Materials with the Court

In accordance with Rule 15.01(3)(b), the notice of motion and supporting affidavit must be filed with the court along with the affidavit of service at least three days before the hearing.

> 15.01(3) The notice of motion and supporting affidavit,
> (b) shall be filed, with proof of service, at least three days before the hearing date.

Remember to check Rule 8 concerning service to determine if additional time must be counted in based on the method of service. For example, if service is by regular mail, service is not considered effective under Rule 8.07(2) until the five days after the date of mailing.

Note that there is also a court fee to be paid for bringing a motion. The fee to file a motion is $40 as of July 17, 2013.

Responding to a Motion

When the person bringing the motion (called the **moving party**) serves his or her motion material on the other party (called the **responding party**), the responding party may have a version of evidence and facts that he or she wishes to rely on to show why the order requested should not be granted. In this case, in accordance with Rule 15.01(4), the responding party has to set out his or her facts in an affidavit in response (Form 15B), serve it on every other party not in default, and file the affidavit and the affidavit of service at least two days prior to the hearing:

> 15.01(4) A party who prepares an affidavit (Form 15B) in response to the moving party's notice of motion and supporting affidavit shall serve it on every party who has filed a claim or defence and file it, with proof of service, at least two days before the hearing date.

The moving party may also file a supplementary affidavit, in accordance with Rule 15.01(5), setting out additional facts and evidence not covered in the moving party's original affidavit. Presumably this will permit the moving party to reply to the contents of the responding party's affidavit, and should be used when the responding party has raised facts and issues in the responding affidavit that are not addressed at all in the moving party's original affidavit. Otherwise, the moving party should avoid the temptation to file a supplementary affidavit in order to simply have the last word. The moving party's supplementary affidavit, like the responding affidavit, must also be filed at least two days prior to the hearing of the motion.

> 15.01(5) The moving party may serve a supplementary affidavit on every party who has filed a claim or defence and file it, with proof of service, at least two days before the hearing date.

It is also possible that a notice of motion and supporting affidavit served by one party on the other may trigger not only an affidavit in response, but a **cross motion,** where in addition to opposing the main motion, the cross motion claims separate remedies. For example, a motion to strike out a plaintiff's claim as having no reasonable cause of action could be met with a cross motion to strike out the defence on the grounds that it is inflammatory and an abuse of process. When this happens, the mover of the cross motion is subject to the same rules for service as the mover of any motion. While cross motions are not prohibited by the Rules, they are not clearly contemplated by them, either, and you may need to use the rules toolbox to help the court untangle the procedural knots, allowing everyone reasonable time to serve and respond to the opposing party's motion material.

Timing Sequence for Serving and Filing Motion Material

As you will see from Figure 9.1 and from reading Rule 15.01, the timeline for both moving and opposing parties to serve and file their material is a short one: eight days prior to the motion (as your motion material must be served at least seven days before the motion date, and the day of service is excluded from your count) for the moving party and four days for an opposing party or for a moving party's supplementary affidavit (as their affidavits must be served and filed at least two days before the motion). Remember that in calculating a time period under the Rules, Rule 3.01 states that (i) you exclude the first day on which you do something and include the last day on which it can be done; and (ii) if the last day of the period of time falls on a holiday, the period ends on the next day that is not a holiday.[1]

A moving party can try to use the motion service and filing rules to his or her advantage by serving material right on the eighth day before the hearing, leaving the respondent only a short time to respond. The moving party, after obtaining a motion date from the court, often has weeks to prepare and serve their motion material. The moving party can generally bring a motion at any time.[2] Once the motion is served, it can be filed five days later; but the responding

---

[1] Rule 1.02 defines holiday to include Saturday and Sunday, as well as all statutory holidays. If the last day of the period falls on a holiday, the next normal business day will become the last day of the time period.

[2] If a party makes numerous motions that are without merit, the court can use Rule 15.04 to make an order prohibiting any further motions unless leave is sought.

FIGURE 9.1: Motion Serving Sequence

Day 1	Moving party serves motion and supporting affidavit at least 7 days before hearing date (Rule 15.01(3)(a)). Rule 3.01 states that the first day (i.e., day of service) is excluded from your count.
Day 2 (Day 1)	In accordance with Rule 3.01, this would be the first day of service.
Day 3	
Day 4	
Day 5	Last day (3 days before the hearing) to file notice of motion and supporting affidavit with the court (Rule 15.01(3)) as Rule 3.01 says not to count first day.
Day 6	Last day (2 days before hearing) to serve and file responding and supplementary affidavits (Rule 15.01(4)).
Day 7	
Day 8 (Day 7)	Motion Hearing Date This is actually the 7th day before the motion as Day 1 was excluded under Rule 3.01. Rule 3.01 states that the last day of the period is included.

party has to scramble, having only five days after service to prepare and serve the respondent's affidavit. Of course, the responding party can also put pressure on the moving party. If the moving party wants to file a supplementary affidavit in response to the moving party's affidavit, there could be only one day to prepare, serve, and file the supplementary affidavit. In all cases, remember Rule 2.01 in your rules toolbox, which can be used to ask the court to accept an abridgement (i.e., shortening) of the time for service. Note that whether you are the moving or responding party, you may have to serve opposing parties or their representatives personally or by fax, as any service method involving mail or courier service means that the effective date of service is five days after mailing or couriering the material; the material may end up being officially served *after* the date of hearing, which does not come close to complying with Rule 15.01's time limits.

However, before a moving party tries to take advantage of the serving and filing times in Rule 15.01 in this way, he or she should consider that that strategy could backfire. An attempt to use the rules to ambush the opposing party will likely result in a request for an adjournment, which, if granted, will result in a delay in having the motion heard, as a new motion date will have to be selected. Also, although your client may like the idea of an ambush, these kinds of practices, if repeated, can damage a legal representative's reputation and credibility with the court. In most cases, it is advisable for the moving party to consult the opposing party to obtain an agreed upon motion date, and to serve his or her motion material well in advance of the motion date in order to give all parties the opportunity to prepare and respond and, by so doing, avoid unnecessary adjournments. If an adjournment does become necessary, the court will adjourn on consent of all parties; otherwise, the adjournment has to be argued. If you request an adjournment from the other party, follow an oral request with one in writing, setting out reasons; notify the clerk of your request; and file a copy of your letter with the court. A timely and well-documented request will help to persuade the court that your request is appropriate and should be granted. If a motion is to be withdrawn, it may be done on consent; otherwise, it must be argued before the court.

Keep in mind that Rule 3.02(1) allows the court to lengthen or shorten any prescribed time on such terms as are just. In other words, this rule also allows you to ask the court to abridge (shorten) the required time for service or lengthen the time to respond. Such a request is often used in emergency situations where strictly following the time guidelines for service would prejudice one of the parties.

Methods of Hearing on Motions with Notice

As we noted in Chapter 7, in the discussion of motions for assessment of damages in an undefended claim, there are types of motion that involves only the moving party and can be made in writing, under Rule 11.03(2)(a), without anyone having to appear on the motion to make oral arguments. Rule 15.02 provides several other methods for hearing a motion in a defended case, but the usual method is for the parties, or their representatives, to appear in person and argue the motion orally, based on their written material, before a judge. On the day appointed for the motion, the parties should arrive at the courthouse at least 30 minutes before their scheduled motion time. The representatives for each party or the parties themselves, if unrepresented, should check in with the court clerk who sits at the front of the courtroom just below the judge's desk. The legal representatives should fill out a counsel slip, which is a form on which they state their name and who they represent. As set out in Figure 9.2, the judge sits at an elevated

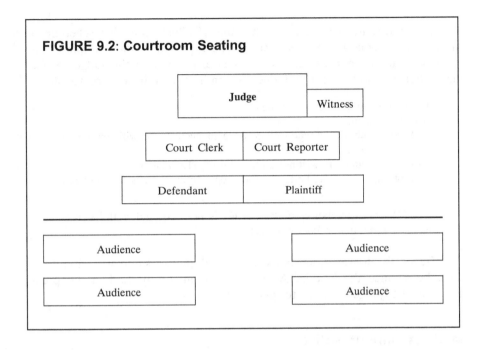

FIGURE 9.2: Courtroom Seating

desk at the front of the courtroom. To the judge's right sits the court clerk, and to the left sits the court reporter, if there is one.[3] Both plaintiff and defendant, as well as their representatives, sit in front of the judge: the plaintiff and his or her representative on the judge's left, and the defendant and his or her representative on the judge's right.

Where a motion is argued in person, the moving party begins by telling the court what relief, remedy, or order the moving party is seeking and the grounds or basis for seeking it. The moving party also identifies the rule, statute, or case law on which he or she relies, with an explanation about how the rule or legal principle should be applied, based on the facts and evidence set out in the affidavit that shows why, in this case, the requested remedy should be granted. Then the responding party presents his or her argument as to why the order sought should not be granted, identifying principles of law or rules that support the opposing party's argument, and referring to facts and evidence in the opposing affidavit. The judge will usually make a decision at the end of the hearing, recording the decision in the order on the endorsement record, a copy of which can later be obtained from the clerk.

---

[3] In many Small Claims Courts, the court clerk also has the task of recording the proceedings using a recording device.

The court, in accordance with Rule 15.02(1), can also schedule a motion by telephone or video conference, provided the equipment is available and the parties request it. It is also open to the judge to use any other method that the judge determines is fair and reasonable.

> 15.02(1) A motion may be heard,
> (a) in person;
> (b) by telephone or video conference in accordance with paragraph 2 of subrule 1.07(1);
> (c) by a judge in writing under clause 11.03(2)(a);
> (d) by any other method that the judge determines is fair and reasonable.
>
> (2) The attendance of the parties is not required if the motion is in writing under clause (1)(c).

Generally, however, motions are heard in the same way that they have been since the Middle Ages — in person, orally, and in the presence of the judge who is to decide the matter.

Motions without Notice

Under Rule 15.03 some motions may be brought without notice to other parties:

> 15.03(1) Despite rule 15.01, a motion may be made without notice if the nature or circumstances of the motion make notice unnecessary or not reasonably possible.

For example, if you bring a motion to assess damages against a defaulting defendant, you do not serve the defaulting party, because having failed to file a defence, he or she is no longer entitled, in most cases, to notice of further proceedings. In addition, in appropriate circumstances, where notice is normally required, you may ask a judge to dispense with notice: for example, if you are unable to locate or contact the party to serve him or her. If you intend to bring a motion without notice, you should remember to ask for leave to dispense with service of the motion in addition to the other relief requested on the motion. A judge will first hear you on the issue of leave to bring the motion without notice, and if the decision is in your favour, he or she will go on to hear the motion. If the judge decides the motion should be heard on notice to the other party, the matter can be adjourned until the material is served. Proceeding without notice to an opponent is a serious issue for the court, and leave is not given lightly. However, when it is, Rule 15.03 goes on to require that any order made without notice shall be served on affected parties, along with a copy of the notice of motion and supporting affidavit within five days of the order being made. In this way, what has been done without notice is brought to the other party's attention, and he or she has 30 days after being served to move to set aside or vary the order.

> 15.03(2) A party who obtains an order on motion without notice shall serve it on every affected party, together with a copy of the notice of motion and supporting affidavit used on the motion, within five days after the order is signed.
>
> (3) A party who is affected by an order obtained on motion without notice may make a motion to set aside or vary the order, within 30 days after being served with the order.

Consent Motions

If all parties consent to the order sought by the moving party, written consents from all parties can be filed with the notice of motion and supporting affidavit. The consents, signed by a party or his or her representative, should state the order that is being consented to or indicate that it is a consent to the order requested in the notice of motion. In this case, the notice of motion should request that the motion be decided on the basis of the documents filed without a hearing.

Consent Motions by Request for a Clerk's Order

Rule 11.2 creates a procedure for a clerk to make a consent order where the relief sought falls into specific categories set out in Rule 11.2.01 and all parties consent to the order. The orders covered are really more administrative than judicial in nature. There is little need for someone with legal training to exercise judicial discretion in most situations set out in the rule. The categories are set out in Rule 11.2.01(1):

> 11.2.01(1) The clerk shall, on the filing of a request for clerk's order on consent (Form 11.2A), make an order granting the relief sought, including costs, if the following conditions are satisfied:
> 1. The relief sought is,
>   i. amending a claim or defence less than 30 days before the originally scheduled trial date,
>   ii. adding, deleting or substituting a party less than 30 days before the originally scheduled trial date,
>   iii. setting aside the noting in default or default judgment against a party and any specified step to enforce the judgment that has not yet been completed,
>   iv. restoring a matter that was dismissed under rule 11.1 to the list,
>   v. noting that payment has been made in full satisfaction of a judgment or terms of settlement, or
>   vi. dismissing an action.

2. The request is signed by all parties (including any party to be added, deleted or substituted) and states,

  i. that each party has received a copy of the request, and

  ii. that no party that would be affected by the order is under disability.

3.,4. Revoked.

(2) The clerk shall serve a copy of an order made under subrule (1) in accordance with subrule 8.01(14) on a party that requests it and provides a stamped, self-addressed envelope.

(3) Where the clerk refuses to make an order, the clerk shall serve a copy of the request for clerk's order on consent (Form 11.2A), with reasons for the refusal, on all the parties.

(4) Where an order is made setting aside a specified step to enforce a judgment under subparagraph 1 iii of subrule (1), a party shall file a copy of the order at each court location where the enforcement step has been requested.

The relief available from a Clerk's Consent Order under Rule 11.2.01(1) can be categorized as follows:

- Amending a claim or defence, where there is less than 30 days before the trial and a motion would otherwise be required

- Adding, deleting, or substituting a party — where, for example, a plaintiff has sued an individual carrying on a business, when in fact the business is incorporated and it is the company that should be served — a common occurrence

- Setting aside noting in default, or a default judgment, and any enforcement step taken, usually in circumstances where it is clear that the default was inadvertent and where it is likely that the judgment will be set aside

- Restoring a matter that was administratively dismissed by a clerk under Rule 11.1, due to delay by the parties in meeting a case management deadline

- Noting and recording that a judgment or settlement has been paid in full

- Dismissing an action

The procedure for obtaining a clerk's consent order is for the moving party to complete a Request for Clerk's Order on Consent (Form 11.2A) in which the category of order requested is identified, with necessary detail. The form must be signed by every party, including any party added or deleted or substituted, and all parties must be given a copy. If any party is under disability, the matter must proceed as an ordinary motion before a judge. Follow the instructions set out on the form for the relief sought. For example, if amending a pleading, two copies of the amended pleading must be provided. If enforcement action is to be withdrawn or terminated, instructions as to what to do with any money collected must be provided.

Once the court has received the material and the order is made, the clerk shall serve a copy of the order on anyone requesting it who also provided a stamped, self-addressed envelope.

If the clerk is uncertain as to whether there is authority to make the order requested, he or she shall refuse to make the order and indicate the reasons on the Request for Clerk's Order on Consent and serve a copy of the request on all parties.

If the order is to set aside a default judgment and an enforcement step, a copy of the order should be sent by the moving party to any court where an enforcement step is being taken: for example, a defendant sued in Toronto may have property that is being subjected to enforcement in Peterborough.

Illustration 9.1 shows a sample Request for Clerk's Order on Consent in the Cruel Credit Ltd. case in Example 7.1 on page 269.

Unnecessary Motions and Costs on Motions

A client with financial resources facing a client who is not as financially able, or a party whose strategy is to prolong proceedings by wearing the other side down, in part by bringing frequent and unnecessary motions, may try to "motion the other side to death". These attempts to delay matters or to wear the other side down are seen to be an abuse of process. Rule 15.04 provides that on the motion of a party, the court may, in the circumstances described here, prohibit a party who brings numerous, unmeritorious motions from bringing any further motions without first obtaining the court's permission:

> 15.04 If the court is satisfied that a party has tried to delay the action, add to its costs or otherwise abuse the court's process by making numerous motions without merit, the court may, on motion, make an order prohibiting the party from making any further motions in the action without leave of the court.

The court may also make a punitive costs award on a motion that constitutes abuse, and, unlike regular motions, there is no specific limit on the amount of such an award. For all other motions, the court, under Rule 15.07, may award the winning party on a motion costs of up to $100, plus disbursements, to cover the court fee to file the motion, the costs of serving it, photocopying, and any other related out-of-pocket payment made to bring the motion. The court has discretion under the rule to award higher costs in the event of special circum-

ILLUSTRATION 9.1: Sample Request for Clerk's Order on Consent (Form 11.2A)

ONTARIO
Superior Court of Justice
Cour supérieure de justice

Request for Clerk's Order on Consent
Demande d'ordonnance du greffier sur consentement
Form / Formule 11.2A Ont. Reg. No. / Règl. de l'Ont. : 258/98

Toronto	**SC-00-42658-00**
Small Claims Court / Cour des petites créances de	Claim No. / N° de la demande

47 Sheppard Ave. E., 3rd Fl.
Toronto, ON M2N 5N1
Address / Adresse

416-326-3554
Phone number / Numéro de téléphone

Plaintiff No. 1 / Demandeur n° 1 ☐ Additional plaintiff(s) listed on attached Form 1A.
Le ou les demandeurs additionnels sont mentionnés sur la formule 1A ci-jointe.

Last name, or name of company / Nom de famille ou nom de la compagnie		
Cruel Credit Ltd.		
First name / Premier prénom	Second name / Deuxième prénom	Also known as / Également connu(e) sous le nom de
Address (street number, apt., unit) / Adresse (numéro et rue, app., unité)		
c/o Paul Paralegal, 27 Milkyway		
City/Town / Cité/ville	Province	Phone no. / N° de téléphone
Somewhere	**ON**	**909-842-5678**
Postal code / Code postal		Fax no. / N° de télécopieur
K2L 3T4		**909-842-5679**
Representative / Représentant(e)		LSUC # / N° du BHC
Paul Paralegal		**P02953**
Address (street number, apt., unit) / Adresse (numéro et rue, app., unité)		
27 Milkyway		
City/Town / Cité/ville	Province	Phone no. / N° de téléphone
Somewhere	**ON**	**909-842-5678**
Postal code / Code postal		Fax no. / N° de télécopieur
K2L 3T4		**909-842-5679**

Defendant No. 1 / Défendeur n° 1 ☐ Additional defendant(s) listed on attached Form 1A.
Le ou les défendeurs additionnels sont mentionnés sur la formule 1A ci-jointe.

Last name, or name of company / Nom de famille ou nom de la compagnie		
DeFaulter		
First name / Premier prénom	Second name / Deuxième prénom	Also known as / Également connu(e) sous le nom de
Donald		
Address (street number, apt., unit) / Adresse (numéro et rue, app., unité)		
2340 Main Street		
City/Town / Cité/ville	Province	Phone no. / N° de téléphone
Newmarket	**ON**	
Postal code / Code postal		Fax no. / N° de télécopieur
L3Y 3H3		
Representative / Représentant(e)		LSUC # / N° du BHC
Address (street number, apt., unit) / Adresse (numéro et rue, app., unité)		
City/Town / Cité/ville	Province	Phone no. / N° de téléphone
Postal code / Code postal		Fax no. / N° de télécopieur

NOTE: This request must be signed by all parties and anyone being added, deleted or substituted.
REMARQUE : La présente demande doit être signée par toutes les parties et par toute personne qui est jointe, radiée ou substituée.

SCR 11.2.01-11.2A (June 1, 2009 / 1er juin 2009) CSD

continues....

Illustration 9.1 (continued)

FORM / *FORMULE* 11.2A   PAGE 2   SC-00-42658-00

Claim No. / *N° de la demande*

TO THE PARTIES:
AUX PARTIES :

THIS REQUEST IS FILED BY: Cruel Credit Ltd.
LA PRÉSENTE DEMANDE EST DÉPOSÉE PAR :   (Name of party / *Nom de la partie*)

I state that:
Je déclare que :

☒ Each party has received a copy of this form.
    Chaque partie a reçu une copie de la présente formule.

☒ No party that would be affected by the order is under disability.
    Aucune partie sur laquelle l'ordonnance aurait une incidence n'est incapable.

☒ This form has been signed and consented to by all parties, including any parties to be added, deleted or substituted.
    Toutes les parties, y compris celles qui doivent être jointes, radiées ou substituées, ont signé la présente formule et y ont consenti.

I request that the clerk make the following order(s) on the consent of all parties:
Je demande au greffier de rendre l'ordonnance ou les ordonnances suivantes sur consentement de toutes les parties :
(Check appropriate boxes. / *Cochez les cases appropriées.*)

☒ set aside the noting in default of   **Donald DeFaulter**
    l'annulation de la constatation du défaut de   (Name of defendant(s) / *Nom du/de la/des défendeur(s)/défenderesse(s)*)

☒ set aside Default Judgment against   **Donald DeFaulter**
    l'annulation du jugement par défaut prononcé contre   (Name of defendant(s) / *Nom du/de la/des défendeur(s)/défenderesse(s)*)

☐ restore to the list the following matter that was dismissed under Rule 11.1: (Specify.)
    la réinscription au rôle de l'affaire suivante qui a été rejetée aux termes de la règle 11.1 :   (*Précisez.*)

☐ cancel the examination hearing regarding
    l'annulation de l'interrogatoire concernant   (Name of person to be examined / *Nom de la personne qui doit être interrogée*)

☐ with respect to the following step(s) taken to enforce the default judgment that are not yet completed:
    à l'égard de la ou des mesures suivantes qui ont été prises pour exécuter le jugement par défaut et qui ne sont pas encore menées à terme :

    ☐ withdraw the Writ of Seizure and Sale of Land issued against: (Name of debtor(s))
        le retrait du bref de saisie-exécution de biens-fonds délivré contre :   (*Nom du/de la/des débiteur(s)/débitrice(s)*)

    and directed to the sheriff of the   :
    et adressé au shérif de   (Name of county/region in which the sheriff(enforcement office) is located / *Nom du comté/de la région où se trouve le shérif (bureau de l'exécution)*)

    (Provide instructions about what is to be done with any proceeds held or property seized by the sheriff. / *Donnez des instructions sur ce qu'il faut faire de tout produit de la vente détenu ou bien saisi par le shérif.*)

SCR 11.2.01-11.2A (June 1, 2009 / *1er juin 2009*) CSD   **Continued on next page / *Suite à la page suivante***

continues....

Illustration 9.1 (continued)

FORM / FORMULE 11.2A   **PAGE 3**   SC-00-42658-00

Claim No. / N° de la demande

☐ withdraw the Writ of Seizure and Sale of Personal Property issued against: (Name of debtor(s))
le retrait du bref de saisie-exécution de biens meubles délivré contre : (Nom du/de la/des débiteur(s)/débitrice(s))

and directed to the bailiff of the .... :
et adressé à l'huissier de   (Small Claims Court location / Emplacement de la Cour des petites créances)

(Provide instructions about what is to be done with any proceeds held by the clerk of the court or property that has been seized by the bailiff. / Donnez des instructions sur ce qu'il faut faire de tout produit de la vente détenu par le greffier du tribunal ou de tout bien saisi par l'huissier.)

☐ terminate the Notice of Garnishment or Notice of Renewal of Garnishment issued against:
la fin de l'avis de saisie-arrêt ou de l'avis de renouvellement de la saisie-arrêt délivré contre :

(Name of debtor(s) / Nom du/de la/des débiteur(s)/débitrice(s))

and directed to .... :
et adressé à   (Name of garnishee / Nom du tiers saisi)

(Provide instructions about what is to be done with any money held by the clerk of the court. / Donnez des instructions sur ce qu'il faut faire de toute somme d'argent détenue par le greffier du tribunal.)

☐ note that payment has been made in full satisfaction of an order or terms of settlement
le constat qu'un paiement intégral a été effectué en exécution d'une ordonnance ou des conditions de la transaction

☐ dismiss the: ☐ Plaintiff's Claim   ☐ Defendant's Claim
le rejet de la :   *demande du demandeur*   *demande du défendeur*

☒ costs in the amount of $ ....200.00..... , to be paid to **Cruel Credit Ltd.**
le versement de   (Amount / Montant)   *$ au titre des dépens à*   (Name of party(ies) / Nom de la ou des parties)

                                 by **Donald DeFaulter**
                                 par   (Name of party(ies) / Nom de la ou des parties)

The originally scheduled trial date is less than 30 days away and I request that the clerk make the following order(s) on the consent of all parties and any person to be added or substituted :
La date du procès fixée à l'origine tombe dans moins de 30 jours et je demande au greffier de rendre l'ordonnance ou les ordonnances suivantes sur consentement de toutes les parties et de toute personne qui doit être jointe ou substituée :
(Check appropriate boxes. / Cochez les cases appropriées.)

☐ amend a Plaintiff's Claim issued on ....
la modification de la demande d'un demandeur délivrée le
(Attach two (2) copies of the amended Plaintiff's Claim. / Annexez deux (2) copies de la demande du demandeur modifiée.)

☐ amend a Defence filed on ....
la modification d'une défense déposée le
(Attach two (2) copies of the amended Defence. / Annexez deux (2) copies de la défense modifiée.)

SCR 11.2.01-11.2A (June 1, 2009 / 1ᵉʳ juin 2009) CSD   Continued on next page / Suite à la page suivante

continues....

Illustration 9.1 (continued)

FORM / *FORMULE* 11.2A	PAGE 4	SC-00-42658-00
		Claim No. / *N° de la demande*

☐ amend a Defendant's Claim issued on _____ .
la modification de la demande d'un défendeur délivrée le
(Attach two (2) copies of the amended Defendant's Claim. / Annexez deux (2) copies de la demande du défendeur modifiée.)

☐ add _____
la jonction de   (Name of party / *Nom de la partie*)

to the   ☐ Plaintiff's Claim   ☐ Defendant's Claim
à la   *demande du demandeur*   *demande du défendeur*

as a   ☐ defendant   ☐ Plaintiff
à titre de   *défendeur/défenderesse*   *demandeur/demanderesse*

☐ delete _____
la radiation de   (Name of party / *Nom de la partie*)

from the   ☐ Plaintiff's Claim   ☐ Defendant's Claim
de la   *demande du demandeur*   *demande du défendeur*

☐ substitute _____
la substitution à   (Name of party / *Nom de la partie*)

with _____
de   (Name of party / *Nom de la partie*)

in the   ☐ Plaintiff's Claim   ☐ Defendant's Claim
dans la   *demande du demandeur*   *demande du défendeur*

July 20, Yr. 0	July 20, Yr. 0
Donald DeFaulter	Per: "Cruel Credit" Pres. Cruel Credit Ltd.
(Signature of party consenting / *Signature de la partie qui consent*)	(Signature of party consenting / *Signature de la partie qui consent*)
Donald DeFaulter	**Cruel Credit Ltd.**
(Name of party consenting / *Nom de la partie qui consent*)	(Name of party consenting / *Nom de la partie qui consent*)
Warren Witness	*Darlene Darling*
(Signature of witness / *Signature du témoin*)	(Signature of witness / *Signature du témoin*)
Warren Witness	**Darlene Darling**
(Name of witness / *Nom du témoin*)	(Name of witness / *Nom du témoin*)
(Signature of party consenting / *Signature de la partie qui consent*)	(Signature of party consenting / *Signature de la partie qui consent*)
(Name of party consenting / *Nom de la partie qui consent*)	(Name of party consenting / *Nom de la partie qui consent*)
(Signature of witness / *Signature du témoin*)	(Signature of witness / *Signature du témoin*)
(Name of witness / *Nom du témoin*)	(Name of witness / *Nom du témoin*)

SCR 11.2.01-11.2A (June 1, 2009 / *1er juin 2009*) CSD

Continued on next page / *Suite à la page suivante*

continues....

Illustration 9.1 (continued)

FORM / *FORMULE* 11.2A   PAGE 5   SC-00-42658-00
....
                                                                   Claim No. / *N° de la demande*

DISPOSITION: *The clerk of the court will complete this section.*
DÉCISION :   Le greffier du tribunal remplit cette partie.

☐ order to go as asked
    ordonnance de procéder comme il a été demandé

☐ order refused because:
    ordonnance refusée pour les motifs suivants :

....
                                                          (Signature of clerk / *Signature du greffier*)

SCR 11.2.01-11.2A (June 1, 2009 / *1ᵉʳ juin 2009*) CSD

stances. For example, a motion for a new trial may require the filing of and reference to transcripts, which would require extra time for the motion. In such cases, the judge may be persuaded to award costs greater than $100.

> 15.07 The costs of a motion, exclusive of disbursements, shall not exceed $100 unless the court orders otherwise because there are special circumstances.

DISCONTINUANCE OF AN UNDEFENDED ACTION

Sometimes a plaintiff may commence a claim, serve the claim, and then have second thoughts about proceeding. If the time to file a defence has passed and a defence has not been filed, the rules now permit a plaintiff to discontinue the claim by serving a Notice of Discontinued Claim (Form 11.3A) on all defendants who were served with the claim. If a defendant is under disability, leave of the court is required to discontinue the claim. The discontinuance of a claim is not a defence to a subsequent action on the matter.

> 11.3.01(1) A plaintiff may discontinue his or her claim against a defendant who fails to file a defence to all or part of the claim with the clerk within the prescribed time by,
> (a) serving a notice of discontinued claim (Form 11.3A) on all defendants who were served with the claim; and
> (b) filing the notice with proof of service.
>
> (2) A claim may not be discontinued by or against a person under disability, except with leave of the court.

> 11.3.02 The discontinuance of a claim is not a defence to a subsequent action on the matter, unless an order granting leave to discontinue provides otherwise.

CHAPTER SUMMARY

In this chapter you were introduced to various resources, procedures, and techniques that can be used to correct errors or make changes in your pleadings, untangle procedural knots, and resolve pre-trial disputes. You were reminded of several general rules in the "Rules Toolbox" that allow the court to flexibly and sensibly use and interpret the Rules in a non-technical way to ensure quick and inexpensive trials on the merits. Rule 12, which allows amendments to pleadings without the necessity of bringing a motion, was examined, as were the steps to take to deal with pleadings that are gravely defective, with a view to forcing their amendment or having them struck out. You were introduced to motions as the chief tool for dealing with procedural issues before and after trial, including an examination of motion procedure and the requirements for drafting clear affidavits. Lastly, you were advised of the procedure to discontinue an undefended claim.

REVIEW QUESTIONS

1. What is the "Rules Toolbox"?

2. You discover an error in your claim 29 days before trial. How can you correct the error?

3. Credit R Us sued Henry Slippery on an unpaid loan. The plaintiff's claim states the following in paragraph 6: "The defendant, having failed to pay, has demonstrated that he is a low-life scoundrel." Is this permissible pleading?

4. Morris has sued Fisher, claiming that Fisher, having been introduced to him, turned on his heel and walked off. Morris has sued for damages for his hurt feelings. If you are acting for Fisher, what would your advice be?

5. Suppose Al sues Bert, and Bert files a defence. Bert also files a defendant's claim in which he makes separate claims against Clem and Dan on matters that are not related to the facts of Al's case. What can Al do if he doesn't want to be tied up in a lengthy case involving the other parties that has nothing to do with him?

6. Al would like to bring a motion. As moving party, what steps does he have to take prior to the hearing? Give the time limits for responding where applicable.

7. If Al brings the motion referred to in the preceding questions, what options are open to the other parties?

8. How may motions be heard?

9. If you sued Leonardo da Vinci over an unfinished painting but discovered that these artistic efforts were carried out by a company, da Vinci Ltd., is there a simple way to substitute the limited company for the individual, if both consent?

10. In anger, you commenced a frivolous claim that has not been defended. How can you discontinue the claim?

DISCUSSION QUESTIONS/CASE STUDIES

1. You act for George Green. You have just received from him a copy of the claim by Robert Brown served on him, claiming return of a lawnmower on the grounds that George failed to return it. You notice that in the claim, Robert states that he lent the lawnmower to George on September 1, Yr. –3. The claim was issued on March 10, Yr. 0, two and a half years after the lawnmower was given to George. Prepare a motion to strike out the claim and have the action dismissed.

2. You received a copy of the following claim from your client, Harriet Hapless, who runs Hapless Beauty School Ltd. Harriet, but not the limited company, has been sued by a student. Critique the claim below with a view to the procedure to be taken in striking it out or moving to have it amended:

> (i) The plaintiff is an indivisual who lives in Toronto.
>
> (ii) Harriet Hapless carries on the operation of a beauty school in Toronto.
>
> (iii) The plaintiff enrolled in the defendant's beauty school and paid tuition of $3,000 on September 6, Yr. 0, to Hapless Beauty School Ltd.
>
> (iv) The plaintiff has been taught nothin by the defendant.
>
> (v) The defendant cheted the plaintiff, and is a disreputable liar and scoundrel.
>
> (vi) The plaintiff was told by other students, that she, the defendant, "couldn't mascara her way out of a paper bag", for which the plaintiff claims damages for hurt feelings for $6,000.
>
> (vii) The plaintiff claims the return of her tuition of $3,000.

Chapter 10

Settlement

LEARNING OBJECTIVES

⇨ Understand the purposes of a settlement conference

⇨ Know how to use settlement conferences to assist your case

⇨ Know settlement conference procedure and how to participate effectively in settlement conferences

⇨ Know how to use the settlement conference for pre-trial discovery

⇨ Know how to use the settlement conference to prepare your case for trial if settlement is not possible

⇨ Know when and how to make a written offer to settle under Rule 14

⇨ Know when to use and how to draft various documents when a legal dispute is settled

INTRODUCTION

After pleadings have been exchanged between the parties, the next procedural step is a settlement conference. The settlement conference is designed to facilitate settlement prior to trial. Failing that, the settlement conference can be used to identify relevant issues for trial, narrow the issues for trial, help the parties to resolve all pre-trial issues, and, generally, get ready for trial. The chapter also explores other aspects of settlement: making offers to settle under Rule 14 and drafting Terms of Settlement (Form 14D), Minutes of Settlement, releases, and other settlement documentation, all focused on settling a dispute before or after an action commences or after judgment.

SETTLEMENT CONFERENCES

Settlement conferences (formerly called pre-trial conferences) are mandatory under Rule 13, in all cases that are defended:

> 13.01(1) A Settlement Conference shall be held in every defended action.
>
> (2) The clerk shall fix a time, date and place for the Settlement Conference and serve a notice of Settlement Conference, together with a list of proposed witnesses (Form 13A), on the parties.
>
> (3) The Settlement Conference shall be held within 90 days after the first defence is filed.
>
> (4) Subrules (1) to (3) do not apply if the defence contains an admission of liability for all of the plaintiff's claim and a proposal of terms of payment under subrule 9.03(1).

If there are several defendants, only those who have defended participate. In accordance with Rule 13.01(4), if a defendant has defaulted or admits liability and makes a payment proposal under Rule 9.03, no settlement conference is required. The reason for this is that there is no need for a settlement conference if the case has ended in a proposal or in a default. But for those parties still in the action, it is a good idea to learn how to use the settlement conference effectively, either to settle an action or to get judicial input and assistance in narrowing issues for trial and in resolving pre-trial disputes so that the trial, when it does occur, is conducted fairly and efficiently, with the parties staying focused on what they need to do.

The purposes of a settlement conference are set out in Rule 13.03(1):

> 13.03(1) The purposes of a Settlement Conference are,
> (a) to resolve or narrow the issues in the action;
> (b) to expedite the disposition of the action;
> (c) to encourage settlement of the action;

(d) to assist the parties in effective preparation for trial; and

(e) to provide full disclosure between the parties of the relevant facts and evidence.

A settlement conference, in addition to encouraging settlement of the action, provides the parties with an opportunity to resolve or narrow the issues in the trial. The conference can also help to ensure that the action is dealt with quickly and inexpensively. As well, the conference will assist the parties in preparing for trial and provide an opportunity, prior to trial, for full discovery or disclosure of relevant facts and evidence, including documents and witness statements.

A settlement conference may be before a judge (who will not hear the trial if the matter does not settle), or a referee, or under Rule 21.01(1) a person assigned the powers of a referee if directed to do so by the Regional Senior Justice or his or her designate.

> 21.01(1) A person assigned the powers and duties of a referee under subsection 73(2) of the *Courts of Justice Act* may, if directed by the regional senior justice or his or her designate,
>
> (a) hear disputes of proposals of terms of payment under rule 9.03;
>
> (b) conduct settlement conferences under rule 13;
>
> (c) hear motions for consolidation orders under rule 20.09; and
>
> (d) assess receipted disbursements for fees paid to the court, a court reporter or a sheriff under the regulations made under the *Administration of Justice Act.*
>
> (2) Except under subrule 9.03(5) (order as to terms of payment), a referee shall not make a final decision in any matter referred to him or her but shall report his or her findings and recommendations to the court.

Encouraging Settlement

The court emphasizes the importance of settling a case rather than litigating to the end in two ways: (i) making the settlement conference mandatory, and (ii) introducing a formal "offer to settle" process with cost consequences for those who refuse to accept reasonable offers. The court has a clear stake in settlement. If every case actually went to trial, it would take years for a case to be heard, and the system would break down and become very expensive to run.[1] But there are other important reasons for the parties to settle. While there are some cases where there are moral or personal issues where a party wants to see

---

[1] The fees paid to the court to file claims, set a matter down for trial, and so on, do not cover the cost of the court's operations. Consequently, the more cases diverted out of the system, the less it costs to run a system that is largely paid for by taxpayers.

justice done, most cases should be approached on a more rational basis:

1. A trial is always something of a gamble, and the outcome cannot be predicted with certainty. A witness who sounded confident in interviews may, for example, come apart on vigorous cross-examination. A settlement is, on the other hand, a sure thing.

2. Parties who negotiate their own settlement tend to live with it more easily than they do with one imposed by a judge. With a judicial decision, there is always a winner and a loser; with a negotiated decision, with results customized to the goals and needs of the parties, both sides can be winners. For example, sometimes an apology can be an important part of the settlement, which may go a long way to helping a party to accept a settlement. Or you may wish to have a party who has breached a contract perform the promised work rather than simply be paid damages for non-performance. As a back-up for non-performance of the promised work, the Minutes of Settlement should provide that the defaulter pay the full amount originally claimed. You can customize a settlement, while judges in the Small Claims Court cannot, given their inability to do more than hand out judgments for the payment of money or the return of personal property.

3. Where there is a settlement, compliance with its terms is more likely, and recovery much more certain. Where you obtain a judgment and try to enforce it against a resistant judgment-debtor, you may spend time and money on enforcement with little to show for your efforts.

4. If it is important for parties to have a continuing relationship after they have resolved a legal dispute, as is often true for businesses, it is better for the parties to work out a solution to their dispute than to have one imposed on them.

5. A settlement, particularly an early settlement, will greatly reduce legal costs and court costs for both parties — an important consideration for claims that are for $25,000 or less, as legal fees can greatly reduce the net value of a judgment.

A commercial client, or a legally sophisticated one, will be aware of the advantages of settling. But an unsophisticated client may have to be sold on the desirability of settling rather than litigating. Settlement is something that should be discussed at an early stage, as early as the time the dispute arises, and certainly when the claim is issued and served and the defence has been received. You and your client should determine what the client wants and what he or she is prepared to take to end the action, establishing a bottom line but being flexible enough to consider various ways of getting to it. Making an offer to settle under Rule 14 at an early stage is generally a good strategy, and having a settlement plan by the time of the settlement conference is extremely important, unless it is the type of case where there is no hope of settlement — but those are relatively rare.

There are also advantages to you as a paralegal in encouraging early settlement as well. Provided you have clients bringing cases forward at a steady rate, the faster you close and bill a file, the better your cash flow is likely to be, and the higher your net income. This is particularly the case where, given the monetary limits of the Small Claims Court, the amount you can bill for a trial may not justify running every case to trial, as it reduces the number of files you can handle. Specialist litigation law firms may be able to make a great deal of money from complex and lengthy trials for large stakes, but smaller law practices and paralegal practices are unlikely to be able to do so where the amounts in dispute are low.

Scheduling of Settlement Conferences

As settlement conferences are mandatory, this is one of the steps in the Small Claims Court process that is not left to the parties to schedule. Once the first defence is filed, the clock begins to run for scheduling a settlement conference. In accordance with Rule 13.01(3), a settlement conference must be held within 90 days of the filing of the first defence. If there are multiple defendants, and some are served late in the pre-trial process or added late in the process, those defendants may find the settlement conference comes on very quickly. Late-added defendants will be expected to move quickly in preparing for the settlement conference, although adjournments may be obtained in appropriate cases.[2] The conference itself will be scheduled by the clerk of the court within the 90-day period. The clerk sends out a notice with the date, time, and place of the conference, together with a blank Form 13A, the List of Proposed Witnesses. You need to list here the names and contact information of all persons whom you think you may call as witnesses, even if you do not in fact call them all at trial. The form

---

[2] If you have not received a Notice of Settlement Conference within two weeks of the filing or receipt of the defence, you should call the court to determine if a conference has been scheduled. The court may have a previous firm address in their document generation computer system despite the fact that a more recent address has been set out on the documents you filed with the court for your present case. As you have obligations to meet with respect to the service of documents prior to the conference, and the client is generally required to attend the conference (and may need to book a day off), it is important that you know well in advance when the mandatory conference will be held.

also asks you to list others who know about the case but who you do not intend to call. Neither the Rules nor the form explain clearly why this second group needs to be listed, but one might include here potential witnesses. Once you know who the other party's witnesses are likely to be, you may contact them and ask them about their evidence. The fact that one party intends to call a person as a witness does not mean that they "own" the witness. Any party can talk to a potential witness, although the witness can refuse to respond or answer questions if he or she so wishes. This is part of the discovery/disclosure process that begins when the claim and supporting documents are filed.

It is often the case that parties attach what they consider to be important documents to their claim or defence, but do not attach all documents that are relevant, including documents that are not favourable. A settlement conference judge will ensure that all documents, including witness statements, expert reports, and lists of witnesses, are disclosed prior to trial so that parties know the case they have to present and meet, and we do not have **trial by ambush**.

Illustrations 10.1 and 10.2 show a sample Notice of Settlement Conference and a sample List of Proposed Witnesses.

Mandatory Attendance and Alternatives to Personal Attendance

A party and his or her representative are required to attend a settlement conference in order to negotiate and, if possible, agree to the terms of settlement. For this reason the Rules are quite specific about attendance at settlement conferences. Rule 13.02 requires both the party and the legal representative, if there is one, to be present:

> 13.02(1) A party and the party's lawyer or agent, if any, shall, unless the court orders otherwise, participate in the Settlement Conference,
> (a) by personal attendance; or
> (b) by telephone or video conference in accordance with rule 1.07.

If there is a legal representative and the court has ordered on consent or after argument that a party does not have to be physically present, the party should be immediately available by phone to give instructions and to consent or agree to any settlement that is worked out. A motion to proceed at the settlement conference without a party can be made in advance of or at the conference. If the party is a corporation, the person attending on behalf of the party must be someone with authority to settle on behalf of the company, such as a manager. Rule 13.02(1)(b) provides that the conference can be held by telephone or video in accordance with Rule 1.07. A party wishing to have a tele-

ILLUSTRATION 10.1: Sample Notice of Settlement Conference

Superior Court of Justice
Cour supérieure de justice

Notice of Settlement Conference
Avis de conférence en vue d'une transaction

Toronto

SC-00-47669-00

Small Claims Court / *Cour des petites créances de*

Claim No. / *N° de la demande*

47 Sheppard Ave. E., 3rd Fl.
Toronto, ON M2N 5N1

Address / *Adresse*

416-326-3554

Phone number / *N° de téléphone*

BETWEEN /*ENTRE*

Albert Oryx

Plaintiff(s) / *Demandeur(s)*

and / *et*

Ophelia Foot

Defendant(s) / *Défendeur(s)*

TO THE PARTIES:
AUX PARTIES :

THIS COURT WILL HOLD A MANDATORY SETTLEMENT CONFERENCE in this defended action on
*LE TRIBUNAL PRÉCITÉ TIENDRA UNE CONFÉRENCE OBLIGATOIRE EN VUE D'UNE TRANSACTION dans
le cadre de la présente action contestée le*

April 27, Yr. 1 , at 10:30 a.m./p.m., or as soon as possible after that time, at
à *(heure), ou dès que possible après, à/au*

47 Sheppard Ave. E., Conference Room 307

(Address of court location & courtroom number / *Adresse du tribunal et numéro de la salle d'audience*)

and thereafter as may be required from time to time.
et par la suite, au besoin.

EACH PARTY and the party's agent or lawyer, if any, must participate in the settlement conference, unless the
court orders otherwise.
*CHAQUE PARTIE et son mandataire ou avocat, le cas échéant, doivent participer à la conférence en vue d'une
transaction, sauf ordonnance contraire du tribunal.*

AT LEAST 14 DAYS BEFORE THE SETTLEMENT CONFERENCE, each party must serve on every other
party and file with the court:
*AU MOINS 14 JOURS AVANT LA DATE DE LA CONFÉRENCE EN VUE D'UNE TRANSACTION, chaque
partie doit signifier aux autres parties et déposer auprès du tribunal ce qui suit :*

- a copy of any document to be relied on at the trial, including an expert report, that was not attached to the
  party's claim or defence; and
  *une copie des documents à l'appui au procès, y compris les rapports d'experts, qui n'étaient pas joints à la
  demande ou à la défense de la partie*

- a List of Proposed Witnesses (Form 13A) and of other persons with knowledge of the matters in dispute in
  the action.
  *une liste des témoins proposés (formule 13A) et des autres personnes qui ont connaissance des questions
  en litige dans l'action.*

SAA 13.01-00 (June 1, 2009 / *1er juin 2009*) CSD
(Non-regulated form / *Formule non prescrite*)

continues....

Illustration 10.1 (continued)

Superior Court of Justice   PAGE 2   **Notice of Settlement Conference**
Cour supérieure de justice   *Avis de conférence en vue d'une*
                                                                 transaction

SC-00-47669-00
....
Claim No. / *N° de la demande*

IF YOU FAIL to serve and file the materials listed above at least 14 days before the settlement conference, or if you attend the settlement conference and are so inadequately prepared as to frustrate the purposes of the conference, the court may award costs against you.

SI VOUS OMETTEZ de signifier et de déposer les documents susmentionnés au moins 14 jours avant la conférence en vue d'une transaction, ou si vous vous présentez à la conférence en étant tellement peu préparé(e) que les objectifs de la conférence en sont contrecarrés, le tribunal peut vous condamner à des dépens.

YOU MAY REQUEST THAT THE SETTLEMENT CONFERENCE BE CONDUCTED BY TELEPHONE OR VIDEO CONFERENCE by filing a Request for Telephone or Video Conference (Form 1B). Where facilities are available and the court permits it, the clerk will make the necessary arrangements for the telephone or video conference and notify the parties of them. You can get forms at court offices or online at www.ontariocourtforms.on.ca

VOUS POUVEZ DEMANDER QUE LA CONFÉRENCE EN VUE D'UNE TRANSACTION SOIT TENUE PAR CONFÉRENCE TÉLÉPHONIQUE OU VIDÉOCONFÉRENCE en déposant une demande de conférence téléphonique ou de vidéoconférence (formule 1B). Si des installations sont disponibles et que le tribunal le permet, le greffier prendra les dispositions nécessaires en vue de la conférence téléphonique ou téléconférence et en avisera les parties. Vous pouvez vous procurer les formules auprès d'un greffe, ou en ligne à l'adresse : www.ontariocourtforms.on.ca.

AT THE SETTLEMENT CONFERENCE, the parties or their representatives must openly and frankly discuss the issues in dispute. The settlement conference is not a trial, so DO NOT bring witnesses with you. The matters discussed at the settlement conference must not be disclosed to others until after the action has been disposed of, unless all parties consent to disclosure.

Lors de la conférence en vue d'une transaction, les parties ou leurs représentants doivent discuter ouvertement et franchement des questions en litige dans l'action. Il ne s'agit pas d'un procès; par conséquent, N'AMENEZ PAS de témoins avec vous. Les questions qui font l''objet d'une discussion lors de la conférence en vue d'une transaction ne doivent pas être divulguées à des tiers tant que l'action n'a pas été décidée, sauf avec le consentement de toutes les parties.

CAUTION TO DEFENDANT:	**IF YOU FAIL TO ATTEND THIS SETTLEMENT CONFERENCE** the court may order costs and other sanctions against you and order that an additional settlement conference be held. **IF YOU FAIL TO ATTEND THIS ADDITIONAL SETTLEMENT CONFERENCE** the court may strike out your defence and dismiss your defendant's claim, if any, or make such other order as is just.
AVERTISSEMENT AU DÉFENDEUR :	*SI VOUS NE VOUS PRÉSENTEZ PAS À CETTE AUDIENCE EN VUE D'UNE TRANSACTION, le tribunal peut vous condamner à des dépens ou vous imposer d'autres sanctions et ordonner qu'une autre conférence en vue d'une transaction soit tenue. SI VOUS NE VOUS PRÉSENTEZ PAS À L'AUDIENCE SUPPLÉMENTAIRE EN VUE D'UNE TRANSACTION, le tribunal peut radier votre défense, le cas échéant, ou rendre une autre ordonnance juste.*

NOTE:	**IF YOU DO NOT SETTLE** your case at the settlement conference, you may go to the court office and request a trial date. There is a fee. Your case can be dismissed by the clerk if more than 150 days have passed since the first defence was filed and your case has not been set down for trial or disposed of by order.
REMARQUE :	*SI VOUS N'EFFECTUEZ AUCUNE TRANSACTION À L'ÉGARD DE votre affaire à l'issue de l'audience en vue d'une transaction, vous pouvez vous présenter au greffe pour demander qu'une date d'audience soit fixée. Des frais s'appliquent. Le greffier peut rejeter votre instance si la première défense a été déposée depuis plus de 150 jours et que votre affaire n'a pas été inscrite pour instruction ni réglée par une ordonnance depuis.*

_____April 8, Yr. 1_____   _____"Iam Clerk"_____
                                  (Signature of clerk / *Signature du greffier*)

SAA 13.01-00 (June 1, 2009 / *1ᵉʳ juin 2009*) CSD
(Non-regulated form / *Formule non prescrite*)

ILLUSTRATION 10.2: Sample List of Proposed Witnesses (Form 13A)

ONTARIO
Superior Court of Justice
Cour supérieure de justice

List of Proposed Witnesses
Liste des témoins proposés
Form / *Formule* 13A Ont. Reg. No. / *Règl. de l'Ont.* : 258/98

Toronto
Small Claims Court / *Cour des petites créances de*

SC-00-47669-00
Claim No. / *N° de la demande*

47 Sheppard Ave. E., 3rd Fl.
Toronto, ON M2N 5N1
Address / *Adresse*

416-326-3554
Phone number / *Numéro de téléphone*

BETWEEN / *ENTRE*

Albert Oryx
Plaintiff(s) / *Demandeur(s)/demanderesse(s)*

and / *et*

Ophelia Foot
Defendant(s) / *Défendeur(s)/défenderesse(s)*

My name is Peter Paralegal
Je m'appelle
(Name of party/representative / *Nom de la partie ou du/de la représentant(e)*)

The following is my list of proposed witnesses in this case:
La liste suivante constitue ma liste des témoins proposés dans la présente cause :

Name of witness / *Nom du témoin*	Address, phone and fax numbers / *Adresse, numéros de téléphone et de télécopieur*
1. Albert Oryx	28 Montrose Ave.
	Toronto, ON
	M4R 1X6
	Tel. 416-221-1234
2. Michael Oryx	1010 — 10 Fairview Rd.
	Toronto, ON
	M2X 3B6
	Tel. 647-345-1234
3. Eatom Shredlu	20 Scarsdale Rd.
	Toronto, ON
	M2R 5B6
	Tel. 416-485-1234
	Fax 416-485-1235

SCR 13.01-13A (June 1, 2009 / *1er juin 2009*) CSD

continues....

Illustration 10.2 (continued)

FORM / *FORMULE 13A*　　　　　　PAGE 2　　　　　　SC-00-47669-00
....
　　　　　　　　　　　　　　　　　　　　　　　　　　Claim No. / *N° de la demande*

4. ....

5. ....

The following is my list of other persons with knowledge of the matter in dispute in this case:
La liste suivante constitue ma liste des autres personnes qui ont connaissance des questions en litige dans la présente cause :

Name of person / *Nom de la personne*	Address, phone and fax numbers / *Adresse, numéros de téléphone et de télécopieur*
1. Peter Pendulum	2301 Yonge Street. — 2nd Fl.
	Toronto, ON
	M4R 1J9
	Tel. 416-485-6891
	Fax 416-485-6892
2.	

(Attach a separate sheet in the above format for additional witnesses or other persons.)
(En cas de témoins ou de personnes additionnels, annexez une autre feuille reproduisant le format ci-dessus.)

April 10, Yr. 1　　　　　　　　　　　　　*Peter Paralegal*
....　..
　　　　　　　　　　　　　　　　(Signature of party or representative / *Signature de la partie ou du/de la représentant(e)*)

　　　　　　　　　　　　　　Peter Paralegal, 41 Yonge Street, #410
　　　　　　　　　　　　　　Toronto ON   M5G 1S1
　　　　　　　　　　　　　　416-597-0048
　　　　　　　　　　　　..
　　　　　　　　　　　　(Name, address and phone number of party or representative / *Nom, adresse et numéro de téléphone de la partie ou du/de la représentant(e)*)

NOTE:	**EACH PARTY MUST SERVE THIS LIST** on all other parties and file it with the court at least fourteen (14) days before the settlement conference [R. 13.03(2)(b)].
REMARQUE :	*CHAQUE PARTIE DOIT SIGNIFIER LA PRÉSENTE LISTE à toutes les autres parties et la déposer auprès du tribunal au moins quatorze (14) jours avant latenue de la conférence en vue d'une transaction [alinéa 13.03 (2) b)].*

SCR 13.01-13A (June 1, 2009 / *1er juin 2009*) CSD

phone or video conference must fill out a request for such a conference using Form 1B and set out the reasons for the request. In deciding whether or not to grant the request, the judge is to consider the balance of convenience between the party requesting it and any party opposing it. The judge is also to consider any other relevant matters. If an order is made for a telephone or video conference, the court makes the necessary arrangements and notifies the parties.

> 1.07(1) If facilities for a telephone or video conference are available at the court, all or part of any of the following may be heard or conducted by telephone or video conference as permitted by subrules (2) and (3):
> 1. A settlement conference.
> 2. A motion.
>
> (1.1) If facilities for a video conference are available at the court, all or part of an examination of a debtor or other person under rule 20.10 may be conducted by video conference as permitted by subrules (2) and (3).
>
> (2) A settlement conference or motion may be heard or conducted by telephone or video conference or all or part of an examination under rule 20.10 may be conducted by video conference if a party files a request for the conference (Form 1B), indicating the reasons for the request, and the court grants the request.
>
> (3) In deciding whether to direct a telephone or video conference, the judge shall consider,
> (a) the balance of convenience between the party that wants the telephone or video conference and any party that opposes it; and
> (b) any other relevant matter.
>
> (4) If an order directing a telephone or video conference is made, the court shall make the necessary arrangements for the conference and notify the parties of them.
>
> (5) A judge presiding at a proceeding or step in a proceeding may set aside or vary an order directing a telephone or video conference.

While there do not seem to be limits on the use of telephone conferences to convey instructions and consents to settle, some judges may take the position that telephone attendance may be used only to prevent hardship, not just for the sake of convenience. For example, if a party is in another province, it might be a hardship to make him or her come to Toronto for a settlement conference, but it would only be a mere inconvenience if the party had to come to Toronto from Newmarket.

The courts have made it clear that legal representatives, who attend alone without being able to get instructions immediately, may face sanctions.[3] There is some flexibility in the rule, however. If a not-for-profit corporation or statutory agency requires board or committee ratification of a settlement worked out at a settlement conference, the company's officer or employee attending should be in a position to work out a settlement, with an undertaking to recommend it to the board or committee for ratification.

Disclosure and Production

As noted earlier in the chapter, the Rules require the parties to make full disclosure with their pleadings by attaching all relevant documents. In practice this rarely happens. But the settlement conference ensures that full disclosure does occur by having a judge or referee use the settlement conference to oversee the discovery process and make sure that there is full disclosure prior to trial. Rule 13.03(2) requires the parties to serve on all other parties and file with the court at least 14 days before the settlement conference copies of every document they intend to rely on at trial, lists of potential witnesses, witness statements, and expert reports:

> 13.03(2) At least 14 days before the date of the Settlement Conference, each party shall serve on every other party and file with the court,
> (a) a copy of any document to be relied on at the trial, including an expert report, not attached to the party's claim or defence; and
> (b) a list of proposed witnesses (Form 13A) and of other persons with knowledge of the matters in dispute in the action.

Even if it was not entirely clear what was relevant when a claim or defence was filed, by the time of the settlement conference a legal representative should be fully familiar with the case and know what documents and evidence they will be relying on at trial so that all relevant documents are before the parties and the judge at the settlement conference.

If you have more than one or two documents to rely on, it is helpful to create a document brief in the following format: copy and bind the documents, tabbing each document as a separate item with a letter or a number. It is also a good idea to include a table of contents, identifying the item by a letter or a page number in the brief where it is to be found.

---

[3] Rule 13 permits costs sanctions of up to $100.00 on settlement conferences, with even higher costs in exceptional circumstances. Normally, no costs are awarded to either party on a settlement conference.

It may be the case that, through settlement discussion or with unrepresented parties, you discover other relevant documents that are required. If so, consider requesting an adjournment to permit each party to serve the other relevant documents prior to re-convening the settlement conference. The request is likely to be granted if the parties are seriously and in good faith trying to negotiate a settlement where the omission was inadvertent.

Adjournments, Non-attendance, Non-cooperation, Unpreparedness, Costs Consequences, and Second Conferences

The Rules contemplate the possibility that it will be necessary to schedule additional settlement conferences in two circumstances. One, as noted in the preceding section, is when additional documents are required to continue negotiations or negotiations are continuing, and more time is needed. This circumstance is usually seen to be benign and does not attract penalties.

The second is where a party does not attend the settlement conference. Because attendance to achieve settlement or provide for a speedy and efficient trial is crucial, the Rules do not permit a party to sidestep the settlement conference by not attending, or by not being properly prepared. Failure to attend may result, under Rule 13.02(5), in the court ordering a new settlement conference or applying cost sanctions, or both:

> 13.02(5) If a party who has received a notice of Settlement Conference fails to attend the conference, the court may,
> (a) impose appropriate sanctions, by way of costs or otherwise; and
> (b) order that an additional Settlement Conference be held, if necessary.
>
> (6) If a defendant fails to attend a first Settlement Conference, receives notice of an additional Settlement Conference and fails to attend the additional Settlement Conference, the court may,
> (a) strike out the defence and dismiss the defendant's claim, if any, and allow the plaintiff to prove the plaintiff's claim; or
> (b) make such other order as is just.
>
> (7) The court may award costs against a person who attends a Settlement Conference if,
> (a) in the opinion of the court, the person is so inadequately prepared as to frustrate the purposes of the conference;
> (b) the person fails to file the material required by subrule 13.03(2).

In the case of a party who fails to attend both the first settlement conference and a second rescheduled one, the penalties under Rule

13.02(6) are increased beyond just costs. As it is usually the defendant who does not cooperate, the defence and any defendant's claim may be struck out and the plaintiff may be allowed to proceed to prove his or her claim. Or the court may make any other order, including dismissing an action where a plaintiff is uncooperative about attendance.

In the case where a party attends but comes unprepared to negotiate or discuss settlement, the court can impose costs sanctions under Rule 13.02(7). This is usually a problem that arises with self-represented litigants who do not really understand what is required. In addition to costs, the court may also order an additional settlement conference under Rule 13.02(3), with specific directions on preparing for the rescheduled hearing:

> 13.02(3) The court may order the parties to attend an additional Settlement Conference.
> (4) The clerk shall fix a time and place for any additional Settlement Conference and serve a notice of Settlement Conference, together with a list of proposed witnesses (Form 13A) on the parties.

Adjournment of Settlement Conference on Consent

As the court clerk schedules the first settlement conference date, sometimes, one or both of the parties or their representatives are not available on that date. The parties may consent to an adjournment of the settlement conference to another date. This can be done by having the parties or their representatives sign a Form 13B Consent and file this with the court in person or by mail or fax. Normally, documents cannot be filed by fax, but most Small Claims Court offices will permit the adjournment of a first settlement conference by the filing of a consent by fax. You should call the court office and find out if this is permitted and obtain the fax number for filing consent adjournments. You can include a letter with dates upon which you and the other party's representative are available for another settlement conference. As a settlement conference must be held in every defended case, an adjournment date may well be two to three months away, so your available dates for adjournment should include dates in that time period.

The Conduct of a Settlement Conference

The Rules do not say much about how a settlement conference is actually conducted, beyond directing the parties, under Rule 13.03(3), "to openly and frankly discuss the issues involved in the action." In fact, the way in which settlement conferences are run varies widely. The meeting may be held before a judge or a referee or a person assigned the duties of a referee (referees are found in large urban centres, such as Toronto, where case volume is very high). Where a judge or referee can do something under the Rules, a rule will often say, "The court may......". If only a judge may do something, the rule will say, "A judge may......",[4] but as Rule 13.03(5) permits a referee's order to be confirmed by a judge, in practical terms a referee can do whatever a judge can do at a settlement conference.

The conference is often in a meeting room rather than a courtroom and, in any case, is fairly informal. Most judges will open by explaining what a settlement conference is. They then will ask the plaintiff to say what he or she thinks are the issues and the relevant facts, in effect summarizing the case from his or her point of view. The defendant will then be asked to do the same thing. As you explain your case, you may want to direct the judge or referee to key documents in your document brief. In order for a party or a representative to set out the issues effectively, he or she needs to be prepared:

1. Know the relevant facts and issues.

2. From the fact/issue base, have a theory of the case developed that guides your view of the case.

3. Know the legal issues: review and update legislation and case law.

4. Work out a settlement position, both to make an offer and to consider one from the other party.

5. Determine the "settlement" point at which you will agree to resolve the dispute and settle the case. This includes not only how much gets paid, but how and when it is paid, if there is a proposal to pay by instalments.

When considering settlements, be prepared to be creative. As noted earlier, a settlement may include things other than payments of money or the return of property. In a consumer or commercial case, granting credits or discounts on future transactions can ensure the continuance of a relationship beneficial to both parties. Providing a letter of apology may be useful, as may be offering to continue to perform and complete a contract to supply goods or services. What you do here will obviously vary from case to case, but there is nothing wrong with being creative and imaginative in solving a problem. But these kinds of arrangements can be complex, and you will need to work them out before the settlement conference. You may wish to present them in

---

[4] The authority of a referee is set out in Rule 21, and includes the authority to conduct a settlement conference. The referee's findings and recommendations can be confirmed by a judge under Rule 13.03(5), effectively permitting a referee to make any order a judge could make.

FIGURE 10.1: Settlement Conference Checklist

Bring with you:

☐ 1. The client, unless the court has ordered otherwise or a conference by phone or video has been approved.

☐ 2. Copy of the claim

☐ 3. Copy of defence

☐ 4. List of documentary evidence

☐ 5. List of proposed witnesses

☐ 6. Statement of facts

☐ 7. Statement of issues to be resolved

☐ 8. Case law, if you are relying on it

☐ 9. Statute law, if you are relying on it

☐ 10. Offer to settle, if one has been made

☐ 11. Copies of all evidence not yet produced, including witness statements, documents, and expert reports, with copies for the court and the other party

☐ 12. Affidavit of Service to prove that you served on the other side, at least 14 days in advance of the settlement conference, the List of Proposed Witnesses (Form 13A), and any documents that you intend to rely upon at trial in accordance with Rule 13.03(2)

☐ 13. A Day-Timer or calendar to check clear days for trial scheduling

☐ 14. A calculator

☐ 15. Small Claims Court Rules

writing as well, so the other side can give them careful consideration. If it leads to further negotiations, do not be afraid to ask to adjourn and reschedule the settlement conference, if the allotted time for the session is running out. Note that the time allotted for the settlement conference may be limited rather than open-ended.

Once a judge or referee has heard the parties, a number of things may happen, depending on the style of the judge or referee and the attitude and abilities of the parties. A judge or referee may try to mediate, discussing settlement possibilities with the parties: usually by shuttling between the two, but sometimes by keeping the parties together and talking to them together. A judge or referee may also give a neutral or open evaluation, where he or she gives a frank assessment of the party's chances at trial based on the law, the facts, and documents presented at the conference. This may be done following an attempt to mediate, or as part of the mediation process. Rule 13.04 permits the court to make recommendations to the parties on any matter relating to the conduct of the action in order to fulfill the purposes of the conference. These may include recommendations to clarify and simplify the issues, to eliminate claims or defences that appear to be unsupported, and to recommend the admission of facts or documents without further proof.

> 13.04 The court may make recommendations to the parties on any matter relating to the conduct of the action, in order to fulfil the purposes of a Settlement Conference, including recommendations as to,
> (a) the clarification and simplification of issues in the action;
> (b) the elimination of claims or defences that appear to be unsupported; and
> (c) the admission of facts or documents without further proof.

Using a Settlement Conference to "Clean Up" an Action

If you do not settle an action, you can use the settlement conference to "clean up" a proceeding prior to trial. While this can also be done by bringing motions, it is often cheaper and quicker to note what has to be fixed either by you or the other party, or what pre-trial issues have to be resolved, and deal with them at the settlement conference, using the court's powers under Rule 13.05:

> 13.05(1) A judge conducting a Settlement Conference may make any order relating to the conduct of the action that the court could make.
>
> (2) Without limiting the generality of subrule (1), the judge may,

(a) make an order,
    (i) adding or deleting parties,
    (ii) consolidating actions,
    (iii) staying the action,
    (iv) amending or striking out a claim or defence under rule 12.02,
    (v) staying or dismissing a claim,
    (vi) directing production of documents,
    (vii) changing the place of trial under rule 6.01,
    (viii) directing an additional Settlement Conference under subrule 13.02(3), and
    (ix) ordering costs; and
(b) at an additional Settlement Conference, order judgment under subrule 13.02(6).

(3) If the Settlement Conference is conducted by a referee, a judge may, on the referee's recommendation, make any order that may be made under subrules (1) and (2).

(4) A judge may order final judgment at a Settlement Conference where the matter in dispute is for an amount under the appealable limit and a party files a consent (Form 13B) signed by all parties before the Settlement Conference indicating that they wish to obtain final determination of the matter at the Settlement Conference if a mediated settlement is not reached.

(5) Within 10 days after the judge signs an order made at a Settlement Conference, the clerk shall serve the order on the parties that were not present at the Settlement Conference in accordance with subrule 8.01(6).

Rule 13.04 allows the court to make recommendations to the parties to clarify and simplify issues, eliminate claims and defences that are without factual support, and admit a fact or the authenticity of a document. This is very useful for voluntarily correcting errors, and narrowing issues for trial when one or both parties are self-represented.

However, if a party refuses to accept a recommendation, a judge has the power under Rule 13.05 to make any order within the judge's jurisdiction and power. (A referee under Rule 13.05 may make a recommendation, which is then confirmed by a judge.) While the power is broad and general, Rule 13.05(2)(a) sets out some of the more common situations where judges do make orders:

1. Adding or deleting parties: This often happens when one party has incorrectly sued an individual carrying on business when it turns out that the business is actually a limited company that should be named as a party.

2. Consolidating actions: *A* may have sued *B* in more than one action, where the facts or events indicate that the actions should be combined or tried together.

3. Staying the action: A judge may order an action not to proceed until a party who has failed to do something, such as supply a document, has done what is required.

4. Amending or striking out a claim or defence under Rule 12.02 where there is no reasonable defence or cause of action, or the pleadings are inflammatory, etc. This is a very drastic remedy, and the Divisional Court has imposed some limits on the use of this remedy, which are discussed below.

5. Staying or dismissing a claim: This power is used to deal with plaintiff's claims where, for example, a plaintiff is a vexatious litigant, frequently suing the same defendant over the same issues, where the matter has already been decided by a court.

6. Directing the production of documents: Where the parties drag their feet in producing documents, the court can order the documents to be produced; if the documents are not produced, the court can tie the order to an order to stay or dismiss. In Illustration 10.3, you can see that Albert Oryx was ordered at the settlement conference to produce an additional document by a set date.

7. Changing the place of trial under Rule 6.01: This permits the court to order compliance with the rule if the action was started in the wrong place, or the balance of convenience indicates it should be tried in a particular place.

8. Directing an additional settlement conference under Rule 13.02(3) where more time is required to negotiate a settlement or produce documents.

9. Order costs: This power is used where a party has been unprepared or does not participate in the settlement conference in good faith.

The court may also dismiss an action or grant judgment where a party has failed to attend a second settlement conference. Settlement conference orders are recorded on an Endorsement Record/Order of the Court, a sample of which appears in Illustration 10.3. Note that any order made at a settlement conference must be served by the clerk on all parties who were not present at the settlement conference.

As noted above, the power to dismiss an action at the settlement conference has been challenged on appeal to the Divisional Court, which has imposed some limits on the use of this power. In *Wan v.*

ILLUSTRATION 10.3: Sample Endorsement Record/ Order of the Court

Superior Court of Justice	**Endorsement Record/Order of the Court**
Cour supérieure de justice	*Fiche d'inscription/Ordonnance judiciaire*

Toronto	SC-00-47669-00
Small Claims Court / *Cour des petites créances de*	Claim No. / *N° de la demande*

47 Sheppard Ave. E., 3rd Fl.

Toronto, ON M2N 5N1

Address / *Adresse*

416-326-3554

Phone number / *Numéro de téléphone*

BETWEEN / *ENTRE*

Albert Oryx

Plaintiff(s) / *Demandeur(s)/demanderesse(s)*

and / *et*

Ophelia Foot

Defendant(s) / *Défendeur(s)/défenderesse(s)*

Representative of the plaintiff(s): Peter Paralegal
Représentant du demandeur :

Representative of the defendant(s): Digbert Fightback
Représentant du défendeur :

Event type: Settlement Conference
Type d'affaire :

On April 27, Yr. 1 , a hearing was held in the above matter and the following order was made:
Le *une audience a eu lieu concernant l'affaire susmentionnée, et l'ordonnance suivante a été rendue :*

The plaintiff is to serve and file the appraisal of diamond enagement ring by PK Jewels Ltd.

dated Nov 1, Yr. −1 on the Defendant by May 15, Yr 1.

"J. Justero"

Signature of judge / *Signature du juge*

Endorsement Record/Order of the Court / *Fiche d'inscription/Ordonnance judiciaire* (June 1, 2009 / *1er Juin 2009*) CSD

Wan, [2005] O.J. 4482, the Divisional Court overturned a judgment of a judge at a settlement conference because in the circumstances of the case, the plaintiff had no notice that the judgment on her claim would be at risk. It follows from this that an order to dismiss (or, as was the case in *Wan*, to set aside a judgment) should be made in circumstances where the parties have notice of the issues and are in a position to argue on the merits — in some cases, the order may be made conditional pending the parties having an opportunity to properly argue the merits or rectify an error. If you are seeking to have your opponent's claim dismissed or a defence struck out at a settlement conference, it is advisable to give your opponent written notice that you intend to raise the issue at the settlement conference. You can do this by letter; there is no form for this.

Obtaining a Final Determination at a Settlement Conference

Rule 13.05(4) permits a judge at a settlement conference to give judgment on the merits without the case going on to trial:

- The claim must be for an amount that is below the threshold amount for an appeal. (As of July 17, 2013, a final order had to be for $2,500 or more if it were to be appealed.)

- All parties must file a consent indicating they wish to have a final determination of the matter at the settlement conference, if mediation does not result in a settlement.

Note that the parties must agree to submit to mediation at the settlement conference — something that will happen anyway — thus, a key reason for being there. In effect, this becomes a mediation that then turns into arbitration. The process is informal, and no formal evidence is called. The parties have already made full disclosure, and from discussion of the facts and issues during mediation the judge should have a pretty good idea about an appropriate outcome.

A party may not move for **summary judgment** by a motion during the settlement conference, before it, or after it. The Superior Court *Rules of Civil Procedure* have a provision, Rule 20, which permits this. The *Rules of the Small Claims Court* do not specifically permit this, although judgments without a trial may occur under Rule 12.02, which, as we have seen, permits parties to bring motions to strike out pleadings where there is no reasonable cause of action or defence, where the pleadings would cause delay or hinder a fair trial, and where a pleading is inflammatory or abusive. This rule is designed to deal with obviously defective pleadings, and in many cases, if repair is possible, the court will allow the pleading to be amended. But if it is clear that there is no viable cause of action (for example, the plaintiff missed the limitation period), judgment may be given dismissing the action without the case going to trial.

Rule 1.03(2) had once been the basis for an argument that the Small Claims Court might proceed in a summary way. The court has now ruled in several cases that there is no such thing as a motion for summary judgment in Small Claims Court.[5]

Concluding a Settlement Conference

At the end of the conference, the judge or referee is required to prepare a memorandum that includes the following:

* Summarizes any recommendations made under Rule 13.04 to clarify or narrow issues, or admit facts or documents.
* Identifies remaining issues in dispute.
* Identifies matters agreed to by parties: facts, admissions, evidence to be called, etc.
* Identifies evidentiary matters that are relevant, including suggestions of the type of evidence required to prove specific facts in issue.
* Sets a timetable for any remaining steps to be taken prior to trial — productions of further evidence, amending pleadings as agreed, supplying amended witness lists, or whatever else might be required.

Note that admissions or settlement discussion material (other than a reference to issues that have been settled or withdrawn) do not appear in the memorandum that is filed with the court and given to the trial judge, who should not be privy to settlement discussions or offers to settle. This is consistent with the requirement that the judge who conducts a settlement conference shall not preside at the trial. At one time, the parties could consent to having the same judge preside, but Rule 13.08 now clearly excludes the settlement conference judge from trying a case:

> 13.08 A judge who conducts a Settlement Conference in an action shall not preside at the trial of the action.

When setting a date for trial, check with the clerk to be sure the presiding judge will not be the same judge as the settlement conference

---

[5] *Fountain v. Ford*, [2009] O.J. No. 562 (S.C.J.) and *Caprio v. Caprio* (2009), 97 O.R. (3d) 312 (S.C.J.). See also J.S. Winny, "Is Summary Judgment Available in the Ontario Small Claims Court" (2009) 36:1 *Advocates' Quarterly* 128.

judge. (Illustration 10.4 provides a sample Settlement Conference Memorandum completed for the *Oryx v. Foot* case.)

Costs

Normally, if both parties are cooperative, there are no costs awarded on a settlement conference. But the Rules seem to contemplate two levels of cost awards to punish parties who have not done what is required by Rule 13. If a party is not well prepared or is not directly available to approve a settlement or give directions to counsel, costs of up to $100 plus disbursements, for example, may be ordered under Rule 13.10 against a party who has prevented, even if unintentionally, an effective settlement conference from taking place. The rule also provides for costs in excess of the $100 cap in "exceptional circumstances". This term is undefined. Arguably, it contemplates situations where a party is inadequately prepared, especially where the lack of preparation is deliberate and wilful.

> 13.10 The costs of a settlement conference, exclusive of disbursements, shall not exceed $100 unless the court orders otherwise because there are special circumstances. O. Reg. 78/06, s. 27.

No Discontinuance of Claim

While parties may settle at a settlement conference, if they have not done so once it is concluded, the party, in accordance with Rule 13.09, may not withdraw a claim against a party who is not in default unless the party consents or a judge on a motion to discontinue so orders. The reason for this rule is that if the parties did not formally settle, the plaintiff should not simply be able to stop the action by withdrawing a claim without having the court be able to assess costs. A defendant who has defended right up to trial can be seen as a successful party if the claim is now withdrawn, and would be eligible to be compensated in costs in a situation where the defendant has "won".

> 13.09 After a settlement conference has been held, a claim against a party who is not in default shall not be withdrawn or discontinued by the party who brought the claim without,
> (a) the written consent of the party against whom the claim is brought; or
> (b) leave of the court.

Moving on to Trial — Notice of Trial

The clerk, under Rule 13.07, is required to give a notice to the parties during or after the settlement conference, informing them that one or the other of them must request a trial date from the clerk

ILLUSTRATION 10.4: Sample Settlement Conference Memorandum

Superior Court of Justice	**Settlement Conference Memorandum**
Cour supérieure de justice	*Procès-verbal de conférence en vue d'une transaction*

Toronto

Small Claims Court / *Cour des petites créances de*
47 Sheppard Ave. E., 3rd Fl.
Toronto, ON M2N 5N1
Address / *Adresse*

416-326-3554
Phone number / *Numéro de téléphone*

Claim No. / *N° de la demande*
SC-00-47669-00

BETWEEN / *ENTRE*

Albert Oryx

Plaintiff(s) / *Demandeur(s)/demanderesse(s)*

and / *et*

Ophelia Foot

Defendant(s) / *Défendeur(s)/défenderesse(s)*

	Lawyer / avocat	Student-at-law / étudiant en droit	Paralegal / parajuristes
Peter Paralegal	☐	☐	☒
Representative of the plaintiff(s) / *Représentant(e) du/de la ou des demandeur(s)/demanderesse(s)*			
Digbert Fightback	☐	☐	☒
Representative of the defendant(s) / *Représentant(e) du/de la ou des défendeur(s)/défenderesse(s)*			

NOTE: All orders to be made on the Endorsement Record.
REMARQUE : *Toutes les ordonnances seront rendues dans la fiche d'inscription.*

SUMMARY OF PLEADINGS
SOMMAIRE DES ACTES DE PROCÉDURE

Claim: / *Demande :*

Claim for return of engagement ring on the basis that it was a conditional gift, condition breached.

Defence/Defendant's Claim: / *Défense/Demande du défendeur :*

Gift of ring unconditional, ring now property of defendant.

Settlement Conference Memorandum / *Procès-verbal de conférence en vue d'une transaction* (June 1, 2009 / *1er juin 2009*) CSD

continues....

Illustration 10.4 (continued)

Superior Court of Justice *Cour supérieure de justice*	PAGE 2	**Settlement Conference Memorandum** *Procès-verbal de conférence en vue* *d'une transaction*

SC-00-47669-00

Claim No. / *N° de la demande*

SUMMARY OF ISSUES
SOMMAIRE DES QUESTIONS EN LITIGE

Issues agreed on: / *Questions sur lesquelles les parties se sont entendues :*

Plaintiff bought ring, possession passed to defendant

Issues in dispute: / *Questions en litige non encore réglées :*

Ownership of ring based on whether conditional or unconditional gift

Evidentiary matters/Recommendations/Other: / *Questions relatives à la preuve/Recommandations/Autres remarques :*

Evidence of parties as to understanding of gift based on conversation between them

Estimated number of witnesses at trial: *Nombre estimatif de témoins au procès :*	Plaintiff(s): 3 *Demandeur(s) :*	Defendant(s): 2 *Défendeur(s) :*

Interpreter required by
Interprète demandé par

☐ Plaintiff(s):   ☐ French/English   ☐ Sign Language   ☐ Other language (to be provided by party)
Demandeur(s)   *Français/Anglais*   *Langage gestuel*   *Autre (doit être fourni par la partie)*

☐ Defendant(s):   ☐ French/English   ☐ Sign Language   ☐ Other language (to be provided by party)
Défendeur(s)   *Français/Anglais*   *Langage gestuel*   *Autre (doit être fourni par la partie)*

Estimated time of trial: 2 hours
Durée estimative du procès :

April 27, Yr. 1	D. Justero	" D. Justero"
(Date)	(Name of official / *nom du fonctionnaire*)	Signature

Settlement Conference Memorandum / *Procès-verbal de conférence en vue d'une transaction* (June 1, 2009 / *1er juin 2009*) CSD

within 30 days of the end of the settlement conference if the case has not settled and pay the fee for **setting the action down for trial**. A Notice to Set Action Down for Trial is usually given to the plaintiff. (See Illustration 10.5 for a sample notice.) As the plaintiff is the one usually most concerned about getting to court, he or she usually notifies the clerk by sending a letter requesting a date for trial. In this letter it may be helpful to indicate what dates you are available so that the clerk doesn't schedule you on a day you are not available. Also consider contacting the other party's representative to see if he or she is available on dates you wish to choose. Doing this may prevent unnecessary adjournments. The party requesting the trial must pay the fee to fix a trial date. The fee is higher for frequent claimants. Once the clerk has received the request, he or she is to fix a trial date and serve a notice of trial by mail or fax on every party who filed a claim or defence. (A sample Notice of Trial for the *Oryx v. Foot* case is given in Illustration 10.6.)

RULE 14 OFFER TO SETTLE — PLAYING "SETTLEMENT ROULETTE"

The parties do not have to wait for a settlement conference to consider the possibility of settling. Both defendants and plaintiffs can make moves to settle a dispute — before or after proceedings are commenced, and even after judgment. Rule 14 sets out the mechanics and terms relating to an offer to settle.

To encourage parties to settle rather than going to trial, Rule 14 contains a subrule that makes a settlement offer work like gambling. If your offer to settle is refused and it turns out to be the same as or better than the judgment at trial, you are rewarded for making a reasonable offer by being compensated with extra costs. Another way of looking at this is that a party who refuses a "good" offer is penalized in costs. In effect, the court is saying that by refusing to accept a good offer, a party has unnecessarily pushed a matter on to trial. The party has then wasted court time and put everyone to the expense and inconvenience of a trial that should never have had to occur.

The Rule 14 Offer Procedure

Who Can Make an Offer?

Rule 14.01 provides that any party can make an offer to any other party or to all other parties to settle an action:

> 14.01 A party may serve on any other party an offer to settle a claim on the terms specified in the offer.

ILLUSTRATION 10.5: Notice to Set Action Down for Trial

Superior Court of Justice *Cour supérieure de justice*	**Notice to Set Action Down for Trial** *Avis d'inscription de l'action au rôle*

Toronto
Small Claims Court / *Cour des petites créances de*

47 Sheppard Ave. E., 3rd Fl.
Toronto, ON M2N 5N1
Address / *Adresse*

416-326-3554
Phone number / *N° de téléphone*

TO THE PARTIES:
AUX PARTIES :

TAKE NOTICE THAT THIS ACTION MAY NOW PROCEED TO TRIAL.
PRENEZ NOTE QUE CETTE ACTION PEUT MAINTENANT ÊTRE INSTRUITE.

IF THIS ACTION DOES NOT SETTLE within 30 days after the settlement conference, a party MUST file a Request to Clerk (Form 9B) requesting a trial date together with the required trial fee. [R. 13.07]. Fees must be paid in Canadian funds and may be paid by cheque payable to the Minister of Finance, or by cash or money order.
SI CETTE ACTION NE SE CONCLUT PAS PAR UNE TRANSACTION dans les 30 jours qui suivent la conférence en vue d'une transaction, une des parties DOIT déposer une requête au greffier (formule 9B) en vue de demander une date de procès, accompagnée des frais nécessaires pour inscrire l'action au rôle [R. 13.07]. Ces frais doivent être payés en monnaie canadienne et peuvent être payés par chèque à l'ordre du ministre des Finances, ou en espèces ou par mandat.

IF YOU FAIL TO SETTLE THE ACTION AND FAIL TO SET THE ACTION DOWN FOR TRIAL, the clerk may make an order dismissing the action as abandoned 150 days after the first defence was filed. The clerk will send all parties a notice of impending dismissal before the dismissal order is made. [R. 11.1.01(2)].
SI VOUS NE CONCLUEZ PAS DE TRANSACTION À L'ÉGARD DE CETTE ACTION ET QUE VOUS NE LA FAITES PAS INSCRIRE POUR INSTRUCTION, le greffier peut rendre une ordonnance rejetant l'action pour cause de désistement après un délai de 150 jours suivant le dépôt de la première défense. Le greffier fera parvenir à chacune des parties un avis concernant le rejet imminent avant que l'ordonnance de rejet soit rendue. [par. 11.1.01(2)].

You can get a list of Small Claims Court fees at court offices and online at: www.attorneygeneral.jus.gov.on.ca.
Vous pouvez vous procurer une liste des frais en vigueur à la Cour des petites créances auprès d'un greffe, ou en ligne à l'adresse : www.attorneygeneral.jus.gov.on.ca.

April 27, Yr. 1	*Iam Clerk*
	(Signature of clerk / *Signature du greffier*)

SAA 13.07-00 (June 1, 2009 / *1ᵉʳ juin 2009*) CSD
(Non-regulated form / *Formule non prescrite*)

ILLUSTRATION 10.6: Sample Notice of Trial

Superior Court of Justice
Cour supérieure de justice

Notice of Trial
Avis de procès

Toronto
Small Claims Court / *Cour des petites créances de*

47 Sheppard Ave. E. – 3rd Fl.
Address / *Adresse*

Toronto, ON M2N 5N1

416-326-3554
Phone number / *N° de téléphone*

SC-00-47669-00
Claim No. / *N° de la demande*

BETWEEN /*ENTRE*

Albert Oryx

Plaintiff(s) / Demandeur(s)

and / *et*

Ophelia Foot

Defendant(s) / Défendeur(s)

TO THE PARTIES:
AUX PARTIES :

THIS COURT WILL HOLD A TRIAL on _____ Sept. 14, Yr. 1 _____ , at ___ 10:00 ___ , a.m./p.m.,
LE TRIBUNAL PRÉCITÉ TIENDRA UN PROCÈS le   , à   *(heure)*

or as soon as possible after that time, at ___ 47 Sheppard Ave. E. ___
ou dès que possible après, àlau

Toronto, ON, Courtroom 31
(Address of court location & courtroom number / *Adresse du tribunal et numéro de la salle d'audience*)

and thereafter as may be required from time to time.
et par la suite, au besoin.

CAUTION:	**IF YOU FAIL TO ATTEND THIS TRIAL,** your claim may be dismissed or judgment may be given against you, with costs, in your absence.
AVERTISSEMENT :	*SI VOUS NE VOUS PRÉSENTEZ PAS À CE PROCÈS, votre demande pourra être rejetée ou un jugement pourra être rendu contre vous, avec dépens, en votre absence.*

May 1, Yr. 1
Le

"Iam Clerk"
(Signature of clerk / *Signature du greffier*)

SAA 13.01-00 (January 25, 2006 / *25 janvier 2006*) CSD
(Non-regulated form / *Formule non prescrite*)

Under this rule, a third party defendant to a defendant's claim can make an offer to the plaintiff in the defendant's claim, which may remove the third party from the action while it continues between the other parties. And, of course, either a defendant or a plaintiff can make an offer to settle.

Requirements for Attracting Cost Consequences

Rules 14.01.1(1), 14.02(1), (2), and 14.07 lay out the requirements for offers if they are to attract cost consequences. An offer to settle may be made at any time; but, if not accepted prior to trial, in order to trigger costs consequences, it must be made in writing and served on the other party at least seven days before trial, and it must remain open until after the trial begins. In order to meet this condition, the usual wording in an offer designed to attract cost consequences is to state that "this offer remains open for acceptance until one minute after the trial commences." You should not refer to an exact trial date, as trials are sometimes postponed to another date, wherein your offer would inadvertently expire and the cost consequences rule would no longer apply.

Written Requirement for Offers

Under Rule 14.01.1, offers must be in writing. However, use of the court forms is not mandatory. A party can make up an offer in any clear and legible format that he or she wishes to use, although it is advisable to put on the offer document the parties' names, court file number, the date, and the fact that it is an offer.

> 14.01.1(1) An offer to settle, an acceptance of an offer to settle and a notice of withdrawal of an offer to settle shall be in writing.
> (2) An offer to settle may be in Form 14A, an acceptance of an offer to settle may be in Form 14B and a notice of withdrawal of an offer to settle may be in Form 14C.
> (3) The terms of an accepted offer to settle may be set out in terms of settlement (Form 14D).

Alternatively, the offer can also be made using Form 14A, setting out all of the terms of the offer. See Illustration 10.7 for a sample Offer to Settle by Ophelia Foot.

Withdrawal of Offer

Under Rule 14.03, an offer may be withdrawn by the offeror at any time before it is accepted by serving a notice of withdrawal of the offer. If the offer contains an expiry date or expires at or some time

ILLUSTRATION 10.7: Sample Offer to Settle (Form 14A)

ONTARIO
Superior Court of Justice
Cour supérieure de justice

Offer to Settle
Offre de transaction
Form / *Formule* 14A Ont. Reg. No. / *Règl. de l'Ont.* : 258/98

Toronto
Small Claims Court / *Cour des petites créances de*

SC-00-47669-00
Claim No. / *Nº de la demande*

47 Sheppard Ave. E., 3rd Fl.
Toronto, ON M2N 5N1

Address / *Adresse*

416-326-3554
Phone number / *Numéro de téléphone*

BETWEEN / ENTRE

Albert Oryx

Plaintiff(s) / *Demandeur(s)/demanderesse(s)*

and / et

Ophelia Foot

Defendant(s) / *Défendeur(s)/défenderesse(s)*

My name is **Digbert Fightback**
Je m'appelle

(Full name / *Nom et prénoms*)

1. In this action, I am the
   Dans la présente action, je suis le/la

   ☐ Plaintiff
   demandeur/demanderesse

   ☐ Defendant
   défendeur/défenderesse

   ☒ representative of **Ophelia Foot**
   représentant(e) de   (Name of party(ies) / *Nom de la ou des parties*)

2. I offer to settle this action against **Ophelia Foot**
   Je présente une offre de transaction dans cette action contre   (Name of party(ies) / *Nom de la ou des parties*)

   on the following terms: *(Set out terms in numbered paragraphs, or on an attached sheet.)*
   selon les conditions suivantes : (Indiquez les conditions sous forme de paragraphes numérotés ou sur une feuille annexée.)

   Pay to the plaintiff by certified cheque within 10 days of acceptance the sum of $1,000 inclusive of costs, pre- and post-judgment interest in full and final settlement of all claims.

   Upon receipt of payment in full under these minutes, the parties shall both consent to a clerk's order to dismiss the action.

SCR 14.01.1-14A (June 1, 2009 / *1er juin 2009*) CSD

continues....

Illustration 10.7 (continued)

FORM / *FORMULE 14A*   PAGE 2   SC-00-47669-00
Claim No. / *N° de la demande*

3.   This offer to settle is available for acceptance until   **one minute after the trial commences.**
L'acceptation de la présente offre de transaction peut se faire jusqu'au

This offer to settle may be accepted by serving an acceptance of offer to settle (Form 14B may be used) on the party who made it, at any time before it is withdrawn or before the court disposes of the claim to which the offer applies [R. 14.05(1)]. You can get forms at court offices or online at <u>www.ontariocourtforms.on.ca</u>.
La présente offre de transaction peut être acceptée en signifiant une acceptation de l'offre de transaction (la formule 14B peut être utilisée) à la partie qui l'a faite, avant que l'offre ne soit retirée ou avant que le tribunal ne décide la demande qui en fait l'objet [par. 14.05 (1)]. Vous pouvez obtenir des formules aux greffes des tribunaux ou en ligne à l'adresse <u>www.ontariocourtforms.on.ca</u>.

June 1, Yr. 1   *Digbert Fightback*

                              (Signature of party or representative making offer / *Signature de la partie ou du/de la représentant(e)*)

                             Digbert Fightback
                             60 My Way, Toronto, ON M6R 8P1
                             Tel. 416-491-5041

                            (Name, address and phone number of party or representative / *Nom, adresse et numéro de téléphone de la partie ou du/de la représentant(e)*)

NOTE:	IF YOU ACCEPT AN OFFER TO SETTLE, THEN FAIL TO COMPLY WITH ITS TERMS, judgment in the terms of the accepted offer may be obtained against you on motion to the court, or the action may continue as if there has been no offer to settle [R. 14.06].
REMARQUE :	*SI VOUS ACCEPTEZ UNE OFFRE DE TRANSACTION MAIS QU'ENSUITE VOUS N'EN OBSERVEZ PAS LES CONDITIONS, un jugement suivant les conditions de l'offre acceptée peut être obtenu contre vous sur présentation d'une motion au tribunal ou l'action peut continuer comme s'il n'y avait jamais eu d'offre de transaction [règle 14.06].*

NOTE:	IF THIS OFFER TO SETTLE IS NOT ACCEPTED, IT SHALL NOT BE FILED WITH THE COURT OR DISCLOSED to the trial judge until all questions of liability and relief (other than costs) have been determined [R. 14.04].
REMARQUE :	*SI LA PRÉSENTE OFFRE DE TRANSACTION N'EST PAS ACCEPTÉE, ELLE NE DOIT PAS ÊTRE DÉPOSÉE AUPRÈS DU TRIBUNAL NI DIVULGUÉE au juge du procès tant que toutes les questions relatives à la responsabilité et aux mesures de redressement (à l'exclusion des dépens) n'ont pas été décidées [règle 14.04].*

SCR 14.01.1-14A (June 1, 2009 / *1ᵉʳ juin 2009*) CSD

after the start of trial, then it is deemed to be withdrawn at that time if it is not accepted. If the offer does not contain an expiry date, it is also deemed to expire when the court disposes of the claim. Keep in mind that if the offer was made to attract costs consequences, the costs consequences rule no longer applies once the offer has been withdrawn, unless a new offer is made at least seven or more days before trial and that offer remains open for acceptance until after the commencement of the trial.

> 14.03(1) An offer to settle may be withdrawn at any time before it is accepted, by serving a notice of withdrawal of an offer to settle on the party to whom it was made.
>
> (2) If an offer to settle specifies a date after which it is no longer available for acceptance, and has not been accepted on or before that date, the offer shall be deemed to have been withdrawn on the day after that date.
>
> (3) An offer may not be accepted after the court disposes of the claim in respect of which the offer is made.

Example 10.1 Withdrawal of Offer to Settle

Ophelia served Albert with an offer to settle on June 1. After waiting for 15 days, and with Albert still showing no interest in settling, Ophelia was getting angry. She demanded that her legal representative, Digbert Fightback, withdraw her offer as she did not wish to continue settlement discussions. Digbert prepared a Notice of Withdrawal of Offer to Settle and was ready to serve it upon Albert when he received a call from Peter Paralegal, accepting the offer on Albert's behalf.

For Ophelia Foot's Notice of Withdrawal of Offer to Settle (Form 14C), which is prepared but not served, see Illustration 10.8.

Acceptance of Offers

An offer may be accepted by serving a notice of acceptance at any time prior to the withdrawal of the offer or before the court disposes of the claim by giving judgment. Note, however, that even after judgment, it is possible to settle if the plaintiff agrees to accept less than he or she is entitled to under a judgment. However, there are some legal formalities that must be observed, which are discussed in the section of this chapter on Settlement Documentation.

Under Rule 14.05, if an offer by a plaintiff is accepted prior to trial and it contains a provision that the settlement amount is to be

ILLUSTRATION 10.8: Sample Notice of Withdrawal of Offer to Settle (Form 14C)

ONTARIO
Superior Court of Justice
Cour supérieure de justice

Notice of Withdrawal of Offer to Settle
Avis de retrait de l'offre de transaction
Form / *Formule* 14C Ont. Reg. No. / *Règl. de l'Ont.* : 258/98

Toronto
Small Claims Court / *Cour des petites créances de*

SC-00-47669-00
Claim No. / *Nº de la demande*

47 Sheppard Ave. E., 3rd. Fl.
Toronto, ON M2N 5N1
Address / *Adresse*

416-326-3554
Phone number / *Numéro de téléphone*

BETWEEN / *ENTRE*

Albert Oryx
Plaintiff(s) / *Demandeur(s)/demanderesse(s)*

and / *et*

Ophelia Foot
Defendant(s) / *Défendeur(s)/défenderesse(s)*

My name is Digbert Fightback
Je m'appelle
(Full name / *Nom et prénoms*)

1.   In this action, I am the
     Dans la présente action, je suis le/la

     ☐ plaintiff
        demandeur/demanderesse

     ☐ defendant
        défendeur/défenderesse

     ☒ representative of **Ophelia Foot**
        représentant(e) de
        (Name of party(ies) / *Nom de la ou des parties*)

2.   I withdraw the offer to settle provided to **Albert Oryx**
     Je retire l'offre de transaction faite à
        (Name of party(ies) / *Nom de la ou des parties*)

     dated **June 1, Yr. 1**, which has not been accepted.
     et datée du, *laquelle n'a pas été acceptée.*

June 15, Yr. 1

     Digbert Fightback
     (Signature of party or representative withdrawing offer / *Signature de la
     partie ou du/de la représentant(e) qui retire l'offre*)

     Digbert Fightback
     60 My Way, Toronto, ON M6R 8P1
     Tel. 416-491-5041

     (Name, address and phone number of party or representative / *Nom,
     adresse et numéro de téléphone de la partie ou du/de la représentant(e)*)

SCR 14.01.1-14C (June 1, 2009 / *1er juin 2009*) CSD

paid into court as a condition of the offer, then the defendant, to accept the offer, must make the payment into court. Similarly, if the defendant makes an offer to pay that is accepted by the plaintiff, the plaintiff may accept the offer and impose a condition that payment be made into court. This condition ensures that the offer is complied with and makes it easier for a plaintiff to move to enforce settlement rights if the defendant fails to do what has been agreed to.

> 14.05(1) An offer to settle may be accepted by serving an acceptance of an offer to settle on the party who made it, at any time before it is withdrawn or before the court disposes of the claim in respect of which it is made.
>
> (2) An offer by a plaintiff to settle a claim in return for the payment of money by a defendant may include a term that the defendant pay the money into court; in that case, the defendant may accept the offer only by paying the money into court and notifying the plaintiff of the payment.
>
> (3) If a defendant offers to pay money to a plaintiff in settlement of a claim, the plaintiff may accept the offer with the condition that the defendant pay the money into court; if the offer is so accepted and the defendant fails to pay the money into court, the plaintiff may proceed as provided in rule 14.06.
>
> (4) If an accepted offer to settle does not deal with costs, the plaintiff is entitled,
> (a) in the case of an offer made by the defendant, to the plaintiff's disbursements assessed to the date the plaintiff was served with the offer;
> (b) in the case of an offer made by the plaintiff, to the plaintiff's disbursements assessed to the date that the notice of acceptance was served.

Example 10.2 Acceptance of an Offer to Settle

Satisfied that he has kept Ophelia on her toes long enough, on June 15, Albert decided to accept Ophelia's offer to settle. Instead of drafting his own acceptance, Peter Paralegal, Albert's legal representative, chose to use an Acceptance of Offer to Settle form (Form 14B). He also recorded the terms of the settlement on a Terms of Settlement form (Form 14D).

Offers can be accepted using Form 14B. If an offer is accepted, its terms may be set out in Form 14D. (See Albert Oryx's Form 14B, Acceptance of Offer, in Illustration 10.9; for Form 14D, the Terms of Settlement between Oryx and Foot, see Illustration 10.10.)

ILLUSTRATION 10.9: Sample Acceptance of Offer to Settle (Form 14B)

ONTARIO
Superior Court of Justice
Cour supérieure de justice

Acceptance of Offer to Settle
Acceptation de l'offre de transaction
Form / *Formule* 14B Ont. Reg. No. / *Règl. de l'Ont.* : 258/98

Toronto
Small Claims Court / *Cour des petites créances de*

SC-00-47669-00
Claim No. / *N° de la demande*

**47 Sheppard Ave. E., 3ʳᵈ Fl.
Toronto, ON M2N 5N1**
Address / *Adresse*

416-326-3554
Phone number / *Numéro de téléphone*

BETWEEN / *ENTRE*

Albert Oryx
Plaintiff(s) / *Demandeur(s)/demanderesse(s)*

and / *et*

Ophelia Foot
Defendant(s) / *Défendeur(s)/défenderesse(s)*

My name is Peter Paralegal
Je m'appelle
(Full name / *Nom et prénoms*)

1. In this action, I am the
Dans la présente action, je suis le/la

☐ plaintiff
demandeur/demanderesse

☐ defendant
défendeur/défenderesse

☒ representative of **Albert Oryx**
représentant(e) de   (Name of party(ies) / *Nom de la ou des parties*)

2. I accept the offer to settle from **Ophelia Foot**
J'accepte l'offre de transaction faite par   (Name of party(ies) / *Nom de la ou des parties*)

dated **June 1, Yr. 1**
et datée du

3. This offer to settle has not expired and has not been withdrawn.
Cette offre de transaction n'est pas expirée et n'a pas été retirée.

June 15, Yr. 1

Peter Paralegal
(Signature of party or representative accepting offer / *Signature de la partie ou du/de la représentant(e) qui accepte l'offre*)

**Peter Paralegal
41 Yonge Street, #410, Toronto, ON M5G 1S1
Tel. 416-597-0048**
(Name, address and phone number of party or representative / *Nom, adresse et numéro de téléphone de la partie ou du/de la représentant(e)*)

CAUTION:	**IF YOU ACCEPT AN OFFER TO SETTLE, THEN FAIL TO COMPLY WITH ITS TERMS,** judgment in the terms of the accepted offer may be obtained against you on motion to the Court, or this action may continue as if there has been no offer to settle [R. 14.06].
AVERTISSEMENT :	*SI VOUS ACCEPTEZ UNE OFFRE DE TRANSACTION MAIS QU'ENSUITE VOUS N'EN OBSERVEZ PAS LES CONDITIONS,* un jugement suivant les conditions de l'offre acceptée peut être obtenu contre vous sur présentation d'une motion au tribunal ou la présente action peut continuer comme s'il n'y avait jamais eu d'offre de transaction [règle 14.06].

SCR 14.01.1-14B (June 1, 2009 / *1ᵉʳ juin 2009*) CSD

ILLUSTRATION 10.10: Sample Terms of Settlement (Form 14D)

ONTARIO
Superior Court of Justice
Cour supérieure de justice

Terms of Settlement
Conditions de la transaction
Form / *Formule* 14D Ont. Reg. No. / *Règl. de l'Ont.* : 258/98

Toronto
Small Claims Court / *Cour des petites créances de*

**47 Sheppard Ave. E., 3rd Fl.
Toronto, ON M2N 5N1**
Address / *Adresse*

416-326-3554
Phone number / *Numéro de téléphone*

SC-00-47669-00
Claim No. / *N° de la demande*

BETWEEN / *ENTRE*

Albert Oryx

Plaintiff(s) / *Demandeur(s)/demanderesse(s)*

and / *et*

Ophelia Foot

Defendant(s) / *Défendeur(s)/défenderesse(s)*

We have agreed to settle this action on the following terms:
Nous avons convenu de régler la présente action selon les conditions suivantes :

1. **Ophelia Foot**
   (Name of party(ies) / *Nom de la ou des parties*)

   Albert Oryx
   (Name of party(ies) / *Nom de la ou des parties*)

   shall pay to
   verse à

   the sum of
   la somme de

   $ **1,000.00** as follows as full and final settlement of the claim, inclusive of interest and costs:
   $ comme suit, à titre de transaction complète et définitive sur la demande, y compris les intérêts et les dépens :

   (Provide terms of payment such as start date, frequency, amount and duration / *Indiquez les modalités de paiement telles que la date de début des versements ainsi que leur fréquence, leur montant et leur durée.*)

   Payment to be made by certified cheque payable to "Peter Paralegal in trust" within 10 days of the execution of the terms of settlement.

   Payment constitutes full and final settlement of all claims by each party against the other.

   Upon payment in full to the plaintiff, the parties' shall sign a consent to clerk's order dismissing the action.

Put a line through any blank space and initial.
Tracez une ligne en travers de tout espace laissé en blanc et apposez vos initiales.

SCR 14D (June 1, 2009 / *1er juin 2009*) CSD

continues....

Illustration 10.10 (continued)

FORM / *FORMULE* 14D	PAGE 2	SC-00-47669-00
		Claim No. / *N° de la demande*

2. This claim (and Defendant's Claim, if any) is withdrawn.
   Cette demande (et celle du défendeur, le cas échéant) est retirée (sont retirées).

3. If a party to these terms of settlement fails to comply, judgment in the terms of settlement may be obtained against that party on motion to the court or this action may continue as if there has been no settlement.
   Si une partie aux présentes conditions de la transaction n'en observe pas les conditions, un jugement suivant les conditions de la transaction peut être obtenu contre cette partie sur présentation d'une motion au tribunal ou la présente action peut continuer comme s'il n'y avait jamais eu de transaction.

4. Provided that the terms of settlement are complied with, the parties above fully and finally release one another from all claims related to the facts and issues raised in this action.
   Pourvu que les conditions de la transaction soient observées, les parties susmentionnées se dégagent l'une et l'autre complètement et définitivement de toutes demandes liées aux faits et questions en litige soulevés dans la présente action.

The parties do not need to sign terms of settlement on the same day, but each must sign in the presence of his or her witness who signs a moment later. (For additional parties' signatures, attach a separate sheet in the below format.)
Les parties ne sont pas tenues de signer les conditions de la transaction le même jour, mais chacune doit les signer en présence de son témoin, qui le signe à son tour aussitôt après. (S'il y a lieu, annexez une autre feuille portant la signature des parties additionnelles présentée selon le format indiqué ci-dessous.)

June 15, Yr. 1	June 16, Yr. 1
Albert Oryx	*Ophelia Foot*
(Signature of party / *Signature de la partie*)	(Signature of party / *Signature de la partie*)
Albert Oryx	**Ophelia Foot**
(Name of Party / *Nom de la partie*)	(Name of Party / *Nom de la partie*)
Peter Paralegal	*Digbert Fightback*
(Signature of witness / *Signature du témoin*)	(Signature of witness / *Signature du témoin*)
Peter Paralegal	**Digbert Fightback**
(Name of witness / *Nom du témoin*)	(Name of witness / *Nom du témoin*)
(Signature of party / *Signature de la partie*)	(Signature of party / *Signature de la partie*)
(Name of Party / *Nom de la partie*)	(Name of Party / *Nom de la partie*)
(Signature of witness / *Signature du témoin*)	(Signature of witness / *Signature du témoin*)
(Name of witness / *Nom du témoin*)	(Name of witness / *Nom du témoin*)

SCR 14D (June 1, 2009 / *1er juin 2009*) CSD

Note that the Rules make the use of these forms permissive: that is, you do not have to use them. You can make, accept, and withdraw offers by letter or other written format. By drafting your own acceptance and settlement, you avoid the standard terms on the Small Claims Court forms, which stipulate that a failure to comply with the offer can result in (i) a motion to enforce the settlement, or (ii) the "wronged" party choosing to take the case to trial. You are limited to judgment based on only the terms of the offer or you have to take your chances at a trial. If you draft your own settlement forms, you can put down that a consequence of failing to abide by the settlement terms means that the other party can obtain judgment for the amount originally sued for.

Costs in Respect of an Offer Accepted before Trial

As set out in the sample Offer to Settle in Illustration 10.7, most offers to settle propose a final payment sum that is inclusive of costs (which would encompass one sum for representation fees and disbursements) and pre- and post-judgment interest. In some cases the offer may be silent as to the issue of costs. In such a case, Rule 14.05(4) provides that the plaintiff is entitled to costs as follows:

- **If the defendant made the offer:** Plaintiff is entitled to all disbursements assessed to the date **the offer** was served on the plaintiff by the defendant.

- **If the plaintiff made the offer:** Plaintiff is entitled to all disbursements to the date the **notice of acceptance** was served on the plaintiff by the defendant.

In either case, the key in determining the payment of disbursements is the date on which the plaintiff knows the defendant has made or accepted an offer. Note that, under Rule 14.05(4), only disbursements are covered. The issue of representation fees arises only if the defendant refused to accept a reasonable offer and the case went to trial.

Enforcement of an Offer to Settle

In accordance with Rule 14.06, if a party fails to comply with an accepted offer, the other party may either bring a motion for judgment on the terms of the offer that was accepted or continue on to trial as if no offer had been made. These two options are reflected in Form 14D, Terms of Settlement (see #3 on Page 2 of the form).

14.06 If a party to an accepted offer to settle fails to comply with the terms of the offer, the other party may,

(a) make a motion to the court for judgment in the terms of the accepted offer; or

(b) continue the proceeding as if there had been no offer to settle.

Where a plaintiff fails to comply, a defendant has the choice of forcing acceptance via a judgment, which is a good strategy if the defendant thinks he or she may not do as well at trial. Similar considerations apply to a plaintiff. Note that it doesn't matter if you made or accepted the offer, the key is whether or not there was an acceptance and whether or not you reneged on the offer. If a plaintiff makes an offer and the defendant accepts it, and the plaintiff then reneges by trying to withdraw the offer or refusing payment when tendered by the defendant, it is the defendant who then has the choice to enforce the settlement or proceed to trial.

It may also be possible for a plaintiff, faced with a defendant who reneges, to move for judgment on the full amount of the claim rather than the amount of the settlement. To do this, you should draft your own Minutes of Settlement, in which you specifically include the right to obtain judgment on the full amount of the claim, rather than use Form 14D, which limits you to enforcing the agreement or continuing on to trial.

Cost Consequences after Judgment on a Rule 14 Offer

If the parties have not settled before trial, then Rule 14 turns the settlement process into "settlement roulette", with Rule 14.07 setting out the cost consequences if an offer is not accepted before trial:

14.07(1) When a plaintiff makes an offer to settle that is not accepted by the defendant, the court may award the plaintiff an amount not exceeding twice the costs of the action, if the following conditions are met:

1. The plaintiff obtains a judgment as favourable as or more favourable than the terms of the offer.

2. The offer was made at least seven days before the trial.

3. The offer was not withdrawn and did not expire before the trial.

(2) When a defendant makes an offer to settle that is not accepted by the plaintiff, the court may award the defendant an amount not exceeding twice the costs awardable to a successful party, from the date the offer was served, if the following conditions are met:

1. The plaintiff obtains a judgment as favourable as or less favourable than the terms of the offer.

2. The offer was made at least seven days before the trial.
3. The offer was not withdrawn and did not expire before the trial.

(3) If an amount is awarded under subrule (1) or (2) to a self-represented party, the court may also award the party an amount not exceeding $500 as compensation for inconvenience and expense.

Note that the costs rules are applied differently, depending on whether a plaintiff or a defendant made an offer. (Figure 10.2 provides a quick summary on the relationship between offer, judgment, and costs.) In both cases, a party must do the following:

- Make an offer in writing
- Serve it on the other party at least seven days before trial
- Leave it open until the trial starts

A judge considers a rejected offer only after the judgment has been given and costs are determined. You must be careful not to disclose terms of an offer during the trial, and you should also not allude to an offer having been made. Rule 14.04 bars all disclosure of anything about an offer until after judgment:

14.04 If an offer to settle is not accepted, no communication about it or any related negotiations shall be made to the trial judge until all questions of liability and the relief to be granted, other than costs, have been determined.

Cost Consequences When a Plaintiff Makes an Offer

If the plaintiff gets a judgment that is *as good as or better than the offer* that he or she made, the plaintiff is entitled to up to *two times the costs of the action* otherwise payable to a successful party.

The following examples demonstrate how this costs rule works:

- The plaintiff sues for $9,000, offers to settle for $7,000, and obtains a judgment for $8,000 at trial. The plaintiff may be awarded up to double costs because the judgment awarded was higher than the amount the plaintiff had offered to settle for. The plaintiff's offer was a good deal for the defendant, who did worse at trial, and should have accepted the offer instead of putting everyone to the unnecessary expense of a trial. Note that it does not matter how much the claim was for, or that the plaintiff recovered less than he or she claimed. The only issue is, did the plaintiff do better than or as well as the terms of the offer at trial?

- The plaintiff sues for $9,000, offers to settle for $7,000, and obtains a judgment for $7,000 at trial. Because the plaintiff's offer was equal

---

FIGURE 10.2: Comparison of Offer, Judgment, and Costs Awarded

Offer Compared to Judgment*	Costs That May Be Awarded
Plaintiff made offer that was less than judgment awarded.	• Up to double costs to the plaintiff
Plaintiff made offer that was equal to the judgment awarded.	• Up to double costs to the plaintiff
Plaintiff made offer that was more than the judgment awarded.	• Regular costs to the plaintiff
Plaintiff made offer; plaintiff lost because the case was dismissed.	• No costs to plaintiff • Regular costs to defendant
Defendant made offer that was more than the judgment awarded.	• Regular costs to the plaintiff up to the date of the offer • Up to double costs to defendant from date the offer was served
Defendant made offer that was equal to the judgment awarded.	• Regular costs to the plaintiff up to the date of the offer • Up to double costs to defendant from the date the offer was served
Defendant made offer that was less than the judgment awarded.	• Regular costs to the plaintiff
Defendant made offer, but plaintiff lost because the case was dismissed.	• Regular costs to the defendant up to the date of the offer • Up to double costs to the defendant from the date the offer was served

* Assume offer made in writing, served seven or more days before trial, not accepted, and remained open until trial started.

---

to the amount awarded in the judgment, he or she may get up to double costs. The defendant would have saved everyone time and money if he or she had accepted the plaintiff's offer.

• The plaintiff sues for $9,000, offers to settle for $7,000, and obtains a judgment for $6,000. Because the judgment was less favourable than the offer, the plaintiff is entitled only to the regular costs awarded to a successful party. Here, the defendant was right to refuse the offer because she did better at trial than she would have

Settlement 10

done under the offer. Still, because the plaintiff was successful on the claim, the usual practice that costs are awarded to the winning party, as permitted by the Rules, prevails.

- The plaintiff sues for $9,000, offers to settle for $7,000, and loses at trial, with the claim being dismissed. In this case, the plaintiff gets no costs at all. But the defendant is entitled to regular costs because she has been successful, winning the case by having the claim dismissed.

Cost Consequences When a Defendant Makes an Offer

If the defendant makes an offer and the plaintiff obtains a judgment that is *as good as or less than* the terms of the offer made by the defendant, the defendant is entitled to up to *two times the costs of the action from the date the offer was served*. Unlike the plaintiff, the defendant gets double costs only from the time the plaintiff behaved "unreasonably" by refusing a "good" offer, not throughout.

The following examples show how Rule 14 works for defendants:

- The defendant offered to settle for $6,000, and the plaintiff obtained a judgment for $5,000 at trial. Because the defendant's offer was better than the result at trial, the defendant may be awarded to up to double costs from the date the offer was made. The plaintiff will usually recover costs from before that date if he or she was successful in obtaining a judgment for some amount, although the Rules are silent on the plaintiff's right of costs recovery here.

- The defendant offered to settle for $6,000, and the plaintiff obtained a judgment for $6,000 at trial. The defendant is entitled to up to double costs from the time the offer was served, as the plaintiff has done no better than the offer, suggesting the trial was a waste of time.

- The defendant offered to settle for $6,000, and the plaintiff obtained a judgment for $7,000. Because the plaintiff was more successful at trial than he would have been if he accepted the offer to settle, the defendant must pay the ordinary costs of the action to the successful plaintiff.

- The defendant offered to settle for $6,000, and the plaintiff's claim was dismissed. Here, the defendant was the winning party and is entitled to ordinary costs up until the time she made the offer to settle, and from that point on, she is entitled to up to double costs.

Note that where a defendant recovers double costs from the time the offer was made, it will also include trial costs, such as the representation fee, which can be up to 15% of the claim if the party was represented by a lawyer, and up to 7.5% of the claim if represented by a paralegal or articling student. If the party is self-represented, the party may get up to double costs on disbursements, which is limited by Rule 14.07(3) to $500 as compensation for inconvenience and expense. As some judges may be reluctant to engage in "mathematical gymnastics" in apportioning costs between the categories of "before an offer was made" and "after an offer was made", the parties should consider bringing to trial an itemized list of all costs broken down into those incurred before they made an offer and those incurred after an offer was made. The list could be submitted to the court in the event that an apportionment of costs between various dates is required. The party should also bring an extra copy of the itemized costs lists for the other side. The division of representation fees may require a breakdown of the number of days that passed from the time the claim was issued to the date of the offer and the number of days that then passed from the date of the offer to the date of the judgment.

SETTLEMENT DOCUMENTATION AND PRACTICE

You can settle a case at any time, whether or not you play "settlement roulette" under Rule 14. You can settle before an action starts, during the action, or after judgment. However, the documentation you use may depend on when you settle.

Settlement Before the Action Begins

If you settle before an action begins, you should not use the Small Claims Court settlement forms, because there is no action. Instead, record the settlement agreement in Minutes of Settlement that you draft, to be signed by all parties who are to be bound by the settlement. The creditor will usually require a lump sum payment, or instalment payments by post-dated cheques delivered to the creditor. The debtor will want a release from any liability arising from the transaction or events that were the subject of the legal dispute so that the creditor does not settle and then turn around and sue anyway. The release should be held by the creditor until the lump sum or instalment payments are made. The creditor may also want to include a provision that says that if the debtor fails to pay, he or she shall consent to judgment for the full amount of the claim or for the settlement amount. This effectively bars the filing of a defence if the plaintiff sues. In determining the settlement amount the parties may consider the actual amount owing, interest on that amount, and collection costs.

Documents Required for Settling Before the Action Begins

There are several documents required for settlement before the action begins:

- Post-dated/certified cheque(s) for creditor
- Minutes of Settlement, including liability release (or include a separate release if it is being held until all payments are made)
- Consent to judgment for creditor (may be included in the Minutes of Settlement)

An example of Minutes of Settlement, including a release and consent to judgment, are set out in Figure 10.3.

Settlement After the Action Begins

Here you can use either the Small Claims Court Form 14D, Terms of Settlement, or draft your own Minutes of Settlement to record the terms. As noted earlier in the chapter, Form 14D is deficient because it does not contain language that allows a creditor to sign judgment for the full amount of the claim where a defendant defaults on the agreement. Form 14D only permits you to move for judgment on the agreement amount or to continue the action, with the defendant having a right to defend as if there had been no settlement agreement. For these reasons it is suggested that the plaintiff opt for Minutes of Settlement so as to have a clear and simple payment structure so that a consent to judgment in the full amount claimed, not just the settlement amount, is available to the plaintiff on default. Some legal representatives in the Toronto Small Claims Court have started to use a fill-in-the-blanks type of Minutes of Settlement form that permits the parties to decide upon themselves the monetary consequences of default. A sample copy of the form is shown in Figure 10.4.

The consent in the Minutes will be a bar to any defence, and a default judgment should follow. If the defendant complies with the settlement, he or she will insist on having the action dismissed once the payments are made. If so, an action may be dismissed on consent by using a Request for Clerk's Order on Consent (Form 11.2A). The form can be completed in advance and held by the plaintiff until the payment is made, on the undertaking by the plaintiff that he or she will file the document and have the action dismissed. If a claim has been issued and the matter settles before a defence has been filed, it is still a good idea to file Minutes of Settlement with the court. Under Rule 11.1.01(5), the court clerk will not dismiss a claim after 180 days if a defence has not been filed but Minutes of Settlement have been filed. Accordingly, if the Minutes are not followed and the plaintiff needs to

FIGURE 10.3: Minutes of Settlement

MINUTES OF SETTLEMENT

B E T W E E N:

ALBERT ORYX

and

OPHELIA FOOT

The parties agree to settle a dispute about the ownership of a diamond engagement ring as follows:

1. Ophelia Foot agrees to pay Albert Oryx by certified cheque payable to "Peter Paralegal in trust" within 10 days of the signing of this agreement, the sum of $1,000 inclusive of interest and legal costs.

2. The payment in paragraph one constitutes a full and final settlement of all claims by either party against the other party.

3. In the event that Ophelia Foot fails to pay Albert Oryx in accordance with the provision of paragraph 1 of this agreement, Foot shall be deemed to consent to judgment by default for $2,000 plus pre- and post-judgment interest and costs as if the claim had been undefended.

Signed this 15th day of June, Yr. 1

Albert Oryx

witness:

Peter Paralegal

Signed this 16th day of June, Yr. 1

Ophelia Foot

witness:

Digbert Fightback

FIGURE 10.4: Toronto Small Claims Court Minutes of Settlement Form

File Number: SC-

IN THE SUPERIOR COURT OF JUSTICE
TORONTO SMALL CLAIMS COURT

B E T W E E N:

_____

PLAINTIFF

AND

_____

DEFENDANT

MINUTES OF SETTLEMENT

The above parties have agreed to settle this action on the following terms:

1. The Defendant shall pay to the Plaintiff the sum of $ _____ as follows:

    _____
    _____
    _____
    _____

2. This Claim (and Defendant's Claim, if any) are dismissed.
3. Should the Defendant default, the Plaintiff may ask the Clerk of the Court to sign judgment, without notice, for $ _____ , plus interest and costs, less any payments made.
4. Provided that the terms of settlement are complied with, the parties above fully and finally release one another from all claims related to the facts and issues raised in this action.

Dated at Toronto, this _____ day of _____ 20 _____.

Witness: _____   Plaintiff: _____

Witness: _____   Plaintirf: _____

go to court to enforce the Minutes or to continue the lawsuit, the claim has not been dismissed. If the claim has been dismissed, the plaintiff will need to pay for a motion to try to restore it to the list.

Documents Required for Settling After the Action Begins

Several documents are required after the action begins:

- Terms of Settlement (Form 14D) or Minutes of Settlement
- Consent to judgment signed by the defendant for default on payment of settlement (may be included in the Minutes of Settlement)
- Request for Clerk's Order on Consent (Form 11.2A), agreeing to dismiss the action after payment has been made

An example of Form 14D, Terms of Settlement, was provided in Illustration 10.10, and Form 11.2A from the *Oryx v. Foot* case is shown in Illustration 10.11.

Settling After Judgment

If a plaintiff obtains a judgment and agrees to settle with the judgment debtor after the judgment, the terms should be recorded in Minutes of Settlement. The debtor will have to provide the usual certified cheque or post-dated cheques. In exchange, once all payments are made, a Request for Clerk's Order on Consent should be filed: (i) to note that payment had been made in full satisfaction of an order and (ii) to request that the clerk withdraw writs of seizure and sale that have been issued and terminate any garnishments. As a debtor, you will not want writs of seizure and sale or other enforcement orders to remain out-standing, as they will affect your credit rating. Alternatively, the judg-ment creditor may provide the debtor with an **Accord and Satisfaction** (sometimes called a Satisfaction Piece). This document acknowledges the payment of the agreed amount, which is declared to be full satisfaction of the judgment — it has been paid and is no longer enforceable. This is the case even if the agreed amount is less than the full amount required under the judgment. The Accord and Satisfac-tion document has largely been replaced in the Small Claims Court by the Request for Clerk's Order on Consent form. However, it is still used in the Superior Court of Justice and some lawyers may still request that it be used in Small Claims Court.

Documents Required for Settling After Judgment

A number of documents are required for settling after judgment, and they are listed below:

ILLUSTRATION 10.11: Sample Request for Clerk's Order on Consent (Form 11.2A)

ONTARIO
Superior Court of Justice
Cour supérieure de justice

Request for Clerk's Order on Consent
Demande d'ordonnance du greffier sur consentement
Form / Formule 11.2A Ont. Reg. No. / Règl. de l'Ont. : 258/98

Toronto
Small Claims Court / *Cour des petites créances de*

SC-00-47669-00
Claim No. / *N° de la demande*

47 Sheppard Ave. E., 3rd Fl.
Toronto, ON M2N 5N1
Address / *Adresse*

416-326-3554
Phone number / *Numéro de téléphone*

Plaintiff No. 1 / *Demandeur n° 1*

☐ Additional plaintiff(s) listed on attached Form 1A.
Le ou les demandeurs additionnels sont mentionnés sur la formule 1A ci-jointe.

Last name, or name of company / *Nom de famille ou nom de la compagnie*		
Oryx		

First name / *Premier prénom*	Second name / *Deuxième prénom*	Also known as / *Également connu(e) sous le nom de*
Albert		

Address (street number, apt., unit) / *Adresse (numéro et rue, app., unité)*		
c/o Peter Paralegal, 41 Yonge Street, #410		

City/Town / *Cité/ville*	Province	Phone no. / *N° de téléphone*
Toronto	ON	416-597-0048

Postal code / *Code postal*		Fax no. / *N° de télécopieur*
M5G 1S1		416-597-0049

Representative / *Représentant(e)*		LSUC # / *N° du BHC*
Peter Paralegal		P02952

Address (street number, apt., unit) / *Adresse (numéro et rue, app., unité)*		
41 Yonge Street, #410		

City/Town / *Cité/ville*	Province	Phone no. / *N° de téléphone*
Toronto	ON	416-597-0048

Postal code / *Code postal*		Fax no. / *N° de télécopieur*
M5G 1S1		416-597-0049

Defendant No. 1 / *Défendeur n° 1*

☐ Additional defendant(s) listed on attached Form 1A.
Le ou les défendeurs additionnels sont mentionnés sur la formule 1A ci-jointe.

Last name, or name of company / *Nom de famille ou nom de la compagnie*		
Foot		

First name / *Premier prénom*	Second name / *Deuxième prénom*	Also known as / *Également connu(e) sous le nom de*
Ophelia		

Address (street number, apt., unit) / *Adresse (numéro et rue, app., unité)*		
c/o Digbert Fightback, 60 My Way		

City/Town / *Cité/ville*	Province	Phone no. / *N° de téléphone*
Toronto	ON	416-491-5041

Postal code / *Code postal*		Fax no. / *N° de télécopieur*
M6R 8P1		416-491-5042

Representative / *Représentant(e)*		LSUC # / *N° du BHC*
Digbert Fightback		P05427

Address (street number, apt., unit) / *Adresse (numéro et rue, app., unité)*		
60 My Way		

City/Town / *Cité/ville*	Province	Phone no. / *N° de téléphone*
Toronto	ON	416-491-5041

Postal code / *Code postal*		Fax no. / *N° de télécopieur*
M6R 8P1		416-491-5042

NOTE: This request must be signed by all parties and anyone being added, deleted or substituted.
REMARQUE : *La présente demande doit être signée par toutes les parties et par toute personne qui est jointe, radiée ou substituée.*

SCR 11.2.01-11.2A (June 1, 2009 / *1er juin 2009*) CSD

continues....

Illustration 10.11 (continued)

FORM / *FORMULE* 11.2A   PAGE 2   SC-00-47669-00
                                                    Claim No. / *N° de la demande*

TO THE PARTIES:
AUX PARTIES :

THIS REQUEST IS FILED BY: Albert Oryx
LA PRÉSENTE DEMANDE EST DÉPOSÉE PAR :   (Name of party / *Nom de la partie*)

I state that:
Je déclare que :

☒ Each party has received a copy of this form.
   Chaque partie a reçu une copie de la présente formule.

☒ No party that would be affected by the order is under disability.
   Aucune partie sur laquelle l'ordonnance aurait une incidence n'est incapable.

☒ This form has been signed and consented to by all parties, including any parties to be added, deleted or
   substituted.
   *Toutes les parties, y compris celles qui doivent être jointes, radiées ou substituées, ont signé la présente
   formule et y ont consenti.*

I request that the clerk make the following order(s) on the consent of all parties:
Je demande au greffier de rendre l'ordonnance ou les ordonnances suivantes sur consentement de toutes les parties :
(Check appropriate boxes. / Cochez les cases appropriées.)

☐ set aside the noting in default of _____
   l'annulation de la constatation du défaut de   (Name of defendant(s) / *Nom du/de la/des défendeur(s)/défenderesse(s)*)

☐ set aside Default Judgment against _____
   l'annulation du jugement par défaut prononcé contre   (Name of defendant(s) / *Nom du/de la/des
                                                              défendeur(s)/défenderesse(s)*)

☐ restore to the list the following matter that was dismissed under Rule 11.1: (Specify.)
   la réinscription au rôle de l'affaire suivante qui a été rejetée aux termes de la règle 11.1 : *(Précisez.)*

_____

☐ cancel the examination hearing regarding _____
   l'annulation de l'interrogatoire concernant   (Name of person to be examined / *Nom de la personne qui doit être interrogée*)

☐ with respect to the following step(s) taken to enforce the default judgment that are not yet completed:
   *à l'égard de la ou des mesures suivantes qui ont été prises pour exécuter le jugement par défaut et qui ne
   sont pas encore menées à terme :*

   ☐ withdraw the Writ of Seizure and Sale of Land issued against: (Name of debtor(s))
      le retrait du bref de saisie-exécution de biens-fonds délivré contre : *(Nom du/de la/des débiteur(s)/débitrice(s))*

   _____

   and directed to the sheriff of the _____ :
   et adressé au shérif de   (Name of county/region in which the sheriff(enforcement office) is located / *Nom du
                                 comté/de la région où se trouve le shérif (bureau de l'exécution)*)

   (Provide instructions about what is to be done with any proceeds held or property seized by the sheriff. / *Donnez des instructions
   sur ce qu'il faut faire de tout produit de la vente détenu ou bien saisi par le shérif.*)

SCR 11.2.01-11.2A (June 1, 2009 / *1er juin 2009*) CSD   Continued on next page / *Suite à la page suivante*

continues....

Illustration 10.11 (continued)

FORM / *FORMULE* 11.2A   PAGE 3   SC-00-47669-00
                                                               Claim No. / *N° de la demande*

☐ withdraw the Writ of Seizure and Sale of Personal Property issued against: (Name of debtor(s)
   le retrait du bref de saisie-exécution de biens meubles délivré contre : (Nom du/de la/des débiteur(s)/débitrice(s))

and directed to the bailiff of the _____ :
et adressé à l'huissier de   (Small Claims Court location / *Emplacement de la Cour des petites créances*)

(Provide instructions about what is to be done with any proceeds held by the clerk of the court or property that has been seized by the bailiff.
/ *Donnez des instructions sur ce qu'il faut faire de tout produit de la vente détenu par le greffier du tribunal ou de tout bien saisi par l'huissier.*)

☐ terminate the Notice of Garnishment or Notice of Renewal of Garnishment issued against:
   la fin de l'avis de saisie-arrêt ou de l'avis de renouvellement de la saisie-arrêt délivré contre :

(Name of debtor(s) / *Nom du/de la/des débiteur(s)/débitrice(s)*)

and directed to _____ :
et adressé à   (Name of garnishee / *Nom du tiers saisi*)

(Provide instructions about what is to be done with any money held by the clerk of the court. / *Donnez des instructions sur ce qu'il
faut faire de toute somme d'argent détenue par le greffier du tribunal.*)

☒ note that payment has been made in full satisfaction of an order or terms of settlement
   le constat qu'un paiement intégral a été effectué en exécution d'une ordonnance ou des conditions de la transaction

☒ dismiss the: ☒ Plaintiff's Claim   ☐ Defendant's Claim
   le rejet de la :   *demande du demandeur*   *demande du défendeur*

☐ costs in the amount of $ _____ to be paid to _____
   le versement de   (Amount / *Montant*) $ au titre des dépens à   (Name of party(ies) / *Nom de la ou des parties*)

_____ by _____
                          par   (Name of party(ies) / *Nom de la ou des parties*)

**The originally scheduled trial date is less than 30 days away and I request that the clerk make the
following order(s) on the consent of all parties and any person to be added or substituted :**
*La date du procès fixée à l'origine tombe dans moins de 30 jours et je demande au greffier de rendre
l'ordonnance ou les ordonnances suivantes sur consentement de toutes les parties et de toute personne
qui doit être jointe ou substituée :*
(Check appropriate boxes. / *Cochez les cases appropriées.*)

☐ amend a Plaintiff's Claim issued on _____ .
   la modification de la demande d'un demandeur délivrée le
   (Attach two (2) copies of the amended Plaintiff's Claim. / *Annexez deux (2) copies de la demande du demandeur modifiée.*)

☐ amend a Defence filed on _____ .
   la modification d'une défense déposée le
   (Attach two (2) copies of the amended Defence. / *Annexez deux (2) copies de la défense modifiée.*)

SCR 11.2.01-11.2A (June 1, 2009 / *1er juin 2009*) CSD   Continued on next page / *Suite à la page suivante*

continues....

Illustration 10.11 (continued)

FORM / *FORMULE* 11.2A PAGE 4 SC-00-47669-00

Claim No. / *N° de la demande*

☐ amend a Defendant's Claim issued on _____ .
la modification de la demande d'un défendeur délivrée le
(Attach two (2) copies of the amended Defendant's Claim. / Annexez deux (2) copies de la demande du défendeur modifiée.)

☐ add _____
la jonction de   (Name of party / *Nom de la partie*)

   to the   ☐ Plaintiff's Claim   ☐ Defendant's Claim
   à la   *demande du demandeur*   *demande du défendeur*

   as a   ☐ defendant   ☐ Plaintiff
   à titre de   *défendeur/défenderesse*   *demandeur/demanderesse*

☐ delete _____
la radiation de   (Name of party / *Nom de la partie*)

   from the ☐ Plaintiff's Claim   ☐ Defendant's Claim
   de la   *demande du demandeur*   *demande du défendeur*

☐ substitute _____
la substitution à   (Name of party / *Nom de la partie*)

   with _____
   de   (Name of party / *Nom de la partie*)

   in the   ☐ Plaintiff's Claim   ☐ Defendant's Claim
   dans la   *demande du demandeur*   *demande du défendeur*

June 29, Yr. 1	June 30, Yr. 1
Albert Oryx	*Ophelia Foot*
(Signature of party consenting / *Signature de la partie qui consent*)	(Signature of party consenting / *Signature de la partie qui consent*)
Albert Oryx	**Ophelia Foot**
(Name of party consenting / *Nom de la partie qui consent*)	(Name of party consenting / *Nom de la partie qui consent*)
Peter Paralegal	*Digbert Fightback*
(Signature of witness / *Signature du témoin*)	(Signature of witness / *Signature du témoin*)
Peter Paralegal	**Digbert Fightback**
(Name of witness / *Nom du témoin*)	(Name of witness / *Nom du témoin*)
(Signature of party consenting / *Signature de la partie qui consent*)	(Signature of party consenting / *Signature de la partie qui consent*)
(Name of party consenting / *Nom de la partie qui consent*)	(Name of party consenting / *Nom de la partie qui consent*)
(Signature of witness / *Signature du témoin*)	(Signature of witness / *Signature du témoin*)
(Name of witness / *Nom du témoin*)	(Name of witness / *Nom du témoin*)

SCR 11.2.01-11.2A (June 1, 2009 / *1er juin 2009*) CSD

Continued on next page / *Suite à la page suivante*

continues....

Illustration 10.11 (continued)

FORM / *FORMULE* 11.2A   PAGE 5   SC-00-47669-00
                                                          Claim No. / *N° de la demande*

DISPOSITION: *The clerk of the court will complete this section.*
DÉCISION :   Le greffier du tribunal remplit cette partie.

☐ order to go as asked
    ordonnance de procéder comme il a été demandé

☐ order refused because:
    ordonnance refusée pour les motifs suivants :

....
                                                          (Signature of clerk / *Signature du greffier*)

SCR 11.2.01-11.2A (June 1, 2009 / *1ᵉʳ juin 2009*) CSD

- Minutes of Settlement
- Accord and Satisfaction, or
- Request for Clerk's Order on Consent (Form 11.2A), indicating that judgment has been paid in full
- Letter to clerk to withdraw any writs of seizure and sale and any other enforcements in place

A sample of an Accord and Satisfaction document is set out in Figure 10.5.

CHAPTER SUMMARY

In this chapter, we focused on the importance of trying to settle a case rather than going to trial, pointing out the advantages to all parties and their legal representatives of trying to settle cases. In this connection we examined the purposes of settlement conferences — to settle a case, usually through mediation, and, failing that, to narrow the issues for trial and prepare for trial. Preparation for settlement conferences was discussed, as were the procedures and requirements for a settlement conference, which include having clients present for negotiation and knowing how to use the settlement conferences — to obtain full discovery and disclosure, identifying issues, evidence, and problems for trial where settlement fails. We then noted how offers to settle under Rule 14 can be used to promote settlement by tying these offers to cost sanctions and rewards, depending on whether an offer was as good as or better than the trial judgment. Last, we examined the various settlement documents that are used when settling a legal dispute, noting that there are different requirements and considerations, depending on whether the settlement takes place before or after an action begins, or after a judgment has been obtained.

FIGURE 10.5: Accord and Satisfaction Document

File no. SC-00-47669-00

The Toronto Small Claims Court

B E T W E E N:

ALBERT ORYX

Plaintiff

and

OPHELIA FOOT

Defendant

ACKNOWLEDGEMENT OF SATISFACTION OF JUDGMENT

Satisfaction is acknowledged of the judgment dated September 14, Yr. 1, in an action in the Small Claims Court in which Albert Oryx was the plaintiff, and Ophelia Foot was the defendant, and it was adjudged that the plaintiff should recover $2,000 and costs.

The plaintiff, Albert Oryx, nominates his legal representative, Peter Paralegal, to witness and attest the plaintiff's acknowledgement of satisfaction of this judgment.

Signed by Albert Oryx on October 29, Yr. 1, in the presence of Peter Paralegal, legal representative of the plaintiff.

Albert Oryx
Albert Oryx

And I, Peter Paralegal, declare myself to be the legal representative for the plaintiff, expressly named by him, and attending at the plaintiff's request to inform the plaintiff of the nature and effect of this acknowledgement of satisfaction of judgment. I so informed the plaintiff before he executed the acknowledgement of satisfaction of judgment.

Peter Paralegal
Peter Paralegal

REVIEW QUESTIONS

1. What is the purpose of a settlement conference?
2. Explain to your client why settlement is generally a good idea.
3. Who calls a settlement conference?
4. If you receive an opponent's witness list, are you prohibited from contacting the witnesses?
5. Who must attend a settlement conference?
6. How does a settlement conference judge ensure that each party has provided full disclosure to other parties?
7. How does a settlement conference judge or referee ensure that the parties cooperate fully in the process?
8. How is a settlement conference conducted?
9. Can a judge dismiss an action at a settlement conference?
10. Can a judge make a final determination of a claim at a settlement conference?
11. Can a summary judgment be obtained at a settlement conference?
12. What happens next, after the settlement conference has been completed?
13. If a defendant makes a Rule 14 offer to settle for $4,000 and a plaintiff obtains a judgment for $7,000 at trial, what is the likely costs award under Rule 14?
14. If a plaintiff makes a Rule 14 offer to settle for $4,000 and obtains a judgment for $7,000 at trial, what is the likely costs award under Rule 14?
15. If a defendant makes a Rule 14 offer to settle for $8,000 and the plaintiff obtains a judgment for $6,000, what is the likely costs award under Rule 14?
16. If the parties settle before an action begins, what settlement documents are required?
17. If an action settles after an action begins, what settlement documents are required?
18. How would your answer be different if the settlement occurred after judgment?

DISCUSSION QUESTIONS/CASE STUDIES

FACTS

You are Paul Paralegal, 27 Milkyway, Somewhere, ON K2L 3TU, phone 909-842-5678. You act for Freda's

Linens, a sole proprietorship operated by Freda Smith. Freda sold $5,000 worth of curtain material to Nopay Windows on June 2, Yr. 0. Nopay's business is located at 12 South Mall, Nowhere, ON L2L 3T4. The Nopays, the partners who run Nopay Windows, retained Delford Defendo, Paralegal, 123 Commerce Road, Nowhere, Ontario L2L 3Y4, Tel. 909-765-4321, Fax 909-765-4322. His Law Society number is P9876. The claim you filed indicated that Freda's Linens sued for $5,000 for curtain material sold on July 2, Yr. 0, to Nopay by Freda's Linens. However, the curtain material was defective. It had defects in the weave, and was different in texture and colour from the sample they had seen when they ordered. They were going to use it to complete an order from the Hotel Nowhere, but when the hotel's manager saw the material he said it was not what he had bargained for with Nopay. The hotel, which would have paid on July 30, Yr. 0, cancelled the $20,000 contract on that date, and Nopay lost the sale and the profit it would have made of $6,000 on the sale. Nopay filed a defence and a defendant's claim for the $6,000 lost profit. You have just completed the settlement conference, and Freda has decided to make an offer to Nopay to settle the action with a payment to Nopay of $2,000 inclusive of interest and costs.

1. Draft the Rule 14 offer, using Form 14A.
2. Assume that Nopay accepts the offer, draft an acceptance in letter format.
3. Draft Minutes of Settlement with mutual releases.
4. Draft the documents required to dismiss all claims by both parties.

Chapter 11

Preparation for Trial and Trial

LEARNING OBJECTIVES

⇨ Know how to take the necessary steps to move a case from the settlement conference to trial

⇨ Know how to obtain an adjournment of the trial date

⇨ Understand that your organization of argument, law, and evidence at trial is based on a clear understanding of your theory of the case

⇨ Know how to develop and, if necessary, revise your theory of the case

⇨ Know the "special" rules governing admissibility of evidence in Small Claims Court

⇨ Know how to summons a witness and how to deal with a situation if the witness does not show up

⇨ Know what to bring to trial and how to conduct the trial

⇨ Understand the *Paralegal Rules of Conduct* related to advocacy

INTRODUCTION

Having completed the settlement conference, the next step is to prepare for trial. In this chapter we discuss some of the things you need to do to try the case.

- **Theory of the case:** Know how to develop and revise the theory of the case to fit the facts you are going to prove, and the evidence available to prove them.
- **Evidence:** You must be knowledgeable about the rules of evidence, common law and statutory, with special attention to the more permissive Small Claims Rules that facilitate the admission of documentary evidence and hearsay evidence.
- **Summonses:** You must know how and when to use summons procedure to ensure that witnesses attend court when required.
- **Organizing and presenting a case:** Know how to present a case in a systematic and orderly way.

PREPARING FOR TRIAL

You have now completed the settlement conference. As noted in the preceding chapter, at the conference or shortly thereafter, the clerk notifies the parties that if they have not settled the case within 30 days of the settlement conference, one of the parties must request that the clerk fix a date for trial and serve a Notice of Trial. You will know the date of trial in advance. Make sure you will have your client and all your witnesses available and your documentary and **demonstrative evidence** properly prepared so that it will be admissible at trial.

Adjourning a Trial and Consequences of Non-attendance

Rules 17.01 and 17.02 contemplate various situations where, after a trial date is fixed, a party needs an adjournment, or simply fails to show up at trial. There are various possible consequences, depending on the circumstances, including opportunities for a "last chance" in the form of a motion to set aside or vary a judgment where a party failed to attend trial.

Adjournments

It is sometimes the case that you find the trial is scheduled for a date on which you have another trial, or some other court appearance, and you are "double booked". Or perhaps your client is not available or a key witness is out of town. If you find you need an adjournment, you should write to the court clerk and to the other parties immediately, explaining that you need an adjournment and why. Rule 17.02(1) implies that a request for a first or even a second adjournment may be granted even where other parties oppose it, but the court may require the party seeking the adjournment to compensate the other party or parties for the inconvenience and expense the adjournment will cause if granted.

> 17.02(1) The court may postpone or adjourn a trial on such terms as are just, including the payment by one party to another of an amount as compensation for inconvenience and expense.
>
> (2) If the trial of an action has been adjourned two or more times, any further adjournment may be made only on motion with notice to all the parties who were served with the notice of trial, unless the court orders otherwise.

If a case has been adjourned two or more times, further adjournments may be obtained only by bringing a motion serving the notice of motion on all parties who received a Notice of Trial. Here, given a number of previous adjournments, you will have to persuade a court that the adjournment should be granted, and again, there may be cost consequences if an adjournment is granted.

Consequences of Non-attendance at Trial

Non-attendance is another matter. Rule 17.01 sets out the consequences of non-attendance at trial:

> 17.01(1) If an action is called for trial and all the parties fail to attend, the trial judge may strike the action off the trial list.
>
> (2) If an action is called for trial and a party fails to attend, the trial judge may,
> (a) proceed with the trial in the party's absence;
> (b) the plaintiff attends and the defendant fails to do so, strike out the defence and dismiss the defendant's claim, if any, and allow the plaintiff to prove the plaintiff's claim, subject to subrule (3);
> (c) if the defendant attends and the plaintiff fails to do so, dismiss the action and allow the defendant to prove the defendant's claim, if any; or
> (d) make such other order as is just.
>
> (2.1) In the case described in clause (2)(b) or (c), the person with the claim is not required to prove liability against the party who has failed to attend but is required to prove the amount of the claim.
>
> (3) In the case described in clause (2)(b), if an issue as to the proper place of trial under subrule 6.01(1) is raised in the defence, the trial judge shall consider it and make a finding.

Rule 17.01 contemplates two situations: one where no one shows up, and the other where one party doesn't show up. If no one shows up, the case is simply struck off the trial list. The case has not been dismissed, but it does have to be rescheduled and put back on the trial list. The rule is silent on the process, but a good place to start is with a written request to the clerk, copied to other parties, to place it back on the trial list with a new trial date. If the reason no one appears is that the case has settled, you should be filing Minutes of Settlement, or Terms of Settlement (Form 14D), with a Request for Clerk's Order on Consent (Form 11.2A) to dismiss the case.

If only one party fails to appear, which is a much more likely scenario, Rule 17.01 is much more specific and detailed as to what should happen. The judge has a great deal of discretion as to how to handle the failure of a party to appear. Much will depend on whether or not there is a history in this proceeding of a party being uncooperative or vexatious, and the judge has the following options:

1. Proceed with the trial in the party's absence. Here a plaintiff will still have to prove liability as well as damages if a defendant fails to show. If a plaintiff fails to show, the defendant can simply give evidence on liability and damages in reference to the plaintiff's case as pleaded. This approach is likely to be used where there are several defendants and one of them doesn't appear at trial.

2. If the defendant fails to show up, a not uncommon occurrence, the judge may strike out the defence and the defendant's claim, if any, and allow the plaintiff to prove damages, as once a defence is struck out, there is no need to prove liability.[1] However, if the defendant in his or her defence claimed that the plaintiff sued in the wrong Small Claims Court, that is an issue that goes to the court's territorial jurisdiction. The court must examine that defence and rule on it before it can consider striking out the defence. If the defendant is correct, then the court has no jurisdiction and cannot make a final judgment or strike out the defence. Instead, he or she must order the case moved to a Small Claims Court with territorial jurisdiction under Rule 6.01. If the judge finds against the defendant on the jurisdictional defence, then he or she can proceed to strike out the defence. The same is true if the defence states that the plaintiff has exceeded the

---

[1] Rule 17.01(2.1), a recent amendment to the Rules, makes it abundantly clear that where a defence is struck out for non-attendance, a finding of liability is automatic, and the only remaining issue is damages.

court's monetary jurisdiction by, for example, splitting a case in two when it is in fact one proceeding. Here the court may order the case to be transferred to the Superior Court.

3. If the plaintiff fails to show up, the judge may dismiss the claim and allow the defendant to prove damages on the defendant's claim, if there is one.

4. A judge may make "any order as is just", suggesting very broad discretion in dealing with "no-shows". For example, a punitive costs order against a "no-show" may be in order if there has been a history of obstructive behaviour, particularly where the other side has spent time and money preparing for trial.

Setting Aside a Judgment for Failure to Attend Trial

While the Rules certainly contemplate severe consequences for wilful non-attendance, sometimes because of illness, accident, or family catastrophes a party is unable to attend, and a judgment is obtained against him or her. In that case Rules 17.01(4) and (5) permit a party to move to vary or set the judgment aside, provided he or she does so within 30 days of becoming aware of the judgment, or makes a motion for an extension of the 30-day time period to file the motion:

> 17.01(4) The court may set aside or vary, on such terms as are just, a judgment obtained against a party who failed to attend at the trial.
>
> (5) The court may make an order under subrule (4) only if,
> (a) the party who failed to attend makes a motion for the order within 30 days after becoming aware of the judgment; or
> (b) the party who failed to attend makes a motion for an extension of the 30-day period mentioned in clause (a) and the court is satisfied that there are special circumstances that justify the extension.

In order to grant the 30-day extension, the court must be satisfied that there are "special circumstances" that would justify the order. "Special circumstances" are not defined and must be determined on the particular facts of each case.

Reviewing and Revising the Theory of the Case Prior to Trial

During the settlement conference, if the case didn't settle, the judge may have given a neutral evaluation (indicating what the judge thinks the outcome at trial will be given his or her understanding of the issues, facts and supporting evidence). The judge may also have summarized facts and commented on the evidence required to prove them, and assessed the evidence provided by each side at the settlement conference. In light of further disclosure and suggestions from the court on the allegations of each party and the evidence required to prove the case, you should review your theory of the case to see if it needs to be revised because facts have changed or a new legal issue has arisen. The thing to remember is that if the facts and evidence don't fit the theory of the case, the theory needs to be revised to fit the facts and evidence. Consider the following example:

Example 11.1 Occupier Liability Case Facts

Morris Misstep, a 24-year-old lathe operator at Crumble Tool and Die Co. Ltd., stopped off at Zeke's Convenience Store on August 2, Yr. 0, on his way home from work. The store is in rented premises owned by Fly By Night Realty.

On entering the store, Morris slipped on some water on the floor near the front door and fell heavily to the ground, striking his left elbow on a counter as he fell. The water came from a dripping air conditioner condensation line that should have gone through the window over the door, but it had slipped and was discharging water on the floor.

As a result of his fall, Morris suffered extensive pain in his lower arm and numbness in his fingers for a period of two weeks following the fall. He required prescription painkillers and anti-inflammatory medication that cost $150.00. He was unable to sleep. He was unable to work, and he lost two weeks' wages at $500.00/week gross, plus expected overtime of about $300 gross for the two-week period. He wants to sue Zeke for damages for negligence.

Initial Theory of the Case for the Plaintiff and Defendant

At this stage, when the plaintiff filed his claim, he analyzed the issues and constructed a theory of the case. (Figure 11.1 shows a theory of the case for the plaintiff and the defendant.)

The theory of Morris's case against Zeke at the point when the claim was filed was threefold: (i) that his injuries arose from his lawful presence on the premises, (ii) that the defendant owed him a duty as an occupier, and (iii) that the defendant breached the duty, and as a result Morris suffered injuries, giving rise to general and special damages.

FIGURE 11.1: Theory of the Case

The Plaintiff's Theory of the Case

What is plaintiff suing for?	• Damages for his injury for pain and suffering, cost of medications, loss of wages
What does he have to prove?	• That he was injured on the defendant's premises and was owed an occupier's duty by plaintiff under the *Occupier's Liability Act* • That he was injured on the premises as a result of occupier's negligence • That there is a causal link between negligence and damages • The amount of his losses

The Defendant's Theory of the Case

What is the defendant being sued for?	• General and special damages based on occupier's liability
What result is the defendant seeking?	• A finding that he is not liable and no money is owing, with the case against Zeke being dismissed
What must defendant prove to win?	• That the plaintiff was not on the premises lawfully or at all (Zeke is unlikely to be able to prove this.) • That, if on the premises, the plaintiff failed to take reasonable care when faced with an obvious risk where the water on floor was plainly visible (Zeke can try proving there was contributory negligence by Morris.) • That the damage was caused by a third party (If a leak caused damage to Morris, it was caused by a third party, such as an air conditioner maintenance company, or Fly By Night Realty, or both, in which case the defendant's claim must state that any liability Zeke might incur is the responsibility of the other defendants, who are directly liable to the plaintiff or liable to indemnify Zeke if Zeke is found liable.)

The theory of the case for Zeke, the defendant, is that Morris was contributorily negligent, or that the negligence is that of others, not the defendant.

After the defence is filed and there is disclosure at the settlement conference, Morris and Zeke should consider whether they need to revise their respective theories of the case.

Consideration of Revisions to Your Theory of the Case

As there is no evidence that Morris was unlawfully on the premises, it should be dropped as an allegation and cease to be part of the theory of Zeke's case. As Zeke is alleging others were responsible for Morris's injuries, and presuming the facts can support this, Zeke should consider defendant's claims against the air conditioner maintenance company and Fly By Night Realty, the owner of the building Zeke rents, so that the facts as alleged fit the theory.

Morris may also need to revise his theory of the case. He may need to introduce evidence to show that he was alert and took care when he entered the premises, and he should stay focused on facts that support that in order to negate the allegation by Zeke that he was contributorily negligent. Morris may also wish to amend his theory of the case and amend his claim to include the air conditioner maintenance company and the building owner as defendants, alleging that they are jointly liable for his injuries. Alternatively, Morri may simply proceed as is against Zeke, if Zeke brings the other parties into the action by way of a defendant's claim.

Each case, of course, is different, but be sure to revisit and, if necessary, revise your theory to fit the facts and the evidence you have to prove those facts, as well as amending pleadings, if necessary. Hopefully, this will be done by the close of the settlement conference. But if it has not been, it should be done as soon as possible thereafter so that you can prepare the case you need to present at trial. If an adjournment is necessary to do this, do not hesitate to ask for one.

Evidentiary Considerations

Once you have reviewed your theory of the case, you will know what facts you have to prove and can determine what evidence you will use to prove them. It is not possible in this text to thoroughly review the common law and statutory rules of evidence, but you should bear in mind that s. 27 of the *Courts of Justice Act* and Rule 18 of the Small Claims Court Rules make the presentation of evidence to prove your case much easier than it would be in a Superior Court trial, by greatly reducing or eliminating many of the barriers to the introduction of evidence. In particular, the hearsay rule is virtually demolished, and almost any kind of documentary evidence can be presented in court, provided it is relevant.

Section 27 of the *Courts of Justice Act*

Under s. 27 of the *Courts of Justice Act*, the court has the authority to admit into evidence any oral testimony and any document or thing. The only requirement is that the evidence must be relevant to the issues in the action before the court. It doesn't matter that the evidence might be inadmissible in other courts, or that the document or the oral testimony is not sworn or affirmed to be true.

> **27.**(1) Subject to subsections (3) and (4), the Small Claims Court may admit as evidence at a hearing and act upon any oral testimony and any document or other thing so long as the evidence is relevant to the subject-matter of the proceeding, but the court may exclude anything unduly repetitious.
>
> (2) Subsection (1) applies whether or not the evidence is given or proven under oath or affirmation or admissible as evidence in any other court.
>
> (3) Nothing is admissible in evidence at a hearing,
> (a) that would be inadmissible by reason of any privilege under the law of evidence; or
> (b) that is inadmissible by any Act.
>
> (4) Nothing in subsection (1) overrides the provisions of any Act expressly limiting the extent to or purposes for which any oral testimony, documents or things may be admitted or used in evidence in any proceeding.
>
> (5) A copy of a document or any other thing may be admitted as evidence at a hearing if the presiding judge is satisfied as to its authenticity.

Section 27 is very broadly drafted, and gives a judge wide discretion in deciding to admit evidence. The section also allows you to use copies of documents rather than originals, relaxing the usual requirement for originals if you have them.[2]

---

[2] If you don't have the original, a copy is usually admissible under the "best evidence" rule; however, in the Small Claims Court this is not an issue, as you can file a copy whether you have the original or not.

Consider what s. 27 will allow you to do in practice:

- Instead of using oral testimony to prove facts, you may use a witness statement, subject to limits in Rule 18. The witness statement need not be sworn.

- You may, in a witness statement, include hearsay that would otherwise be inadmissible.

- You may file as evidence all kinds of documents that are unsworn or that contain hearsay, including the reports of expert witnesses which normally have certain tests governing admissibility. There are, however, certain limitations set out in Rule 18, as discussed below.

Note, however, that the discretion to admit, under s. 27, belongs to the judge, not the party. Just because you wish to file and use an unsworn statement does not guarantee it will be admitted — there are some limitations. A judge may refuse to admit testimony or documents for the following reasons:

- The judge is of the view that the evidence is not relevant.

- The evidence is unduly repetitious — you have already filed other evidence that is relevant to the same fact or issue.

- It would be unfair or unjust to admit the evidence. This is very broad, and might be used to exclude evidence, which, for example, is so inflammatory that its prejudicial impact outweighs its probative value.

- The evidence is, by statute, inadmissible in any court, or its admissibility is limited. For example, s. 11 of the Ontario *Evidence Act*, R.S.O. 1990, c. E.23 (the federal counterpart being the *Canada Evidence Act*, R.S.C. 1985, c. C-5), prohibits the introduction in evidence of a statement by one spouse against the other unless the spouse agrees to give evidence.

- The evidence is privileged under the common law. Correspondence between the legal representative and the client about the action cannot be introduced in evidence unless the client waives the privilege. Similarly, documents headed "without prejudice" are not admissible — these are usually letters discussing settlement that may directly or by implication contain admissions. If they are admissions made on a without prejudice basis, they are privileged and inadmissible. Note that if a document is privileged, the client can waive the privilege. But in this case it should be done early enough to be disclosed to other parties at the settlement conference, and certainly no later than other documents you intend to submit in evidence at trial under Rule 18.

Rules 18.01 and 18.02: Controls and Protections on the Admission of Evidence

While s. 27 of the *Courts of Justice Act* opens the evidentiary door, Rule 18 of the Small Claims Court contains some controls over what comes through it. Rule 18.01 allows you to prove a case without calling witnesses but by using affidavit evidence instead, if the case is not defended:

> 18.01 At the trial of an undefended action, the plaintiff's case may be proved by affidavit, unless the trial judge orders otherwise.

We have already seen this rule in operation in default judgment proceedings to allow the plaintiff to prove damages where no defence has been filed. It is also available if a defence is filed, but the defendant fails to show up at trial and a judge, under Rule 17, allows the plaintiff to proceed.

ADMISSION OF WRITTEN STATEMENTS, DOCUMENTS, AND RECORDS AS EVIDENCE

Rule 18.02 sets out a procedural code you must follow to have written records, documents, or statements admitted in evidence instead of either calling a witness to give oral testimony or calling a witness to identify a documentary record prior to its being admitted in evidence.

- Rule 18.02(1) requires that a document, written statement of a witness, or an audio or visual record (a tape, DVD, CD) must be served on every party to the action who has received a Notice of Trial at least 30 days before the date of the trial:

> 18.02(1) A document or written statement or an audio or visual record that has been served, at least 30 days before the trial date, on all parties who were served with the notice of trial, shall be received in evidence, unless the trial judge orders otherwise.

- Rule 18.02(2) provides a list of written documents and statements (and presumably audio or visual records) that are covered by Rule 18.02(1):

> 18.02(2) Subrule (1) applies to the following written statements and documents:
>   1. The signed written statement of any witness, including the written report of an expert, to the extent that the statement relates to facts and opinions to which the witness would be permitted to testify in person.
>   2. Any other document, including but not limited to a hospital record or medical report made in the course of care and treatment, a financial record, a receipt, a bill, documentary evidence of loss of income or property damage, and a repair estimate.

The list of documents includes the following:

- *Signed* written witness statements
- Written reports of experts (also signed), provided the contents relate to facts and opinions to which the witness could testify in person (evidence given within his or her expertise, including answers to speculative or hypothetical questions)
- Other documents, including hospital records or medical reports, financial records, receipts, bills, documentary evidence of loss of income or property, and repair estimates. Note that these are merely examples of documents. The category is in fact open-ended. The specific inclusion of medical reports and financial records in Rule 18.02 indicates that the usual rules in s. 52 (medical records and reports) and s. 35 (business records), of the Ontario *Evidence Act* respectively, governing admissibility of these kinds of records do not apply here. However, the point may be moot, as the 30-day notice period in Rule 18.02 would more than comply with the much shorter notice periods in s. 52 and s. 35. When you comply with Rule 18, you will have complied with the Ontario *Evidence Act* notice periods.

- If a document has been properly served, 30 days before trial, it will be admitted in evidence on proof of service by affidavit of service unless the judge, considering the s. 27 factors previously discussed, orders otherwise.

- If you serve a written witness statement or other document you, must include, in accordance with Rule 18.02(3), the name, telephone number, and address for service of the witness or author or maker of the document. In the case of business or medical records, the person named should be the person you would normally call as a witness to introduce a business or other record, such as a hospital records clerk or a bank clerk. Such a person may not know much about the content of the record but can testify as to how it was made and started. Where the record or statement is one where an identifiable individual actually has knowledge of the contents, that person should be named.

- If you serve an expert report, in addition to the contact information above, Rule 18.02(3)(b) states that you also need to supply information about the expert's qualifications so that the other party can determine whether or not to challenge the witness's status as an expert. An easy way to do this is to attach the expert's resume.

18.02(3) A party who serves on another party a written statement or document described in subrule (2) shall append to or include in the statement or document,
  (a) the name, telephone number and address for service of the witness or author; and
  (b) if the witness or author is to give expert evidence, a summary of his or her qualifications.

Once the document, report, or statement is served on other parties, the other party or parties must decide whether to let the evidence be filed without doing anything further, or summons the witness in order to cross-examine him or her on the statement, report, or document. If the document concerns facts or issues that are not seriously in dispute, the parties served with the document need not do anything further. The judge, provided he or she has not otherwise excluded the evidence, will assess its weight and probative value with respect to the facts in issue. However, if there are credibility issues about the contents of the document or if the contents are disputed or contentious, then the party who questions the evidence may call the maker of the document as a witness, using the normal procedure for summonsing witnesses, in order to cross-examine on the contents of the report or document.

If you decide to challenge the document, witness, or report, you can use the contact information provided by the other party to call the witness prior to trial and question him or her about the evidence. The witness may answer your questions and tell you what you need to know so that you can decide whether or not you need to formally cross-examine the witness at trial. But the witness is under no obligation to talk to you about his or her proposed evidence in advance. In this case, or if you already have concerns about the contents or the witness's credibility, you should serve a summons on the witness. The summons procedure is discussed in the next section of this chapter.

If you serve a summons on a witness who has given a signed statement under Rule 18.02(5), you should serve a copy on all other parties so that they know you intend to cross-examine this witness and have notice of that fact. Failure to serve other parties may result in an adjournment with costs against you. When you serve the summons, comply with all of the rules about summonses, including payment of attendance money as required by Rule 18.03.

Procedure for Summonsing Witnesses

The procedure for summonsing witnesses is set out in Rule 18.03:

18.03(1) A party who requires the attendance of a person in Ontario as a witness at a trial may serve the person with a summons to witness (Form 18A) requiring him or her to attend the trial at the time and place stated in the summons.

(2) The summons may also require the witness to produce at the trial the documents or other things in his or her possession, control or power relating to the matters in question in the action that are specified in the summons.

(3) A summons to witness (Form 18A) shall be served in accordance with subrule 8.01(7).

(4) Service of a summons and the payment or tender of attendance money may be proved by affidavit (Form 8A).

(5) A summons to witness continues to have effect until the attendance of the witness is no longer required.

Briefly, then, if you wish to have someone attend trial and give evidence, you need to serve him or her with a summons to attend. (See Illustration 11.1 for a Summons to Witness issued to Muriel Mouthe served by Albert Oryx.) Similarly, if you wish to compel the production at trial of documentary evidence in the control of someone else, where you cannot obtain copies voluntarily, you need to serve a summons on that person and include in the summons a direction to produce specific documents or items to get them before the court.

Generally, unless a witness is a close relative who loves you (and even then, he or she can be detained by a car accident on the way to trial), you should not depend on a witness's promise to appear without being summonsed. If a witness does not appear at trial, and his or her evidence is important, you will have to request an adjournment. The judge will ask to see the summons and the affidavit of service. If you did not summons the witness, the judge may not grant the adjournment. If you did use a summons, as we will see, the judge will likely grant the adjournment and may issue a warrant for the arrest of the witness, requiring him or her to be brought to court (this rarely happens in practice). At this stage, the arrest of a witness is not for contempt, but to get him or her before the court. But a summons is an order from the court requiring the named witness to appear to give evidence. Continued disobedience to the order by refusing to give evidence is contempt of court and can result in punishment up to and including imprisonment.

Once you know who will be giving evidence at trial you need to do the following:

- Prepare a summons in Form 18A. Indicate in the summons the date and time of the trial, and the place where the court is located. Also include a description of specific documents you wish the witness to bring to court. If there are no specific documents you require, put a line through the blank space given to list documents. Even without specifying documents, there is a **basket clause** that contains a general direction to bring all relevant documents. There has been a practice of putting several witness names on the summons so that you only

ILLUSTRATION 11.1: Sample Summons to Witness (Form 18A)

ONTARIO
Superior Court of Justice
Cour supérieure de justice

Summons to Witness
Assignation de témoin
Form / *Formule* 18A Ont. Reg. No. / *Règl. de l'Ont.* : 258/98

Seal / *Sceau*

Toronto
Small Claims Court / *Cour des petites créances de*

SC-00-47669-00
Claim No. / *N° de la demande*

**47 Sheppard Ave. E., 3rd Fl.
Toronto, ON M2N 5N1**
Address / *Adresse*

416-326-3554
Phone number / *Numéro de téléphone*

BETWEEN / *ENTRE*

Albert Oryx
Plaintiff(s) / *Demandeur(s)/demanderesse(s)*

and / *et*

Ophelia Foot
Defendant(s) / *Défendeur(s)/défenderesse(s)*

TO: Muriel Mouthe
DESTINATAIRE :
(Name of witness / *Nom du témoin*)

YOU ARE REQUIRED TO ATTEND AND TO GIVE EVIDENCE IN COURT at the trial of this action on
VOUS ÊTES REQUIS(E) DE VOUS PRÉSENTER DEVANT LE TRIBUNAL POUR TÉMOIGNER à l'instruction de cette action le

September 14, Yr. 1   **at** **10:00 a.m.**   **, at**
à   (Time / *heure*)   *à/au*

47 Sheppard Ave. E., 3rd Fl., Toronto, ON M2N 5N1
(Address of court location / *Adresse du tribunal*)

and to remain until your attendance is no longer required. You may be required to return to court from time to time. *et d'y demeurer jusqu'à ce que votre présence ne soit plus requise. Vous pourriez être requis(e) de vous présenter à nouveau devant le tribunal à l'occasion.*

YOU ARE ALSO REQUIRED TO BRING WITH YOU AND PRODUCE AT THE TRIAL the following documents or other things in your possession, control or power: (Identify and describe particular documents and other things required)
VOUS ÊTES EN OUTRE REQUIS(E) D'APPORTER AVEC VOUS ET DE PRODUIRE LORS DE L'INSTRUCTION les documents ou autres objets suivants dont vous avez la garde, la possession ou le contrôle :
(Indiquez et décrivez les documents et autres objets particuliers qui sont requis)
Your notes of your conversation with Ophelia Foot, January 27, Yr. 1.

SCR 18.03-18A (June 1, 2009 / *1er juin 2009*) CSD

continues....

Illustration 11.1 (continued)

FORM / *FORMULE* 18A   PAGE 2   SC-00-47669-00
                                                           Claim No. / *N° de la demande*

and all other documents or other things in your possession, control or power relating to the action.
ainsi que tous les autres documents ou autres objets dont vous avez la garde, la possession ou le contrôle et qui se rapportent à l'action.

Albert Oryx   has requested the clerk to issue this summons.
.... *a demandé au greffier de délivrer la présente*
                (Name of party / *Nom de la partie*)   *assignation.*

August 5, Yr. 1   *Iam Clerk*
.... _____
                                                          (Signature of clerk / *Signature du greffier*)

NOTE:	THIS SUMMONS MUST BE SERVED personally, at least 10 days before the trial date, on the person to be summoned together with attendance money calculated in accordance with the Small Claims Court Schedule of Fees, which is a regulation under the *Administration of Justice Act*. To obtain a copy of the regulation, attend the nearest Small Claims Court or access the following website: www.e-laws.gov.on.ca .
REMARQUE :	*LA PRÉSENTE ASSIGNATION DOIT ÊTRE SIGNIFIÉE à personne, au moins 10 jours avant la date du procès, à la personne devant être assignée, avec l'indemnité de présence calculée conformément au barème des honoraires et frais de la Cour des petites créances qui constitue un règlement pris en application de la Loi sur l'administration de la justice Vous pouvez obtenir un exemplaire du règlement auprès de la Cour des petites créances de votre localité ou en consultant le site Web suivant : www.lois-en-ligne.gouv.on.ca.*

CAUTION:	IF YOU FAIL TO ATTEND OR REMAIN IN ATTENDANCE AS REQUIRED BY THIS SUMMONS, A WARRANT MAY BE ISSUED FOR YOUR ARREST.
AVERTISSEMENT :	*SI VOUS NE VOUS PRÉSENTEZ PAS OU SI VOUS NE DEMEUREZ PAS PRÉSENT(E) COMME L'EXIGE LA PRÉSENTE ASSIGNATION, UN MANDAT D'ARRÊT PEUT ÊTRE DÉLIVRÉ CONTRE VOUS.*

SCR 18.03-18A (June 1, 2009 / *1ᵉʳ juin 2009*) CSD

have one summons to issue and pay only one fee for issuing it. Then, when you serve the summons on each individual, serve a copy showing that individual's name only, with the names of the other witnesses being blanked out in the copy. The original shows all the names and is never altered after it is issued. However, note that the form itself seems to contemplate an individual witness per form.

- Prepare a Form 9B, Request to Clerk Form (see sample on page 277), checking off the last box labelled "other", then writing in "Issue a Summons to Witness".

- Take the completed form to the court to pay the fee to have the clerk issue the summons. The fees are set out in O. Reg. 432/93, *Small Claims Court — Fees and Allowances*, made under the *Administration of Justice Act*.[3] Use the website version of the fees so that you have the most recent version of the fees (as fees change from time to time and almost always in an upward direction). Note that the fees are divided into schedules: Schedule 1 sets out court fees charged to frequent users as well as occasional ones. Schedule 2 sets out fees paid to the court bailiffs, usually for services connected to enforcement of orders, and Schedule 3 lists fees paid to witnesses who are summonsed to court.

- Have the summons served *personally* on the witness, following the directions in Rule 8.01(7):

    8.01(7) A summons to witness (Form 18A) shall be served personally by the party who requires the presence of the witness, or by the party's lawyer or agent, at least 10 days before the trial date; at the time of service, attendance money calculated in accordance with the regulations made under the *Administration of Justice Act* shall be paid or tendered to the witness.

    In accordance with Rule 8.01(7), you must serve the summons at least 10 days before trial and serve or tender (offer) **attendance money** with the summons. The amounts required are set out in Schedule 3 of the *Small Claims Court — Fees and Allowances*, which covers attendance money to be paid to a witness. Note that some experts (but not all) are paid a higher per diem witness fee. Note

---

[3] See the Bibliography section of this book for the citation for the Court Fees and Allowances. Note that the up-to-date e-version of the court fees is on the Attorney General's website: <http://www.attorneygeneral.jus.gov.on.ca/>, click on Court Services, and follow the link to Small Claims Court Fees. The attendance money amounts are laughably low, like something out of the 19th century — the witness fee would barely cover the cost of a cup of coffee and a sandwich.

that this is a required minimum. Experts are entitled to charge fees for the services they provide in writing the report and preparing to give evidence, which are far in excess of the minimum fee for attendance money. The witness is also entitled to travel expenses, provided these do not exceed the kilometrage expenses set out in R.R.O. 1990, Reg. 11, made under the *Administration of Justice Act*. You can review this regulation online through the e-Laws site (<http://www.e-laws.gov.on.ca/index.html>) by clicking on the "+" sign in front of the *Administration of Justice Act*, which will then list the various regulations made under the Act, including R.R.O. 1990, Reg. 11. If the person travels by car, kilometrage payments are based on the distance from the witness's normal residence to the court, and back. If the person has to come by air or train or from a great distance, you may have to pay air or train fare to get them to court, and this will be more than the standard kilometrage payment under R.R.O. 1990, Reg. 11.

Rule 19 and the Schedule of Court Fees do not make clear when it is necessary for you to provide air or train fare. In deciding this, you may wish to argue that Tariff A of the Rules of Civil Procedure provides appropriate guidance. Tariff A indicates that a witness who resides more than 300 km from the court should be entitled to reasonable airfare to get to court, including a kilometrage allowance to get to and from the airport at either end. If the witness is required to attend trial for more than one day, reasonable accommodation costs should be provided. In either case, the amount can be determined by checking websites that give information about cheap flights and hotel rates. The reasoning used here can also be used to justify these disbursements when costs are assessed under Rule 19. If you win, try to recover what you paid as a reasonable expense incurred to try the case, under Rule 19.01(1). The same applies to expert witness fees.

- If the witness is not fluent in either English or French, the party calling the witness must provide an interpreter at the party's expense pursuant to Rule 18.03(5.1):

  18.03(5.1) If a party serves a summons on a witness who requires an interpreter, the party shall arrange for a qualified interpreter to attend at the trial unless the interpretation is from English to French or French to English and an interpreter is provided by the Ministry of the Attorney General.

  (5.2) If a party does not comply with subrule (5.1), every other party is entitled to request an adjournment of the trial, with costs.

If the person speaks French, contact the clerk so as to arrange for an interpreter to be supplied by the Ministry of the Attorney General at no expense to you as provided for in Rule 18.03(5.1). Note that under the *French Language Services Act* a party may apply for a trial in French, which may cause delays while interpreters are arranged and a Francophone judge is assigned to the case.

If you did need an interpreter and failed to make arrangements, the case may be adjourned, but you will have to pay costs as determined by the trial judge for causing an unnecessary delay, and inconvenience and expense to other parties.

RULES OF PROFESSIONAL CONDUCT
CONCERNING WITNESSES

The *Paralegal Rules of Conduct* must be adhered to in all matters concerning the use of witnesses, whether for written statements or oral testimony. Rules 4.02 and 4.03 set out a code of conduct for paralegals in their dealings with witnesses.

Rule 4.02 deals with the interviewing of witnesses. In all circumstances the paralegal must disclose his or her interest in the case and must not subvert or suppress any evidence or procure the witness to stay out of the way. To meet the requirements of Rule 4.02, a paralegal must disclose his or her interest in the case. A witness must be told that the paralegal is the legal representative of the plaintiff or defendant, as the case may be. If the witness has a legal representative, the consent of the legal representative to speak to that witness is required. Evidence must not be suppressed. An example of suppression would be where a paralegal keeps secret the existence of a piece of evidence. If Zeke, the defendant in our earlier example, did not disclose a town work order requiring him to fix his air conditioner to stop the dripping water, he would be suppressing evidence. Under Rule 4.02(1), a paralegal must not procure a witness to stay out of the way. For example, a paralegal should not give a witness a plane ticket to go on vacation during the period in which the trial will take place.

Rule 4.03 sets out the permitted conduct for dealing with a witness giving testimony. It is important to note that a paralegal must not discuss evidence with a witness who is in the process of testifying or who is between examination-in-chief and cross-examination.

Interviewing Witnesses
4.02(1) A paralegal may seek information from any potential witness, whether under subpoena or not, but shall disclose the paralegal's interest and take care not to subvert or suppress any evidence or procure the witness to stay out of the way.

Communication with Witnesses Giving Testimony
4.03(1) Subject to the direction of the tribunal, a paralegal shall observe the following rules respecting communication with witnesses giving evidence:

1. During examination-in-chief, the examining paralegal may discuss with the witness any matter that has not been covered in the examination up to that point.
2. During examination-in-chief by another licensee of a witness who is unsympathetic to the paralegal's cause, the paralegal not conducting the examination-in-chief may discuss the evidence with the witness.
3. Between completion of examination-in-chief and commencement of cross-examination of the paralegal's own witness, the paralegal ought not to discuss the evidence given in chief or relating to any matter introduced or touched on during the examination-in-chief.
4. During cross-examination by an opposing licensee, the witness's own representative ought not to have any conversation with the witness about the witness's evidence or any issue in the proceeding.
5. Between completion of cross-examination and commencement of a re-examination, a paralegal who is going to re-examine the witness ought not to have any discussion about evidence that will be dealt with on re-examination.
6. During cross-examination by the representative of a witness unsympathetic to the cross-examiner's cause, the paralegal may discuss the witness's evidence with the witness.
7. During cross-examination by the representative of a witness who is sympathetic to that licensee's cause, any conversations ought to be restricted in the same way as communications during examination-in-chief of one's own witness.
8. During re-examination of a witness called by an opposing licensee, if the witness is sympathetic to the paralegal's cause, the paralegal ought not to discuss the evidence to be given by that witness during re-examination. The paralegal may, however, properly discuss the evidence with a witness who is adverse in interest.

(2) With the consent of the opposing licensee or with leave of the tribunal, a paralegal may enter into discussions with a witness that might otherwise raise a question under this rule as to the propriety of the discussions.

(3) This rule applies, with necessary modifications, to examinations out of court. **(THE PARALEGAL RULES)**

Witness Management

Most witnesses would rather be somewhere other than in court giving evidence. If the witness is a stranger, such as a witness to a barroom brawl, he or she is likely to be indifferent and unwilling to attend court. There are some things you can do to gain cooperation. Presumably you will have talked to the witness beforehand, interviewing him or her and, hopefully, having him or her sign a statement (which you may be able to file as evidence under Rule 18.02, rather than calling the witness). Try to establish a friendly relationship that encourages the witness to cooperate. Show some sympathy with the fact that the witness is being inconvenienced, and try to make it easier for him or her. Obtain a contact phone number — a cell phone, if possible, and give the witness yours. In this way, you can quickly inform the witness of a settlement or adjournment where his or her presence is no longer required, or not required at the date and time set out in the summons. In this connection, note that you usually make the time and date in the summons the same as it is in the Notice of Trial. At that point you really don't know what time you will actually need the witness to give evidence. You can tell the witness to be nearby in phone contact, so that he or she can come directly to court when needed, instead of having to hang around at the court house, waiting. If you haven't been able to meet with the witness in advance, you can send a letter conveying these messages to gain cooperation: attach it to the copy of the summons that is to be served and tuck in with the attendance money. Note that if the case is adjourned and the witness has not yet been called, ask the judge to "**bind the witness over**": in effect, remind the witness that he or she is still subject to the summons and must attend on the return date as scheduled by the court. The judge binds the witness over by writing on the Endorsement Record/Order of the Court that the witnesses are bound over. This endorsement is an order that the witnesses must return to court on the date the trial resumes.

If it turns out that the witness's evidence was not necessary and that his or her presence was not really required, the judge may order the party who issued the summons to pay the witness an amount over and above the witness fee and attendance money to compensate him or her for inconvenience and expense.

What to Do If the Witness Fails to Appear

If a witness, properly summonsed, fails to appear, you may need an adjournment. The judge will ask to see that you served the summons personally on the witness, so the affidavit of service should be in the file you bring to court. Personal service is required by the Rules because if the witness is found in contempt, he or she can be arrested and jailed. But no judge will deprive a subject of his or her liberty unless it is clear that personal service has been effected. However, at your request (and sometimes without it) the judge, pursuant to Rule 18.03(6), may issue a warrant for the individual's arrest in Form 18B (see Illustration 11.2 for the Warrant for Arrest of Muriel Mouthe, who failed to show up in court):

ILLUSTRATION 11.2: Sample Warrant for Arrest of Defaulting Witness (Form 18B)

ONTARIO

Superior Court of Justice
Cour supérieure de justice

Warrant for Arrest of Defaulting Witness
Mandat d'arrêt d'un témoin défaillant
Form / *Formule* 18B Ont. Reg. No. / *Régl. de l'Ont.* : 258/98

Seal / Sceau

Toronto
Small Claims Court / *Cour des petites créances de*

SC-00-47669-00
Claim No. / *N° de la demande*

47 Sheppard Ave. E., 3rd Fl.
Toronto, ON M2N 5N1
Address / *Adresse*

416-326-3554
Phone number / *Numéro de téléphone*

BETWEEN / ENTRE

Albert Oryx

Plaintiff(s) / *Demandeur(s)/demanderesse(s)*

and / et

Ophelia Foot

Defendant(s) / *Défendeur(s)/défenderesse(s)*

TO ALL POLICE OFFICERS IN ONTARIO AND TO THE OFFICERS OF ALL CORRECTIONAL INSTITUTIONS IN ONTARIO:
À TOUS LES AGENTS DE POLICE DE L'ONTARIO ET AUX AGENTS DE TOUS LES ÉTABLISSEMENTS CORRECTIONNELS DE L'ONTARIO :

The witness **Muriel Mouthe**
Le témoin   (Name / *Nom*)

of **123, 4th Street, Somewhere, ON N5Q 5L3**
de   (Address / *Adresse*)

was served with a Summons to Witness (Form 18A) to give evidence at the trial of this action, and the prescribed attendance money was paid or tendered.
a reçu signification d'une assignation de témoin (formule 18A) pour témoigner à l'instruction de la présente action, et l'indemnité de présence prescrite lui a été versée ou offerte.

The witness failed to attend or to remain in attendance at the trial, and I am satisfied that the evidence of this witness is material to this proceeding.
Le témoin ne s'est pas présenté ou n'est pas demeuré présent au procès, et je suis convaincu(e) que son témoignage est essentiel à l'instance.

YOU ARE ORDERED TO ARREST AND BRING this person before the court to give evidence in this action, and if the court is not then sitting or if the person cannot be brought before the court immediately, to deliver the person to a provincial correctional institution or other secure facility, to be admitted and detained there until the person can be brought before the court.
JE VOUS ORDONNE D'ARRÊTER CETTE PERSONNE ET DE L'AMENER devant le tribunal afin qu'elle témoigne dans l'action et, si le tribunal ne siège pas ou si la personne ne peut être amenée devant le tribunal immédiatement, de la livrer à un établissement correctionnel provincial ou à un autre établissement de garde en milieu fermé, afin qu'elle y soit admise et détenue jusqu'à ce qu'elle puisse être amenée devant le tribunal.

I FURTHER ORDER YOU TO HOLD this person in custody and to detain him/her only so long as necessary to bring this person before a court as ordered above.
JE VOUS ORDONNE EN OUTRE DE MAINTENIR cette personne sous garde et de la détenir tant et aussi longtemps qu'il sera nécessaire pour l'amener devant un tribunal, comme il est ordonné ci-dessus.

September 14, Yr. 1

A. W. Smith
(Signature of judge / *Signature du juge*)

SCR 18.03-20.11-18B (June 1, 2009 / *1er juin 2009*) CSD

18.03(6) If a witness whose evidence is material to the conduct of an action fails to attend at the trial or to remain in attendance in accordance with the requirements of a summons to witness served on him or her, the trial judge may, by warrant (Form 18B) directed to all police officers in Ontario, cause the witness to be apprehended anywhere within Ontario and promptly brought before the court.

(6.1) The party who served the summons on the witness may file with the clerk an identification form (Form 20K) to assist the police in apprehending the witness.

(7) On being apprehended, the witness may be detained in custody until his or her presence is no longer required or released on such terms as are just, and may be ordered to pay the costs arising out of the failure to attend or remain in attendance.

The warrant does not result in an immediate contempt finding. It is directed to all police officers in Ontario, and directs them to apprehend the witness and bring him or her before the court for the purpose of giving evidence. You may also, pursuant to Rule 18.03(6.1), complete Form 20K, an identification form containing descriptive information about the witness, for use by the police in tracking down the witness (the form is also used in other enforcement proceedings). Illustration 11.3 shows an identification form of Muriel Mouthe completed by Albert Oryx.

An arrest warrant might sound like an effective measure to get your witness to show up in court; in practice, the opposite is the case. Although the law is clear that the police can be directed to enforce orders of civil courts, such as this one, the police do not make it a high priority. The police have a variety of public duties to perform, and this one is low on the list. You may do better if you know exactly where the witness is and can direct the police to that location. Otherwise, apprehension is more likely to occur by accident than by design, where, for example, the witness is the subject of a traffic offence stop, and the warrant turns up on a police computer check.

If a person is actually detained, the police, pursuant to Rule 18.03(7), can hold him or her in custody in order to bring him or her before the court, where the witness may be ordered detained until his or her presence is no longer required, or released on conditions, and may be made to pay the costs of the adjournment to all parties. If the witness refuses to testify, however, he or she can be held in contempt, and the court will schedule a contempt hearing.

When your witnesses do come to court, they will probably come into the courtroom. If they stay during the trial and hear what other witnesses have to say, they may tailor their evidence. If they are your witnesses, you might like the idea of all the witnesses being consistent in what they say on an issue, but the other parties won't be happy. Nor will you be if the other party's witnesses are sitting in the courtroom,

ILLUSTRATION 11.3: Sample Identification Form (Form 20K)

ONTARIO
Superior Court of Justice
Cour supérieure de justice

Identification Form
Formule de renseignements signalétiques
Form / Formule 20K Ont. Reg. No. / Règl. de l'Ont. : 258/98

Toronto
Small Claims Court / *Cour des petites créances de*

SC-00-47669-00
Claim No. / *N° de la demande*

47 Sheppard Ave. E., 3ʳᵈ Fl.
Toronto, ON M2N 5N1
Address / *Adresse*

416-326-3554
Phone number / *Numéro de téléphone*

BETWEEN / ENTRE

Albert Oryx
Plaintiff(s)/Creditor(s) / *Demandeur(s)/demanderesse(s)/Créancier(s)/créancière(s)*

and / et

Ophelia Foot
Defendant(s)/Debtor(s) / *Défendeur(s)/défenderesse(s)/Débiteur(s)/débitrice(s)*

TO HELP PROCESS A CIVIL WARRANT FOR COMMITTAL, the following information, or **as much information as is reasonably available should be provided**. This is necessary for the police to identify the person to be arrested. Without this information it will be difficult to enforce the warrant.
POUR FACILITER LA DÉLIVRANCE D'UN MANDAT DE DÉPÔT AU CIVIL, les renseignements suivants ou autant de renseignements qui sont raisonnablement disponibles devraient être fournis. Ces renseignements sont nécessaires pour que la police puisse identifier la personne à arrêter. Sans ces renseignements, il sera difficile d'exécuter le mandat.

1. Name **Mouthe**   **Muriel**   **Azrat**
   Nom   (Last name of individual / *Nom de famille*   (First name / *Premier prénom*)   (Second name / *Deuxième prénom*)
              du particulier)

2. Also known as names (if any) **"Mouthy Muriel"**
   Nom(s) sous lequel/lesquels la personne est également connue (le cas échéant)

3. Last known address and telephone number
   Dernière adresse connue et dernier numéro de téléphone connu
   123, 4ᵗʰ Street, Somewhere, ON N5Q 5L3
   Tel. 905-123-4567
   Cell 905-201-4001

4. (a) Date of birth *(d, m, y)* **04-11-84**
       Date de naissance (j, m, a)

5. Physical description
   Description physique

   (a) Gender **F**   (b) Height **1.5 M**   (c) Weight **46 kg.**   (d) Build **Medium**
       Sexe   *Taille*   *Poids*   *Corpulence*

   (e) Colour of eyes **Blue**   (f) Hair colour **Light Brown**   (g) Complexion **Fair**
       Couleur des yeux   *Couleur des cheveux*   *Teint*

   (h) Clean-shaven **N/A**   (i) Wears glasses **No**
       Rasé de près   *Porte des lunettes*

   (j) Clothing habits and tastes **Casual dresser, nothing matches**
       Habitudes et goûts vestimentaires

SCR 20.11-20K (June 1, 2009 / *1ᵉʳ juin 2009*) CSD

continues....

Illustration 11.3 (continued)

FORM / FORMULE 20K	**PAGE 2**	**SC-00-47669-00**
		Claim No. / *N° de la demande*

(k) Distinguishing marks, scars, tattoos, etc. **Scar under right eye**
   Marques distinctives, cicatrices, tatouages, etc.

(l) Other **Irritating nasal voice**
   Autre   (Specify / *Précisez.*)

6. Usual occupation **Freelance illustrator**
   Profession habituelle

7. Last known place of employment **N/A**
   Dernier lieu de travail connu

8. Vehicle description
   Description du véhicule

   (a) Make, model and year **Does not own an automobile**   (b) Colour
      Marque, modèle et année   *Couleur*

   (c) Licence plate number   Province or state
      Numéro de la plaque d'immatriculation   *Province ou État*

   (d) Driver's licence number   Province or state
      Numéro du permis de conduire   *Province ou État*

   (e) Distinguishing features on the vehicle (dents, car stereo, etc.)
      Caractéristiques distinctives du véhicule (bosses, autoradio, etc.)

      Uses an old, black 10-speed bicycle in rusty condition, with a red seat and
9. Other information **streamers on handle bars.**
   Autres renseignements

10. Photograph of the person provided in the box below, if available.
    Une photographie de la personne figure dans la case ci-dessous, si elle est disponible.

   The information supplied above is true to the best of my knowledge
   and belief.
   Au mieux de ma connaissance et de ce que je tiens pour véridique,
   les renseignements ci-dessus sont exacts.

   (Signature of party / *Signature de la partie*)

   Albert Oryx
   (Name of party / *Nom de la partie*)

   September 14, Yr. 1

SCR 20.11-20K (June 1. 2009 / *1er juin 2009*) CSD

listening to the evidence and orchestrating a common story. It is generally a good idea at the start of the trial to make a motion for an order to exclude witnesses. With motions at trial, there is no need to serve a notice of motion. Just stand up and tell the judge you have a motion to exclude witnesses — assuming the judge doesn't make the order on his or her own motion. Then, the witnesses have to sit outside of the court, to be called in by court staff when their presence is required. Once they give their evidence, witnesses may remain in the court if they wish.

PRESENTING THE CASE AT TRIAL — A STEP-BY-STEP OVERVIEW

Trial preparation is usually part of the general topic of advocacy, and a detailed discussion is beyond the scope of this text, as far as techniques are concerned, but here is an organizational overview that should be helpful to you in preparing for trial:[4]

1. Review and revise, if necessary, your theory of the case.

2. Identify the facts you have to prove to succeed.

3. Identify the evidence — documentary, demonstrative, and oral — that you will need to prove the facts and to refute the version of the case presented by the other party.

4. Serve your documents and witness statements, under Rule 18.02, at least 30 days prior to the date fixed for trial.

5. In presenting your case, you may find a trial brief useful. It need not be elaborate. You can use tabs so that you can easily find what you need during the trial. The trial brief may contain the following:
   - A tab for opening argument, with the points you wish to make in outline form. Use a large font, and double-space, so that you can see what you have written from a distance but you don't appear to be reading from the text.
   - A tab for each witness you will call, with an outline of the issues and facts you wish to examine them on. Write your outline points on the left half of the page, and leave the right side blank to make notes and comments on answers to your ques-

---

[4] See also, M.A. Zuker, "The Trial — Evidence and Best Strategies", *The Small Claims Court Rules: Hot Spots One Year Later*, June 2007, Department of Continuing Education, Law Society of Upper Canada.

tions, as well as questions on cross-examination, as you may want to ask questions on **redirect**.

- A tab for each witness examined by the opposing party, with the issues you wish to cover on cross-examination written on the left, with additional points added during examination-in-chief.
- Tabs for copies of legal authorities: case and statute law.
- A tab for the outline of your closing argument.
- A tab for submissions, to make after judgment is rendered, concerning interest and costs.

6. At trial, remember to stand when speaking to the judge or making an objection. Small Claims Court judges are referred to as "Your Honour".

7. Prior to making opening statements, rise and introduce yourself, saying and spelling your name, and indicating that you are a paralegal, lawyer, etc., as the case may be, representing the plaintiff (or defendant).

8. The plaintiff usually makes an opening statement indicating what the case is about, identifying the basic facts and the issues that arise from them — in essence, a very brief summary of the case. Do not argue the case at this point or describe the evidence; the defendant may follow with his or her opening statement, or the defendant may make it after the conclusion of the plaintiff's case as a way of opening his or her own case prior to calling defence witnesses. If the judge asks both parties to make their opening statements at the beginning of the trial, then follow the judge's suggestion. If one or both parties are unrepresented, opening statements may be skipped, particularly if the plaintiff commences the statement by starting to present his or her case evidence saying what happened to him or her. As the judge would prefer to hear this as sworn testimony, the judge will ask the plaintiff to take the witness stand and give sworn testimony. Occasionally, if a defendant believes that a plaintiff has not proven his/her case, the defendant may elect to call no witnesses and would set out how the plaintiff has not made out his/her case in his/her own closing submissions. The defendant would ask the court to dismiss the claim with costs payable to the defendant. The defendant in such a case does not need to wait until trial. The defendant can bring a motion under Rule 12.02(1) to strike out the claim for disclosing no reasonable cause of action.

9. No matter how irritated or angry you are with opposing legal representatives, parties, or the judge, maintain a polite tone and calm demeanour.

10. The art of examination and cross-examination of witnesses is beyond the scope of this text. However, where you do call oral evidence or cross-examine another party's witness, there are a number of problems that commonly[5] occur in Small Claims Court proceedings, which you need to be able to deal with:

- Hearsay evidence, submitted in accordance with Rule 18.02, is potentially admissible in Small Claims Courts through signed witness statements, although the evidence of the witness may be subject to cross-examination if a party wishes to test the truth and reliability of hearsay evidence:

> 18.02(1) A document or written statement or an audio or visual record that has been served, at least 30 days before the trial date, on all parties who were served with the notice of trial, shall be received in evidence, unless the trial judge orders otherwise.
>
> (2) Subrule (1) applies to the following written statements and documents:
>
> 1. The signed written statement of any witness, including the written report of an expert, to the extent that the statement relates to facts and opinions to which the witness would be permitted to testify in person.
> 2. Any other document, including but not limited to a hospital record or medical report made in the course of care and treatment, a financial record, a receipt, a bill, documentary evidence of loss of income or property damage, and a repair estimate.
>
> (3) A party who serves on another party a written statement or document described in subrule (2) shall append to or include in the statement or document,
>
> (a) the name, telephone number and address for service of the witness or author; and
> (b) if the witness or author is to give expert evidence, a summary of his or her qualifications.
>
> (4) A party who has been served with a written statement or document described in subrule (2) and wishes to cross-examine the witness or author may summon him or her as a witness under subrule 18.03(1).

If served with a witness statement 30 days before trial, you need to assess the evidence and decide if you wish to call the

---

[5] Identified as common problems with oral testimony in Small Claims Courts by Laura S. Ntoukas, Deputy Judge, Small Claims Court, Toronto, "The Small Claims Court Rules — One Year Later: Common Pitfalls", in *The Small Claims Court Rules Hot Spots One Year Later*, p. 4b, 5–7 (The Law Society of Upper Canada, Dept of Continuing Education, June 2007).

witness and cross-examine him or her, in which case you must serve the witness with the summons and attendance money at least 10 days before trial.

- If a witness is giving oral testimony, you may object to hearsay evidence. Be aware of the principal exceptions, such as evidence to show that a hearsay statement was made, but not that the statement is true; this kind of hearsay is generally admissible.

- Only expert witnesses may give opinion evidence and speculate about a hypothetical situation; other witnesses have to stick to what they have seen or heard or know directly.

- Refreshing a witness's memory from notes made by the witness (where, for example, one person has taken down another's evidence in a statement, the writer can refresh his memory as to what was written) or by someone else, and verified by the witness, at or near the time the event recorded in the notes took place, is permissible. Witnesses may not be able to remember the details of the facts they are giving evidence about. But if they had made notes at the time, you can ask them to look at their notes to refresh their memory. Note that the opposing party then also has a right to look at the notes.

- A witness statement given to you before trial can be used to contradict a witness's evidence. If you interview your potential witnesses prior to trial, ask him or her to review and sign a statement of the evidence, making any necessary corrections. If at trial the witness deviates from the story he or she told you earlier, you can use the earlier written statement to contradict the current oral testimony. But if you are going to use a prior inconsistent statement to contradict the witness, you need to point out the contradiction, and permit the witness to offer an explanation, if he or she has one.

11. Closing arguments should briefly summarize the case you have presented or refuted, with brief allusions to the evidence given and a reference to the law on which you rely. You should give the judge and the representative of the other party a copy of any cases you rely on, with key portions underlined. It makes the judge's job much easier than it would be if he or she had to simply take notes on your argument. But even without case citations, Small Claims Court judges have the power and authority to apply the law that is relevant to the evidence presented in the case, despite whether or not specific principles and rules of law have been pleaded in the claim or defence, provided it is not unfair to do so or would not take the other party by surprise. Appeal courts recognize that in a court where large numbers of self-

represented parties appear, the pleadings are not likely to cite the law with specificity or even clarity.[6] This is some assurance that if your pleadings were deficient, you may be able to remedy the situation in closing argument.

12. Judgment will be discussed in detail in Chapter 12; however, you should prepare your submissions on interest and costs for two scenarios: one in the event that you obtained the relief sought, and one to use in the event that a decision is made against your client. Refer to any Rule 14 offers to settle made, and have a copy of the offer and affidavit of service on hand. Judges have a largely blank Endorsement Record/Order of the Court form to complete; therefore, clear, concise submissions as to costs and interest, with rules and calculations to back up your submissions, may be welcome. Submission of a draft bill of costs, which will be discussed in Chapter 12, is recommended as well.

PROFESSIONAL CONDUCT IN COURT PROCEEDINGS

A paralegal should keep in mind, at all times, his or her duties under the *Paralegal Rules of Conduct*: to act with integrity and honesty and in good faith, and to uphold the integrity of the justice system. Rules 6 and 7 of the *Paralegal Rules of Conduct* (the Paralegal Rules) set out these duties. Rule 6 sets out the duty owed to the administration of justice. A paralegal must encourage public respect for the administration of justice. The paralegal shall also try to improve the administration of justice and must, without breaching confidentiality, inform the police of a potentially dangerous situation at a court facility.

General Duty
6.01(1) A paralegal shall encourage public respect for, and try to improve, the administration of justice.

(2) A paralegal shall take care not to weaken or destroy public confidence in legal institutions or authorities by making irresponsible allegations or comments particularly when commenting on judges or members of a tribunal.

Security of Court Facilities
(3) Subject to Rule 3.03 relating to confidentiality, a paralegal who has reasonable grounds for believing that a dangerous situation is likely to develop at a court facility shall inform the local police force and give particulars. **(THE PARALEGAL RULES)**

---

[6] Ntoukas, *op. cit.*, p. 4b–7; see also the case cited there *936464 Ontario Ltd. v. Mungo Bear Ltd.* (2003), 74 O.R. (3d) 45 (Sup. Ct. J. (Div. Ct.)).

Media Statements and Public Comment on Court Cases

A paralegal is permitted to comment to the media on a court case; however, the provisions of Rules 6.01(4) and (4.1) must be adhered to:

> *Public Appearances and Statements*
> 6.01(4) So long as there is no infringement of the paralegal's obligation to the client, the paralegal profession, the courts, or the administration of justice, a paralegal may communicate information to the media and may make public appearances and statements.
>
> (4.1) A paralegal shall not communicate information to the media or make public statements about a matter before a tribunal if the paralegal knows or ought to know that the information or statement will have a substantial likelihood of materially prejudicing a party's right to a fair trial or hearing. (**THE PARALEGAL RULES**)

In all cases, paralegals should be careful not to infringe upon their obligations to their client. They must not communicate information to the public that could prejudice a party's right to a fair hearing. For example, a paralegal who tells a newspaper reporter that his client was "at a party but was not the person who started the brawl at the party" may be revealing too much information as it is the job of the Crown attorney to prove that the accused was at the party. To state to a reporter that the client was there may prejudice the accused person's right to a fair trial.

Duty to Report Persons Not Authorized to Practise Law

From time to time a paralegal may encounter representatives in a court case who are not legally authorized to practise law. Rules 6.01(5) and (6) impose a positive duty upon the paralegal to assist in preventing the unauthorized practice of law. If you encounter a person practising law whom you suspect is not authorized to practise, you should check the list of lawyers and paralegals online in the Lawyer and Paralegal Directory on the Law Society of Upper Canada website at <http://www.lsuc.on.ca>. If the representative's name does not appear as an actively licensed representative, you should notify the Law Society of Upper Canada of the person's name and your observation that he or she appears to be practising law without a licence.

> *Working With or Employing Unauthorized Persons*
> 6.01(5) A paralegal shall assist in preventing the unauthorized practice of law and the unauthorized provision of legal services.
>
> (6) Without the express approval of a committee of Convocation appointed for the purpose, a paralegal shall not retain, occupy

office space with, use the services of, partner or associate with, or employ in any capacity having to do with the provision of legal services any person who, in Ontario or elsewhere,

(a) is disbarred and struck off the Rolls,

(b) is a person whose license to practice law or to provide legal services is revoked,

(c) as a result of disciplinary action, has been permitted to resign his or her membership in the Law Society or to surrender his or her licence to practise law or to provide legal services, and has not had his or her license restored,

(d) is suspended,

(e) is a person whose license to practise law or to provide legal services is suspended, or

(f) is subject to an undertaking not to practise law or to provide legal services. **(THE PARALEGAL RULES)**

There are persons exempt from licensing, such as a union representative in court on union business or a legal aid case worker. However, it is better to err on the side of caution and report the matter to the Law Society if the representative is not a lawyer or a licensed paralegal. A sample letter to report the person to the Law Society is provided in Figure 11.2.

General Courtesy and Good Faith Towards Others Involved in the Administration of Justice

The paralegal, under Rule 7 of the Paralegal Rules, owes a duty of courtesy and good faith to other legal licensees. Communication between licensees should be done in a professional manner. Communications that are abusive, offensive, and otherwise inappropriate must be avoided. If you receive such communications, whether verbally or in writing, you should remind the licensee of his or her duty of civility under the Paralegal Rules and contact the Law Society of Upper Canada to report such behaviour. As well, paralegals should agree to reasonable requests from other licensees and parties for adjournments. Any undertakings made should be answered in a prompt manner.

Courtesy and Good Faith
7.01(1) A paralegal shall avoid sharp practice and shall not take advantage of or act without fair warning on slips, irregularities or mistakes on the part of other licensees not going to the merits or involving the sacrifice of a client's rights.

(2) A paralegal shall agree to reasonable requests concerning trial dates, adjournments, waiver of procedural formalities and similar matters that do not prejudice the rights of the client.

(3) A paralegal shall not, in the course of [] providing legal services, communicate, in writing or otherwise, with a client, another

FIGURE 11.2: Reporting an Unauthorized Paralegal

Peter Paralegal
410 — 41 Yonge Street
Toronto, ON   M5G 1S1
Tel.: (416) 597-0048
Fax: (416) 597-0049
peterparalegal@email.com

June 1, Year 0

SENT BY FAX TO: 416-947–5263

The Law Society of Upper Canada
Client Service Centre, Osgoode Hall
130 Queen Street West
Toronto, ON   M5H 2N6

Dear Sir/Madam:

Re: I.M. Power

Pursuant to my understanding of my obligation to do so, I am notifying the Law Society of my inability to find an LSUC Directory listing for the above referenced person, who has identified himself both to me and to the court last week, as a paralegal licensee.

I have enclosed copies of my searches of the LSUC Directory that were conducted this morning, all of which show NO RECORDS returned.

In addition, I have enclosed copies of correspondence (with any confidential information blacked out) that I received in today's mail from Mr. Power, as well as a copy of one page of a court document; in both of which he has identified himself as 'I.M. Power', with an LSUC # P28453 set out after his name.

My P1 Licence number is P02952.

In the event that you require any further information, please feel free to contact me.

Yours very truly,

Peter Paralegal
Peter Paralegal

enclosures

Source: The authors would like to thank Fredrick Goodman, licensed paralegal, of Toronto for providing this sample letter of complaint to the LSUC concerning possible unauthorized practice.

licensee, or any other person in a manner that is abusive, offensive, or otherwise inconsistent with the proper tone of a professional communication from a paralegal.

(4) A paralegal shall not engage in ill-considered or uninformed criticism of the competence, conduct, advice or charges of other licensees, but should be prepared, when requested, to represent a client in a complaint involving another licensee.

(5) A paralegal shall answer with reasonable promptness, all professional letters and communications from other licensees that require an answer, and a paralegal shall be punctual in fulfilling all commitments.

(6) A paralegal shall not use a tape recorder or other device to record a conversation between the paralegal and a client or another licensee, even if lawful, without first informing the other person of the intention to do so. (**THE PARALEGAL RULES**)

CHAPTER SUMMARY

This chapter focused on the steps that must be taken to prepare for trial and to conduct the trial.

In preparing for trial, you review and, if necessary, revise your theory of the case, in light of all of the evidence disclosed by both parties, in light of the facts and the advice from the settlement conference judge. In organizing the evidence, be aware that the Small Claims Court Rules facilitate the presentation of evidence, both oral and documentary, under Rule 18. The procedure for summonsing witnesses was examined to ensure that the witnesses you need to give oral evidence will be in court when you need them. You were also introduced to the procedures necessary to deal with a witness who fails to show up, despite being served with a summons. Having taken the steps to prepare for trial, we made observations about some of the things you should do in organizing and preparing for trial and looked at the Paralegal Rules concerning conduct towards witnesses and legal representatives.

REVIEW QUESTIONS

1. What do you need to do to obtain an adjournment of the trial prior to the hearing of the case?

2. What can happen if you fail to attend trial on the scheduled date?

3. How do the Small Claims Court Rules make it easier to present evidence at trial in a Small Claims Court than in other courts?

4. Suppose you are acting for Albert Oryx, and you wish to file a copy of a jeweller's appraisal of the diamond engagement ring he gave to Ophelia Foot, instead of calling the jeweller as a witness. Can you do this? If so, how?

5. If Ophelia's legal representative receives a copy of the appraisal, what should he or she do?

6. How do you make certain that your witnesses show up at trial?

7. What steps should you take in preparing for trial?

DISCUSSION QUESTIONS/CASE STUDIES

FACTS

You are Delford Defendo, Paralegal, 123 Commerce Rd., Nowhere, Ontario L2L 3Y4, tel. 909-765-4321, fax 909-765-4322. Your Law Society Number is P09876. Your client, Albert Oregano, has sued Bertram Sage as a result of Albert having been injured on Sage's property. The claim number is SC-00-19325-00. Sage is representing himself, and he lives at 141 Avenue Road, Toronto, Ontario M4P 1J6. His telephone number is 416-123-4567. Albert's uncle, Barry Boar, saw Albert right after Albert was injured and took some photos of his injuries. We want Uncle Barry to come to give evidence at the trial in Toronto and bring his photos with him. The trial is set for September 14, Yr. 0. It is now August 5, Yr. 0.

Uncle Barry lives at 23 Eaglesnout Rd., Pig's Backside, Ontario L0N 1A5. This is in southern Ontario. His phone number is 705-456-1234. Barry lives 120 km from Toronto. The trial is expected to last one day, and it begins at 10:00 a.m. on September 14. Uncle Barry is a big guy, 1.8 metres in height, and he is quite obese, at 125 kg. In fact, his nickname is "Big Barry". He has hazel eyes, light brown hair, and a florid or ruddy complexion. He is clean-shaven and doesn't wear glasses. Barry always dresses casually, usually wearing sweat shirts and sweat pants. He is also unemployed and doesn't own a car.

1. Draft a summons to get Uncle Barry to attend court and give evidence on September 14.
2. Indicate how much attendance money you have to pay Uncle Barry.
3. Suppose Uncle Barry doesn't show up. Prepare a warrant for his arrest and an identification form.

III

Judgment and Enforcement

Unless otherwise specified, all rules discussed in
this section are Small Claims Court Rules.

Chapter 12

Judgment, Post-Judgment Motions, and Appeals

LEARNING OBJECTIVES

⇨ Know how to calculate a judgment, pre- and post-judgment interest, and costs

⇨ Know how to amend a judgment

⇨ Know under what circumstances an appeal or motion for a new trial should be filed

INTRODUCTION

Once the case has been tried, the judge will record the judgment in an endorsement record that will include pre-judgment interest and costs and provide for post-judgment interest. You need to know how to calculate both types of interest, and you must also present a claim for costs if you are the successful party (or if you are the defendant and you served a Rule 14 Offer to Settle on the plaintiff, which was equal to or greater than the judgment).

If you think the judge has made an error in deciding the case, you need to consider what you should do. You may file an appeal for major errors of fact or errors of law. Where there is a calculation error in the amount of the judgment, or there is new evidence that was not and could not have been available for trial, you may wish to consider the quicker and cheaper method of bringing a motion for a new trial.

JUDGMENT, PRE- AND POST-JUDGMENT INTEREST, AND COSTS

When a small claims case ends, the judge will usually tell you what the judgment is, recording the decision on an Endorsement Record/Order form. The record should indicate if the case has been dismissed with or without costs and, if it has not been dismissed, the amount of money awarded on the claim, pre-judgment interest on that amount, and the costs.[1] It should also indicate the post-judgment interest rate that will be applied to calculate interest on the total judgment (including damages, pre-judgment interest, and costs) from the day of judgment to the date of payment. Usually, the judge will give the decision orally at the end of the trial. If, however, the judge is not sure of the decision, he or she may give a **reserved judgment**, handing down the judgment at a later date. Sometimes, in addition to the judgment, the judge may give written reasons for judgment. This may occur if the case raises an important issue of law or a finding of importance of interest to more than just the parties to the action. But it is rare to receive written reasons from a Small Claims Court judge. Reasons for judgment from higher courts have some value as precedents. But Small Claims Court decisions have little precedent value, as they are not binding on other courts. Small Claims Court decisions are merely persuasive for other

---

[1] The record can also be used to note adjournments and other orders and decisions associated with the case as it moves to trial. Note that it is also used on an assessment of damages for a default judgment.

Small Claims Court judges and are rarely even considered by higher courts.

While the judge determines and calculates the damages, pre-judgment interest, and costs on the judgment, you need to know how to do this to check the calculations in case there is an error. If there is a mathematical error in calculating damages, it may be corrected on a motion for a new trial (which will not necessarily result in a new trial), which is discussed later in this chapter.

Judgment

This is the monetary amount awarded for general and special damages as totalled on the endorsement record. The general damages component cannot be calculated precisely using a formula, but you can check components of special damages, such as a list of expenses for prescription drugs. However, the endorsement record does not provide for an itemized list of components of the judgment, although there is space on the form to provide this information if a judge wishes to do so. But generally the judgment amount will be set out as a single figure.

Pre- and Post-Judgment Interest

Pre-judgment and post-judgment interest, and how to calculate interest, is discussed in detail in Chapter 5. Pre-judgment interest on the judgment amount, not including costs, is available from the time the cause of action arises to the day before judgment. The rate for that period is the rate agreed to by contract between the parties, as is the case on personal loans. If there is no agreed rate, then it will be the relevant rate (for the quarter of the year in which the claim is issued) as set out in the pre-judgment interest rate table pursuant to s. 127 of the *Courts of Justice Act*.

Once a judgment has been given, the plaintiff is also entitled to post-judgment interest on the entire amount of the judgment, starting on the day of the judgment and running up to and including the date of payment. The rate used is the contract rate if there is an agreement between the parties. If so, it is likely to be the same rate as the pre-judgment interest rate; however, it is rare for post-judgment interest to be stipulated in a contract. If there is no agreed rate, the rate is to be found in the *CJA* post-judgment interest rate table (using the rate in place for the quarter of the year in which judgment is made). This rate is usually higher than the pre-judgment interest rate, as it is calculated using a different formula. Note that you do not have to calculate the rate yourself — just use the rate from the table. You can find up-to-date pre- and post-judgment interest tables at the Ministry of the Attorney General website at <http://www.attorneygeneral.jus.gov.on.ca>; click on Court Services and follow the links to pre- and post-judgment interest tables (under Court Fees). Some lawyers and paralegals may calculate pre- and post-judgment interest based on different start and end dates. Some of this variation can trace its origin to different commercial practices in various industries and a lack of agreement on any one approach within the legal professions. For example, some take the position that post-judgment interest begins the day after the judgment has been granted. However, in all circumstances, to ensure that your default judgment and judgment enforcement requests are signed by the court clerk, you should check with your local Small Claims Court office to determine their method of date calculation for pre- and post-judgment interest. The Toronto Small Claims Court clerks, for example, will sign default judgments where pre-judgment interest is calculated beginning with the date the cause of action arose to and including the day before judgment. They then start post-judgment interest on the date of judgment. Figure 12.1 sets out the interest calculation start and end dates based on this method of calculation.

Pre-Judgment Interest

Pre-judgment interest begins to be charged on the day the cause of action arises up to and including the day before judgment. The day the cause of action begins to run is the day on which acts of the defendant give rise to the right to a remedy: the day on which a debt is past due, or the day the defendant damaged your property. In the case of Albert Oryx, it is the day on which Ophelia refused to return the engagement ring to Albert.

If there is a contractual rate of interest, use that rate for pre-judgment interest. If there is no contract or the contract is silent as to interest, use the rate in the *Courts of Justice Act* pre-judgment interest rate table for the quarter in which the claim is issued. Note that this may be different from the rate for the quarter in which the cause of action arose. The rules for how to choose the rate and how to determine the interest period are set out in ss. 127 and 128 of the *Courts of Justice Act*.

Post-Judgment Interest

Post-judgment interest is calculated on the full amount of the judgment, including pre-judgment interest and costs. This is one situation where interest is calculated on interest (the pre-judgment interest component of the total judgment). Post-judgment interest begins to accrue on the day of judgment up to and including the day of payment,

FIGURE 12.1: Pre- and Post-Judgment Interest Information

Type of Interest	Where to Find Rate of Interest	Start Date of Interest	End Date of Interest
Pre-judgment	In the parties' contract or in the *CJA* table for pre-judgment interest, using the quarter in which the claim is issued.	The date the cause of action arose, which would be the date the debt is overdue or, in the case of "net 30 day" terms, the date interest starts to be charged on the debt (Day 31), or, in the case of a tort, the date the "wrong" was committed.	The day before judgment.
Post-judgment	In the parties' contract or in the *CJA* table for post-judgment interest, using the quarter in which the judgment is made.	The date of judgment.	The date of payment or, for enforcement document purposes, the date you prepare the enforcement request document.

at either the contract rate or, if there is no agreed contract rate,[2] at the rate set out in the post-judgment interest table for the quarter in which the judgment is given. The rules for how to choose the rate and how to determine the interest period are set out in ss. 127–129 of the *Courts of Justice Act*.

---

[2] Note that a properly drafted commercial contract should state the interest rate applicable to pre-judgment interest, post-judgment interest, and interest on costs. Such contracts are rarely seen in Small Claims Court. On occasion, a business contract may deal with pre-judgment interest and interest on a judgment but neglect to mention costs. In that situation you would use the *CJA* post-judgment interest rate on the costs portion.

Example 12.1 provides an example of a calculation for both pre- and post-judgment interest.

Example 12.1 Pre- and Post-judgment Interest

(a) Pre-judgment interest
Albert sued Ophelia for $2,000 or the return of an engagement ring on January 16, Yr. 1. Albert had demanded the return of the ring on December 11, Yr. 0. He successfully obtained judgment on September 14, Yr. 1. How much is the pre-judgment interest, assuming there is no agreement as to a rate?

Solution:

1. Determine principal amount: $2,000.00.

2. Check the pre-judgment interest rate for the quarter in which the claim was issued. As the claim was issued on January 16, Yr. 1, you would check the rate for the first quarter of Yr. 1. *CJA* interest rates can be found on-line at <http://www.attorneygeneral.jus.gov.on.ca> (click on Court Services and follow the links to pre- and post-judgment interest tables). Assume the rate for the first quarter of Yr. 1 is 6.0% as claimed and that Yr. 1 is not a leap year.

3. Calculate the pre-judgment interest on $2,000 from the day the cause of action arose (December 11, Yr. 0) to the day before judgment, which would be September 13, Yr. 1:

   December 11 to December 31, Yr. 0 = 21 days
   January 1 to September 13, Yr. 1 = 256 days
   Total = 256 + 21 = 277 days

   Calculate pre-judgment interest:
   $2,000 × .006 × 277/365 = $91.07

Pre-judgment interest of $91.07 is claimed and becomes part of the judgment.

(b) Post-judgment interest
Assume, for this example, Albert's judgment against Ophelia, obtained on September 14, Yr. 1, totalled $2,500, including pre-judgment interest and costs. Assume Ophelia finally decided to pay Albert on November 30, Yr. 1, so that she

Example continues....

> **Example 12.1 (continued)**
>
> could get on with her life. How much is the post-judgment interest, assuming there is no agreement as to a rate? And how much does Ophelia owe Albert in total as of November 30, Yr. 1? Assume for this example that she has not made any payments to him.
>
> *Solution:*
>
> 1. Determine the principal amount: $2,500.00.
>
> 2. Check the post-judgment interest rate in the table on the Attorney General's website for the third quarter of Yr. 1 as the judgment was made on September 14, Yr. 1. Assume rate for the second quarter is 5.0%.
>
> 3. Calculate the post-judgment interest on $2,500 from and including the judgment day of September 14 up to and including the payment date of November 30, Yr. 1:
>
>   September 14 to November 30, Yr. 1 = 78 days
>
>   Calculate simple post-judgment interest:
> $2,500 \times .05 \times 78/365 = \$26.71$
>
>   Post-judgment interest to November 30 is $26.71.
>
> 4. Calculate the total amount owed. The total amount owed is the judgment, including pre-judgment interest, plus post-judgment interest:
> $2,500 + $26.71 = $2,526.71.

Instalment Orders

Section 28 of the *Courts of Justice Act* and Rule 20.02 give the court the power to order payments on a judgment by instalments. This is in keeping with the Small Claims Court's long involvement as a forum handling high volumes of consumer debt cases. As noted earlier in the text, the instalment initiative may come from a debtor who makes a proposal to pay by instalments in the defence. But it may also come after judgment is given on a motion to pay the judgment by instalments. It is clear that the court has the power to order instalment payments of a judgment, and it also has the power to vary that order if the judgment debtor's situation changes. Once such an order is in force and the payments under it are made, the creditor may not take any other steps to enforce the judgment. Rule 20.02(2), however, does permit the creditor to issue and file a writ of seizure and sale of land.

If the judgment debtor goes into default on the instalment payments, the creditors may serve a Notice of Default of Payment

(Form 20L) on the debtor, indicating that there has been a default of payment. If payment is not made within 15 days of serving the notice, an Affidavit of Default of Payment (Form 20M), in which the creditor swears to the fact of the default and the amounts owing must be filed.

The instalment order terminates 15 days after the Notice of Default is served, unless the creditor, during the 15-day period, files a Consent (Form 13B), indicating that he or she has waived the default. A creditor will often file the consent if the judgment debtor brings the instalment payments into good standing before the 15-day period has expired. From a creditor's point of view, having some kind of voluntary payment may be preferable to spending time and money on enforcement remedies that generally are not as cost effective as simply taking the restored voluntary payments. However, if an instalment order terminates, the judgment creditor is at liberty to use any and all of the enforcement remedies available under Rule 20.

A factual example using these forms is set out in Example 12.2 and shown in Illustrations 12.1, 12.2, and 12.3. Note that as instalment payments are made, post-judgment interest has to be calculated from time to time on the declining balance.

Example 12.2 Instalment Orders and Default

Assume, for this example, that a judgment was made against Ophelia Foot on September 14 for $2,568.65. She was permitted to pay by instalments of $200 per week beginning on September 21, and continuing on September 28, and so on. She defaulted on September 28.

Albert decides initially to consent to the default, and a consent is prepared. (A sample consent is provided in Illustration 12.1.) Before the consent is filed, he instructs his representative to disregard the consent and serve a notice of default instead, as he believes that Ophelia has no intention to voluntarily pay. (A sample notice of default is provided in Illustration 12.2.)

The Notice of Default was served on October 1. Because the account had not been brought into good standing within 15 days of service of the Notice of Default, an Affidavit of Default of Payment dated October 16, including post-judgment interest to that was filed. The post-judgment interest rate was 5%.

Unless the parties have agreed to contractual terms of interest, post-judgment interest is simple, annual interest calculated from time to time on the balance on the judgment. In this case, post-judgment inter-

ILLUSTRATION 12.1: Consent (Form 13B)

ONTARIO
Superior Court of Justice
Cour supérieure de justice

Consent
Consentement
Form / *Formule* 13B Ont. Reg. No. / *Régl. de l'Ont.* : 258/98

Toronto
Small Claims Court / *Cour des petites créances de*
47 Sheppard Ave. E., 3rd Fl.
Toronto, ON M2N 5N1
Address / *Adresse*

416-326-3554
Phone number / *Numéro de téléphone*

SC-00-47669-00
Claim No. / *N° de la demande*

BETWEEN / *ENTRE*

Albert Oryx

Plaintiff(s) / *Demandeur(s)/demanderesse(s)*

and / *et*

Ophelia Foot

Defendant(s) / *Défendeur(s)/défenderesse(s)*

I/We, **Albert Oryx**
Je/Nous soussigné(e)(s),

(Name of party(ies) / *Nom de la ou des parties*)

consent to the following:
consens/consentons à ce qui suit :

To waive the default of instalment order.

The parties do not need to sign this consent on the same day, but each must sign in the presence of his or her witness who signs a moment later. (For additional parties' signatures, attach a separate sheet in the format below.)
Les parties ne sont pas tenues de signer le présent consentement le même jour, mais chacune doit le signer en présence de son témoin, qui le signe à son tour aussitôt après. (S'il y a lieu, annexez une autre feuille portant la signature des parties additionnelles présentée selon le format suivant.)

September 30, Yr. 1

Albert Oryx
(Signature of party consenting / *Signature de la partie qui consent*)

Albert Oryx
(Name of party consenting / *Nom de la partie qui consent*)

Peter Paralegal
(Signature of witness / *Signature du témoin*)

(Name of witness / *Nom du témoin*)

(Signature of party consenting / *Signature de la partie qui consent*)

(Name of party consenting / *Nom de la partie qui consent*)

(Signature of witness / *Signature du témoin*)

(Name of witness / *Nom du témoin*)

SCR 3-8-11-14-20-13B (September 1, 2010 / *1er septembre 2010*) CSD

ILLUSTRATION 12.2: Sample Notice of Default of Payment (Form 20L)

ONTARIO
Superior Court of Justice
Cour supérieure de justice

Notice of Default of Payment
Avis de défaut de paiement
Form / *Formule* 20L Ont. Reg. No. / *Règl. de l'Ont.* : 258/98

Toronto
Small Claims Court / *Cour des petites créances de*

SC-00-47669-00
Claim No. / *N° de la demande*

47 Sheppard Ave. E., 3rd Fl.
Toronto, ON M2N 5N1
Address / *Adresse*

416-326-3554
Phone number / *Numéro de téléphone*

BETWEEN / *ENTRE*

Albert Oryx
Plaintiff(s)/Creditor(s) / *Demandeur(s)/demanderesse(s)/Créancier(s)/créancière(s)*

and / *et*

Ophelia Foot
Defendant(s)/Debtor(s) / *Défendeur(s)/défenderesse(s)/Débiteur(s)/débitrice(s)*

TO: Ophelia Foot
DESTINATAIRE(S) :   (Name of defendant(s)/debtor(s) / *Nom du/de la/des défendeur(s)/défenderesse(s)/débiteur(s)/débitrice(s)*)

TAKE NOTICE that you defaulted in your payment(s) to
VEUILLEZ PRENDRE NOTE *que vous n'avez pas effectué le ou les paiements que vous deviez verser à*

Albert Oryx
(Name of plaintiff(s)/creditor(s) / *Nom du/de la/des demandeur(s)/demanderesse(s)/créancier(s)/créancière(s)*)

(Check appropriate box. / Cochez la case appropriée.)

☒ under an order for periodic payment, dated **September 14, Yr. 1**   .
   en vertu d'une ordonnance prescrivant des versements périodiques datée du

   According to Rule 20.02(4) of the *Rules of the Small Claims Court*, the order for periodic payment terminates
   on the day that is 15 days after the creditor serves the debtor with this notice, unless before that date, a
   Consent (Form 13B) is filed in which the creditor waives the default.
   Conformément au paragraphe 20.02 (4) des Règles de la Cour des petites créances, l'ordonnance
   prescrivant des versements périodiques prend fin le 15ᵉ jour qui suit la signification par le créancier au
   débiteur du présent avis, sauf si, avant cette date, le créancier dépose le consentement (formule 13B) dans
   lequel il renonce à la constatation du défaut.

☐ under a proposal of terms of payment in the Defence (Form 9A) dated ....
   en vertu d'une proposition à l'égard des modalités de paiement dans la défense (formule 9A) datée du

   According to Rule 9.03(2)(c) the clerk may sign judgment for the unpaid balance of the undisputed amount
   on the day that is 15 days after the plaintiff serves the defendant with this notice.
   Conformément à l'alinéa 9.03 (2) c), le greffier peut consigner un jugement relativement au solde impayé de
   la somme non contestée le 15ᵉ jour qui suit la signification par le demandeur au défendeur du présent avis.

SCR 20.02-20L (June 1, 2009 / *1ᵉʳ juin 2009*) CSD

continues....

Illustration 12.2 (continued)

FORM / *FORMULE* 20L	PAGE 2	SC-00-47669-00
		Claim No. / *N° de la demande*

You can get forms and self-help materials at the Small Claims Court or online at: www.ontariocourtforms.on.ca.
Vous pouvez obtenir les formules et la documentation à l'usage du client auprès de la Cour des petites créances ou en ligne à l'adresse : www.ontariocourtforms.on.ca.

NOTE TO DEFENDANT/DEBTOR: / *REMARQUE AU DÉFENDEUR/DÉBITEUR :*

If you / *Si, selon le cas :*

> failed to make payments but intend to do so; or
> *vous n'avez pas effectué de paiements mais vous avez l'intention de le faire;*

> made payments but the payments were not received by the creditor;
> *vous avez effectué des paiements mais le créancier ne les a pas reçus;*

contact the plaintiff/creditor to make payment arrangements or correct the reason for non-receipt of payments. You may obtain the plaintiff/creditor's written consent (Form 13B may be used) to waive the default and file it with the court within 15 days of being served with this notice. Failure to do so may result in the following:
communiquez avec le demandeur/créancier pour prendre les dispositions de paiement ou pour régler le motif de la non-réception des paiements. Vous pouvez obtenir le consentement écrit du demandeur/créancier (vous pouvez utiliser la formule 13B) pour renoncer à la constatation du défaut et le déposer au tribunal dans les 15 jours de la signification du présent avis. Si vous ne le faites pas, vous pourriez subir l'une ou l'autre des conséquences suivantes :

- in the case of default under a proposal of terms of payment in the Defence (Form 9A), the plaintiff may obtain default judgment for the unpaid balance of the undisputed amount; or
  si vous n'effectuez pas les paiements conformément aux modalités de paiement proposées dans la défense (formule 9A), le demandeur pourra obtenir un jugement par défaut relativement au solde impayé de la somme non contestée;

- in the case of default under an order for periodic payment, the order will terminate and the creditor may take other steps to enforce the order.
  si vous n'effectuez pas les paiements conformément à une ordonnance prescrivant des versements périodiques, l'ordonnance prendra fin et le créancier pourra prendre d'autres mesures en vue de l'exécution forcée de l'ordonnance.

October 1, Yr. 1

Peter Paralegal

(Signature of plaintiff/creditor or representative / *Signature du demandeur/de la demanderesse/du créancier/de la créancière ou du/de la représentant(e)*)

Peter Paralegal
41 Yonge Street, #410, Toronto, ON M5G 1S1
Tel. 416-597-0048

(Name, address and phone number of plaintiff/creditor or representative /
Nom, adresse et numéro de téléphone du demandeur/de la demanderesse/du créancier/de la créancière ou du/de la représentant(e))

SCR 20.02-20L (June 1, 2009 / *1ᵉʳ juin 2009*) CSD

ILLUSTRATION 12.3: Sample Affidavit of Default of Payment (Form 20M)

ONTARIO
Superior Court of Justice
Cour supérieure de justice

Affidavit of Default of Payment
Affidavit de défaut de paiement
Form / *Formule* 20M Ont. Reg. No. / *Règl. de l'Ont.* : 258/98

Toronto
Small Claims Court / *Cour des petites créances de*

SC-00-47669-00
Claim No. / *N° de la demande*

47 Sheppard Ave. E., 3rd Fl.,
Toronto, ON M2N 5N1
Address / *Adresse*

416-326-3554
Phone number / *Numéro de téléphone*

BETWEEN / *ENTRE*

Albert Oryx
Plaintiff(s)/Creditor(s) / *Demandeur(s)/demanderesse(s)/Créancier(s)/créancière(s)*

and / *et*

Ophelia Foot
Defendant(s)/Debtor(s) / *Défendeur(s)/défenderesse(s)/Débiteur(s)/débitrice(s)*

My name is Peter Paralegal
Je m'appelle
(Full name / *Nom et prénoms*)

I live in Toronto, Ontario
J'habite à
(Municipality & province / *Municipalité et province*)

and I swear/affirm that the following is true:
et je déclare sous serment/j'affirme solennellement que les renseignements suivants sont véridiques :

1. In this action, I am the
   Dans la présente action, je suis le/la

   (Check one box only. / Cochez une seule case.)

   ☐ plaintiff/creditor.
   demandeur/demanderesse/créancier/créancière.

   ☒ representative of the
   plaintiff(s)/creditor(s) **Albert Oryx**
   représentant(e) du/de la/des demandeur(s)/demanderesse(s)
   ou du/de la/des créancier(s)/créancière(s)
   (Name of plaintiff(s)/creditor(s) / *Nom du/de la/des demandeur(s)/demanderesse(s) ou du/de la/des créancier(s)/créancière(s)*)

2. To date, I have received from the defendant(s)/debtor(s) $ ____200.00____ , the last payment being made
   À ce jour, j'ai reçu du ou des défendeurs/débiteurs   (Amount / *Montant*)   *$, soit le dernier paiement ayant*
   on or about **September 21, Yr. 1** .
   été effectué le ou vers le

3. I make this affidavit in support of a request that:
   Je fais le présent affidavit à l'appui d'une demande visant à :

   (Check appropriate box and complete paragraph. / Cochez la case appropriée et remplissez le point.)

   ☐ the clerk of the court issue a Default Judgment (Form 11B) [R. 9.03(2)(c)]. The defendant(s)
   enjoindre au greffier du tribunal de rendre un jugement par défaut (formule 11B) [alinéa 9.03 (2) c)].
   Le ou les défendeurs

   _____
   (Name(s) of defendant(s) / *Nom du/de la/des défendeur(s)/défenderesse(s)*)

   failed to make payment in accordance with the proposed terms of payment in the Defence
   n'ont pas effectué les paiements conformément aux modalités de paiement proposées dans la défense
   (Form 9A) dated _____ and fifteen (15) days have passed since the
   (formule 9A) datée du *et quinze (15) jours se sont écoulés depuis*

   defendant was served with a Notice of Default of Payment (Form 20L) at the following address(es):
   la signification de l'avis de défaut de paiement au défendeur (formule 20L) à l'adresse (aux adresses)
   suivante(s) :

   _____
   (Address(es) of defendant(s) / *Adresse(s) du/de la/des défendeur(s)/défenderesse(s)*)

SCR 9.03-20M (April 11, 2012 / *11 avril 2012*) CSD

continues....

Illustration 12.3 (continued)

FORM / *FORMULE* 20M   PAGE 2   SC-00-47669-00
                                                              Claim No. / *N° de la demande*

☐ the clerk of the court issue a Default Judgment (Form 11B) [R. 9.03(7)]. The defendant(s)
enjoindre au greffier du tribunal de rendre un jugement par défaut (formule 11B) [par. 9.03 (7)]. Le ou les défendeurs

_____
(Name of defendant(s) / *Nom du/de la/des défendeur(s)/défenderesse(s)*)

failed to make payment in accordance with the terms of payment order
n'ont pas effectué les paiements conformément à l'ordonnance relative aux modalités de paiement

(Check appropriate box and complete paragraph. / Cochez la case appropriée et remplissez le point.)

dated _____
datée du

☒ I may enforce the judgment [R. 20.02(3)]. The debtor(s)
m'autoriser à exécuter le jugement [par. 20.02 (3)]. Le ou les débiteurs

Ophelia Foot
_____
(Name(s) of debtor(s) / *Nom du/de la/des débiteur(s)/débitrice(s)*)

failed to make payment in accordance with the order for periodic payment dated
n'ont pas effectué les paiements conformément à l'ordonnance prescrivant des versements périodiques datée du

September 14, Yr. 1 _____, and fifteen (15) days have passed since the debtor(s) has/have
                                      et quinze (15) jours se sont écoulés depuis la signification de

been served with a Notice of Default of Payment (Form 20L) at the following address(es):
l'avis de défaut de paiement (formule 20L) au ou aux débiteurs à l'adresse (aux adresses) suivante(s) :

_____
(Address(es) of debtor(s) / *Adresse(s) du/de la/des débiteur(s)/débitrice(s)*)

A Consent (Form 13B) in which the creditor waives the default has not been filed.
Un consentement (formule 13B) dans lequel le créancier renonce à la constatation du défaut n'a pas été déposé.

4.   The unpaid balance is calculated as follows:
     Le solde impayé est calculé de la façon suivante :

(A)   **DEBT** $ _____ 2,000.00
      LA CRÉANCE $

(B)   **PRE-JUDGMENT INTEREST** calculated
      LES INTÉRÊTS ANTÉRIEURS AU JUGEMENT calculés

      on the sum of $ _____ 2,000.00 at the rate of **6.0** %
      sur la somme de $ *au taux de*   *pour cent*

      per annum from **December 11, Yr. 0** to **September 13, Yr. 1** ,
      par an du   *au*

      being **277** days. $ _____ 91.07
      soit   *jours.* $

NOTE:	Calculation of interest is always on the amount owing from time to time as payments are received. This is true for both pre-judgment and post-judgment interest. Attach a separate sheet setting out how you calculated the total amount of any pre/post-judgment interest.
REMARQUE :	*Les intérêts doivent toujours être calculés sur la somme due. Le calcul doit tenir compte des paiements reçus de temps à autre. Ceci s'applique autant aux intérêts antérieurs au jugement qu'aux intérêts postérieurs au jugement. Annexez une feuille distincte indiquant comment vous avez calculé le montant total des intérêts antérieurs et postérieurs au jugement.*

                                    SUBTOTAL (amount of judgment) $ _____ 2,091.07
                                      TOTAL PARTIEL *(montant du jugement)* $

SCR 9.03-20M (April 11, 2012 / *11 avril 2012*) CSD   Continued on next page / *Suite à la page suivante*

continues....

Illustration 12.3 (continued)

FORM / *FORMULE* 20M   PAGE 3   SC-00-47669-00
                                                      Claim No. / *N° de la demande*

(C) **COSTS** to date of judgment $ 477.58
      LES DÉPENS *à la date du jugement* $

(D) **TOTAL AMOUNT OF PAYMENTS RECEIVED FROM DEBTOR**
      after judgment (if any)   (minus) $ 200.00
      LE MONTANT TOTAL DES PAIEMENTS REÇUS DU DÉBITEUR *(moins)*
      après le jugement (le cas échéant) $

(E) **POST-JUDGMENT INTEREST** to date calculated
      LES INTÉRÊTS POSTÉRIEURS AU JUGEMENT *à ce jour, calculés*
                    See Exhibit "C"
      on the sum of $ attached   at the rate of **5.00**   %
      sur la somme de $ *au taux de*   *pour cent*

      per annum from   to
      par an du   *au*

      being   days. $ 10.92
      soit   *jours.* $

(F) **SUBSEQUENT COSTS** incurred after judgment (including the cost of serving
      the Notice of Default of Payment (Form 20L)) $ Nil
      LES DÉPENS SUBSÉQUENTS *engagés après le jugement (y compris le coût de*
      signification de l'avis de défaut de paiement (formule 20L)) $

                                              TOTAL DUE $ 2,379.57
                                            SOLDE DÛ $

Sworn/Affirmed before me at **Toronto**
Déclaré sous serment/Affirmé
solennellement devant moi à   (Municipality / *municipalité*)

in **Ontario**
en/à/au   (Province, state, or county / *province, État ou pays*)

on **October 16, Yr. 1**   "I. Shredlu"
le   Commissioner for taking affidavits
                                      Commissaire aux affidavits
                                 (Type or print name below if signature is
                                      illegible.)
                             (Dactylographiez le nom ou écrivez-le en
                             caractères d'imprimerie ci-dessous si la
                             signature est illisible.)

Peter Paralegal
                        Signature
(This form is to be signed in front of a
lawyer, justice of the peace, notary public
or commissioner for taking affidavits.)
(La présente formule doit être signée en
présence d'un avocat, d'un juge de paix,
d'un notaire ou d'un commissaire aux
affidavits.)

WARNING:	IT IS AN OFFENCE UNDER THE CRIMINAL CODE TO KNOWINGLY SWEAR OR AFFIRM A FALSE AFFIDAVIT.
AVERTISSEMENT :	*FAIRE SCIEMMENT UN FAUX AFFIDAVIT CONSTITUE UNE INFRACTION AU CODE CRIMINEL.*

SCR 9.03-20M (April 11, 2012 / *11 avril 2012*) CSD

continues....

Illustration 12.3 (continued)

**Exhibit "C" to the Affidavit of Default of Peter Paralegal
sworn October 16, Yr. 1
Post-judgment interest calculations
per item E, p. 3 of the Affidavit of Default**

Interest rate: 5% per *Courts of Justice Act*

Period	Calculation	Interest
Sept. 14–21 = 8 days	$2,568.65 × .05 × 8/365 =	$2.81
Sept. 22–Oct. 16 = 25 days	$2,368.65 × .05 × 25/365 =	$8.11
	Total post-judgment interest as of Oct. 16 =	$10.92

est is calculated on, and added to, the balance. Do not include post-judgment costs of enforcement or accrued post-judgment interest in the amounts on which you calculate post-judgment interest. Just calculate it on the amount of the judgment. If instalment payments are made on the judgment so that the balance due on it is reduced, calculate post-judgment interest on that reduced balance, doing a new calculation each time the balance changes as a result of a payment. This type of calculation is discussed in more detail in Chapter 13, in the section entitled "Enforcement Remedies".

Costs

Costs will usually be awarded to the successful party by the judge at the end of trial. On the basis of that award, a clerk may review and assess the **disbursements** that include fees paid to the court on various filings and reasonable expenses connected with conducting the case, as permitted by the Rules. For disbursements, where you have incurred expenses, attach receipts, where they are available, to prove the costs were incurred. If you submitted a favourable Rule 14 offer to settle, be sure to advise the judge after the decision has been made but prior to the judge making a decision on costs, as this may double your costs as assessed from the beginning of the proceeding (plaintiff) or from the date the offer was made (defendant). Offers to Settle that meet the requirements of Rule 14 are dealt with in Chapter 10.

Generally, costs are said to "follow the event" in common law jurisdictions. This means that the winner usually gets costs that include a representation fee and disbursements. Costs provide partial coverage of the winner's total costs. In the Superior Court, the judge has a very broad discretion in terms of who is awarded costs and how much they receive, and whether costs should be awarded at all. In the Small Claims Court, s. 29 of the *Courts of Justice Act* limits costs awards for the representation fee for lawyers, paralegals, and students-at-law (collectively known as legal representatives) to 15% of the amount claimed:

> **29.** An award of costs in the Small Claims Court, other than disbursements, shall not exceed 15 per cent of the amount claimed or the value of the property sought to be recovered unless the court considers it necessary in the interests of justice to penalize a party or a party's representative for unreasonable behaviour in the proceeding.

Under Rule 19.05, an unrepresented party may be awarded up to $500 in compensation for inconvenience and expense if she or he wins the claim.

> 19.05 The court may order an unsuccessful party to pay to a successful party who is self-represented an amount not exceeding $500 as compensation for inconvenience and expense.

Disbursements, if reasonable, may be recovered in full. A discussion of witness travel expenses can be found in Chapter 11. Section 29 lifts the limit on costs if an award is made to punish a party or legal representative who has behaved improperly in the action. In this case the cap is removed, and costs may be awarded in any amount that a judge thinks is appropriate.

The decision to award costs at all is that of a judge. A judge will usually determine the representation fee at trial following the decision, and may determine the disbursements as well. Or the judge may refer the disbursements to the clerk for assessment. The Superior Court has a process where the parties can argue about the amount of the costs award on an item-by-item basis if the losing party thinks the costs claimed by the winner are excessive. In the Small Claims Court there is no specific procedure outlined in the Rules, but Rule 19.04 contemplates an assessment hearing. Bearing in mind that a judge has a broad jurisdiction to award costs and can consider a variety of factors in deciding on an amount, you may wish to request an assessment hearing at the end of the trial, for example, in the following circumstances:

- One party has behaved unreasonably or, in an unduly complicated way, prolonged the proceeding.
- The upper limits for costs and the representation fee are too high considering the outcome of the case and the extent of the winning party's success.
- Because of the winning party's behaviour, you wish to argue that he or she should be deprived of costs.

You also need to consider the impact of a reasonable offer to settle under Rule 14, which can double the amount of costs awarded for a plaintiff, and double them from the time an offer was made by a defendant. In the latter case, in particular, an assessment hearing may be required to determine what proportion of costs were incurred or can be assigned to the time periods before and after a defendant made an offer.

Whether you are asking the judge to assess costs at the end of trial, or asking for an assessment hearing, or having the clerk assess disbursements, it is a good idea to file a **bill of costs,** which is a list setting out the cost components. There is a standard form in the Superior Court for a bill of costs, but no form in the Small Claims Court. But that doesn't mean you shouldn't make one up. Having every item set down on a sheet of paper, with attached receipts where relevant, can be very helpful to the court. One way to do this is to set out the costs using the five costs elements noted in the next section of this text, with each item that you claim set out under one of the five headings, with a total at the bottom of the document. A sample Bill of Costs is shown in Figure 12.2.[3] HST applies to legal fees, which in the past were exempt from PST. The Law Society of Upper Canada asked that legal fees be exempted from HST. An exemption, however, was not granted. In the Bill of Costs, HST was added to legal fees. Some disbursements, such as copies, would have HST applied to them and would be set out as such on the Bill of Costs. Disbursements for court fees are not subject to HST.

1. Disbursements and Expenses

Rule 19.01 allows you to include in your costs all reasonable disbursements incurred in making a claim or defending against one. The rule goes on to describe the types of things that may be included in disbursements without specifically limiting costs to just those items listed in the rule — the test for inclusion is that they be reasonable,

---

[3] Some lawyers add the $50 LawPro Errors and Omissions Insurance Litigation File Processing fee to their clients accounts and to Bills of Costs.

FIGURE 12.2: Sample Bill of Costs

Superior Court of Justice   File no. SC-00-47669-00

The Toronto Small Claims Court

BETWEEN:

Albert Oryx

Plaintiff

and

Ophelia Foot

Defendant

BILL OF COSTS

SUMMARY OF FEES AND DISBURSEMENT

FEES:

Preparation Fee under
Rule 19.01(4) for Plaintiff's Claim $100.00

Representation Fee for Peter Paralegal
in accordance with Rule 19.04 and
s. 29 of the *Courts of Justice Act*
(15% of Plaintiff's Claim for $2,000) $300.00

HST on Fees $52.00

TOTAL FEES, including HST: $452.00

DISBURSEMENTS:

Paid to issue claim (infrequent claimant) $75.00

Paid to serve claim (maximum allowed
under Rule 19.01(3) claimed for
each person served) $60.00

Paid to issue a summons for one
witness (Muriel Mouthe) $19.00

Paid one day attendance fee for one
witness (Muriel Mouthe) $6.00

Mileage for 10 km at 30 cents a km
paid for one witness (Muriel Mouthe) $3.00

Paid to serve summons on Muriel Mouthe $60.00

Paid to fix trial date $100.00

TOTAL DISBURSEMENTS: $323.00

TOTAL FEES AND DISBURSEMENTS
(Firm HST No. 345678) $775.00

THIS BILL assessed and allowed at $ this   day of   , Yr. 1.

_____

TO: Digbert Fightback
60 My Way
Toronto, ON M6R 8P1
Paralegal for the Defendant

and incurred to pursue or defend the case. The rule specifically permits you to include the following:

- Cost of serving documents, including postage — however, note that Rule 19.01(3) limits your costs for service of each person to $60, unless there are "special circumstances" — these are not defined, but could include the costs of service overseas.

  > 19.01(3) The amount of disbursements assessed for effecting service shall not exceed $60 for each person served unless the court is of the opinion that there are special circumstances that justify assessing a greater amount.

- Travel expenses, either as an amount per kilometre by car or air, bus, or train fare, as the case may be. Note that R.R.O. 1990, Reg. 11 of the *Administration of Justice Act* restricts this to a kilometrage fee:

  > REGULATION 11
  > **1.** If payment of a travel or kilometre allowance is authorized and the authorizing instrument states that the allowance shall be in accordance with or as set out in this Regulation, the allowance for each kilometre actually travelled is,
  > (a) in northern Ontario, 30.5 cents; and
  > (b) in southern Ontario, 30 cents.
  >
  > **2.** For the purpose of section 1, northern Ontario is comprised of,
  > (a) all of The District Municipality of Muskoka;
  > (b) everything lying north of the line consisting of Healey Lake (Municipal) Road from Healey Lake easterly to its junction with Highway 612; and
  > (c) everything lying north of the line consisting of Highway 60 easterly to its junction with Highway 62 at Killaloe Station and Highway 62 to Pembroke.

- Accommodation costs for witnesses or for a legal representative, where out of town travel is required, where it would be reasonable to stay in a hotel.

- Photocopying costs, per page — some photocopiers allow you to use a client account number to activate a photocopier, allowing you to keep track of client photocopying.

- Expenses for experts' reports.

There are other items not specifically listed in Rule 19.02(1) that are customarily included. Long distance telephone charges, postal charges, and the cost of using a legal research site, such as Quicklaw, are some examples of what could be included here.

Note that with the exception of the costs of serving documents and the costs of witness travel expenses, it may be possible to recover disbursements in full on a dollar-for-dollar basis, unless they are so high as to be unreasonable. Here, "unreasonable" may mean that the cost actually paid was higher than it should have been, or it may mean that the cost paid was too high in terms of the amounts at stake in the case. For example, paying $4,000 for an expert report in a case where the claim was $5,000 might be considered unreasonable so that the cost award in respect of this item might be considerably reduced on assessment.

You should also include in your disbursements all fees and allowances paid by you, in the amounts set out in the Small Claims Court Schedule of Fees and Allowances. As the schedule changes from time to time, you should check the current version online at <http://www.attorneygeneral.jus.gov.on.ca>: click on Court Services and follow the links to Court Fees and Small Claims Court Fees and Allowances. (For convenience, the schedule as it was at the time of writing is set out in Appendix 4 to this book.) In determining which fees to include, you need to scan the list in the first schedule for fees you have paid and for which you should have receipts. If you filed more than 10 claims in the year in this court, you are a frequent claimant and pay a higher fee than an infrequent claimant does on some items: filing the claim, fixing the date for trial and entering a default judgment.[4]

The typical case will have the following fees charged:

Plaintiff	*Defendant*
• Filing a claim	• Filing a defence
• Issuing a summons	• Issuing a summons
• Fixing a date for trial	

Schedule 3 sets out allowances for witnesses: As of July 17, 2013, a witness allowance is $6 per day, with $15 per day for expert witnesses. An amount is also allowed for travel to court, but it is limited to the amount per kilometre in R.R.O. 1990, Reg. 11. This regulation sets a kilometrage rate, which, as of July 17, 2013, is 30 cents per kilometre in the southern part of the province (30.5 cents in northern Ontario). Always update the rate by checking the latest version of the regulation online on e-laws at <http://www.e-laws.gov.on.ca/index.html>: click on *Administration of Justice Act* in consolidated law; under the Act, click on Reg. 11. Be aware that you may pay an expert more for his or her report than the allowance provides, but the allowance determines what you will recover if you are awarded costs.

---

[4] Note that the frequent claimant designation applies to a party, not to the legal representatives.

2. Preparation Fee

Under Rule 19.01(4) you may be paid up to $100 for the time and effort involved in preparing pleadings. This is available to both represented parties and unrepresented ones. And it is available if a case is settled or if the defendant defaults before it ever reaches a trial, as well as after a trial.

> 19.01(4) The amount of disbursements assessed for preparing a plaintiff's or defendant's claim or a defence shall not exceed $100.

3. The Representation Fee

Rule 19.04 allows a costs award to include a representation fee in a reasonable amount. If a party requests an assessment hearing or a judge orders one, the fee will be set at the assessment hearing.

> 19.04 If a successful party is represented by a lawyer, student-at-law or agent, the court may award the party a reasonable representation fee at trial or at an assessment hearing.

If you are represented by a lawyer, paralegal, or articling student, reading Rule 19.04 with s. 29 of the *Courts of Justice Act*, you may be awarded a representation fee of up to 15% of the amount of the claim. This means if the claim is for $25,000, you may be awarded a representation fee of $3,750, to which will be added disbursements and other allowed fees.

4. Compensation for Inconvenience and Expense If Unrepresented

If you represent yourself, you are still entitled to costs for the bother and inconvenience to you of preparing and presenting your case. If you are successful in the suit, you are allowed for an amount up to $500 for inconvenience, per Rule 19.05.

> 19.05 The court may order an unsuccessful party to pay to a successful party who is self-represented an amount not exceeding $500 as compensation for inconvenience and expense.

5. Costs Penalty

In addition to a normal cost award, the court may order one party to compensate another under Rule 19.06 for behaviour that is unreasonable, or where one party unduly prolonged or complicated an action:

> 19.06 If the court is satisfied that a party has unduly complicated or prolonged an action or has otherwise acted unreasonably, the court may order the party to pay an amount as compensation to another party.

There is no limit imposed by the rule or s. 29 of the *Courts of Justice Act* on the amount of compensation. However, the compensation should bear some relationship to the damage or harm caused and could be as much as or more than the actual amount of the claim in the case.

> **29.** An award of costs in the Small Claims Court, other than disbursements, shall not exceed 15 per cent of the amount claimed or the value of the property sought to be recovered unless the court considers it necessary in the interests of justice to penalize a party or a party's representative for unreasonable behaviour in the proceeding.

Certificates of Judgment

If a judgment is recorded on an endorsement record, that judgment is an internal document used only by the court for its own administrative purpose, including enforcement proceedings carried out in that court.

If the court's judgment is to be used for enforcement in another Small Claims Court in Ontario, you must prepare a Certificate of Judgment (Form 20A), with an Affidavit for Enforcement Request (Form 20P), to verify the amount currently owing on the judgment as set out in the Certificate of Judgment.

The certificate of judgment recites the details of the judgment, which should be the same as on the endorsement record. The rate of post-judgment interest is also set out. An example of a completed Certificate of Judgment in the *Oryx v. Foot* case is set out in Illustration 12.5, using information from the Endorsement Record in Illustration 12.4. An example using a more complex default situation is set out in Chapter 13.

APPEALS AND MOTIONS FOR A NEW TRIAL

As Yogi Berra is reputed to have said, "It ain't over 'til it's over." If your client isn't happy with the trial results, it may be possible to either appeal the judgment or bring a motion for a new trial. However, appeals and motions for a new trial are relatively rare because the costs of these proceedings, particularly appeals, are relatively expensive, given the amounts of the claim. However, there are situations and times when you should resort to these remedies.

Appeals

Under s. 31 of the *Courts of Justice Act*, appeal of a Small Claims Court trial decision can be made to the Divisional Court of the Superior

ILLUSTRATION 12.4: Endorsement Record/Order of the Court

Superior Court of Justice
Cour supérieure de justice

Endorsement Record/Order of the Court
Fiche d'inscription/Ordonnance judiciaire

Toronto

SC-00-47669-00

Small Claims Court / *Cour des petites créances de*

Claim No. / *N° de la demande*

47 Sheppard Ave. E., 3rd Fl.

Toronto, ON M2N 5N1

Address / *Adresse*

416-326-3554

Phone number / *Numéro de téléphone*

BETWEEN / ENTRE

Albert Oryx

Plaintiff(s) / *Demandeur(s)/demanderesse(s)*

and / et

Ophelia Foot

Defendant(s) / *Défendeur(s)/défenderesse(s)*

Representative of the plaintiff(s):   *Peter Paralegal*
Représentant du demandeur :

Representative of the defendant(s):   *Digbert Fightback*
Représentant du défendeur :

Event type: Trial and Assessment
Type d'affaire :

On   *September 14, Yr. 1*   , a hearing was held in the above matter and the following order was made:
Le   *une audience a eu lieu concernant l'affaire susmentionnée, et l'ordonnance suivante a été rendue :*

Judgment for Albert Oryx, against Ophelia Foot for $2,000.00 plus $477.58 costs.
Pre-judgment interest at 6.0% from December 11, Yr. 0 to September 13, Yr. 1, and
post-judgment interest at 5%.

A. W. Smith

Signature of judge / *Signature du juge*

Endorsement Record/Order of the Court / *Fiche d'inscription/Ordonnance judiciaire* (June 1, 2009 / 1ᵉʳ *juin* 2009) CSD

ILLUSTRATION 12.5: Sample Certificate of Judgment (Form 20A)

ONTARIO
Superior Court of Justice
Cour supérieure de justice

Certificate of Judgment
Certificat de jugement

Form / *Formule* 20A Ont. Reg. No. / *Régl. de l'Ont.* : 258/98

Seal / *Sceau*

Toronto
Small Claims Court / *Cour des petites créances de*

47 Sheppard Ave. E., 3rd Fl.
Toronto, ON M2N 5N1
Address / *Adresse*

416-326-3554
Phone number / *Numéro de téléphone*

SC-00-47669-00
Claim No. / *N° de la demande*

BETWEEN / *ENTRE*

Albert Oryx

Creditor(s) / *Créancier(s)/créancière(s)*

and / *et*

Ophelia Foot

Debtor(s) / *Débiteur(s)/débitrice(s)*

A judgment was made in this action on ___**September 14, Yr. 1**___ , in the
Un jugement a été rendu dans la présente action le , *à la*

Toronto

(Name of court where judgment was made / *Nom de la cour où le jugement a été rendu*)

against / *contre*

Last name of debtor, or name of company / *Nom de famille du débiteur/de la débitrice ou nom de la compagnie*		
Foot		
First name / *Premier prénom*	Second name / *Deuxième prénom*	Third name / *Troisième prénom*
Ophelia		
Address / *Adresse*		
c/o Digbert Fightback, 60 My Way, Toronto, ON M6R 8P1		

Last name of debtor, or name of company / *Nom de famille du débiteur/de la débitrice ou nom de la compagnie*		
First name / *Premier prénom*	Second name / *Deuxième prénom*	Third name / *Troisième prénom*
Address / *Adresse*		

Last name of debtor, or name of company / *Nom de famille du débiteur/de la débitrice ou nom de la compagnie*		
First name / *Premier prénom*	Second name / *Deuxième prénom*	Third name / *Troisième prénom*
Address / *Adresse*		

☐ Additional debtor(s) and also known as names are listed on attached Form 1A.1.
Le ou les débiteur(s) additionnel(s) et le ou les noms sous lesquels les débiteurs sont également connus sont mentionnés sur la formule 1A.1 ci-jointe.

SCR 20.04-20A (September 1, 2010 / *1er septembre 2010*) CSD

continues....

Illustration 12.5 (continued)

FORM / *FORMULE* 20A   PAGE 2   SC-00-47669-00
....
Claim No. / *N° de la demande*

Judgment was made for the following sums:
Un jugement a été rendu à l'égard des sommes suivantes :

(A) **AMOUNT OF JUDGMENT** (debt and pre-judgment interest) $ 2,091.07
    LE MONTANT DU JUGEMENT (créance et intérêts antérieurs au jugement) $

(B) **COSTS** to date of judgment $ 477.58
    LES DÉPENS à la date du jugement $

Post-judgment interest continues to accrue at **5.00**   % per annum.
Les intérêts postérieurs au jugement continuent   (Interest rate /   % par an.
à courir au taux de   Taux d'intérêt)

October 30, Yr. 1   *"I. M. Clerk"*
....
(Signature of clerk / *Signature du greffier*)

TO THE CLERK OF THE Hamilton   **SMALL CLAIMS COURT:**
AU GREFFIER DE LA COUR DES PETITES   (Name of court to where the judgment is to be filed
CRÉANCES DE   / *Nom du tribunal où le jugement doit être déposé*)

The person requesting this certificate is **Albert Oryx**
La personne qui demande le présent certificat est   (Name of party requesting certificate / *Nom de la partie qui demande le certificat*)

c/o **Peter Paralegal, 41 Yonge Street, #410, Toronto, ON M5G 1S1**
(Address of party requesting certificate / *Adresse de la partie qui demande le certificat*)

SCR 20.04-20A (September 1, 2010 / *1er septembre 2010*) CSD

Court of Justice if the final order was for an amount in excess of $2,500 or for the recovery of personal property exceeding $2,500 in value:

> **31.** An appeal lies to the Divisional Court from a final order of the Small Claims Court in an action,
> (a) for the payment of money in excess of the prescribed amount, excluding costs; or
> (b) for the recovery of possession of personal property exceeding the prescribed amount in value.

The provision for the monetary amount for an order for appeals is set out in O. Reg. 626/00 made under the *Courts of Justice Act.*

The Divisional Court is composed of one to three Superior Court judges assigned to this court on rotation. This court was established to review decisions of administrative boards and tribunals to make sure that boards and tribunals behave judicially when they make legal decisions. The court also functions as a lower level appellate court, as is the case for the Small Claims Court.

As the appeal court is a superior court, only lawyers may appear there, which means that if your client wishes to appeal, you must retain a lawyer to handle the appeal, which proceeds under Rule 61 of the Superior Court *Rules of Civil Procedure*, rather than the Small Claims Court Rules.[5]

Note that under the *Rules of Civil Procedure*, Rule 61, the process begins with a Notice of Appeal in Form 61A, which must be filed within 30 days of the date of the appealed decision. However, you may bring a motion to the Divisional Court to extend the time for filing the Notice of Appeal, if necessary. Included with the Notice of Appeal must be a certificate of agreement respecting the evidence to be used. Rule 61 is complex and must be interpreted in accordance with a variety of practice directions. The proper way to proceed is to retain the services of a lawyer to file the notice, order the evidence and prepare appeal books and factums. If time is short, you may wish to prepare and serve the Notice of Appeal. A sample Notice of Appeal is set out in Figure 12.3. This document normally contains a back sheet, which has been omitted here.

Most appeals do not succeed. An error of fact or law is required, and it must be serious and substantial and have resulted in an incorrect decision. An appellate court will not intervene if the error, even if serious, caused no miscarriage of justice. In the case of *Polito v. 1201553 Ontario Ltd. (Tri-Bear Construction)*, 2007 CanLII 54969 (Ont.

---

[5] *Walford v. Stone and Webster Canada LP* (2006), 217 O.A.C. 166, 152 A.C.W.S. (3d) 602 (Div. Ct.).

FIGURE 12.3: Notice of Appeal

ONTARIO
SUPERIOR COURT OF JUSTICE
DIVISIONAL COURT

B E T W E E N:

ALBERT ORYX

Plaintiff (Respondent)

AND

OPHELIA FOOT

Defendant (Appellant)

NOTICE OF APPEAL

THE DEFENDANT APPEALS to the Divisional Court from the judgment of Her Honour Deputy Judge A.W. Smith of the Toronto Small Claims Court, dated September 14, Yr. 1, made at Toronto.

THE APPELLANT ASKS that the judgment be set aside and the action dismissed.

THE GROUNDS OF APPEAL are as follows:

1. The learned trial judge erred in that she completely misapprehended the evidence.

2. The learned trial judge erred in that she misapprehended and misapplied the law.

3. The learned trial judge's behaviour was such during the trial as to create a reasonable apprehension of bias.

THE BASIS OF THE APPELLATE COURT'S JURISDICTION IS: s. 31 of the *Courts of Justice Act.*

The appellant requests that this appeal be heard at Osgoode Hall, Toronto.

October 2, Yr. 1.

I.M. Law
LSUC No. 333145R
Barrister and Solicitor
123 Yonge Street
Toronto, ON M1G 4X1
Tel: 416-597-0001
Fax 416-597-0012
Lawyer for the Appellant

TO: Albert Oryx
111 First Avenue,
Toronto, ON M4R 1X6
Respondent

Sup. Ct.), Tri-Bear Construction appealed a Small Claims Court decision wherein the court made a finding that the homeowners had not
agreed to further extend the start date of their home renovation project. The Politos sued in Small Claims Court for the return of their
deposit of $4,000. Tri-Bear Construction counterclaimed for the sum of
$4,384 for the costs of construction designs made for the renovation.
The court granted the Politos judgment for $4,000 and dismissed the
counterclaim. Tri-Bear Construction appealed to the Superior Court of
Justice. Justice Reilly stated in his reasons for denying the appeal that
"[i]t is trite law to observe that the standard of review with respect to
a matter of law is one of 'correctness'. The standard of review with
respect to the facts is whether the trial judge made a 'palpable and
overriding error' regarding the facts." Quoting the Supreme Court of
Canada decision in *Housen v. Nikolaisen*, [2002] 2 S.C.R. 235, he
stated that "[i]t is not the role of the appellate courts to second-guess
the weight to be assigned to the various items of evidence. If there is
no palpable and overriding error with respect to the underlying facts
that the trial judge relies on to draw the inference, then it is only
where the inference-drawing process itself is palpably in error that an
appellate court can interfere with the factual conclusion. The appellate
court is not free to interfere with a factual conclusion that it disagrees
with where such disagreement stems from a difference of opinion over
the weight to be assigned to the underlying facts." Justice Reilly went
on to state that "[i]t is not appropriate for this court to say what
conclusions I might have come to on that evidence. Deputy Judge
Breithaupt was the trial judge and he was entitled to come to his own
conclusions based on the evidence before him as long as there were
facts that would justify his conclusions. Indeed there were. This court
must therefore give deference to his conclusions." Justice Reilly made
some comments concerning the counterclaim expressing his opinion
that "[i]t would have been preferable if the trial judge had expressed
cogent reasons in some greater detail for dismissing the counterclaims
based on unjust enrichment and quantum meruit. However, from his
statement I conclude that the trial judge determined that the plaintiff
did not derive a benefit from the plans.... While further reasons would
have been preferable, I conclude they were not necessary in the context of a Small Claims Court action and their absence does not justify
a direction for a new trial."

With respect to an error of fact, the court will look at irrational
conclusions from proven facts as a basis of appeal, but it will not interfere with findings of credibility by the trial judge. The appellate court
only has the transcript of evidence to go on, and, as it didn't see or
observe the witness, it will not substitute its decision for that of the
trial judge on an issue of credibility.

With respect to bias, the Divisional Court recognizes that the Small Claims Court judge, dealing often with unskilled and self-represented parties, must intervene to clarify issues and guide case presentations to an extent that would not be permitted in other courts where lawyers, rather than self-represented parties, present cases. So there will be some tolerance for judicial intervention, although if the intervention goes beyond guidance in presenting a case to taking over its presentation, the court will intervene.[6]

Appeals require the filing of a variety of documents, including transcripts of the trial, which can be expensive; and as most appeals are not successful, you should be sure your client understands the appellate facts of life before going down this road.

Motions for a New Trial

In addition to moving to set aside a judgment due to an inability to attend trial, Rule 17.04 permits a party to move to set aside the judgment and obtain a new trial, a kind of poor man's appeal, provided that one of the following conditions are met:

- There was a purely arithmetical error in the determination of the amount of damages awarded at trial — where interest is improperly calculated or an error is made in totalling up the damages.

- There is relevant evidence now available that was not available to the party at the time of trial and could not reasonably have been expected to be available at trial. Note that this does not provide an option for a re-trial where, on consideration, you realize there was some evidence you should have presented but did not. The evidence in question has to have been unavailable despite reasonable efforts to find or obtain it.

> 17.04(4) On the hearing of the motion, the court may,
> (a) if the party demonstrates that a condition referred to in subrule (5) is satisfied,
>   (i) grant a new trial, or
>   (ii) pronounce the judgment that ought to have been given at trial and order judgment accordingly; or
> (b) dismiss the motion.
>
>   (5) The conditions referred to in clause (4)(a) are:
> 1. There was a purely arithmetical error in the determination of the amount of damages awarded.

---

[6] *Mak v. T.D. Waterhouse Canada* (2005), 198 O.A.C. 92, 139 A.C.W.S. (3d) 5 (Div. Ct.).

> 2. There is relevant evidence that was not available to the party at the time of the original trial and could not reasonably have been expected to be available at that time.

The moving party must bring an ordinary motion requesting a new trial before the court (but not necessarily the judge) that gave the original judgment within 30 days of the making of the judgment. Rule 17.04 requires you to serve and file a notice of motion and supporting affidavit along with proof that a request has been made for a transcript of the reasons for judgment and any other part of the proceeding that is relevant.

> 17.04(1) A party may make a motion for a new trial within 30 days after a final order is made.
>
> (2) In addition to serving and filing the notice of motion and supporting affidavit (Form 15A) required under rule 15.01, the moving party shall serve and file proof that a request has been made for a transcript of,
> (a) the reasons for judgment; and
> (b) any other portion of the proceeding that is relevant.
>
> (3) If available, a copy of the transcript shall, at least three days before the hearing date,
> (a) be served on all parties who were served with the original notice of trial; and
> (b) be filed, with proof of service.

The supporting affidavit should set out the circumstances that fit one of the two grounds for moving for a new trial. Where possible, particularly with arithmetical errors, indicate what the correct amount in the judgment should have been. The motion material and proof that a transcript has been requested must be served on all other parties to the action. You should try and have the relevant transcript served and filed at least three days before the hearing; but transcript preparation is in the hands of the court reporter and it does take time to do. When fixing a hearing date for the motion with the court, get the reporter's estimate of when the transcript will be ready, prior to fixing a date.

On the motion, the court may order a new trial; this is likely if the court is persuaded that the new evidence is relevant to the issues and that, if proved, it might result in a different decision from that in the original judgment. In the case of an arithmetical error, if you can demonstrate what the "right answer" is from your affidavit material at the hearing, the motion judge may order the error corrected and grant a new judgment in the right amount, without requiring a new trial. If a judge is not persuaded the new evidence is really new or relevant, or would make a difference, or that there is an arithmetical error, he or she can dismiss the motion.

CHAPTER SUMMARY

This chapter deals with the mechanics of determining the amounts due on the judgment, including interest and costs, and with appeals and motions for a new trial. Once a judgment is given, you need to know how to calculate post-judgment interest, structure and administer instalment payments, and present a claim for costs. Also in this chapter, we noted the steps that must be taken to file an appeal, noting that the grounds for appeal are relatively narrow and that appeals are not usually successful. We also noted the alternative to appeals, which is a motion for a new trial where there is new evidence or an error in calculating the damages. At this point the trial and judgment process is complete, and if the plaintiff is successful, he or she can start to think about enforcing payment on the judgment.

REVIEW QUESTIONS

1. The court granted judgment against Alan in favour of Edward on July 6, Year 0. Alan called Edward on October 23, Year 0, and said he was going to come over and pay Edward that day. How many days of post judgment interest are there?

2. Jennifer obtained judgment against Pat's Pancake House on October 5, Year 0. Jennifer has an examination in aid of execution booked against Pat's on January 3, Year 1. How many days of post-judgment interest are there as of the date of the examination?

3. Suppose Morris Mildew sued Art Dodger for $5,000 for injuries sustained when Morris stepped on a banana peel in Art's store. The accident happened on April 18, 2006. The action started on June 13, 2006, and judgment was given on February 4, 2007. There was no contractual agreement between them about interest. Assuming Morris was successful, calculate the pre-judgment interest he should receive.

4. Assume on the facts of the preceding question that Art finally agreed to pay the judgment of $5,600 (including pre-judgment interest and costs), on March 20, 2007. How much post-judgment interest should be added to the amount due under the judgment?

5. Suppose you won at trial and you, as plaintiff, made a successful Rule 14 offer, which the defendant refused. You were represented by counsel, and neither party behaved inappropriately. What cost elements can you include in your costs award?

6. Can you recover costs for the following:
   (a) The other party prolonged the proceeding.
   (b) It cost you $55.00 to serve the claim.
   (c) You had to stay in a hotel overnight at your expense.
   (d) You had to pay airfare for a witness to come from Thunder Bay to Toronto.

7. When do you need to use a Certificate of Judgment after the trial?

8. Under what circumstances would you file an appeal? A motion for a new trial?

9. Is there anything you can do for a client facing a judgment for an amount he or she cannot pay all at once?

DISCUSSION QUESTIONS/CASE STUDIES

Date: February 1, 2007

Memo to: Paul Paralegal

Re: Orlando Gibbon v. John Dowland

Our client, Gibbon, sued Dowland for $8,000.00 on August 3, 2006, for a trespass and damage to property that occurred on December 18, 2005. The trial occurred January 27, 2007, judgment being given on that date, to our client for $8,000. I want you to check the costs and the pre-judgment interest as set out on the endorsement record to see that they are accurate. The plaintiff is an infrequent claimant. In addition to issuing the claim, we issued summonses to three witnesses, all of whom live in Toronto and walked to court, so no travel allowance was required. We also set the matter down for trial. We incurred telephone charges of $14.00 and photocopying charges of $35.00. There were also postal charges of $8.00. Personal service of the claim cost $65.00; the legal representative was Peter Paralegal.

---

1. How much is the pre-judgment interest?
2. What costs is the plaintiff entitled to?
3. After checking the endorsement record, you notice that the post-judgment interest rate is set at 4.5%, but it should be set for the first quarter, when the post-judgment rate was, in fact, 6.0%. It appears that whoever entered the rate on the endorsement was looking at the pre-judgment interest table when he or she should have been looking at the post-judgment interest table. Draft the document required to correct the error.

Chapter 13

Post-Judgment Considerations

LEARNING OBJECTIVES

⇨ Know the options available to you in enforcing a judgment

⇨ Know how to develop and implement a strategy to collect a judgment debt in a cost-effective way

⇨ Know how to set up and conduct an examination in aid of execution

⇨ Know how to determine the amount due and owing on a judgment from time to time

⇨ Understand contempt of court proceedings in relation to judgment enforcement

⇨ Know about instalment orders and consolidation orders

INTRODUCTION

Having obtained a judgment, we are now faced with the task of enforcing it. Remember that the court has limited powers: it can order the payment of money or the return of property, provided the amount claimed or the value of the property is $25,000 or less, exclusive of interest and costs. Not surprisingly, the remedies for enforcing a judgment that are available in Small Claims Court are limited (under Rule 20.03), and they are as follows:

1. Seizing and selling real property of the judgment debtor, using a writ of seizure and sale of land, and paying the judgment debt out of the money from the sale(s)

2. Seizing and selling personal property of the judgment debtor, using a writ of seizure and sale of personal property, and paying the judgment debt out of the money from the sale(s)

3. Seizing and returning to the judgment creditor personal property belonging to the judgment creditor that the court has ordered a defendant to return, using a writ of delivery

4. Using a notice of garnishment to obtain monies owing to the judgment debtor from a third party, such as a bank or an employer, to pay the judgment

5. Using a notice of examination to set up and conduct an examination of the **judgment debtor** to discover his means, assets, obligations, and ability to pay

> 20.03 In addition to any other method of enforcement provided by law,
> (a) an order for the payment or recovery of money may be enforced by,
>   (i) a writ of seizure and sale of personal property (Form 20C) under rule 20.06,
>   (ii) a writ of seizure and sale of land (Form 20D) under rule 20.07, and
>   (iii) garnishment under rule 20.08; and
> (b) a further order as to payment may be made under subrule 20.10(7).

Sometimes the defendant will pay the judgment debt right after the trial. More often the plaintiff, now known as the **judgment creditor**, will have to press the defendant, now known as the judgment debtor, to pay the money that is owing, using one of the collection remedies referred to above.

If the judgment debtor is relatively sophisticated, she may have "judgment proofed" herself by transferring valuable assets to relatives and friends, or by moving property to other jurisdictions, or by arranging business affairs to make it difficult to tell who owns an asset that might be seized. As a judgment creditor's claim in the first place was never more than $25,000, even with added interest and costs it makes little sense to spend vast sums to recover relatively small judgment debts. It is a fact of life that the judgment creditor will sometimes find that the court's remedies are not effective in collecting what is owing, and he or she will have to write off the debt.

At other times, the judgment creditor will discover that the debtor simply is unable to pay what is owing now or in the future, and the debt will have to be written off. For example, the judgment creditor may discover, in questioning the judgment debtor at an examination, that the judgment debtor has a permanent and serious disability that prevents her from ever working again and, therefore, limits her income to CPP disability payments, which cannot be garnished to pay an ordinary judgment. If there does not appear to be any property or other means of realizing a judgment, it may be better for the judgment creditor to write off the debt than to spend any more time or money attempting to collect the debt.

In between these extremes are those judgment debts that you will have to develop some strategies to collect, using the available court collection remedies to recover what is owing to the judgment creditor. The balance of this chapter is about assessing collection prospects, developing strategies to collect from uncooperative judgment debtors, and using the examination in aid of execution to obtain information that will assist the creditor in collecting from the debtor. We also examine how to determine the amount owing from time to time after judgment and information that we will need to complete the various enforcement forms.

DEVELOPING A STRATEGY TO COLLECT A JUDGMENT DEBT

Rare is the case where, by the time you obtain a judgment, you know nothing about the judgment debtor. Either you, in preparing the case, or your client, in his or her dealings with the defendant, carried out some or all of the investigation processes that we discussed in Chapter 3: execution searches, PPSA searches, credit reporting searches, bankruptcy searches, and so on. Those searches had two main purposes at the beginning of a case — to verify the location and identification of the debtor as the proper party to sue, and to determine whether the defendant was worth suing: would there be assets available to enforce a judgment? If the lawsuit went ahead, there probably were assets thought to be available to satisfy a judgment.

It is wise to review the results of those initial investigations now and, in some cases, to update them. If, for example, the debtor defaulted on other debts after being sued and seems to have disappeared, you can use some of the identification and debtor-locating techniques described in Chapter 3 to locate the debtor (and, hopefully, the debtor's assets). It is especially useful to review and, if necessary, update the credit report you obtained from Equifax or a similar credit reporting agency: the credit report often contains location information, identifies other judgment creditors, and may have information that will help you locate assets you can seize, as well as giving the names of banks and employers you can garnish.

If the debtor was on the edge of financial ruin, update your bankruptcy search. If the debtor has gone bankrupt, enforcement will involve filing a claim with the trustee in bankruptcy so that your claim will be included with those of other unsecured creditors, as you will not be able to otherwise enforce the judgment.

Once you have determined where the debtor is and what assets might satisfy a judgment, you will have an idea of what enforcement procedures will be effective. Prepare to move quickly to begin enforcement. The longer you delay, the less likely you are to recover what is owing on the judgment.

Specific Steps to Take After Obtaining Judgment

There are some things you should do in nearly every case:

1. File a Writ of Seizure and Sale of Personal Property immediately upon obtaining a judgment. If the debtor resides in the jurisdiction of another court or has property elsewhere, file writs in those courts as well. Remember, if you are filing in a court other than the one that gave the judgment, obtain and file a Certificate of Judgment. Even if you don't know whether there is property to seize, filing a writ is useful: e.g., if another creditor seizes and sells something, you will get to share proportionally in the net amount from the sale — all without doing much more than filing the writ. The writ also has the effect of creating credit problems for the judgment debtor. The writ will turn up on searches that any lender is likely to carry out, and the presence of the writ can result in a downgrading of a credit rating. In effect, filing the writ is a bit like fishing. You bait the hook, cast your line, and wait to see what bites.

2. File a Writ of Seizure and Sale of Land immediately upon obtaining a judgment. This stops the judgment debtor from re-financing or selling an existing property and from obtaining financing for a

new property. Note that in the event that the debtor obtains a consolidation order (as discussed later in this chapter), the Writ of Seizure and Sale of Land is the only enforcement remedy that the judgment creditor is allowed to obtain or keep on file if he or she has already obtained the writ.

3. Obtain a Writ of Delivery where applicable. If the court ordered the judgment debtor to return the judgment creditor's property and the judgment debtor has not done so, the judgment creditor may ask the court to issue a Writ of Delivery to permit the bailiff of the court to seize the judgment creditor's property from the judgment debtor.

4. Garnish the judgment debtor's income and bank accounts where applicable. If you know who the judgment debtor's employer is or where he or she banks, immediately move to garnish wages and/or bank accounts. If the judgment debtor is a business and you know its current customers, who may owe the judgment debtor money, send out garnishment notices to them. As judgment debtors usually do not want third parties to know about their financial difficulties, this may prompt payment.

5. If your initial efforts with garnishment and filing writs of seizure and sale were unsuccessful, you can carry out an examination of the judgment debtor. In addition to finding out about things that can be seized or garnished to satisfy a judgment, the main reason to hold the examination is to be able to sit down with the judgment debtor to persuade him or her to come to an arrangement to pay the judgment debt voluntarily. You may also discover, from questioning the judgment debtor and obtaining documents from the judgment debtor (such as income tax returns and pay stubs), other sources of assets or income to seize or garnish.

ENFORCEMENT REMEDIES

As noted, there are five main enforcement remedies: writs of seizure and sale of personal property, writs of seizure and sale of land, writs of delivery, garnishment proceedings, and examinations of judgment debtors. Remedies available in Superior Court, particularly equitable remedies, such as mandatory injunctions requiring a defendant to do or refrain from doing certain things, or orders for specific performance of contracts, or orders to appoint a receiver, are not available in Small Claims Court.

There are some remedies available to judgment debtors that can ease the impact of enforcement, such as instalment payment orders and consolidation orders. Consolidation orders allow several judgments against a judgment debtor to be joined together with instalment payments made by the judgment debtor to be shared by the judgment creditors equally.

Basic Enforcement Procedure

Specific enforcement procedures for each of the main types of enforcement are provided in later chapters; however, a quick summary is provided here for reference purposes. When you are ready to use an enforcement remedy, you will not only need to complete the relevant enforcement form, for example, a Writ of Seizure and Sale, but you will also need to prepare other supporting documents:

1. If you are enforcing a judgment given by one court in a different geographical location, you will have to prepare a Certificate of Judgment (Form 20A), in addition to other required documents.

2. If you are obtaining a Certificate of Judgment, garnishing a debt, issuing a Writ of Seizure and Sale of Personal Property or of Land, issuing a Writ of Delivery, or issuing a Notice of Examination, you must also file an Affidavit for Enforcement Request (Form 20P). A Direction to Enforce a Writ of Seizure and Sale of Personal Property (Form 20O) is required to seize personal property. This writ is enforced by the bailiff of the Small Claims Court.

3. If you are enforcing a default on an instalment payment order under Rule 20.02, you must prepare an Affidavit of Default in Payment (Form 20M) and a Notice of Default of Payment (Form 20L). Both documents were discussed in detail in Chapter 12.

Enforcement documents are filed with the clerk of the court, but as you will see when you examine the forms, the Small Claims Court bailiff carries out the seizure of a debtor's property under a Writ of Seizure and Sale of Personal Property or a Writ of Delivery. For the other enforcement remedies, the court clerk will administer payment procedures for garnishment and consolidation orders and will set up examinations in aid of execution, also known as judgment debtor exams. Enforcement of writs of seizure and sale of land are carried out by the Superior Court of Justice's Sheriff's Office.

For each enforcement remedy there are enforcement costs. You will need to pay the court fee for issuing a writ or other enforcement remedy, as set out in schedule 1 of the Small Claims Court Fees and Allowances. There are fees for sending a bailiff out to seize property, and you also have to pay the bailiff for reasonable expenses incurred in enforcing the writ. These costs may be added to the judgment debt.

Calculating the Amount Owing after Judgment: Step by Step

Calculating the amount owing after judgment involves calculating and adding post-judgment interest to the total judgment, and then adding on any post-judgment enforcement costs, for example, the court fee to issue a Writ of Seizure and Sale. In cases where the defendant has not paid anything on the judgment, this is easy enough. But if the debtor pays part of what is due over time, the amount on which post-judgment interest is calculated will have to be recalculated on the new balance owing. The resulting new balance will then become the amount on which post-judgment interest continues to accrue.

The calculations on a fluctuating post-judgment debt must be done for every enforcement remedy, usually by way of an Affidavit for Enforcement Request (Form 20P) or an Affidavit of Default of Payment (Form 20M), used for defaults on instalment orders or on a payment proposal filed on a Defence (Form 9A). All of these forms are set up in the same way for the calculations of amounts owing post-judgment. If you can successfully complete one, then you should easily be able to complete the others. Step-by-step instructions for completing the calculation section in Form 20P are provided in Figure 13.1.

FIGURE 13.1: Steps to Completing Form 20P

Form 20P, Affidavit for Enforcement Request, is the most common enforcement document. The process for completing Section 3 on Pages 3 and 4 of this form is set out below. (Most of the information required for this form can be found in the judgment or the endorsement record.) A number has been placed on each part of the form to correspond to the steps set out below, followed by an example using actual figures.

1. Determine the debt, which is the monetary amount (before interest is added) awarded on the claim.

2. Calculate the pre-judgment interest awarded, and provide the following information:
   (a) The principal amount of the debt awarded by the judge (#1)
   (b) The rate of pre-judgment interest awarded
   (c) The start date of pre-judgment interest (usually the date the cause of action arose)
   (d) The last day for pre-judgment interest to be charged, which is usually the day before judgment date

continues....

Figure 13.1 (continued)

(e) The number of days from and including the date pre-judgment interest starts up to and including the day before judgment date

At line 2, fill in the monetary amount of pre-judgment interest that you calculated.

3. Add numbers from #1 and #2 for a subtotal of the debt plus pre-judgment interest.

4. State the costs awarded.

5. Set out any payments received from the judgment debtor after the judgment. Attach a separate calculations sheet for such payments and post-judgment interest on those payments. (Note: You would add the accrued post-judgment interest to the amount owing at the time of the payment, then deduct the payment to get a new balance, then calculate your post-judgment interest on this new subtotal going forward, and repeat this calculation each time a payment is received.)

6. Calculate post-judgment interest on the subtotal (#3) plus costs (#4) and provide the following information:

   (a) The new subtotal (#3 + #4) less any payments made post-judgment (#5)

   (b) The rate of post-judgment interest awarded as set out on the judgment/endorsement (This rate can be found on the judgment and is usually the *Courts of Justice Act* post-judgment interest rate for the quarter in which the judgment was made. Post-judgment interest rates can be found in Appendix 5 to this book.)

   (c) The judgment date

   (d) The date that you are filing the form with the court

   (e) The total number of days, from and including judgment date to and including the day the form is filed with the court (inclusive)

   At line 6, calculate and fill in the amount of post-judgment interest.

7. Calculate any costs incurred since the judgment. You can include the cost of issuing the requested enforcement (e.g., the cost of a Writ of Seizure and Sale of Personal Property).

8. Calculate the total due by adding numbers 3, 4, 6, and 7 together (having deducted any amount of payments made set out in #5 and, in that case, having added a schedule showing your calculations and how interest was applied on the declining balance). Note that the total-due figure must match the total figure identified in the enforcement process. For example, on a Writ of Seizure and Sale of Personal Property, the total-due amount must match the total-due amount on the Affidavit for Enforcement Request form.

continues....

Figure 13.1 (continued)

FORM / *FORMULE* **20P**   **PAGE 3**   _____
                                                                    Claim No. / *N° de la demande*

(A) **DEBT** $ _____ **1**
     LA CRÉANCE $

(B) **PRE-JUDGMENT INTEREST** calculated
     LES INTÉRÊTS ANTÉRIEURS AU JUGEMENT calculés

     on the sum of $ _____ **2(a)** ____ at the rate of __ **2(b)** __ %
     sur la somme de $ *au taux de*   *pour cent*

     per annum from __ **2(c)** ____ , 20 ___ to __ **2(d)** ____ , 20 ____ ,
     par an du   *au*

     being **2(e)** _____ days. $ _____ **2**
     soit   *jours.* $

                            SUBTOTAL (Amount of Judgment) $ _____ **3**
                            TOTAL PARTIEL (montant du jugement) $

(C) **COSTS** to date of judgment $ _____ **4**
     LES DÉPENS à la date du jugement $

FORM / *FORMULE* **20P**   **PAGE 4**   _____
                                                                    Claim No. / *N° de la demande*

(D) **TOTAL AMOUNT OF PAYMENTS RECEIVED FROM DEBTOR**
     after judgment (if any)   (minus) $ _____ **5**
     LE MONTANT TOTAL DES PAIEMENTS REÇUS DU   *(moins)* $
     DÉBITEUR après le jugement (le cas échéant)

(E) **POST-JUDGMENT INTEREST** to date calculated
     LES INTÉRÊTS POSTÉRIEURS AU JUGEMENT à ce jour, calculés

     on the sum of $ _____ **6(a)** ____ at the rate of **6(b)** __ %
     sur la somme de $ *au taux de*   *pour cent*

     per annum from __ **6(c)** ____ , 20 ___ to __ **6(d)** ____ , 20 ____ ,
     par an du   *au*

     being __ **6(e)** _____ days. $ _____ **6**
     soit   *jours.* $

     ┌───┐
     │ **NOTE:** Calculation of interest is always on the amount owing from time to time as payments are │
     │ received. This is true for both pre-judgment and post-judgment interest. Attach a separate │
     │ sheet setting out how you calculated the total amount of any pre/post-judgment interest. │
     │ *REMARQUE: Les intérêts doivent toujours être calculés sur la somme due. Le calcul doit tenir* │
     │ *compte des paiements reçus de temps à autre. Ceci s'applique autant aux intérêts antérieurs au* │
     │ *jugement qu'aux intérêts postérieurs au jugement. Annexez une feuille distincte indiquant comment* │
     │ *vous avez calculé le montant total des intérêts antérieurs et postérieurs au jugement.* │
     └───┘

(F) **SUBSEQUENT COSTS** incurred after judgment (including the cost of issuing
     the requested enforcement(s)) $ _____ **7**
     LES DÉPENS SUBSÉQUENTS engagés après le jugement (y compris le $
     coût de la délivrance de la ou des mesures d'exécution forcée demandées)

                                            TOTAL DUE $ _____ **8**
                                            SOLDE DÛ $

SCR 20.04-10-20P (June 1, 2009 / *1ᵉʳ juin 2009*) CSD

Because the calculations on the amount owing after judgment are not always straightforward, and the forms are somewhat less than informative in offering guidance, we have also included a detailed step-by-step example, Example 13.1, for calculating the amount owing on a judgment at any time, with a completed Form 20P, Affidavit for Enforcement Request.

Example 13.1 Affidavit for Enforcement Request
                Scenario

Irene Murphy is a caterer who works out of her home. On December 15, Year 0, Irene catered a large party for Gloria Glitz at her home. The arrangement was that Gloria would give Irene a deposit of $500 in early December (which she did) and give Irene the balance on the date of the party. At the end of the party, Irene presented Gloria with a bill for $3,200 ($3,700 minus the $500 deposit). Gloria did not pay the bill.

After several phone calls to Gloria, and a demand letter from you, you sued Gloria in Small Claims Court. She did not respond, and you got default judgment for $3,200, plus pre-judgment interest and costs on February 16, Year 1. Assume Year 1 is not a leap year. The court also awarded post-judgment interest. Since there were no agreed contract rates, you used the *Courts of Justice Act* rates, which were 4.5% for pre-judgment interest and 6.0% for post-judgment interest. Assume costs were $420.

After receiving a copy of the judgment, Gloria paid Irene $1,200 on February 28, Year 1, and a further $500 on March 15. Since then Irene has received nothing, and she would like you to enforce the judgment. Prepare an Affidavit for Enforcement Request as of April 10, Year 1, to enable Irene to file a Writ of Seizure and Sale of Personal Property. As of April 10, Year 1, there are post-judgment enforcement costs of $100.

Here is how to determine the amounts owing.

Steps
1. From the endorsement record,
   - determine the amount of the judgment debt: $3,200
   - determine the amount of the costs: $420

Example continues....

Example 13.1 (continued)

> - determine the pre-judgment interest from the date
>   the cause of action arose until the day before judg-
>   ment:
>   December 16–February 15 = 62 days
> $3,200 × .045 × 62/365 = $24.46
>
> Judgment total: $3,644.46 (= $3,200 + $420 + $24.46)

2. Enter the judgment debt, pre-judgment interest, and costs
   on Lines A, B, and C on Page 3 of the Affidavit for
   Enforcement Request. Add up the amounts in A and B,
   and enter them on the line for the subtotal. Enter costs
   on Line C.

3. Enter the total amount of payments received from the
   debtor after judgment on Line D:

   > February 28: $1,200
   > March 15: $500
   > Total payments received (Line D): $1,700

4. Post-judgment interest
   Because payments have been made after judgment, as
   noted in #3 above, you have to calculate post-judgment
   interest, adding it to the amount of the judgment until a
   payment is made. Then deduct the payment to create a
   new balance, and begin calculating post-judgment interest
   on the new balance until the next payment is made, and
   so on.

   Note that when you have a changing balance due on
   the judgment, the box on Page 4 tells you to show your
   calculations on a separate sheet. Attach this sheet to the
   affidavit. Write "see attached calculation" on the last line
   of Section E.

   The sheet should be headed, "Schedule A to the
   Affidavit of Irene Murphy, sworn (April 10, Year 1): Cal-
   culation of Post-Judgment Interest Taking into Account
   Payments made".

   Post-judgment interest rate: 6.0% pursuant to ss. 127–9
   of the *Courts of Justice Act*.

   > - February 16–28 = 13 days
   > $3,644.46 × .06 × 13/365 = $7.79
   >
   >   Total owing as of February 28:
   > $3,644.46 + $7.79 = $3,652.25
   >   Less payment of $1,200
   >   Balance as of February 28 = $2,452.25

Example continues....

Example 13.1 (continued)

- March 1–March 15 = 15 days
  $2,452.25 × .06 × 15/365 = $6.05

  Total owing as of March 15:
  $2,452.25 + $6.05 = $2,458.30
  Less payment of $500
  Balance as of March 15 = $1,958.30

- March 16–April 10 = 26 days
  $1,958.30 × .06 × 26/365 = $8.37

  Amount owing on April 10:
  $1,958.30 + $8.37 = $1,966.67

5. Determine post-judgment enforcement costs, if any, and add them together, and enter the total on Line F.

   Post-judgment enforcement costs: $100

6. Add post-judgment enforcement costs to the amount owing on the judgment on April 10, Year 1 = $1,966.67 + $100 = $2,066.67. Enter this amount as "Total Due" on Page 4.

7. Note that subsequent post-judgment interest continues to accrue on the amount owing as of April 10. To calculate the per diem (daily) interest on the amount owing on April 10, use the "Total Due" amount minus post-judgment enforcement costs and multiply it by the post-judgment interest rate multiplied by one day of interest (i.e., 1/365):

   $1,966.67 × .06 × 1/365 = $0.32 per day

   Note that if further payments are received, the per diem post-judgment interest will have to be recalculated on the new balance.

The Affidavit for Enforcement Request is set out in Illustration 13.1.

Certificates of Judgment

Before you use any of the court's enforcement remedies, consider whether you first need to obtain a Certificate of Judgment (Form 20A) from the clerk of the court that gave judgment, directed to the clerk of the court in which you wish to enforce your judgment. As noted earlier, pursuant to Rule 20.04, you will need a Certificate of Judgment to enforce a judgment in a Small Claims Court other than the one that gave the judgment:

ILLUSTRATION 13.1: Affidavit for Enforcement Request (Form 20P)

ONTARIO

Superior Court of Justice
Cour supérieure de justice

Affidavit for Enforcement Request
Affidavit relatif à une demande d'exécution forcée
Form / *Formule* 20P Ont. Reg. No. / *Règl. de l'Ont.* : 258/98

Toronto
Small Claims Court / *Cour des petites créances de*

SC-00-48669-12
Claim No. / *N° de la demande*

47 Sheppard Ave. E., 3rd Fl.
Toronto, ON M2N 5N1
Address / *Adresse*

416-326-3554
Phone number / *Numéro de téléphone*

BETWEEN / *ENTRE*

Irene Murphy
Plaintiff(s)/Creditor(s) / *Demandeur(s)/demanderesse(s)/Créancier(s)/créancière(s)*

and / *et*

Gloria Glitz
Defendant(s)/Debtor(s) / *Défendeur(s)/défenderesse(s)/Débiteur(s)/débitrice(s)*

My name is Irene Murphy
Je m'appelle
(Full name / *Nom et prénoms*)

I live in Toronto, Ontario
J'habite à
(Municipality & province / *Municipalité et province*)

and I swear/affirm that the following is true:
et je déclare sous serment/j'affirme solennellement que les renseignements suivants sont véridiques :

1. **In this action, I am the**
   Dans la présente action, je suis le/la

   (Check one box only. / *Cochez une seule case.*)

   ☒ plaintiff/creditor.
   demandeur/demanderesse/créancier/créancière.

   ☐ representative of the plaintiff(s)/creditor(s).
   représentant(e) du/de la/des demandeur(s)/demanderesse(s)/créancier(s)/créancière(s).

   I make this affidavit in support of a request that the clerk of the court issue the following enforcement process(es):
   Je fais le présent affidavit à l'appui d'une demande visant à enjoindre au greffier du tribunal de délivrer l'acte ou les actes de procédure portant exécution forcée suivants :

   ☐ Certificate of Judgment (Form 20A) to the clerk of the
   Certificat de jugement (formule 20A), au greffier de la Cour des petites créances de
   (Name of court where the judgment is to be filed / *Nom du tribunal où le jugement doit être déposé*)

   Small Claims Court.

   ☒ Writ of Seizure and Sale of Personal Property (Form 20C) directed to the bailiff of
   Bref de saisie-exécution de biens meubles (formule 20C) adressé à l'huissier de la Cour des petites créances de

   Brampton
   (Name of court location / *Emplacement du tribunal*)
   Small Claims Court.

   ☐ Writ of Seizure and Sale of Land (Form 20D) directed to the sheriff of
   Bref de saisie-exécution de biens-fonds (formule 20D) adressé au shérif du/de la
   (Name of county/region in which the enforcement office is located / *Comté/région où est situé le bureau de l'exécution*)

SCR 20.04-10-20P (June 1, 2009 / *1er juin 2009*) CSD

Illustration 13.1 (continued)

FORM / *FORMULE* 20P   PAGE 2   SC-00-48669-12
....
Claim No. / *N° de la demande*

☐ Notice of Garnishment (Form 20E)/Notice of Renewal of Garnishment (Form 20E.1).
Avis de saisie-arrêt (formule 20E)/Avis de renouvellement de la saisie-arrêt (formule 20E.1).

I believe that the garnishee ....
Je crois que le tiers saisi   (Name of garnishee / *Nom du tiers saisi*)

at ....
à/au   (Address of garnishee / *Adresse du tiers saisi*)

is indebted to the debtor or will become indebted to the debtor for the following reasons:
est ou sera redevable d'une dette au débiteur pour les motifs suivants :

The Notice will be served on the debtor ....
L'avis sera signifié au débiteur,   (Name of debtor / *Nom du débiteur/de la débitrice*)

at ....
à/au   (Address of debtor for service / *Adresse du débiteur/de la débitrice aux fins de signification*)

within five days of serving it on the garnishee.
dans les cinq jours qui suivent sa signification au tiers saisi.

☐ Notice of Examination (Form 20H).
Avis d'interrogatoire (formule 20H).

☐ Writ of Delivery (Form 20B).
Bref de délaissement (formule 20B).

☐ Other *(Set out the nature of your request)*:
Autre (Indiquez la nature de votre demande) :

Complete this section if you are requesting a Writ of Delivery.
Remplissez la présente section si vous demandez un bref de délaissement.

2. An order for the delivery of the following personal property:
    Une ordonnance de délaissement des biens meubles suivants :
    (According to the court order, set out a description of the property to be delivered. Identify any marks or serial numbers. Selon l'ordonnance du
    tribunal, donnez la description des biens qui doivent être restitués. Indiquez toute marque d'identification ou tout numéro de série y figurant.)

SCR 20.04-10-20P (June 1, 2009 / *1er juin 2009*) CSD   Continued on next page / *Suite à la page suivante*

* The calculations are set out on p. 507.

Illustration 13.1 (continued)

FORM / *FORMULE* 20P	PAGE 3	SC-00-48669-12
		Claim No. / *N° de la demande*

was made in this action against: ....
a été rendue dans l'action contre :   (Name of person against whom the order was made / *Nom de la personne contre qui*
                                                                                    l'ordonnance a été rendue)

on ...., in the ....
le ....   *à la Cour des petites* (Name of court location where order was made / *Emplacement*
                                                       créances de   *du tribunal où l'ordonnance a été rendue)*

Small Claims Court. Since the above listed personal property has not been delivered, I make this affidavit in
support of a request that the clerk of the court issue a Writ of Delivery (Form 20B) to the bailiff of the
Étant donné que les biens meubles susmentionnés n'ont pas été restitués, je fais le présent affidavit à l'appui
d'une demande visant à enjoindre au greffier du tribunal de délivrer un bref de délaissement (formule 20B) à
l'huissier de la Cour des petites créances de

.... Small Claims Court.
                    (Name of court location / *Emplacement du tribunal)*

Complete this section if you are requesting a Certificate of Judgment, Writ of Seizure
and Sale of Personal Property, Writ of Seizure and Sale of Land, Notice of
Garnishment, Notice of Renewal of Garnishment or Notice of Examination.
Remplissez la présente section si vous demandez un certificat de jugement, un bref de
saisie-exécution de biens meubles, un bref de saisie-exécution de biens-fonds, un avis
de saisie-arrêt, un avis de renouvellement de la saisie-arrêt ou un avis d'interrogatoire.

3. A judgment was made in this action against **Gloria Glitz**
   Un jugement a été rendu dans l'action contre   (Name of debtor(s) / *Nom du/de la/des débiteur(s)/débitrice(s))*

   on **February 16, Yr. 1**   in the
   le   *à la Cour des petites créances de*

   Toronto .... Small Claims Court
        (Name of court where judgment was made / *Nom du tribunal où le jugement a été rendu)*

   for the following sums:
   à l'égard des sommes suivantes :

   (A) **DEBT** $ 3,200.00
       LA CRÉANCE $

   (B) **PRE-JUDGMENT INTEREST** calculated
       LES INTÉRÊTS ANTÉRIEURS AU JUGEMENT calculés

       on the sum of $ .... 3,200.00   at the rate of **4.5**   %
       sur la somme de $ *au taux de*   *pour cent*

       per annum from **Dec. 16, Yr. 0**   to **Feb. 15, Yr. 1** .... ,
       par an du   *au*

       being **62** .... days. $ 24.46
       soit   *jours.* $

                                   SUBTOTAL (Amount of Judgment) $ 3,224.46
                                   TOTAL PARTIEL (montant du jugement) $

   (C) **COSTS** to date of judgment $ 420.00
       LES DÉPENS *à la date du jugement* $

SCR 20.04-10-20P (June 1, 2009 / *1er juin 2009*) CSD   Continued on next page / *Suite à la page suivante*

continues....

Illustration 13.1 (continued)

FORM / *FORMULE* 20P   PAGE 4   SC-00-48669-12

Claim No. / *N° de la demande*

(D) **TOTAL AMOUNT OF PAYMENTS RECEIVED FROM DEBTOR**
after judgment (if any)   (minus) $ 1,700.00
LE MONTANT TOTAL DES PAIEMENTS REÇUS DU   *(moins)* $
DÉBITEUR après le jugement (le cas échéant)

(E) **POST-JUDGMENT INTEREST** to date calculated
LES INTÉRÊTS POSTÉRIEURS AU JUGEMENT à ce jour, calculés

on the sum of $ _____ at the rate of _____ %
sur la somme de   *$ au taux de*   *pour cent*

per annum from _____ to _____ ,
par an du   *au*

                                      22.21
                               (See attached
being _____ days. $ calculations)
soit   *jours.* $

> **NOTE:** Calculation of interest is always on the amount owing from time to time as payments are received. This is true for both pre-judgment and post-judgment interest. Attach a separate sheet setting out how you calculated the total amount of any pre/post-judgment interest.
> **REMARQUE :** *Les intérêts doivent toujours être calculés sur la somme due. Le calcul doit tenir compte des paiements reçus de temps à autre. Ceci s'applique autant aux intérêts antérieurs au jugement qu'aux intérêts postérieurs au jugement. Annexez une feuille distincte indiquant comment vous avez calculé le montant total des intérêts antérieurs et postérieurs au jugement.*

(F) **SUBSEQUENT COSTS** incurred after judgment (including the cost of issuing
the requested enforcement(s)) $ 100.00
LES DÉPENS SUBSÉQUENTS engagés après le jugement (y compris le $
coût de la délivrance de la ou des mesures d'exécution forcée demandées)

                       TOTAL DUE $ 2,066.67
                       SOLDE DÛ $

Sworn/Affirmed before me at **Toronto**
Déclaré sous serment/Affirmé   (Municipality / *municipalité*)
solennellement devant moi à

in **Ontario**
en/à/au   (Province, state or country / *province, État ou pays*)

on **April 10, Yr. 1**   **"I.M.A. Signer"**
le   Commissioner for taking affidavits
                      Commissaire aux affidavits
                      (Type or print name below if signature is illegible.)
                      (Dactylographiez le nom ou écrivez-le en caractères d'imprimerie ci-dessous si la signature est illisible.)

"Irene Murphy"
Signature
(This form is to be signed in front of a lawyer, justice of the peace, notary public or commissioner for taking affidavits.)
(La présente formule doit être signée en présence d'un avocat, d'un juge de paix, d'un notaire ou d'un commissaire aux affidavits.)

WARNING: IT IS AN OFFENCE UNDER THE *CRIMINAL CODE* TO KNOWINGLY SWEAR OR AFFIRM A FALSE AFFIDAVIT.
AVERTISSEMENT :   *FAIRE SCIEMMENT UN FAUX AFFIDAVIT CONSTITUE UNE INFRACTION AU* CODE CRIMINEL.

SCR 20.04-10-20P (June 1, 2009 / *1er juin 2009*) CSD

continues....

Illustration 13.1 (continued)

SCHEDULE "A"
TO THE AFFIDAVIT OF IRENE MURPHY
SWORN APRIL 10, YR. 1
CALCULATION OF POST-JUDGMENT INTEREST TAKING INTO
ACCOUNT PAYMENTS MADE

Judgment, including costs and pre-judgment interest	$3,644.46		
Post-Judgment Interest			
(a) Feb. 16–Feb. 28, Yr. 1 = 13 days $3,644.46 × .06 × 13/365 =		+ $7.79	$7.79
Less payment of $1,200		– $1,200	
Balance as of February 28, Yr. 1 =		$2,452.25	
(b) Mar. 1–Mar. 15, Yr. 1 = 15 days $2,452.25 × .06 × 15/365 =		+ $6.05	$6.05
Less payment of $500		– $500	
Balance as of Mar. 15, Yr. 1 =		$1,958.30	
(c) Mar. 16–Apr. 10, Yr. 1 = 26 days $1,958.30 × .06 × 26/365 =		+ $8.37	$8.37
Amount owing on April 10, Yr. 1 $1,958.30 + $8.37 = $1,966.67		$1,966.67	
Total Post-Judgment Interest			$22.21

20.04(1)   If there is default under an order for the payment or recovery of money, the clerk shall, at the creditor's request, supported by an affidavit for enforcement request (Form 20P) stating the amount still owing, issue a certificate of judgment (Form 20A) to the clerk at the court location specified by the creditor.

(2) The certificate of judgment shall state,
(a) the date of the order and the amount awarded;
(b) the rate of post-judgment interest payable; and
(c) the amount owing, including post-judgment interest.

You will also need to file an Affidavit for Enforcement Request (Form 20P) to show how much is owing on the judgment at the time you file to enforce. If you look at the Certificate of Judgment (Form 20A), you will see that the information required to complete the "Judgment was made for the following sums" section on Page 2 is also required in the Affidavit for Enforcement Request. Therefore, once you complete the affidavit, you need only transfer the relevant amounts to the relevant lines on Page 2 of the Certificate of Judgment. See Page 3 of the Affidavit for Enforcement Request (Illustration 13.1) sworn by Irene Murphy in the previous step-by-step example and Page 2 of the Certificate of Judgment set out in Illustration 13.2. If the defendant is listed on the claim as having a second name (an aka name), ensure that the judgment has both names on it.

Examination Hearing

Immediately upon getting a judgment, the creditor, in addition to immediately filing Writs of Seizure and Sale, should, as a passive enforcement strategy, consider if he or she has enough information to effectively enforce the judgment. Here, a credit report or information from the creditor may be enough to find the debtor and assets to enforce against. But if that is not the case and you know very little about the judgment debtor's financial situation, an examination hearing, also known as an examination in aid of execution, also known as a judgment debtor examination, may be in order. Rule 20.10 governs examination hearings:

> 20.10(1) If there is default under an order for the payment or recovery of money, the clerk of a court in the territorial division in which the debtor or other person to be examined resides or carries on business shall, at the creditor's request, issue a notice of examination (Form 20H) directed to the debtor or other person.
>
> (2) The creditor's request shall be accompanied by,
> (a) an affidavit for enforcement request (Form 20P) setting out,
>   (i) the date of the order and the amount awarded,
>   (ii) the territorial division in which the order was made,
>   (iii) the rate of post-judgment interest payable,
>   (iv) the total amount of any payments received since the order was granted, and
>   (v) the amount owing, including post-judgment interest; and
> (b) a certificate of judgment (Form 20A), if the order was made in another territorial jurisdiction.

The purpose of the examination is to allow you to question the debtor on his or her assets and means to see what sources of income you can garnish or what assets may be available for seizure and sale. You may also question the debtor on his or her debts, liabilities, and expenses. This will give you some idea of your chances of successfully finding unencumbered assets that you can seize, but it also gives you information that will be useful in making arrangements with a debtor to pay off the judgment by instalments on an instalment payment order or a consolidation order. In the course of questioning the debtor, you may

ILLUSTRATION 13.2: Certificate of Judgment (Form 20A)

ONTARIO

Superior Court of Justice
Cour supérieure de justice

Certificate of Judgment
Certificat de jugement
Form / *Formule* 20A Ont. Reg. No. / *Régl. de l'Ont.* : 258/98

Seal / *Sceau*

Toronto
Small Claims Court / *Cour des petites créances de*

SC-00-48669-12
Claim No. / *Nº de la demande*

47 Sheppard Ave. E., 3rd Fl.
Toronto, ON M2N 5N1
Address / *Adresse*

416-326-3554
Phone number / *Numéro de téléphone*

BETWEEN / *ENTRE*

Irene Murphy

Creditor(s) / *Créancier(s)/créancière(s)*

and / *et*

Gloria Glitz

Debtor(s) / *Débiteur(s)/débitrice(s)*

A judgment was made in this action on   Feburary 16, Yr. 1   , in the
Un jugement a été rendu dans la présente action le   , *à la*

Toronto Small Claims Court
(Name of court where judgment was made / *Nom de la cour où le jugement a été rendu*)

against / *contre*

Last name of debtor, or name of company / *Nom de famille du débiteur/de la débitrice ou nom de la compagnie*		
Glitz		
First name / *Premier prénom*	Second name / *Deuxième prénom*	Third name / *Troisième prénom*
Gloria		
Address / *Adresse*		

Last name of debtor, or name of company / *Nom de famille du débiteur/de la débitrice ou nom de la compagnie*		
First name / *Premier prénom*	Second name / *Deuxième prénom*	Third name / *Troisième prénom*
Address / *Adresse*		

Last name of debtor, or name of company / *Nom de famille du débiteur/de la débitrice ou nom de la compagnie*		
First name / *Premier prénom*	Second name / *Deuxième prénom*	Third name / *Troisième prénom*
Address / *Adresse*		

☐ Additional debtor(s) and also known as names are listed on attached Form 1A.1.
Le ou les débiteur(s) additionnel(s) et le ou les noms sous lesquels les débiteurs sont également connus sont mentionnés sur la formule 1A.1 ci-jointe.

SCR 20.04-20A (September 1, 2010 / *1er septembre 2010*) CSD

continues....

Illustration 13.2 (continued)

FORM / *FORMULE* 20A   PAGE 2   SC-00-48669-12
                                                          Claim No. / *N° de la demande*

Judgment was made for the following sums:
Un jugement a été rendu à l'égard des sommes suivantes :

(A) **AMOUNT OF JUDGMENT** (debt and pre-judgment interest) $ 3,224.46
    LE MONTANT DU JUGEMENT (créance et intérêts antérieurs au jugement) $

(B) **COSTS** to date of judgment $ 420.00
    LES DÉPENS à la date du jugement $

Post-judgment interest continues to accrue at **6.0** .... % per annum.
Les intérêts postérieurs au jugement continuent   (Interest rate /   % *par an.*
à courir au taux de   *Taux d'intérêt*)

April 10, Yr. 1   "I. M. Clerk"
                                                (Signature of clerk / *Signature du greffier*)

TO THE CLERK OF THE Brampton   **SMALL CLAIMS COURT:**
AU GREFFIER DE LA COUR DES PETITES   (Name of court to where the judgment is to be filed
CRÉANCES DE   / *Nom du tribunal où le jugement doit être déposé*)

The person requesting this certificate is Irene Murphy
La personne qui demande le présent certificat est   (Name of party requesting certificate / *Nom de la partie qui demande le certificat*)

20 Gershman Way, Toronto, ON M5R 1P6
         (Address of party requesting certificate / *Adresse de la partie qui demande le certificat*)

SCR 20.04-20A (September 1, 2010 / *1er septembre 2010*) CSD

Note: See Example 13.1 on p. 507 for the calculation of the "Judgment was made for the following sums" section.

also ask questions to see if the debtor has been transferring assets to relatives, or selling off assets, or engaging in other fraudulent transfers. Generally, any question relevant to the enforcement of the judgment is permitted, which gives the judgment creditor a great deal of leeway in asking questions.

The judgment debtor, under Rule 20.10(4.1), has a duty, once served with a notice of examination, to assemble information on the matters to be examined, including particulars of his or her income, property, debts, and the disposal of property (i.e., matters generally set out in Rule 20.10(4)):

> 20.10(4) The debtor, any other persons to be examined and any witnesses whose evidence the court considers necessary may be examined in relation to,
> (a) the reason for nonpayment;
> (b) the debtor's income and property;
> (c) the debts owed to and by the debtor;
> (d) the disposal the debtor has made of any property either before or after the order was made;
> (e) the debtor's present, past and future means to satisfy the order;
> (f) whether the debtor intends to obey the order or has any reason for not doing so; and
> (g) any other matter pertinent to the enforcement of the order.
>
> (4.1) A person who is served with a notice of examination shall,
> (a) inform himself or herself about the matters mentioned in subrule (4) and be prepared to answer questions about them; and
> (b) in the case of an examination of a debtor who is an individual, complete a financial information form (Form 20I) and,
> (i) serve it on the creditor requesting the examination, but not file it with the court, and
> (ii) provide a copy of it to the judge presiding at the examination hearing.

The examination takes place in a courtroom, but it may not be open to the public. Sometimes examinations are held in a room adjoining the courtroom. Rule 20.10(6) states that the examination is to be conducted under oath and will be recorded:

> 20.10(6) The examination shall be,
> (a) held in the absence of the public, unless the court orders otherwise;
> (b) conducted under oath; and
> (c) recorded.

Under Rule 1.07(1.1) an examination in aid of execution can be carried out via video conference.

A judge oversees the examination. Where the court has referees, a referee rather than a judge may supervise the examination. A judge or referee may take part in putting questions to the judgment debtor or guide the judgment creditor in asking questions. He or she may also make suggestions informally with respect to settlement, the possibility of instalment payments, or, where applicable, a consolidation order.

If you are to examine a judgment debtor, you do not need to re-invent the wheel in framing your questions. In the past, the Law Society's Bar Admission Course had published an outline of questions to be asked of individuals or representatives of corporations for use on judgment debtor examinations. A question outline similar to the Bar Admission course one appears in Figure 13.2. In addition, if the judgment debtor is an individual, he or she is supposed to provide you with a Financial Information Form (Form 20I), setting out monthly income and expenses, debts, and the value of assets. According to Rule 20.10(4.2), the judgment debtor is to bring a copy of the form and documents to support the information in the form to the court.

> 20.10(4.2) A debtor required under clause (4.1)(b) to complete a financial information form (Form 20I) shall bring such documents to the examination hearing as are necessary to support the information that he or she provides in the financial information form.

You can use this information to further question the debtor and as a basis for settlement and determination of an order to pay by instalments. If you are examining someone on behalf of a corporate judgment debtor, you can find a question outline in Figure 13.3.

A debtor cannot prevent a creditor from suing, but he or she may not respond to the suit with the result that the creditor obtains a default judgment. In the silence from the debtor that often follows this event, the creditor may serve a Notice of Examination. If the debtor ignored the claim, he or she may ignore this, too. Or the judgment debtor may show up and refuse to answer questions, or give evasive, long-winded answers, or otherwise misbehave. Much of Rule 20.10, which governs judgment debtor examinations, focuses on the steps to be taken to compel cooperation and obedience from the judgment debtor, with incarceration for contempt as the ultimate "persuader".

Procedure for Examination of Judgment Debtor

Rule 20.10 governs the procedure for examinations. In most cases, an examination in aid of execution is held after a judgment has been obtained. Note, however, that Rule 20.10(1) states that an examination may be held "[i]f there is a default under an order for the payment or recovery of money". Therefore, any party, or even a non-party, who has an outstanding order in his or her favour may request an examination

FIGURE 13.2: Questions Used in Examining an Individual Debtor

Date of judgment: _____

Date Writ of Seizure and Sale filed: _____

Date Writ of Seizure and Sale of Land filed: _____

Total owed as of today: _____

_____

I.   PERSONAL DETAILS

A. Personal History

Full name: _____ Birth date: _____

Telephone: _____ Cell: _____

E-mail: _____

Residence address: _____

Do you ever use any other name(s)? _____

If so, what name(s)? _____

Do you have any identification — for example, a driver's licence? _____

Spousal Status

Married: _____ Common Law: _____ Single: _____

Divorced: _____ Living Apart: _____

Family Information

Children: _____ No.: _____ Other Dependants: _____

Total family group equals _____ persons.

B. Employment Status

Unemployed: _____ Employed: _____ Self-Employed: _____

Full-Time or Part-Time? _____

What is your occupation? _____

Who is your superior? _____

Name and address of employer: _____

Position: _____

Present Wages (hourly rate or salary): _____

Overtime? — hours per week/month: _____ rate: _____

How long have you held this position? _____

When are you paid (obtain day of week)? _____

Bonus schemes (when paid, etc.): _____

Commissions: _____

Are you in any way related to your employer? _____

continues....

Figure 13.2 (continued)

Previous Employers:

Name: _____ Address: _____

How Long? _____

Have you ever been in business on your own? _____

When? _____ Where? _____

Inventory? _____ What? _____

Where kept? _____

Have you ever had any employees? _____

Have you been involved in any partnership? _____

When? _____ Where? _____

Have you ever carried on business under any trade or business name? _____

If so, what name? _____

Inventory? _____ What? _____

Where kept? _____

Are you an Officer or Director of any corporation? _____

If so, which corporation(s)? _____

Do you have other jobs? _____

If so, where? (*name and address*) _____

If unemployed, are you subject to recall? _____

— When? _____

— Are you receiving EI? _____

    Lump sum or other severance amount? _____

II.   DETAILS OF PLACE OF RESIDENCE

A. Type of Accommodation

Description of property (i.e., 2-storey, garage, number of bedrooms):

_____

Municipal address: _____

Legal description (Lot + plan #): _____

Do you own it? _____

continues....

Figure 13.2 (continued)

B. If Residence Is Owned

Describe ownership (absolute, beneficial, joint tenant, or tenant in common).

_____

Date of purchase: _____

— reporting letter: _____

Amount paid: _____

— present value: _____

— air conditioning: _____

— type of heating (oil, gas, or coal): _____

— number of square feet per floor: _____

— number of bathrooms: _____

— unfinished areas: _____

Do you own the furniture? _____ Value: $ _____

Any notices to repossess? _____

Who lives there? _____

Particulars of mortgage, including

— amount: _____

— balance owing: _____

— terms: _____

C. If Residence Is Not Owned

Name of building's owner: _____

Address: _____

Do you pay rent? _____ How much? $ _____

When is rent due? _____

Is landlord related to you? _____

Is rent paid up to date? _____

To whom do you give the rent? _____

Do you pay rent by cash or cheque? _____

Who signs the cheque? _____

Is there a lease? _____

Who signed the lease? _____

Rent receipts? _____

continues....

Figure 13.2 (continued)

III.   DETAILS ABOUT DEBTOR'S SPOUSE / COMMON LAW PARTNER

Full Name: _____

Birth Name: _____

Address: _____

Date of Birth: _____ Telephone: _____

Employment Status

Unemployed: _____ Self-employed: _____ Part-Time: _____

Name of Employer: _____

Address: _____

Position: _____

Salary: ($) _____

When paid: _____

How long has he/she worked there? _____

Where did he/she last work? _____

Name: _____

Address: _____

Wages/salary: ($) _____

IV.   CHILDREN — DETAILS

	Name	Age	Address	Employed	School
1.				Yes/No	Yes/No
2.				Yes/No	Yes/No
3.				Yes/No	Yes/No
4.				Yes/No	Yes/No
5.				Yes/No	Yes/No

continues....

Figure 13.2 (continued)

V. **DETAILS OF PERSONAL BUDGET**
  (CHECK FINANCIAL INFORMATION FORM, FORM 20I)

Sources of Income and Expense

Income (per Month)		*Expenses (per Month)*	
1. Weekly Salary	$	1. Groceries	$
2. Weekly Salary	$	2. Meals Out	$
3. Room and Board from Others	$	3. Housing:	
		— Rent or Mortgage	$
4. Pensions	$	— Taxes	$
5. Employment Insurance	$	— Fuel	$
6. Workers' Compensation	$	— Telephone	$
7. Annuities	$	— Cable/Internet	$
8. Inheritances	$	4. Transportation	$
9. Other	$	5. Insurance	$
		6. Education and Recreation	$
		7. Medical and Dental	$
		8. Bank Loans	$
		9. Other	$
Total $			$

continues....

Figure 13.2 (continued)

VI.   ASSETS OTHER THAN INCOME

A. Real Estate

Other than your current residence, do you own any other real estate? _____
If yes,

Street Address	City	Tenants?	Rent $
1.			
2.			
3.			

(Obtain municipal address and legal description.)

If not, when did you last own a real estate? _____

How did you transfer it? _____

When? _____ To whom? _____ How much? $ _____

Who was the lawyer acting on your behalf? _____

B. Vehicles

1. Do you own (and/or lease) a car or truck? _____ (Yes/No)

   Make _____ Year _____ Model _____

   For each:
   Licence No. _____ V.I.N. _____ Plate No. _____

   Where is it kept? _____

   What use is made of it? _____

   Value: ($) _____

   How much do you still owe on it? $ _____

   To whom? _____ (Name)

   Address: _____

   What is the vehicle worth now? $ _____

   What type of security is there for this debt? _____

2. If you do not own an automobile, do you drive an automobile? ____ (Yes/No)
   (If yes, ask who owns the car and above particulars.)

   When did you last own an automobile? _____

   To whom did you sell it? _____

   For what amount? $ _____

   Were there any liens on the car? _____

   To whom? _____

continues....

Figure 13.2 (continued)

3. Do you own, lease, or have the use of a tractor? A snowmobile? An airplane? A motorcycle? A motor boat? _____ (Yes/No) (If yes to any one or more, ask particulars above.)

C. Bank Accounts

1. Do you have any bank accounts or trust company accounts? _____ (Yes/No) If yes, give the following information:

	Bank	Address	Type and account number	Balance
a.	....	....	....	....
b.	....	....	....	....
c.	....	....	....	....
d.	....	....	....	....

(Obtain statements and entry books if possible.)

If no, when did you last have a bank account? _____

Where? _____

When did you close it? _____

When did you last have any claim to or interest in any bank account in any name? _____

When did you last write a cheque? _____

To whom was that cheque payable? _____

Amount: $ _____

What was it given for? _____

Have you ever had the right of access to any safe deposit box? _____

Box No.: _____ Bank: _____

Address: _____

When was the last time you had a safe deposit box? _____

Do you have any term deposits? _____

When was the last time you had a term deposit? _____

continues....

Figure 13.2 (continued)

D. Specific Assets

		Yes	No	Describe
1.	Mortgages	....	....	....
2.	Promissory notes/IOUs	....	....	....
3.	Loan agreements	....	....	....
4.	Other security for payment of money	....	....	....
5.	Government bonds	....	....	....
6.	Other bonds	....	....	....
7.	Common stock in public and private corporations	....	....	....
8.	Preferred stock in public and private corporations	....	....	....
9.	RRSP	....	....	....
10.	RHOSP	....	....	....
11.	RDSP	....	....	....
12.	RESP	....	....	....
13.	Mutual funds	....	....	....
14.	Television set	....	....	....
15.	Refrigerator	....	....	....
16.	Stove	....	....	....
17.	Washer and dryer	....	....	....
18.	Furniture	....	....	....
19.	Computers	....	....	....
20.	Fur coats	....	....	....
21.	Jewellery	....	....	....
22.	Silver- or goldware	....	....	....
23.	Works of art	....	....	....
24.	Horses and/or boats	....	....	....
25.	Any interest in any patent, copyright, process, formula, invention, or royalties	....	....	....
26.	Pensions	....	....	....
27.	Lottery tickets	....	....	....
28.	Coins and stamps	....	....	....
29.	Liquor	....	....	....

continues....

Figure 13.2 (continued)

E. Life Insurance

Do you carry life insurance on yourself? _____ (Yes/No)
(Check whether term, group, or whole life.)

If yes, please give following information:

Name of Insurance Company	Policy No.	Amount of Policy	Beneficiary	Premium	Who Pays Premium	Cash Surrender Value
1.						
2.						
3.						
4.						

Do you carry life insurance on your wife or any person in which you have an interest? _____

If yes, please give following information:

Name of Insurance Company	Policy No.	Amount of Policy	Beneficiary	Premium	Who Pays Premium	Cash Surrender Value
1.						
2.						
3.						
4.						

F. Moneys Owing to Defendant

Is there money owing to you? _____ (Yes/No)

If yes, give the following information:

Name of Debtor	Address	Amount	Security Held
1.			
2.			

G. Miscellaneous

1. How much money are you carrying right now? $ _____
2. Have you any income from any other source? _____
3. Have you made a will? _____
4. Have you any interest as beneficiary, or otherwise under any will, trust, or in any estate? _____

continues....

Figure 13.2 (continued)

5. Have you ever been a party to a trust agreement or other trust instrument? Did you at any time put any money or property of any kind in trust for yourself or anyone else?

   _____

6. Have you received any money or property of any kind under any will or by inheritance or from any estate? _____

7. Do you have any business deals pending which will likely give you money?

   _____

   _____

VII. ASSETS OF SPOUSE AND CHILDREN

A. Real Estate

Does your spouse own any real estate? _____ (Yes/No)

Do your children own any real estate? _____ (Yes/No)

Locations

	Street Address	City	Tenants
1.	....	....	....
2.	....	....	....
3.	....	....	....

When did they last own real estate? (Give details above.)

B. Automobiles

1. Does your spouse own an automobile? _____ (Yes/No)

   Make _____ Year _____ Model _____

   Licence No. _____ V.I.N. _____ Plate No. _____

   Where is it kept? _____

   What use is made of it? _____

   How much does he/she still owe on it? $ _____

   To whom? _____ (Name)

   Address: _____

   Equity in owned auto? _____

   What type of security is there for this debt? _____

   Does he/she own any other cars? _____

2. If he/she does not own an automobile, does he/she drive an automobile? _____ (Yes/No) (If yes, ask who owns the car and above particulars.)

   continues....

Figure 13.2 (continued)

3. When did he/she last own an automobile? _____ (Date)

    To whom did he/she sell it? _____ (Name)

    Telephone: _____

    Amount: $ _____ Security taken: _____

C. Bank Accounts

1. Do your spouse or children have any bank accounts? _____ (Yes/No)

    If yes, give the following information:

	Bank	Address	Type and Account Number	Balance
a.	....	....	....	....
b.	....	....	....	....
c.	....	....	....	....
d.	....	....	....	....

    Do you give them any money to put in the account(s)? _____

    If yes, how much? _____

    If no, where did they get it? _____

VIII. LIST OF CREDITORS

Present debts (approximate) $ _____

Please list your debts for me, giving the following information:

	Name of Creditor	Address	Amount	Security Held	Judgment
1.	....	....	....	....	....
2.	....	....	....	....	....
3.	....	....	....	....	....
4.	....	....	....	....	....
5.	....	....	....	....	....
6.	....	....	....	....	....
7.	....	....	....	....	....
8.	....	....	....	....	....
9.	....	....	....	....	....
10.	....	....	....	....	....

continues....

Figure 13.2 (continued)

Give details of payments to other creditors:

Who? _____

How much? _____

When? _____

Why? _____

What is the cause of your financial difficulty? Explain briefly: _____

_____

1. Do you hold property in trust for anyone else? (particulars)

   _____

2. During the past year did you guarantee anyone's debt?

   _____

3. When did you last apply for or obtain a loan at any bank, finance company, or other lending institution or from any non-lender, corporation, or person whatsoever?

   _____

4. Are you holding in your name or possession for the benefit of anyone else any property of any kind, whether real property, personal property or otherwise?

   _____

5. Is anyone holding your property in trust for you?

   _____

_____

IX. MISCELLANEOUS MATTERS

1. Do you have any judgment, or interest in any judgment, in your favour?

   _____

2. Do you have any claim of any kind against anyone? _____

3. Do you have any interest of any kind in any mortgage or any lease or interest in any leasehold on any real or personal property? _____

4. Are you a party to any agreement of any kind with anyone? _____

5. Are you a party to any action now pending in the courts? _____

6. Have you filed your income tax return for the past two years? _____ (Obtain a copy.) Any tax refunds? _____

7. Have you ever been bankrupt? (If so, obtain particulars.)

   _____

8. When did you take your last vacation? _____

continues....

Figure 13.2 (continued)

X. DISPOSAL OF ASSETS

1. Have you sold any of the assets you have identified from the debt date to present? _____

2. Have you transferred any of the assets you have identified from the debt date to present? _____
   (A debtor should be able to account for every asset that he/she had at the debt date and every asset he/she acquired from that date to the present.)

3. Have you allowed anyone to use your land or property free of charge? For a nominal charge? _____

4. Have you assigned or transferred any of your property to anyone by way of security? _____

XI. PROPOSED SETTLEMENT

The amount owing to our client is $ _____ . Is there any possibility that you may be able to get the money together to pay this debt? _____ (Yes/No)

If yes: When? _____ What terms? _____

Suggested payments: $ _____ per week, month; payments to be made starting _____ .

What arrangements have you made for paying this judgment?

_____

Why has the judgment not been paid? _____

Source: Adapted from F. Bennett, *Collections*, 5th ed. (Aurora: Carswell, 2003).

**FIGURE 13.3: Questions Used in Examining an Officer/
Representative of a Corporate Judgment Debtor**

I.   INTRODUCTION

1. Name of the officer.
2. Officer's address.
3. Is this the notice of appointment that was served upon you?
4. Are you aware of the amount owing to his creditor as a result of judgment?
5. What is your position with the company?
6. How long have you been with the company?

II.   MINUTE BOOK

1. Location of minute book.
2. Would you please make minute books available to me if I want to examine them? (Yes/No)

III.   FINANCIAL STATEMENTS

1. For present period: books of accounting, general ledger, etc.
2. For five years prior.
3. Particulars of revenues.
4. Particulars of expenses.
5. Particulars of loans, advances, or dividends to shareholders.
6. Salaries paid to officers and directors.
7. Any extraordinary expenses or revenues from time action commenced.
8. Has the company during the past five years returned any goods to creditors or paid creditors out of the normal course of business?
9. Copy of bank statements.
10. Who are the company's auditors/accountants/solicitors?

IV.   PARTICULARS OF CORPORATION

1. Date of incorporation.
2. What kinds of shares were originally issued by the company? What was their original value? How many shares were originally issued?
3. Who were the original shareholders?
4. Who are the present shareholders?
5. Could you please give me the particulars of the transfer of shares?
6. Were the shares paid for in full?
7. Who were the original directors?
8. Who are the present directors?
9. Who were the original officers?
10. Who are the present officers?
11. Where is the company's head office?
12. Are the premises owned or leased?
13. Were premises ever owned by the company?
14. Could you please describe the type of business?
15. What was the cause for financial difficulties?

continues....

Figure 13.3 (continued)

V.   CREDITORS OF COMPANY
1. Are there any other creditors?
2. What is the status of their claims — that is, do they have secured claims or judgments?
3. Do any creditors have any form of security on the company's assets?
4. If so, what type, when given, and circumstances at time when given?
5. Please provide a list of all the creditors.
6. Does the company owe the bank any money, either on a loan or overdraft?
7. How does the bank secure its indebtedness, i.e., assignment of accounts receivable, section 178 security, personal guarantees, or security agreement?
8. Are there any mortgages or liens against automobiles, equipment, furniture, trade fixtures, or general equipment or inventory of the company?
9. Are any of the company's goods taken on consignment or sold on consignment?

VI.   ASSETS OF COMPANY
1. Furniture.
2. Office and plant equipment.
3. Vehicles — type, when acquired, how used.
4. Trade fixtures.
5. Inventory.
6. Accounts receivable — obtain list.
7. Lease for office or other leases owned by company.
8. Any holdings outside Canada.
9. If so, with whom did the company deal?
10. Does the company own any bonds?
11. Are any mortgages payable to the company?
12. Are any loan agreements payable to the company?
13. Are any securities payable to the company?
14. Does the company own any common stock in other corporations?
15. Does the company own any other personal property — that is, TV or refrigerator?
16. Does the company own any real property?
17. Does the company own any other property?

Source: Adapted from F. Bennett, *Collections*, 5th ed. (Aurora: Carswell, 2003).

in aid of execution to assist in enforcing the order. For example, one of the parties may have received a costs order in his or her favour at a motion or at a settlement conference. In some cases, a witness who was improperly summonsed to court may have been awarded costs under Rule 18.03(8). He or she may request an examination hearing to assist in the enforcement of this costs order. Also, in some cases, examinations may be requested under Rule 20 to assist in enforcing orders of other courts and tribunals. Orders made by the Ontario Rental Housing Tribunal are often brought to the Small Claims Court for enforcement. Certain criminal and provincial offences court orders may also be enforced in the Small Claims Court, as provided under s. 68 of the *Provincial Offences Act*, s. 19 of the *Statutory Powers of Procedures Act*, and s. 74.1(1) of the Canadian *Criminal Code*. You may examine a judgment debtor, or a party who has been ordered to pay money, in a court in the territorial division where the debtor resides or carries on business. The court in the division located closest to where the debtor resides or carries on business should be selected. The creditor must do the following to conduct a judgment debtor examination:

- As usual, prepare an Affidavit for Enforcement Request (Form 20P), indicating details of the judgment.

- If the examination is to be held in a court other than the court that gave the judgment, obtain a Certificate of Judgment (Form 20A). The fee for a certificate of judgment, as of July 17, 2013, is $19.

- Prepare a Notice of Examination (Form 20H) to be issued by the clerk. Obtain a date, time, and courtroom from the clerk prior to preparing the notice. Be sure the total outstanding on the judgment is the same as in the Affidavit for Enforcement Request. Note that under Rule 20.10(5.1), in some places the debtor may attend by video conference in accordance with Rule 1.07. The debtor must file a Request for Telephone or Video Conference (Form 1B) with the court, setting out the reasons for the request.

- If the judgment debtor is an individual, be sure to attach a blank Financial Information Form (Form 20I).

- Pay the prescribed court fee for the examination. The fee, as of July 17, 2013, is $35.

- Serve the Notice of Examination (Form 20H) and, if required, the Financial Information Form (Form 20I) on the debtor or the person to be examined in the case of a partnership or corporation. Service is covered by Rule 20.10(3):

    20.10(3) The notice of examination shall be served in accordance with subrules 8.01(10), (11) and (12).

Under Rule 8.01(10), the notice must be personally served on the debtor or by an alternative to personal service. In accordance with Rule 8.01(12)(a), the Notice of Examination and the Financial Information Form, if applicable, must be served at least 30 days before the examination date.

• File the notice and affidavit of service at least three days before the examination in accordance with Rule 8.01(12)(b).

Rule 20.10(5) sets out who may be examined on behalf of the judgment debtor. In the case of a corporation, you may examine an officer or a director. In the case of a partnership or sole proprietorship, you may examine the sole proprietor or any partner.

> 20.10(5) An officer or director of a corporate debtor, or, in the case of a debtor that is a partnership or sole proprietorship, the sole proprietor or any partner, may be examined on the debtor's behalf in relation to the matters set out in subrule (4).

The completed Affidavit for Enforcement Request (Form 20P), the Notice of Examination (Form 20H), and the Financial Information Form (Form 20I), required to conduct a judgment debtor examination, for *Oryx v. Foot* are shown in Illustrations 13.3, 13.4, and 13.5. (Note: For the rest of the enforcement documents in the *Oryx* case, starting with Illustration 13.3, assume that no instalment payments were made after the judgment was granted.)

Examination of a Person Other Than the Judgment Debtor

Rule 20.10, titled as Examination of Debtor or Other Person, provides also for the examination of someone other than the debtor. Throughout Rule 20.10, the words "the debtor or other person" are used. Accordingly, if you cannot find the debtor, or the debtor is not cooperating in providing answers to the questions asked, the court will permit the examination of someone else.

Service must be by personal service or by an alternative to personal service. If the judgment debtor is a corporation, you may serve an officer or director of the company, where the person to be examined resides, regardless of where the company is located. If the judgment debtor is a partnership, you may serve and examine any of the partners where they reside. If the judgment debtor is a sole proprietorship, you may examine the proprietor where he or she resides. You may obtain the names of officers and directors, partners or sole proprietors, as the case may be, by conducting an online corporate or business name search using the techniques discussed in Chapter 3.

ILLUSTRATION 13.3: Affidavit for Enforcement Request (Form 20P) for *Oryx v. Foot*

ONTARIO

Superior Court of Justice
Cour supérieure de justice

Affidavit for Enforcement Request
Affidavit relatif à une demande d'exécution forcée
Form / Formule 20P Ont. Reg. No. / Règl. de l'Ont. : 258/98

Toronto
Small Claims Court / *Cour des petites créances de*

SC-00-47669-00
Claim No. / N° de la demande

47 Sheppard Ave. E., 3rd Fl.
Toronto, ON M2N 5N1
Address / *Adresse*

416-326-3554
Phone number / *Numéro de téléphone*

BETWEEN / *ENTRE*

Albert Oryx
Plaintiff(s)/Creditor(s) / *Demandeur(s)/demanderesse(s)/Créancier(s)/créancière(s)*

and / *et*

Ophelia Foot
Defendant(s)/Debtor(s) / *Défendeur(s)/défenderesse(s)/Débiteur(s)/débitrice(s)*

My name is Peter Paralegal
Je m'appelle
(Full name / *Nom et prénoms*)

I live in Toronto, Ontario
J'habite à
(Municipality & province / *Municipalité et province*)

and I swear/affirm that the following is true:
et je déclare sous serment/j'affirme solennellement que les renseignements suivants sont véridiques :

1. **In this action, I am the**
    Dans la présente action, je suis le/la

    (Check one box only. / *Cochez une seule case.*)

    ☐ plaintiff/creditor.
    demandeur/demanderesse/créancier/créancière.

    ☒ representative of the plaintiff(s)/creditor(s).
    représentant(e) du/de la/des demandeur(s)/demanderesse(s)/créancier(s)/créancière(s).

    I make this affidavit in support of a request that the clerk of the court issue the following enforcement process(es):
    Je fais le présent affidavit à l'appui d'une demande visant à enjoindre au greffier du tribunal de délivrer l'acte ou les actes de procédure portant exécution forcée suivants :

    ☐ Certificate of Judgment (Form 20A) to the clerk of the _____
    Certificat de jugement (formule 20A), au greffier   (Name of court where the judgment is to be filed / *Nom du tribunal*
    de la Cour des petites créances de   *où le jugement doit être déposé*)

    Small Claims Court.

    ☐ Writ of Seizure and Sale of Personal Property (Form 20C) directed to the bailiff of
    Bref de saisie-exécution de biens meubles (formule 20C) adressé à l'huissier de la Cour des petites créances de

    _____ Small Claims Court.
    (Name of court location / *Emplacement du tribunal*)

    ☐ Writ of Seizure and Sale of Land (Form 20D) directed to the sheriff of _____
    Bref de saisie-exécution de biens-fonds (formule 20D) adressé   (Name of county/region in which the
    au shérif du/de la   enforcement office is located / *Comté/région où
                                                                        est situé le bureau de l'exécution*)

SCR 20.04-10-20P (June 1, 2009 / *1er juin 2009*) CSD

continues....

Illustration 13.3 (continued)

FORM / *FORMULE* 20P   **PAGE 2**   SC-00-47669-00
                                                                   Claim No. / *N° de la demande*

☐ Notice of Garnishment (Form 20E)/Notice of Renewal of Garnishment (Form 20E.1).
   Avis de saisie-arrêt (formule 20E)/Avis de renouvellement de la saisie-arrêt (formule 20E.1).

I believe that the garnishee ....
Je crois que le tiers saisi   (Name of garnishee / *Nom du tiers saisi*)

at ....
à/au   (Address of garnishee / *Adresse du tiers saisi*)

is indebted to the debtor or will become indebted to the debtor for the following reasons:
est ou sera redevable d'une dette au débiteur pour les motifs suivants :

The Notice will be served on the debtor ....
L'avis sera signifié au débiteur,   (Name of debtor / *Nom du débiteur/de la débitrice*)

at ....
à/au   (Address of debtor for service / *Adresse du débiteur/de la débitrice aux fins de signification*)

within five days of serving it on the garnishee.
dans les cinq jours qui suivent sa signification au tiers saisi.

☒ Notice of Examination (Form 20H).
   Avis d'interrogatoire (formule 20H).

☐ Writ of Delivery (Form 20B).
   Bref de délaissement (formule 20B).

☐ Other *(Set out the nature of your request):*
   Autre (Indiquez la nature de votre demande) :

Complete this section if you are requesting a Writ of Delivery.
Remplissez la présente section si vous demandez un bref de délaissement.

2. An order for the delivery of the following personal property:
   Une ordonnance de délaissement des biens meubles suivants :
   (According to the court order, set out a description of the property to be delivered. Identify any marks or serial numbers. *Selon l'ordonnance du tribunal, donnez la description des biens qui doivent être restitués. Indiquez toute marque d'identification ou tout numéro de série y figurant.*)

SCR 20.04-10-20P (June 1, 2009 / *1er juin 2009*) CSD   Continued on next page / *Suite à la page suivante*

continues....

Illustration 13.3 (continued)

FORM / *FORMULE* 20P   **PAGE 3**   SC-00-47669-00
                                                                    Claim No. / *N° de la demande*

was made in this action against: ....
a été rendue dans l'action contre :   (Name of person against whom the order was made / *Nom de la personne contre qui*
                                                    l'ordonnance a été rendue)

on .... , in the ....
le   *à la Cour des petites*   (Name of court location where order was made / *Emplacement*
                                        créances de   *du tribunal où l'ordonnance a été rendue*)

Small Claims Court. Since the above listed personal property has not been delivered, I make this affidavit in support of a request that the clerk of the court issue a Writ of Delivery (Form 20B) to the bailiff of the
Étant donné que les biens meubles susmentionnés n'ont pas été restitués, je fais le présent affidavit à l'appui d'une demande visant à enjoindre au greffier du tribunal de délivrer un bref de délaissement (formule 20B) à l'huissier de la Cour des petites créances de

.... Small Claims Court.
                    (Name of court location / *Emplacement du tribunal*)

Complete this section if you are requesting a Certificate of Judgment, Writ of Seizure and Sale of Personal Property, Writ of Seizure and Sale of Land, Notice of Garnishment, Notice of Renewal of Garnishment or Notice of Examination.
Remplissez la présente section si vous demandez un certificat de jugement, un bref de saisie-exécution de biens meubles, un bref de saisie-exécution de biens-fonds, un avis de saisie-arrêt, un avis de renouvellement de la saisie-arrêt ou un avis d'interrogatoire.

3. A judgment was made in this action against **Ophelia Foot** ....
   Un jugement a été rendu dans l'action contre   (Name of debtor(s) / *Nom du/de la/des débiteur(s)/débitrice(s)*)

   on **September 14, Yr. 1** .... in the
   le   *à la Cour des petites créances de*

   Toronto .... Small Claims Court
          (Name of court where judgment was made / *Nom du tribunal où le jugement a été rendu*)

   for the following sums:
   à l'égard des sommes suivantes :

   (A) **DEBT** $ 2,000.00
        LA CRÉANCE $

   (B) ***PRE-JUDGMENT INTEREST*** calculated
        LES INTÉRÊTS ANTÉRIEURS AU JUGEMENT *calculés*

        on the sum of $ .... 2,000.00 at the rate of **6.0** %
        sur la somme de $ *au taux de*   *pour cent*

        per annum from **Dec. 11, Yr. 0** .... to **Sept. 13, Yr. 1** .... ,
        par an du   *au*

        being **277** .... days. $ 91.07
        soit   *jours.* $

                              SUBTOTAL (Amount of Judgment) $ 2,091.07
                              TOTAL PARTIEL (montant du jugement) $

   (C) **COSTS** to date of judgment $ 477.58
        LES DÉPENS *à la date du jugement* $

SCR 20.04-10-20P (June 1, 2009 / *1ᵉʳ juin 2009*) CSD   Continued on next page / *Suite à la page suivante*

continues....

Illustration 13.3 (continued)

FORM / *FORMULE* 20P PAGE 4 SC-00-47669-00
Claim No. / *N° de la demande*

(D) **TOTAL AMOUNT OF PAYMENTS RECEIVED FROM DEBTOR**
after judgment (if any) (minus) $ ....
LE MONTANT TOTAL DES PAIEMENTS REÇUS DU *(moins)* $
DÉBITEUR après le jugement (le cas échéant)

(E) **POST-JUDGMENT INTEREST** to date calculated
LES INTÉRÊTS POSTÉRIEURS AU JUGEMENT à ce jour, calculés

on the sum of $ .... 2,568.65 .... at the rate of **5.0** %
sur la somme de $ *au taux de* *pour cent*

per annum from **Sept. 14, Yr. 1** .... to **Oct. 12, Yr. 1** .... ,
par an du *au*

being **29** .... days. $ 10.20
soit *jours.* $

NOTE: Calculation of interest is always on the amount owing from time to time as payments are
received. This is true for both pre-judgment and post-judgment interest. Attach a separate sheet
setting out how you calculated the total amount of any pre/post-judgment interest.
REMARQUE : *Les intérêts doivent toujours être calculés sur la somme due. Le calcul doit tenir
compte des paiements reçus de temps à autre. Ceci s'applique autant aux intérêts antérieurs au
jugement qu'aux intérêts postérieurs au jugement. Annexez une feuille distincte indiquant comment
vous avez calculé le montant total des intérêts antérieurs et postérieurs au jugement.*

(F) **SUBSEQUENT COSTS** incurred after judgment (including the cost of issuing
the requested enforcement(s)) $ 54.00*
LES DÉPENS SUBSÉQUENTS engagés après le jugement (y compris le $
coût de la délivrance de la ou des mesures d'exécution forcée demandées)

*Certificate of Judgement $19 + Notice of Examination $35 **TOTAL DUE** $ 2,632.85
SOLDE DÛ $

Sworn/Affirmed before me at **Toronto**
Déclaré sous serment/Affirmé (Municipality / *municipalité*)
solennellement devant moi à

in **Ontario**
en/à/au (Province, state or country / *province, État ou pays*)

on **October 12, Yr. 1** "I. Shredlu"
le Commissioner for taking affidavits
Commissaire aux affidavits
(Type or print name below if signature is illegible.)
*(Dactylographiez le nom ou écrivez-le en caractères
d'imprimerie ci-dessous si la signature est illisible.)*

Peter Paralegal
Signature
(This form is to be signed in front of a
lawyer, justice of the peace, notary public
or commissioner for taking affidavits.)
*(La présente formule doit être signée en
présence d'un avocat, d'un juge de paix, d'un
notaire ou d'un commissaire aux affidavits.)*

WARNING: **IT IS AN OFFENCE UNDER THE** *CRIMINAL CODE* **TO KNOWINGLY SWEAR OR
AFFIRM A FALSE AFFIDAVIT.**
AVERTISSEMENT : FAIRE SCIEMMENT UN FAUX AFFIDAVIT CONSTITUE UNE INFRACTION AU CODE
CRIMINEL.

SCR 20.04-10-20P (June 1, 2009 / *1er juin 2009*) CSD

Note: (F), Subsequent Costs, include Certificate of Judgment, $19, and Notice of
Examination, $35.

ILLUSTRATION 13.4: Notice of Examination (Form 20H) for
Oryx v. Foot

ONTARIO
Superior Court of Justice
Cour supérieure de justice

Notice of Examination
Avis d'interrogatoire
Form / *Formule* 20H Ont. Reg. No. / *Règl. de l'Ont.* : 258/98

(Seal / *Sceau*)

Toronto
Small Claims Court / *Cour des petites créances de*

SC-00-47669-00
Claim No. / *N° de la demande*

**47 Sheppard Ave. E., 3rd Fl.,
Toronto, ON M2N 5N1**
Address / *Adresse*

416-326-3554
Phone number / *Numéro de téléphone*

BETWEEN / *ENTRE*

Albert Oryx

Creditor(s) / *Créancier(s)/créancière(s)*

and / *et*

Ophelia Foot

Debtor(s) / *Débiteur(s)/débitrice(s)*

TO: Ophelia Foot
DESTINATAIRE :   (Name of person to be examined / *Nom de la personne qui doit être interrogée*)

of **83 Greengrove Rd., Toronto, ON M6R 4O5**
de/du   (Address of person to be examined / *Adresse de la personne qui doit être interrogée*)

The creditor **Albert Oryx**
Le créancier (Name of creditor / *Nom du/de la créancier/créancière*)

c/o Peter Paralegal, 41 Yonge Street, #410,
of **Toronto, ON M5G 1S1**
de (Address of creditor / *Adresse du/de la créancier/créancière*)

has obtained a judgment against **Ophelia Foot**
a obtenu un jugement contre (Name of debtor / *Nom du débiteur/de la débitrice*)

on **September 14**
le

Y1 , in the **Toronto**
à la Cour des petites créances de (Name of court where judgment was made /
Nom du tribunal où le jugement a été rendu)

Small Claims Court.

According to the supporting affidavit filed by the creditor, the total due on the judgment is
Selon l'affidavit à l'appui déposé par le créancier, le solde somme due aux termes du jugement s'élève à

$ __2,520.41__ .   *(This amount must match the total amount identified in the supporting affidavit.)*
(Total)   **$.** *(Ce montant doit correspondre au montant total énoncé dans l'affidavit à l'appui.)*

This total due takes into account all money received, accrued post-judgment interest and costs to
Ce solde somme due tient compte de toutes les sommes reçues, des intérêts postérieurs au jugement courus et des dépens

this date: **October 12, Yr. 1**   . *(This date must match the date of the supporting affidavit.)*
à cette date :   *(Cette date doit correspondre à celle de l'affidavit à l'appui.)*

YOU ARE REQUIRED TO ATTEND AN EXAMINATION HEARING to explain how the debtor will pay this judgment and if there are any reasons for not doing so.
VOUS ÊTES REQUIS(E) DE VOUS PRÉSENTER À UN INTERROGATOIRE *pour expliquer de quelle façon le débiteur acquittera la somme due aux termes de ce jugement et s'il existe quelque motif que ce soit de ne pas le faire.*

SCR 20.10-20H (April 11, 2012 / *11 avril 2012*) CSD

Continued on next page / *Suite à la page suivante*

continues....

Illustration 13.4 (continued)

FORM / *FORMULE* 20H   PAGE 2   SC-00-47669-00
Claim No. / N° de la demande

THIS COURT WILL HOLD AN EXAMINATION HEARING
LE TRIBUNAL PRÉCITÉ TIENDRA UN INTERROGATOIRE

on   November 29, Yr. 1   , at   10:30 a.m.   or as soon as possible after that time, at
le   , à   (Time / *heure*)   *ou dès que possible par la suite à/au*

45 Sheppard Ave. E., Toronto, ON
(Address of court location / Adresse du tribunal)

306
(Courtroom number / Numéro de la salle d'audience)

October 12, Yr. 1   "I.M. Clerk"
(Signature of clerk / Signature du greffier)

CAUTION TO PERSON BEING EXAMINED: *AVERTISSEMENT À LA PERSONNE QUI EST INTERROGÉE :*	If you fail to attend the examination hearing or attend and refuse to answer questions or produce documents, you may be ordered to attend a contempt hearing. At the contempt hearing, you may be found in contempt of court and the court may order you to be jailed. *Si vous ne vous présentez pas à l'interrogatoire ou si vous vous présentez mais que vous refusez de répondre aux questions ou de produire des documents, le tribunal peut ordonner que vous vous présentiez à une audience pour outrage. Lors de l'audience pour outrage, vous pouvez être reconnu(e) coupable d'outrage au tribunal et le tribunal peut ordonner que vous soyez incarcéré(e).*
NOTE TO DEBTOR: *REMARQUE AU DÉBITEUR :*	A debtor who is an individual must serve on the creditor a completed Financial Information Form (Form 20I) prior to the hearing. This form must **not** be filed with the court. The debtor must provide a completed copy of this form to the judge at the examination hearing. The debtor must also bring to the hearing documents that support the information given in this form. *Le débiteur qui est un particulier doit signifier au créancier une formule de renseignements financiers remplie (formule 20I) avant l'interrogatoire. Cette formule ne doit **pas** être déposée auprès du tribunal. Le débiteur doit remettre la formule dûment remplie au juge chargé de l'audience. Le débiteur doit aussi apporter à l'audience les documents qui appuient l'information donnée sur cette formule.*

SCR 20.10-20H (April 11, 2012 / *11 avril 2012*) CSD

ILLUSTRATION 13.5: Financial Information Form (Form 20I)

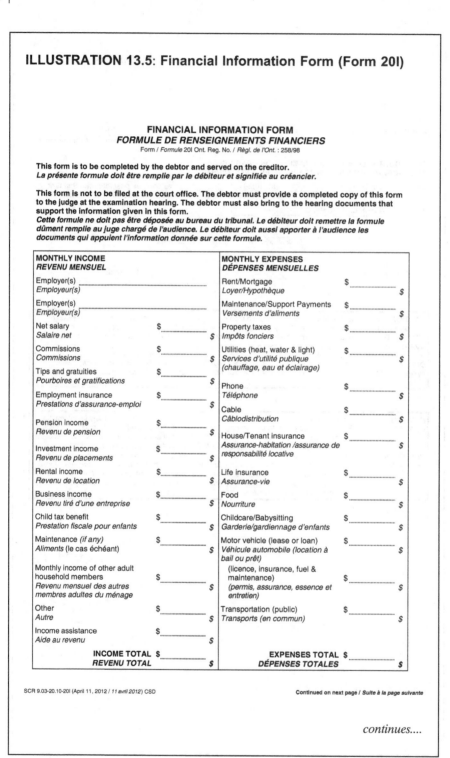

FINANCIAL INFORMATION FORM
FORMULE DE RENSEIGNEMENTS FINANCIERS
Form / Formule 20I Ont. Reg. No. / Règl. de l'Ont. : 258/98

This form is to be completed by the debtor and served on the creditor.
La présente formule doit être remplie par le débiteur et signifiée au créancier.

This form is not to be filed at the court office. The debtor must provide a completed copy of this form to the judge at the examination hearing. The debtor must also bring to the hearing documents that support the information given in this form.
Cette formule ne doit pas être déposée au bureau du tribunal. Le débiteur doit remettre la formule dûment remplie au juge chargé de l'audience. Le débiteur doit aussi apporter à l'audience les documents qui appuient l'information donnée sur cette formule.

MONTHLY INCOME / *REVENU MENSUEL*		**MONTHLY EXPENSES** / *DÉPENSES MENSUELLES*	
Employer(s) / *Employeur(s)*		Rent/Mortgage / *Loyer/Hypothèque*	$ $
Employer(s) / *Employeur(s)*		Maintenance/Support Payments / *Versements d'aliments*	$ $
Net salary / *Salaire net*	$ $	Property taxes / *Impôts fonciers*	$ $
Commissions / *Commissions*	$ $	Utilities (heat, water & light) / *Services d'utilité publique (chauffage, eau et éclairage)*	$ $
Tips and gratuities / *Pourboires et gratifications*	$ $	Phone / *Téléphone*	$ $
Employment insurance / *Prestations d'assurance-emploi*	$ $	Cable / *Câblodistribution*	$ $
Pension income / *Revenu de pension*	$ $	House/Tenant insurance / *Assurance-habitation /assurance de responsabilité locative*	$ $
Investment income / *Revenu de placements*	$ $	Life insurance / *Assurance-vie*	$ $
Rental income / *Revenu de location*	$ $	Food / *Nourriture*	$ $
Business income / *Revenu tiré d'une entreprise*	$ $	Childcare/Babysitting / *Garderie/gardiennage d'enfants*	$ $
Child tax benefit / *Prestation fiscale pour enfants*	$ $	Motor vehicle (lease or loan) / *Véhicule automobile (location à bail ou prêt)*	$ $
Maintenance *(if any)* / *Aliments (le cas échéant)*	$ $	(licence, insurance, fuel & maintenance) / *(permis, assurance, essence et entretien)*	$ $
Monthly income of other adult household members / *Revenu mensuel des autres membres adultes du ménage*	$ $	Transportation (public) / *Transports (en commun)*	$ $
Other / *Autre*	$ $		
Income assistance / *Aide au revenu*	$ $		
INCOME TOTAL / *REVENU TOTAL*	$ $	**EXPENSES TOTAL** / *DÉPENSES TOTALES*	$ $

SCR 9.03-20.10-20I (April 11, 2012 / *11 avril 2012*) CSD

Continued on next page / *Suite à la page suivante*

continues....

Illustration 13.5 (continued)

FORM / *FORMULE* **20I**   PAGE 2

MONTHLY DEBTS / *DETTES MENSUELLES*	VALUE OF ASSETS / *VALEUR DES AVOIRS*
Credit card(s) payments *(please specify)*: / *Paiements de carte(s) de crédit* (Veuillez préciser.)	Real estate equity / *Valeur nette réelle des biens immobiliers* $ ___ $
$ ___ $	Market value $ ___ / *Valeur marchande* $
$ ___ $	Mortgage balance $ ___ / *Solde de l'hypothèque* $
$ ___ $	Automobile equity $ ___ / *Valeur nette réelle des véhicules automobiles* $
Bank or finance company loan payments *(please specify)*: / *Remboursement de prêt(s) d'une banque ou d'une compagnie de financement* (Veuillez préciser.)	Make and year ___ / *Marque et année*
	Loan balance $ ___ / *Solde du/des prêts* $
$ ___ $	Bank or other account balance(s) (include RRSPs) / *Solde de compte(s) bancaire(s) ou autre(s) compte(s)* (Incluez les REÉR.) $ ___ $
$ ___ $	
Department store(s) payments *(please specify)*: / *Versements à un ou des grands magasins* (Veuillez préciser.)	Stocks & bonds / *Actions et obligations* $ ___ $
$ ___ $	Life insurance (cash value) / *Assurance-vie (valeur de rachat)* $ ___ $
$ ___ $	Money owing to you / *Sommes qui vous sont dues* $ ___ $
	Name of debtor ___ / *Nom du débiteur/de la débitrice*
DEBTS TOTAL $ ___ / *DETTES TOTALES* $	Personal property / *Biens meubles* $ ___ $
	Cash / *Argent comptant* $ ___ $
	Other / *Autre* $ ___ $
	TOTAL VALUE OF ASSETS $ ___ / *VALEUR TOTALE DES AVOIRS* $

_____ (Name / *Nom*)   _____ (Signature)

SCR 9.03-20.10-20I (April 11, 2012 / *11 avril 2012*) CSD

If you have sued in the business name, as you have a right to do, you should obtain a provincial business name search, if you had not previously done so, to link the individual you are examining to the business debtor you have sued in order to obtain a contempt order if the person later fails to appear at the hearing. Before a court will commit an individual for contempt who was served as a representative of a party, it will want to be assured that the individual is a partner of a partnership, or the sole proprietor, or an officer or director of a company, as the case may be. Be ready to produce a government search abstract or report to prove the connection on a contempt hearing.

The Judgment Debtor's Obligations at the Examination

The person to be examined is expected to inform himself or herself about his or her assets, means, ability to pay, expenses, debts, and liabilities. If the person is an individual, he or she is expected to serve a completed copy of the Financial Information Form on the creditor prior to the examination. It is not necessary to file a copy with the court. The judgment debtor must bring a copy of the completed Financial Information Form to court to give to the judge. Be prepared for the fact that judgment debtors, particularly when self-represented, often show up without completing the form, let alone serving it prior to the examination. To get cooperation, in addition to serving the form, also send the debtor a letter reminding him or her to complete the form and bring supporting documents, such as credit card statements, leases, rent receipts, a statement of wages, or salary cheque stubs.

The examination is conducted in court or in chambers, in private, unless otherwise ordered, and is under oath, with a court monitor recording the examination and maintaining the list of examinations and photocopying documents. A less busy court may make do with one monitor. It may be necessary to order a copy of the transcript of the record if the client is uncooperative or refuses to answer proper questions, or is evasive or disruptive. The transcript can then be used as evidence in a subsequent motion for contempt. The Rules contemplate that at the end of the hearing, or on consent, a judge or referee will make a payment order, which may be a lump sum or instalment payments. The judgment debtor will be given an opportunity to comply with the order. Rule 20.10(7) stipulates that with the debtor's consent, or after the examination, an order as to payment can be made:

> 20.10(7) After the examination or if the debtor's consent is filed, the court may make an order as to payment.

Aside from filing a Writ of Seizure and Sale of Land with the sheriff, Rule 20.10(8) provides that, while an order for payment is in force, no further enforcement action may be taken by the creditor until the time for payment expires. The wise creditor will have also filed a Writ of Seizure and Sale of Personal Property prior to the examination, and that writ may remain on file.

> 20.10(8) While an order as to payment is in force, no step to enforce the judgment may be taken or continued against the debtor by a creditor named in the order, except issuing a writ of seizure and sale of land and filing it with the sheriff.

Contempt Proceedings

Contempt proceedings are governed by Rule 20.11 and depend on the type of contempt committed. At common law, a lower court, such as the Small Claims Court, could deal with contempt only *in facie* — that is, contempt in the face of the court, committed in the courtroom when the judge is present. This, however, has been modified by legislative changes that permit deputy judges to make an *ex facie* contempt order if the debtor fails to appear at an examination.[1]

In the Small Claims Court, inappropriate behaviour in the pre-trial and trial stage is usually *in facie* and is dealt with by a Small Claims Court judge. It is customary for a judge other than the judge before whom the contempt occurred to hear the contempt motion in order to preserve the appearance of impartiality, objectivity, and fairness. However, contempt proceedings are rare prior to judgment. When they do crop up, it is usually with respect to examinations:

- Contempt *in facie*: The judgment debtor appears at the hearing, but refuses to answer questions; is disruptive; gives evasive, meandering, uninformative answers; fails, if an individual, to complete the Financial Information Form; or fails to produce documents. This kind of contempt will be dealt with by a Small Claims Court judge.

- Contempt *ex facie*: Having been served with a Notice of Examination, the judgment debtor fails to appear on the date of the hearing.

---

[1] Section 30 of the *CJA* was revised with the intention of permitting deputy judges to make *ex facie* contempt orders. However, in 2013, deputy judges were advised to stop making *ex facie* contempt orders until the legislation could be further clarified. In some jurisdictions contempt orders may still be made, so it is best to check with local court offices as to their current practice for contempt orders. In most jurisdictions, if a judgment debtor fails to show up for a second examination, a contempt hearing will be set before a deputy judge; however, if the debtor fails to show up at the contempt hearing, the matter must then be sent to a Superior Court judge for a contempt order.

Section 30 of the *CJA* has been amended to confirm that deputy judges may preside at contempt hearings for debtors who fail to attend an examination in aid of execution. A deputy judge can order that the judgment debtor be jailed for up to five days.

Under Rule 20.11(1), the Small Claims Court may order a person to attend before the court for a contempt hearing if, having appeared, he or she failed to answer questions or produce documents. Note that "failed to answer questions" may encompass uncooperative or disruptive behaviour, as well as standing mute. This means that there will be another hearing at a separate time or place. The clerk will give the creditor a notice of this hearing, and the creditor shall serve it personally on the debtor or person summoned to the examination. Because a contempt hearing may lead to a jail sentence, personal service is required when the liberty of the subject is in issue.

> 20.11(1) If a person on whom a notice of examination has been served under rule 20.10 attends the examination but refuses to answer questions or to produce records or documents, the court may order the person to attend before it for a contempt hearing.

Rule 20.11(2) says that if a person served with a Notice of Examination fails to appear, the court may order the person to appear for a contempt hearing:

> 20.11(2) If a person on whom a notice of examination has been served under rule 20.10 fails to attend the examination, the court may order the person to attend before it for a contempt hearing under subsection 30(1) of the *Courts of Justice Act*.

Pursuant to Rule 20.11(6), when a contempt hearing is held under s. 30(1) of the *CJA*, a judge may find the person in contempt if satisfied that the person failed to attend as required by the notice of examination and that the failure to attend was wilful.

> 20.11(6) The finding of contempt at a hearing held under subsection 30(1) of the *Courts of Justice Act* is subject to subsection 30(2) of that Act.

Rule 20.11(3) provides that the court clerk shall provide the creditor with a notice of contempt hearing if an order for such a hearing is made. The creditor is to serve the notice on the debtor or other person.

> 20.11(3) If the court makes an order for a contempt hearing,

(a) the clerk shall provide the creditor with a notice of contempt hearing setting out the time, date and place of the hearing; and

(b) the creditor shall serve the notice of contempt hearing on the debtor or other person in accordance with subrule 8.01(13) and file the affidavit of service at least seven days before the hearing.

The creditor must file the affidavit of service of the contempt hearing seven days before the contempt hearing, showing that the person was personally served. Using Rule 20.11(4), the debtor or party to be examined may move to set aside the order to attend a contempt hearing, and the court may order another hearing if it appears that the debtor or person to be examined had a good excuse for not attending:

> 20.11(4) A person who has been ordered to attend a contempt hearing under subsection 30(1) of the *Courts of Justice Act* may make a motion to set aside the order, before or after receiving the notice of contempt hearing but before the date of the hearing and, on the motion, the court may set aside the order and order that the person attend another examination under rule 20.10.

At the contempt hearing under Rule 20.11(5), the burden is on the party to be examined to show cause why he or she should not be held in contempt. This means he or she should have a good reason for failing to appear or for not answering questions or producing documents: for example, the questions asked or the documents demanded were not relevant.

> 20.11(5) At a contempt hearing held under subrule (1), the court may find the person to be in contempt of court if the person fails to show cause why the person should not be held in contempt for refusing to answer questions or produce records or documents.

A completed Notice of Contempt Hearing for Small Claims Court is provided in Illustration 13.6.

In the court, the person must demonstrate that the failure to attend at the examination was not wilful. If the court is persuaded that there is a reasonable excuse for not answering or not attending, the court may schedule a new hearing. If the court makes a finding of contempt, it has broad powers to order the person to purge him or herself of contempt. A deputy judge will be able to make an order that the person in contempt be jailed for up to five days. In theory, the person can then be ordered to attend before the judge and be made to do what he or she was required to do — attend the examination and answer questions. If the person still refuses, he or she can be jailed

ILLUSTRATION 13.6: Notice of Contempt Hearing

Superior Court of Justice
Cour supérieure de justice

Notice of Contempt Hearing
Avis d'audience pour outrage

Toronto

SC-00-47669-00

<u>Small Claims Court / *Cour des petites créances de*</u>

Claim No. / *N° de la demande*

47 Sheppard Ave. E., 3rd Fl.
Address / *Adresse*

Toronto, ON M2N 5N1

416-326-3554
Phone number / *N° de téléphone*

BETWEEN /*ENTRE*

Albert Oryx

Plaintiff(s) / *Demandeur(s)*

and / *et*

Ophelia Foot

Defendant(s) / *Défendeur(s)*

TO:
À :

Ophelia Foot

(Name of person examined / *Nom de la personne interrogée*)

THIS COURT WILL HOLD A CONTEMPT HEARING on December 5, Yr. 1 , at 10:00
CE TRIBUNAL TIENDRA UNE AUDIENCE POUR OUTRAGE le

à

a.m./p.m., or as soon as possible after that time, at Toronto Small Claims Court
h ou dès que possible après, à l'endroit suivant :

(address as above), Courtroom 306
(Name of court, address of court location & courtroom number / *Nom et adresse de la cour et numéro de la salle d'audience*)

because you refused to answer questions or produce documents or records at the examination hearing.
parce que vous avez refusé de répondre aux questions ou de produire des documents ou dossiers lors de l'interrogatoire.

At the contempt hearing, the court may order that you:
À l'issue de l'audience pour outrage, le tribunal peut ordonner, selon le cas :

(a) attend an examination under Rule 20.10; or
a) *que vous vous présentiez à un interrogatoire aux termes de la règle 20.10;*

(b) be jailed for a period not exceeding 40 days; or
b) *que vous soyez incarcéré(e) pour une période maximale de 40 jours;*

(c) attend an additional contempt hearing; or
c) *que vous vous présentiez à une autre audience pour outrage;*

(d) comply with any other order that the judge considers necessary or just.
d) *que vous vous conformiez à toute autre ordonnance que le juge estime juste ou nécessaire.*

THIS NOTICE SHALL BE SERVED by the creditor on the debtor or other person to be examined personally as provided in Rule 8.02 of the *Rules of the Small Claims Court*, unless the court orders otherwise.
CET AVIS EST SIGNIFIÉ par le créancier au débiteur ou à toute autre personne devant être interrogée en personne conformément à la règle 8.02 des Règles de la Cour des petites créances, sauf ordonnance contraire du tribunal.

SAA 20.11-00 (January 25, 2006 / *25 janvier 2006*) CSD
(Non-regulated form / *Formule non prescrite*)

continues....

Illustration 13.6 (continued)

PAGE 2

SC-00-47669-00
Claim No. / *N° de la demande*

If you are found in contempt of court at the contempt hearing and a warrant is issued for your committal to jail, you or your representative may ask the court to reverse the finding of contempt by filing a motion (Form 15A) and an affidavit (Form 15B) at the Small Claims Court office. In your affidavit, and at the motion hearing, explain to the judge the reasons why the contempt order should be set aside.

Si vous êtes trouvé(e) coupable d'outrage au tribunal à l'issue de l'audience pour outrage et qu'un mandat de dépôt est délivré à votre entroit, vous ou votre représentant pouvez demander au tribunal d'annuler la condamnation d'outrage en déposant une motion (Formulaire 15A) et un affidavit (Formulaire 15B) au greffe de la Cour des petites créances. Dans votre affidavit et à l'audition de la motion, il vous faut expliquer au juge les raisons pour lesquelles l'ordonnance d'outrage devrait être annulée.

To obtain forms and self-help materials, attend the nearest Small Claims Court or access the following website: www.ontariocourtforms.on.ca.
Vous pouvez obtenir les formulaires et la documentation explicative auprès de la Cour des petites créances de votre localité ou en consultant le site Web suivant : www.ontariocourtforms.on.ca.

Le ____ Nov. 26, Yr. 1 ____
(Date)

____ "I.M. Clerk" ____
(Signature of clerk / *Signature du greffier*)

SAA 20.11-00 (January 25, 2006 / *25 janvier 2006*) CSD
(Non-regulated form / *Formule non prescrite*)

again, though this is rare. Rule 20.11(7) sets out some of the orders that the court may make at a contempt hearing:

> 20.11(7) At a contempt hearing, the court may order that the person,
> (a) attend an examination under rule 20.10;
> (b) be jailed for a period of not more than five days;
> (c) attend an additional contempt hearing under subrule (1) or subsection 30(1) of the *Courts of Justice Act*, as the case may be; or
> (d) comply with any other order that the judge considers necessary or just.

If the judge orders the person to be jailed, he or she issues a Warrant of Committal (Form 20J). Warrants are covered by Rule 20.11(8):

> 20.11(8) If a committal is ordered under clause (7)(b),
> (a) the creditor may complete and file with the clerk an identification form (Form 20K) to assist the police in apprehending the person named in the warrant of committal; and
> (b) the clerk shall issue a warrant of committal (Form 20J), accompanied by the identification form, if any, directed to all police officers in Ontario to apprehend the person named in the warrant anywhere in Ontario and promptly bring the person to the nearest correctional institution.

The creditor should complete an Identification Form (Form 20K) to assist the police, using the Warrant of Committal, to arrest the person found in contempt and bring the person to the nearest jail to be held until the time set out in the warrant has expired, or until further order of the court. (See Illustrations 13.7 and 13.8 for the Warrant of Committal and Identification Form for Ophelia Foot, who failed to show up at the contempt hearing.)

The arrest warrant remains in force for 12 months and, on expiry, may be renewed by the creditor by bringing a motion for renewal. There is no limit on the number of times the warrant may be renewed. If the warrant is issued by a Superior Court judge, it must be renewed or discharged only by a Superior Court judge. Do not assume that the police will quickly apprehend the person named in the warrant. While the police are obliged to enforce civil orders of the court when asked to do so, it is not their highest priority. If the person is apprehended, it is most likely because he or she was caught in a R.I.D.E. ("Reduce Impaired Driving Everywhere") stop or a speed trap and the warrant came up when the officer ran the driver's licence or vehicle registration through the computer.

ILLUSTRATION 13.7: Warrant of Committal (Form 20J)

ONTARIO
Superior Court of Justice
Cour supérieure de justice

Warrant of Committal
Mandat de dépôt
Form / *Formule* 20J Ont. Reg. No. / *Règl. de l'Ont.* : 258/98

Seal / *Sceau*

Toronto
Small Claims Court / *Cour des petites créances de*

SC-00-47669-00
Claim No. / *N° de la demande*

47 Sheppard Ave. E., 3rd Fl.
Toronto, ON M2N 5N1
Address / *Adresse*

416-326-3554
Phone number / *Numéro de téléphone*

BETWEEN / *ENTRE*

Albert Oryx
Plaintiff(s) / *Demandeur(s)/demanderesse(s)*

and / *et*

Ophelia Foot
Defendant(s) / *Défendeur(s)/défenderesse(s)*

TO ALL POLICE OFFICERS IN ONTARIO AND TO THE OFFICERS OF ALL CORRECTIONAL INSTITUTIONS IN ONTARIO:
À TOUS LES AGENTS DE POLICE DE L'ONTARIO ET AUX AGENTS DE TOUS LES ÉTABLISSEMENTS CORRECTIONNELS DE L'ONTARIO :

THIS WARRANT IS FOR THE COMMITTAL OF / *LE PRÉSENT MANDAT EST DÉCERNÉ POUR L'INCARCÉRATION DE*

Last name / *Nom de famille* **Foot**		
First name / *Premier prénom* **Ophelia**	Second name / *Deuxième prénom*	Also known as / *Également connu(e) sous le nom de*
Address (street number, apt., unit) / *Adresse (numéro et rue, app., unité)* **c/o Digbert Fightback, 60 My Way**		
City/Town / *Cité/ville* **Toronto**	Province **ON**	Phone no. / *N° de téléphone* **416-491-5041**
Postal code / *Code postal* **M6R 8P1**		Fax no. / *N° de télécopieur* **416-491-5042**

A Notice of Contempt Hearing was issued from this court which required
Un avis d'audience pour outrage a été délivré par le tribunal précité ordonnant à

Ophelia Foot
(Name of person required to attend contempt hearing / *Nom de la personne tenue de se présenter à l'audience pour outrage*)

to attend the sittings of this court at **10:00 a.m.** on **December 15, Yr. 1** .
de se présenter aux séances du (Time / *Heure*) *le* (Date)
tribunal à

At the contempt hearing, it was duly proven that the Notice of Contempt Hearing was properly served, and
Lors de l'audience pour outrage, il a été dûment prouvé que l'avis d'audience pour outrage a été signifié en bonne et due forme et

SCR 20.11-20J (September 1, 2010 / *1er septembre 2010*) CSD

continues....

Illustration 13.7 (continued)

FORM / *FORMULE* 20J   PAGE 2   SC-00-47669-00
                                                          Claim No. / *Nº de la demande*

this court found this person to be in contempt of court because he/she:
d'autre part, le tribunal a reconnu la personne susmentionnée coupable d'outrage au tribunal pour l'un des motifs suivants :

(Check appropriate box. / Cochez la case appropriée.)

☒ wilfully failed to attend an examination hearing as required by a Notice of Examination (Form 20H), which was properly served.
elle a délibérément omis de se présenter à un interrogatoire comme l'exigeait un avis d'interrogatoire (formule 20H), qui a été signifié en bonne et due forme.

☐ attended the examination hearing, refused to answer questions or produce documents or records, and failed to show cause why he/she should not be held in contempt for refusing to answer questions or produce documents or records.
elle s'est présentée à l'interrogatoire mais a refusé de répondre aux questions ou de produire des documents ou des dossiers et a omis de justifier pourquoi elle ne devrait pas être accusée pour outrage pour avoir refusé de répondre aux questions ou de produire des documents ou des dossiers.

At the contempt hearing, a judge of this court ordered this person to be committed.
Lors de l'audience pour outrage, un juge du tribunal a ordonné l'incarcération de la personne susmentionnée.

YOU ARE ORDERED to take the person named above to the nearest correctional institution and admit and
IL VOUS EST ORDONNÉ *d'amener la personne susmentionnée à l'établissement correctionnel le plus proche*

detain him or her there for **5**   days.
et de l'y admettre et l'y détenir pendant   *jours.*

This warrant expires twelve (12) months from the date of issue, unless renewed by court order. If renewed, the warrant expires twelve (12) months from the date of the renewal.
Le présent mandat expire douze (12) mois à compter de la date de sa délivrance, sauf si le tribunal le renouvelle par ordonnance. S'il est renouvelé, le mandat expire douze (12) mois à compter de la date du renouvellement.

December 17, Yr. 1   "I.M. Clerk"
                                          (Signature of clerk / *Signature du greffier*)

SCR 20.11-20J (September 1, 2010 / *1ᵉʳ septembre 2010*) CSD

ILLUSTRATION 13.8: Identification Form (Form 20K)

ONTARIO
Superior Court of Justice
Cour supérieure de justice

Identification Form
Formule de renseignements signalétiques
Form / Formule 20K Ont. Reg. No. / Règl. de l'Ont. : 258/98

Toronto
Small Claims Court / *Cour des petites créances de*

SC-00-47669-00
Claim No. / *N° de la demande*

47 Sheppard Ave. E., 3rd Fl.
Toronto, ON M2N 5N1

Address / *Adresse*

416-326-3554
Phone number / *Numéro de téléphone*

BETWEEN / *ENTRE*

Albert Oryx
Plaintiff(s)/Creditor(s) / *Demandeur(s)/demanderesse(s)/Créancier(s)/créancière(s)*

and / *et*

Ophelia Foot
Defendant(s)/Debtor(s) / *Défendeur(s)/défenderesse(s)/Débiteur(s)/débitrice(s)*

TO HELP PROCESS A CIVIL WARRANT FOR COMMITTAL, the following information, or **as much information as is reasonably available should be provided**. This is necessary for the police to identify the person to be arrested. Without this information it will be difficult to enforce the warrant.
POUR FACILITER LA DÉLIVRANCE D'UN MANDAT DE DÉPÔT AU CIVIL, les renseignements suivants ou autant de renseignements qui sont raisonnablement disponibles devraient être fournis. Ces renseignements sont nécessaires pour que la police puisse identifier la personne à arrêter. Sans ces renseignements, il sera difficile d'exécuter le mandat.

1. Name **Foot**   **Ophelia**   **Mabel**
   Nom (Last name of individual / *Nom de famille du particulier*)   (First name / *Premier prénom*)   (Second name / *Deuxième prénom*)

2. Also known as names (if any) **N/A**
   Nom(s) sous lequel/lesquels la personne est également connue (le cas échéant)

3. Last known address and telephone number
   Dernière adresse connue et dernier numéro de téléphone connu
   83 Greengrove Rd., Toronto, ON M6R 4Q5, 416-482-1234

4. (a) Date of birth *(d, m, y)* **12-04-Yr–20**
   Date de naissance (j, m, a)

5. Physical description
   Description physique

   (a) Gender **F**   (b) Height **1.57 m**   (c) Weight **54.4 kgs**   (d) Build **Medium**
   Sexe   *Taille*   *Poids*   *Corpulence*

   (e) Colour of eyes **Brown**   (f) Hair colour **Brown**   (g) Complexion **Sallow**
   Couleur des yeux   *Couleur des cheveux*   *Teint*

   (h) Clean-shaven **N/A**   (i) Wears glasses **No**
   Rasé de près   *Porte des lunettes*

   (j) Clothing habits and tastes **Favours casual sportswear**
   Habitudes et goûts vestimentaires

SCR 20.11-20K (June 1, 2009 / *1ᵉʳ juin 2009*) CSD

continues....

Illustration 13.8 (continued)

FORM / *FORMULE* 20K PAGE 2 SC-00-47669-00
Claim No. / *N° de la demande*

(k) Distinguishing marks, scars, tattoos, etc. **Acne scars on cheeks**
Marques distinctives, cicatrices, tatouages, etc.

(l) Other **Missing front tooth, upper**
Autre (Specify / *Précisez.*)

6. Usual occupation **Office Manager**
Profession habituelle

7. Last known place of employment **Fly by Night Construction Ltd.**
Dernier lieu de travail connu

8. Vehicle description
Description du véhicule

(a) Make, model and year **None** (b) Colour
Marque, modèle et année *Couleur*

(c) Licence plate number Province or state
Numéro de la plaque d'immatriculation *Province ou État*

(d) Driver's licence number Province or state
Numéro du permis de conduire *Province ou État*

(e) Distinguishing features on the vehicle (dents, car stereo, etc.)
Caractéristiques distinctives du véhicule (bosses, autoradio, etc.)

9. Other information **May be found in company of sister, Penelope Foot, 185 Smith St., Toronto, ON M4R 1Q6**
Autres renseignements

10. Photograph of the person provided in the box below, if available.
Une photographie de la personne figure dans la case ci-dessous, si elle est disponible.

The information supplied above is true to the best of my knowledge
and belief.
Au mieux de ma connaissance et de ce que je tiens pour véridique,
les renseignements ci-dessus sont exacts.

Albert Oryx
(Signature of party / *Signature de la partie*)

Albert Oryx
(Name of party / *Nom de la partie*)

December 5, Yr. 1

SCR 20.11-20K (June 1. 2009 / *1er juin 2009*) CSD

The debtor held in custody on a warrant can be discharged under Rule 20.11(9) by the earlier of an order of the court or when the time prescribed in the warrant expires. Under Rule 20.11(10), a warrant remains in force for 12 months from its date of issue. Warrants may be renewed by order of the court, on a motion, for 12 months.

> 20.11(9) A person in custody under a warrant issued under this rule shall be discharged from custody on the order of the court or when the time prescribed in the warrant expires, whichever is earlier.
>
> (10) A warrant issued under this rule remains in force for 12 months after the date of issue and may be renewed by order of the court on a motion made by the creditor for 12 months at each renewal, unless the court orders otherwise.

Relief for Judgment Debtors

The enforcement procedure recognizes that debtors, particularly consumer debtors, cannot always pay a judgment outright, but could pay if they were permitted to pay the judgment in a series of instalment payments. At the conclusion of a judgment debtor's examination, the payment order that the court can make may very well feature instalment payments under Rule 20.02 or a Consolidation Order under Rule 20.09.

Instalment Orders

We have already examined a procedure where a debtor can pay by instalments. If served with a claim, a debtor could file a defence admitting the claim and making a proposal to pay by instalments. The instalment payment scheme here is similar, except that it comes after a judgment, usually as part of the enforcement process, and often following a judgment debtor exam. Under Rule 20.02, the court may order payments to be made by instalment on a judgment, and may vary the amounts of payments, the length of time between payments, and the number of payments if the debtor's circumstances change. The court may also stay enforcement of the judgment if it is appropriate to do so, for a period of time, and on terms.

> 20.02(1) The court may,
> (a) stay the enforcement of an order of the court, for such time and on such terms as are just; and
> (b) vary the times and proportions in which money payable under an order of the court shall be paid, if it is satisfied that the debtor's circumstances have changed.
>
> (2) While an order for periodic payment is in force, no step to enforce the judgment may be taken or continued against the debtor

by a creditor named in the order, except issuing a writ of seizure and sale of land and filing it with the sheriff.

(3) The creditor may serve the debtor with a notice of default of payment (Form 20L) in accordance with subrule 8.01(14) and file a copy of it, together with an affidavit of default of payment (Form 20M), if the debtor fails to make payments under an order for periodic payment.

(4) An order for periodic payment terminates on the day that is 15 days after the creditor serves the debtor with the notice of default of payment, unless a consent (Form 13B) in which the creditor waives the default is filed within the 15-day period.

One might wonder why a debtor would agree to pay by instalments after judgment. One inducement is that no further steps may be taken to enforce the judgment except to permit a Writ of Seizure and Sale of Land to be filed with the sheriff. As a debtor may have been subjected to vigorous enforcement by the creditor, a stay of enforcement while instalment payments are being made might seem preferable to dodging the bailiff.

Should the debtor fail to make instalment payments as ordered, the creditor serves on the debtor a Notice of Default of Payment (Form 20L). The debtor then has 15 days from the date of service to bring the payments into good standing or to obtain a consent in Form 13B from the creditor, waiving the default. If payment is not made in 15 days, the creditor can file the notice of default and an Affidavit of Default of Payment (Form 20M) with the court. Once the instalment order terminates, the creditor may resume using all of the enforcement remedies available against the judgment debtor.

Consolidation Orders

A consolidation order is a type of instalment order that is restricted to situations where a debtor has two or more unsatisfied money judgments against him or her. In this case a debtor may make a motion for a consolidation order. Under Rule 20.09(1), debtors with two or more judgments against them may seek a consolidation order if they are subjected to enforcement by multiple creditors, where property is being seized and wages garnished. Such an order may also arise following a judgment debtor examination when it becomes apparent that there are multiple judgments in favour of different creditors.

20.09(1) A debtor against whom there are two or more unsatisfied orders for the payment of money may make a motion to the court for a consolidation order.

To obtain a consolidation order, the debtor must do the following:

- A judgment debtor with two or more judgments against him or her must prepare a notice of motion and supporting affidavit in accordance with Rule 20.09(2):

  > 20.09(2) The debtor's notice of motion and supporting affidavit (Form 15A) shall set out, in the affidavit portion,
  >
  > (a) the names and addresses of the creditors who have obtained an order for the payment of money against the debtor;
  >
  > (b) the amount owed to each creditor;
  >
  > (c) the amount of the debtor's income from all sources, identifying them; and
  >
  > (d) the debtor's current financial obligations and any other relevant facts.

  The affidavit must set out the names and addresses of the creditors with the judgments, the amount owing to each creditor, and the amount of the debtor's income from all sources, with each source identified, as well as the debtor's current debts and expenses and other relevant facts. In preparing the supporting affidavit, you can use the format in the Financial Information Form (Form 20I) as a guide, or even attach it, completed, as an exhibit to the affidavit to provide information on income and expenses.

- The debtor, under Rule 20.09(3), must serve the notice of motion and supporting affidavit on each judgment creditor at least seven days before the hearing date to give the creditors time to review the material and respond if they intend to oppose the motion:

  > 20.09(3) For the purposes of clause 15.01(3)(a), the notice of motion and supporting affidavit shall be served on each of the creditors mentioned in it at least seven days before the hearing date.

  At the hearing the judge can deny the motion or grant it. If granted, the order, in accordance with Rule 20.09(4), will record a list of unsatisfied judgments with the details of the court, date, judgment amount, and amounts still owing. The order will also specify the amount of the instalment payments and the times they are to be paid. As per subrule (5), the total amount to be paid under the order cannot exceed the portion of wages subject to seizure under s. 7 of the *Wages Act*. Under the *Wages Act*, for an ordinary judgment, no more than 20% of a person's net wages can be seized.

  > 20.09(4) At the hearing of the motion, the court may make a consolidation order setting out,
  >
  > (a) a list of unsatisfied orders for the payment of money against the debtor, indicating in each case the date, court and amount and the amount unpaid;

    (b) the amounts to be paid into court by the debtor under the
consolidation order; and

    (c) the times of the payments.

      (5) The total of the amounts to be paid into court by the
debtor under a consolidation order shall not exceed the portion of
the debtor's wages that are subject to seizure or garnishment under
section 7 of the *Wages Act.*

A creditor is permitted, under Rule 20.09(6), to make submissions at the consolidation motion hearing as to the amount and timing of payments:

> 20.09(6) At the hearing of the motion, a creditor may make submissions as to the amount and times of payment.

- The debtor then pays those amounts to the court for distribution to the judgment creditors named in the order. Rule 20.09(12) provides that the creditors share equally in the payments. Under Rule 20.09(13) the clerk must distribute the funds paid under the consolidation order to the creditors at least once every six months, although the court may forward payments more often than that:

> 20.09(12) All payments into a consolidation account belong to the creditors named in the consolidation order, who shall share equally in the distribution of the money.
>
>   (13) The clerk shall distribute the money paid into the consolidation account at least once every six months.

- While the consolidation order is in force, the creditors covered by the order must, in accordance with Rule 20.09(9), cease enforcement against the debtor, except for issuing and filing a Writ of Seizure and Sale of Land with the sheriff:

> 20.09(9) While the consolidation order is in force, no step to enforce the judgment may be taken or continued against the debtor by a creditor named in the order, except issuing a writ of seizure and sale of land and filing it with the sheriff.

- The consolidation order terminates when the final payment due under the order is made, in which case the debtor asks the creditors, under Rule 20.12, to file a Request for a Clerk's Order on Consent indicating that payment has been made in full and that the judgment or order has been satisfied. If one or more of the creditors does not consent to this, the debtor can bring a motion for an order confirming that the judgment has been satisfied. This can be useful in restoring a debtor's credit rating. The debtor should notify the credit bureau once payment in full has been made.

> 20.12 If payment is made in full satisfaction of an order,

(a) where all parties consent, a party may file a request for clerk's order on consent (Form 11.2A) indicating that payment has been made in full satisfaction of the order or terms of settlement; or

(b) the debtor may make a motion for an order confirming that payment has been made in full satisfaction of the order or terms of settlement.

- As a consolidation order is a benefit for a debtor, it terminates immediately in two situations, under Rules 20.09(10) and 20.09(8):
  - The debtor is in default of payment on the order for more than 21 days (the debtor can pay "late" without an automatic termination, provided the lateness does not extend beyond 21 days):

    20.09(10) A consolidation order terminates immediately if the debtor is in default under it for 21 days.

  - A creditor obtains judgment on a date *after* the consolidation order was made for a debt incurred *after* the consolidation order was made. In this case it is implied that the debtor is not being financially responsible and that he or she should not have the benefit of the order:

    20.09(8) A consolidation order terminates immediately if an order for the payment of money is obtained against the debtor for a debt incurred after the date of the consolidation order.

- If a creditor obtains a judgment against the debtor *after* the consolidation order was made, on a debt incurred *before* the consolidation order was made, under Rule 20.09(7) this is seen as part of the financial situation that led to the consolidation order, rather than as new financial irresponsibility. In this case, the "new" judgment creditor may file a certified copy of the "new judgment" with the clerk, who shall add the new judgment to the consolidation order so that the "new" judgment creditor shares equally with the other judgment creditors in the distribution of payments. The consolidation order does not terminate but continues, although its terms may be varied by the court.

    20.09(7) If an order for the payment of money is obtained against the debtor after the date of the consolidation order for a debt incurred before the date of the consolidation order, the creditor may file with the clerk a certified copy of the new order; the creditor shall be added to the consolidation order and shall share in the distribution under it from that time.

- If a consolidation order terminates, under Rule 20.09(11), the clerk serves notice that the order has terminated. Pursuant to Rule

20.09(11.1), the notice may be served by mail or fax to the judgment creditors, who are then at liberty to re-start enforcement:

> 20.09(11) If a consolidation order terminates under subrule (8) or (10), the clerk shall notify the creditors named in the consolidation order, and no further consolidation order shall be made in respect of the debtor for one year after the date of termination.
>
> (11.1) The notice that the consolidation order is terminated shall be served by mail or fax.

- If the order terminates, as set out in Rule 20.09(11) above, the debtor must wait one year from termination before he or she can apply for a new consolidation order.

(See Illustration 13.9 for a completed Termination of Consolidation Order for *Oryx v. Foot.*)

CHAPTER SUMMARY

In this chapter, we discussed enforcement strategies and tactics, which depend on the debtor's means, assets, and debts to determine which enforcement techniques should be used to enforce the judgment creditor's right to payment. We noted that the enforcement techniques available are slow, cumbersome, and not very effective against a sophisticated judgment debtor who is determined not to pay. As a rule, it is a good idea to file a Writ of Seizure and Sale of Personal Property and a Writ of Seizure and Sale of Land, and to garnish wages and bank accounts, if you know of any. The court's enforcement remedies are limited to Writs of Delivery of Personal Property, Writs of Seizure and Sale of personal property and land, and garnishment. The specific procedures for obtaining these remedies are covered in later chapters. If you need more information about a debtor's financial situation, you may conduct a judgment debtor examination, where, if the debtor refuses to attend or answer questions, you may proceed to have him or her found in contempt. If a debtor is not able to pay a judgment, the court may facilitate payment by ordering the judgment to be paid by instalments. If the debtor has multiple judgments against him or her, he or she may ask for a consolidation order to spread payments over time while stopping creditors from continuing to enforce the judgment.

ILLUSTRATION 13.9: Termination of Consolidation Order for *Oryx v. Foot*

Superior Court of Justice	**Termination of Consolidation Order**
Cour supérieure de justice	*Résiliation de l'ordonnance de consolidation*

Toronto

Small Claims Court / *Cour des petites créances de*

47 Sheppard Ave. E., 3rd Fl.

Address / *Adresse*

Toronto, ON M2N 5N1

416-326-3554

Phone number / *N° de téléphone*

SC-00-47669-00

Claim No. / *N° de la demande*

BETWEEN /*ENTRE*

Albert Oryx

Plaintiff(s) / *Demandeur(s)*

and / *et*

Ophelia Foot

Defendant(s) / *Défendeur(s)*

TO THE CREDITORS NAMED IN THE CONSOLIDATION ORDER:

AUX CRÉANCIERS NOMMÉS DANS L'ORDONNANCE DE CONSOLIDATION :

The consolidation order is terminated immediately because:

À l'issue de l'audience pour outrage, le tribunal peut ordonner, selon le cas :

X (a)   an order for the payment of money has been obtained against the debtor for a debt incurred after the date of the consolidation order;

   a)   *une ordonnance de paiement d'une somme d'argent a été obtenue contre le débiteur à l'égard d'une dette contractée après la date de l'ordonnance de consolidation;*

OR / *OU*

  (b)   according to the supporting affidavit filed by the creditor, the debtor has defaulted under the consolidation order for 21 days.

   b)   *selon l'affidavit à l'appui déposé par le créancier, le débiteur est en défaut à l'égard de l'ordonnance de consolidation depuis 21 jours.*

Notice of termination is hereby given to the creditors named in the consolidation order. No further consolidation order shall be made in respect of the debtor for one year after the date of termination.

Avis est donné par les présentes aux créanciers nommés dans l'ordonnance de consolidation que celle-ci a pris fin. Le débiteur ne peut obtenir de nouvelle ordonnance de consolidation pendant la période d'un an qui suit la date à laquelle l'ordonnance a pris fin.

Le   April 2, Yr. 2

            (Date)

"I.M. Clerk"

(Signature of clerk / *Signature du greffier*)

SAA 20.09-00 (January 25, 2006 / *25 janvier 2006*) CSD

(Non-regulated form / *Formule non prescrite*)

REVIEW QUESTIONS

1. What steps should you take to enforce a judgment immediately after obtaining it?

2. What remedies are available to enforce money judgments?

3. What documents do you have to file in support of the following?
   (a) Certificate of Judgment
   (b) Notice of Examination

4. Where do you examine a judgment debtor? What happens if he or she does not show up? What happens if he or she does show up, but refuses to answer questions?

5. When might the court order instalment payments? What happens if the debtor defaults?

6. When might the court make a consolidation order? When might it end one?

DISCUSSION QUESTIONS/CASE STUDIES

FACTS

You are a paralegal working at Seneca Paralegals, 1750 Finch Avenue East, Toronto, Ontario M2J 2X5. You are representing Wilbur Watson, who lives at 364 Maple Blvd., Toronto, Ontario M3H 4F1, in an action against B & J Contracting (B & J), a partnership owned by Bradley and Jordan Ames. Their business is located at 487 Regency Blvd., Richmond Hill, Ontario L4A 3B8.

Wilbur hired B & J to put a sunroom on the back of his house. The partnership did a terrible job, and finished on August 1, Year 0. It cost Wilbur $6,800 to have the sunroom fixed. The claim was issued on November 1, Year 0. You acted for Wilbur when he sued B & J in Small Claims Court, and got judgment on January 26, Year 1, for $6,800, costs of $670, and post-judgment interest pursuant to the *Courts of Justice Act*.

Wilbur has no idea what assets B & J owns, but he wants to enforce his judgment. You decide that the first step should be a judgment debtor examination of Bradley Ames. Assume for these questions that you have expanded your enforcement rights under Rule 5 so that you can enforce against the partners as well as the partnership.

Prepare the necessary documents for an examination on March 19, Year 1. Today is February 15, Year 1.

Chapter 14

Writs of Delivery and Writs of Seizure and Sale

LEARNING OBJECTIVES

⇨ Understand what writs of delivery and writs of seizure and sale are

⇨ Know when to use writs of delivery and writs of seizure and sale

⇨ Know how to obtain writs of delivery and writs of seizure and sale

INTRODUCTION

Having learned about the various methods of enforcing a judgment, we are now faced with the task of selecting the most effective remedy or remedies to enforce our judgment. From our searches or from information obtained from an examination in aid of execution, we may have discovered that the judgment debtor has real or personal property, or both, that could be seized and sold to satisfy the judgment. In some cases the judgment debtor may have been ordered by the court to return property belonging to the judgment creditor but has not done so. In that situation a writ of delivery may be required to secure the return of the property. This chapter will detail the steps required to obtain a writ of delivery and writs of seizure and sale of personal property and of land.

WRITS OF DELIVERY

Writs of delivery are used when you seek to have personal property wrongfully held by the defendant returned to the plaintiff. Writs of delivery are permitted under Rule 20.05:

> 20.05(1) An order for the delivery of personal property may be enforced by a writ of delivery (Form 20B) issued by the clerk to a bailiff, on the request of the person in whose favour the order was made, supported by an affidavit of that person or the person's agent stating that the property has not been delivered.
>
> (2) If the property referred to in a writ of delivery cannot be found or taken by the bailiff, the person in whose favour the order was made may make a motion to the court for an order directing the bailiff to seize any other personal property of the person against whom the order was made.
>
> (3) Unless the court orders otherwise, the bailiff shall keep personal property seized under subrule (2) until the court makes a further order for its disposition.
>
> (4) The person in whose favour the order is made shall pay the bailiff's storage costs, in advance and from time to time; if the person fails to do so, the seizure shall be deemed to be abandoned.

In his original claim, Albert Oryx was seeking the return of the engagement ring, which he claimed Ophelia Foot was not entitled to keep, rather than damages for its loss. The property should be described in enough detail in the claim so that the description can be included in the endorsement record at the end of the trial. As well, if it is likely that the property is located in a residence, you should ask the judge to endorse on the record that reasonable force may be used pursuant to s. 20(2) of the *Execution Act*. It is also useful to request an order that states that if the lock cannot be picked then the lock may be drilled out if necessary. The reason for this is that, in some jurisdictions, if a lock cannot be picked then entry cannot be gained without an order permitting the drilling of a lock. When an order is sought for the return of property with reasonable force to be used if necessary, the claim or the motion for a writ of delivery should request:

> An order authorizing the use of reasonable force, if necessary, to enter a private dwelling to execute the writ, in accordance with section 20(2) of the Execution Act and a further order that if the lock cannot be picked, that the lock, if necessary, may be drilled out.

Once you have your order, you should first demand the return of the specific property. If the property is not returned, then complete an Affidavit for Enforcement Request (Form 20P) and a Writ of Delivery (Form 20B) and bring three copies of the documents to the court that made the order for the return of property or the order for a writ of delivery to have the writ issued along with the fee of $35 for issuance of a writ of delivery. The clerk will review the draft writ of delivery and compare it to the judge's endorsement. If the endorsement provides that reasonable force may be used for entry, then he or she will check off the box on page 2 noting that such force may be used. The clerk will emboss the court seal on one copy of the writ and stamp the other two copies and return the original embossed one and a copy to you for enforcement, and have the clerk issue the writ.

Content of the Writ of Delivery

The writ is addressed on Form 20B to the bailiff; however, sheriff's offices in each jurisdiction have taken over the enforcement of writs of delivery. The current form still names a bailiff. The court will accept these forms, as updated ones have not been made at this time. The writ describes the property to be seized with as much detail as possible. If the property was referred to in detail in the claim, attach the claim. Provide serial numbers for the items, if applicable. If the parties had a signed lease, attach a copy of the lease (which should have been attached to the claim). Indicate where the property is to be found; if that does not provide enough detail, include a map. If the endorsement record indicates that reasonable force may be used to seize the property, the clerk will indicate this at the foot of the form. The endorsement will be necessary if entry to a private residence is required. If it is not a private residence, reasonable force may be used without an order. Note also that the court cannot order that the defendant fix or repair an item that is to be returned. If you wish to do that, you need to sue in the Superior Court, where the court has the power to make that kind of order. However, if the property has been damaged or your loss of its use has resulted in a monetary loss to you, then you can also claim money damages, together with an order for return of the property. Illustration 14.1 shows the Writ of Delivery for the *Oryx v. Foot* case.

Enforcement of the Writ of Delivery

Once the writ of delivery has been issued, the original writ and a copy must be filed with the sheriff's office in the jurisdiction in which the defendant resides. If, for example, the order for the return of property was made by the Brampton Small Claims Court and the defendant resided in Newmarket then the writ would need to be filed with the Sheriff's Office in Newmarket. Most sheriff's offices require the legal representative enforcing the writ to provide a letter of direction on their letterhead requesting the sheriff's assistance in enforcing the writ of delivery. The letter should provide the paralegal's full address and contact information, the details of the order and the writ of delivery. The original writ must be submitted for enforcement along with payment of the local tariff and mileage to cover the sheriff's trip to and from the courthouse to enforce the writ.

The legal representative should call the sheriff's office to inquire as to what their tariff is, as the amount varies in each region, as does the rate of mileage that is charged, with some offices charging a flat fee and others requesting mileage based on the distance to and from the court to the enforcement site. The writ, letter, and payment to the Minister of Finance may be sent to the sheriff's office by courier. Your letter should be sent to the attention of the enforcement office. The sheriff's office will assign their own file number to the matter. Once the letter and writ are filed and payment of the tariff and mileage is made, the sheriff's office will contact the legal representative to set up a time for enforcement. The legal representative may attend with the sheriff and should arrange for a locksmith to attend at the same time if one will be required. After the writ of delivery has been executed the sheriff's office will send the legal representative a report as to the details of the execution of the writ and will return the original writ.

Taking Other Property "Hostage"

It is important to give as much information about the property and where it is to be found as you can. The enforcement office will not engage in creative interpretation of writs or carry out investigations

ILLUSTRATION 14.1: Writ of Delivery (Form 20B) for *Oryx v. Foot*

ONTARIO
Superior Court of Justice
Cour supérieure de justice

Writ of Delivery
Bref de délaissement
Form / *Formule* 20B Ont. Reg. No. / *Règl. de l'Ont.* : 258/98

Seal / *Sceau*

<u>Toronto</u>
Small Claims Court / *Cour des petites créances de*

<u>SC-00-47669-00</u>
Claim No. / *N° de la demande*

47 Sheppard Ave. E., 3rd Fl.
Toronto, ON M2N 5N1
Address / *Adresse*

<u>416-326-3554</u>
Phone number / *Numéro de téléphone*

BETWEEN / *ENTRE*

Albert Oryx
Plaintiff(s) / *Demandeur(s)/demanderesse(s)*

and / *et*

Ophelia Foot
Defendant(s) / *Défendeur(s)/défenderesse(s)*

TO THE BAILIFF OF <u>Toronto</u>   **SMALL CLAIMS COURT:**
À L'HUISSIER DE LA COUR   (Name of Small Claims Court location / *Emplacement de la Cour*
DES PETITES CRÉANCES DE   *des petites créances*)

Under an order of this court made on <u>Sept. 14, Yr. 1</u>
En vertu d'une ordonnance rendue par le tribunal précité le

YOU ARE DIRECTED to seize from <u>Ophelia Foot</u>
NOUS VOUS ENJOIGNONS *de saisir auprès de*   (Name of person against whom the order was made / *Nom de la personne*
contre qui l'ordonnance a été rendue)

and to deliver without delay to
et de remettre sans retard à

Name of person in whose favour the order was made / *Nom de la personne en faveur de qui l'ordonnance a été rendue* **Albert Oryx**
Street and number / *Numéro et rue* **c/o Peter Parelegal, 41 Yonge Street, #410**
City, province, postal code / *Ville, province, code postal* **Toronto, ON M5G 1S1**
Phone number and fax number, if any / *Numéro de téléphone et numéro de télécopieur, le cas échéant* **Tel. 416-597-0048; Fax 416-597-0049**

possession of the following personal property:
la possession des biens meubles suivants :
(According to the court order, set out a description of the property to be delivered. Identify any marks or serial numbers. If the order refers to items set out in the issued claim, attach a copy of the issued claim.)
(Conformément à l'ordonnance du tribunal, donnez la description des biens qui doivent être remis. Indiquez toute marque d'identification ou tout numéro de série y figurant. Si l'ordonnance vise des articles énoncés dans la demande délivrée, annexez une copie de la demandedélivrée.)

1. Silver engagement ring, single 1k diamond in contemporary setting

SCR 20.05-20B (June 1, 2009 / *1er juin 2009*) CSD

continues....

Illustration 14.1 (continued)

FORM / *FORMULE* 20B PAGE 2 SC-00-47669-00
Claim No. / *N° de la demande*

The above personal property is located at: <u>83 Greengrove Rd., Toronto, ON M6R 4Q5</u>
Les biens meubles susmentionnés se trouvent à/au : (Address / *Adresse*)

If the address provided does not clearly identify where the items are located, please attach a detailed map that shows the nearest intersection.
Si l'adresse fournie n'indique pas clairement l'emplacement des articles, veuillez annexer un plan détaillé qui montre l'intersection la plus rapprochée.

(To be completed by the clerk of the court. / Section à remplir par le greffier du tribunal.)	☒ **THE COURT HAS EXPRESSLY ORDERED** that you are authorized to use reasonable force to enter a private dwelling to execute this writ of delivery, if necessary [*Execution Act*, s. 20(2)]. A copy of the court's order on the endorsement record is attached. *EN VERTU D'UNE ORDONNANCE EXPRESSE DU TRIBUNAL, vous êtes autorisé(e) à avoir recours à la force raisonnable pour pénétrer dans un logement privé pour exécuter le présent bref de délaissement, si cela est nécessaire [Loi sur l'exécution forcée, par. 20 (2)]. Une copie de l'ordonnance du tribunal qui figure au dossier des inscriptions est annexée.*

December 12, Yr. 1

"I.M. Clerk"
(Signature of clerk / *Signature du greffier*)

SCR 20.05-20B (June 1, 2009 / *1ᵉʳ juin 2009*) CSD

to locate the property. If they can't find it where you tell them it is located, they will report that fact. If it turns out that the property has been moved to another location, you may need to obtain another writ authorizing a search of those premises.

Where it is apparent that the judgment debtor is not being co-operative and the property cannot be found, Rule 20.05(3) provides a solution. You may bring a motion requesting an order authorizing seizure of any other personal property belonging to the judgment debtor. The property will then be seized and held until the court authorizes its disposition by sale or, possibly, by delivery to the debtor. Your affidavit in support of the motion should describe the unsuccessful efforts to recover the property and, if possible, identify in as much detail as possible other personal property that clearly belongs to the judgment debtor. The process works better if you provide maximum information about what to seize and where it might be located. If you have a choice, identify property of roughly equivalent value to the property you are trying to recover — although this is not a requirement.

Note that when personal property is seized, the judgment creditor, in accordance with Rule 20.05(4), is responsible for paying the reasonable enforcement expenses, in addition to a set fee (tariff) for each attempt at seizure. These expenses may include towing or shipping charges, kilometrage fees, storage charges, and other relevant costs. If the judgment creditor does not pay the costs, the seizure may be deemed abandoned, and the property may then be disposed of to recover the costs.

WRITS OF SEIZURE AND SALE — PERSONAL PROPERTY

There are two different Writs for seizing and selling a judgment debtor's property — one for seizing personal property, and one for seizing an interest in land. Both are sometimes referred to as Writs of Execution as well as Writs of Seizure and Sale.

The process for seizing and selling personal property is set out in Rule 20.06:

> 20.06(1) If there is default under an order for the payment or recovery of money, the clerk shall, at the creditor's request, supported by an affidavit for enforcement request (Form 20P) stating the amount still owing, issue to a bailiff a writ of seizure and sale of personal property (Form 20C), and the bailiff shall enforce the writ for the amount owing, post-judgment interest and the bailiff's fees and expenses.

(1.1) If more than six years have passed since the order was made, a writ of seizure and sale of personal property may be issued only with leave of the court.

(1.2) If a writ of seizure and sale of personal property is not issued within one year after the date on which an order granting leave to issue it is made,
(a) the order granting leave ceases to have effect; and
(b) a writ of seizure and sale of personal property may be issued only with leave of the court on a subsequent motion.

(1.3) A writ of seizure and sale of personal property shall show the creditor's name, address and telephone number and the name, address and telephone number of the creditor's lawyer or agent, if any.

(2) A writ of seizure and sale of personal property remains in force for six years after the date of its issue and for a further six years after each renewal.

(3) A writ of seizure and sale of personal property may be renewed before its expiration by filing a request to renew a writ of seizure and sale (Form 20N) with the bailiff.

(4) The creditor may request enforcement of a writ of seizure and sale of personal property by filing a direction to enforce writ of seizure and sale of personal property (Form 20O) with the bailiff.

(5) Within a reasonable time after a request is made by the debtor or the debtor's agent, the bailiff shall deliver an inventory of personal property seized under a writ of seizure and sale of personal property.

(6) Personal property seized under a writ of seizure and sale of personal property shall not be sold by the bailiff unless notice of the time and place of sale has been,
(a) mailed, at least 10 days before the sale,
(i) to the creditor at the address shown on the writ, or to the creditor's lawyer or agent, and
(ii) to the debtor at the debtor's last known address; and
(b) advertised in a manner that is likely to bring it to the attention of the public.

To use this process you will need to file an Affidavit for Enforcement Request (Form 20P), setting out the amount owing on the judgment at the time the affidavit is signed, including accrued post-judgment interest and enforcement costs. With the affidavit also file a Writ of Seizure and Sale of Personal Property (Form 20C). The information about the amount owing set out in the writ should be the same as in the affidavit. The writ is directed to the bailiff of the Small Claims Court. The bailiff will enforce the writ for the amount in the writ, plus his reasonable costs in enforcing the writ. In any sale, the net enforcement costs (enforcement costs minus any deposit paid to cover the bailiff's costs) will be deducted before the judgment creditors receive any money from the sale. The writ should be issued within six years of the order. If more than six years have passed, an order granting leave to issue the writ can be sought. You then have up to one more year to issue the writ. If the writ is not issued in that time, a further motion seeking leave to issue the writ is required.

Contents of the Writ of Seizure and Sale — Personal Property

The writ records the date of the judgment, name, address, and phone number of the creditor, and the creditor's lawyer or agent, if any, and then directs the bailiff to seize the personal property of the named judgment debtor. Note that the name of the judgment debtor must be given as accurately as possible. If the debtor is an individual, then in addition to the last name, you are also asked for first and second names, and any names they are also known as so that the bailiffs have as much information as possible to locate the correct individual judgment debtor, especially if the name is a common name. It also provides information for other judgment creditors, who are searching writs, to determine if your judgment debtor is one and the same as the one they are searching. If, in addition to filing the Writ of Seizure and Sale, you also wish to send the bailiff to seize property, you will need to identify the property to be seized in as much detail as possible and give its location, if known, just as you would do for a Writ of Delivery.

Illustration 14.2 shows a completed Writ of Seizure and Sale of Personal Property (Form 20C) for the *Oryx v. Foot* case.

Seizure and Sale Procedure

A writ of seizure and sale of personal property is enforced when the creditor files a Direction to Enforce Writ of Seizure and Sale of Personal Property (Form 20O) with the bailiff under Rule 20.06(4). A sample Direction to Enforce is set out in Illustration 14.3. The direction gives the bailiff the details of the property to be seized and its location.

If a bailiff seizes personal property of a judgment debtor, he or she, if asked to do so by the debtor or the debtor's agent, is obliged to furnish under Rule 20.06(5), within a reasonable time, an inventory of the property seized and give said inventory to the debtor or the debtor's agent if requested. If a bailiff has entered a residence and seized more than one item of personal property, for example, it would be wise to obtain a list in order to know what was taken. A bailiff,

ILLUSTRATION 14.2: Writ of Seizure and Sale of Personal Property (Form 20C)

ONTARIO

Superior Court of Justice
Cour supérieure de justice

Writ of Seizure and Sale of Personal Property
Bref de saisie-exécution de biens meubles
Form / *Formule* 20C Ont. Reg. No. / *Règl. de l'Ont.* : 258/98

Seal / *Sceau*

Toronto		SC-00-47669-00
Small Claims Court / *Cour des petites créances de*		Claim No. / *N° de la demande*

47 Sheppard Ave. E., 3rd Fl.
Toronto, ON M2N 5N1
Address / *Adresse*

416-326-3554
Phone number / *Numéro de téléphone*

Creditor No. 1 / *Créancier n° 1*

☐ Additional party(ies) listed on attached Form 1A.
La ou les parties additionnelles sont mentionnées sur la formule 1A ci-jointe.

Last name, or name of company / *Nom de famille ou nom de la compagnie*		
Oryx		
First name / *Premier prénom* **Albert**	Second name / *Deuxième prénom*	Also known as / *Également connu(e) sous le nom de*
Address (street number, apt., unit) / *Adresse (numéro et rue, app., unité)* **c/o Peter Paralegal, 41 Yonge Street, #410**		
City/Town / *Cité/ville* **Toronto**	Province **ON**	Phone no. / *N° de téléphone* **416-597-0048**
Postal code / *Code postal* **M5G 1S1**		Fax no. / *N° de télécopieur* **415-597-0049**
Representative / *Représentant(e)* **Peter Paralegal**		LSUC # / *N° du BHC* **P02952**
Address (street number, apt., unit) / *Adresse (numéro et rue, app., unité)* **41 Yonge Street, #410**		
City/Town / *Cité/ville* **Toronto**	Province **ON**	Phone no. / *N° de téléphone* **416-597-0048**
Postal code / *Code postal* **M5G 1S1**		Fax no. / *N° de télécopieur* **416-597-0049**

Debtor No. 1 / *Débiteur n° 1*

☐ Additional party(ies) listed on attached Form 1A.
La ou les parties additionnelles sont mentionnées sur la formule 1A ci-jointe.

Last name, or name of company / *Nom de famille ou nom de la compagnie*		
Foot		
First name / *Premier prénom* **Ophelia**	Second name / *Deuxième prénom*	Also known as / *Également connu(e) sous le nom de*
Address (street number, apt., unit) / *Adresse (numéro et rue, app., unité)* **c/o Digbert Fightback, 60 My Way**		
City/Town / *Cité/ville* **Toronto**	Province **ON**	Phone no. / *N° de téléphone* **416-491-5041**
Postal code / *Code postal* **M6R 8P1**		Fax no. / *N° de télécopieur* **416-491-5042**
Representative / *Représentant(e)* **Digbert Fightback**		LSUC # / *N° du BHC* **P05427**
Address (street number, apt., unit) / *Adresse (numéro et rue, app., unité)* **60 My Way**		
City/Town / *Cité/ville* **Toronto**	Province **ON**	Phone no. / *N° de téléphone* **416-491-5041**
Postal code / *Code postal* **M6R 8P1**		Fax no. / *N° de télécopieur* **416-491-5042**

SCR 20.06-20C (June 1, 2009 / *1er juin 2009*) CSD

continues....

Illustration 14.2 (continued)

FORM / *FORMULE* 20C   **PAGE 2**   SC-00-47669-00

                                                              Claim No. / *N° de la demande*

TO THE BAILIFF OF THE Toronto   **SMALL CLAIMS COURT:**
À L'HUISSIER DE LA COUR   (Small Claims Court location / *Emplacement de la Cour des*
DES PETITES CRÉANCES DE   *petites créances)*

Under an order of this court made on **September 14, Yr. 1**   , in favour of
En vertu d'une ordonnance rendue par ce tribunal le   *, en faveur de*

Albert Oryx

                          (Name of creditor(s) / *Nom du/de la/des créancier(s)/créancière(s)*

YOU ARE DIRECTED to seize and sell the personal property of
NOUS VOUS ENJOIGNONS de saisir les biens meubles de

Last name, or name of company / *Nom de famille ou nom de la compagnie*		
Foot		
First name / *Premier prénom*	Second name / *Deuxième prénom*	Third name / *Troisième prénom*
Ophelia	Mabel	Mary

☐ Additional debtor(s) and also known as names listed on attached Form 1A.1.
    Le ou les débiteurs additionnels et le ou les noms sous lesquels ils sont également connus sont mentionnés
    sur la formule 1A.1 ci-jointe.

situated within your jurisdiction and to realize from the seizure and sale the following sums:
qui se trouvent dans votre ressort et de procéder à leur vente pour réaliser les sommes suivantes :

(A) **AMOUNT OF JUDGMENT** (debt and pre-judgment interest) $ 2,091.07
     LE MONTANT DU JUGEMENT *(créance et intérêts antérieurs au jugement)* $

(B) **COSTS** to date of judgment $ 477.58
     LES DÉPENS *à la date du jugement* $

(C) **TOTAL AMOUNT OF PAYMENTS RECEIVED FROM DEBTOR** after
    judgment (if any) $ Nil
     LE MONTANT TOTAL DES PAIEMENTS REÇUS DU DÉBITEUR *après le* $
     jugement (le cas échéant)

     Post-judgment interest continues to accrue
     Les intérêts postérieurs au jugement continuent à courir

     at the rate of **5.0**   % per annum from **September 14, Yr. 1**   .
     au taux de   % par an à compter du

(D) **SUBSEQUENT COSTS** incurred after judgment (including the cost of issuing this writ) $ 124.00
     LES DÉPENS SUBSÉQUENTS *engagés après le jugement (y compris le coût* $
     de délivrance du présent bref)

(E) Your fees and expenses in enforcing this writ.
     Les honoraires et frais qui vous sont dus pour l'exécution forcée du présent bref.

SCR 20.06-20C (June 1, 2009 / *1ᵉʳ juin 2009*) CSD   **Continued on next page /** *Suite à la page suivante*

Note: (D), Subsequent Costs, include Certificate Judgment, $19; Notice of Examination, $35; Writ of Delivery, $35; Personal Property Writ of Seizure and Sale, $35.

continues....

Illustration 14.2 (continued)

FORM / *FORMULE* 20C	PAGE 3	SC-00-47669-00
		Claim No. / *N° de la demande*

YOU ARE DIRECTED to calculate the amount owing at the time of enforcement and to pay the proceeds over to the clerk of this court for the creditor.
ET NOUS VOUS ENJOIGNONS *de calculer la somme due au moment de l'exécution forcée et de verser le produit de la vente au greffier du tribunal précité pour le compte du créancier.*

October 12, Yr. 1   "I. M. Clerk"

(Signature of clerk / *Signature du greffier*)

Reasonable disbursements necessarily incurred to enforce this writ	$	
Débours raisonnables qui ont dû être engagés pour exécuter le présent bref		(filled in and initialled by the enforcement office / *à remplir et à parapher par le bureau de l'exécution*) $
(Bailiff (enforcement office) fees and expenses / *Honoraires et frais de l'huissier (bureau de l'exécution)*)		

NOTE: **THIS WRIT REMAINS IN FORCE FOR SIX YEARS** after the date of its issue and for a further six years after each renewal. The writ may be renewed before it expires by filing a Request to Renew a Writ of Seizure and Sale (Form 20N) with the bailiff (enforcement office).

REMARQUE :   ***LE PRÉSENT BREF RESTE EN VIGUEUR PENDANT SIX ANS*** *après la date de sa délivrance ou après chaque renouvellement. Le bref peut être renouvelé avant qu'il n'expire en déposant une demande de renouvellement du bref de saisie-exécution (formule 20N) auprès de l'huissier (bureau de l'exécution).*

SCR 20.06-20C (June 1, 2009 / *1ᵉʳ juin 2009*) CSD

ILLUSTRATION 14.3: Direction to Enforce Writ of Seizure and Sale of Personal Property (Form 20O)

ONTARIO
Superior Court of Justice
Cour supérieure de justice

Direction to Enforce Writ of Seizure and Sale of Personal Property
Ordre d'exécution d'un bref de saisie-exécution de biens meubles
Form / *Formule* 20O Ont. Reg. No. / *Règl. de l'Ont.* : 258/98

Toronto
Small Claims Court / *Cour des petites créances de*

47 Sheppard Ave. E., 3rd Fl.
Toronto, ON M2N 5N1

Address / *Adresse*

416-326-3554
Phone number / *Numéro de téléphone*

SC-00-47669-00
Claim No. / *N° de la demande*

BETWEEN / *ENTRE*

Albert Oryx

Creditor(s) / *Créancier(s)/créancière(s)*

and / *et*

Ophelia Foot

Debtor(s) / *Débiteur(s)/débitrice(s)*

My name is **Albert Oryx**
Je m'appelle

(Full name / *Nom et prénoms*)

1. In this action, I am the
   Dans la présente action, je suis le/la

   (Check one box only. / *Cochez une seule case.*)

   ☒ creditor.
   créancier/créancière.

   ☐ representative of the creditor(s).
   représentant(e) du/de la/des créancier(s)/créancière(s).

   A Writ of Seizure and Sale of Personal Property (Form 20C) directed to the bailiff of the
   Un bref de saisie-exécution de biens meubles (formule 20C) adressé à l'huissier de la Cour des petites créances de

   Toronto _____ Small Claims Court was issued on:
   (Small Claims Court location / *emplacement de la Cour des petites créances*) *a été délivré le :*

   September 14, Yr. 1 _____, in favour of **Albert Oryx**
   , en faveur de   (Name of creditor / *Nom du/de la créancier/créancière*)

2. I am filing this direction to enforce the Writ of Seizure and Sale of Personal Property, and direct the bailiff to seize and sell (if required) the personal property belonging to the following debtor(s):
   Je dépose le présent ordre d'exécution du bref de saisie-exécution de biens meubles et ordonne à l'huissier de saisir et de vendre (s'il y a lieu) les biens meubles appartenant au(x) débiteur(s) suivant(s) :

Last name, or name of company / *Nom de famille ou nom de la compagnie*		
Foot		
First name / *Premier prénom*	Second name / *Deuxième prénom*	Third given name (individual only) (if applicable) / *Troisième prénom (particulier seulement) (s'il y a lieu)*
Ophelia	**Mabel**	**Mary**

☐ Additional debtor(s) and also known as names are listed on attached Form 1A.1.
   Le ou les débiteurs additionnels et le ou les noms sous lesquels les débiteurs sont également connus sont mentionnés sur la formule 1A.1 ci-jointe.

Set out a description of the property to be seized. *Identify any marks or serial numbers.*
Donnez la description des biens qui doivent être saisis. Indiquez toute marque d'identification ou tout numéro de série y figurant.

1. Silver engagement ring, single 1k diamond in contemporary setting

SCR 20.06-20O (June 1, 2009 / *1er juin 2009*) CSD

continues....

Illustration 14.3 (continued)

FORM / *FORMULE* 20O   PAGE 2   SC-00-47669-00

Claim No. / *N° de la demande*

3. The above personal property is located at: **83 Greengrove Rd., Toronto, ON M6R 4Q5**
Les biens meubles susmentionnés se trouvent à/au :   (Address / *Adresse*)

If the address provided does not clearly identify where the property is located, please attach a detailed map showing the nearest intersection.
Si l'adresse fournie n'indique pas clairement l'emplacement des biens, veuillez annexer un plan détaillé qui montre l'intersection la plus rapprochée.

4. From the date that the Writ of Seizure and Sale of Personal Property was issued, the following payments have been received from the debtor and/or subsequent costs incurred by the creditor:
Depuis la date de délivrance du bref de saisie-exécution de biens meubles, les paiements suivants ont été reçus du débiteur ou les dépens subséquents engagés par le créancier :

(A) **PAYMENTS RECEIVED FROM DEBTOR**
PAIEMENTS REÇUS DU DÉBITEUR

Date of Payment *Date du paiement*	Payment Amount *Montant du paiement*
$	NIL $
$	$
$	$
$	$

☐ List of additional payments attached
Liste de paiements additionnels ci-jointe

(B) **SUBSEQUENT COSTS** incurred since issuance of Writ of Seizure and Sale of Personal Property
DÉPENS SUBSÉQUENTS engagés depuis la délivrance du bref de saisie-exécution de biens meubles

Reason cost was incurred *Raison pour laquelle les dépens ont été engagés*	Cost Amount *Montant des dépens*
$	$
$	$
$	$
$	$

☐ List of additional costs attached
Liste de dépens additionnels ci-jointe

The bailiff will calculate the amount owing based on the information provided within the Writ of Seizure and Sale of Personal Property and the details provided above. This amount will include any reasonable disbursements necessarily incurred to enforce this writ.
L'huissier calculera la somme due en fonction des renseignements donnés dans le bref de saisie-exécution de biens meubles et des précisions données ci-dessus. Cette somme inclura les débours raisonnables qui ont dû être engagés pour exécuter ce bref.

October 12, Yr. 1

Peter Paralegal

(Signature of creditor or representative / *Signature du créancier/de la créancière ou du/de la représentant(e)*)

Peter Paralegal, 41 Yonge Street, #410
Toronto ON   M5G 1S1
416-597-0048

(Name, address and phone number of creditor or representative /*Nom, adresse et numéro de téléphone du créancier/de la créancière ou du/de la représentant(e)*)

SCR 20.06-20O (June 1, 2009 / *1er juin 2009*) CSD

having seized goods, is responsible for keeping the property safe until it is sold or until the debtor pays the debt, in which case the goods must be returned to the judgment debtor.

The property must be advertised for sale in such a way as to bring it to the public's attention. Placing a notice of sale in the legal notices section of a local newspaper at least 10 days prior to the sale is the usual way to do this. The creditor and debtor also must be mailed copies of the notice of sale. The sale itself is usually done by auction, using a private auctioneer retained by the bailiff. The bailiff is not required to get the best price possible, or even fair market value. So long as the bailiff conducts a public sale as required by Rule 20.06(6), he or she will have met his or her obligations. As noted, the bailiff will deduct his or her costs from the amounts received on the sale and remit the balance to the clerk of the court for distribution to creditors.

If there are several **execution creditors** who have filed writs against the judgment debtor and one of them has successfully seized and sold property, that execution creditor must share the net proceeds of sale on a *pro rata* basis with the other execution creditors who filed writs in the same court, in accordance with the provisions of the *Creditors' Relief Act, 2010*.[1] A **pro rata distribution** requires that the execution creditor who is owed the most money gets the largest share of the net sale proceeds, even if another creditor takes all the steps to seize and sell property. Example 14.1 shows how the net sale proceeds are divided among several execution creditors.

Example 14.1 Pro-rata Distribution

A is owed $100
B is owed $200
C is owed $300
Total owed: $600

All three have filed their Writs of Seizure and Sale in the same court. *A* enforces his writ, and the net proceeds of sale are $200.

A gets 100/600 of $200, which is 16.67% × $200 = $ 33.33
B gets 200/600 of $200, which is 33.33% × $200 = $ 66.66
C gets 300/600 of $200, which is 50.00% × $200 = $100.00

---

[1] Under s. 10 of *Creditor's Relief Act, 2010*, an execution creditor with a Superior Court judgment can direct the sheriff to seize any money or property collected or held by the clerk or bailiff of the Small Claims Court.

Note that although *A* did all the work, she recovers less than the others do, even though they did nothing other than file their writs. This illustrates the value of filing a writ even when you do not know whether there is property to seize. Another creditor might know, and you may reap a windfall as a result.

Writs of Seizure and Sale expire at the end of six years, but may be renewed for further six-year terms. You should diarize the renewal date and not depend on the court to provide you with notice that the writ is about to expire. The appropriate form to use to renew a writ of seizure and sale is Form 20N, and it is to be filed with the bailiff. (See Illustration 14.4 for a completed Form 20N.)

Considerations in Seizing and Selling Property

Filing a writ is useful as a passive enforcement technique because you may get some money under the provisions of the *Creditors' Relief Act, 2010*, as set out above, if another creditor seizes something. More often, the existence of a filed writ will damage the judgment debtor's credit rating, and that may motivate him or her to pay what is owing so as to get the writ vacated. Before sending out a bailiff to seize something, consider the following:

- The buyers who attend these sales generally perceive a bailiff's sale as a distress sale. It is difficult to get high prices on such sales. This is reinforced by the fact that the goods you seek to sell are used. Considering the cost of the sale, selling the judgment debtor's used chattels may not be worthwhile.

- If the judgment debtor resists the seizure or says he doesn't own a particular chattel, the bailiff will retreat rather than seize goods where the title is unclear. A further court order to determine legal ownership may be necessary to get the bailiff to act. This drives up costs and causes further delay.

- Valuable items such as cars, recreational vehicles, and boats are often subject to security interests that give the secured lender priority over any sale proceeds. There may be little or nothing left for the execution creditor who caused the sale.

- Many items you would seize are subject to exemptions — these are discussed in the next section.

Unless the judgment debtor owns a car or a boat, or has an art collection, or something else of value that is not subject to a security interest or statutory exemption, sending the bailiff out to seize property may not be worth the effort. You will need to do a *Personal Property*

ILLUSTRATION 14.4: Renewal of Writ (Form 20N)

ONTARIO
Superior Court of Justice
Cour supérieure de justice

Request to Renew Writ of Seizure and Sale
Demande de renouvellement du bref de saisie-exécution
Form / Formule 20N Ont. Reg. No. / Règl. de l'Ont. : 258/98

Toronto
Small Claims Court / *Cour des petites créances de*

47 Sheppard Ave. E., 3rd Fl.
Toronto, ON M2N 5N1
Address / *Adresse*

416-326-3554
Phone number / *Numéro de téléphone*

SC-00-47669-00
Claim No. / *N° de la demande*

BETWEEN / *ENTRE*

Albert Oryx
Creditor(s) / *Créancier(s)/créancière(s)*

and / *et*

Ophelia Foot
Debtor(s) / *Débiteur(s)/débitrice(s)*

TO THE SHERIFF/BAILIFF OF Toronto   :
AU SHÉRIF/À L'HUISSIER DU/DE LA (Name of county/region and city/town in which the enforcement office is located / *Nom du comté/de la région et de la cité/ville où est situé le bureau de l'exécution*)

YOU ARE REQUESTED TO RENEW the   ☒ Writ of Seizure and Sale of Personal Property (Form 20C)
VOUS ÊTES PRIÉ(E) DE RENOUVELER le   *bref de saisie-exécution de biens meubles (formule 20C)*

☐ Writ of Seizure and Sale of Land (Form 20D)
    bref de saisie-exécution de biens-fonds (formule 20D)

issued on October 12, Yr. 1   , in this proceeding and filed in your office for a period of
délivré le   *dans la présente instance et déposé à votre bureau, pour*

six years from the date of renewal.
une période de six ans à compter de la date du renouvellement.

September 10, Yr. 7

Peter Paralegal
(Signature of creditor or representative / *Signature du créancier/de la créancière ou du/de la représentant(e)*)

Peter Paralegal, 41 Yonge Street, #410
Toronto ON   M5G 1S1
416-597-0048
(Name, address and phone number of creditor or representative / *Nom, adresse et numéro de téléphone du créancier/de la créancière ou du/de la représentant(e)*)

NOTE: **A WRIT OF SEIZURE AND SALE OF LAND OR OF PERSONAL PROPERTY** remains in force for six years after the date of its issue and for a further six years after each renewal.
REMARQUE :   *LE BREF DE SAISIE-EXÉCUTION DE BIENS-FONDS OU DE BIENS MEUBLES reste en vigueur pendant six ans après la date de sa délivrance ou après chaque renouvellement.*

SCR 20.06-20.07-20N (June 1, 2009 / *1er juin 2009*) CSD

Security Act search, along with some of the other searches we looked at when considering whether or not to sue a debtor, to verify whether there are assets available with enough value and equity in them to make a seizure and sale worthwhile.

Personal Property Exempt from Seizure

Even if the property is valuable, it may be exempt from seizure under s. 2 of the *Execution Act* and O. Reg. 657/05 under the Act. Section 2 identifies the classes of assets covered by exemptions; the regulations prescribe exempt amounts for these classes. You should check the regulations from time to time, as the exemption limits may increase. As of July 17, 2013, they are as follows:

- Necessary clothing of the debtor and the debtor's dependants worth less than $5,650 are exempt from seizure.

- Household furnishings and appliances worth less than $11,300 are exempt from seizure.

- Tools and other personal property of the debtor that are used by the debtor to earn income from the debtor's occupation other than in agriculture, worth less than $11,300, are exempt from seizure. However, if the monies owed to the judgment creditor were used to purchase such tools, they are not exempt from seizure.

- Tools, equipment, livestock, and crops of a debtor engaged in agriculture worth $28,300 or less are exempt from seizure.

- One motor vehicle(s) owned by the judgment debtor worth less than $5,650 is exempt from seizure.

On October 25, 2010, several amendments made to the *Execution Act* under Bill 68, Ontario *Open for Business Act, 2010*, came into force, and the following items became exempt from seizure and sale:

- The principal residence of a debtor if the value of the debtor's equity in the principal residence does not exceed the prescribed amount.

- Aids and devices owned by a debtor that are required by the debtor or the debtors dependants to assist with a disability or a medical or dental condition.

You can quickly see that the exemption limits are sufficiently high that you may find it difficult to seize any personal property. For example, if you have a judgment for $3,000 and the debtor has a used car worth $4,000, seizing and selling the car might satisfy the judgment, except for the fact that the car is worth less than the exemption limit, so that it is not available to seize and sell. Under the newly in force revisions to the *Execution Act*, the debtor can select from his or her personal property the property to be exempted from seizure and sale. In the event an exemption is claimed for household furnishing or an appliance that has a value in excess of the prescribed amount and other personal property is not available for seizure and sale, the item is subject to seizure and sale, and the prescribed exemption amount shall be paid to the debtor. These exemptions are not available to corporations but are available to sole proprietorships and partnerships, as well as individuals. If a chattel falls into an exempt category but is also collateral on a security agreement, the secured creditor may seize the asset. The exemptions do not apply to secured creditors who sue a secured debtor.

There are other assets that are not available for seizure and sale or, for that matter, for garnishment:

- Compensation paid to a victim under victims of crime legislation, such as the *Compensation for Victims of Crime Act*, R.S.O. 1990, c. C.24, is exempt.

- Pensions — most pensions are exempt under various pension-related statutes, except to satisfy a family support order.

- *Workplace Safety and Insurance Act* benefits are exempt.

- Welfare payments are exempt.

- Rights of an insured in an insurance contract for payments and the rights of a designated beneficiary of a life insurance policy to payments are protected from seizure under s. 196(2) of the *Insurance Act*, R.S.O. 1990, c. I.8, if the beneficiary is a close family member (spouse, child, grandchild, or parent).

- Wages — 80% of net wages are exempt from seizure unless it is a family support order, in which case the exemption is 50%. The exemption limit can be varied up or down by the court on the motion of either the creditor or debtor under s. 7 of the *Wages Act*, R.S.O. 1990, c. W.1.

- Federal pensions, both general and for various federal employees, are exempt, although they are not exempt from garnishment by a creditor on a family support order.

- Under the *Indian Act*, R.S.C. 1985, c. I-5, the real and personal property of Status Natives cannot, in most circumstances, be seized by a non-Native creditor.

WRITS OF SEIZURE AND SALE — REAL PROPERTY

If the judgment debtor owns or has an interest in real property, you can move to seize and sell it. The judgment debtor does not have to occupy the property in order for the writ to attach to the judgment debtor's interest in the property. An interest in property can take various forms:

- Sole ownership of a freehold interest in land: a house, condominium, etc.

- Co-ownership of an interest in land as a co-tenant or joint tenant

- Ownership of units or shares in cooperative housing

- Mortgage lender's interest in land

- Landlord's interest in rented premises

- Tenant's interest in a tenancy on a long-term commercial lease (Acquiring and then assigning or subletting a commercial lease where the premises are in demand can generate a reasonable amount of profit. Residential leases technically are also interests in land, but there is little value in acquiring an interest in residential leases because subletting residential premises will generate little or no net income.)

Because interests in land tend to have relatively high value compared to the amount of a small claims judgment, a judgment debtor's interest may well be worth seizing and selling. Establishing an ownership interest is relatively easy, as virtually every kind of interest in property is registered in one of the two land registration systems: the Registry system or the Land Titles system. Interests in land are not subject to exemption limits, as is the case for chattels, except for the principal residence of a debtor. Under October 2010 amendments to the *Execution Act*, s. 2(2), the principal residence of a debtor is exempt from seizure and sale if the equity in the property does not exceed a prescribed amount. As of July 17, 2013, the regulation setting the prescribed amount has not been proclaimed. If you look at notices of sheriff's sales in the newspaper, they frequently involve the sale of an interest in land. Because an interest in land is often a judgment debtor's biggest asset, and because he or she may reside in that asset, an attempt to seize and sell that interest will often inspire prompt payment.

Procedure for Writs of Seizure and Sale of Land

Writs of Seizure and Sale of Land are issued from the Small Claims Court, but are sent to the sheriff of the county or region where the land you have identified for seizure is located. The Small Claims Court bailiffs have no authority to seize or sell interests in land. Writs of Seizure and Sale of Land are covered under Rule 20.07:

> 20.07(1) If an order for the payment or recovery of money is unsatisfied, the clerk shall at the creditor's request, supported by an affidavit for enforcement request (Form 20P) stating the amount still owing, issue to the sheriff specified by the creditor a writ of seizure and sale of land (Form 20D).
>
> (1.1) If more than six years have passed since the order was made, a writ of seizure and sale of land may be issued only with leave of the court.
>
> (1.2) If a writ of seizure and sale of land is not issued within one year after the date on which an order granting leave to issue it is made,
> (a) the order granting leave ceases to have effect; and
> (b) a writ of seizure and sale of land may be issued only with leave of the court on a subsequent motion.
>
> (2) A writ of seizure and sale of land issued under subrule (1) has the same force and effect and may be renewed or withdrawn in the same manner as a writ of seizure and sale issued under rule 60 of the Rules of Civil Procedure.
>
> (3) A writ of seizure and sale of land remains in force for six years after the date of its issue and for a further six years after each renewal.
>
> (4) A writ of seizure and sale of land may be renewed before its expiration by filing a request to renew a writ of seizure and sale (Form 20N) with the sheriff

You need to complete an Affidavit for Enforcement Request (Form 20P). A sample Affidavit for Enforcement Request is shown in Illustration 13.3. Check off at the bottom of Page 1 your request for a writ of seizure and sale of land, and fill in the county or region where the property wish you to sell is located. Then complete Part 3 beginning at Page 3. You must also prepare a Writ of Seizure and Sale of Land (Form 20D). This writ contains the same information as the Writ of Seizure and Sale for Personal Property: the precise name of the judgment debtor and the amount owing on the judgment as of the time the writ is filed. As with other enforcement procedures, the amount of the outstanding judgment should be the same on the affidavit and the writ. A completed Form 20D for the *Oryx v. Foot* case is provided in Illustration 14.5. If you have more than one debtor to list on your writ of seizure of land or personal property or for a certificate of judgment, or your debtors are known by other names, list this infor-

ILLUSTRATION 14.5: Writ of Seizure and Sale of Land (Form 20D) for *Oryx v. Foot*

ONTARIO
Superior Court of Justice
Cour supérieure de justice

Writ of Seizure and Sale of Land
Bref de saisie-exécution de biens-fonds
Form / Formule 20D Ont. Reg. No. / Règl. de l'Ont. : 258/98

Seal / Sceau

Toronto
Small Claims Court / Cour des petites créances de

47 Sheppard Ave. E., 3rd Fl.
Toronto, ON M2N 5N1
Address / Adresse

416-326-3554
Phone number / Numéro de téléphone

SC-00-47669-00
Claim No. / N° de la demande

Creditor No. 1 / *Créancier n° 1*

☐ Additional party(ies) listed on attached Form 1A.
La ou les parties additionnelles sont mentionnées sur la formule 1A ci-jointe.

Last name, or name of company / Nom de famille ou nom de la compagnie		
Oryx		
First name / Premier prénom **Albert**	Second name / Deuxième prénom	Also known as / Également connu(e) sous le nom de
Address (street number, apt., unit) / Adresse (numéro et rue, app., unité) **c/o Peter Paralegal, 41 Yonge Street, #410**		
City/Town / Cité/ville **Toronto**	Province **ON**	Phone no. / N° de téléphone **416-597-0048**
Postal code / Code postal **M5G 1S1**		Fax no. / N° de télécopieur **416-597-0049**
Representative / Représentant(e) **Peter Paralegal**		LSUC # / N° du BHC **P02962**
Address (street number, apt., unit) / Adresse (numéro et rue, app., unité) **41 Yonge Street, #410**		
City/Town / Cité/ville **M5G 1S1**	Province **ON**	Phone no. / N° de téléphone **416-597-0048**
Postal code / Code postal **M5G 1S1**		Fax no. / N° de télécopieur **416-597-0049**

Debtor No. 1 / *Débiteur n° 1*

☐ Additional party(ies) listed on attached Form 1A.
La ou les parties additionnelles sont mentionnées sur la formule 1A ci-jointe.

Last name, or name of company / Nom de famille ou nom de la compagnie		
Foot		
First name / Premier prénom **Ophelia**	Second name / Deuxième prénom	Also known as / Également connu(e) sous le nom de
Address (street number, apt., unit) / Adresse (numéro et rue, app., unité) **c/o Digbert Fightback, 60 My Way**		
City/Town / Cité/ville **Toronto**	Province **ON**	Phone no. / N° de téléphone **416-491-5041**
Postal code / Code postal **M6R 8P1**		Fax no. / N° de télécopieur **416-491-5042**
Representative / Représentant(e) **Digbert Fightback**		LSUC # / N° du BHC **P05427**
Address (street number, apt., unit) / Adresse (numéro et rue, app., unité) **60 My Way**		
City/Town / Cité/ville **M6R 8P1**	Province **ON**	Phone no. / N° de téléphone **416-491-5041**
Postal code / Code postal **M6R 8P1**		Fax no. / N° de télécopieur **416-491-5042**

NOTE:	**THIS WRIT REMAINS IN FORCE FOR SIX YEARS** after the date of its issue and for a further six years after each renewal. The writ may be renewed before it expires by filing a Request to Renew a Writ of Seizure and Sale (Form 20N) with the sheriff (enforcement office).
REMARQUE :	*LE PRÉSENT BREF RESTE EN VIGUEUR PENDANT SIX ANS* après la date de sa délivrance ou après chaque renouvellement. Le bref peut être renouvelé avant qu'il n'expire en déposant une demande de renouvellement du bref de saisie-exécution (formule 20N) auprès du shérif (bureau de l'exécution).

SCR 20.07-20D (June 1, 2009 / 1er juin 2009) CSD

continues....

Illustration 14.5 (continued)

FORM / *FORMULE* 20D   PAGE 2   SC-00-47669-00
                                                                   Claim No. / *N° de la demande*
                                                                                                    :

TO THE SHERIFF OF _Toronto_
AU SHÉRIF DE   (Name of county/region in which the enforcement office is located / *Nom du comté/de la région où est situé*
                                        le bureau de l'exécution)

Under an order of this court made on **September 14, Yr. 1**_____, in favour of
En vertu d'une ordonnance rendue par ce tribunal le   , *en faveur de*

Albert Oryx
                        (Name of creditor(s) / *Nom du/de la/des créancier(s)/créancière(s)*)

YOU ARE DIRECTED to seize and sell the real property of
NOUS VOUS ENJOIGNONS de saisir les biens immeubles de

Last name, or name of company / *Nom de famille ou nom de la compagnie*		
Foot		
First name / *Premier prénom*	Second name / *Deuxième prénom*	Third name / *Troisième prénom*
Ophelia	**Mabel**	**Mary**

☐ Additional debtor(s) and also known as names listed on attached Form 1A.1.
   Le ou les débiteurs additionnels et le ou les noms sous lesquels ils sont également connus sont mentionnés
   sur la formule 1A.1 ci-jointe.

situated within your jurisdiction and to realize from the seizure and sale the following sums:
qui se trouvent dans votre ressort et de procéder à leur vente pour réaliser les sommes suivantes :

(A) **AMOUNT OF JUDGMENT** (debt and pre-judgment interest) $ _____2,091.07_____
    MONTANT DU JUGEMENT *(créance et intérêts antérieurs au jugement)* $

(B) **COSTS** to date of judgment $ _____477.58_____
    LES DÉPENS *à la date du jugement* $

(C) **TOTAL AMOUNT OF PAYMENTS RECEIVED FROM DEBTOR** after
    judgment (if any) $ _____Nil_____
    LE MONTANT TOTAL DES PAIEMENTS REÇUS DU DÉBITEUR *après le* $
    jugement (le cas échéant)

    Post-judgment interest continues to accrue
    Les intérêts postérieurs au jugement continuent à courir

    at the rate of **5.0**_____ % per annum from **September 14, Yr. 1**_____.
    au taux de   *% par an à compter du*

(D) **SUBSEQUENT COSTS** incurred after judgment (including the cost of issuing this writ) $ _____159.00_____
    LES DÉPENS SUBSÉQUENTS *engagés après le jugement (y compris le coût* $
    de délivrance du présent bref)

(E) Your fees and expenses in enforcing this writ.
    Les honoraires et frais qui vous sont dus pour l'exécution forcée du présent bref.

YOU ARE DIRECTED to calculate the amount owing at the time of enforcement and pay out the proceeds
according to law and to report on the execution of this writ if required by a party who filed this writ.
ET NOUS VOUS ENJOIGNONS de calculer la somme due au moment de l'exécution forcée et de verser le
produit de la vente conformément à la loi et de faire un rapport sur l'exécution forcée du présent bref si la partie
qui l'a déposé l'exige.

October 12, Yr. 1   "I. M. Clerk"
_____   _____
                                  (Signature of clerk / *Signature du greffier*)

SCR 20.07-20D (June 1, 2009 / *1ᵉʳ juin 2009*) CSD

Note: (D), Subsequent Costs, include Certificate of Judgment, $19; Notice of
Examination, $35; Writ of Delivery, $35; Writ of Seizure and Sale of Personal
Property, $35; and Writ of Seizure and Sale of Land, $35.

mation on a Form 1A.1, Additional Debtors, and attach it to your main form.

Once a sheriff receives a copy of the writ, the Small Claims Court Rules cease to apply, and the sheriff follows the procedures set out in Rule 60 of the *Rules of Civil Procedure* of the Superior Court, in particular, Rule 60.07(17)–(24). Details of the actual writ are dealt with in subrules (1) to (14), set out below. The sale of land provisions are dealt with in (18) to (24), set out in the next section. Subrules (15) to (16) have been omitted because they deal with the sale of personal property seized under a Superior Court writ and are not applicable to Small Claims Court writs of seizure and sale of personal property.

ENFORCEMENT OF ORDERS — WRIT OF SEIZURE AND SALE
(*RULES OF CIVIL PROCEDURE*, current as of July 17, 2013)

Where Available Without Leave

60.07(1) Where an order may be enforced by a writ of seizure and sale, the creditor is entitled to the issue of one or more writs of seizure and sale (Form 60A), on filing with the registrar where the proceeding was commenced a requisition setting out,

  (a) the date and amount of any payment received since the order was made; and

  (b) the amount owing and the rate of postjudgment interest,

together with a copy of the order as entered and any other evidence necessary to establish the amount awarded and the creditor's entitlement.

Electronic Issue of Writ

(1.1) Where an order may be enforced by a writ of seizure and sale, a creditor is entitled to the electronic issue of one or more writs of seizure and sale on filing electronically under subrule 4.05.1(2) a requisition setting out,

  (a) the date and amount of any payment received since the order was made; and

  (b) the amount owing and the rate of postjudgment interest.

(1.2) Where the Workplace Safety and Insurance Board is entitled to file a certificate under section 139 of the *Workplace Safety and Insurance Act, 1997*, the Board is entitled to the electronic issue of one or more writs of seizure and sale on filing electronically a requisition setting out,

  (a) the date and amount of any payment received since the order was made; and

  (b) the amount owing and the rate of postjudgment interest.

Order Deemed Entered

(1.3) Where a creditor files a requisition under subrule (1.1), the order to which the requisition relates shall be deemed to have been entered as an order of the Superior Court of Justice.

(1.4) Where the Workplace Safety and Insurance Board files a requisition under subrule (1.2), the certificate referred to in that subrule shall be deemed to have been entered as an order of the Superior Court of Justice.

Where Leave is Required

(2) If six years or more have elapsed since the date of the order, or if its enforcement is subject to a condition, a writ of seizure and sale shall not be issued unless leave of the court is first obtained.

(3) An order granting leave to issue a writ of seizure and sale ceases to have effect if the writ is not issued within one year after the date of the order granting leave, but the court may grant leave again on a subsequent motion.

Order for Payment into Court

(4) Where an order is for the payment of money into court, the writ of seizure and sale shall contain a notice that all money realized by the sheriff under the writ is to be paid into court.

Order for Payment at Future Time

(5) Where an order is for payment at or after a specified future time, the writ of seizure and sale shall not be issued until after the expiration of that time.

Duration and Renewal

(6) A writ of seizure and sale remains in force for six years from the date of its issue and for a further six years from each renewal.

(7) Revoked.

(8) A writ of seizure and sale that is filed with a sheriff may be renewed before its expiration by filing a request to renew (Form 60E) with the sheriff, who shall record the date of renewal.

(8.1) A creditor may file electronically under subrule 4.05.1(2) a request to renew under subrule (8).

(9) A writ of seizure and sale that is not filed with a sheriff may be renewed before its expiration by filing with the registrar who issued it a requisition to renew the writ, and the registrar shall renew the writ and record the date of renewal.

Change or Variation of Debtor's Name

(10) Where a debtor named in a writ of seizure and sale,

(a) changes his, her or its name after the writ is issued;
(b) uses an alias; or
(c) uses a variation of spelling of the name,

the creditor may on motion made without notice seek a change or variation to the writ.

(11) On a motion referred to in subrule (10), the court may order the sheriff to,

(a) amend the writ by adding the words "now or also known as", followed by the new name of the debtor, the alias or the spelling variation;

(b) amend the index of writs to show the new name, the alias or the spelling variation; and

(c) if a copy of the writ was sent to the land registrar for filing under the *Land Titles Act*, send a copy of the amended writ to the land registrar.

(11.1) On a motion referred to in subrule (10), the court may grant the creditor leave to file an amendment to the writ electronically under subrule 4.05.1(2) to show the new name, the alias or the spelling variation.

Writ to Bear Creditor's Address

(12) Every writ of seizure and sale shall bear the name and address of the creditor and the creditor's lawyer, if any.

Change of Address

(12.1) If the address of the creditor or the creditor's lawyer changes after the writ is issued, the creditor may have the new address noted on the writ by filing a requisition to that effect with the sheriff.

(12.2) If the address of the creditor or the creditor's lawyer changes after the writ is issued, the creditor may have the new address recorded by filing a change of address form electronically under subrule 4.05.1(2).

Direction to Enforce

(13) Where an order may be enforced by a writ of seizure and sale, a creditor who has filed a writ of seizure and sale with a sheriff may file with the sheriff a copy of the order as entered, together with a direction to enforce (Form 60F) setting out,

(a) the date of the order and the amount awarded;

(b) the rate of postjudgment interest payable;

(c) the costs of enforcement to which the creditor is entitled under rule 60.19;

(d) the date and amount of any payment received since the order was made; and

(e) the amount owing, including postjudgment interest,

and directing the sheriff to enforce the writ for the amount owing, subsequent interest and the sheriff's fees and expenses.

Sheriff may Decline to Enforce

(13.1) The sheriff may decline to enforce the writ of seizure and sale, and the creditor may make a motion to the court for directions, where the sheriff is uncertain whether the writ of seizure and sale has been properly issued or filed.

Property in Hands of Receiver
(14) A writ of seizure and sale shall not be enforced against property in the hands of a receiver appointed by a court.

Some points to note:

- When you file the writ with the sheriff, it goes into the sheriff's file where it binds or affects land in the Land Registry System, although those searching title in the registry system must check the sheriff's file. The sheriff will also file the writ, if requested and if the appropriate fee is paid, in the office of the Registrar of Land Titles, if the land is registered in that system.[2] Under the recently enacted amendments to the *Execution Act*, once a writ of execution is filed with the sheriff, it will be entered into the index of writs of execution electronic database, which will indicate that the writ affects real property governed by the *Land Titles Act*, R.S.O. 1990, c. L.5. Once you have filed a writ of execution, a search of sheriff's certificates along with a title search in the Land Titles system will reveal any executions against the land in Land Titles. If the debtor is trying to sell his or her interest, any buyer or mortgage lender will know that your Writ has priority over later interests. A buyer or **mortgagee** will then refuse to complete the transaction unless arrangements are made to pay off the execution creditor. However, the sheriff will not move to sell the land until you formally notify him in writing to move to sell the land. And as you will see below, you cannot do this as soon as you file your writ.

- Unlike a writ to seize and sell personal property, you cannot ask the sheriff to seize and sell land until at least four months after the writ has been filed with the sheriff. It is, therefore, important to file the writ as soon as possible to start the time running. Many lawyers and paralegals obtain a writ of execution right after judgment has been granted.

- No land may be sold by the sheriff until six months after the writ has been filed. In effect, you can file the writ immediately, ask the sheriff to give notice to seize and sell the land four months later,

---

[2] There are two land registration systems, the older being the Registry system. The more modern one, the Land Titles System, was introduced starting in the late 19th century. In the future, the province's intention is to gradually move all land registrations from the Registry Office to the Land Titles Office. However, in some locations, both systems exist side by side, and land in the county and region could be in either system. You can generally tell which system land is in by reading property documents for the affected land, such as deeds or transfers, where the short description will tell you which system it is in.

and sell it two months after that. The timeline of such a writ, as prescribed in Subrules (17) and (18), is shown below:

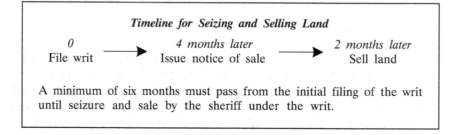

Timeline for Seizing and Selling Land

| 0 | 4 months later | 2 months later |
| File writ | Issue notice of sale | Sell land |

A minimum of six months must pass from the initial filing of the writ until seizure and sale by the sheriff under the writ.

The idea here is to give the judgment debtor lots of opportunity to pay the judgment and have the writ withdrawn.

The time requirements for the notice of sale and the selling of real property are found in Rule 60.07(17)–(24):

ENFORCEMENT OF ORDERS — WRIT OF SEIZURE AND SALE
(*RULES OF CIVIL PROCEDURE*, **current as of July 17, 2013**)

60.07(17) A creditor may not take any step to sell land under a writ of seizure and sale until four months after the writ was filed with the sheriff or, where the writ has been withdrawn, four months after the writ was re-filed.

(18) No sale of land under a writ of seizure and sale may be held until six months after the writ was filed with the sheriff or, where the writ has been withdrawn, six months after the writ was re-filed.

(19) A sale of land shall not be held under a writ of seizure and sale unless notice of the time and place of sale has been,

(a) mailed to the creditor at the address shown on the writ or to the creditor's solicitor and to the debtor at the debtor's last known address, at least thirty days before the sale;

(b) published in *The Ontario Gazette* once at least thirty days before the sale and in a newspaper of general circulation in the place where the land is situate, once each week for two successive weeks, the last notice to be published not less than one week nor more than three weeks before the date of sale; and

(c) posted in a conspicuous place in the sheriff's office for at least thirty days before the sale.

(20) The notice shall set out,

(a) a short description of the property to be sold;
(b) the short title of the proceeding;
(c) the time and place of the intended sale; and
(d) the name of the debtor whose interest is to be sold.

(21) The sheriff may adjourn a sale to a later date where the sheriff considers it necessary in order to realize the best price that can be obtained in all the circumstances, and where the sale is adjourned, it may be conducted on the later date with such further notice, if any, as the sheriff considers advisable.

(22) Where notice of a sale of land under a writ of seizure and sale is published in *The Ontario Gazette* before the writ expires, the sale may be completed by a sale and transfer of the land after the writ expires.

Abortive Sale

(23) Where personal property or land seized under a writ of seizure and sale remains unsold for want of buyers, the sheriff shall notify the creditor of the date and place of the attempted sale and of any other relevant circumstances.

(24) On receipt of a notice under subrule (23), the creditor may instruct the sheriff in writing to sell the personal property or land in such manner as the sheriff considers will realize the best price that can be obtained.

- No sale may occur unless notice of the sale has been mailed to the creditor and the debtor or their legal representatives, and the Notice of Sale has been published in the *Ontario Gazette* (the official government publication where public notices required by statute are posted, among other things) at least 30 days prior to the sale.

- Notice must also be published in a newspaper of general circulation (an ordinary daily paper aimed at the general public) in the area where the land is located, once a week for two successive weeks. The last notice must be published no more than three weeks before the sale, and no less than one week before the sale. This is a more stringent requirement than under Rule 20 for the sale of personal property.

- A notice of the sale must also be posted in an open, public area in the sheriff's office for at least 30 days prior to the sale. Note that there is no requirement that this be posted on a government website. As far as notice is concerned, we are still in the 19th century.

- The notice must contain the short title of the proceeding, a short description of the land, usually by lot and plan number used to identify the parcel in either of the two land registration systems, and by inclusion of the municipal or street address if there is one. The notice also contains the place, date, and time of the sale, and the name of the debtor whose land is being sold.

- The sheriff is obliged to obtain the best price possible in the circumstances (the circumstances being a sheriff's sale and not a sale by a high end real estate broker on the open market). Because the sheriff has a duty not to dump the property at any price, he or she may adjourn the sale if bids or offers are not sufficiently high, and reschedule the sale for a later time, with notice being given of the rescheduled sale. If the property still doesn't sell, the sheriff must notify the creditor of the aborted sale, with necessary details. The creditor may then instruct the sheriff to sell the land for the best price possible. This notice to the sheriff must be in writing and provides some protection to the sheriff from an action in negligence by an irate debtor whose land is sold for a pittance.

This writ expires at the end of six years after it is filed; it may be renewed using the same Request to Renew Writ of Seizure and Sale (Form 20N) that is used for writs to seize and sell personal property. Once a property is sold and the judgment creditor paid, the writ must be withdrawn in accordance with the provisions of Rule 60.

CHAPTER SUMMARY

In this chapter, we discussed the use of writs of delivery and writs of seizure and sale of personal property and land to enforce a judgment. We saw how writs of delivery can be obtained and used to secure the return of the creditor's property. We learned that writs of seizure and sale of personal property can be used to seize the debtor's personal property assets; however, we also learned that the seizure of such property is subject to some exemptions under the *Execution Act*. The procedures for obtaining and executing a writ of seizure and sale of land were covered, with detail provided on the sheriff's role.

REVIEW QUESTIONS

1. What documents do you have to file in support of the following?
   (a) Writ of Delivery
   (b) Writ of Seizure and Sale — personal property
   (c) Writ of Seizure and Sale — land

2. What are some common problems in using the Writ of Seizure and Sale?

3. If you file a Writ of Seizure and Sale of Land, how long is it in force, and how soon can you move to sell the debtor's interest in land?

DISCUSSION QUESTIONS/CASE STUDIES

FACTS

You are a paralegal working at Seneca Paralegals, 1750 Finch Avenue East, Toronto, Ontario M2J 2X5. You are representing Wilbur Watson, who lives at 364 Maple Blvd., Toronto, Ontario M3H 4F1, in an action against B & J Contracting (B & J), a partnership owned by Bradley and Jordan Ames. Their business is located at 487 Regency Blvd., Richmond Hill, Ontario L4A 3B8.

Wilbur hired B & J to put a sunroom on the back of his house. B & J did a terrible job and finished on August 1, Yr. 0. It cost Wilbur $6,800 to have the sunroom fixed. The claim was issued on November 1, Yr. 0. You acted for Wilbur when he sued B & J in Small Claims Court, and got judgment on January 26, Yr. 1, for $6,800, costs of $670, and post-judgment interest pursuant to the *Courts of Justice Act* (6%). Pre-judgment interest was 4.5%.

You conduct an examination in aid of execution. At the examination, you find out that Bradley owns a fancy powerboat, a Maxum 500S, with boat licence number LN 56789123, which he stores behind the partnership premises. A PPSA search reveals that it is unencumbered.

1. Prepare the necessary documents to allow the bailiff to seize the boat. Today is March 26, Yr. 1.

ADDITIONAL FACTS

You also find out that Jordan owns a cottage in the District Municipality of Muskoka. It is located on Muskeg Road, Moosepuss Township. On March 28, Yr. 1, B & J paid Wilbur $1,000. Today is April 10, Yr. 1.

2. Prepare the necessary documents to file a Writ of Seizure and Sale of Land in Muskoka.

Chapter 15

Garnishment

LEARNING OBJECTIVES

⇨ Understand what garnishment is

⇨ Know when to use a garnishment to enforce a judgment

⇨ Know the procedure for using garnishments

INTRODUCTION

In the previous chapter we learned procedures for seizing property wrongfully detained, and for seizing personal property and land in order to sell the property and use the sale proceeds to satisfy a judgment. But sometimes you can cut to the chase and intercept money owing to the debtor, diverting it to pay the creditor's judgment. This is done by using one of the most common judgment enforcement methods, garnishment, which is examined in this chapter. After looking at when a garnishment should be used, the procedure for obtaining a garnishment is set out.

WHEN TO USE A GARNISHMENT

Garnishment can be used where you know that another person, called the **garnishee**, owes the judgment debtor money at the time of the garnishment, or will owe the judgment debtor money in the next six years. The garnishment notice will attach to the debt owed by the garnishee, causing the garnishee to pay some or all of the debt owed to the judgment debtor into court for the benefit of the judgment creditor.

Possible targets for garnishment include the following:

- **Wages:** Note that under s. 7 of the *Wages Act*, 20% of the net wages (gross wages less some deductions) may be garnished. If garnishment is in respect of a support order, 50% of the net wages may be subject to garnishment. The example below will give you an idea of how the deductions affect the amount payable:

  Ophelia Foot is paid $1,000 a week, gross, subject to the following deductions:

–	$200	income tax withheld
–	10	Employment Insurance deduction
–	20	Canada Pension Plan deduction
–	50	group life insurance — employee contribution
–	100	drug/medical plan
=	25	pension — employee contribution
=	$405	total deductions

  Net wages: $1,000 – $405 = $595
  $595 × .20 = $119, available for garnishment each week.

- **Money in bank accounts of any financial institutions:** Money in a judgment debtor's bank account or money held in other investments, such as a GIC, that is payable by the bank to the judgment debtor on demand may be garnished. If the account is joint, Rule 20.08(2) makes a presumption that half that amount is subject to garnishment, although the presumption can be rebutted. Because the joint owner of the account's rights may be affected, they are entitled to notice of the proceedings and may participate in the proceedings to defend their interest. There is a note to joint holders (or co-owners of the debt) at the bottom of Page 2 of the Garnishee's Statement (see Illustration 15.2).

- **Accounts receivable of a business, including corporations, sole proprietorships, or partnerships:** You can find out who the judgment debtor's customers are on a judgment debtor examination and ask for a list of accounts receivable or even recent invoices that have been sent out or are due to be sent out in order to see who owes your judgment debtor money. Notices of Garnishment could then be served on these customers.

- **Estate or trust benefits:** You may garnish payments that are to be paid by an estate trustee out of an estate under a will or court order to the judgment debtor who is the beneficiary of the estate or the trust.

- **Payment under a family law property settlement:** While periodic support payments are exempt from garnishment, a judgment debtor's right to payment under a family law property settlement or division of property under a court order is not exempt.

- **Investment income:** Stock dividends, interest, or other investment income paid by a trustee, bank, or trust company to a judgment debtor may be garnished. Also includes mortgage payments to the debtor.

- **Any amount that a trust is obliged to pay a trust beneficiary:** Payments to be made by a trust to a beneficiary may be garnished. Note that if the payment is discretionary so that it is up to the trustee whether or not to pay the beneficiary, you cannot compel the trustee to exercise his or her discretion to make the payment.

- **Rental income:** Rent paid to a judgment debtor who is a landlords may be garnished.

- **Income from intellectual property:** Copyright licensing fees and royalties payable to inventors, franchisors, authors, or other creators of written, cinematic or musical works may be garnished.

- **Other employment income:** Tips and commissions due to a judgment debtor who is a server or salesperson may be garnished.

- **RRSPs/RRIFs:** Payout of money from an RRSP/RRIF to a judgment debtor may be garnished. (Currently there is a discussion about provincial legislation to exempt RRSPs from seizure by creditors.)

> **Example 15.1 Determining What to Garnish**
>
> Remember Julie the babysitter in Chapter 9? At an Examination in Aid of Execution, she learns that Marie is employed, has a bank account, and owns a rental property from which she collects rents. Julie, as the judgment creditor, can garnish Marie's employment income, bank account, and rents owed to her to satisfy the judgment.

GARNISHMENT PROCEDURE

Garnishment involves a judgment creditor, a judgment debtor, and a garnishee who owes money to the judgment debtor. There are never fewer than three parties to the process, and there may be more. If the garnishee owes a debt to a judgment debtor and a co-owner of that debt, the co-owner of the debt becomes involved in the process to determine how much of the debt owed by the garnishee belongs to the co-owner of the debt, and how much is available for payment into court for the benefit of the judgment creditor. An example of a co-owned debt would be where the garnishee owes money to a law partnership, where only one of the partners is liable to the judgment creditor. In this case, the garnishee needs to know how much of the payment he owes to the partnership can be attributed to the judgment debtor, which has to be paid into court. Other examples would include a joint bank account or other jointly held investment. As we will see, the co-owner of a debt is entitled to notice of garnishment proceedings in order to protect his or her interest in the debt.

Commencement of Garnishment Proceedings

Garnishment is dealt with under Rule 20.08:

> 20.08(1) A creditor may enforce an order for the payment or recovery of money by garnishment of debts payable to the debtor by other persons.
>
> (2) If a debt is payable to the debtor and to one or more co-owners, one-half of the indebtedness or a greater or lesser amount specified in an order made under subrule (15) may be garnished.

(2.1) If more than six years have passed since the order was made, or if its enforcement is subject to a condition, a notice of garnishment may be issued only with leave of the court.

(2.2) If a notice of garnishment is not issued within one year after the date on which an order granting leave to issue it is made,
(a) the order granting leave ceases to have effect; and
(b) a notice of garnishment may be issued only with leave of the court on a subsequent motion.

(2.3) A notice of renewal of garnishment may be issued under subrule (5.3) without leave of the court before the original notice of garnishment or any subsequent notice of renewal of garnishment expires.

(3) A creditor who seeks to enforce an order by garnishment shall file with the clerk of a court in the territorial division in which the debtor resides or carries on business,
(a) an affidavit for enforcement request (Form 20P) naming one debtor and one garnishee and stating,
  (i) the date of the order and the amount awarded,
  (ii) the territorial division in which the order was made,
  (iii) the rate of post-judgment interest payable,
  (iv) the total amount of any payments received since the order was granted,
  (v) the amount owing, including post-judgment interest,
  (vi) the name and address of the named garnishee to whom a notice of garnishment is to be directed,
  (vii) the creditor's belief that the named garnishee is or will become indebted to the debtor, and the grounds for the belief, and
  (viii) any particulars of the debts that are known to the creditor; and
(b) a certificate of judgment (Form 20A), if the order was made in another territorial division.

(4) On the filing of the documents required by subrule (3), the clerk shall issue a notice of garnishment (Form 20E) naming as garnishee the person named in the affidavit.

(5) A notice of garnishment issued under subrule (4) shall name only one debtor and only one garnishee.

(5.1) A notice of garnishment remains in force for six years from the date of its issue and for a further six years from each renewal.

(5.2) A notice of garnishment may be renewed before its expiration by filing with the clerk of the court in which the notice of garnishment was issued a notice of renewal of garnishment (Form 20E.1), together with an affidavit for enforcement request (Form 20P).

(5.3) On the filing of the notice and affidavit required by subrule (5.2), the clerk shall issue the notice of renewal of garnishment (Form 20E.1) naming as garnishee the person named in the affidavit.

(5.4) The provisions of these rules that apply with respect to notices of garnishment also apply with respect to notices of renewal of garnishment.

(6) The notice of garnishment (Form 20E) shall be served by the creditor in accordance with subrule 8.01(8).

(6.1) The creditor shall serve the notice of garnishment on the debtor within five days of serving it on the garnishee.

(6.2) If the garnishee is a financial institution, the notice of garnishment and all further notices required to be served under this rule shall be served at the branch at which the debt is payable.

(6.3) Service of the notice of garnishment may be proved by affidavit.

(7) The garnishee is liable to pay to the clerk any debt of the garnishee to the debtor, up to the amount shown in the notice of garnishment, within 10 days after service of the notice on the garnishee or 10 days after the debt becomes payable, whichever is later.

(8) For the purpose of subrule (7), a debt of the garnishee to the debtor includes,
 (a) a debt payable at the time the notice of garnishment is served; and
 (b) a debt payable (whether absolutely or on the fulfilment of a condition) after the notice is served and within six years after it is issued.

(9) A garnishee who admits owing a debt to the debtor shall pay it to the clerk in the manner prescribed by the notice of garnishment, and the amounts paid into court shall not exceed the portion of the debtor's wages that are subject to seizure or garnishment under section 7 of the *Wages Act*.

(10) If the clerk has issued notices of garnishment in respect of a debtor at the request of more than one creditor and receives payment under any of the notices of garnishment, he or she shall distribute the payment equally among the creditors who have filed a request for garnishment and have not been paid in full.

(11) A garnishee referred to in subrule (12) shall, within 10 days after service of the notice of garnishment, file with the court a statement (Form 20F) setting out the particulars.

(12) Subrule (11) applies to a garnishee who,
 (a) wishes to dispute the garnishment for any reason; or

(b) pays to the clerk less than the amount set out in the notice of garnishment as owing by the garnishee to the debtor, because the debt is owed to the debtor and to one or more co-owners of the debt or for any other reason.

(13) The garnishee shall serve a copy of the garnishee's statement on the creditor and the debtor.

(14) A creditor who is served with a garnishee's statement under subrule (13) shall forthwith send to any co-owners of the debt, in accordance with subrule 8.01(14), a notice to co-owner of debt (Form 20G) and a copy of the garnishee's statement.

(15) At the request of a creditor, debtor, garnishee, co-owner of the debt or any other interested person, the clerk shall fix a time and place for a garnishment hearing.

(15.1) After having obtained a hearing date from the clerk, the party requesting the garnishment hearing shall serve the notice of garnishment hearing (Form 20Q) in accordance with subrule 8.01(9).

(15.2) At the garnishment hearing, the court may,
(a) if it is alleged that the garnishee's debt to the debtor has been assigned or encumbered, order the assignee or encumbrancer to appear and state the nature and particulars of the claim;
(b) determine the rights and liabilities of the garnishee, any co-owner of the debt, the debtor and any assignee or encumbrancer;
(c) vary or suspend periodic payments under a notice of garnishment; or
(d) determine any other matter in relation to a notice of garnishment.

(16) A person who has been served with a notice to co-owner of debt is not entitled to dispute the enforcement of the creditor's order for the payment or recovery of money or a payment made by the clerk unless the person requests a garnishment hearing within 30 days after the notice is sent.

(17) If the garnishee does not pay to the clerk the amount set out in the notice of garnishment and does not send a garnishee's statement, the creditor is entitled to an order against the garnishee for payment of the amount set out in the notice, unless the court orders otherwise.

(18) If, after service of a notice of garnishment, the garnishee pays a debt attached by the notice to a person other than the clerk, the garnishee remains liable to pay the debt in accordance with notice.

(19) Payment of a debt by a garnishee in accordance with a notice of garnishment is a valid discharge of the debt as between the garnishee and the debtor and any co-owner of the debt, to the extent of the payment.

(20) When proof is filed that the notice of garnishment was served on the debtor, the clerk shall distribute a payment received under a notice of garnishment to a creditor in accordance with subrule (20.1), unless,

(a) a hearing has been requested under subrule (15);

(b) a notice of motion and supporting affidavit (Form 15A) has been filed under rule 8.10, 11.06 or 17.04; or

(c) a request for clerk's order on consent (Form 11.2A) has been filed seeking the relief described in subparagraph 1 iii of subrule 11.2.01(1)

(20.1) The clerk shall distribute the payment,

(a) in the case of the first payment under the notice of garnishment, 30 days after the date it is received; and

(b) in the case of every subsequent payment under the notice of garnishment, as they are received.

(20.2) Once the amount owing under an order that is enforced by garnishment is paid, the creditor shall immediately serve a notice of termination of garnishment (Form 20R) on the garnishee and on the clerk.

(21) If a payment of a debt owed to the debtor and one or more co-owners has been made to the clerk, no request for a garnishment hearing is made and the time for doing so under subrule (16) has expired, the creditor may file with the clerk, within 30 days after that expiry,

(a) proof of service of the notice to co-owner; and

(b) an affidavit stating that the creditor believes that no co-owner of the debt is a person under disability, and the grounds for the belief.

(22) The affidavit required by subrule (21) may contain statements of the deponent's information and belief, if the source of the information and the fact of the belief are specified in the affidavit.

(23) If the creditor does not file the material referred to in subrule (21) the clerk shall return the money to the garnishee.

In order to understand how garnishment works as a process, we will assume Albert Oryx has received a judgment against Ophelia Foot. To garnish a debt owing to Ophelia currently or within the next six years, Albert must take the following steps under Rule 20.08:

1. Albert will have to complete an Affidavit for Enforcement Request (Form 20P). He needs to check off the Notice of Garnishment Box on Page 2 of the form and set out the name and address of the garnishee and debtor, along with the reasons why he believes the garnishee is or will become indebted to the debtor. (For example, that the judgment debtor is employed by the garnishee, or that the judgment debtor has a demand savings

account with the garnishee.) Details of the judgment and post-judgment interest are filled in on Pages 3 and 4. If there is more than one garnishee, he will need to file a separate affidavit for each one.

2. The affidavit will be filed in the court office in the territorial division closest to where the judgment debtor resides or carries on business. This could be a different court from the one that gave judgment. If so, Albert will have to prepare a Certificate of Judgment and have it issued from the court where the original judgment was made.

3. On filing the Affidavit for Enforcement Request, and if necessary, the Certificate of Judgment, the clerk will issue the Notice of Garnishment (Form 20E) as prepared by Albert. On Page 1, the usual heading that is used in all other documents is not used here. Instead, a special form of general heading is used, which also includes the garnishee's name, address, and phone number. At the back of the notice (Page 4) is a page for the garnishee to complete and send in to the court with each payment. Note that the form anticipates that the garnishee may make any number of payments to the court in respect of any payments due to the judgment debtor over the next six years. It is a good idea for the garnishee in this situation to make several copies of the back page to send in to the court for future payments.

4. On payment of the prescribed fee, the clerk will issue the Notice of Garnishment. (A completed Form 20E for *Oryx v. Foot* is shown in Illustration 15.1.)

Service of the Notice of Garnishment

Service is governed by Rule 20.08(6)–(7). Albert is responsible for serving the Notice of Garnishment on the garnishee and the judgment debtor. It is presumed at this stage that if there is a co-owner of the debt being garnished, Albert knows nothing of it. Service may be by mail, courier, an alternative to personal service, or personal service. When possible, use personal service, as there is less likelihood of hearing arguments about someone's not being served, since a process server can swear an affidavit of service that he or she served the debtor or garnishee.

Albert must take the steps below to serve the Notice of Garnishment:

1. The judgment debtor is to be served with the Notice of Garnishment, and the Affidavit for Enforcement Request within five days

ILLUSTRATION 15.1: Notice of Garnishment (Form 20E) for *Oryx v. Foot*

ONTARIO
Superior Court of Justice
Cour supérieure de justice

Notice of Garnishment
Avis de saisie-arrêt
Form / *Formule* 20E Ont. Reg. No. / *Régl. de l'Ont.* : 258/98

Toronto
Small Claims Court / *Cour des petites créances de*

SC-00-47669-00
Claim No. / *N° de la demande*

(Seal / *Sceau*)

**47 Sheppard Ave. E., 3rd Fl.
Toronto, ON M2N 5N1**
Address / *Adresse*

416-326-3554
Phone number / *Numéro de téléphone*

☐ Additional creditor(s) listed on the attached Form 1A.
Le ou les créanciers additionnels sont mentionnés sur la formule 1A ci-jointe.

Creditor / *Créancier*

Last name, or name of company / *Nom de famille ou nom de la compagnie*		
Oryx		
First name / *Premier prénom* **Albert**	Second name / *Deuxième prénom*	Also known as / *Également connu(e) sous le nom de*
Address (street number, apt., unit) / *Adresse (numéro et rue, app., unité)* **c/o Peter Paralegal, 41 Yonge Street, #410**		
City/Town / *Cité/ville* **Toronto**	Province **ON**	Phone no. / *N° de téléphone* **416-597-0048**
Postal code / *Code postal* **M5G 1S1**		Fax no. / *N° de télécopieur* **416-597-0049**
Representative / *Représentant(e)* **Peter Paralegal**		LSUC # / *N° du BHC* **P02952**
Address (street number, apt., unit) / *Adresse (numéro et rue, app., unité)* **41 Yonge Street, #410**		
City/Town / *Cité/ville* **Toronto**	Province **ON**	Phone no. / *N° de téléphone* **416-597-0048**
Postal code / *Code postal* **M5G 1S1**		Fax no. / *N° de télécopieur* **416-597-0049**

Debtor / *Débiteur*

Last name, or name of company / *Nom de famille ou nom de la compagnie*		
Foot		
First name / *Premier prénom* **Ophelia**	Second name / *Deuxième prénom*	Also known as / *Également connu(e) sous le nom de*
Address (street number, apt., unit) / *Adresse (numéro et rue, app., unité)* **c/o Digbert Fightback, 60 My Way**		
City/Town / *Cité/ville* **Toronto**	Province **ON**	Phone no. / *N° de téléphone* **416-491-5041**
Postal code / *Code postal* **M6R 8P1**		Fax no. / *N° de télécopieur* **416-491-5042**

Garnishee / *Tiers saisi*

Last name, or name of company / *Nom de famille ou nom de la compagnie*		
The Caring Bank		
First name / *Premier prénom*	Second name / *Deuxième prénom*	Also known as / *Également connu(e) sous le nom de*
Address (street number, apt., unit) / *Adresse (numéro et rue, app., unité)* **4800 Trustme Rd.**		
City/Town / *Cité/ville* **Toronto**	Province **ON**	Phone no. / *N° de téléphone* **416-485-6811**
Postal code / *Code postal* **M6R 1J6**		Fax no. / *N° de télécopieur*

NOTE: **THE CREDITOR SHALL SERVE THIS NOTICE** on the debtor with an Affidavit for Enforcement Request (Form 20P) and serve on the garnishee this notice with a blank Garnishee's Statement (Form 20F).

REMARQUE : *LE CRÉANCIER SIGNIFIE LE PRÉSENT AVIS au débiteur conjointement avec un affidavit en vue d'une demande d'exécution (formule 20P) et signifie au tiers saisi le présent avis avec une déclaration du tiers saisi (formule 20F) en blanc.*

SCR 20.08-20E (September 1, 2010 / *1ᵉʳ septembre 2010*) CSD

continues....

Illustration 15.1 (continued)

FORM / *FORMULE* 20E   PAGE 2   SC-00-47669-00

Claim No. / *N° de la demande*

TO THE GARNISHEE:
AU TIERS SAISI :

The creditor has obtained a court order against the debtor. The creditor claims that you owe or will owe the debtor a debt in the form of wages, salary, pension payments, rent, annuity or other debt that you pay out in a lump-sum, periodically or by instalments. (A debt to the debtor includes both a debt payable to the debtor alone and a joint debt payable to the debtor and one or more co-owners.)
Le créancier a obtenu une ordonnance du tribunal contre le débiteur. Le créancier prétend que vous êtes ou serez redevable au débiteur d'une dette sous forme de salaire, de prestations de retraite, de loyer, de rente ou autre que vous payez par somme forfaitaire, périodiquement ou par versements échelonnés. (Une dette envers le débiteur comprend à la fois une dette payable au débiteur seul et une dette payable conjointement au débiteur et à un ou plusieurs autres cotitulaires de la créance.)

YOU ARE REQUIRED TO PAY to the clerk of the Toronto Small Claims Court
VOUS ÊTES REQUIS(E) DE PAYER au greffier (Garnishment issuing court / *Tribunal qui prononce la*
de la Cour des petites créances de   *saisie-arrêt)*

(a)   all debts now payable by you to the debtor, **within 10 days** after this notice is served on you; **and**
       d'une part, toutes les dettes dont vous êtes maintenant redevable au débiteur, dans les 10 jours qui suivent la signification du présent avis;

(b)   all debts that become payable by you to the debtor after this notice is served on you and **within 6 years** after this notice is issued, **within 10 days** after they become payable.
       d'autre part, toutes les dettes dont vous deviendrez redevable au débiteur après la signification du présent avis et dans les 6 années qui suivent sa délivrance, dans les 10 jours qui suivent la date à laquelle elles deviennent exigibles.

The total amount of all your payments to the clerk is not to exceed $ 2,772.85 .
La totalité des paiements que vous ferez au greffier ne doit pas dépasser   (Amount unsatisfied / **$.**
                                                   Montant impayé)

THIS NOTICE IS LEGALLY BINDING ON YOU until it expires or is changed, renewed, terminated or satisfied. If you do not pay the total amount or such lesser amount as you are liable to pay, you must serve a Garnishee's Statement (Form 20F) on the creditor and debtor, and file it with the clerk within 10 days after this notice is served on you.
LE PRÉSENT AVIS VOUS LIE LÉGALEMENT jusqu'à ce qu'il expire ou qu'il soit modifié, renouvelé ou résilié, ou qu'il y soit satisfait. Si vous ne payez pas le montant total ou le montant moindre dont vous êtes redevable, vous devez signifier une déclaration du tiers saisi (formule 20F) au créancier et au débiteur et la déposer auprès du greffier dans les 10 jours qui suivent la signification du présent avis.

EACH PAYMENT, payable to the Minister of Finance, MUST BE SENT with a copy of the attached garnishee's payment notice to the clerk at the above court address.
CHAQUE PAIEMENT, libellé à l'ordre du ministre des Finances, DOIT ÊTRE ENVOYÉ au greffier, à l'adresse du tribunal indiquée ci-dessus, avec une copie de l'avis de paiement du tiers saisi ci-joint.

If your debt is jointly owed to the debtor and to one or more co-owners, you must pay the debtor's appropriate share of the amount now payable, or which becomes payable, or such a percentage as the court may order.
Si votre dette est payable conjointement au débiteur et à un ou plusieurs autres cotitulaires de la créance, vous devez payer la quote-part appropriée du débiteur du montant dont vous êtes maintenant redevable, ou qui devient redevable, ou le pourcentage que le tribunal ordonne.

SCR 20.08-20E (September 1, 2010 / *1ᵉʳ septembre 2010*) CSD   Continued on next page / *Suite à la page suivante*

continues....

Illustration 15.1 (continued)

FORM / *FORMULE* **20E**   **PAGE 3**   SC-00-47669-00
Claim No. / *N° de la demande*

The amounts paid into court shall not exceed the portion of the debtor's wages that are subject to seizure or garnishment under Section 7 of the *Wages Act* (information available at: www.attorneygeneral.jus.gov.on.ca and www.e-laws.gov.on.ca). The portion of wages that can be garnished may be increased o decreased only by order of the court. If such a court order is attached to this notice or is served on you, you must follow the direction in that court order.
Les montants consignés au tribunal ne doivent pas dépasser la partie du salaire du débiteur qui peut faire l'objet d'une saisie ou d'une saisie-arrêt aux termes de l'article 7 de la Loi sur les salaires (pour de plus amples renseignements, reportez-vous aux adresses : www.attorneygeneral.jus.gov.on.ca et www.lois-en-ligne.gouv.on.ca). La partie saisissable du salaire ne peut être augmentée ou réduite que sur ordonnance du tribunal. Si une telle ordonnance du tribunal est annexée au présent avis ou vous est signifiée, vous devez vous conformer à la directive qui y est énoncée.

October 12, Yr. 1   "I. M. Clerk"
(Signature of clerk / *Signature du greffier*)

CAUTION TO GARNISHEE:	IF YOU FAIL TO PAY to the clerk the amount set out in this notice and do not file a Garnishee's Statement (Form 20F) disputing garnishment, JUDGMENT MAY BE OBTAINED AGAINST YOU BY THE CREDITOR for payment of the amount set out above, plus costs. If you make a payment to anyone other than the clerk of the court, you may be liable to pay again [R. 20.08(17) and (18)].
AVERTISSEMENT AU TIERS SAISI :	*SI VOUS NE VERSEZ PAS au greffier le montant précisé dans le présent avis et ne déposez pas la déclaration du tiers saisi (formule 20F) contestant la saisie-arrêt, LE CRÉANCIER PEUT OBTENIR CONTRE VOUS UN JUGEMENT ordonnant le paiement du montant précisé ci-dessus et des dépens. Si vous effectuez un paiement à une personne qui n'est pas le greffier du tribunal, vous pouvez être tenu(e) de payer de nouveau [par. 20.08 (17) et (18)].*

NOTE:	Any party or interested person may complete and serve a Notice of Garnishment Hearing (Form 20Q) to determine any matter related to this notice. To obtain forms and self-help materials, attend the nearest Small Claims Court or access the following website: www.ontariocourtforms.on.ca.
REMARQUE :	*Toute partie ou personne intéressée peut remplir et signifier un avis d'audience sur la saisie-arrêt (formule 20Q) en vue de décider une question relative au présent avis. Vous pouvez obtenir les formules et la documentation à l'usage du client auprès de la Cour des petites créances de votre localité ou en consultant le site Web suivant : www.ontariocourtforms.on.ca.*

CR 20.08-20E (September 1, 2010 / *1ᵉʳ septembre 2010*) CSD   Continued on next page / *Suite à la page suivante*

continues....

Illustration 15.1 (continued)

FORM / *FORMULE* 20E   PAGE 4   SC-00-47669-00
Claim No. / *N° de la demande*

The top portion of the garnishee's payment notice, below, is to be completed by the creditor before the Notice of Garnishment is issued. Where it is anticipated that more than one payment will be made by the garnishee, the creditor should supply extra copies of the garnishee's payment notice. Additional copies of the garnishee's payment notice are available at court offices or online at www.ontariocourtforms.on.ca (see Form 20E or 20E.1).
Le créancier doit remplir la partie supérieure de l'avis de paiement du tiers saisi figurant ci-dessous avant la délivrance de l'avis de saisie-arrêt. S'il est prévu que le tiers saisi fera plus d'un paiement, le créancier doit fournir des exemplaires supplémentaires de l'avis de paiement du tiers saisi. Vous pouvez obtenir des exemplaires supplémentaires de l'avis de paiement du tiers saisi aux greffes des tribunaux ou en ligne à l'adresse www.ontariocourtforms.on.ca (consultez la formule 20E ou 20E.1).

GARNISHEE'S PAYMENT NOTICE / *AVIS DE PAIEMENT DU TIERS SAISI*

Make payment by cheque or money order payable to the Minister of Finance and send it, along with this payment notice to the clerk of the court at the following address:
Effectuez le paiement par chèque ou mandat-poste à l'ordre du ministre des Finances et envoyez-le, avec une copie du présent avis de paiement, au greffier du tribunal à l'adresse suivante :

Court address: **47 Sheppard Ave. E., 3rd Fl. Toronto, ON M2N 5N1**
Adresse du tribunal :

Claim No.:   **SC-00-47669-00**
N° de la demande :

Creditor: **Albert Oryx**
Créancier/créancière :

Debtor: **Ophelia Foot**
Débiteur/débitrice :

Garnishee: **The Caring Bank**
Tiers saisi :

TO BE COMPLETED BY GARNISHEE FOR EACH PAYMENT
À REMPLIR PAR LE TIERS SAISI LORS DE CHAQUE PAIEMENT

Date of payment: ....
Date du paiement :

Amount enclosed: $ ....
Montant inclus : $

CR 20.08-20E (September 1, 2010 / *1er septembre 2010*) CSD

of the garnishee being served with the Notice of Garnishment. In this way, the judgment debtor has notice of the amount in issue, not that this should come as a surprise.

2. The garnishee is served with the Notice of Garnishment (Form 20E) and a blank Garnishee's Statement (Form 20F).

3. Peter Paralegal, or the process server, should prepare an Affidavit of Service.

4. It is usual to serve the garnishee first in order to attach the debt before the judgment debtor knows it has been done. Otherwise, if the judgment debtor and garnishee are not at **arm's length**, a knowing judgment debtor might collude with the garnishee to advance a payment to the judgment debtor so that nothing is owing by the garnishee when he or she is finally served. In any event, if the garnishee is served first, the judgment debtor must be served within the next five days.

5. If the garnishee is a financial institution, the notice must be served on the branch where the debt is payable. This is designed to cut through the confusion that might result if the head office of the bank was served, and the account got emptied by Ophelia before the bank could locate the account and sequester the amount required for garnishment. This may make life easier for banks but may create problems for Albert if he only knows that Ophelia has a Caring Bank account without knowing the branch.

    In an age of Internet banking, this rule hardly seems necessary. Nor does it make sense if the judgment debtor deals with a bank like ING Direct, where banking is done electronically on the Internet and with automatic tellers, and where there is no individual branch for customers. In situations where you are having difficulty locating a branch, consider bringing a motion using the "Toolbox Rules" to ask the court not to apply and enforce this rule (20.08(6.2)).

6. Once the garnishee is served, he or she is liable to pay, up to the amount in the notice, any amount payable to the judgment debtor within 10 days of service, or within 10 days of the debt becoming due in the next six years, whichever is later.

GARNISHEE'S RESPONSE

The garnishee's response depends on whether or not a debt is payable at all, whether the debt represents wages, whether the garnishee is paying less than the full amount in the notice, and whether there is a co-

---

**FIGURE 15.1: Calculating the Net Amount of Wages
Available for Garnishment**

Gross wages: $2,000   per week

Permitted deductions
    From gross: 600   Income Tax
                  20   Canada Pension Plan
                  40   Employment Insurance
                       Employee Contribution to an
               100   Employer Pension Plan
                       Employee Contribution to a
                  40   Group Health Benefits Insurance
                       Employee Contribution to a
                  <u>60</u>   Group Life Insurance
              $ 860   Total Permitted Deductions

Net pay is $2,000 – $860 = $1,140
Amount available for garnishment: $1,140 × 0.20 = $228.00 per week.

---

owner of the debt. If less than the full amount is to be paid, the garnishee must file a Garnishee's Statement to explain why he or she is not paying the full amount. If the garnishee also wishes to dispute the garnishment for any reason, he or she must file the Garnishee's Statement, obtain a date for a garnishment hearing, and serve a Notice of Garnishment hearing on all interested parties.

If the garnishee agrees, there is a debt payable to the judgment debtor within the next six years after service of the notice, the garnishee must make the payment directly to the clerk of the court that issued the notice, as indicated in the notice.

If the debt is in respect of wages, the garnishee must only pay out 20% of the net wages payable. Set out in Figure 15.1 is an illustration of the permitted deductions from gross wages for garnishment calculation purposes. The judgment creditor or debtor on a motion to the court can apply to vary the exempt percentage of wages upward or downward. Of course, if such an order is made, it must be served on the garnishee, who is then obliged to follow it. Note that the garnishee may be remitting payments to the court for many pay periods over the next six years, until the debt is paid, and even longer if the garnishment is renewed.

If several judgment creditors have all issued Notices of Garnishment in that territorial division in respect of a single debtor, and any garnishee makes a payment, that payment shall be shared equally under Rule 20.08(10) among the creditors who filed a request for garnishing money to the extent any creditor remains unpaid. This will also be the case if all creditors of a debtor serve notices on the same garnishee. Note the difference between equal sharing here, and pro rata sharing on Writs of Seizure and Sale under the *Execution Act*.

If a garnishee does not owe any money to the judgment debtor, or will not owe any money in the next six years, or owes less than the amount claimed by the creditor in the notice, or is aware of a co-owner of the debt, or has any question or issue about the garnishment process of any kind, the garnishee must file with the court a Garnishee's Statement (Form 20F) within 10 days of being served with the Notice of Garnishment. The statement is designed to be completed easily, using check-off boxes covering all of the possible reasons why the garnishee is not going to pay the full amount in the notice. Note that if, for example, the debtor is owed wages, the full amount may be paid over time as wages become due or payable. Because the garnishee is not paying the full amount in the notice, even though that amount will be paid over time, the garnishee still needs to explain a payment that is less than the total amount in the notice and must file a statement. This is important. A garnishee who fails to pay the full amount in the notice and who does not file a statement explaining why may become liable to the creditor for the full amount of the judgment outstanding.

The options listed on the Garnishee's Statement regarding "no payment" or less than full payment should be examined carefully:

- The garnishee does not owe money now and does not, in good faith, *expect* to owe anything to the judgment debtor in the next six years.

- The debtor never worked for the garnishee.

- The debtor quit. In this case, give the date. However, if the debtor has not received all his pay before the Garnishee Notice was served, it is payable to the court, subject to the *Wages Act*. If the debtor quit and had been paid off, the garnishee should also check the box that says nothing is due and that the debtor has been paid in full, with the date.

- The garnishee is a bank or financial institution or trust company, and it holds no funds of any kind belonging to the debtor.

- The amount payable to the debtor is less than the amount in the notice. The garnishee should check off the appropriate box on the statement in respect of the type of partial payment:

- Payment is in respect of wages (set out the pay period, gross, net, and *Wages Act* amounts).
- Payment is not being made now because the debtor has been laid off but may return to work later.
- Payment is not being made in full because some of the debt is owed to a co-owner of the debt.
- We have been served with other garnishee notices in respect of the same debtor (list the particulars of each garnishment notice).

Illustration 15.2 gives a completed Form 20F, Garnishee's Statement, for *Oryx v. Foot*. The form was filed by the Caring Bank, where Ophelia Foot and her sister, Penelope, held a joint bank account.

GARNISHMENT DISPUTES AND HEARINGS

The Garnishee's Statement must be served and filed if the garnishee is paying less than the full amount in the notice. But if the garnishee or any party or person affected by the garnishment proceeding wishes to dispute the garnishment altogether, he or she must obtain a time and date for a hearing from the clerk and then serve a Notice of Garnishment Hearing (Form 20Q) on all concerned parties by mail, courier, personally, or by an alternative to personal service. On the Hearing Notice, the person asking for the hearing will indicate briefly what the basis is for his or her dispute. Note that Page 1 setting out the parties actually extends to two or more pages to include everyone: judgment creditor, debtor, garnishee, co-owner of a debt, other interested parties, if any.

A garnishee or, indeed, any party may dispute or challenge the garnishment. For example, if a garnishee has received notice that the debtor's right to payment has been assigned to someone else, then that money arguably is no longer due to be paid to the debtor. On the other hand, the "assignment" may be a non-arm's length transaction that is nothing more than an attempt to defraud a creditor. This kind of issue can be settled at a garnishment hearing. In this case the assignee should be served with the Notice of Garnishment Hearing, and should appear to explain his or her position. Note that the court has the power at the hearing, under Rule 20.08(15.2), to order that person to appear at the hearing, and in general to hear and determine any issue in regard to the garnishment proceeding raised by any party.

If the garnishee has indicated in the Garnishee's Statement that there is a co-owner of a debt, the creditor must serve a Notice to Co-owner of a Debt (Form 20G) on the co-owner of the debt, together with a copy of the Garnishee's Statement. Service may be by mail, courier, personal service, or an alternative to personal service. The co-

ILLUSTRATION 15.2: Garnishee's Statement (Form 20F) for *Oryx v. Foot*

ONTARIO
Superior Court of Justice
Cour supérieure de justice

Garnishee's Statement
Déclaration du tiers saisi
Form / *Formule* 20F Ont. Reg. No. / *Règl. de l'Ont.* : 258/98

Toronto
Small Claims Court / *Cour des petites créances de*

SC-00-47669-00
Claim No. / *N° de la demande*

**47 Sheppard Ave. E., 3rd Fl.,
Toronto, ON M2N 5N1**
Address / *Adresse*

416-326-3554
Phone number / *Numéro de téléphone*

BETWEEN / *ENTRE*

Albert Oryx

Creditor(s) / *Créancier(s)/créancière(s)*

and / *et*

Ophelia Foot

Debtor(s) / *Débiteur(s)/débitrice(s)*

Name of Garnishee The Caring Bank
Nom du tiers saisi

(Full legal name of garnishee / *Nom et prénoms officiels du tiers saisi*)

A Notice of Garnishment was issued on **October 12, Yr. 1** , naming me/us as garnishee
Un avis de saisie-arrêt a été délivré le , *me/nous désignant comme tiers saisi(s)*

in relation to the debtor **Ophelia Foot**
en rapport avec le débiteur

(Name of debtor / *Nom du/de la débiteur/débitrice*)

☐ **I/WE DO NOT OWE** and do not expect to owe to the debtor the amount set out in the Notice of Garnishment
for the following reason(s):
*JE NE SUIS/NOUS NE SOMMES PAS REDEVABLE(S) et je ne m'attends/nous ne nous attendons pas à
être redevable(s) au débiteur du montant énoncé dans l'avis de saisie-arrêt pour le ou les motifs suivants :*

☒ **I/WE OWE OR WILL OWE** the debtor (or the debtor and one or more co-owners), wages or periodic
payments based on the terms explained below:
*JE SUIS OU SERAI/NOUS SOMMES OU SERONS REDEVABLE(S) au débiteur (ou au débiteur et à un ou
plusieurs autres cotitulaires de la créance) des montants suivants exigibles à titre de salaire ou de
versements périodiques et selon les modalités suivantes :*

(State the amount(s) and how often the debtor is paid. If the debtor is paid wages, state the gross amount of the debtor's wages before
any deductions required by law and the net amount after those deductions, and attach a copy of a pay slip. If you owe or will owe the
debtor a lump sum, state when and how much will be paid.)
(Indiquez le ou les montants et la fréquence des paiements faits au débiteur. Si le débiteur touche un salaire, indiquez son salaire brut
avant les retenues que vous êtes tenu(e)(s) de déduire, selon la loi, ainsi que le montant net après les retenues, et annexez une copie
d'un bordereau de paie. Si vous êtes ou serez redevable(s) d'une somme forfaitaire au débiteur, indiquez-en le montant et à quel
moment le paiement sera effectué.)

SCR 20.08-20F (April 11, 2012 / *11 avril 2012*) CSD

Continued on next page / *Suite à la page suivante*

continues....

Illustration 15.2 (continued)

FORM / *FORMULE* 20F	PAGE 2	SC-00-47669-00
		Claim No. / *N° de la demande*

☒ **I/We are making payment of less than** the amount stated because the debt is owed to the debtor and to one or more co-owners, or for another reason explained below:
J'effectue/Nous effectuons un paiement inférieur au montant indiqué parce qu'il s'agit d'une dette envers le débiteur et envers un ou plusieurs autres cotitulaires de la créance, ou pour un autre motif indiqué ci-dessous :

Debtor -- 50% -- $750.00; co-owner -- 50% -- $750.00

(Identify the amount(s) and percentage owed to the debtor and each co-owner / *Précisez le ou les montants et le pourcentage redevable au débiteur et à chaque autre cotitulaire de la créance*)

Co-owner(s) of the debt: **Penelope Foot**
Cotitulaire(s) de la créance :   (Full legal name(s) / *Nom et prénoms officiels*)

185 Smith St., Toronto, ON M4R 1Q6

(Address (street & number, unit, municipality, province) / *Adresse (numéro et rue, unité, municipalité, province)*)

☐ **I/We are not making a payment at this time or are making a payment of less than the amount stated** because I/we have been served with other notice(s) of garnishment against the debtor. (Provide details below.)
Je n'effectue/Nous n'effectuons aucun paiement présentement ou j'effectue/nous effectuons un paiement inférieur au montant indiqué parce que j'ai/nous avons reçu signification d'un ou de plusieurs autres avis de saisie-arrêt contre le débiteur. (Donnez-en les détails ci-dessous.)

Name of creditor / *Nom du créancier*	Name of issuing court / *Nom du tribunal délivreur*	Location of court or Sheriff's Office where payment is currently being made / *Emplacement du tribunal ou bureau du shérif où le paiement est actuellement effectué*	Date Notice of Garnishment received / *Date de réception de l'avis de saisie-arrêt*

☐ **I/We will dispute the garnishment** by completing and serving a Notice of Garnishment Hearing (Form 20Q) on the creditor, debtor and co-owner(s) of the debt (if any) and any other interested person, and filing it with the clerk of the court.
Je contesterai/Nous contesterons la saisie-arrêt en remplissant et en signifiant un avis d'audience sur la saisie-arrêt (formule 20Q) au créancier, au débiteur et au(x) cotitulaire(s) de la créance (le cas échéant) et à tout autre intéressé et en le déposant auprès du greffier du tribunal.

October 15, Yr. 1   **"I. M. Prudent"**

(Signature of garnishee or representative / *Signature du tiers saisi ou du/de la représentant(e)*)

4800 Trustme Rd., Toronto ON M6R 1J6
Tel. 416-485-6811

(Address, phone and fax number of garnishee or representative /*Adresse, numéro de téléphone et de télécopieur du tiers saisi ou du/de la représentant(e)*)

NOTE TO GARNISHEE: *REMARQUE AU TIERS SAISI :*	The garnishee must serve a copy of the Garnishee's Statement on the creditor and the debtor and file it with the court. You can get an electronic version of this form online at www.ontariocourtforms.on.ca. *Le tiers saisi doit signifier une copie de la déclaration du tiers saisi au créancier et au débiteur et la déposer auprès du tribunal. Vous pouvez obtenir une version électronique de la présente formule en ligne à l'adresse www.ontariocourtforms.on.ca.*
NOTE TO CREDITOR: *REMARQUE AU CRÉANCIER :*	A creditor who is served with a Garnishee's Statement must send it to the co-owners of the debt, if any, together with a Notice to Co-owner of Debt (Form 20G). You can get forms at court offices or online at www.ontariocourtforms.on.ca. *Le créancier qui reçoit signification de la déclaration du tiers saisi doit la faire parvenir aux cotitulaires de la créance, le cas échéant, avec l'avis au cotitulaire d'une créance (formule 20G). Vous pouvez obtenir des formules aux greffes des tribunaux ou en ligne à l'adresse www.ontariocourtforms.on.ca.*

SCR 20.08-20F (April 11, 2012 / *11 avril 2012*) CSD

owner may then request a garnishment hearing to determine his or her rights in the debt, and the amount, if any, to be paid by the garnishee to the creditor. However, a co-owner who wishes to dispute payment cannot hang about but must make a request for a hearing from the clerk within 30 days of being served with the Notice to Co-owner of a Debt.

In general, you should remember that if there is any dispute raised by any party having to do with garnishment, you should request a hearing from the clerk and serve the Notice of Garnishment Hearing on every relevant party.

Illustration 15.3 is a completed Notice to Co-owner of Debt (Form 20G) served on Penelope Foot, co-owner of a joint account in the garnishee, the Caring Bank. Penelope disputed the payment and requested a hearing. Her Notice of Garnishment Hearing (Form 20Q) is shown in Illustration 15.4.

GARNISHMENT PAYMENTS AND DISTRIBUTIONS TO CREDITORS

The garnishee must pay the full amount in the Notice of Garnishment directly to the clerk. If he or she pays nothing, or less than the full amount, and does not file a Garnishee's Statement or pays someone other than the clerk, the garnishee may be liable to pay the full amount of the judgment to the creditor.

When the clerk has received a payment, it is deemed to be a valid discharge of the debt between the garnishee and the debtor and co-owner of the debt, if any, to the extent of the payment. Or, to put it another way, the debtor can't sue the garnishee because the garnishee didn't pay the debtor money that was owing to the debtor. The amounts received by the clerk shall be distributed as follows:

- For the first payment, 30 days after it was received by the clerk. This gives co-owners of debts and other interested persons the necessary time to file motions, or request a garnishment hearing, or otherwise dispute the garnishment.

- For subsequent payments, immediately after the payment is received by the clerk.

Rule 20.08(20) uses the word "distribute" rather than "pay" because there may be more than one creditor entitled to a share of the proceeds. Remember that if there are several garnishment notices filed against the same debtor, the clerk must distribute any payment received from any garnishee equally among the judgment creditors who filed requests for garnishment.

ILLUSTRATION 15.3: Notice to Co-owner of Debt (Form 20G) for *Oryx v. Foot*

ONTARIO
Superior Court of Justice
Cour supérieure de justice

Notice to Co-owner of Debt
Avis au cotitulaire d'une créance
Form / Formule 20G Ont. Reg. No. / Régl. de l'Ont. : 258/98

Toronto Small Claims Court / Cour des petites créances de	SC-00-47669-00 Claim No. / N° de la demande

47 Sheppard Ave. E., 3rd Fl.
Toronto, ON M2N 5N1
Address / Adresse

416-326-3554
Phone number / Numéro de téléphone

☐ Additional creditor(s) listed on the attached Form 1A.
Le ou les créanciers additionnels sont mentionnés
sur la formule 1A ci-jointe.

Creditor / Créancier

Last name, or name of company / Nom de famille ou nom de la compagnie **Oryx**		
First name / Premier prénom **Albert**	Second name / Deuxième prénom	Also known as / Également connu(e) sous le nom de
Address (street number, apt., unit) / Adresse (numéro et rue, app., unité) **c/o Peter Paralegal, 41 Yonge Street, #410**		
City/Town / Cité/ville **Toronto**	Province **ON**	Phone no. / N° de téléphone **416-597-0048**
Postal code / Code postal **M5G 1S1**		Fax no. / N° de télécopieur **416-597-0049**
Representative / Représentant(e) **Peter Paralegal**		LSUC # / N° du BHC **P02952**
Address (street number, apt., unit) / Adresse (numéro et rue, app., unité) **41 Yonge Street, #410**		
City/Town / Cité/ville **Toronto**	Province **ON**	Phone no. / N° de téléphone **416-597-0048**
Postal code / Code postal **M5G 1S1**		Fax no. / N° de télécopieur **416-597-0049**

Debtor / Débiteur

Last name, or name of company / Nom de famille ou nom de la compagnie **Foot**		
First name / Premier prénom **Ophelia**	Second name / Deuxième prénom	Also known as / Également connu(e) sous le nom de
Address (street number, apt., unit) / Adresse (numéro et rue, app., unité) **c/o Digbert Fightback, 60 My Way**		
City/Town / Cité/ville **Toronto**	Province **ON**	Phone no. / N° de téléphone **416-491-5041**
Postal code / Code postal **M6R 8P1**		Fax no. / N° de télécopieur

Garnishee / Tiers saisi

Last name, or name of company / Nom de famille ou nom de la compagnie **The Caring Bank — Trustme Rd. Branch**		
First name / Premier prénom	Second name / Deuxième prénom	Also known as / Également connu(e) sous le nom de
Address (street number, apt., unit) / Adresse (numéro et rue, app., unité) **4800 Trustme Rd.**		
City/Town / Cité/ville **Toronto**	Province **ON**	Phone no. / N° de téléphone **416-485-6811**
Postal code / Code postal **M6R 1J6**		Fax no. / N° de télécopieur

NOTE:	**THIS NOTICE SHALL BE SERVED BY THE CREDITOR** on each co-owner of debt together with a copy of the Garnishee's Statement (Form 20F) received from the garnishee.
REMARQUE :	*LE CRÉANCIER SIGNIFIE LE PRÉSENT AVIS à chaque cotitulaire d'une créance conjointement avec une copie de la déclaration du tiers saisi (formule 20F) qu'il reçoit du tiers saisi.*

SCR 20.08-20G (September 1, 2010 / 1er septembre 2010) CSD

continues....

Illustration 15.3 (continued)

FORM / *FORMULE* 20G   PAGE 2   SC-00-47669-00

Claim No. / *Nº de la demande*

TO:

DESTINATAIRE :

Name of co-owner(s) of debt / *Nom du ou des cotitulaires de la créance*
Penelope Foot

(Attach a separate sheet, in the same format, for additional co-owners of debt. / Annexez une autre feuille, présentée selon le même format, en cas d'autres cotitulaires de la créance.)

Street and number / *Numéro et rue*
185 Smith St.

City, province, postal code / *Ville, province, code postal*
Toronto, ON M4R 1Q6

The creditor has obtained a court order against the debtor. The creditor has served a Notice of Garnishment
Le créancier a obtenu une ordonnance du tribunal contre le débiteur. Le créancier a signifié un avis de saisie-arrêt

(Form 20E), dated **October 12, Yr. 1** , on **The Caring Bank** ,
(formule 20E), daté du   *à*   (Name of garnishee / *Nom du tiers saisi*)

claiming that the garnishee owes or will owe the debtor a debt in the form of wages, salary, pension payments, rent, annuity, or other debt that the garnishee pays out in a lump-sum, periodically or by instalments. (A debt to the debtor includes both a debt payable to the debtor alone and a joint debt payable to the debtor and one or more co-owners.)
dans lequel il prétend que le tiers saisi est ou sera redevable au débiteur d'une dette sous forme de salaire, de prestations de retraite, de loyer, de rente ou autre que le tiers saisi paie par somme forfaitaire, périodiquement ou par versements échelonnés. (Une dette envers le débiteur comprend à la fois une dette payable au débiteur seul et une dette payable conjointement au débiteur et à un ou plusieurs autres cotitulaires de la créance.)

The garnishee has set out in the attached Garnishee's Statement (Form 20F) that you are a co-owner of debt. Under the Notice of Garnishment, the garnishee has paid or will pay to the clerk of the Small Claims Court the appropriate share of the amount payable or such a percentage as the court may order.
Le tiers saisi a indiqué dans la déclaration du tiers saisi annexée (formule 20F) que vous êtes un cotitulaire de la créance. Aux termes de l'avis de saisie-arrêt, le tiers saisi a payé ou paiera au greffier de la Cour des petites créances la quote-part appropriée du montant redevable ou le pourcentage que le tribunal ordonne.

IF YOU HAVE A CLAIM to the money being paid to the clerk of the Small Claims Court by the garnishee, you have 30 days from service of this notice to request a garnishment hearing by completing and serving a Notice of Garnishment Hearing (Form 20Q) on the creditor, debtor and garnishee, and filing it with the clerk. If you fail to do so, you are not entitled to dispute the enforcement of the creditor's order for the payment or recovery of money and the funds may be paid out to the creditor unless the court orders otherwise.
SI VOUS PRÉTENDEZ AVOIR UN DROIT sur l'argent que le tiers saisi verse au greffier de la Cour des petites créances, vous disposez de 30 jours à compter de la signification du présent avis pour demander une audience sur la saisie-arrêt en remplissant et en signifiant un avis d'audience sur la saisie-arrêt (formule 20Q) au créancier, au débiteur et au tiers saisi, et en le déposant auprès du greffier. Si vous ne le faites pas, vous n'aurez pas le droit par la suite de contester l'exécution forcée de l'ordonnance obtenue par le créancier en vue du paiement ou du recouvrement de sommes d'argent et ces sommes pourront être remises au créancier, sauf ordonnance contraire du tribunal.

To obtain forms and self-help materials, attend the nearest Small Claims Court or access the following website: www.ontariocourtforms.on.ca.
Vous pouvez obtenir les formules et la documentation à l'usage du client auprès de la Cour des petites créances de votre localité ou en consultant le site Web suivant : www.ontariocourtforms.on.ca.

October 18, Yr. 1   *Peter Paralegal*

(Signature of creditor or representative / *Signature du créancier/de la créancière ou du/de la représentant(e)*)

| NOTE: | Within seven (7) calendar days of changing your address for service, notify the court and all other parties in writing. |
| *REMARQUE :* | *Dans les sept (7) jours civils qui suivent tout changement de votre adresse aux fins de signification, veuillez en aviser par écrit le tribunal et les autres parties.* |

SCR 20.08-20G (September 1, 2010 / *1er septembre 2010*) CSD

ILLUSTRATION 15.4: Notice of Garnishment Hearing (Form 20Q) for *Oryx v. Foot*

ONTARIO
Superior Court of Justice
Cour supérieure de justice

Notice of Garnishment Hearing
Avis d'audience sur la saisie-arrêt
Form / *Formule* 20Q Ont. Reg. No. / *Règl. de l'Ont.* : 258/98

Toronto
Small Claims Court / *Cour des petites créances de*

SC-00-47669-00
Claim No. / *N° de la demande*

47 Sheppard Ave. E., 3rd Fl.
Toronto, ON M2N 5N1
Address / *Adresse*

416-326-3554
Phone number / *Numéro de téléphone*

☐ Additional creditor(s) listed on the attached Form 1A.
*Le ou les créanciers additionnels sont mentionnés
sur la formule 1A ci-jointe.*

Creditor / *Créancier*

Last name, or name of company / *Nom de famille ou nom de la compagnie*		
Oryx		
First name / *Premier prénom*	Second name / *Deuxième prénom*	Also known as / *Également connu(e) sous le nom de*
Albert		
Address (street number, apt., unit) / *Adresse (numéro et rue, app., unité)*		
c/o Peter Paralegal, 41 Yonge Street, #410		
City/Town / *Cité/ville*	Province	Phone no. / *N° de téléphone*
Toronto	ON	416-597-0048
Postal code / *Code postal*		Fax no. / *N° de télécopieur*
M5G 1S1		416-597-0049
Representative / *Représentant(e)*		LSUC # / *N° du BHC*
Peter Paralegal		P02952
Address (street number, apt., unit) / *Adresse (numéro et rue, app., unité)*		
41 Yonge Street, #410		
City/Town / *Cité/ville*	Province	Phone no. / *N° de téléphone*
Toronto	ON	416-597-0048
Postal code / *Code postal*		Fax no. / *N° de télécopieur*
M5G 1S1		416-597-0049

Debtor / *Débiteur*

Last name, or name of company / *Nom de famille ou nom de la compagnie*		
Foot		
First name / *Premier prénom*	Second name / *Deuxième prénom*	Also known as / *Également connu(e) sous le nom de*
Ophelia		
Address (street number, apt., unit) / *Adresse (numéro et rue, app., unité)*		
c/o Digbert Fightback, 60 My Way		
City/Town / *Cité/ville*	Province	Phone no. / *N° de téléphone*
Toronto	ON	416-491-5041
Postal code / *Code postal*		Fax no. / *N° de télécopieur*
M6R 8P1		416-491-5042
Representative / *Représentant(e)*		LSUC # / *N° du BHC*
Digbert Fightback		P05427
Address (street number, apt., unit) / *Adresse (numéro et rue, app., unité)*		
60 My Way		
City/Town / *Cité/ville*	Province	Phone no. / *N° de téléphone*
Toronto	ON	416-491-5041
Postal code / *Code postal*		Fax no. / *N° de télécopieur*
M6R 8P1		416-491-5042

NOTE:	The Notice of Garnishment Hearing must be served by the person requesting the hearing on the creditor, debtor, garnishee, co-owner of debt, if any, and any other interested person [R. 8.01(9)].
REMARQUE :	*L'avis d'audience sur la saisie-arrêt doit être signifié par la personne qui demande l'audience au créancier, au débiteur, au tiers saisi et au cotitulaire de la créance, le cas échéant, et à tout autre intéressé [par. 8.01 (9)].*

SCR 20.08-20Q (September 1, 2010 / *1er septembre 2010*) CSD

continues....

Illustration 15.4 (continued)

FORM / *FORMULE* **20Q**   **PAGE 2**   SC-00-47669-00
                                                                            Claim No. / *N° de la demande*

Garnishee / *Tiers saisi*

Last name, or name of company / *Nom de famille ou nom de la compagnie*			
The Caring Bank			
First name / *Premier prénom* **Trustme Rd. Branch**	Second name / *Deuxième prénom*		Also known as / *Également connu(e) sous le nom de*
Address (street number, apt., unit) / *Adresse (numéro et rue, app., unité)* **4800 Trustme Rd.**			
City/Town / *Cité/ville* **Toronto**	Province **ON**		Phone no. / *N° de téléphone* **416-485-6811**
Postal code / *Code postal* **M6R 1J6**			Fax no. / *N° de télécopieur*
Representative / *Représentant(e)*			LSUC # / *N° du BHC*
Address (street number, apt., unit) / *Adresse (numéro et rue, app., unité)*			
City/Town / *Cité/ville*	Province		Phone no. / *N° de téléphone*
Postal code / *Code postal*			Fax no. / *N° de télécopieur*

Co-Owner of Debt (if any) /   ☐ Additional co-owner(s) listed on attached Form 1A.
Cotitulaire d'une créance (le cas échéant)   *Le ou les cotitulaires additionnels sont mentionnés sur la formule 1A ci-jointe.*

Last name, or name of company / *Nom de famille ou nom de la compagnie*			
Foot			
First name / *Premier prénom* **Penelope**	Second name / *Deuxième prénom*		Also known as / *Également connu(e) sous le nom de*
Address (street number, apt., unit) / *Adresse (numéro et rue, app., unité)* **185 Smith St.**			
City/Town / *Cité/ville* **Toronto**	Province **ON**		Phone no. / *N° de téléphone*
Postal code / *Code postal*			Fax no. / *N° de télécopieur*
Representative / *Représentant(e)*			LSUC # / *N° du BHC*
Address (street number, apt., unit) / *Adresse (numéro et rue, app., unité)*			
City/Town / *Cité/ville*	Province		Phone no. / *N° de téléphone*
Postal code / *Code postal*			Fax no. / *N° de télécopieur*

Other Interested Person (if any) /   ☐ Additional interested person(s) listed on attached Form 1A.
Autre intéressé (le cas échéant)   *Le ou les intéressés additionnels sont mentionnés sur la formule 1A ci-jointe.*

Last name, or name of company / *Nom de famille ou nom de la compagnie*			
First name / *Premier prénom*	Second name / *Deuxième prénom*		Also known as / *Également connu(e) sous le nom de*
Address (street number, apt., unit) / *Adresse (numéro et rue, app., unité)*			
City/Town / *Cité/ville*	Province		Phone no. / *N° de téléphone*
Postal code / *Code postal*			Fax no. / *N° de télécopieur*
Representative / *Représentant(e)*			LSUC # / *N° du BHC*
Address (street number, apt., unit) / *Adresse (numéro et rue, app., unité)*			
City/Town / *Cité/ville*	Province		Phone no. / *N° de téléphone*
Postal code / *Code postal*			Fax no. / *N° de télécopieur*

SCR 20.08-20Q (September 1, 2010 / *1ᵉʳ septembre 2010*) CSD   **Continued on next page /** *Suite à la page suivante*

continues....

Illustration 15.4 (continued)

FORM / *FORMULE* 20Q   PAGE 3   SC-00-47669-00
Claim No. / *N° de la demande*

TO THE PARTIES:
AUX PARTIES :
(The person requesting this garnishment hearing or the person's representative must contact the clerk of the court to choose a time and date when the court could hold this garnishment hearing. / *La personne qui demande l'audience sur la saisie-arrêt ou son représentant doit communiquer avec le greffier du tribunal pour choisir la date et l'heure où le tribunal pourrait tenir cette audience.*)

THIS COURT WILL HOLD A GARNISHMENT HEARING on December 15, Yr. 1 , at
LE TRIBUNAL PRÉCITÉ TIENDRA UNE AUDIENCE SUR LA SAISIE-ARRÊT le , à

10:00 a.m. , or as soon as possible after that time, at (Address of court location and courtroom number)
(Time / *heure*) , ou dès que possible par la suite, à/au (*Adresse du tribunal et numéro de la salle d'audience*)

47 Sheppard Ave. E., Courtroom 301

because (Check the appropriate box.)
parce que (Cochez la case appropriée.)

☐ the creditor   ☐ the debtor   ☐ the garnishee   ☒ the co-owner of debt
  le créancier   *le débiteur*   *le tiers saisi*   *le cotitulaire d'une créance*

☐ other interested person: ....
  une autre personne intéressée :   (Specify / *Précisez.*)

states the following: (In numbered paragraphs, provide details of your dispute and the order(s) requested.)
déclare ce qui suit : (Donnez, sous forme de paragraphes numérotés, le détail de votre contestation et l'ordonnance ou les ordonnances demandées.)

I am listed as a co-owner of joint savings account #5678 at the Caring Bank with my sister Ophelia. Ophelia has no beneficial interest in the monies in the account and was listed on the account for estate succession reasons so that she would inherit monies in the account by right of survivorship in the event of my death.

☐ **Additional pages are attached because more space was needed.**
  Des feuilles supplémentaires sont annexées en raison du manque d'espace.

October 28, Yr. 1   "Penelope Foot"
(Signature of party or representative / *Signature de la partie ou du/de la représentant(e)*)

NOTE: If you fail to attend this garnishment hearing, an order may be made in your absence and enforced against you.
REMARQUE : *Si vous ne vous présentez pas à cette audience sur la saisie-arrêt, une ordonnance peut être rendue en votre absence et être exécutée contre vous.*

SCR 20.08-20Q (September 1, 2010 / *1er septembre 2010*) CSD

There are some situations where the clerk may not distribute monies received from a garnishee. Under Rule 20.08(20), no distribution may take place under any of the following circumstances:

- A garnishment hearing has been requested.
- A person has filed a motion under Rule 8.10 (document served failed to reach or come to the attention of the person served).
- A party has filed a motion to set aside default judgment on which the garnishment was based, under Rule 11.06.
- A party has obtained consent to set aside default judgment under Rule 11.2.01(1)1(iii).
- A party has brought a motion for a new trial under Rule 17.04. Note that filing an appeal does not result in a stay of a clerk's distribution. A motion under the *Rules of Civil Procedure* to stay a judgment pending appeal would be required.
- The court has ordered a stay of enforcement proceedings: for example, if a consolidation order has been made, or if instalment payments were ordered.

If the debt owed by the garnishee involves a co-owner of the debt, before distribution of the payment the clerk must satisfy himself or herself that the following conditions have been met:

- The creditor has served a Notice to Co-owner of a Debt on the co-owner and provided proof of service of the Notice.
- There is no request for a garnishment hearing, and the time for doing so has expired.
- The creditor provides an affidavit indicating that he or she believes, stating the basis for that belief, that the co-owner of the debt is not a person under disability. If the co-owner of the debt is a person under disability, the creditor should request a garnishment hearing to determine the conditions for distribution, as the court is concerned with protecting the legal rights of persons under disability.

If the creditor cannot prove service on the co-owner, or provide the affidavit, or take any other step, Rule 20.08(23) states that the payment shall be returned to the garnishee by clerk.

RENEWAL OF GARNISHMENT

A notice of garnishment may be renewed within six years of its issue date by filing an Affidavit for Enforcement Request (Form 20P) and a Notice of Renewal of Garnishment (Form 20E.1). A sample Notice of

Renewal of Garnishment is found in Illustration 15.5. The Notice of Renewal and a blank Garnishee's Statement (Form 20F) must be served on the garnishee and the debtor.

TERMINATION OF GARNISHMENT

Once the judgment has been paid in full, you must serve a Notice of Termination of Garnishment (Form 20R) on the garnishee and the court clerk. A sample Notice of Termination of Garnishment is provided in Illustration 15.6.

CHAPTER SUMMARY

In this chapter, using the method of garnishment to enforce a judgment was covered. We looked at what a garnishment is, when to use one, and the steps to obtain a garnishment. We also examined how a party questioning the garnishment process can dispute the garnishment and how to renew and terminate a garnishment.

ILLUSTRATION 15.5: Notice of Renewal of Garnishment (Form 20E.1) for *Oryx v. Foot*

ONTARIO
Superior Court of Justice
Cour supérieure de justice

(Seal / *Sceau*)

Notice of Renewal of Garnishment
Avis de renouvellement de la saisie-arrêt
Form / *Formule* 20E.1 Ont. Reg. No. / *Règl. de l'Ont.* : 258/98

Toronto
Small Claims Court / *Cour des petites créances de*

SC-00-47669-00
Claim No. / *N° de la demande*

47 Sheppard Ave. E., 3rd Fl.
Toronto, ON M2N 5N1
Address / *Adresse*

416-326-3554
Phone number / *Numéro de téléphone*

☐ Additional creditor(s) listed on the attached Form 1A.
Le ou les créanciers additionnels sont mentionnés sur la formule 1A ci-jointe.

Creditor / *Créancier*

Last name, or name of company / *Nom de famille ou nom de la compagnie*		
Oryx		
First name / *Premier prénom* **Albert**	Second name / *Deuxième prénom*	Also known as / *Également connu(e) sous le nom de*
Address (street number, apt., unit) / *Adresse (numéro et rue, app., unité)* **c/o Peter Paralegal, 41 Yonge Street, #410**		
City/Town / *Cité/ville* **Toronto**	Province **ON**	Phone no. / *N° de téléphone* **416-597-0048**
Postal code / *Code postal* **M2G 1S1**		Fax no. / *N° de télécopieur* **416-597-0049**
Representative / *Représentant(e)* **Peter Paralegal**		LSUC # / *N° du BHC* **P02952**
Address (street number, apt., unit) / *Adresse (numéro et rue, app., unité)* **41 Yonge Street, #410**		
City/Town / *Cité/ville* **Toronto**	Province **ON**	Phone no. / *N° de téléphone* **416-597-0048**
Postal code / *Code postal* **M5G 1S1**		Fax no. / *N° de télécopieur* **416-597-0049**

Debtor / *Débiteur*

Last name, or name of company / *Nom de famille ou nom de la compagnie*		
Foot		
First name / *Premier prénom* **Ophelia**	Second name / *Deuxième prénom*	Also known as / *Également connu(e) sous le nom de*
Address (street number, apt., unit) / *Adresse (numéro et rue, app., unité)* **c/o Digbert Fightback, 60 My Way**		
City/Town / *Cité/ville* **Toronto**	Province **ON**	Phone no. / *N° de téléphone* **416-491-5041**
Postal code / *Code postal* **M6R 8P1**		Fax no. / *N° de télécopieur*

Garnishee / *Tiers saisi*

Last name, or name of company / *Nom de famille ou nom de la compagnie*		
The Caring Bank — Trustme Rd. Branch		
First name / *Premier prénom*	Second name / *Deuxième prénom*	Also known as / *Également connu(e) sous le nom de*
Address (street number, apt., unit) / *Adresse (numéro et rue, app., unité)* **4800 Trustme Rd.**		
City/Town / *Cité/ville* **Toronto**	Province **ON**	Phone no. / *N° de téléphone* **416-485-6811**
Postal code / *Code postal* **M6R 1J6**		Fax no. / *N° de télécopieur*

SCR 20.08-20E.1 (September 1, 2010 / *1er septembre 2010*) CSD

continues....

Illustration 15.5 (continued)

FORM / *FORMULE* 20E.1   PAGE 2   SC-00-47669-00
                                                                      Claim No. / *N° de la demande*

TO THE GARNISHEE:
AU TIERS SAISI :

The creditor has renewed the garnishment issued or last renewed on December 15, Yr. 1 ,
Le créancier a renouvelé la saisie-arrêt prononcée ou renouvelée   (Date)
la dernière fois le

against the debtor. The creditor claims that you owe or will owe the debtor a debt in the form of wages, salary, pension payments, rent, annuity or other debt that you pay out in a lump-sum, periodically or by instalments. (A debt to the debtor includes both a debt payable to the debtor alone and a joint debt payable to the debtor and one or more co-owners.)
contre le débiteur. Le créancier prétend que vous êtes ou serez redevable au débiteur d'une dette sous forme de salaire, de prestations de retraite, de loyer, de rente ou autre que vous payez par somme forfaitaire, périodiquement ou par versements échelonnés. (Une dette envers le débiteur comprend à la fois une dette payable au débiteur seul et une dette payable conjointement au débiteur et à un ou plusieurs autres cotitulaires de la créance.)

YOU ARE REQUIRED TO PAY to the clerk of the   Toronto   Small Claims Court
VOUS ÊTES REQUIS(E) DE PAYER au greffier (Garnishment issuing court / *Tribunal qui prononce la*
de la Cour des petites créances de   *saisie-arrêt*)

(a)   all debts now payable by you to the debtor, **within 10 days** after this notice is served on you; **and**
       *d'une part, toutes les dettes dont vous êtes maintenant redevable au débiteur, **dans les 10 jours** qui suivent la signification du présent avis;*

(b)   all debts that become payable by you to the debtor after this notice is served on you and **within 6 years** after this notice is issued, **within 10 days** after they become payable.
       *d'autre part, toutes les dettes dont vous deviendrez redevable au débiteur après la signification du présent avis et **dans les 6 années** qui suivent sa délivrance, **dans les 10 jours** qui suivent la date à laquelle elles deviennent exigibles.*

The total amount of all your payments to the clerk is not to exceed $ $1,000.00 .
La totalité des paiements que vous ferez au greffier ne doit pas dépasser   (Amount unsatisfied /   **$.**
                                                               Montant impayé)

THIS NOTICE IS LEGALLY BINDING ON YOU until it expires or is changed, renewed, terminated or satisfied. If you do not pay the total amount or such lesser amount as you are liable to pay, you must serve a Garnishee's Statement (Form 20F) on the creditor and debtor, and file it with the clerk within 10 days after this notice is served on you.
LE PRÉSENT AVIS VOUS LIE LÉGALEMENT jusqu'à ce qu'il expire ou qu'il soit modifié, renouvelé ou résilié, ou qu'il y soit satisfait. Si vous ne payez pas le montant total ou le montant moindre dont vous êtes redevable, vous devez signifier une déclaration du tiers saisi (formule 20F) au créancier et au débiteur et la déposer auprès du greffier dans les 10 jours qui suivent la signification du présent avis.

EACH PAYMENT, payable to the Minister of Finance, MUST BE SENT with a copy of the attached garnishee's payment notice to the clerk at the above court address.
CHAQUE PAIEMENT, libellé à l'ordre du ministre des Finances, DOIT ÊTRE ENVOYÉ au greffier, à l'adresse du tribunal indiquée ci-dessus, avec une copie de l'avis de paiement du tiers saisi ci-joint.

If your debt is jointly owed to the debtor and to one or more co-owners, you must pay the debtor's appropriate share of the amount now payable, or which becomes payable, or such a percentage as the court may order.
Si votre dette est payable conjointement au débiteur et à un ou plusieurs autres cotitulaires de la créance, vous devez payer la quote-part appropriée du débiteur du montant dont vous êtes maintenant redevable, ou qui devient redevable, ou le pourcentage que le tribunal ordonne.

SCR 20.08-20E.1 (September 1, 2010 / *1er septembre 2010*) CSD   **Continued on next page / *Suite à la page suivante***

continues....

Illustration 15.5 (continued)

FORM / *FORMULE* 20E.1   PAGE 3   SC-00-47669-00
                                              Claim No. / *N° de la demande*

The amounts paid into court shall not exceed the portion of the debtor's wages that are subject to seizure or garnishment under Section 7 of the Wages Act (information available at: www.attorneygeneral.jus.gov.on.ca and www.e-laws.gov.on.ca). The portion of wages that can be garnished may be increased or decreased only by order of the court. If such a court order is attached to this notice or is served on you, you must follow the direction in that court order.

Les montants consignés au tribunal ne doivent pas dépasser la partie du salaire du débiteur qui peut faire l'objet d'une saisie ou d'une saisie-arrêt aux termes de l'article 7 de la Loi sur les salaires (pour de plus amples renseignements, reportez-vous aux adresses : www.attorneygeneral.jus.gov.on.ca et www.lois-en-ligne.gouv.on.ca). La partie saisissable du salaire ne peut être augmentée ou réduite que sur ordonnance du tribunal. Si une telle ordonnance du tribunal est annexée au présent avis ou vous est signifiée, vous devez vous conformer à la directive qui y est énoncée.

July 12, Yr. 7   "I. M. Clerk"
                                     (Signature of clerk / *Signature du greffier*)

CAUTION TO GARNISHEE:	**IF YOU FAIL TO PAY** to the clerk the amount set out in this notice and do not file a Garnishee's Statement (Form 20F) disputing garnishment, **JUDGMENT MAY BE OBTAINED AGAINST YOU BY THE CREDITOR** for payment of the amount set out above, plus costs. If you make a payment to anyone other than the clerk of the court, you may be liable to pay again [R. 20.08(17) and (18)].
AVERTISSEMENT AU TIERS SAISI :	*SI VOUS NE VERSEZ PAS au greffier le montant précisé dans le présent avis et ne déposez pas la déclaration du tiers saisi (formule 20F) contestant la saisie-arrêt, LE CRÉANCIER PEUT OBTENIR CONTRE VOUS UN JUGEMENT ordonnant le paiement du montant précisé ci-dessus et des dépens. Si vous effectuez un paiement à une personne qui n'est pas le greffier du tribunal, vous pouvez être tenu(e) de payer de nouveau [par. 20.08 (17) et (18)].*

NOTE:	Any party or interested person may complete and serve a Notice of Garnishment Hearing (Form 20Q) to determine any matter related to this notice. To obtain forms and self-help materials, attend the nearest Small Claims Court or access the following website: www.ontariocourtforms.on.ca.
REMARQUE :	*Toute partie ou personne intéressée peut remplir et signifier un avis d'audience sur la saisie-arrêt (formule 20Q) en vue de décider une question relative au présent avis. Vous pouvez obtenir les formules et la documentation à l'usage du client auprès de la Cour des petites créances de votre localité ou en consultant le site Web suivant : www.ontariocourtforms.on.ca.*

SCR 20.08-20E.1 (September 1, 2010 / *1ᵉʳ septembre 2010*) CSD

Continued on next page / *Suite à la page suivante*

continues....

Illustration 15.5 (continued)

FORM / *FORMULE* 20E.1   PAGE 4   SC-00-47669-00
                                                                                Claim No. / *N° de la demande*

The top portion of the garnishee's payment notice, below, is to be completed by the creditor before the Notice of Renewal of Garnishment (Form 20E.1) is issued. Where it is anticipated that more than one payment will be made by the garnishee, the creditor should supply extra copies of the garnishee's payment notice. Additional copies of the garnishee's payment notice are available at court offices or online at www.ontariocourtforms.on.ca (see Form 20E or 20E.1).
Le créancier doit remplir la partie supérieure de l'avis de paiement du tiers saisi figurant ci-dessous avant la délivrance de l'avis de renouvellement de la saisie-arrêt (formule 20E.1). S'il est prévu que le tiers saisi fera plus d'un paiement, le créancier doit fournir des exemplaires supplémentaires de l'avis de paiement du tiers saisi. Vous pouvez obtenir des exemplaires supplémentaires de l'avis de paiement du tiers saisi aux greffes des tribunaux ou en ligne à l'adresse www.ontariocourtforms.on.ca (consultez la formule 20E ou 20E.1).

GARNISHEE'S PAYMENT NOTICE / *AVIS DE PAIEMENT DU TIERS SAISI*

Make payment by cheque or money order payable to the Minister of Finance and send it, along with this payment notice to the clerk of the court at the following address:
Effectuez le paiement par chèque ou mandat-poste à l'ordre du ministre des Finances et envoyez-le, avec une copie du présent avis de paiement, au greffier du tribunal à l'adresse suivante :

Court address: **47 Sheppard Ave. E., 3rd Fl. Toronto, ON M2N 5N1**
Adresse du tribunal :

Claim No.:   **SC-00-47669-00**
N° de la demande :

Creditor: **Albert Oryx**
Créancier/créancière :

Debtor: **Ophelia Foot**
Débiteur/débitrice :

Garnishee: **The Caring Bank — Trustme Branch**
Tiers saisi :

TO BE COMPLETED BY GARNISHEE FOR EACH PAYMENT
À REMPLIR PAR LE TIERS SAISI LORS DE CHAQUE PAIEMENT

Date of payment:
Date du paiement :

Amount enclosed: $
Montant inclus : $

SCR 20.08-20E.1 (September 1, 2010 / *1ᵉʳ septembre 2010*) CSD

ILLUSTRATION 15.6: Notice of Termination of Garnishment (Form 20R) for *Oryx v. Foot*

ONTARIO

Superior Court of Justice
Cour supérieure de justice

Notice of Termination of Garnishment
Avis de mainlevée de la saisie-arrêt
Form / Formule 20R Ont. Reg. No / Régl. de l'Ont : 258/98

Toronto
Small Claims Court / *Cour des petites créances de*

SC-00-47669-00
Claim No. / *N° de la demande*

47 Sheppard Ave. E., 3rd Fl.
Toronto, ON M2N 5N1
Address / *Adresse*

416-326-3554
Phone number / *Numéro de téléphone*

BETWEEN / *ENTRE*

Albert Oryx

Creditor(s) / *Créancier(s)/créancière(s)*

and / *et*

Ophelia Foot

Debtor(s) / *Débiteur(s)/débitrice(s)*

TO   **The Caring Bank**
À

(Name of garnishee / *Nom du tiers saisi*)

AND TO the clerk of the   **Toronto**   Small Claims Court:
ET AU greffier de la Cour
des petites créances de

(Name of court location / *Emplacement du tribunal*)

The Notice of Garnishment/Notice of
Renewal of Garnishment dated   **October 12, Yr 1**   , served on you with respect to the debt of
L'avis de saisie-arrêt/l'avis de   *qui vous a été signifié à l'égard de la*
renouvellement de la saisie-arrêt daté du   *créance de :*

Last name of debtor, or name of company / *Nom de famille du débiteur/de la débitrice ou nom de la compagnie*		
Foot		
First name / *Premier prénom*	Second name / *Deuxième prénom*	Also known as / *Également connu(e) sous le nom de*
Ophelia		
Address / *Adresse*		
c/o Digbert Fightback, 60 My Way, Toronto, ON M6R 8P1		

is terminated and you are not to make any further payments under it.
prend fin et vous n'avez pas besoin de faire d'autres paiements aux termes de celui-ci.

October 20, Yr 4

Peter Paralegal

(Signature of creditor or representative / *Signature du créancier/de la*
créancière ou du/de la représentant(e))

Peter Paralegal, 41 Yonge Street, #410
Toronto ON   M5G 1S1
416-597-0048

(Name, address and phone number of creditor or representative / *Nom,*
adresse et numéro de téléphone du créancier/de la créancière ou du/de la
représentant(e))

NOTE: The creditor must serve this notice on the garnishee and on the court clerk.
REMARQUE :   *Le créancier doit signifier le présent avis au tiers saisi et au greffier du tribunal.*

SCR 20.08-20R (September 1, 2010 / *1ᵉʳ septembre 2010*) CSD

REVIEW QUESTIONS

1. What documents do you have to file in support of a garnishment?

2. Albert wants to garnish Ophelia's savings accounts at the Caring Bank. What steps does he need to take to do this? What happens if the account turns out to be a joint account with Ophelia's new husband, Ben?

3. In Albert's garnishment process, what is likely to happen in the following circumstances?

    (a) Albert garnishes Ophelia's wages.

    (b) Albert discovers that there are two other people with garnishments against Ophelia's wages.

4. In what circumstances should the bank file a Garnishee's Statement or ask for a garnishment hearing?

5. When should payments be distributed by the clerk?

6. What sources are exempt from garnishment?

DISCUSSION QUESTIONS/CASE STUDIES

FACTS

You are a paralegal working at Seneca Paralegals, 1750 Finch Avenue East, Toronto, Ontario M2J 2X5. You are assigned the Ames file. In this case, you are representing Wilbur Watson, who lives at 364 Maple Blvd., Toronto, Ontario M3H 4F1. Mr. Watson has obtained a small claims judgment against B & J Contracting (B & J), a partnership owned by Bradley and Jordan Ames. Their business is still located at 487 Regency Blvd., Richmond Hill, Ontario L4A 3B8. Assume that you have expanded your enforcement rights under Rule 5 to claim against the individuals as well as the partnership that you have sued.

The claim was issued on November 1, Yr. 0. The claim involves payment in the principal sum of $6,800 for work done in the past for which interest started to be charged on August 1, Yr. 0. The pre-judgment *Courts of Justice Act* interest rate was 4.5%. You acted for Wilbur when he sued B & J in the Richmond Hill Small Claims Court and got judgment on January 26, Yr. 1, for $6,800, plus pre-judgment interest, costs of $670, and post-judgment interest at the rate of 6% pursuant to the *Courts of Justice Act*. You conducted a judgment debtor examination on March 19, Yr. 1. Today is March 26, Yr. 1.

You have discovered during the judgment debtor examination that Wilbur was not the defendants' only customer. You now know that B & J completed some work for Quinius Quilp, who lives at 123 Green Road, Toronto, Ontario M6E 1Z5 (telephone: 416-123-4567). The contract amount due from Quilp to the defendants is $1,500. It is payable now, and it is still outstanding. You don't know anything further about the contract.

Prepare the documents necessary to garnish the debt owing from Quilp to the defendant.

Appendices
Glossary
Bibliography
Index

Appendices

Appendix 1: Days of the Year Chart

Instructions for Using the Days of the Year Chart

General Instructions

1. In most cases, use as your start date the day BEFORE interest begins to run unless your interest start date is January 1, in which case you would use January 1. For example, if interest began to be charged on June 1, you would use May 31, as your start date for counting, using the Days of the Year Chart.

2. Look up the day of the year for the last day interest is being calculated, and deduct that number from the number obtained in (1), above. For example, if the day before interest started was May 31, and you were calculating interest up to and including September 30, you would subtract 151 (the number of May 31) from 273 (the number for September 30) for a total of 122 days.

Leap Year Instructions

1. If February 29 is included in your interest calculation period, adjust the days on the table to make February 29 Day 60 and then increase the numbers after February 29 by adding 1 to them. For example, if interest began on February 1 and you were counting to April 1, you would make Day 91 (April 1) Day 92 and subtract 31 (January 31 as you backed up a day) for a total of 60 days.

2. If you are counting days in a leap year after February 29, you do not need to adjust your numbers to account for the leap day.

The Chart

Day of month	Jan	Feb	Mar	Apr	May	Jun	July	Aug	Sep	Oct	Nov	Dec	Day of month
					The number of each day of the year								
1	1	32	60	91	121	152	182	213	244	274	305	335	**1**
2	2	33	61	92	122	153	183	214	245	275	306	336	**2**
3	3	34	62	93	123	154	184	215	246	276	307	337	**3**
4	4	35	63	94	124	155	185	216	247	277	308	338	**4**
5	5	36	64	95	125	156	186	217	248	278	309	339	**5**
6	6	37	65	96	126	157	187	218	249	279	310	340	**6**
7	7	38	66	97	127	158	188	219	250	280	311	341	**7**
8	8	39	67	98	128	159	189	220	251	281	312	342	**8**
9	9	40	68	99	129	160	190	221	252	282	313	343	**9**
10	10	41	69	100	130	161	191	222	253	283	314	344	**10**
11	11	42	70	101	131	162	192	223	254	284	315	345	**11**
12	12	43	71	102	132	163	193	224	255	285	316	346	**12**
13	13	44	72	103	133	164	194	225	256	286	317	347	**13**
14	14	45	73	104	134	165	195	226	257	287	318	348	**14**
15	15	46	74	105	135	166	196	227	258	288	319	349	**15**
16	16	47	75	106	136	167	197	228	259	289	320	350	**16**
17	17	48	76	107	137	168	198	229	260	290	321	351	**17**
18	18	49	77	108	138	169	199	230	261	291	322	352	**18**
19	19	50	78	109	139	170	200	231	262	292	323	353	**19**
20	20	51	79	110	140	171	201	232	263	293	324	354	**20**
21	21	52	80	111	141	172	202	233	264	294	325	355	**21**
22	22	53	81	112	142	173	203	234	265	295	326	356	**22**
23	23	54	82	113	143	174	204	235	266	296	327	357	**23**
24	24	55	83	114	144	175	205	236	267	297	328	358	**24**
25	25	56	84	115	145	176	206	237	268	298	329	359	**25**
26	26	57	85	116	146	177	207	238	269	299	330	360	**26**
27	27	58	86	117	147	178	208	239	270	300	331	361	**27**
28	28	59	87	118	148	179	209	240	271	301	332	362	**28**
29	29		88	119	149	180	210	241	272	302	333	363	**29**
30	30		89	120	150	181	211	242	273	303	334	364	**30**
31	31		90		151		212	243		304		365	**31**

Appendix 2: **Rules of the Small Claims Court**

Courts of Justice Act, O. Reg. 258/98, as am. by O. Reg. 400/12
(Current as of July 17, 2013)

RULE 1 GENERAL

Citation

1.01 These rules may be cited as the Small Claims Court Rules. O. Reg. 258/ 98, r. 1.01.

Definitions

1.02(1) In these rules,

"court" means the Small Claims Court;

"disability", where used in respect of a person or party, means that the person or party is,

(a) a minor,

(b) mentally incapable within the meaning of section 6 or 45 of the *Substitute Decisions Act, 1992* in respect of an issue in the proceeding, whether the person or party has a guardian or not, or

(c) an absentee within the meaning of the *Absentees Act*;

"document" includes data and information in electronic form;

"electronic" includes created, recorded, transmitted or stored in digital form or in other intangible form by electronic, magnetic or optical means or by any other means that has capabilities for creation, recording, transmission or storage similar to those means, and "electronically" has a corresponding meaning;

"holiday" means,

(a) any Saturday or Sunday,

(b) New Year's Day,

(b.1) Family Day,

(c) Good Friday,

(d) Easter Monday,

(e) Victoria Day,

(f) Canada Day,

(g) Civic Holiday,

(h) Labour Day,

(i) Thanksgiving Day,

(j) Remembrance Day,

(k) Christmas Day,

(l) Boxing Day, and

(m) any special holiday proclaimed by the Governor General or the Lieutenant Governor,

and if New Year's Day, Canada Day or Remembrance Day falls on a Saturday or Sunday, the following Monday is a holiday, and if Christmas Day falls on a Saturday or Sunday, the following Monday and Tuesday are holidays, and if Christmas Day falls on a Friday, the following Monday is a holiday;

"order" includes a judgment;

"self-represented", when used in reference to a person, means that the person is not represented by a lawyer, student-at-law or agent. O. Reg. 258/98, r. 1.02; O. Reg. 461/01, s. 1(1); O. Reg. 78/06, s. 2(1, 2); O. Reg. 574/07, s. 1.

"territorial division" means,

(a) a county, a district or a regional municipality, and

(b) each of the following, as they existed on December 31, 2002:

(i) The combined area of County of Brant and City of Brantford.

(ii) Municipality of Chatham-Kent.

    (iii) Haldimand County.
    (iv) City of Hamilton.
    (v) City of Kawartha Lakes.
    (vi) Norfolk County.
    (vii) City of Ottawa.
    (viii) County of Prince Edward.
    (ix) City of Toronto.

    (2) Revoked: O. Reg. 78/06, s. 2(3).

General Principle
1.03(1) These rules shall be liberally construed to secure the just, most expeditious and least expensive determination of every proceeding on its merits in accordance with section 25 of the *Courts of Justice Act*. O. Reg. 258/98, r. 1.03(1).

Matters Not Covered in Rules
    (2) If these rules do not cover a matter adequately, the court may give directions and make any order that is just, and the practice shall be decided by analogy to these rules, by reference to the *Courts of Justice Act* and the Act governing the action and, if the court considers it appropriate, by reference to the Rules of Civil Procedure. O. Reg. 78/06, s. 3.

Orders on Terms
1.04 When making an order under these rules, the court may impose such terms and give such directions as are just. O. Reg. 258/98, r. 1.04.

Standards for Documents
1.05 A document in a proceeding shall be printed, typewritten, written or reproduced legibly. O. Reg. 78/06, s. 4.

Forms
1.06(1) The forms prescribed by these rules shall be used where applicable and with such variations as the circumstances require. O. Reg. 78/06, s. 4.

Table of Forms
    (2) In these rules, when a form is referred to by number, the reference is to the form with that number that is described in the Table of Forms at the end of these rules and is available on the Internet through www.ontariocourtforms.on.ca. O. Reg. 78/06, s. 4.

Additional Parties
    (3) If a form does not have sufficient space to list all of the parties to the action on the first page, the remaining parties shall be listed in Form 1A, which shall be appended to the form immediately following the first page. O. Reg. 78/06, s. 4.

Additional Debtors
    (4) If any of the following forms do not have sufficient space to list all of the debtors in respect of which the form applies, the remaining debtors shall be listed in Form 1A.1, which shall be appended to the form:
  1. Certificate of judgment (Form 20A).
  2. Writ of seizure and sale of personal property (Form 20C).
  3. Writ of seizure and sale of land (Form 20D).

4. Direction to enforce writ of seizure and sale of personal property (Form 20O). O. Reg. 393/09, s. 2(2).

Affidavit

(5) If these rules permit or require the use of an affidavit, Form 15B may be used for the purpose unless another form is specified. O. Reg. 393/09, s. 2(2).

Telephone and Video Conferences — Where Available

1.07(1) If facilities for a telephone or video conference are available at the court, all or part of any of the following may be heard or conducted by telephone or video conference as permitted by subrules (2) and (3):

1. A settlement conference.
2. A motion. O. Reg. 78/06, s. 4.

(1.1) If facilities for a video conference are available at the court, all or part of an examination of a debtor or other person under rule 20.10 may be conducted by video conference as permitted by subrules (2) and (3). O. Reg. 393/09, s. 3(1).

Request to be Made

(2) A settlement conference or motion may be heard or conducted by telephone or video conference or all or part of an examination under rule 20.10 may be conducted by video conference if a party files a request for the conference (Form 1B), indicating the reasons for the request, and the court grants the request. O. Reg. 78/06, s. 4.

Balance of Convenience

(3) In deciding whether to direct a telephone or video conference, the judge shall consider,

(a) the balance of convenience between the party that wants the telephone or video conference and any party that opposes it; and
(b) any other relevant matter. O. Reg. 78/06, s. 4.

Arrangements for Conference

(4) If an order directing a telephone or video conference is made, the court shall make the necessary arrangements for the conference and notify the parties of them. O. Reg. 78/06, s. 4.

Setting Aside or Varying Order

(5) A judge presiding at a proceeding or step in a proceeding may set aside or vary an order directing a telephone or video conference. O. Reg. 78/06, s. 4.

RULE 2 NON-COMPLIANCE WITH THE RULES

Effect of Non-Compliance

2.01 A failure to comply with these rules is an irregularity and does not render a proceeding or a step, document or order in a proceeding a nullity, and the court may grant all necessary amendments or other relief, on such terms as are just, to secure the just determination of the real matters in dispute. O. Reg. 258/98, r. 2.01.

Court May Dispense With Compliance
2.02 If necessary in the interest of justice, the court may dispense with compliance with any rule at any time. O. Reg. 258/98, r. 2.02.

RULE 3 TIME

Computation
3.01 If these rules or an order of the court prescribe a period of time for the taking of a step in a proceeding, the time shall be counted by excluding the first day and including the last day of the period; if the last day of the period of time falls on a holiday, the period ends on the next day that is not a holiday. O. Reg. 258/98, r. 3.01.

Powers of Court
3.02(1) The court may lengthen or shorten any time prescribed by these rules or an order, on such terms as are just. O. Reg. 258/98, r. 3.02(1).

Consent
(2) A time prescribed by these rules for serving or filing a document may be lengthened or shortened by filing the consent of the parties. O. Reg. 258/98, r. 3.02(2); O. Reg. 461/01, s. 3.

RULE 4 PARTIES UNDER DISABILITY

Plaintiff's Litigation Guardian
4.01(1) An action by a person under disability shall be commenced or continued by a litigation guardian, subject to subrule (2). O. Reg. 258/98, r. 4.01(1).

Exception
(2) A minor may sue for any sum not exceeding $500 as if he or she were of full age. O. Reg. 258/98, r. 4.01(2).

Consent
(3) A plaintiff's litigation guardian shall, at the time of filing a claim or as soon as possible afterwards, file with the clerk a consent (Form 4A) in which the litigation guardian,
(a) states the nature of the disability;
(b) in the case of a minor, states the minor's birth date;
(c) sets out his or her relationship, if any, to the person under disability;
(d) states that he or she has no interest in the proceeding contrary to that of the person under disability;
(e) acknowledges that he or she is aware of his or her liability to pay personally any costs awarded against him or her or against the person under disability; and
(f) states whether he or she is represented by a lawyer or agent and, if so, gives that person's name and confirms that the person has written authority to act in the proceeding. O. Reg. 258/98, r. 4.01(3).

Defendant's Litigation Guardian
4.02(1) An action against a person under disability shall be defended by a litigation guardian. O. Reg. 258/98, r. 4.02(1).

(2) A defendant's litigation guardian shall file with the defence a consent (Form 4A) in which the litigation guardian,
(a) states the nature of the disability;
(b) in the case of a minor, states the minor's birth date;
(c) sets out his or her relationship, if any, to the person under disability;
(d) states that he or she has no interest in the proceeding contrary to that of the person under disability; and
(e) states whether he or she is represented by a lawyer or agent and, if so, gives that person's name and confirms that the person has written authority to act in the proceeding. O. Reg. 258/98, r. 4.02(2); O. Reg. 78/06, s. 5.

(3) If it appears to the court that a defendant is a person under disability and the defendant does not have a litigation guardian the court may, after notice to the proposed litigation guardian, appoint as litigation guardian for the defendant any person who has no interest in the action contrary to that of the defendant. O. Reg. 258/98, r. 4.02(3).

Who May Be Litigation Guardian
4.03(1) Any person who is not under disability may be a plaintiff's or defendant's litigation guardian, subject to subrule (2). O. Reg. 258/98, r. 4.03(1).

(2) If the plaintiff or defendant,
(a) is a minor, in a proceeding to which subrule 4.01(2) does not apply,
  (i) the parent or person with lawful custody or another suitable person shall be the litigation guardian, or
  (ii) if no such person is available and able to act, the Children's Lawyer shall be the litigation guardian;
(b) is mentally incapable and has a guardian with authority to act as litigation guardian in the proceeding, the guardian shall be the litigation guardian;
(c) is mentally incapable and does not have a guardian with authority to act as litigation guardian in the proceeding, but has an attorney under a power of attorney with that authority, the attorney shall be the litigation guardian;
(d) is mentally incapable and has neither a guardian with authority to act as litigation guardian in the proceeding nor an attorney under a power of attorney with that power,
  (i) a suitable person who has no interest contrary to that of the incapable person may be the litigation guardian, or
  (ii) if no such person is available and able to act, the Public Guardian and Trustee shall be the litigation guardian;
(e) is an absentee,
  (i) the committee of his or her estate appointed under the *Absentees Act* shall be the litigation guardian,
  (ii) if there is no such committee, a suitable person who has no interest contrary to that of the absentee may be the litigation guardian, or
  (iii) if no such person is available and able to act, the Public Guardian and Trustee shall be the litigation guardian;
(f) is a person in respect of whom an order was made under subsection 72(1) or (2) of the *Mental Health Act* as it read before April 3, 1995, the Public Guardian and Trustee shall be the litigation guardian. O. Reg. 258/98, r. 4.03(2).

Duties of Litigation Guardian

4.04(1) A litigation guardian shall diligently attend to the interests of the person under disability and take all steps reasonably necessary for the protection of those interests, including the commencement and conduct of a defendant's claim. O. Reg. 258/98, r. 4.04(1).

Public Guardian and Trustee, Children's Lawyer

(2) The Public Guardian and Trustee or the Children's Lawyer may act as litigation guardian without filing the consent required by subrule 4.01(3) or 4.02(2). O. Reg. 258/98, r. 4.04(2).

Power of Court

4.05 The court may remove or replace a litigation guardian at any time. O. Reg. 258/98, r. 4.05.

Setting Aside Judgment, etc.

4.06 If an action has been brought against a person under disability and the action has not been defended by a litigation guardian, the court may set aside the noting of default or any judgment against the person under disability on such terms as are just, and may set aside any step that has been taken to enforce the judgment. O. Reg. 258/98, r. 4.06.

Settlement Requires Court's Approval

4.07 No settlement of a claim made by or against a person under disability is binding on the person without the approval of the court. O. Reg. 258/98, r. 4.07.

Money to be Paid into Court

4.08(1) Any money payable to a person under disability under an order or a settlement shall be paid into court, unless the court orders otherwise, and shall afterwards be paid out or otherwise disposed of as ordered by the court. O. Reg. 258/98, r. 4.08(1).

(2) If money is payable to a person under disability under an order or settlement, the court may order that the money shall be paid directly to the person, and payment made under the order discharges the obligation to the extent of the amount paid. O. Reg. 258/98, r. 4.08(2).

Supporting Affidavit

(3) A motion for an order under this rule shall be supported by an affidavit in Form 4B rather than an affidavit in Form 15A. O. Reg. 400/12, s. 1.

Costs

(4) In making an order under this rule, the court may order that costs payable to the moving party be paid out of the money in court directly to the person representing that party in the proceeding. O. Reg. 400/12, s. 1.

RULE 5 PARTNERSHIPS AND SOLE PROPRIETORSHIPS

Partnerships

5.01 A proceeding by or against two or more persons as partners may be commenced using the firm name of the partnership. O. Reg. 258/98, r. 5.01.

Defence
5.02 If a proceeding is commenced against a partnership using the firm name, the partnership's defence shall be delivered in the firm name and no person who admits being a partner at any material time may defend the proceeding separately, except with leave of the court. O. Reg. 258/98, r. 5.02.

Notice to Alleged Partner
5.03(1) In a proceeding against a partnership using the firm name, a plaintiff who seeks an order that would be enforceable personally against a person as a partner may serve the person with the claim, together with a notice to alleged partner (Form 5A). O. Reg. 258/98, r. 5.03(1).

(2) A person served as provided in subrule (1) is deemed to have been a partner at the material time, unless the person defends the proceeding separately denying having been a partner at the material time. O. Reg. 258/98, r. 5.03(2).

Disclosure of Partners
5.04(1) If a proceeding is commenced by or against a partnership using the firm name, any other party may serve a notice requiring the partnership to disclose immediately in writing the names and addresses of all partners constituting the partnership at a time specified in the notice; if a partner's present address is unknown, the partnership shall disclose the last known address. O. Reg. 258/98, r. 5.04(1).

(1.1), (1.1.1) Revoked: O. Reg. 78/06, s. 6.

Partnership's Failure to Comply
(2) If a partnership fails to comply with a notice under subrule (1), its claim may be dismissed or the proceeding stayed or its defence may be struck out. O. Reg. 258/98, r. 5.04(2).

Enforcement of Order
5.05(1) An order against a partnership using the firm name may be enforced against the partnership's property. O. Reg. 258/98, r. 5.05(1).

(2) An order against a partnership using the firm name may also be enforced, if the order or a subsequent order so provides, against any person who was served as provided in rule 5.03 and who,
(a) under that rule, is deemed to have been a partner at the material time;
(b) has admitted being a partner at that time; or
(c) has been adjudged to have been a partner at that time. O. Reg. 258/98, r. 5.05(2).

Against Person not Served as Alleged Partner
(3) If, after an order has been made against a partnership using the firm name, the party obtaining it claims to be entitled to enforce it against any person alleged to be a partner other than a person who was served as provided in rule 5.03, the party may make a motion for leave to do so; the judge may grant leave if the person's liability as a partner is not disputed or, if disputed, after the liability has been determined in such manner as the judge directs. O. Reg. 258/98, r. 5.05(3); O. Reg. 78/06, s. 7.

Sole Proprietorships

5.06(1) If a person carries on business in a business name other than his or her own name, a proceeding may be commenced by or against the person using the business name. O. Reg. 258/98, r. 5.06(1).

(2) Rules 5.01 to 5.05 apply, with necessary modifications, to a proceeding by or against a sole proprietor using a business name, as though the sole proprietor were a partner and the business name were the firm name of a partnership. O. Reg. 258/98, r. 5.06(2).

RULE 6 FORUM AND JURISDICTION

Place of Commencement and Trial

6.01(1) An action shall be commenced,
 (a) in the territorial division,
   (i) in which the cause of action arose, or
   (ii) in which the defendant or, if there are several defendants, in which any one of them resides or carries on business; or
 (b) at the court's place of sitting that is nearest to the place where the defendant or, if there are several defendants, where any one of them resides or carries on business. O. Reg. 78/06, s. 8(1).

(2) An action shall be tried in the place where it is commenced, but if the court is satisfied that the balance of convenience substantially favours holding the trial at another place than those described in subrule (1), the court may order that the action be tried at that other place. O. Reg. 78/06, s. 8(1).

(3) If, when an action is called for trial or settlement conference, the judge finds that the place where the action was commenced is not the proper place of trial, the court may order that the action be tried in any other place where it could have been commenced under this rule. O. Reg. 78/06, s. 8(1).

6.02 A cause of action shall not be divided into two or more actions for the purpose of bringing it within the court's jurisdiction. O. Reg. 258/98, r. 6.02.

6.03 Revoked: O. Reg. 78/06, s. 8(2).

RULE 7 COMMENCEMENT OF PROCEEDINGS

Plaintiff's Claim

7.01(1) An action shall be commenced by filing a plaintiff's claim (Form 7A) with the clerk, together with a copy of the claim for each defendant. O. Reg. 258/98, r. 7.01(1).

Contents of Claim, Attachments

(2) The following requirements apply to the claim:
1. It shall contain the following information, in concise and non-technical language:
   i. The full names of the parties to the proceeding and, if relevant, the capacity in which they sue or are sued.
   ii. The nature of the claim, with reasonable certainty and detail, including the date, place and nature of the occurrences on which the claim is based.

iii. The amount of the claim and the relief requested.
iv. The name, address, telephone number, fax number if any, and Law Society of Upper Canada registration number if any, of the lawyer or agent representing the plaintiff or, if the plaintiff is self-represented, the plaintiff's address, telephone number and fax number if any.
v. The address where the plaintiff believes the defendant may be served.

2. If the plaintiff's claim is based in whole or in part on a document, a copy of the document shall be attached to each copy of the claim, unless it is unavailable, in which case the claim shall state the reason why the document is not attached. O. Reg. 461/01, s. 5; O. Reg. 78/06, s. 9(1); O. Reg. 56/08, s. 1.

(3) Revoked: O. Reg. 78/06, s. 9(2).

7.02 Revoked: O. Reg. 461/01, s. 6.

Issuing Claim
7.03(1) On receiving the plaintiff's claim, the clerk shall immediately issue it by dating, signing and sealing it and assigning it a court file number. O. Reg. 258/98, r. 7.03(1).

(2) The original of the claim shall remain in the court file and the copies shall be given to the plaintiff for service on the defendant. O. Reg. 258/98, r. 7.03(2).

RULE 8 SERVICE

Service of Particular Documents Plaintiff's or Defendant's Claim
8.01(1) A plaintiff's claim or defendant's claim (Form 7A or 10A) shall be served personally as provided in rule 8.02 or by an alternative to personal service as provided in rule 8.03. O. Reg. 258/98, r. 8.01(1).

Time for Service of Claim
(2) A claim shall be served within six months after the date it is issued, but the court may extend the time for service, before or after the six months has elapsed. O. Reg. 258/98, r. 8.01(2).

Defence
(3) A defence shall be served by the clerk, by mail or by fax. O. Reg. 258/98, r. 8.01(3).

(3.1) Revoked: O. Reg. 78/06, s. 10.

Default Judgment
(4) A default judgment (Form 11B) shall be served by the clerk, by mail or by fax, on all parties named in the claim. O. Reg. 78/06, s. 10.

(4.1), (4.1.1) Revoked: O. Reg. 78/06, s. 10.

Assessment Order
(5) An order made on a motion in writing for an assessment of damages under subrule 11.03(2) shall be served by the clerk to the moving party if the party provides a stamped, self-addressed envelope with the notice of motion and supporting affidavit. O. Reg. 78/06, s. 10.

Settlement Conference Order

(6) An order made at a settlement conference shall be served by the clerk by mail or by fax, on all parties that did not attend the settlement conference. O. Reg. 78/06, s. 10.

Summons to Witness

(7) A summons to witness (Form 18A) shall be served personally by the party who requires the presence of the witness, or by the party's lawyer or agent, at least 10 days before the trial date; at the time of service, attendance money calculated in accordance with the regulations made under the *Administration of Justice Act* shall be paid or tendered to the witness. O. Reg. 78/06, s. 10.

Notice of Garnishment

(8) A notice of garnishment (Form 20E) shall be served by the creditor,
(a) together with a sworn affidavit for enforcement request (Form 20P), on the debtor, by mail, by courier, personally as provided in rule 8.02 or by an alternative to personal service as provided in rule 8.03; and
(b) together with a garnishee's statement (Form 20F), on the garnishee, by mail, by courier, personally as provided in rule 8.02 or by an alternative to personal service as provided in rule 8.03. O. Reg. 78/06, s. 10.

Notice of Garnishment Hearing

(9) A notice of garnishment hearing (Form 20Q) shall be served by the person requesting the hearing on the creditor, debtor, garnishee and co-owner of the debt, if any, and any other interested persons by mail, by courier, personally as provided in rule 8.02 or by an alternative to personal services as provided in rule 8.03. O. Reg. 78/06, s. 10.

Notice of Examination

(10) A notice of examination (Form 20H) shall be served by the creditor on the debtor or person to be examined personally as provided in rule 8.02 or by an alternative to personal service as provided in rule 8.03. O. Reg. 78/06, s. 10.

Financial Statement

(11) If the person to be examined is the debtor and the debtor is an individual, the creditor shall serve the notice of examination on the debtor together with a blank financial information form (Form 20I). O. Reg. 78/06, s. 10.

(12) The notice of examination,
(a) shall be served, together with the financial information form if applicable, at least 30 days before the date fixed for the examination; and
(b) shall be filed, with proof of service, at least three days before the date fixed for the examination. O. Reg. 393/09, s. 4(3).

Notice of Contempt Hearing

(13) A notice of a contempt hearing shall be served by the creditor on the debtor or person to be examined personally as provided in rule 8.02. O. Reg. 78/06, s. 10.

Other Documents

(14) A document not referred to in subrules (1) to (13) may be served by mail, by courier, by fax, personally as provided in rule 8.02 or by an alternative to personal service as provided in rule 8.03, unless the court orders otherwise. O. Reg. 78/06, s. 10.

Personal Service

8.02 If a document is to be served personally, service shall be made,

Individual

(a) on an individual, other than a person under disability, by leaving a copy of the document with him or her;

Municipality

(b) on a municipal corporation, by leaving a copy of the document with the chair, mayor, warden or reeve of the municipality, with the clerk or deputy clerk of the municipality or with a lawyer for the municipality;

Corporation

(c) on any other corporation, by leaving a copy of the document with,
    (i) an officer, a director or agent of the corporation, or
    (ii) a person at any place of business of the corporation who appears to be in control or management of the place of business;

Board or Commission

(d) on a board or commission, by leaving a copy of the document with a member or officer of the board or commission;

Person Outside Ontario Carrying on Business in Ontario

(e) on a person outside Ontario who carries on business in Ontario, by leaving a copy of the document with anyone carrying on business in Ontario for the person;

Crown in Right of Canada

(f) on Her Majesty the Queen in right of Canada, in accordance with subsection 23(2) of the *Crown Liability and Proceedings Act* (Canada);

Crown in Right of Ontario

(g) on Her Majesty the Queen in right of Ontario, in accordance with section 10 of the *Proceedings Against the Crown Act*;

Absentee

(h) on an absentee, by leaving a copy of the document with the absentee's committee, if one has been appointed or, if not, with the Public Guardian and Trustee;

Minor

(i) on a minor, by leaving a copy of the document with the minor and, if the minor resides with a parent or other person having his or her care or lawful custody, by leaving another copy of the document with the parent or other person;

Mentally Incapable Person

(j) on a mentally incapable person,
    (i) if there is a guardian or an attorney acting under a validated power of attorney for personal care with authority to act in the proceeding, by leaving a copy of the document with the guardian or attorney,

     (ii) if there is no guardian or attorney acting under a validated power of attorney for personal care with authority to act in the proceeding but there is an attorney under a power of attorney with authority to act in the proceeding, by leaving a copy of the document with the attorney and leaving an additional copy with the person,

     (iii) if there is neither a guardian nor an attorney with authority to act in the proceeding, by leaving a copy of the document bearing the person's name and address with the Public Guardian and Trustee and leaving an additional copy with the person;

Partnership

  (k) on a partnership, by leaving a copy of the document with,

     (i) any one or more of the partners, or

     (ii) a person at the principal place of business of the partnership who appears to be in control or management of the place of business; and

Sole Proprietorship

  (l) on a sole proprietorship, by leaving a copy of the document with,

     (i) the sole proprietor, or

     (ii) a person at the principal place of business of the sole proprietorship who appears to be in control or management of the place of business. O. Reg. 258/98, r. 8.02; O. Reg. 56/12, s. 1.

Alternatives to Personal Service

8.03(1) If a document is to be served by an alternative to personal service, service shall be made in accordance with subrule (2), (3) or (5); in the case of a plaintiff's claim or defendant's claim served on an individual, service may also be made in accordance with subrule (7). O. Reg. 258/98, r. 8.03(1).

At Place of Residence

    (2) If an attempt is made to effect personal service at an individual's place of residence and for any reason personal service cannot be effected, the document may be served by,

  (a) leaving a copy in a sealed envelope addressed to the individual at the place of residence with anyone who appears to be an adult member of the same household; and

  (b) on the same day or the following day, mailing or sending by courier another copy of the document to the individual at the place of residence. O. Reg. 258/98, r. 8.03(2); O. Reg. 78/06, s. 11(1).

Corporation

    (3) If the head office or principal place of business of a corporation or, in the case of an extra-provincial corporation, the attorney for service in Ontario cannot be found at the last address recorded with the Ministry of Government Services, service may be made on the corporation,

  (a) by mailing or sending by courier a copy of the document to the corporation or to the attorney for service in Ontario, as the case may be, at that address; and

  (b) by mailing or sending by courier a copy of the document to each director of the corporation as recorded with the Ministry of Government Services, at the director's address as recorded with that Ministry. O. Reg. 78/06, s. 11(2).

When Effective

(4) Service made under subrule (2) or (3) is effective on the fifth day after the document is mailed or verified by courier that it was delivered. O. Reg. 258/98, r. 8.03(4); O. Reg. 78/06, s. 11(3).

Acceptance of Service by Lawyer

(5) Service on a party who is represented by a lawyer may be made by leaving a copy of the document with the lawyer or an employee in the lawyer's office, but service under this subrule is effective only if the lawyer or employee endorses on the document or a copy of it an acceptance of service and the date of the acceptance. O. Reg. 258/98, r. 8.03(5).

(6) By accepting service the lawyer is deemed to represent to the court that he or she has the client's authority to accept service. O. Reg. 258/98, r. 8.03(6).

Service of Claim by Mail to Last Known Address

(7) Service of a plaintiff's claim or defendant's claim on an individual against whom the claim is made may be made by sending a copy of the claim by registered mail or by courier to the individual's place of residence, if the signature of the individual or any person who appears to be a member of the same household, verifying receipt of the copy, is obtained. O. Reg. 393/09, s. 5(4); O. Reg. 440/10, s. 1(1).

(8) Service under subrule (7) is effective on the date on which receipt of the copy of the claim is verified by signature, as shown in a delivery confirmation provided by or obtained from Canada Post or the commercial courier, as the case may be. O. Reg. 393/09, s. 5(4); O. Reg. 440/10, s. 1(2).

(9) Revoked: O. Reg. 393/09, ss. 5(4), 26.

Substituted Service

8.04 If it is shown that it is impractical to effect prompt service of a claim personally or by an alternative to personal service, the court may allow substituted service. O. Reg. 258/98, r. 8.04.

Service Outside Ontario

8.05 If the defendant is outside Ontario, the court may award as costs of the action the costs reasonably incurred in effecting service of the claim on the defendant there. O. Reg. 258/98, r. 8.05; O. Reg. 78/06, s. 12.

Proof of Service

8.06 An affidavit of service (Form 8A) made by the person effecting the service constitutes proof of service of a document. O. Reg. 78/06, s. 13.

Service by Mail

8.07(1) If a document is to be served by mail under these rules, it shall be sent, by regular lettermail or registered mail, to the last address of the person or of the person's lawyer or agent that is,

 (a) on file with the court, if the document is to be served by the clerk;

 (b) known to the sender, if the document is to be served by any other person. O. Reg. 258/98, r. 8.07(1); O. Reg. 78/06, s. 14.

When Effective

(2) Service of a document by mail is deemed to be effective on the fifth day following the date of mailing. O. Reg. 258/98, r. 8.07(2).

Exception
(3) This rule does not apply when a claim is served by registered mail under subrule 8.03(7). O. Reg. 393/09, s. 6.

Service by Courier
8.07.1(1) If a document is to be served by courier under these rules, it shall be sent by means of a commercial courier to the last address of the person or of the person's lawyer or agent that is on file with the court or known to the sender. O. Reg. 78/06, s. 15.

When Effective
(2) Service of a document sent by courier is deemed to be effective on the fifth day following the date on which the courier verifies to the sender that the document was delivered. O. Reg. 78/06, s. 15.

Exception
(3) This rule does not apply when a claim is served by courier under subrule 8.03(7). O. Reg. 78/06, s. 15.

Service by Fax
8.08(1) Service of a document by fax is deemed to be effective,
(a) on the day of transmission, if transmission takes place before 5 p.m. on a day that is not a holiday;
(b) on the next day that is not a holiday, in any other case. O. Reg. 258/98, r. 8.08(1).

(2) A document containing 16 or more pages, including the cover page, may be served by fax only between 5 p.m. and 8 a.m. the following day, unless the party to be served consents in advance. O. Reg. 258/98, r. 8.08(2).

Notice of Change of Address
8.09(1) A party whose address for service changes shall serve notice of the change on the court and other parties within seven days after the change takes place. O. Reg. 78/06, s. 16.
(2) Service of the notice may be proved by affidavit if the court orders that proof of service is required. O. Reg. 78/06, s. 16.

Failure to Receive Document
8.10 A person who has been served or who is deemed to have been served with a document in accordance with these rules is nevertheless entitled to show, on a motion to set aside the consequences of default, on a motion for an extension of time or in support of a request for an adjournment, that the document,
(a) did not come to the person's notice; or
(b) came to the person's notice only at some time later than when it was served or is deemed to have been served. O. Reg. 461/01, s. 9(1).

RULE 9 DEFENCE

Defence
9.01(1) A defendant who wishes to dispute a plaintiff's claim shall file a defence (Form 9A), together with a copy for each of the other parties with the clerk within 20 days of being served with the claim. O. Reg. 258/98,

r. 9.01(1); O. Reg. 461/01, s. 10(1); O. Reg. 440/03, s. 2; O. Reg. 78/06, s. 17(1); O. Reg. 440/10, s. 2(1).

Service of Copy by Clerk

(2) On receiving the defence, the clerk shall retain the original in the court file and shall serve a copy in accordance with subrule 8.01(3) on each of the other parties. O. Reg. 258/98, r. 9.01(2); O. Reg. 461/01, s. 10(2); O. Reg. 78/06, s. 17(2); O. Reg. 440/10, s. 2(2).

(3) Revoked: O. Reg. 78/06, s. 17(3).

Contents of Defence, Attachments

9.02(1) The following requirements apply to the defence:
1. It shall contain the following information:
    i. The reasons why the defendant disputes the plaintiff's claim, expressed in concise non-technical language with a reasonable amount of detail.
    ii. If the defendant is self-represented, the defendant's name, address and telephone number, and fax number if any.
    iii. If the defendant is represented by a lawyer or agent, that person's name, address and telephone number, and fax number if any, and Law Society of Upper Canada registration number if any.
2. If the defence is based in whole or in part on a document, a copy of the document shall be attached to each copy of the defence, unless it is unavailable, in which case the defence shall state the reason why the document is not attached. O. Reg. 461/01, s. 11; O. Reg. 78/06, s. 18; O. Reg. 56/12, s. 2.

(2) Revoked: O. Reg. 78/06, s. 19.

Admission of Liability and Proposal of Terms of Payment

9.03(1) A defendant who admits liability for all or part of the plaintiff's claim but wishes to arrange terms of payment may in the defence admit liability and propose terms of payment. O. Reg. 258/98, r. 9.03(1).

Where No Dispute

(2) If the plaintiff does not dispute the proposal within the 20-day period referred to in subrule (3),
 (a) the defendant shall make payment in accordance with the proposal as if it were a court order;
 (b) the plaintiff may serve a notice of default of payment (Form 20L) on the defendant if the defendant fails to make payment in accordance with the proposal; and
 (c) the clerk shall sign judgment for the unpaid balance of the undisputed amount on the filing of an affidavit of default of payment (Form 20M) by the plaintiff swearing,
     (i) that the defendant failed to make payment in accordance with the proposal,
     (ii) to the amount paid by the defendant and the unpaid balance, and
     (iii) that 15 days have passed since the defendant was served with a notice of default of payment. O. Reg. 258/98, r. 9.03(2); O. Reg. 78/06, s. 20(1).

Dispute

(3) The plaintiff may dispute the proposal within 20 days after service of the defence by filing with the clerk and serving on the defendant a request to clerk (Form 9B) for a terms of payment hearing before a referee or other person appointed by the court. O. Reg. 78/06, s. 20(2).

(4) The clerk shall fix a time for the hearing, allowing for a reasonable notice period after the date the request is served, and serve a notice of hearing on the parties. O. Reg. 258/98, r. 9.03(4).

Manner of Service

(4.1) The notice of hearing shall be served by mail or fax. O. Reg. 330/02, s. 8(1).

Financial Information Form, Defendant an Individual

(4.2) The clerk shall serve a financial information form (Form 20I) on the defendant, together with the notice of hearing, if the defendant is an individual. O. Reg. 78/06, s. 20(3).

(4.3) Where a defendant receives a financial information form under subrule (4.2), he or she shall complete it and serve it on the creditor before the hearing, but shall not file it with the court. O. Reg. 78/06, s. 20(3).

Order

(5) On the hearing, the referee or other person may make an order as to terms of payment by the defendant. O. Reg. 258/98, r. 9.03(5); O. Reg. 78/06, s. 20(4).

Failure to Appear, Default Judgment

(6) If the defendant does not appear at the hearing, the clerk may sign default judgment against the defendant for the part of the claim that has been admitted and shall serve a default judgment (Form 11B) on the defendant in accordance with subrule 8.01(4). O. Reg. 78/06, s. 20(5).

(6.1) Revoked: O. Reg. 78/06, s. 20(5).

Failure to Make Payments

(7) Unless the referee or other person specifies otherwise in the order as to terms of payment, if the defendant fails to make payment in accordance with the order, the clerk shall sign judgment for the unpaid balance on the filing of an affidavit by the plaintiff swearing to the default and stating the amount paid and the unpaid balance. O. Reg. 258/98, r. 9.03(7).

RULE 10 DEFENDANT'S CLAIM

Defendant's Claim

10.01(1) A defendant may make a claim,
 (a) against the plaintiff;
 (b) against any other person,
   (i) arising out of the transaction or occurrence relied upon by the plaintiff, or
   (ii) related to the plaintiff's claim; or
 (c) against the plaintiff and against another person in accordance with clause (b). O. Reg. 258/98, r. 10.01(1).

(2) The defendant's claim shall be in Form 10A and may be issued,

(a) within 20 days after the day on which the defence is filed; or

(b) after the time described in clause (a) but before trial or default judgment, with leave of the court. O. Reg. 78/06, s. 21(1).

Copies

(3) The defendant shall provide a copy of the defendant's claim to the court. O. Reg. 258/98, r. 10.01(3); O. Reg. 461/01, s. 13(1).

Contents of Defendant's Claim, Attachments

(4) The following requirements apply to the defendant's claim:

1. It shall contain the following information:
   i. The full names of the parties to the defendant's claim and, if relevant, the capacity in which they sue or are sued.
   ii. The nature of the claim, expressed in concise non-technical language with a reasonable amount of detail, including the date, place and nature of the occurrences on which the claim is based.
   iii. The amount of the claim and the relief requested.
   iv. If the defendant is self-represented, the defendant's name, address and telephone number, and fax number if any.
   v. If the defendant is represented by a lawyer or agent, that person's name, address and telephone number, and fax number if any, and Law Society of Upper Canada registration number if any.
   vi. The address where the defendant believes each person against whom the claim is made may be served.
   vii. The court file number assigned to the plaintiff's claim.
2. If the defendant's claim is based in whole or in part on a document, a copy of the document shall be attached to each copy of the claim, unless it is unavailable, in which case the claim shall state the reason why the document is not attached. O. Reg. 461/01, s. 13(2); O. Reg. 78/06, s. 21(2, 3); O. Reg. 56/12, s. 3.

(5) Revoked: O. Reg. 78/06, s. 21(4).

Issuance

(6) On receiving the defendant's claim, the clerk shall immediately issue it by dating, signing and sealing it, shall assign it the same court file number as the plaintiff's claim and shall place the original in the court file. O. Reg. 258/98, r. 10.01(6); O. Reg. 461/01, s. 13(3).

(7), (8) Revoked: O. Reg. 78/06, s. 21(4).

Service

10.02 A defendant's claim shall be served by the defendant on every person against whom it is made, in accordance with subrules 8.01(1) and (2). O. Reg. 258/98, r. 10.02.

Defence

10.03(1) A party who wishes to dispute the defendant's claim or a third party who wishes to dispute the plaintiff's claim may, within 20 days after service of the defendant's claim, file a defence (Form 9A) with the clerk, together with a copy for each of the other parties or persons against whom the defendant's or plaintiff's claim is made. O. Reg. 78/06, s. 22.

Service of Copy by Clerk

(2) On receiving a defence under subrule (1), the clerk shall retain the original in the court file and shall serve a copy on each party in accordance with subrule 8.01(3). O. Reg. 78/06, s. 22.

Defendant's Claim to be Tried with Main Action

10.04(1) A defendant's claim shall be tried and disposed of at the trial of the action, unless the court orders otherwise. O. Reg. 258/98, r. 10.04(1).

Exception

(2) If it appears that a defendant's claim may unduly complicate or delay the trial of the action or cause undue prejudice to a party, the court may order separate trials or direct that the defendant's claim proceed as a separate action. O. Reg. 258/98, r. 10.04(2).

Rights of Third Party

(3) If the defendant alleges, in a defendant's claim, that a third party is liable to the defendant for all or part of the plaintiff's claim in the action, the third party may at the trial contest the defendant's liability to the plaintiff, but only if the third party has filed a defence in accordance with subrule 10.03(1). O. Reg. 258/98, r. 10.04(3); O. Reg. 78/06, s. 23.

Application of Rules to Defendant's Claim

10.05(1) These rules apply, with necessary modifications, to a defendant's claim as if it were a plaintiff's claim, and to a defence to a defendant's claim as if it were a defence to a plaintiff's claim. O. Reg. 258/98, r. 10.05(1).

Exception

(2) However, when a person against whom a defendant's claim is made is noted in default, judgment against that person may be obtained only in accordance with rule 11.04. O. Reg. 258/98, r. 10.05(2); O. Reg. 56/08, s. 2.

RULE 11 DEFAULT PROCEEDINGS

Noting Defendant in Default

11.01(1) If a defendant to a plaintiff's claim or a defendant's claim fails to file a defence to all or part of the claim with the clerk within the prescribed time, the clerk may, when proof is filed that the claim was served within the territorial division, note the defendant in default. O. Reg. 78/06, s. 24.

Leave Required for Person under Disability

(2) A person under disability may not be noted in default under subrule (1), except with leave of the court. O. Reg. 78/06, s. 24.

Service Outside Territorial Division

(3) If all the defendants have been served outside the court's territorial division, the clerk shall not note any defendant in default until it is proved by an affidavit for jurisdiction (Form 11A) submitted to the clerk, or by evidence presented before a judge, that the action was properly brought in that territorial division. O. Reg. 78/06, s. 24.

Default Judgment, Plaintiff's Claim, Debt or Liquidated Demand
11.02(1) If a defendant has been noted in default, the clerk may sign default judgment (Form 11B) in respect of the claim or any part of the claim to which the default applies that is for a debt or liquidated demand in money, including interest if claimed. O. Reg. 78/06, s. 24.

(2) The fact that default judgment has been signed under subrule (1) does not affect the plaintiff's right to proceed on the remainder of the claim or against any other defendant for all or part of the claim. O. Reg. 78/06, s. 24.

Manner of Service of Default Judgment
(3) A default judgment (Form 11B) shall be served in accordance with subrule 8.01(4). O. Reg. 78/06, s. 24.

Default Judgment, Plaintiff's Claim, Unliquidated Demand
11.03(1) If all defendants have been noted in default, the plaintiff may obtain judgment against a defendant noted in default with respect to any part of the claim to which rule 11.02 does not apply. O. Reg. 78/06, s. 24.

(2) To obtain judgment, the plaintiff may,
(a) file a notice of motion and supporting affidavit (Form 15A) requesting a motion in writing for an assessment of damages, setting out the reasons why the motion should be granted and attaching any relevant documents; or
(b) file a request to clerk (Form 9B) requesting that an assessment hearing be arranged. O. Reg. 78/06, s. 24.

Inadequate Supporting Affidavit
(3) On a motion in writing for an assessment of damages under clause (2)(a), a judge who finds the plaintiff's affidavit inadequate or unsatisfactory may order that,
(a) a further affidavit be provided; or
(b) an assessment hearing be held. O. Reg. 78/06, s. 24.

Assessment Hearing
(4) If an assessment hearing is to be held under clause (2)(b) or (3)(b), the clerk shall fix a date for the hearing and send a notice of hearing to the plaintiff, and the assessment hearing shall proceed as a trial in accordance with rule 17. O. Reg. 78/06, s. 24.

Matters to be Proved
(5) On a motion in writing for an assessment of damages or at an assessment hearing, the plaintiff is not required to prove liability against a defendant noted in default, but is required to prove the amount of the claim. O. Reg. 78/06, s. 24.

Service of Order
(6) An order made on a motion in writing for an assessment of damages shall be served by the clerk in accordance with subrule 8.01(5). O. Reg. 78/06, s. 24.

No Assessment where Defence Filed

(7) If one or more defendants have filed a defence, a plaintiff requiring an assessment of damages against a defendant noted in default shall proceed to a settlement conference under rule 13 and, if necessary, a trial in accordance with rule 17. O. Reg. 78/06, s. 24.

Default Judgment, Defendant's Claim

11.04 If a party against whom a defendant's claim is made has been noted in default, judgment may be obtained against the party only at trial or on motion. O. Reg. 78/06, s. 24.

Consequences of Noting in Default

11.05(1) A defendant who has been noted in default shall not file a defence or take any other step in the proceeding, except making a motion under rule 11.06, without leave of the court or the plaintiff's consent. O. Reg. 78/06, s. 24.

(2) Any step in the proceeding may be taken without the consent of a defendant who has been noted in default. O. Reg. 78/06, s. 24.

(3) A defendant who has been noted in default is not entitled to notice of any step in the proceeding and need not be served with any other document, except the following:
1. Subrule 11.02(3) (service of default judgment).
2. Rule 12.01 (amendment of claim or defence).
3. Subrule 15.01(6) (motion after judgment).
4. Postjudgment proceedings against a debtor under rule 20. O. Reg. 78/06, s. 24.

Setting Aside Noting of Default by Court on Motion

11.06 The court may set aside the noting in default or default judgment against a party and any step that has been taken to enforce the judgment, on such terms as are just, if the party makes a motion to set aside and the court is satisfied that,
 (a) the party has a meritorious defence and a reasonable explanation for the default; and
 (b) the motion is made as soon as is reasonably possible in all the circumstances. O. Reg. 78/06, s. 24.

RULE 11.1 DISMISSAL BY CLERK

Dismissal — Undefended Actions

11.1.01(1) The clerk shall make an order dismissing an action as abandoned if the following conditions are satisfied, unless the court orders otherwise:
1. More than 180 days have passed since the date the claim was issued or an order was made extending the time for service of the claim under subrule 8.01(2).
2. No defence has been filed.
3. The action has not been disposed of by order and has not been set down for trial.
4. The clerk has given 45 days notice to the plaintiff that the action will be dismissed as abandoned. O. Reg. 78/06, s. 24; O. Reg. 56/08, s. 3(1).

Dismissal — Defended Actions

(2) The clerk shall make an order dismissing an action as abandoned if the following conditions are satisfied, unless the court orders otherwise:

1. More than 150 days have passed since the date the first defence was filed.
2. All settlement conferences required under Rule 13 have been held.
3. The action has not been disposed of by order and has not been set down for trial.
4. The clerk has given 45 days notice to all parties to the action that the action will be dismissed as abandoned. O. Reg. 78/06, s. 24; O. Reg. 56/08, s. 3(2); O. Reg. 393/09, s. 10 (2); O. Reg. 56/12, s. 4.

Transition

(3) If an action was started before July 1, 2006, the following applies:

1. The action or a step in the action shall be carried on under these rules on or after July 1, 2006.
2. Despite paragraph 1, if a step in the action is taken on or after July 1, 2006, the timetable set out in subrules (1) and (2) shall apply as if the action started on the date on which the step was taken. O. Reg. 78/06, s. 24.

Same

(4) If an action was commenced before July 1, 2006 and no step is taken in the action on or after that date, the clerk may make an order dismissing it as abandoned if,

(a) where an action is undefended, more than two years have passed since the date the claim was issued and the conditions set out in paragraphs 2, 3 and 4 of subrule (1) are satisfied; or
(b) more than two years have passed since the date the first defence was filed and the conditions set out in paragraphs 3 and 4 of subrule (2) are satisfied. O. Reg. 78/06, s. 24; O. Reg. 56/08, s. 3(3).

Exception Where Terms of Settlement Signed

(5) Subrules (1), (2) and (4) do not apply if terms of settlement (Form 14D) signed by all parties have been filed. O. Reg. 78/06, s. 24.

Exception Where Admission of Liability

(6) Subrule (2) and clause (4)(b) do not apply if the defence contains an admission of liability for the plaintiff's claim and a proposal of terms of payment under subrule 9.03(1). O. Reg. 78/06, s. 24.

Service of Orders

(7) The clerk shall serve a copy of an order made under subrule (1) or clause (4)(a) on the plaintiff and a copy of an order made under subrule (2) or clause (4)(b) on all parties to the action. O. Reg. 78/06, s. 24.

RULE 11.2 REQUEST FOR CLERK'S ORDER ON CONSENT

Consent Order

11.2.01(1) The clerk shall, on the filing of a request for clerk's order on consent (Form 11.2A), make an order granting the relief sought, including costs, if the following conditions are satisfied:

1. The relief sought is,
    i. amending a claim or defence less than 30 days before the originally scheduled trial date,
    ii. adding, deleting or substituting a party less than 30 days before the originally scheduled trial date,
    iii. setting aside the noting in default or default judgment against a party and any specified step to enforce the judgment that has not yet been completed,
    iv. restoring a matter that was dismissed under rule 11.1 to the list,
    v. noting that payment has been made in full satisfaction of a judgment or terms of settlement, or
    vi. dismissing an action.
2. The request is signed by all parties (including any party to be added, deleted or substituted) and states,
    i. that each party has received a copy of the request, and
    ii. that no party that would be affected by the order is under disability.
3. Revoked: O. Reg. 393/09, ss. 11(3), 26.
4. Revoked: O. Reg. 393/09, ss. 11(3), 26.

Service of order

(2) The clerk shall serve a copy of an order made under subrule (1) in accordance with subrule 8.01(14) on a party that requests it and provides a stamped, self-addressed envelope. O. Reg. 78/06, s. 24.

Same, Refusal to Make Order

(3) Where the clerk refuses to make an order, the clerk shall serve a copy of the request for clerk's order on consent (Form 11.2A), with reasons for the refusal, on all the parties. O. Reg. 78/06, s. 24.

Notice of Setting Aside of Enforcement Step

(4) Where an order is made setting aside a specified step to enforce a judgment under subparagraph 1 iii of subrule (1), a party shall file a copy of the order at each court location where the enforcement step has been requested. O. Reg. 78/06, s. 24.

RULE 11.3 DISCONTINUANCE

Discontinuance by Plaintiff in Undefended Action

11.3.01(1) A plaintiff may discontinue his or her claim against a defendant who fails to file a defence to all or part of the claim with the clerk within the prescribed time by,
(a) serving a notice of discontinued claim (Form 11.3A) on all defendants who were served with the claim; and
(b) filing the notice with proof of service. O. Reg. 393/09, s. 12.

(2) A claim may not be discontinued by or against a person under disability, except with leave of the court. O. Reg. 393/09, s. 12.

Effect of Discontinuance on Subsequent Action

11.3.02(1) The discontinuance of a claim is not a defence to a subsequent action on the matter, unless an order granting leave to discontinue provides otherwise. O. Reg. 393/09, s. 12.

RULE 12 AMENDMENT

Right to Amend
12.01(1) A plaintiff's or defendant's claim and a defence to a plaintiff's or defendant's claim may be amended by filing with the clerk a copy that is marked "Amended", in which any additions are underlined and any other changes are identified. O. Reg. 258/98, r. 12.01(1).

Service
(2) The amended document shall be served by the party making the amendment on all parties, including any parties in default, in accordance with subrule 8.01(14). O. Reg. 258/98, r. 12.01(2); O. Reg. 78/06, s. 25(1).

Time
(3) Filing and service of the amended document shall take place at least 30 days before the originally scheduled trial date, unless,
(a) the court, on motion, allows a shorter notice period; or
(b) a clerk's order permitting the amendment is obtained under subrule 11.2.01 (1). O. Reg. 393/09, s. 13.

Service on Added Party
(4) A person added as a party shall be served with the claim as amended, except that if the person is added as a party at trial, the court may dispense with service of the claim. O. Reg. 258/98, r. 12.01(4).

No Amendment Required in Response
(5) A party who is served with an amended document is not required to amend the party's defence or claim. O. Reg. 78/06, s. 25(3).

Motion to Strike out or Amend a Document
12.02(1) The court may, on motion, strike out or amend all or part of any document that,
(a) discloses no reasonable cause of action or defence;
(b) may delay or make it difficult to have a fair trial; or
(c) is inflammatory, a waste of time, a nuisance or an abuse of the court's process. O. Reg. 78/06, s. 26.

(2) In connection with an order striking out or amending a document under subrule (1), the court may do one or more of the following:
1. In the case of a claim, order that the action be stayed or dismissed.
2. In the case of a defence, strike out the defence and grant judgment.
3. Impose such terms as are just. O. Reg. 78/06, s. 26.

RULE 13 SETTLEMENT CONFERENCES

Settlement Conference Required in Defended Action
13.01(1) A settlement conference shall be held in every defended action. O. Reg. 78/06, s. 27.

Duty of Clerk
(2) The clerk shall fix a time, date and place for the settlement conference and serve a notice of settlement conference, together with a list of proposed witnesses (Form 13A), on the parties. O. Reg. 78/06, s. 27.

Timing

(3) The settlement conference shall be held within 90 days after the first defence is filed. O. Reg. 78/06, s. 27.

Exception

(4) Subrules (1) to (3) do not apply if the defence contains an admission of liability for all of the plaintiff's claim and a proposal of terms of payment under subrule 9.03(1). O. Reg. 78/06, s. 27.

Attendance

13.02(1) A party and the party's lawyer or agent, if any, shall, unless the court orders otherwise, participate in the settlement conference,

(a) by personal attendance; or

(b) by telephone or video conference in accordance with rule 1.07. O. Reg. 78/06, s. 27.

Authority to Settle

(2) A party who requires another person's approval before agreeing to a settlement shall, before the settlement conference, arrange to have ready telephone access to the other person throughout the conference, whether it takes place during or after regular business hours. O. Reg. 78/06, s. 27.

Additional Settlement Conferences

(3) The court may order the parties to attend an additional settlement conference. O. Reg. 78/06, s. 27.

(4) The clerk shall fix a time and place for any additional settlement conference and serve a notice of settlement conference, together with a list of proposed witnesses (Form 13A) on the parties. O. Reg. 78/06, s. 27.

Failure to Attend

(5) If a party who has received a notice of settlement conference fails to attend the conference, the court may,

(a) impose appropriate sanctions, by way of costs or otherwise; and

(b) order that an additional settlement conference be held, if necessary. O. Reg. 78/06, s. 27.

(6) If a defendant fails to attend a first settlement conference, receives notice of an additional settlement conference and fails to attend the additional settlement conference, the court may,

(a) strike out the defence and dismiss the defendant's claim, if any, and allow the plaintiff to prove the plaintiff's claim; or

(b) make such other order as is just. O. Reg. 78/06, s. 27.

Inadequate Preparation, Failure to File Material

(7) The court may award costs against a person who attends a settlement conference if,

(a) in the opinion of the court, the person is so inadequately prepared as to frustrate the purposes of the conference;

(b) the person fails to file the material required by subrule 13.03(2). O. Reg. 78/06, s. 27.

Purposes of Settlement Conference

13.03(1) The purposes of a settlement conference are,

(a) to resolve or narrow the issues in the action;
(b) to expedite the disposition of the action;
(c) to encourage settlement of the action;
(d) to assist the parties in effective preparation for trial; and
(e) to provide full disclosure between the parties of the relevant facts and evidence. O. Reg. 78/06, s. 27.

Disclosure

(2) At least 14 days before the date of the settlement conference, each party shall serve on every other party and file with the court,
(a) a copy of any document to be relied on at the trial, including an expert report, not attached to the party's claim or defence; and
(b) a list of proposed witnesses (Form 13A) and of other persons with knowledge of the matters in dispute in the action. O. Reg. 78/06, s. 27.

(3) At the settlement conference, the parties or their representatives shall openly and frankly discuss the issues involved in the action. O. Reg. 78/06, s. 27.

Further Disclosure Restricted

(4) Except as otherwise provided or with the consent of the parties (Form 13B), the matters discussed at the settlement conference shall not be disclosed to others until after the action has been disposed of. O. Reg. 78/06, s. 27.

Recommendations to Parties

13.04 The court may make recommendations to the parties on any matter relating to the conduct of the action, in order to fulfil the purposes of a settlement conference, including recommendations as to,
(a) the clarification and simplification of issues in the action;
(b) the elimination of claims or defences that appear to be unsupported; and
(c) the admission of facts or documents without further proof. O. Reg. 78/06, s. 27.

Orders at Settlement Conference

13.05(1) A judge conducting a settlement conference may make any order relating to the conduct of the action that the court could make. O. Reg. 78/06, s. 27.

(2) Without limiting the generality of subrule (1), the judge may,
(a) make an order,
   (i) adding or deleting parties,
   (ii) consolidating actions,
   (iii) staying the action,
   (iv) amending or striking out a claim or defence under rule 12.02,
   (v) staying or dismissing a claim,
   (vi) directing production of documents,
   (vii) changing the place of trial under rule 6.01,
   (viii) directing an additional settlement conference under subrule 13.02(3), and
   (ix) ordering costs; and
(b) at an additional settlement conference, order judgment under subrule 13.02(6). O. Reg. 78/06, s. 27.

Recommendations to Judge

(3) If the settlement conference is conducted by a referee, a judge may, on the referee's recommendation, make any order that may be made under subrules (1) and (2). O. Reg. 78/06, s. 27.

Consent to Final Judgment

(4) A judge may order final judgment at a settlement conference where the matter in dispute is for an amount under the appealable limit and a party files a consent (Form 13B) signed by all parties before the settlement conference indicating that they wish to obtain final determination of the matter at the settlement conference if a mediated settlement is not reached. O. Reg. 78/06, s. 27.

Service of Order

(5) Within 10 days after the judge signs an order made at a settlement conference, the clerk shall serve the order on the parties that were not present at the settlement conference in accordance with subrule 8.01(6). O. Reg. 78/06, s. 27.

Memorandum

13.06(1) At the end of the settlement conference, the court shall prepare a memorandum summarizing,

(a) recommendations made under rule 13.04;
(b) the issues remaining in dispute;
(c) the matters agreed on by the parties;
(d) any evidentiary matters that are considered relevant; and
(e) information relating to the scheduling of the remaining steps in the proceeding. O. Reg. 78/06, s. 27.

(2) The memorandum shall be filed with the clerk, who shall give a copy to the trial judge. O. Reg. 78/06, s. 27.

Notice of Trial

13.07 At or after the settlement conference, the clerk shall provide the parties with a notice stating that one of the parties must request a trial date if the action is not disposed of within 30 days after the settlement conference, and pay the fee required for setting the action down for trial. O. Reg. 78/06, s. 27.

Judge Not To Preside At Trial

13.08 A judge who conducts a settlement conference in an action shall not preside at the trial of the action. O. Reg. 78/06, s. 27.

Withdrawal of Claim

13.09 After a settlement conference has been held, a claim against a party who is not in default shall not be withdrawn or discontinued by the party who brought the claim without,

(a) the written consent of the party against whom the claim is brought; or
(b) leave of the court. O. Reg. 78/06, s. 27.

Costs

13.10 The costs of a settlement conference, exclusive of disbursements, shall not exceed $100 unless the court orders otherwise because there are special circumstances. O. Reg. 78/06, s. 27.

RULE 14 OFFER TO SETTLE

14.01 A party may serve on any other party an offer to settle a claim on the terms specified in the offer. O. Reg. 258/98, r. 14.01.

Written Documents

14.01.1(1) An offer to settle, an acceptance of an offer to settle and a notice of withdrawal of an offer to settle shall be in writing. O. Reg. 78/06, s. 28.

Use of Forms

(2) An offer to settle may be in Form 14A, an acceptance of an offer to settle may be in Form 14B and a notice of withdrawal of an offer to settle may be in Form 14C. O. Reg. 78/06, s. 28.

Terms of Settlement

(3) The terms of an accepted offer to settle may be set out in terms of settlement (Form 14D). O. Reg. 78/06, s. 28.

Time for Making Offer

14.02(1) An offer to settle may be made at any time. O. Reg. 78/06, s. 29.

Costs Consequences

(2) The costs consequences referred to in rule 14.07 apply only if the offer to settle is served on the party to whom it is made at least seven days before the trial commences. O. Reg. 78/06, s. 29.

Withdrawal

14.03(1) An offer to settle may be withdrawn at any time before it is accepted, by serving a notice of withdrawal of an offer to settle on the party to whom it was made. O. Reg. 78/06, s. 29.

Deemed Withdrawal

(2) If an offer to settle specifies a date after which it is no longer available for acceptance, and has not been accepted on or before that date, the offer shall be deemed to have been withdrawn on the day after that date. O. Reg. 78/06, s. 29.

Expiry When Court Disposes of Claim

(3) An offer may not be accepted after the court disposes of the claim in respect of which the offer is made. O. Reg. 78/06, s. 29.

No Disclosure to Trial Judge

14.04 If an offer to settle is not accepted, no communication about it or any related negotiations shall be made to the trial judge until all questions of liability and the relief to be granted, other than costs, have been determined. O. Reg. 78/06, s. 29.

Acceptance of an Offer to Settle

14.05(1) An offer to settle may be accepted by serving an acceptance of an offer to settle on the party who made it, at any time before it is withdrawn or before the court disposes of the claim in respect of which it is made. O. Reg. 78/06, s. 30.

Payment Into Court As Condition

(2) An offer by a plaintiff to settle a claim in return for the payment of money by a defendant may include a term that the defendant pay the money into court; in that case, the defendant may accept the offer only by paying the money into court and notifying the plaintiff of the payment. O. Reg. 258/98, r. 14.05(2).

(3) If a defendant offers to pay money to a plaintiff in settlement of a claim, the plaintiff may accept the offer with the condition that the defendant pay the money into court; if the offer is so accepted and the defendant fails to pay the money into court, the plaintiff may proceed as provided in rule 14.06. O. Reg. 258/98, r. 14.05(3).

Costs

(4) If an accepted offer to settle does not deal with costs, the plaintiff is entitled,

(a) in the case of an offer made by the defendant, to the plaintiff's disbursements assessed to the date the plaintiff was served with the offer;

(b) in the case of an offer made by the plaintiff, to the plaintiff's disbursements assessed to the date that the notice of acceptance was served. O. Reg. 258/98, r. 14.05(4).

Failure to Comply With Accepted Offer

14.06 If a party to an accepted offer to settle fails to comply with the terms of the offer, the other party may,

(a) make a motion to the court for judgment in the terms of the accepted offer; or

(b) continue the proceeding as if there had been no offer to settle. O. Reg. 258/98, r. 14.06.

Costs Consequences of Failure to Accept

14.07(1) When a plaintiff makes an offer to settle that is not accepted by the defendant, the court may award the plaintiff an amount not exceeding twice the costs of the action, if the following conditions are met:

1. The plaintiff obtains a judgment as favourable as or more favourable than the terms of the offer.
2. The offer was made at least seven days before the trial.
3. The offer was not withdrawn and did not expire before the trial. O. Reg. 258/98, r. 14.07(1).

(2) When a defendant makes an offer to settle that is not accepted by the plaintiff, the court may award the defendant an amount not exceeding twice the costs awardable to a successful party, from the date the offer was served, if the following conditions are met:

1. The plaintiff obtains a judgment as favourable as or less favourable than the terms of the offer.
2. The offer was made at least seven days before the trial.
3. The offer was not withdrawn and did not expire before the trial. O. Reg. 258/98, r. 14.07(2).

(3) If an amount is awarded under subrule (1) or (2) to a self-represented party, the court may also award the party an amount not exceeding $500 as compensation for inconvenience and expense. O. Reg. 78/06, s. 31.

RULE 15 MOTIONS

Notice of Motion and Supporting Affidavit

15.01(1) A motion shall be made by a notice of motion and supporting affidavit (Form 15A). O. Reg. 393/09, s. 14(1).

(2) The moving party shall obtain a hearing date from the clerk before serving the notice of motion and supporting affidavit under subrule (3). O. Reg. 78/06, s. 32.

(3) The notice of motion and supporting affidavit,
 (a) shall be served on every party who has filed a claim and any defendant who has not been noted in default, at least seven days before the hearing date; and
 (b) shall be filed, with proof of service, at least three days before the hearing date. O. Reg. 78/06, s. 32.

Supporting Affidavit in Response

(4) A party who prepares an affidavit (Form 15B) in response to the moving party's notice of motion and supporting affidavit shall serve it on every party who has filed a claim or defence and file it, with proof of service, at least two days before the hearing date. O. Reg. 78/06, s. 32.

Supplementary Affidavit

(5) The moving party may serve a supplementary affidavit on every party who has filed a claim or defence and file it, with proof of service, at least two days before the hearing date. O. Reg. 78/06, s. 32.

Motion After Judgment Signed

(6) A motion that is made after judgment has been signed shall be served on all parties, including those who have been noted in default. O. Reg. 78/06, s. 32.

Method of Hearing

15.02(1) A motion may be heard,
 (a) in person;
 (b) by telephone or video conference in accordance with paragraph 2 of subrule 1.07(1);
 (c) by a judge in writing under clause 11.03(2)(a);
 (d) by any other method that the judge determines is fair and reasonable. O. Reg. 78/06, s. 32.

(2) The attendance of the parties is not required if the motion is in writing under clause (1)(c). O. Reg. 78/06, s. 32.

Motion Without Notice

15.03(1) Despite rule 15.01, a motion may be made without notice if the nature or circumstances of the motion make notice unnecessary or not reasonably possible. O. Reg. 78/06, s. 32.

Service of Order

(2) A party who obtains an order on motion without notice shall serve it on every affected party, together with a copy of the notice of motion and

supporting affidavit used on the motion, within five days after the order is signed. O. Reg. 78/06, s. 32.

Motion to Set Aside or Vary Motion Made Without Notice
(3) A party who is affected by an order obtained on motion without notice may make a motion to set aside or vary the order, within 30 days after being served with the order. O. Reg. 78/06, s. 32.

No Further Motions Without Leave
15.04 If the court is satisfied that a party has tried to delay the action, add to its costs or otherwise abuse the court's process by making numerous motions without merit, the court may, on motion, make an order prohibiting the party from making any further motions in the action without leave of the court. O. Reg. 78/06, s. 32.

Adjournment of Motion
15.05 A motion shall not be adjourned at a party's request before the hearing date unless the written consent of all parties is filed when the request is made, unless the court orders otherwise. O. Reg. 78/06, s. 32.

Withdrawal of Motion
15.06 A motion shall not be withdrawn without,
(a) the written consent of all the parties; or
(b) leave of the court. O. Reg. 78/06, s. 32.

Costs
15.07 The costs of a motion, exclusive of disbursements, shall not exceed $100 unless the court orders otherwise because there are special circumstances. O. Reg. 78/06, s. 32.

RULE 16 NOTICE OF TRIAL

Clerk Fixes Date and Serves Notice
16.01(1) The clerk shall fix a date for trial and serve a notice of trial on each party who has filed a claim or defence if,
(a) a settlement conference has been held; and
(b) a party has requested that the clerk fix a date for trial and has paid the required fee. O. Reg. 78/06, s. 32.

Manner of Service
(2) The notice of trial shall be served by mail or fax. O. Reg. 78/06, s. 32.

RULE 17 TRIAL

Failure to Attend
17.01(1) If an action is called for trial and all the parties fail to attend, the trial judge may strike the action off the trial list. O. Reg. 258/98, r. 17.01(1).

(2) If an action is called for trial and a party fails to attend, the trial judge may,
(a) proceed with the trial in the party's absence;

(b) the plaintiff attends and the defendant fails to do so, strike out the defence and dismiss the defendant's claim, if any, and allow the plaintiff to prove the plaintiff's claim, subject to subrule (3);

(c) if the defendant attends and the plaintiff fails to do so, dismiss the action and allow the defendant to prove the defendant's claim, if any; or

(d) make such other order as is just. O. Reg. 258/98, r. 17.01(2).

(2.1) In the case described in clause (2)(b) or (c), the person with the claim is not required to prove liability against the party who has failed to attend but is required to prove the amount of the claim. O. Reg. 78/06, s. 33(1).

(3) In the case described in clause (2)(b), if an issue as to the proper place of trial under subrule 6.01(1) is raised in the defence, the trial judge shall consider it and make a finding. O. Reg. 258/98, r. 17.01(3).

Setting Aside or Variation of Judgment

(4) The court may set aside or vary, on such terms as are just, a judgment obtained against a party who failed to attend at the trial. O. Reg. 258/98, r. 17.01(4).

Conditions to Making of Order under Subrule (4)

(5) The court may make an order under subrule (4) only if,

(a) the party who failed to attend makes a motion for the order within 30 days after becoming aware of the judgment; or

(b) the party who failed to attend makes a motion for an extension of the 30-day period mentioned in clause (a) and the court is satisfied that there are special circumstances that justify the extension. O. Reg. 78/06, s. 33(2).

Adjournment

17.02(1) The court may postpone or adjourn a trial on such terms as are just, including the payment by one party to another of an amount as compensation for inconvenience and expense. O. Reg. 258/98, r. 17.02.

(2) If the trial of an action has been adjourned two or more times, any further adjournment may be made only on motion with notice to all the parties who were served with the notice of trial, unless the court orders otherwise. O. Reg. 78/06, s. 34.

Inspection

17.03 The trial judge may, in the presence of the parties or their representatives, inspect any real or personal property concerning which a question arises in the action. O. Reg. 258/98, r. 17.03.

Motion for New Trial

17.04(1) A party may make a motion for a new trial within 30 days after a final order is made. O. Reg. 78/06, s. 35.

Transcript

(2) In addition to serving and filing the notice of motion and supporting affidavit (Form 15A) required under rule 15.01, the moving party shall serve and file proof that a request has been made for a transcript of,

(a) the reasons for judgment; and

(b) any other portion of the proceeding that is relevant. O. Reg. 393/09, s. 16(1).

Service and Filing of Transcript

(3) If available, a copy of the transcript shall, at least three days before the hearing date,

(a) be served on all parties who were served with the original notice of trial; and

(b) be filed, with proof of service. O. Reg. 78/06, s. 35.

Powers of Court on Motion

(4) On the hearing of the motion, the court may,

(a) if the party demonstrates that a condition referred to in subrule (5) is satisfied,

  (i) grant a new trial, or

  (ii) pronounce the judgment that ought to have been given at trial and order judgment accordingly; or

(b) dismiss the motion. O. Reg. 78/06, s. 35.

Conditions

(5) The conditions referred to in clause (4)(a) are:

1. There was a purely arithmetical error in the determination of the amount of damages awarded.

2. There is relevant evidence that was not available to the party at the time of the original trial and could not reasonably have been expected to be available at that time. O. Reg. 78/06, s. 35.

RULE 18 EVIDENCE AT TRIAL

Affidavit

18.01 At the trial of an undefended action, the plaintiff's case may be proved by affidavit, unless the trial judge orders otherwise. O. Reg. 258/98, r. 18.01.

Written Statements, Documents and Records

18.02(1) A document or written statement or an audio or visual record that has been served, at least 30 days before the trial date, on all parties who were served with the notice of trial, shall be received in evidence, unless the trial judge orders otherwise. O. Reg. 78/06, s. 36(1).

(2) Subrule (1) applies to the following written statements and documents:

1. The signed written statement of any witness, including the written report of an expert, to the extent that the statement relates to facts and opinions to which the witness would be permitted to testify in person.

2. Any other document, including but not limited to a hospital record or medical report made in the course of care and treatment, a financial record, a receipt, a bill, documentary evidence of loss of income or property damage, and a repair estimate. O. Reg. 258/98, r. 18.02(2); O. Reg. 78/06, s. 36(2).

Details about Witness or Author

(3) A party who serves on another party a written statement or document described in subrule (2) shall append to or include in the statement or document,

(a) the name, telephone number and address for service of the witness or author; and

(b) if the witness or author is to give expert evidence, a summary of his or her qualifications. O. Reg. 78/06, s. 36(3).

(4) A party who has been served with a written statement or document described in subrule (2) and wishes to cross-examine the witness or author may summon him or her as a witness under subrule 18.03(1). O. Reg. 258/98, r. 18.02(4).

Where Witness or Author is Summoned

(5) A party who serves a summons to witness on a witness or author referred to in subrule (3) shall, at the time the summons is served, serve a copy of the summons on every other party. O. Reg. 78/06, s. 36(4).

(6) Service of a summons and the payment or tender of attendance money under this rule may be proved by affidavit (Form 8A). O. Reg. 78/06, s. 36(4).

Adjournment

(7) A party who is not served with a copy of the summons in accordance with subrule (5) may request an adjournment of the trial, with costs. O. Reg. 78/06, s. 36(4).

Summons to Witness

18.03(1) A party who requires the attendance of a person in Ontario as a witness at a trial may serve the person with a summons to witness (Form 18A) requiring him or her to attend the trial at the time and place stated in the summons. O. Reg. 258/98, r. 18.03(1).

(2) The summons may also require the witness to produce at the trial the documents or other things in his or her possession, control or power relating to the matters in question in the action that are specified in the summons. O. Reg. 258/98, r. 18.03(2).

(3) A summons to witness (Form 18A) shall be served in accordance with subrule 8.01(7). O. Reg. 78/06, s. 37(1).

(4) Service of a summons and the payment or tender of attendance money may be proved by affidavit (Form 8A). O. Reg. 78/06, s. 37(1).

(5) A summons to witness continues to have effect until the attendance of the witness is no longer required. O. Reg. 258/98, r. 18.03(5).

Interpreter

(5.1) If a party serves a summons on a witness who requires an interpreter, the party shall arrange for a qualified interpreter to attend at the trial unless the interpretation is from English to French or French to English and an interpreter is provided by the Ministry of the Attorney General. O. Reg. 78/06, s. 37(2).

(5.2) If a party does not comply with subrule (5.1), every other party is entitled to request an adjournment of the trial, with costs. O. Reg. 78/06, s. 37(2).

Failure to Attend or Remain in Attendance

(6) If a witness whose evidence is material to the conduct of an action fails to attend at the trial or to remain in attendance in accordance with the requirements of a summons to witness served on him or her, the trial judge may, by warrant (Form 18B) directed to all police officers in Ontario, cause the witness to be apprehended anywhere within Ontario and promptly brought before the court. O. Reg. 258/98, r. 18.03(6).

Identification Form

(6.1) The party who served the summons on the witness may file with the clerk an identification form (Form 20K) to assist the police in apprehending the witness. O. Reg. 78/06, s. 37(3).

(7) On being apprehended, the witness may be detained in custody until his or her presence is no longer required or released on such terms as are just, and may be ordered to pay the costs arising out of the failure to attend or remain in attendance. O. Reg. 258/98, r. 18.03(7).

Abuse of Power to Summon Witness

(8) If satisfied that a party has abused the power to summon a witness under this rule, the court may order that the party pay directly to the witness an amount as compensation for inconvenience and expense. O. Reg. 258/98, r. 18.03(8).

RULE 19 COSTS

Disbursements

19.01(1) A successful party is entitled to have the party's reasonable disbursements, including any costs of effecting service or preparing a plaintiff's or defendant's claim or a defence and expenses for travel, accommodation, photocopying and experts' reports, paid by the unsuccessful party, unless the court orders otherwise. O. Reg. 78/06, s. 38(1); O. Reg. 440/10, s. 3(1).

(2) The clerk shall assess the disbursements in accordance with the regulations made under the *Administration of Justice Act* and in accordance with subrules (3) and (4)); the assessment is subject to review by the court. O. Reg. 258/98, r. 19.01(2); O. Reg. 440/10, s. 3(2).

(3) The amount of disbursements assessed for effecting service shall not exceed $60 for each person served unless the court is of the opinion that there are special circumstances that justify assessing a greater amount. O. Reg. 258/98, r. 19.01(3); O. Reg. 78/06, s. 38(2); O. Reg. 440/10, s. 3(3).

(4) The amount of disbursements assessed for preparing a plaintiff's or defendant's claim or a defence shall not exceed $100. O. Reg. 440/10, s. 3(4).

Limit

19.02 Any power under this rule to award costs is subject to section 29 of the *Courts of Justice Act*, which limits the amount of costs that may be awarded. O. Reg. 78/06, s. 39.

Preparation and Filing

19.03 Revoked: O. Reg. 440/10, s. 4.

Representation Fee

19.04 If a successful party is represented by a lawyer, student-at-law or agent, the court may award the party a reasonable representation fee at trial or at an assessment hearing. O. Reg. 440/10, s. 5.

Compensation for Inconvenience and Expense

19.05 The court may order an unsuccessful party to pay to a successful party who is self-represented an amount not exceeding $500 as compensation for inconvenience and expense. O. Reg. 440/10, s. 5.

Penalty

19.06 If the court is satisfied that a party has unduly complicated or prolonged an action or has otherwise acted unreasonably, the court may order the party to pay an amount as compensation to another party. O. Reg. 78/06, s. 39.

RULE 20 ENFORCEMENT OF ORDERS

Definitions

20.01 In rules 20.02 to 20.12,

"creditor" means a person who is entitled to enforce an order for the payment or recovery of money;

"debtor" means a person against whom an order for the payment or recovery of money may be enforced. O. Reg. 258/98, r. 20.01; O. Reg. 78/06, s. 40.

Power of Court

20.02(1) The court may,

(a) stay the enforcement of an order of the court, for such time and on such terms as are just; and

(b) vary the times and proportions in which money payable under an order of the court shall be paid, if it is satisfied that the debtor's circumstances have changed. O. Reg. 258/98, r. 20.02(1).

Enforcement Limited While Periodic Payment Order in Force

(2) While an order for periodic payment is in force, no step to enforce the judgment may be taken or continued against the debtor by a creditor named in the order, except issuing a writ of seizure and sale of land and filing it with the sheriff. O. Reg. 258/98, r. 20.02(2).

Service of Notice of Default of Payment

(3) The creditor may serve the debtor with a notice of default of payment (Form 20L) in accordance with subrule 8.01(14) and file a copy of it, together with an affidavit of default of payment (Form 20M), if the debtor fails to make payments under an order for periodic payment. O. Reg. 78/06, s. 41.

Termination on Default

(4) An order for periodic payment terminates on the day that is 15 days after the creditor serves the debtor with the notice of default of payment, unless a consent (Form 13B) in which the creditor waives the default is filed within the 15-day period. O. Reg. 78/06, s. 41.

General

20.03 In addition to any other method of enforcement provided by law,
  (a) an order for the payment or recovery of money may be enforced by,
      (i) a writ of seizure and sale of personal property (Form 20C) under rule 20.06,
      (ii) a writ of seizure and sale of land (Form 20D) under rule 20.07, and
      (iii) garnishment under rule 20.08; and
  (b) a further order as to payment may be made under subrule 20.10(7). O. Reg. 258/98, r. 20.03.

Certificate of Judgment

20.04(1) If there is default under an order for the payment or recovery of money, the clerk shall, at the creditor's request, supported by an affidavit for enforcement request (Form 20P) stating the amount still owing, issue a certificate of judgment (Form 20A) to the clerk at the court location specified by the creditor. O. Reg. 393/09, s. 17.

(2) The certificate of judgment shall state,
  (a) the date of the order and the amount awarded;
  (b) the rate of postjudgment interest payable; and
  (c) the amount owing, including postjudgment interest. O. Reg. 258/98, r. 20.04(2).

Delivery of Personal Property

20.05(1) An order for the delivery of personal property may be enforced by a writ of delivery (Form 20B) issued by the clerk to a bailiff, on the request of the person in whose favour the order was made, supported by an affidavit of that person or the person's agent stating that the property has not been delivered. O. Reg. 258/98, r. 20.05(1).

Seizure of Other Personal Property

(2) If the property referred to in a writ of delivery cannot be found or taken by the bailiff, the person in whose favour the order was made may make a motion to the court for an order directing the bailiff to seize any other personal property of the person against whom the order was made. O. Reg. 258/98, r. 20.05(2).

(3) Unless the court orders otherwise, the bailiff shall keep personal property seized under subrule (2) until the court makes a further order for its disposition. O. Reg. 258/98, r. 20.05(3); O. Reg. 78/06, s. 42.

Storage Costs

(4) The person in whose favour the order is made shall pay the bailiff's storage costs, in advance and from time to time; if the person fails to do so, the seizure shall be deemed to be abandoned. O. Reg. 258/98, r. 20.05(4).

Writ of Seizure and Sale of Personal Property

20.06(1) If there is default under an order for the payment or recovery of money, the clerk shall, at the creditor's request, supported by an affidavit for enforcement request (Form 20P) stating the amount still owing, issue to a bailiff a writ of seizure and sale of personal property (Form 20C), and the bailiff shall enforce the writ for the amount owing, postjudgment interest and the bailiff's fees and expenses. O. Reg. 258/98, r. 20.06(1); O. Reg. 78/06, s. 43(1).

(1.1) If more than six years have passed since the order was made, a writ of seizure and sale of personal property may be issued only with leave of the court. O. Reg. 78/06, s. 43(2).

(1.2) If a writ of seizure and sale of personal property is not issued within one year after the date on which an order granting leave to issue it is made,
(a) the order granting leave ceases to have effect; and
(b) a writ of seizure and sale of personal property may be issued only with leave of the court on a subsequent motion. O. Reg. 393/09, s. 18(2).

(1.3) A writ of seizure and sale of personal property shall show the creditor's name, address and telephone number and the name, address and telephone number of the creditor's lawyer or agent, if any. O. Reg. 393/09, s. 18(2).

Duration of Writ
(2) A writ of seizure and sale of personal property remains in force for six years after the date of its issue and for a further six years after each renewal. O. Reg. 78/06, s. 43(3).

Renewal of Writ
(3) A writ of seizure and sale of personal property may be renewed before its expiration by filing a request to renew a writ of seizure and sale (Form 20N) with the bailiff. O. Reg. 78/06, s. 43(3).

Direction to Enforce
(4) The creditor may request enforcement of a writ of seizure and sale of personal property by filing a direction to enforce writ of seizure and sale of personal property (Form 20O) with the bailiff. O. Reg. 393/09, s. 18(4).

Inventory of Property Seized
(5) Within a reasonable time after a request is made by the debtor or the debtor's agent, the bailiff shall deliver an inventory of personal property seized under a writ of seizure and sale of personal property. O. Reg. 258/98, r. 20.06(5).

Sale of Personal Property
(6) Personal property seized under a writ of seizure and sale of personal property shall not be sold by the bailiff unless notice of the time and place of sale has been,
(a) mailed, at least 10 days before the sale,
   (i) to the creditor at the address shown on the writ, or to the creditor's lawyer or agent, and
   (ii) to the debtor at the debtor's last known address; and
(b) advertised in a manner that is likely to bring it to the attention of the public. O. Reg. 78/06, s. 43(4).

Writ of Seizure and Sale of Land
20.07(1) If an order for the payment or recovery of money is unsatisfied, the clerk shall at the creditor's request, supported by an affidavit for enforcement request (Form 20P) stating the amount still owing, issue to the sheriff specified by the creditor a writ of seizure and sale of land (Form 20D). O. Reg. 258/98, r. 20.07(1); O. Reg. 78/06, s. 44(1).

(1.1) If more than six years have passed since the order was made, a writ of seizure and sale of land may be issued only with leave of the court. O. Reg. 393/09, s. 19(2).

(1.2) If a writ of seizure and sale of land is not issued within one year after the date on which an order granting leave to issue it is made,
 (a) the order granting leave ceases to have effect; and
 (b) a writ of seizure and sale of land may be issued only with leave of the court on a subsequent motion. O. Reg. 393/09, s. 19(2)

(2) A writ of seizure and sale of land issued under subrule (1) has the same force and effect and may be renewed or withdrawn in the same manner as a writ of seizure and sale issued under rule 60 of the Rules of Civil Procedure. O. Reg. 258/98, r. 20.07(2).

Duration of Writ

(3) A writ of seizure and sale of land remains in force for six years after the date of its issue and for a further six years after each renewal. O. Reg. 78/06, s. 44(2).

Renewal or Writ

(4) A writ of seizure and sale of land may be renewed before its expiration by filing a request to renew a writ of seizure and sale (Form 20N) with the sheriff. O. Reg. 393/09, s. 19(3).

Garnishment

20.08(1) A creditor may enforce an order for the payment or recovery of money by garnishment of debts payable to the debtor by other persons. O. Reg. 258/98, r. 20.08(1).

Joint Debts Garnishable

(2) If a debt is payable to the debtor and to one or more co-owners, one-half of the indebtedness or a greater or lesser amount specified in an order made under subrule (15) may be garnished. O. Reg. 258/98, r. 20.08(2).

Where Leave Required

(2.1) If more than six years have passed since the order was made, or if its enforcement is subject to a condition, a notice of garnishment may be issued only with leave of the court. O. Reg. 393/09, s. 20(1).

(2.2) If a notice of garnishment is not issued within one year after the date on which an order granting leave to issue it is made,
 (a) the order granting leave ceases to have effect; and
 (b) a notice of garnishment may be issued only with leave of the court on a subsequent motion. O. Reg. 393/09, s. 20(1).

(2.3) A notice of renewal of garnishment may be issued under subrule (5.3) without leave of the court before the original notice of garnishment or any subsequent notice of renewal of garnishment expires. O. Reg. 393/09, s. 20(1).

Obtaining Notice of Garnishment

(3) A creditor who seeks to enforce an order by garnishment shall file with the clerk of a court in the territorial division in which the debtor resides or carries on business,

(a) an affidavit for enforcement request (Form 20P) naming one debtor and one garnishee and stating,

(i) the date of the order and the amount awarded,

(ii) the territorial division in which the order was made,

(iii) the rate of postjudgment interest payable,

(iv) the total amount of any payments received since the order was granted,

(v) the amount owing, including postjudgment interest,

(vi) the name and address of the named garnishee to whom a notice of garnishment is to be directed,

(vii) the creditor's belief that the named garnishee is or will become indebted to the debtor, and the grounds for the belief, and

(viii) any particulars of the debts that are known to the creditor; and

(b) a certificate of judgment (Form 20A), if the order was made in another territorial division. O. Reg. 78/06, s. 45(1).

(4) On the filing of the documents required by subrule (3), the clerk shall issue a notice of garnishment (Form 20E) naming as garnishee the person named in the affidavit. O. Reg. 78/06, s. 45(1).

(5) A notice of garnishment issued under subrule (4) shall name only one debtor and only one garnishee. O. Reg. 258/98, r. 20.08(5).

Duration and Renewal

(5.1) A notice of garnishment remains in force for six years from the date of its issue and for a further six years from each renewal. O. Reg. 393/09, s. 20(3).

(5.2) A notice of garnishment may be renewed before its expiration by filing with the clerk of the court in which the notice of garnishment was issued a notice of renewal of garnishment (Form 20E.1), together with an affidavit for enforcement request (Form 20P). O. Reg. 393/09, s. 20(3).

(5.3) On the filing of the notice and affidavit required by subrule (5.2), the clerk shall issue the notice of renewal of garnishment (Form 20E.1) naming as garnishee the person named in the affidavit. O. Reg. 393/09, s. 20(3).

(5.4) The provisions of these rules that apply with respect to notices of garnishment also apply with respect to notices of renewal of garnishment. O. Reg. 393/09, s. 20(3).

Service of Notice of Garnishment

(6) The notice of garnishment (Form 20E) shall be served by the creditor in accordance with subrule 8.01(8). O. Reg. 78/06, s. 45(2).

(6.1) The creditor shall serve the notice of garnishment on the debtor within five days of serving it on the garnishee. O. Reg. 78/06, s. 45(2).

Financial Institution

(6.2) If the garnishee is a financial institution, the notice of garnishment and all further notices required to be served under this rule shall be served at the branch at which the debt is payable. O. Reg. 78/06, s. 45(2).

Proof of Service

(6.3) Service of the notice of garnishment may be proved by affidavit. O. Reg. 78/06, s. 45(2).

Garnishee Liable From Time of Service

(7) The garnishee is liable to pay to the clerk any debt of the garnishee to the debtor, up to the amount shown in the notice of garnishment, within 10 days after service of the notice on the garnishee or 10 days after the debt becomes payable, whichever is later. O. Reg. 258/98, r. 20.08(7).

(8) For the purpose of subrule (7), a debt of the garnishee to the debtor includes,
(a) a debt payable at the time the notice of garnishment is served; and
(b) a debt payable (whether absolutely or on the fulfilment of a condition) after the notice is served and within six years after it is issued. O. Reg. 258/98, r. 20.08(8); O. Reg. 78/06, s. 45(3).

Payment by Garnishee

(9) A garnishee who admits owing a debt to the debtor shall pay it to the clerk in the manner prescribed by the notice of garnishment, and the amounts paid into court shall not exceed the portion of the debtor's wages that are subject to seizure or garnishment under section 7 of the *Wages Act*. O. Reg. 78/06, s. 45(4).

Equal Distribution Among Creditors

(10) If the clerk has issued notices of garnishment in respect of a debtor at the request of more than one creditor and receives payment under any of the notices of garnishment, he or she shall distribute the payment equally among the creditors who have filed a request for garnishment and have not been paid in full. O. Reg. 258/98, r. 20.08(10); O. Reg. 461/01, s. 18.

Disputing Garnishment

(11) A garnishee referred to in subrule (12) shall, within 10 days after service of the notice of garnishment, file with the court a statement (Form 20F) setting out the particulars. O. Reg. 258/98, r. 20.08(11).

(12) Subrule (11) applies to a garnishee who,
(a) wishes to dispute the garnishment for any reason; or
(b) pays to the clerk less than the amount set out in the notice of garnishment as owing by the garnishee to the debtor, because the debt is owed to the debtor and to one or more co-owners of the debt or for any other reason. O. Reg. 258/98, r. 20.08(12); O. Reg. 78/06, s. 45(5).

Service on Creditor and Debtor

(13) The garnishee shall serve a copy of the garnishee's statement on the creditor and the debtor. O. Reg. 78/06, s. 45(6).

Notice to Co-Owner of Debt

(14) A creditor who is served with a garnishee's statement under subrule (13) shall forthwith send to any co-owners of the debt, in accordance with subrule 8.01(14), a notice to co-owner of debt (Form 20G) and a copy of the garnishee's statement. O. Reg. 258/98, r. 20.08(14); O. Reg. 78/06, s. 45(7).

Garnishment Hearing

(15) At the request of a creditor, debtor, garnishee, co-owner of the debt or any other interested person, the clerk shall fix a time and place for a garnishment hearing. O. Reg. 78/06, s. 45(8).

Service of Notice of Garnishment Hearing

(15.1) After having obtained a hearing date from the clerk, the party requesting the garnishment hearing shall serve the notice of garnishment hearing (Form 20Q) in accordance with subrule 8.01(9). O. Reg. 78/06, s. 45(8).

Powers of Court at Hearing

(15.2) At the garnishment hearing, the court may,

(a) if it is alleged that the garnishee's debt to the debtor has been assigned or encumbered, order the assignee or encumbrancer to appear and state the nature and particulars of the claim;

(b) determine the rights and liabilities of the garnishee, any co-owner of the debt, the debtor and any assignee or encumbrancer;

(c) vary or suspend periodic payments under a notice of garnishment; or

(d) determine any other matter in relation to a notice of garnishment. O. Reg. 78/06, s. 45(8).

Time to Request Hearing

(16) A person who has been served with a notice to co-owner of debt is not entitled to dispute the enforcement of the creditor's order for the payment or recovery of money or a payment made by the clerk unless the person requests a garnishment hearing within 30 days after the notice is sent. O. Reg. 258/98, r. 20.08(16).

Enforcement Against Garnishee

(17) If the garnishee does not pay to the clerk the amount set out in the notice of garnishment and does not send a garnishee's statement, the creditor is entitled to an order against the garnishee for payment of the amount set out in the notice, unless the court orders otherwise. O. Reg. 258/98, r. 20.08(17).

Payment to Person other than Clerk

(18) If, after service of a notice of garnishment, the garnishee pays a debt attached by the notice to a person other than the clerk, the garnishee remains liable to pay the debt in accordance with notice. O. Reg. 258/98, r. 20.08(18).

Effect of Payment to Clerk

(19) Payment of a debt by a garnishee in accordance with a notice of garnishment is a valid discharge of the debt as between the garnishee and the debtor and any co-owner of the debt, to the extent of the payment. O. Reg. 258/98, r. 20.08(19).

Distribution of Payments

(20) When proof is filed that the notice of garnishment was served on the debtor, the clerk shall distribute a payment received under a notice of garnishment to a creditor in accordance with subrule (20.1), unless,

(a) a hearing has been requested under subrule (15);

(b) a notice of motion has been filed under rule 8.10 or 11.06, subparagraph 1 iii of subrule 11.2.01(1) or rule 17.04. O. Reg. 78/06, s. 45(9).

(20.1) The clerk shall distribute the payment,

(a) in the case of the first payment under the notice of garnishment, 30 days after the date it is received; and

(b) a notice of motion and supporting affidavit (Form 15A) has been filed under rule 8.10, 11.06 or 17.04; or

(c) a request for clerk's order on consent (Form 11.2A) has been filed seeking the relief described in subparagraph 1 iii of subrule 11.2.01(1).

(20.1) The clerk shall distribute the payment,

(a) in the case of the first payment under the notice of garnishment, 30 days after the date it is received; and

(b) in the case of every subsequent payment under the notice of garnishment, as they are received. O. Reg. 78/06, s. 45(9).

Notice Once Order Satisfied

(20.2) Once the amount owing under an order that is enforced by garnishment is paid, the creditor shall immediately serve a notice of termination of garnishment (Form 20R) on the garnishee and on the clerk. O. Reg. 393/09, s. 20(6).

Payment if Debt Jointly Owned

(21) If a payment of a debt owed to the debtor and one or more co-owners has been made to the clerk, no request for a garnishment hearing is made and the time for doing so under subrule (16) has expired, the creditor may file with the clerk, within 30 days after that expiry,

(a) proof of service of the notice to co-owner; and

(b) an affidavit stating that the creditor believes that no co-owner of the debt is a person under disability, and the grounds for the belief. O. Reg. 258/98, r. 20.08(21).

(22) The affidavit required by subrule (21) may contain statements of the deponent's information and belief, if the source of the information and the fact of the belief are specified in the affidavit. O. Reg. 258/98, r. 20.08(22).

(23) If the creditor does not file the material referred to in subrule (21) the clerk shall return the money to the garnishee. O. Reg. 258/98, r. 20.08(23).

Consolidation Order

20.09(1) A debtor against whom there are two or more unsatisfied orders for the payment of money may make a motion to the court for a consolidation order. O. Reg. 258/98, r. 20.09(1).

(2) The debtor's notice of motion and supporting affidavit (Form 15A) shall set out, in the affidavit portion,

(a) the names and addresses of the creditors who have obtained an order for the payment of money against the debtor;

(b) the amount owed to each creditor;

(c) the amount of the debtor's income from all sources, identifying them; and

(d) the debtor's current financial obligations and any other relevant facts. O. Reg. 258/98, r. 20.09(2).

Notice of Motion

(3) For the purposes of clause 15.01 (3) (a), the notice of motion and supporting affidavit shall be served on each of the creditors mentioned in it at least seven days before the hearing date. O. Reg. 393/09, s. 21(2).

Contents of Consolidation Order

(4) At the hearing of the motion, the court may make a consolidation order setting out,

(a) a list of unsatisfied orders for the payment of money against the debtor, indicating in each case the date, court and amount and the amount unpaid;

(b) the amounts to be paid into court by the debtor under the consolidation order; and

(c) the times of the payments. O. Reg. 258/98, r. 20.09(4).

(5) The total of the amounts to be paid into court by the debtor under a consolidation order shall not exceed the portion of the debtor's wages that are subject to seizure or garnishment under section 7 of the *Wages Act*. O. Reg. 78/06, s. 46(1).

Creditor May Make Submissions

(6) At the hearing of the motion, a creditor may make submissions as to the amount and times of payment. O. Reg. 258/98, r. 20.09(6).

Further Orders Obtained After Consolidation Order

(7) If an order for the payment of money is obtained against the debtor after the date of the consolidation order for a debt incurred before the date of the consolidation order, the creditor may file with the clerk a certified copy of the new order; the creditor shall be added to the consolidation order and shall share in the distribution under it from that time. O. Reg. 258/98, r. 20.09(7).

(8) A consolidation order terminates immediately if an order for the payment of money is obtained against the debtor for a debt incurred after the date of the consolidation order. O. Reg. 258/98, r. 20.09(8).

Enforcement Limited While Consolidation Order in Force

(9) While the consolidation order is in force, no step to enforce the judgment may be taken or continued against the debtor by a creditor named in the order, except issuing a writ of seizure and sale of land and filing it with the sheriff. O. Reg. 258/98, r. 20.09(9).

Termination on Default

(10) A consolidation order terminates immediately if the debtor is in default under it for 21 days. O. Reg. 258/98, r. 20.09(10).

Effect of Termination

(11) If a consolidation order terminates under subrule (8) or (10), the clerk shall notify the creditors named in the consolidation order, and no further consolidation order shall be made in respect of the debtor for one year after the date of termination. O. Reg. 258/98, r. 20.09(11); O. Reg. 461/01, s. 19(1).

Manner of Sending Notice

(11.1) The notice that the consolidation order is terminated shall be served by mail or fax. O. Reg. 330/02, s. 12(1).

(11.2), (11.3) Revoked: O. Reg. 78/06, ss. 46(2).

Equal Distribution Among Creditors
(12) All payments into a consolidation account belong to the creditors named in the consolidation order, who shall share equally in the distribution of the money. O. Reg. 258/98, r. 20.09(12).

(13) The clerk shall distribute the money paid into the consolidation account at least once every six months. O. Reg. 258/98, r. 20.09(13).

Examination of Debtor or Other Person
20.10(1) If there is default under an order for the payment or recovery of money, the clerk of a court in the territorial division in which the debtor or other person to be examined resides or carries on business shall, at the creditor's request, issue a notice of examination (Form 20H) directed to the debtor or other person. O. Reg. 258/98, r. 20.10(1).

(2) The creditor's request shall be accompanied by,
(a) an affidavit for enforcement request (Form 20P) setting out,
  (i) the date of the order and the amount awarded,
  (ii) the territorial division in which the order was made,
  (iii) the rate of postjudgment interest payable,
  (iv) the total amount of any payments received since the order was granted, and
  (v) the amount owing, including postjudgment interest; and
(b) a certificate of judgment (Form 20A), if the order was made in another territorial jurisdiction. O. Reg. 258/98, r. 20.10(2); O. Reg. 78/06, s. 47(1).

Service of Notice of Examination
(3) The notice of examination shall be served in accordance with subrules 8.01(10), (11) and (12). O. Reg. 78/06, s. 47(2).

(4) The debtor, any other persons to be examined and any witnesses whose evidence the court considers necessary may be examined in relation to,
(a) the reason for nonpayment;
(b) the debtor's income and property;
(c) the debts owed to and by the debtor;
(d) the disposal the debtor has made of any property either before or after the order was made;
(e) the debtor's present, past and future means to satisfy the order;
(f) whether the debtor intends to obey the order or has any reason for not doing so; and
(g) any other matter pertinent to the enforcement of the order. O. Reg. 258/98, r. 20.10(4).

Duties of Person to be Examined
(4.1) A person who is served with a notice of examination shall,
(a) inform himself or herself about the matters mentioned in subrule (4) and be prepared to answer questions about them; and
(b) in the case of an examination of a debtor who is an individual, complete a financial information form (Form 20I) and,
  (i) serve it on the creditor requesting the examination, but not file it with the court, and
  (ii) provide a copy of it to the judge presiding at the examination hearing. O. Reg. 78/06, s. 47(3); O. Reg. 440/10, s. 6(1).

(4.2) A debtor required under clause (4.1)(b) to complete a financial information form (Form 20I) shall bring such documents to the examination hearing as are necessary to support the information that he or she provides in the financial information form. O. Reg. 440/10, s. 6(2).

Who May Be Examined

(5) An officer or director of a corporate debtor, or, in the case of a debtor that is a partnership or sole proprietorship, the sole proprietor or any partner, may be examined on the debtor's behalf in relation to the matters set out in subrule (4). O. Reg. 258/98, r. 20.10(5).

Attendance

(5.1) A person required to attend an examination may attend,

(a) in person; or

(b) by video conference in accordance with rule 1.07. O. Reg. 393/09, s. 22(3).

Examinations Private, Under Oath and Recorded

(6) The examination shall be,

(a) held in the absence of the public, unless the court orders otherwise;

(b) conducted under oath; and

(c) recorded. O. Reg. 78/06, s. 47(4).

Order As To Payment

(7) After the examination or if the debtor's consent is filed, the court may make an order as to payment. O. Reg. 258/98, r. 20.10(7); O. Reg. 461/01, s. 20(1).

Enforcement Limited while Order as to Payment in Force

(8) While an order as to payment is in force, no step to enforce the judgment may be taken or continued against the debtor by a creditor named in the order, except issuing a writ of seizure and sale of land and filing it with the sheriff. O. Reg. 258/98, r. 20.10(8).

(9)–(15) Revoked: O. Reg. 78/06, s. 47(5).

Contempt Hearing

20.11(1) If a person on whom a notice of examination has been served under rule 20.10 attends the examination but refuses to answer questions or to produce records or documents, the court may order the person to attend before it for a contempt hearing. O. Reg. 440/10, s. 7(1).

Same

(2) If a person on whom a notice of examination has been served under rule 20.10 fails to attend the examination, the court may order the person to attend before it for a contempt hearing under subsection 30(1) of the *Courts of Justice Act*. O. Reg. 440/10, s. 7(1).

Notice of Contempt Hearing

(3) If the court makes an order for a contempt hearing,

(a) the clerk shall provide the creditor with a notice of contempt hearing setting out the time, date and place of the hearing; and

(b) the creditor shall serve the notice of contempt hearing on the debtor or other person in accordance with subrule 8.01(13) and file the affidavit of service at least seven days before the hearing. O. Reg. 78/06, s. 48; O. Reg. 440/10, s. 7(2).

Setting Aside Order for Contempt Hearing

(4) A person who has been ordered to attend a contempt hearing under subsection 30(1) of the *Courts of Justice Act* may make a motion to set aside the order, before or after receiving the notice of contempt hearing but before the date of the hearing and, on the motion, the court may set aside the order and order that the person attend another examination under rule 20.10. O. Reg. 78/06, s. 48; O. Reg. 440/10, s. 7(3).

Finding of Contempt of Court

(5) At a contempt hearing held under subrule (1), the court may find the person to be in contempt of court if the person fails to show cause why the person should not be held in contempt for refusing to answer questions or produce records or documents. O. Reg. 78/06, s. 48.

Same

(6) The finding of contempt at a hearing held under subsection 30(1) of the *Courts of Justice Act* is subject to subsection 30(2) of that Act. O. Reg. 440/10, s. 7(4).

Other Powers of Court at Contempt Hearing

(7) At a contempt hearing, the court may order that the person,
 (a) attend an examination under rule 20.10;
 (b) be jailed for a period of not more than five days;
 (c) attend an additional contempt hearing under subrule (1) or subsection 30(1) of the *Courts of Justice Act*, as the case may be; or
 (d) comply with any other order that the judge considers necessary or just. O. Reg. 78/06, s. 48; O. Reg. 440/10, s. 7(5–7).

Warrant of Committal

(8) If a committal is ordered under clause (7)(b),
 (a) the creditor may complete and file with the clerk an identification form (Form 20K) to assist the police in apprehending the person named in the warrant of committal; and
 (b) the clerk shall issue a warrant of committal (Form 20J), accompanied by the identification form, if any, directed to all police officers in Ontario to apprehend the person named in the warrant anywhere in Ontario and promptly bring the person to the nearest correctional institution. O. Reg. 78/06, s. 48; O. Reg. 440/10, s. 7(8).

Discharge

(9) A person in custody under a warrant issued under this rule shall be discharged from custody on the order of the court or when the time prescribed in the warrant expires, whichever is earlier. O. Reg. 78/06, s. 48; O. Reg. 440/10, s. 7(9).

Duration and Renewal of Warrant of Committal

(10) A warrant issued under this rule remains in force for 12 months after the date of issue and may be renewed by order of the court on a motion made by the creditor for 12 months at each renewal, unless the court orders otherwise. O. Reg. 78/06, s. 48; O. Reg. 440/10, s. 7(10).

(11) Revoked: O. Reg. 440/10, s. 7(11).

Satisfaction of Order
20.12 If payment is made in full satisfaction of an order,
  (a) where all parties consent, a party may file a request for clerk's order on consent (Form 11.2A) indicating that payment has been made in full satisfaction of the order or terms of settlement; or
  (b) the debtor may make a motion for an order confirming that payment has been made in full satisfaction of the order or terms of settlement. O. Reg. 78/06, s. 48.

RULE 21 REFEREE

21.01(1) A person assigned the powers and duties of a referee under subsection 73(2) of the *Courts of Justice Act* may, if directed by the regional senior justice or his or her designate,
  (a) hear disputes of proposals of terms of payment under rule 9.03;
  (b) conduct settlement conferences under rule 13;
  (c) hear motions for consolidation orders under rule 20.09; and
  (d) assess receipted disbursements for fees paid to the court, a court reporter or a sheriff under the regulations made under the *Administration of Justice Act*. O. Reg. 78/06, s. 49.

(2) Except under subrule 9.03(5) (order as to terms of payment), a referee shall not make a final decision in any matter referred to him or her but shall report his or her findings and recommendations to the court. O. Reg. 78/06, s. 49.

RULE 22 PAYMENT INTO AND OUT OF COURT

Definitions
22.01 In this Rule,

"Accountant" means the Accountant of the Superior Court of Justice; ("comptable")

"clerk" means the clerk in the location where the proceeding was commenced. ("greffier") O. Reg. 400/12, s. 2.

Non-Application of Rule
22.02 This Rule does not apply to money paid or to be paid into court,
  (a) under an order or proposal for payment made under rule 9.03;
  (b) under an offer to settle a claim in return for the payment of money; or
  (c) for the enforcement of an order for the payment or recovery of money under Rule 20, including enforcement by garnishment. O. Reg. 400/12, s. 2.

Payment into Court
22.03(1) Subject to subrule (7), a party who is required to pay money into court shall do so in accordance with subrules (2) to (6). O. Reg. 400/12, s. 2.

Filing with Clerk or Accountant
(2) The party shall file the following documents with the clerk or the Accountant:
  1. If the payment into court is under a statutory provision or rule, a written request for payment into court that refers to that provision or rule.

2. If the payment into court is under an order, a written request for payment into court and a copy of the order that bears the court's seal. O. Reg. 400/12, s. 2.

Direction

(3) On receiving the documents required to be filed under subrule (2), the clerk or Accountant shall give the party a direction to receive the money, addressed to a bank listed in Schedule I or II to the *Bank Act* (Canada) and specifying the account in the Accountant's name into which the money is to be paid. O. Reg. 400/12, s. 2.

Clerk to Forward Documents

(4) If the documents are filed with the clerk, the clerk shall forward the documents to the Accountant. O. Reg. 400/12, s. 2.

Payment

(5) On receiving the direction referred to in subrule (3), the party shall pay the money into the specified bank account in accordance with the direction. O. Reg. 400/12, s. 2.

Bank's Duties

(6) On receiving the money, the bank shall give a receipt to the party paying the money and immediately send a copy of the receipt to the Accountant. O. Reg. 400/12, s. 2.

Payment to Accountant by Mail

(7) A party may pay money into court by mailing to the Accountant the applicable documents referred to in subrule (2), together with the money that is payable; the written request for payment into court referred to in that subrule shall include the party's name and mailing address. O. Reg. 400/12, s. 2.

Accountant to Provide Receipt

(8) On receiving money under subrule (7), the Accountant shall send a receipt to the party paying the money. O. Reg. 400/12, s. 2.

Proof of Payment

(9) A party who pays money into court shall, immediately after receiving a receipt from the bank under subrule (6) or from the Accountant under subrule (8), as the case may be, send to every other party a copy of the receipt and file a copy of the receipt with the court. O. Reg. 400/12, s. 2.

Payment Out of Court

22.04(1) Money may only be paid out of court under an order. O. Reg. 400/12, s. 2.

Documents to be Filed

(2) A person who seeks payment of money out of court shall file with the Accountant,

 (a) a written request for payment out and supporting affidavit, in the form provided by the Ministry; and

 (b) a copy of the order for payment out that bears the court's seal. O. Reg. 400/12, s. 2.

Payment Out, Children's Lawyer or Public Guardian and Trustee

(3) If the person seeking payment out is the Children's Lawyer or the Public Guardian and Trustee,

(a) the written request need not be in the form provided by the Ministry and a supporting affidavit is not required; and

(b) a single written request that deals with more than one proceeding may be filed. O. Reg. 400/12, s. 2.

Payment Out, Minor Attaining Age of Majority

(4) Despite subrule (2), money in court to which a party is entitled under an order once the party attains the age of majority may be paid out to the party on filing with the Accountant, in the forms provided by the Accountant,

(a) a written request for payment out; and

(b) an affidavit proving the identity of the party and that the party has attained the age of majority. O. Reg. 400/12, s. 2.

Accountant's Duties

(5) If the requirements of subrule (2) or (4), as the case may be, are met, the Accountant shall pay the money to the person named in the order for payment out, and the payment shall include any accrued interest, unless a court orders otherwise. O. Reg. 400/12, s. 2.

Transition

22.05 This Rule applies to the payment into and out of court of money paid into court on and after the day on which Ontario Regulation 400/12 comes into force. O. Reg. 400/12, s. 2.

23. Omitted (provides for coming into force of provisions of this Regulation). O. Reg. 258/98, s. 23.

Appendix 3: Table of Forms

(See Rule 1.06 and http://www.ontariocourtforms.on.ca)

Form No.	Form Title	Effective Date
1A	Additional Parties	2010-01-01
1A.1	Additional Debtors	2010-01-01
1B	Request for Telephone or Video Conference	2011-01-01
4A	Consent to Act as Litigation Guardian	2010-01-01
4B	Affidavit (Motion for Payment Out of Court)	2013-01-01
5A	Notice to Alleged Partner	2010-01-01
7A	Plaintiff's Claim	2011-01-01
8A	Affidavit of Service	2011-01-01
9A	Defence	2011-01-01
9B	Request to Clerk	2010-01-01
10A	Defendant's Claim	2010-01-01
11A	Affidavit for Jurisdiction	2010-01-01
11B	Default Judgment	2011-01-01
11.2A	Request for Clerk's Order on Consent	2010-01-01
11.3A	Notice of Discontinued Claim	2011-01-01
13A	List of Proposed Witnesses	2010-01-01
13B	Consent	2011-01-01
14A	Offer to Settle	2010-01-01
14B	Acceptance of Offer to Settle	2010-01-01
14C	Notice of Withdrawal of Offer to Settle	2010-01-01
14D	Terms of Settlement	2010-01-01
15A	Notice of Motion and Supporting Affidavit	2011-01-01
15B	Affidavit	2010-01-01
18A	Summons to Witness	2010-01-01
18B	Warrant for Arrest of Defaulting Witness	2010-01-01
20A	Certificate of Judgment	2011-01-01
20B	Writ of Delivery	2010-01-01
20C	Writ of Seizure and Sale of Personal Property	2010-01-01
20D	Writ of Seizure and Sale of Land	2010-01-01
20E	Notice of Garnishment	2011-01-01
20E.1	Notice of Renewal of Garnishment	2011-01-01
20F	Garnishee's Statement	2012-07-01
20G	Notice to Co-owner of Debt	2011-01-01
20H	Notice of Examination	2012-07-01
20I	Financial Information Form	2012-07-01
20J	Warrant of Committal	2011-01-01
20K	Identification Form	2010-01-01
20L	Notice of Default of Payment	2010-01-01
20M	Affidavit of Default of Payment	2012-07-01
20N	Request to Renew Writ of Seizure and Sale	2010-01-01
20O	Direction to Enforce Writ of Seizure and Sale of Personal Property	2010-01-01
20P	Affidavit for Enforcement Request	2010-01-01
20Q	Notice of Garnishment Hearing	2011-01-01
20R	Notice of Termination of Garnishment	2011-01-01

O. Reg. 393/09, s. 25; O. Reg. 505/09, s. 1; O. Reg. 440/10, s. 8; O. Reg. 56/12, s. 5; O. Reg. 400/12, s. 3. FORMS 1A-20J Revoked: O. Reg. 78/06, s. 51.

Appendix 4: Schedule of Small Claims Court Fees and Allowances

This is current as of July 17, 2013. As fees and allowances change from time to time, current information about fees and allowances is available online at:

http://www.e-laws.gov.on.ca/html/regs/english/elaws_regs_930432_e.htm

Administration of Justice Act
ONTARIO REGULATION 432/93
SMALL CLAIMS COURT — FEES AND ALLOWANCES

Consolidation Period: From September 1, 2012, to the e-Laws currency date.
Last amendment: O. Reg. 248/12.
This is the English version of a bilingual regulation.

1.(1) The fees set out in Schedule 1 are payable to clerks of the Small Claims Court.

(2) In this section and Schedule 1,

"claim" does not include a defendant's claim;

"claimant" includes an individual, a sole proprietorship, a partnership, an unincorporated organization and a corporation.

(3) For the purposes of Schedule 1, a claimant who files a claim in a Small Claims Court office on or after January 1 in any calendar year and who has already filed 10 or more claims in the same office in that calendar year is a frequent claimant.

(4) For the purposes of Schedule 1, a claimant who is not a frequent claimant under subsection (3) is an infrequent claimant.

2. The fees and allowances set out in Schedule 2 are payable to bailiffs of the Small Claims Court.

3. The fees and allowances set out in Schedule 3 are payable to witnesses appearing before the Small Claims Court.

4. Omitted (revokes other Regulations).

5. Omitted (provides for coming into force of provisions of the English version of this Regulation).

Schedule 1
CLERK'S FEES

1. Filing of a claim by an infrequent claimant	$ 75.00
2. Filing of a claim by a frequent claimant	145.00
3. Filing of a defendant's claim	75.00
4. Filing a notice of motion served on another party, a notice of motion without notice or a notice of motion for a consent order (except a notice of motion under the *Wages Act*)	40.00
5. Filing a defence	40.00
6. Issuing a summons to a witness	19.00
7. Receiving for enforcement a process from the Ontario Court (Provincial Division) or an order or judgment as provided by statute	25.00
8. Issuing a certificate of judgment	19.00
9. Issuing a writ of delivery, a writ of seizure and sale or a notice of examination	35.00
10. Issuing a notice of garnishment	100.00
11. Preparing and filing a consolidation order	75.00
12. Forwarding a court file to Divisional Court for appeal	20.00
13. Issuing a certified copy of a judgment or other document, per page	3.50
14. Transmitting a document other than by mail	Cost of transmission
15. For the inspection of a court file,	
i. by a solicitor or party in the proceeding	no charge
ii. by a person who has entered into an agreement with the Attorney General for the bulk inspection of court files, per file	1.00
iii. by any other person, per file	10.00
16. Making a photocopy of a document not requiring certification, per page	1.00
17. For a copy on compact disc (CD) of a digital recording of a court hearing in respect of a case, if such a recording exists and a copy is available:	
i. For a single day's recording	22.00
ii. For each additional day's recording, if the request is made at the same time as a request under subitem i	10.50
18. In an application under the *Repair and Storage Liens Act*,	
i. on the filing of,	
A. an application	100.00
B. a notice of objection	35.00
C. a waiver of further claim and a receipt	no charge
ii. on the issuing of,	
A. an initial certificate	35.00
B. a final certificate	35.00
C. a writ of seizure	35.00
19. Fixing of a date for a trial or an assessment hearing by an infrequent claimant	100.00
20. Fixing of a date for a trial or an assessment hearing by a frequent claimant	130.00
21. Entering of a default judgment by an infrequent claimant	35.00
22. Entering of a default judgment by a frequent claimant	50.00

O. Reg. 214/97, s. 2; O. Reg. 488/98, s. 2; O. Reg. 17/00, s. 1; O. Reg. 11/05, s. 1; O. Reg. 271/05, s. 1; O. Reg. 363/06, s. 1; O. Reg. 248/12, s. 1.

Schedule 2
BAILIFF'S FEES

1. Revoked: O. Reg. 363/06, s. 2.

2. For each attempt, whether successful or not, to enforce a writ of delivery — 36.00

3. For each attempt, whether successful or not, to enforce a writ of seizure and sale of personal property,

   i. where no sale is necessary — 36.00

   ii. where a sale is necessary — 60.00

4. For each attempt, whether successful or not, to enforce a writ of seizure under the *Repair and Storage Liens Act* — 36.00

5. Enforcing a writ of delivery or a writ of seizure and sale of personal property, removing property seized, advertising the sale of personal property, including obtaining assistance in seizing, securing or retaining property — Reasonable disbursements necessarily incurred, including appraisers' fees

O. Reg. 11/05, s. 2; O. Reg. 363/06, s. 2.

Schedule 3
FEES AND ALLOWANCES TO WITNESSES

1. For attendance in court, unless item 2 applies, per day — $6.00

2. For attendance in court by a barrister, solicitor, physician, surgeon, engineer or veterinary surgeon who is not a party to the action, to give evidence of a professional service rendered or to give a professional opinion, per day — 15.00

   For travel to court — Reasonable travelling expenses actually incurred, but not exceeding the kilometre allowance set out in Regulation 11 of the Revised Regulations of Ontario, 1990*

O. Reg. 432/93, Sched. 3.

---

* As of July 17, 2013, R.R.O. 1990, Reg. 11 set the kilometre allowances at 30 cents per km for southern Ontario, and 30.5 cents per km for northern Ontario. Northern Ontario is defined in s. 2 of the regulation.

Appendix 5: Post-judgment and Pre-judgment Interest Rates
(Courts of Justice Act, s. 127)

Note that the tables produced here are for the purpose of illustration, showing what they look like and how they work. These show the current rates as of July 17, 2013. Note that the rates are set for each quarter, so you must check the Attorney General's website to see what the current rates are. (From http://www.ontario.ca/welcome-ontario, click Government, then click on Government Ministries, then click on Attorney General. Once you are in the Attorney General site, click on Court Services, then click on pre- and post-judgment interest under Court Fees.)

1. Post-judgment interest rates for causes of action arising on or before October 23, 1989, are as follows:

	1st Quarter	2nd Quarter	3rd Quarter	4th Quarter
1985	12.00%	13.00%	11.00%	11.00%
1986	11.00%	13.00%	10.00%	10.00%
1987	10.00%	9.00%	10.00%	11.00%
1988	10.00%	10.00%	11.00%	12.00%
1989	13.00%	13.00%	14.00%	14.00%
1990	14.00%	15.00%	15.00%	14.00%
1991	14.00%	11.00%	11.00%	10.00%
1992	9.00%	9.00%	8.00%	7.00%
1993	10.00%	8.00%	7.00%	6.00%
1994	6.00%	6.00%	8.00%	7.00%
1995	8.00%	10.00%	9.00%	8.00%
1996	8.00%	7.00%	6.00%	6.00%
1997	5.00%	5.00%	5.00%	5.00%
1998	5.00%	6.00%	6.00%	7.00%
1999	7.00%	7.00%	6.00%	6.00%
2000	6.00%	7.00%	7.00%	7.00%
2001	7.00%	7.00%	6.00%	6.00%
2002	4.00%	4.00%	4.00%	4.00%
2003	4.00%	4.00%	5.00%	5.00%
2004	4.00%	4.00%	4.00%	4.00%
2005	4.00%	4.00%	4.00%	4.00%
2006	5.00%	5.00%	6.00%	6.00%
2007	6.00%	6.00%	6.00%	6.00%
2008	6.00%	6.00%	5.00%	5.00%
2009	4.00%	3.00%	2.00%	2.00%
2010	2.00%	2.00%	2.00%	2.00%
2011	3.00%	3.00%	3.00%	3.00%
2012	3.00%	3.00%	3.00%	3.00%
2013	3.00%	3.00%	3.00%	

2. Pre-judgment interest rates for causes of action arising after October 23, 1989, are as follows:

	1st Quarter	2nd Quarter	3rd Quarter	4th Quarter
1989				12.40%
1990	12.50%	13.50%	13.90%	12.90%
1991	12.30%	10%	9.10%	8.80%
1992	7.70%	7.50%	6.30%	5.10%
1993	8.30%	6.10%	5.10%	5.00%
1994	4.30%	4.10%	6.60%	5.60%
1995	6.00%	8.00%	7.60%	6.60%
1996	6.10%	5.60%	5.00%	4.30%
1997	3.30%	3.30%	3.30%	3.50%
1998	4.00%	5.00%	5.00%	6.00%
1999	5.30%	5.30%	4.80%	4.80%
2000	5.00%	5.30%	6.00%	6.00%
2001	6.00%	5.80%	4.80%	4.30%
2002	2.50%	2.30%	2.50%	3.00%
2003	3.00%	3.00%	3.50%	3.30%
2004	3.00%	2.80%	2.30%	2.30%
2005	2.80%	2.80%	2.80%	2.80%
2006	3.30%	3.80%	4.50%	4.50%
2007	4.50%	4.50%	4.50%	4.80%
2008	4.80%	4.30%	3.30%	3.30%
2009	2.50%	1.30%	0.50%	0.50%
2010	0.50%	0.50%	0.80%	1.00%
2011	1.30%	1.30%	1.30%	1.30%
2012	1.30%	1.30%	1.30%	1.30%
2013	1.30%	1.30%	1.30%	

Appendix 6: Ontario Small Claims Court List

To find the mailing address of the court, you can call the court directly or check online at <http://www.attorneygeneral.jus.gov.on.ca/english/courts/Court_Addresses/>. Note, however, that this website lists all of the courts of all types in Ontario, so you must pick the municipality and then pull down the list of courts for that place to determine if there is a small claims court in that municipality. The list in this appendix narrows down the search by listing places in Ontario that actually do have small claims courts.

PLACE OF SMALL CLAIMS COURT	TELEPHONE NUMBER
Alexandria	613-525-4330
Arnprior	613-732-8581
Attawapiskat	705-272-4256
Bancroft	613-962-9106
Barrie	705-739-6111
Belleville	613-962-9106
Blind River	705-848-2383
Bracebridge	705-645-8793
Brampton (two locations)	905-456-4700
Brantford	519-752-7828
Brighton	905-372-3751
Brockville	613-341-2800
Burks Falls	705-382-2571
Burlington	905-637-4125
Campbellford	905-372-3751
Cayuga	905-772-3335
Chapleau	705-360-4231
Chatham	519-355-2200
Cobourg	905-372-3751
Cochrane	705-272-4256
Collingwood	705-445-9332
Cornwall	613-933-7500
Dryden	807-223-2348
Elliot Lake	705-848-2383
Espanola	705-869-4334
Fort Frances	807-274-5961
Geraldton	807-854-1488
Goderich	519-524-7322
Gore Bay	705-282-2461

PLACE OF SMALL CLAIMS COURT	TELEPHONE NUMBER
Guelph	519-824-4100
Haileybury	705-672-3321
Hamilton	905-645-5252
Hearst	705-337-1477
Huntsville	705-645-8793
Iroquois Falls	705-272-4256
Kaladar	613-354-3845
Kapuskasing (two locations)	705-337-1477
Kenora	807-468-2842
Kingston	613-548-6811
Kirkland Lake	705-567-9381
Kitchener	519-741-3270
Leamington	519-973-6620
Lindsay	705-324-1400
Listowel	519-271-4940
London	519-660-3000
L'Orignal	613-675-4567
Markham	905-731-2664
Midland	705-526-0251
Milton	905-878-7285
Minden	705-324-1400
Morrisburg	613-543-2193
Mount Forest	519-824-4169
Napanee	613-354-3845
Newmarket	905-853-4809
Nipigon	807-887-3829
North Bay	705-495-8309
Orangeville	519-941-5802
Orillia	705-326-2671
Oshawa	905-743-2630
Ottawa	613-267-1079
Owen Sound	519-370-2430
Parry Sound	705-746-4237
Pembroke	613-732-8581
Perth	613-267-2021
Peterborough	705-876-3816
Picton	613-476-6236
Port Hope	905-372-3751

PLACE OF SMALL CLAIMS COURT	TELEPHONE NUMBER
Red Lake	807-727-2376
Renfrew	613-732-8581
Richmond Hill	905-731-2664
Sarnia	519-333-2950
Sault Ste. Marie	705-945-8000
Sharbot Lake	613-548-6811
Simcoe	519-426-6550
St. Catharines	905-988-6200
St. Thomas (two locations)	519-631-3530
Stratford	519-271-9252
Stratford (Perth County)	519-271-1850
Sturgeon Falls	705-753-1090
Sudbury	705-564-7600
Sundridge	705-746-4237
Thunder Bay	807-343-2710
Timmins	705-360-4231
Toronto	416-326-3554
Walkerton	519-881-1772
Wawa	705-945-8000
Welland	905-735-0010
Windsor	519-973-6620
Woodstock	519-539-6187

Glossary

accelerate (ch. 4) A common loan term whereby if the debtor misses one payment all future payments become due.

accord and satisfaction (ch. 10) A document executed by a judgment creditor and judgment debtor where the creditor has agreed to take less than the full amount under the judgment as settlement, and acknowledges that the judgment has been satisfied.

affidavit (ch. 1) A sworn statement by an individual made in writing.

arm's length (ch. 15) A phrase used to describe parties dealing with each other in the ordinary course of business in the open market. Parties not at arm's length include family members, close friends, and associates.

assets (ch. 3) Real or personal property or any interest in it.

attendance money (ch. 11) The money that the fee schedule requires to be paid to a witness, consisting of a fee and reasonable travel expenses; sometimes also referred to by an older name, i.e., conduct money.

bailiff (ch. 4) An officer of the court who enforces orders of the court, including orders to seize personal property. Private, provincially licensed bailiffs seize secured property for creditors outside the court process.

balance of convenience (ch. 6) A test used by judges to determine if it is just and fair to try a case in one place rather than another, based on the facts of the case, where the cause of action arose, where the witnesses have to come from, and so on.

basket clause (ch. 11) A clause in a contract or other document that contains an inclusive, general direction to do something, rather than a specific and particularized direction.

bill of costs (ch. 12) A list of legal fees and disbursements used to determine a costs award. The term is usually used in connection with costs issues in the Superior Court.

bind the witness over (ch. 11) A phrase meaning that a judge instructs a witness, when the case is adjourned, that he or she is still subject to the summons and must appear on the scheduled return date.

cause of action (ch. 5) The legal reason for suing and seeking a remedy based on a legal breach.

claim (ch. 1) The plaintiff's case against the defendant. The plaintiff sets out his or her case on a Plaintiff's Claim (Form 7A). It is issued by the court and then served on the defendant.

collateral (ch. 4) An asset pledged to secure a debt that may be seized by a creditor to satisfy a debt if the debtor fails to pay the debt when it is due.

concurrently liable (ch. 5) Two or more persons are concurrently liable when they each separately cause damage but it is not possible to determine which of them caused specific damage.

conditional sale contract (ch. 4) A contract where the seller of goods finances the sale by lending the purchaser all or part of the price of the goods. To secure the loan, the seller takes a security interest in the goods sold so that if the debtor fails to pay, the creditor can seize and sell the goods to satisfy the debt.

consolidation order (ch. 1) Where a defendant has two or more judgments against him, he can ask the court to bring them together as one order with one monthly payment to be made.

consumer note/consumer paper (ch. 4) Trade terms used to describe conditional sale contracts and other documents where a consumer agrees to pay a seller for goods and where the right of payment can be assigned to a third party by the retail seller. See **negotiable instrument**.

counterclaim (ch. 1, ch. 8) A claim made by a defendant against a plaintiff in regard to the same matter in the plaintiff's claim. In Small Claims Court, counterclaim is made in a Defendant's Claim (Form 10A).

crossclaim (ch. 1, ch. 8) A claim by one defendant against a co-defendant in regard to the same matter in the plaintiff's claim. In Small Claims Court, crossclaim is made in a Defendant's Claim (Form 10A).

cross motion (ch. 9) A motion brought by the responding party in addition to any other response to the main motion brought by the moving party.

defence (ch. 1) The defendant's response to the plaintiff's claim. The defendant completes a Defence Form (9A). It is served on the plaintiff and filed with the court.

default judgment (ch. 1) Where a defendant fails to file a defence on time, he or she has defaulted on the defence, and a judgment may be made against him or her without further notice, and without the right to defend the action, based on the failure to file the defence on time.

demonstrative evidence (ch. 11) Models, diagrams, and other things, such as photos, as opposed to oral evidence or documents, are often referred to by this term.

deponent (ch. 9) The person whose sworn, written statement appears in the affidavit. Also called the maker of the affidavit.

disbursements (ch. 1) Out-of-pocket expenses that are paid by a party for court fees, experts' reports, and other services or things. They do not include the representation fee paid to a legal representative for legal and advocacy services.

domiciled (ch. 6) A person is domiciled in a country, or political subdivision of said country, to which a person is permanently connected, even when he or she is not physically present. It differs from residence, as this requires physical presence, and, while a person can have more than one place where he or she is resident, a person cannot have more than one domicile.

examination in aid of execution (ch. 14) A procedure that allows a judgment creditor to ask questions of a judgment debtor under oath in court for the purposes of enforcing an unpaid judgment. Also referred to as examination hearing.

execution creditor (ch. 14) The person, usually a plaintiff, who has filed a writ of seizure and sale or other enforcement remedy against a judgment debtor.

fiduciary (ch. 6) A person who is a trustee and who must act with the utmost good faith in representing the interest of the other person whose interests always take precedence over those of the fiduciary.

forum (ch. 6) Court office or location.

garnish (ch. 1) The process whereby someone that owes money to a judgment debtor redirects the money to the court for the benefit of the judgment creditor.

garnishee (ch. 15) The person who owes money to a judgment debtor, and who is directed to pay some or all of it for the benefit of the judgment creditor.

garnishment (ch. 15) A court procedure for enforcing judgments in which a person who owes money to a debtor is ordered not to pay the debtor, but to pay the money to the court for the benefit of the debtor's judgment creditors.

general security agreement (ch. 4) A contract between a creditor and a debtor wherein, in exchange for providing financing to the debtor, the creditor takes security over the debtor's present and future inventory. Terms of the security, along with what constitutes a breach and procedures for seizing collateral, are also set out.

improvident (ch. 6) Unwise, foolish, disadvantageous.

individually liable (ch. 5) Two are more persons are individually liable when they each separately cause damage and it is possible to determine which of them caused specific damage.

injunction (ch. 3) A mandatory order from the court ordering a party to do or refrain from doing something.

issuing a court document (ch. 1) A process that occurs when the fee for filing the document is paid to the court, and the court clerk signs it, assigns the case a claim number, and affixes the court's seal to the document on behalf of the court. The document is then said to be issued.

jointly liable (ch. 5) Two or more persons are jointly liable when each is liable for the full amount of the plaintiff's claim.

judgment creditor (ch. 13) The person, usually a plaintiff, who is owed money under a judgment.

judgment debtor (ch. 13) The person, usually a defendant, who owes money as the result of a judgment against him or her.

judgment proof (ch. 3) A debtor or judgment debtor whose circumstances are such that a judgment cannot be enforced against him or her because he or she has no assets or has successfully blocked access to them.

liquidated damages (ch. 7) Damages that can be easily calculated using objective methods and simple mathematics, where anyone assessing the damages should come up with the same amount. Also known as special damages.

memos to the file (ch. 2) An office term referring to writing a note for the file that details who spoke to, when you spoke to them, and the nature of your conversation or meeting.

minutes of settlement (ch. 10) An agreement setting out the terms of settlement.

mortgagee (ch. 14) The lender on a mortgage. The borrower is the mortgagor.

motion (ch. 1) A proceeding sometimes described as "a trial within a trial", where procedural issues that have arisen prior to trial are resolved by the court. Using the motion process, the parties argue their positions on the issue, and the court makes an order that resolves the issue.

moving party (ch. 9) The person who brings a motion.

narrow question (ch. 2) A question that is designed to obtain specific information on a particular issue from a witness.

negotiable instrument (ch. 4) A document that creates a right of payment to a person, where the right to be paid can be assigned to a third party. See **consumer note / consumer paper**.

notice of garnishment (ch. 1) A court document obtained by a judgment creditor from the court to set up a garnishment. It is served on a person, the garnishee, who owes money to the judgment debtor. The garnishee is required to remit payment of some or all of the money he would otherwise owe the judgment debtor to the court to satisfy some or all of the outstanding judgment.

notice of motion (ch. 1) The document used to bring a motion to court. It sets out the issues raised by the moving party, and the reasons why the motion should be granted.

NSF cheque (ch. 3) A cheque that has been presented for payment to a bank by a payee but has been returned marked "not sufficient funds" because there is not enough money in the drawer's chequing account to pay the amount on the cheque.

open-ended questions (ch. 2) Questions that permit the witness to choose what to say in a response to the interviewer.

originating document (ch. 6) The document that begins a lawsuit or first sets out a party's claim.

paralegals (ch. 1) Legal professionals licensed by the Law Society of Upper Canada and permitted to represent clients in the Small Claims Court, some criminal courts, and before various tribunals.

per annum (ch. 5) Latin for "per year".

per diem (ch. 5) Latin for "per day"; the interest owing shown as a daily amount.

pro rata **distribution (ch. 14):** A distribution of sale proceeds to execution creditors based on the amount owed to each creditor; the more an execution creditor is owed, the larger his or her share in the sale proceeds.

perfect (ch. 4) A security interest is perfected when the secured party has taken all the necessary steps that will allow the party to enforce the security agreement. In the PPSR system, perfection is achieved when the creditor registers a financing statement.

perfect the cause of action (ch. 6) A cause of action is perfected when the all of the required elements that make up the whole cause of action have occurred.

pleadings (ch. 1) The court documents that set out or "plead" a party's claim or defence, including claims, crossclaims, counterclaims, and third party claims.

power of attorney (ch. 6)   A document in which an individual grants to another person the power to act as his or her agent in specific matters. A power of attorney for property grants the appointed person the power to act in financial matters, such as enter into contracts, buy and sell property, or borrow or lend money. In some cases, a power of attorney, known as a continuing power of attorney, may continue after a person has become mentally incapable and may include the power to act as a litigation guardian in court proceedings. A power of attorney for personal care allows an individual to appoint someone to make health and other personal care decisions when that individual becomes unable to do so.

purchaser in good faith (ch. 3)   A buyer who pays a price, even if a low one, without notice that another person, other than the seller, might have an interest in the item purchased; also called a purchaser for value without notice.

quarter (ch. 5)   The year may be divided into quarters, consisting of three-month periods.

receivable (ch. 4)   A term used to describe an amount due and payable to a creditor.

receiving order (ch. 3)   An order from the court whereby a receiver is appointed to manage a debtor's business and/or sell off the assets of the business.

redirect (ch. 11)   Refers to questions asked by a legal representative of his or her own witness after cross-examination to deal with issues raised on cross-examination that did not arise on the examination-in-chief.

relief and indemnity over (ch. 8)   A phrase used to describe a situation where a defendant states that if the defendant is found liable, that liability should be transferred to another party, and the defendant should be indemnified by that party.

reserved judgment (ch. 12)   A judgment that is not handed down at the end of the trial, but at a later date.

responding party (ch. 9)   The person who wishes to oppose a motion.

retainer (ch. 2)   An agreement between the client and the paralegal as to the scope of the work that will be carried out by the paralegal. A retainer also stipulates what the fee will be or how it will be calculated. The term can refer to the actual agreement or to the state of being available to provide services to the client; it can also refer to the amount of money that the client has put up as a deposit to secure the paralegal's services.

reverse search (ch. 3)   Instead of searching by name to locate someone, this kind of search permits you to submit an address or phone number and find a name linked to the phone or address.

running account (ch. 5)   Also called a revolving credit account. It is a credit arrangement where the debtor is not required to pay off outstanding balances before incurring further debt; payments are made on the account and further debits incurred, so the balance due changes from time to time.

set off (ch. 8)   A situation of mutual debts where each party claims the other owes him or her money, in which case the mutual claims may be set off, one against the other.

setting the action down for trial (ch. 10)   An action is "set down" when all pre-trial steps have been completed and a party gives notice that he or she is ready for trial.

specific security agreement (ch. 4)   A contract between a debtor and a creditor wherein the terms of financing are set out along with the details of the particular item given as collateral. What constitutes a breach of the agreement is also set out along with details as to how the collateral can be seized in the event of a breach.

statute barred (ch. 2)   If a limitation period expires, the statute in which the limitation period appears bars you from doing now what you could have done before the limitation period expired.

stay proceedings (ch. 9)   Stop or bring a halt to proceedings, until a step or a process occurs or is completed.

stayed (ch. 3)   A stayed lawsuit is one that stops at the stage it happens to be at and cannot continue until the Rules or a court order lifts the stay.

summary hearing (ch. 1)   A hearing in which justice is to be done relatively quickly and inexpensively. Rules and procedures are more relaxed than in a formal court.

summary judgment (ch. 10)   A judgment given on a motion at the pre-trial stage, where on the pleadings and supporting affidavits, there does not appear to be a genuine issue for trial.

third party (ch. 8)   A person who is not a party to the action but who the defendant thinks is responsible for the plaintiff's damages, and who the defendant makes a party to the plaintiff's action, as a third party (after the plaintiff and defendant).

third party claim (ch. 1)   Where a plaintiff has sued a defendant and the defendant believes a party who the plaintiff has not sued is responsible for the plaintiff's loss, the defendant may bring that party into the lawsuit by making a third party claim against him or her, using a defendant's claim (Form 10A).

tickler system (ch. 2)   A date recording and reminder system to alert you to upcoming deadlines, such as limitation periods.

title (ch. 3)   the right to a fee simple (the highest right, i.e., ownership) interest in property.

traverse and denial (ch. 8)   A defence that simply denies all allegations without setting out the defendant's version of the facts.

trial by ambush (ch. 10)   A term used by lawyers to describe a trial strategy where one party avoids pre-trial disclosure of evidence so as to take the other party by surprise at trial. This strategy is not usually productive and is largely prohibited by the Rules.

unliquidated damages, aka general damages (ch. 7)   Damages that must be determined subjectively by applying general principles to facts, and where there is no simple formula to determine the amount.

writ of delivery (ch. 1)   A document issued by the court directing the bailiff to seize from the judgment debtor's property the item that the court ordered the debtor to return.

writ of seizure and sale (ch. 1)   A document issued by the court directed to its enforcement officer (sheriff for land/bailiff for personal property) to seize and sell assets of the judgment-debtor to satisfy the judgment.

Bibliography

This section is divided into three categories: Legislation, Books/Articles, and Websites. Chapter reference(s) enclosed in square brackets indicates where a resource is of significance to that chapter.

Legislation

Absentees Act, R.S.O. 1990, c. A.3. [ch. 6]

Administration of Justice Act, R.S.O. 1990, c. A.6. [ch. 1, ch. 6, ch. 7, ch. 11, ch. 12]

    Kilometre Allowances, R.R.O. 1990, Reg. 11. [ch. 11, ch. 12]

    Fee Waiver, O. Reg. 2/05, as am. by O. Reg. 671/05. [ch. 1, ch. 6]

    Small Claims Court — Fees and Allowances, O. Reg. 432/93. [ch. 6, ch. 11]

Bank Act, S.C. 1991, c. 46. [ch. 3]

Bankruptcy and Insolvency Act, R.S.C. 1985, c. B-3. [ch. 3]

Bills of Exchange Act, R.S.C. 1985, c. B-4. [ch. 4]

Bulk Sales Act, R.S.O. 1990, c. B.14. [ch. 3]

Business Names Act, R.S.O. 1990, c. B.17. [ch. 3]

Canada Evidence Act, R.S.C. 1985, c. C-5. [ch. 11]

Collection Agencies Act, R.S.O. 1990, c. C.14. [ch. 4, ch. 6]

Condominium Act, 1998, S.O. 1998, c. 19, [ch. 1]

Compensation for Victims of Crime Act, R.S.O. 1990, c. C.24. [ch. 14]

Consumer Protection Act, 2002, S.O. 2002, c. 30, Sched. A. [ch. 4]

Courts of Justice Act, R.S.O. 1990, c. C.43, as am. by S.C. 2009, c. 33, Sched. 2. [ch. 1, ch. 5, ch. 11, ch. 12]

    Small Claims Court Jurisdiction, O. Reg. 626/00, as amended by O. Reg. 439/08. [ch. 1, ch. 12]

Creditors' Relief Act, 2010, S.O. 2010, c. 16, Sch. 4. [ch. 3, ch. 14]

Criminal Code, R.S.C. 1985, c. C-46, s. 347. [ch. 5]

Crown Liability and Proceedings Act, R.S.C. 1985, c. C-50. [ch. 6]

Evidence Act, R.S.O. 1990, c. E.23, ss. 35–36, s. 52 (business records, medical reports and records). [ch. 11]

Execution Act, R.S.O. 1990, c. E.24, as am. by 2010, c. 16, Sched. 2, ss. 3, 22. [ch. 3, ch. 6, ch. 14, ch. 15]
   Exemptions, O. Reg. 657/05. [ch. 14]

Family Law Act, R.S.O. 1990, c. F.3, Part V. [ch. 5]

Indian Act, R.S.C. 1985, c. I-5. [ch. 14].

Insurance Act, R.S.O. 1990, c. I.8. [ch. 14]

Interest Act, R.S.C. 1985, c. I-15. [ch. 5]

Law Society Act, R.S.O. 1990, c. L.8. [ch. 1]

Limitations Act, 2002, S.O. 2002, c. 24, Sched. B. [ch. 1, ch. 2]

Parental Responsibility Act, 2000, S.O. 2000, c. 4, s. 2(1). [ch. 1]

Payday Loans Act, 2008, S.O. 2008, c. 9. [ch. 5]

Personal Property Security Act, R.S.O. 1990. c. P.10 (PPSA). [ch. 3, ch. 4, ch. 14]

Rules of Civil Procedure, R.R.O. 1990, Reg. 194.
   Rule 20 (Summary Judgment) [ch. 10]
   Rule 25 (Pleadings in an Action) [ch. 6]
   Rule 60 (Enforcement of Orders) [ch. 14]
   Rule 61 (Appeals to an Appellate Court) [ch. 12]

Rules of the Small Claims Court, O. Reg. 258/98, as am. by O. Reg. 400/12. [ch. 1, ch. 3, chs. 6–15]

Wages Act, R.S.O. 1990, c. W.1. [ch. 13, ch. 14, ch. 15]

Books/Articles

Bennett, F., *Collections*, 5th ed. (Aurora: Carswell, 2003). [ch. 13]

Connolly, John R., and Susan A. Koprich (chairs), *The Small Claims Court Rules: Hotspots One Year Later* (Toronto: Law Society of Upper Canada, Dept. of Continuing Education, 2007).
   Connolly, John R. "Settlement Conferences". [ch. 10]
   Libman, P.K., "Examinations and Contempt Proceedings". [ch. 13]
   Ntoukas, L.S. "The Small Claims Court Rules — One Year Later: Common Pitfalls". [ch. 11]
   Parsons, B., "Thoughts on Collections and Recovery". [ch. 13]
   Zuker, M.A. "The Trial — Evidence and Best Strategies". [ch. 11]

Olivo, L.M., and D. Gonsalves, *Debtor Creditor Law and Procedure* 4th ed. (Toronto: Emond Montgomery Publications, 2012). [ch. 13]

Zuker, Marvin, *Small Claims Court Practice* (Toronto: Carswell, 1997). [ch. 1]

Websites

Law Society of Upper Canada website: <http://www.lsuc.on.ca> [Follow links to paralegals and Paralegal Rules of Conduct and By-laws.]

Ministry of the Attorney General website: <http://www.attorneygeneral.jus.gov.on.ca>
   Office of the Children's Lawyer
     <http://www.attorneygeneral.jus.gov.on.ca/english/family/ocl/>
   Office of the Public Guardian and Trustee
     <http://www.attorneygeneral.jus.gov.on.ca/english/family/pgt/>

Pre- and Post-Judgment Interest
      <http://www.attorneygeneral.jus.gov.on.ca/english/courts/interestrates.asp>
Small Claims Court Fees
      <http://www.e-laws.gov.on.ca/html/regs/english/elaws_regs_930432_e.htm>
Small Claims Court Offices
      <http://www.attorneygeneral.jus.gov.on.ca/english/courts/Court_Addresses/>
      [Choose a municipality under "Choose a municipality" and choose Small
      Claims under "Choose a court office".]

Rules of the Small Claims Court Forms: <http://www.ontariocourtforms.on.ca/english/scc>
      Courts of Justice Act, R.S.O. 1990, c. C.43, as amended. Available at <http://www.e-laws.gov.on.ca/html/statutes/english/elaws_statutes_90c43_e.htm>

ServiceOntario e-Laws site
      Statute and regulation reference site: <http://www.e-laws.gov.on.ca/index.html>

Financial Consumer Agency of Canada
      <http://www.fcac-acfc.gc.ca/>

Index

Where a footnote is indexed, it is identifed by the page number and the note number with an "*n*": e.g., *35n31* means note 31 on page 35. Where illustrations and figures are indexed, they are identified by page number appended with an "*F*": e.g., *324F–327F* means illustrations appear on page 316 to page 319. Not all definitions of terms found in the glossary are indexed here.